The
Psychology of
Attitude Change
and Social Influence

McGraw-Hill Series in Social Psychology

CONSULTING EDITOR, Philip G. Zimbardo

Sharon Brehm:	Intimate Relationships
Susan T. Fiske and Shelley E. Taylor:	Social Cognition
Ayala Pines and Christina Maslach:	Experiencing Social Psychology
Lee Ross and Richard E. Nisbett:	The Person and the Situation: Perspectives of Social Psychology
Philip G. Zimbardo and Michael R. Leippe:	The Psychology of Attitude Change and Social Influence

The
Psychology
of
Attitude Change
and
Social Influence

Philip G. Zimbardo
Stanford University

Michael R. Leippe
Adelphi University

McGraw-Hill, Inc.

New York St. Louis San Francisco Auckland Bogotá Caracas Hamburg
Lisbon London Madrid Mexico Milan Montreal New Delhi Paris San Juan
São Paulo Singapore Sydney Tokyo Toronto

This book was set in Palatino by the College Composition Unit
in cooperation with Waldman Graphics, Inc.
The editors were Christopher Rogers and Sheila H. Gillams;
the production supervisor was Louise Karam.
The cover was designed by Carla Bauer / Joan E. O'Connor.
The photo researcher was Debra Hershkowitz.
Arcata Graphics/Halliday was printer and binder.

Cover painting: Pieter the Younger Brueghel, "A Flemish Kormesse" (Superstock).

The Psychology of Attitude Change and Social Influence

1 2 3 4 5 6 7 8 9 0 HAL HAL 9 0 9 8 7 6 5 4 3 2 1

ISBN 0-07-072877-1

Library of Congress Cataloging-in-Publication Data

Zimbardo, Philip G.
    The psychology of attitude change and social influence / Philip G.
  Zimbardo, Michael R. Leippe.
      p.   cm.—(The McGraw-Hill series in social psychology)
    Includes bibliographical references and index.
    ISBN 0-07-072877-1
    1. Attitude change.   2. Influence (Psychology)   3. Attribution
  (Social psychology)   I. Leippe, Michael R.   II. Title.
  III. Series.
  HM261.Z56   1991
  303.3'8—dc20   90-22689

About the Authors

❖

Philip G. Zimbardo has been a professor of social psychology at Stanford University since 1968. He earned his advanced degrees from Yale University in the late 1950s, working with Carl Hovland in the Yale Attitude Change Program. Later, at New York University, Zimbardo went on to study social influence within the cognitive dissonance–public compliance paradigm. His brand of experimental social psychology can be seen in laboratory investigations of affiliation, deindividuation, aggression, and motivational consequences of dissonance. This work was supplemented with field studies, simulations and correlational analyses of anonymity, vandalism, and shyness. Like his New York City high school classmate, Stanley Milgram, Zimbardo is known for research demonstrations that illustrate the power of the situation, as in his classic Stanford Prison study.

Currently, Dr. Zimbardo is working on a model of the process by which normal people begin to develop pathological explanations for some of their behavior, and on understanding the ways in which time perspective biases influence much individual and collective action. Zimbardo's *Psychology and Life* is the oldest, continuously selling textbook in psychology. His latest work, the PBS-TV series *Discovering Psychology* (1990), was created and hosted by Zimbardo for both students and the general public. The twenty-six-program series explores the significance of the science of psychology and its practical relevance for improving the quality of our lives.

*M*ichael R. Leippe is a professor of psychology at Adelphi University, where he has taught since 1982. He earned his Ph.D. from Ohio State University in 1979. Leippe was inspired by and highly involved in the influential research and theorizing on cognitive responses taking place at Ohio State in the 1970s. He worked with Anthony Greenwald on research into the cognitive processes that underlie persuasion in mass media-like settings, and with Thomas Ostrom on applying social psychology to psycholegal problems such as eyewitness testimony. Since then, Leippe has been carrying out inventive research on attitude change and influence in persuasion, cognitive dissonance, and legal settings.

Dr. Leippe has published more than twenty-five journal articles and book chapters. Recently, he has been engaged in federally funded research on the credibility of children's eyewitness testimony, and on how jurors and other factfinders can be helped to distinguish between accurate and inaccurate memory messages from witnesses. He is also working on a model of audience involvement in persuasion situations.

To the Zimbardo clan: Chris, Adam, Zara, and Tanya—
Always there for me

To Raeanne and Beth Leippe—
Inspirations and so much more

Contents

❖

FOREWORD   xv

PREFACE   xvii

1   *A WORLD OF INFLUENCE*   *1*

Social Influence Processes and Settings   *3*

Tales from the Influence Hall of Fame (and Shame)   *5*

Interpersonal Influence: Conversion and the Personal
Touch 5 / Communication and Persuasion: "Say It Again,
Sam" 12 / Mass Media Influence: Where There's Smoke,
There's Fire (and Advertising) 21

ABCs of Influence: Attitudes, Behavior, and Cognitions   *30*

Attitude Systems 32 / An Organizing Theme: Change Begets
Change 34 / Further Themes Based on the Central Role
of Attitudes 34

A Social Psychological Perspective   *36*

A Look Ahead   *38*

2   *INFLUENCING BEHAVIOR: TAKING DIRECT APPROACHES*   *42*

Learning When Actions Pay Off   *44*

Instrumental Learning and Contingent Reinforcement 44 /
Social Learning Theory 45 / Modeling Aggression 49 /
The Yin and Yang of Modeling 51

Approval and Disapproval: The Power of Social Rewards   *53*

Conformity: Saving Face and Gaining Grace—and Knowledge   55
The Causes of Conformity 57 /   Conformity: Bad or Good? 64

Obedience: Basing Behavior on Authority   65
Milgram's Scenario: Would You Shock a Stranger if Hitler Asked
You? 65 /   Explaining Extraordinary Behavior by Looking
at the Ordinary 69 /   Pushing the Disobedience Exit Button 75

Kneejerk Psychology: Influence through Heuristics   76
The Rule of Reciprocity 76 /   The Rule of Commitment 79

*Point of Departure: When Inner Changes Flow
from External Influence*   83

**3   INFLUENCING ATTITUDES THROUGH BEHAVIOR:
WHEN DOING BECOMES BELIEVING**   87
Attribution and Self-Attribution   89
Attribution Theory 89 /   Self-Perception and Self-Attribution 95

Self-Persuasion and Role-Playing   102
All the World's a Stage...and We're Just Role-Players 102 /
More Self-Persuasion: TV or Not TV 105

The Psychology of Self-Justification: Dissonance Theory   108
Factors Affecting the Magnitude of Dissonance 109 /   Dissonance
and Insufficient Justification: Less Is More 110 /   Modes of
Dissonance Reduction 117 /   Dissonance and an Unethical
Business Decision 120

*Dissonance, Self-Attribution, and Self-Affirmation:
Similarities and Separate Identities*   121
Overjustification 122 /   Similar Effects from Different
Processes 123 /   Affirming One's Self-Regard 123

A Concluding Note   123

**4   CHANGING ATTITUDES THROUGH PERSUASION:
TAKE MY WORDS FOR IT**   127
Seeking Out Influence: Social Comparison Processes   130
Similarity on Related Attributes 130 /   Opinion   132 /
Dissimilarity as a Basis for Comparison 133

Being Sought as a Target: Persuasive Appeals   134
Steps in the Persuasion Process 135 /   Initial and Final Steps 136

Presentation and Exposure   136
Idea Filtration 137 / Media Mind Management 139

Attention   142
Tuning Out 144 / Tuning In and Out 147

Comprehension   148

Acceptance: The Biggest Hurdle   149
Cognitive Responses: It's the Thought That Counts 149 /
Shortcuts to Acceptance: Using Heuristics Instead of Systematic
Analysis 152 / Televised Images 158 / Objectivity and Bias
in Systematic Processing 162

An Interim Stop on the Road to Lasting Persuasion   164

**5 MAKING PERSUASION LAST: THE PERSISTENCE
AND BEHAVIORAL CONSEQUENCES OF ATTITUDE
CHANGE**   168

*Sowing the Seeds of Retention: Creating Strong, Clear,
and Extreme Attitudes*   170
Decent Exposure 171 / Repetition of Complex Messages 176

Retention: Persuasion over Time   179
Hit It Again, Harder, Again and Again 179 / Systematic
Analysis: Active Minds Make Durable Attitudes 181 /
Attitudes: Autonomous Dependents 183 / Primacy and Recency:
Me First or Me Second? 186

Translating Attitudes into Behavior: Ultimate Persuasion   188
The Power of the Situation To Override Attitudes 188 / When
Attitudes Yield Actions: The Conditions of Consistency 192

The Hard-Earned Rewards of Persuasion   198

**6 RESISTING AND EMBRACING INFLUENCE:
THE YIN AND YANG OF PERSUASION**   202

The Stubborn Mind: Resisting and Selective Bending   204
Strength in Structure: The Cognitive Bases of Perseverance 204 /
States of Involvement: Motivational Bases of Resistance
and Openness to Persuasion 208

Overcoming Resistance: Liberating the Totalitarian Ego   217
Facing the Fire (of Accountability) 217 / Playing Devil's Advocate

Is No Sin 217 /   Where Questions Lead, We May Follow—Even
to Paradox 221 /   Striking the Right Chord 223

The Other Extreme: Persuasion Pushovers   225

Lack of Resistance: Cases in Point 226 /   Building
Resistance 229 /   Marshaling the Forces for Good 232

Prejudice: An Attitude That Can Kill   233

The Time Is Now 234 /   The Time Is Then 234 /   Social
Psychological Interest in Prejudice 235 /   Some Origins
of Prejudiced Attitudes 236

A Final Note: On Having an Open Mind without Being a Pushover   239

**7   INFLUENCE, AWARENESS, AND THE UNCONSCIOUS:
WHEN WHAT YOU DON'T KNOW MAY CHANGE YOU**   244

Awareness and Consciousness of Influence   247

Awareness, Associations, and Affect 248 /   Awareness and
''Higher-Order'' Mental Processes 254 /
Shifting into Automatic 257

Nonverbal (and Not Necessarily Conscious) Messages   259

People Reading: Forming Impressions from Voice and Face 262 /
The Sights and Sounds of Feelings and Lies 268 /   Persuasion and
Nonverbal Communication 274 /   The Self-Perception of
Nonverbal Acts: I Nod, Therefore I Agree 275

Subliminals: Inconspicuous Influence   276

The Mind-Altering Possibilities of Subliminal ''Visuals'' 277 /
Subaudible and Print-Embedded Messages: Less Likely
Influences 281 /   The Ethics of Influence—In and Out
of Awareness 284

Awareness and Consciousness: A Closing Perspective   286

8   INFLUENCE AND THE LEGAL SYSTEM: TRYING EXPERIENCES   290

*The Adversarial Approach: Does Competitive Persuasion
Yield Justice?*   292

Fairness and Bias: A Question of Balance 293 /   The More Subtle
Social Psychology of the Adversarial System 294

The Police Station: Gathering Evidence from People   297

Eyewitness Testimony: But I Saw It with My Own Eyes 297 /
What's a Little Confession between Friends? 303

In the Courtroom: The Persuasion Battleground   *308*
Trial Lawyers on Trial 308 /   Identifying Witnesses 313

The Jury Room   *317*
Majorities Rule Most of the Time 318 /   The Occasional Power
of the Few 322 /   When Things That Shouldn't Influence
Do Influence 324

The Case of Psychology and Law: A Closing Statement   *326*

9 *SOCIAL INFLUENCE IN THE SERVICE OF HEALTH
AND HAPPINESS*   *330*

Pro-Environmental Influence: Can Persuasion Preserve the Planet?   *331*
Environmental Attitudes: Weak Links in the Action Chain 333 /
Enhancing Motivation: Pro-Environmental Acts Whose Rewards
Outweigh Costs 334 /   Enhancing Salience: Keeping
Pro-Environmental Behavior in Mind 336 /   From Personal Habits
to Global Pollution: The Generalization Gap 339

The Promotion of Health   *340*
Mass Persuasion: Is an Informed Public a Healthier One? 342 /
Doctor's Orders: Why Don't Patients Do As They're Told? 352

Social Psychological Roads to Mental Health   *358*
Therapy by Any Other Name…Is Influence 359 /   Therapy
as Persuasive Communication 360 /   Cognitive-Behavioral Therapy
and Attribution Therapy: Think and Do Yourself Better 361 /
Dissonance and Therapy: Commitment, Choice, and Effort 365

Social Influence, the Good Life, and Your Future   *367*

APPENDIX A: Research and the Experimental Method   *A.1*
APPENDIX B: Measuring Attitudes and Their Components   *B.1*
REFERENCES   *R.1*
INDEXES
    Name Index   *I.1*
    Subject Index   *I.9*

Foreword

❖

During the many decades when American psychology was held captive by a limited scientific doctrine of behaviorism, the pathfinders who dared to venture beyond these intellectual boundaries and explore new horizons were largely social psychologists. They valued the personal perspectives of the human actor in life's dramas, honored the alternative interpretations of reality held by different observers, and defended the subtle interplay of dynamic forces between and within cultures, social situations, and individual psyches.

Long relegated to a subordinate position within psychology's status hierarchy for these points of view, social psychology has steadily moved to the center of contemporary psychology. It did so by establishing a cognitively flavored brand of psychology, which, in recent years, has become the banner flown by mainstream psychology. Social psychology was the home of generalists within psychology, a haven for scholars interested in understanding the depth and breadth of the nature of human nature. It was neither too shy to ask the big questions that have intrigued social philosophers for centuries, nor too orthodox to venture into alien territories with new methodologies that have provided empirically grounded answers to the more vital questions of our time. Finally, social psychologists have become the vanguard of the movement to extend the boundaries of traditional psychology into realms vital to contributing solutions for real-world problems, the areas of health, ecology, education, law, peace and conflict resolution, and much more. Indeed, it is not immodest to declare that nothing of human nature is too alien to social psychological inquiry and concern.

Our **McGraw-Hill Series in Social Psychology** celebrates the fundamental contributions being made by researchers, theorists, and practitioners of social psychology to a richer understanding of the human condition. The authors of each book in the series are not only distinguished researchers and dedicated teachers, but are committed to sharing a vision of the excitement inherent in their particular area of investigation with their colleagues, graduate students, and seriously curious undergraduates. Taken as a whole, the series titles will cover a wide path of social psychological interests, allowing instructors to use any of them as supplements to their basic textbook, or for the more daring, to organize a challenging course around a collection of them.

The idea of writing a book about principles of attitude change emerged from a seminar I taught at Columbia University, part of which involved observing the dynamics of students role-playing agents and targets of influence. With graduate students the likes of Lee Ross and Judy Rodin to stimulate my interest in formalizing the conceptual and practical aspects of attitude change, I decided to write a "primer" on the subject. At Stanford, the next year, I persuaded Ebbe Ebbesen, then a graduate student, to collaborate on the project. The result, *Influencing Attitudes and Changing Behavior* (1970), offered students a basic introduction to the study of persuasion, attitude change, and behavior modification. The range of practical applications was broadened in our second edition (1977), with the expert collaboration of Christina Maslach, now professor of psychology at the University of California, at Berkeley.

Michael Leippe believed that the time had come to update and refocus this little book to integrate much more of the "new cognitive look" in attitudes and social influence—his heritage from training at Ohio State with Tony Greenwald. But as we began doing so, a different, better book surfaced. What was retained was the core value that the processes of social influence, persuasion, and attitude change are not only central to social psychology, but to many of our everyday interactions in the "real world." Now what emerges is the depth of the empirical foundation of our knowledge about how people are changed by their contacts with other people and the media, as well as the wide-ranging pragmatic utility of that knowledge to students living in the complex world of the 1990s.

Philip G. Zimbardo
Series Editor

Preface

———— ❖ ————

These are exciting times for those of us who study and think about attitude change and social influence. A veritable explosion of research and theory on these topics—on the basic question of how people change—has occurred within the past ten years or so. The emphasis on social cognition that began in the 1970s has yielded new and important insights about the cognitive processes and structures that lie behind persuasion and compliance. Now, renewed interest in motivation, affect, and involvement is generating research that promises a truly integrated understanding of the interplay of attitudes, cognitions, behaviors, and feelings. And, on top of the great strides in basic research and theory, social scientists are applying the psychology of influence to important aspects of everyday life. Social influence is at the heart of many pressing societal issues—promotion of healthful lifestyles, the raising of environmental consciousness, the effects of censorship, "image-processing" in politics, ultrasophisticated advertising and marketing, just to name a few. More and more, both basic and problem-solving research is being aimed increasingly at these issues and the settings in which they arise.

This confluence of exciting developments inspired our book. We wanted to bring together under one cover an integrated treatment of a wide range of research, theory, and application in the realm of social influence. In fact, one of our goals was to combine, in one reasonably short volume, the fine coverage of persuasion and attitude change theories that one finds in a book such as Richard Petty and John Cacioppo's *Attitudes and Persuasion: Classic and Contemporary Approaches* (1981), with the equally excellent treatment of compliance and conformity in Robert Cialdini's *Influence: Science and Practice* (1988).

The result is a book that covers all the major social influence topics, including persuasion, compliance, conformity, obedience, dissonance and self-attribution, conditioning and social learning, attitude-behavior relations, attitude involvement, prejudice, nonverbal communication, and even subliminal influence. The coverage is wide, but also integrated through the use of the recurring theme of "attitude systems" in which attitudes, cognitions, behaviors, and intentions can all be affected by *external* agents of influence, and all can be influenced *internally* by each other.

We also devote two full chapters to applications of social influence principles that we see as decided "growth areas" now and in the near future. One applications chapter focuses on influence in the legal system and the other on improving the quality of life (the environment, personal health, and mental well-being).

Our major goals, naturally, concern the students who will read this book. We wanted to communicate the exciting advances in knowledge gained through the scientific study of social influence to students in a way that gets *them* excited, interested, and cognizant of the relevance this knowledge has for them personally and for society as a whole. To that end, we have tried to write in a style that students will find engaging. Practical issues, applications, and everyday examples are continually worked into the flow of research examples and theoretical viewpoints that we describe. The main focus is on selected social psychological experiments and field studies (both new ones and classics) which are described in lively detail and always brought back to events and experiences we think are interesting and that college students can relate to. The hoped-for result is a text that is both scholarly and enjoyable to read.

This book is intended primarily for undergraduates. A previous course in introductory psychology would be helpful but is not at all necessary in order to enjoy and learn from the book. The book should serve handsomely as one of several paperbacks in a survey course in social psychology, as a supplement to a larger text in a survey course, or as the central text in psychology courses and seminars that might be titled, "Persuasion and Attitude Change," "Social Influence," or even "Mind Control." Professors teaching in the disciplines of sociology, communications, and business might consider using the book in courses such as "Media Environments," "Propaganda and Communications," "Social Influence in Small and Large Groups," and "Fundamentals of Advertising." We have included material relevant to and taken from each of these disciplines.

Graduate students in psychology, sociology, and communications should also find the book interesting and informative. We hope that the many examples and applications will broaden their perspective on the relevance and interconnectedness of what they plan to study as a career. We would be particularly gratified if reading our book helped to inspire some students to contribute to the knowledge base about which we write.

ACKNOWLEDGMENTS

We wish to thank a number of people for various contributions they made to the completion of this book. Rochelle Diogenes, formerly of

McGraw-Hill, deserves much thanks for "teaming us up," and for providing unflagging encouragement and reinforcement during the early stages of our work. Rochelle genuinely saw—and helped shape further—our vision for this book. We also thank Chris Rogers, executive editor of psychology at McGraw-Hill, for enthusiasm and support almost beyond the call of duty. Sheila Gillams, as editing supervisor, and Melissa Mashburn, as editorial assistant, provided patient and constructive assistance, and Elaine Romano did a wonderful and instructive job of technical editing the first drafts of six chapters.

Several colleagues read all or part of the second draft and provided valuable insights, suggestions, and criticisms. They were Gary Wells, Iowa State University; Wendy Wood, Texas A & M University; Mark Zanna, University of Waterloo; and Paul Rosenfeld, Navy Personnel Research and Development Center (who read the entire book and provided a most detailed list of excellent comments). Colleagues like these never cease to amaze us by how much they know and care about social psychology.

We also thank our colleagues, graduate students, and secretaries at Stanford and Adelphi for their support and encouragement. Among graduate students at Adelphi, Andrew Manion was indispensable. He computer-drew the first drafts of all the figures in the book and co-authored the test item file.

Finally, we cannot thank our families enough for the support, love, and joy they give us. On the Leippe side, Beth, Raeanne, and Pat put up with all the ups-n-downs of writing a book. Their presence was quietly encouraging when Mike needed to work, and so very much appreciated at *all* times. On the Zimbardo side, the family gracefully endured yet another A.W.O.L. as dear old dad descended into the writing pit.

Michael R. Leippe
Philip G. Zimbardo

The
Psychology of
Attitude Change
and Social Influence

1

A World of Influence

❖

Social Influence Processes and Settings ◆ *Tales from the Influence Hall of Fame (and Shame)* ◆ *ABCs of Influence: Attitudes, Behavior and Cognitions* ◆ *A Social Psychological Perspective* ◆ *A Look Ahead*

When you woke up this morning, your mind was probably filled with thoughts and plans about the upcoming day. First you have to do this, then that, and later (don't forget) something else. Perhaps you want to have lunch with a friend, but to do so would require ducking out of a class or slipping away from work early. It's your decision. Perhaps you also have to decide how to spend your evening. You don't have to work, and so you could finally go see that movie all your friends are raving about. Or you could drop by the party you were invited to. It's your decision. But, first things first. What's for breakfast? Cereal and juice may sound better than toast and coffee, and if you're concerned about cholesterol and calories, maybe you think you've already had your weekly quota of bacon and eggs. It's up to you.

If you think about it, there are so many things that are really up to you. What to wear, what to watch on television, who to vote for, what to major in, where to live, who to marry—the choices are endless. For most people in countries like the United States, life is a supermarket of options, just waiting for us to select them; people have a lot of control over how they live their lives. Indeed, we become more aware of the lifelong freedoms we have enjoyed—and perhaps have taken too much for granted—when our television screens suddenly explode, as they did in 1989, with the life-and-death struggle of Chinese college students to gain basic freedoms from their authoritarian government. But we also marvel at the profound human need for freedom and democracy when we witness the sudden transformations taking place throughout eastern Europe as the tyranny of oppressive Communist control is overthrown by the people.

No doubt about the considerable degree of personal control we have over our own lives. Yet, with so many people having so much freedom, how do we manage to stay out of each other's way most of the time, as we pursue our individual goals and dreams? How is it that, in the face of countless options, so many people share so many similarities? And how is it that, to further some of your own goals, you often have to get others to do what you want them to—usually without resorting to obvious forces like law, money, physical power, or privilege? And how do others constrain your choices, shape your likes and dislikes, and direct your actions?

Haven't you, like us, at times complied with suggestions or demands from authorities that went against the grain, were not in line with your personal values? And surely you have belonged to groups that exerted pressure on you to dress or act in ways that only later you realize were not "the real you." Did you ever buy an advertised product you didn't really need because of the persuasive appeal of the ad?

These are questions of social influence—the changes in people caused by what others do. We certainly are free to make many decisions, but immersed as all of us are in a social world, we cannot escape the subtle or strong inputs from others that may tip our decisional scales in favor of one option over another. Indeed, we often do not want to escape the influence of others who are wise, just, and concerned about our well-being. To be part of the human condition is to be engaged in the give-and-take of social interaction, to be enmeshed in the fabric of the social context that gives meaning to our lives. And, of course, there is the flip side, that part of ourselves which functions as the influence agent, attempting to influence others—to be our friends, to study or go to the movies with us, to give us a job, to share our views, and even our lives.

Social influence is pervasive. It goes on everywhere, all the time. It's the way of the world. In order to function most effectively in this world, it pays to know how and when to use social influence, to be able to recognize social influence attempts directed at you, and to have a well-tuned sense of whether to accept or reject particular influence attempts. This book is all about the psychology of social influence. It will give you practical advice on how to resist unwanted sources of influence and how to be more effective in your personal quests as an influence agent. But the foundation of those ideas comes from the vast amount of research on persuasion and compliance conducted by researchers in the areas of social and political psychology and in communications. We will examine the empirical research and theories coming out of academic settings and go beyond them to integrate points of view and information that come to us from influence professionals, those who make a living by being good at their craft, be it in marketing, advertising, selling, polling, lobbying, fund-raising, and even recruiting for the military or for cults.

SOCIAL INFLUENCE PROCESSES AND SETTINGS

A social influence process involves behavior by one person that has the effect—or even just the intention—of changing the way another person behaves, feels, or thinks about a stimulus. The stimulus might be a political issue (for example, abortion), a product (such as diet soft drinks), or an activity (for instance, cheating on exams). Thus, you might try to talk an uncertain friend into agreeing with your position on abortion. You may encourage another friend to try a new soft drink you like. And when someone who looks up to you confesses to feeling tempted to cheat, your own record of honesty in test taking may serve as a model to help the friend resist the temptation. In all three cases, you have served as an agent of possible social influence.

In each instance, you changed or attempted to change some target person's behaviors, feelings, or thoughts about an issue, object, or action. In other cases, the stimulus can be yourself: the influence agent. For example, through charming behavior and a winning smile, you might try to get a new acquaintance to like you. In still other cases, the stimulus can be your target, as when you give a depressed friend a pep talk that encourages the friend to think more highly of himself or herself. Counselors and psychotherapists are professional influence agents whose goal is often to change the target's self-image. Finally, you may be both target and agent of influence when you decide to put into practice specific strategies of change designed to transform those New Year's resolutions into the reality of losing weight, making new friends, getting work done on time, and so forth.

There are many techniques of social influence, but they all tap into a relatively few basic influence processes that hinge on the ways in which human beings think, remember, feel, and make decisions. Before focusing on *what* to do and *how* best to achieve your influence objectives, it is essential to focus on *why* it works—understanding the psychology of influence.

That is precisely what we attempt to do in this book. Our general academic goal is to provide a foundation of information about the nature of social influence in its various forms. At the practical level, we expect that this knowledge will prove valuable in your everyday life by making you a more successful agent of social influence and a wiser citizen schooled in detecting and resisting unwanted types of influence and obedience to unjust authority.

But first, we will set the stage with some specific and dramatic examples of social influence occurring in three quite different kinds of settings: interpersonal, persuasion, and mass media. One way in which these influence settings differ is in how personal or *individualized* they are, while a second way is in the *size, or scope, of the target audience* at whom the influence is directed.

The most individualized influence situations are *interpersonal settings,* in which the number of people immediately involved is small and there is one-to-one communication between influence agent and target. The efforts of your two best friends to convince you to go to the movies with them is an instance of an interpersonal influence attempt. So is a mother's efforts to get her busy teenage son to clean up his room, and a car salesperson's pitch to get you to buy a specific car.

Persuasion settings are also common. Here a communicator, typically a speech maker, attempts to sway an audience to agree with him or to take some action he endorses. Persuasion involves one influence agent attempting to influence simultaneously many target people in the audience. Evangelical ministers offer us a prototype of the persuasive pulpit communicator influencing attitudes and changing behavior. Persuasion settings are more impersonal than interpersonal settings. Nevertheless, some communicators are marvelously effective at moving an audience, so powerful and passionate in delivering their message that we label them as *charismatic.*

Influence also takes place in *mass media settings.* Messages and images conveyed over TV, radio, and printed publications reach millions of people around the globe. By nature, they are highly impersonal; not only are they designed to be meaningful to many individuals, but they are also communicated *through* a medium. The communicator is neither physically present nor often explicitly identifiable as a single person or entity. Yet influence through the mass media can be potent. The tens of billions spent on commercial advertising each year attest to the effectiveness of the media in promoting a seemingly endless array of products and in packaging political candidates.

To introduce you to the three major types of settings in which influence takes place, let's look at some current and historical examples of each of these forms of social influence in action. For interpersonal influence, we will examine the techniques used by Moonie recruiters to get young people, like you, to join their cult. For communication and persuasion, we will review the sources of power of charismatic communicators such as the Reverend Martin Luther King, Jr., Ronald Reagan, Adolph Hitler, and the Peoples Temple cult leader Jim Jones. For mass media influence, our focus will be on the strategies and tactics currently being used by cigarette companies to get people to start smoking and already addicted smokers to resist encouragement to stop smoking. These examples, and the theoretical overview that will follow them, illustrate themes and principles that we will elaborate upon in subsequent chapters. The examples also provide some solid real-world substance to what can mistakenly seem to some students like nothing more than an abstract academic exercise.

*T*ALES FROM THE INFLUENCE HALL OF FAME (AND SHAME)

Interpersonal Influence: Conversion and the Personal Touch

You've probably heard about the Moonies, religious cult extraordinaire of the 1970s. *Moonie* is the popular name for members of the Unification Church of Korean Reverend Sun Myung Moon, a very wealthy businessman who calls himself the new messiah. The Moonies became one of the foremost nontraditional religious movements that actively recruited young people on college campuses and in urban centers—obtaining dramatic conversions by the thousands. Keep reading and you will discover that the Moonies are alive and well in the 1990s, probably recruiting on your campus and in local high schools—but in a new disguise, and perhaps more effective than ever.

The typical Moonie recruitment effort unfolds as follows. A church member approaches a potential recruit on the street and hands him a leaflet. The recruiter might explain that she represents an "international student organization for young people concerned about the future of the world." They chat for a while, and apparently impressed with the young man's sensitivity, she invites the potential recruit to a free, or inexpensive, dinner being given that night. "Who is giving the dinner?" he might ask. And the answer she might give is "CARP, the Collegiate Association for Research on Principle." The name has a good ring to it, and it's hard to object to any of those terms, singly or in combination. The bright-eyed and clean-cut young woman gushes over how much fun and how meaningful these dinners are and suggests that "If you're not doing anything special tonight, why not join us?"

Should he take her up on the offer, the would-be recruit finds himself in a pleasantly decorated "visitors' center" and in the company of ten to twenty other young people, a half-dozen of whom might be guests like himself—the rest, well-trained influence agents. The meal is delicious, and the environment filled with gaiety and "unconditional acceptance." That means open demonstrations of affection and respect for the guest and anything he has to say, well almost anything, as he will soon see. The old members—in the majority—deftly guide conversation, describing the worldwide good deeds of the organization and its beliefs regarding the many woes of modern life. Although the world's social, economic, and political problems are complex, there are simple solutions.

After dinner, the dishes are cleared and out come the folk guitars. Festive singing and dancing go on for an hour or so, before a lecture and slide show is given by a smiling and articulate senior member. The new recruit is asked whether he would like to be happier, and whether the source of any aimlessness and discontent he may feel could be the result of living in a misguided and unhappy society. When he says what they want to hear, they are all smiles and hang on to his every word; negatives and uncertainties elicit frowns, loss of eye contact, and a cloud over paradise. At some point he may learn that he is among followers of a religious movement, but that is played down—for now. The slide show proceeds at a rapid pace, showing lovely scenes of happy people in the beautiful mountain farm village operated by the Unification Church. When it's over, the new recruits are invited to come and spend the weekend, or even a whole week at the village. "We have a van leaving tonight!" People are touching, holding hands, being embraced. Do you want more of that good stuff, or do you want to end it and return to your solitary, unappreciated, and isolated existence? That is the question running through the minds of the happy targets.

If our recruit signs on for the weekend, as some of the other guests seem to be doing, he is engaged in gentle conversation about his religious beliefs while en route to the village. The next two days follow a rigid and totally filled schedule that runs from 8 a.m. to 11 p.m. After being awakened by a band of singing campers, the newcomers share in morning exercises and prayers, then breakfast, then song practice, then two lectures expounding the principles and beliefs of the Unification Church, and then lunch. After lunch, it's sports, more songs, another lecture, dinner, and evening discussion groups. Everything is upbeat. It's a return to summer camp at its best, except there is no chance for an intimate encounter; this is serious fun. Regular members, seen in the midst of their work-a-day lives, seem so content. Yet the recruit hears lectures and discussions on heavy topics—the Bible, Jesus Christ, the meaning of life. The constant pitch is for love, trust, and morality; the theme is that society has gone awry—because of the evils of Communism, lust, greed, and other assorted ills—and that following Reverend Moon's philosophy can set it all straight.

The recruits are never left by themselves. At least one member, often an attractive person of the opposite sex, accompanies them everywhere. Discussion and meal groups always have a ratio of at least one member per recruit. The perceptive observer would note that the ever-present members carefully manage communication—outlining the church's beliefs, discouraging statements and ideas that don't bear on their themes, stopping smiling when a guest shows signs of negativity, and beaming with those potent love bombs at positivity. Together, members help one another to create the appearance of agreement and wisdom. And yet the recruit is made to feel very special—liked, a "member of the family," part of something big and important, privy to profound information. As the weekend draws to a close, he receives the invitation to stay the week or longer, to "learn more about us" and gain new insights "we didn't have time to get into."

A Hare Krishna using a Moonie line—on a captive audience.

You can see how "up close and personal" the whole experience is. The potential recruit is face-to-face with influence agents for hours and days, whose mission is to change his beliefs and behavior—to get him to join their organization, to be part of the cult. It seems as if you were being invited and encouraged to come into heaven itself and to leave behind the hell of your previous existence. It sounds like a great deal, right? How could you go wrong?

The chances are about 1 in 3 that, having spent the weekend, our recruit will take his Moonie hosts up on the offer to stay longer, and about 1 in 10 that he will ultimately seek to join the cult as a full-fledged member (Galanter, 1989). Do these statistics impress you? Thirty and ten percent may not seem like a lot, but any advertiser or door-to-door salesperson would gladly accept these rates of compliance because over time and with lots of attempts, they translate into many successful "hits." And make no mistake; this is major league social influence. The typical pattern of those who do convert has been to quit school, give all their money and possessions to the cause, reject their family and closest friends, and devote themselves entirely to the goals of conquering evil and spreading goodwill—mostly through begging and hustling for new members. Converted members even are willing to let Reverend Moon decide whom they should marry. In 1982, he performed a mass wedding of 2,100 couples at Madison Square Garden—all of whom he personally paired and many of whom had never met before.

Conversion to Unificationist beliefs tends to be rather thorough. Indeed, in the 1970s, cults became viewed as a menace to society. They were accused of "brainwashing." Many colleges included, as part of freshman orientation, workshops on how to resist cult recruiters. Some parents attempted to "kidnap" back their converted adolescents, sometimes hiring strong-arms to forcibly remove them from the cult community. A new service emerged known as "deprogramming," and many families purchased it, for as much as $20,000 for one series of these intense counterinfluence encounters (without any guarantee of success). The recaptured recruit would be put in the "care" of a "deprogrammer," who would attempt to undo whatever social influence had led to the conversion, often using techniques very similar to those used by the Moonies to "retrofit" the convert and gain the reconversion. Court decisions against this kidnapping-deprogramming have curtailed its use in recent times (*San Francisco Examiner and Chronicle*, 2/12/90).

Back to the future. Although they draw less popular attention today, the Moonies and literally thousands of other cults are still with us.

The Rev. Sun Myung Moon marries over four thousand Moonies en masse at Madison Square Garden on July 1, 1982. All of these young people accepted the person whom the Rev. Moon personally picked to be their spouse—in some cases a total stranger until this very wedding day. (*UPI/Bettmann Newsphotos*)

In fact, a great deal of our recruitment description was drawn from a feature article in the *San Francisco Chronicle* that ran in August 1989 and was written by a reporter who was "recruited" in the summer of 1989 (Nix, 1989). The Moonies never left; they just switched to a quieter style and kept up with the times. Although their indoctrination techniques remain similar, they are couched in rhetoric tuned to the more conservative outlook of today's youth and cloaked in an aura of mainstream respectability. Moonies call themselves "Unificationists" now. Their youth branches and urban centers long ago switched from hippie-sounding names like the "Creative Community Project" to the mainstream-sounding "Collegiate Association for the Research of Principle." Who can carp about that? More extreme aspects of their indoctrination programs have been eliminated, largely for legal reasons. For example, the deceptive practice of not revealing who they are until after the recruit is at the church retreat—called "heavenly deception"—and the extreme daily regimen of weeklong retreats that sometimes resulted in sleep and food deprivation have been modified. Unification Church politics are now openly conservative. The organization gives millions to conservative political causes, engages in political lobbying in the Congress, and owns (since 1982) the ultraconservative daily newspaper the *Washington Times*.

But recruitment continues as always. Upwards of 10,000 disciples in the United States are engaged in the classic style of recruiting new members. Another 40,000 to 50,000 Unificationists live mainstream lives in neighborhoods across the country, and their numbers are swelling in Korea and other countries.

Extremely normal social influence. What makes Moonie recruitment methods as effective as they are? It isn't mass hypnosis or brainwashing. Moonies do not walk around like zombies. And it isn't physical force. Contrary to some popular myths, there are no barbed wire fences or armed guards surrounding Moonie farms and retreats. Nor is there a spellbinding charismatic orator who lures the youth away to this alternate lifestyle; most recruits are never in direct contact with Reverend Moon, and he is not a particularly strong communicator. The social influence techniques that lead to this relatively rapid religious conversion can be understood in terms of normal psychological processes. The conversions seem dramatic and "abnormal" for two reasons. First, most of the young people who enter the indoctrination process feel somewhat alienated and lonely, or anxious about their uncertain future. Indeed, Moonie recruiters deliberately target for approach individuals who look forlorn or without purpose, especially foreign students or those traveling on vacation. Hence, potential recruits are especially susceptible to all the attention and "love bombing," and to the message that there is a better path for them through a life in the Moon organization. Second, the sheer quantity and diversity of ordinary influence techniques that recruiters apply make for extreme effects. Usually, in any given situation, we get hit with just one influence tactic. Moonie recruiters fire away with their entire arsenal of influence weapons on each and every potential recruit.

In subsequent chapters we will explore at length the psychology of these influence tactics. Perhaps you recognized some as you read about this typical recruitment effort. Among them are (1) building an initially small commitment into progressively bigger commitments that the recruit must justify to himself or herself (come to dinner, come for the weekend, stay the week, give us your money), (2) repeated persuasive arguments that offer straightforward solutions to vexing personal problems, (3) the power of groups dynamics, both the numbers and personal attractiveness of all those agreeing and agreeable members, (4) the denial of the opportunity to counterargue by keeping the recruit busily occupied with information and activities (and never alone), (5) positive reinforcements (smiles and good food and that special brand of attention that makes one feel individuated), and more.

The concerted application of multiple interpersonal influence techniques is by no means restricted to religious cults. Similarities may be drawn between how cults recruit and retain members and how Alcoholics Anonymous chapters convert many confirmed alcoholics to sobriety and keep them that way (Galanter, 1989). All kinds of commitment rituals and group-to-individual persuasion to a strict dogma and new lifestyle occur in this highly successful self-help group. Similarly, closely knit athletic teams do a lot of interpersonal influence among themselves. On the downside, indoctrination into terrorist groups often resembles the Moonie system. An extremist group of Iranian terrorist recruiters have a lot of raw material to work with in a 14-year-old youngster raised in a strict Shiite Islamic tradition in which martyrdom is seen as a direct path to God.

It's influence, but is it legal? Religious cults in general, and the Moonies in particular, recently returned to the news in a dramatic way in 1988—as the objects of a California Supreme Court decision concerning the lawsuit of former Moonies David Molko and Tracy Leal. These individuals were separately recruited and indoctrinated in basically the classic fashion we have outlined here. They spent months as willing and involved recruits at a Moonie farm in northern California, and eventually became formal Church members. Both traveled to different camps and villages for specialized lectures and training. Both returned to urban areas to raise money for the Church by selling flowers on the streets.

Molko, a 27-year-old recent law school graduate, spent 6 months with the Moonies, gave 6,000 dollars of his own money to Church leaders, and took a law bar-review course and the law bar examination with the sponsorship and financial support of the Church. Leal, a 19-year-old college student, spent 4 months as a Moonie. While on Church assignments, Molko and Leal were abducted by deprogrammers hired by their parents. Both were persuaded through the deprogramming experience to give up their membership. In turn, they decided to sue the Unification Church for using fraud and brainwashing to get them to join the church, for inflicting emotional distress, and for falsely imprisoning them.

The trial court threw out these lawsuits on the grounds that they were unconstitutional. The First Amendment forbids interference with the free expression of religious preferences and ideas. And the Unification Church, as a bona fide religion, was expressing its religious ideas and, like other religions, seeking converts. A court of appeals agreed with this judgment. In October 1988, however, the California Supreme Court reversed this decision. It ruled that Molko and Leal have a right to sue for fraud and infliction of emotional distress, but not for false imprisonment. It acknowledged that the Church may have rendered Molko and Leal "incapable of deciding not to join the Church, by subjecting them, without their knowledge or consent, to an intense program of coercive persuasion or mind control" (*Molko/Leal v. Holy Spirit Association*, 1988; *San Francisco Chronicle*, 10/18/88).

This ruling has vast ramifications. What constitutes "coercion"? What is "mind control"? And it raises basic questions for psychologists as well as for all citizens of a democracy: When are our choices guided by our free will, and when are they determined by overwhelming situational forces? Think about this case for a moment. It is true that, during both Molko's and Leal's recruitment, their Moonie hosts practiced their heavenly deception and failed to reveal their identity as members of the Unification Church, despite queries from the recruits. But both were told after several days with whom they were hanging out. And both then stayed on for months, and openly admitted in court that they had been informed they were free to leave if they wished. There is no evidence, or claim, that physical force was ever applied to either former member. Both Molko and Leal recount how, early on, *they* struggled with decisions of whether or not to stay, and then decided themselves to stay longer. They recount the *social* pressure they faced and, in doing so, acknowledge that they were aware of the pressure at the time. Since they saw it coming, were they not free to resist it? Paradoxically, in the end, they had to be forcibly separated from the "captors."

Statistics can be revealing, sometimes. You will recall that 10 percent or fewer Moonie recruits stay on as members for any length of time. Further studies show that a sizable number of recruits who make up this 10 percent were leaning toward Moonie-like ideas and lifestyles to begin with (Barker, 1984). It is hard to conclude from this that Molko and Leal faced some magically overwhelming coercion unique to their indoctrination experience that made virtually anyone vulnerable to its power. Many traditional churches sided with the Unification Church on this issue, fearing an erosion of religious freedom. Some "friends of the court" filed legal briefs contending that there is no such thing as "coercive persuasion" unless the target person is physically confined or in a life-threatening setting.

Although we will not take sides at this point on the coercion issue, we can say with certainty that the Unification Church does use a number of interpersonal influence techniques, in coordinated fashion, to gain conversions. These techniques are known to be effective, especially when carefully programmed into coordinated scripts that can induce extreme changes in some people some of the time. But the Moonie tactics are not "exotic" or peculiar to this group; they are used in thousands of influence settings that few would consider coercive or even a little bit "mind controlling." From high-pressure sales to concerted efforts to get people not to drive after drinking, to say no to drugs, and to have safe sex, *effective* social influence tactics are deliberately and liberally applied every day to virtually every one of us.

The real issues concern (1) the point at which "typical and usual" psychological pressure becomes extraordinary and unfair, or too forceful for the average person to resist, and (2) whether an individual can be said to have lost his or her freedom to resist or to flee in a situation in which physical restraint is totally absent. But then again, isn't it the subjective interpretation of the situation, how someone construes it, that guides behavior, making a "hell of heaven or a heaven of hell"? As you read about social influence processes, these issues will be well worth pondering. For now, the Molko/Leal ruling highlights the potential power and complexities of social influence, which we will attempt to explain and unravel in this book.

Communication and Persuasion: "Say It Again, Sam"

It takes less "person power" to influence many with a powerful speech than to influence people one by one. Interpersonal influence is not very efficient because it is so labor intensive. But effectively influencing large numbers of people with the careful use of words, through what is often called *rhetoric*, is a skill that few master. Those who do can be world movers in positive or, unfortunately, negative ways. Let us look at a few masters of persuasion, including a pair the world admires and a pair it has come to despise.

The words shall make us free: Martin Luther King, Jr. His speeches still ring in the ears of millions. "I've been to the mountaintop...and seen the promised land." "We shall overcome." "I

A communicator who made deep connections with multiple audiences: the Reverend Martin Luther King, Jr., delivers his famous "I have a dream" speech in 1963. (*UPI/Bettmann Newsphotos*)

have a dream." "Free at last, free at last, thank God Almighty, I'm free at last." It is an understatement to say that Dr. Martin Luther King, Jr., was a great orator. Dr. King was the essential leader of the civil rights movement of the 1950s and 1960s. His leadership and contributions took many forms. He wrote books, led marches, organized peaceful protests and boycotts, suffered at the hands of bigots, and went to jail for his beliefs. But it was his rhetorical skill, his ability to strike a deep emotional chord in large audiences of people both black and white, poor and middle class—to *move people to action* by the power of his words alone—that did more than anything else to create a social revolution in American race relations. His speeches convinced masses of people to engage in nonviolence or civil disobedience, to face guns, dogs, and nightsticks without weapons. Like Gandhi, the architect of nonviolent resistance against the British in India, King proved that the word was indeed mightier than the sword.

What was it about Martin Luther King's speech-making skills that made him so uniquely effective as a communicator? He was, of course, a fluid and dynamic speaker, a trained and practiced preacher who made the roller-coaster cadence and emotional appeals of the church pulpit work at the convention center podium as well. King was adept at sending the right nonverbal "vibes" to his audience. His facial expressions and ringing tones of voice—of anger, compassion, joy—closely matched the words he was saying. Watching or listening to him, you never got a feeling of insincerity or disinterest. Quite the contrary, here was a man totally dedicated to an ideal, impassioned with a vision of how society could change for the better. King also seemed to read his audience well. The well-timed pause to let something sink into a suddenly awestruck crowd, the rising climactic tone of voice carrying the crowd to a rising crescendo of vocal approval—these were trademarks of his oratory. Like other great orators, he kept his message simple and direct, and repeated key phrases that the audience could soon anticipate and join in the refrain. The importance of nonverbal signals (voice tone, facial expressions, and the like) will receive careful scrutiny later in the book.

The content of King's speeches was also crucial to the powerful and lasting influence of his speeches. The man was a shrewd and gifted speaker. King knew that his live audiences pretty much already agreed with his positions and shared his goals. He put this to use by using "we" and "our" when expressing *his* hopes and beliefs, and by using key phrases, in-group allusions that made these people feel that they were privileged members of an important movement—insiders on the threshold of a dream. This helped turn mere agreement into willing action. It also brought out the cheers, which became infectious and probably moved many a fence sitter to openly vocal approval; it gave him the "home court advantage."

Out there in TV and radio land, there was a much larger audience, not as unanimously or as fervently tuned in to King's cause—the silent masses. King's real brilliance as a persuader may well be how he brought the masses to sympathy and support for civil rights for African Americans. In his speeches and sermons, King *emphasized what they had in common with him and the movement:* their Christianity and their citizenship in the United States—a nation synonymous with belief in personal freedom. King continually reminded his audiences that freedom and liberty are Judeo-Christian and American ideals, that the push for racial equality is no less noble and righteous a pursuit than the admired struggles of the Israelites, the early Christians, and the Pilgrims. His speeches are laced with biblical passages, as well as paraphrases of memorable statements by famous black preachers and popular political figures like John F. Kennedy. These familiar, often borrowed, themes resonated with large segments of the population. It was an exquisite use of the rhetorical strategy of associating one's new ideas with other, positively valued, familiar ones (Bettinghaus, 1980). In short, King employed audience-approved language to make his message appear consistent with religious, cultural, and patriotic values (K. D. Miller, 1986). Two major determinants of successful persuasion, so well practiced by

King, are (1) establishing perceived similarity of the speaker to the audience and (2) creating positive associations in people's minds. We will discuss these features later in more detail.

Getting one's message understood in the first place is even more fundamental. And King was adept at ensuring message comprehension. Rhetoricians have observed that, although he himself was highly educated and articulate, King's rhetoric usually blended everyday language and what is called a "biblical vernacular" (Marbury, 1989). He spoke in common terms and deftly mixed in the biblical quotes and themes that would communicate clearly to his large religious following. He made his points easy to follow, repeated them, and encouraged the audience—his following—to serve as the chorus, restating and endorsing what they were hearing—a technique referred to as "call and response." They heard the message, believed, were changed, and moved to action.

The Great Communicator: Ronald Reagan. Former President Ronald Reagan's speeches were also easy to follow, and this helps account for his fame as "The Great Communicator." Reagan sent the simple message that if we just behave like good old Americans and get back to the basics, everything will be all right. The optimism theme, according

A straightforward message and a look of sincerity helped make former President Reagan the "Great Communicator." (*UPI/Bettmann Newsphotos*)

to a number of recent psychological studies, plays well with people (Zullow et al., 1988). But it was the way Reagan delivered this message that really made him and his policies so popular. His face beams sincerity and a slightly befuddled look that seems to say, "I don't know why people make this seem so complicated; anyone with common sense realizes that...." In the 1980s, there were a lot of voters out there who felt that *they* had the common sense and were glad to have a leader on their wavelength (instead of lost in abstract intellectual clouds). The steady, soothing voice of Mr. Reagan didn't hurt either. Also, Reagan had a quality that seems to typify many charismatic communicators (Baron and Byrne, 1981). He was highly sensitive to social trends and changes. In his time, it was the middle-American backlash against big government, liberalism, and the "unpatriotic" sentiment of the Vietnam era. He masterfully weaved a "get back your pride, values, and patriotism" theme into his public addresses. It was low-key and unprofound—but effective.

To all this must be added Reagan's training as a professional actor, which made him especially at ease when talking into the same TV lens that rattled so many of his political opponents, like Jimmy Carter and Walter Mondale. When he looked into the camera, he saw Nancy's smiling face that he could talk to. His political opponents, on the other hand, seemed to be looking into a black hole, like their glove compartment.

And so in Martin Luther King, Jr., and Ronald Reagan we have two highly influential mass communicators. They are strikingly different in the emotional force of their speeches, with King being the fiery preacher, and Reagan the soft-spoken soother. But beneath this difference in delivery style, we see major similarities in the optimism of their messages, their visible sincerity, the sense they exude of identification and similarity with the audience, and the elegant clarity of their message. History shows over and over that, mixed together in the right proportion, these components are powerful people movers.

The rhetoric of ruination: Adolph Hitler. On the down side, the power of persuasion can have a truly devastating influence. Consider Hitler. This little man was not nearly as bright or as physically impressive as Martin Luther King., Jr. And to say the least, his dreams and deeds prove him to have been King's opposite in terms of humanity and goodness. But Adolph Hitler resembled King in one way. He moved audiences—enormous audiences. He was an emotional speaker who used the rise and fall of his voice to maximal effect. He connected with German sentiments of the time—wounded patriotic pride, the resentments and frustrations over the humiliating penalties imposed on the nation after World War I. And like other formidable persuaders, Hitler followed an adage that today seems to be a sacred maxim of political speech making: keep it simple. In Hitler's own words:

Hitler magnified the emotional pitch of his messages by surrounding himself with awesome spectacles. (*UPI/Bettmann Newsphotos*)

The receptive ability of the masses is very limited, their understanding small; on the other hand, they have a great power of forgetting. This being so, all effective propaganda must be confined to a very few points which must be brought out in the form of slogans until the very last man is enabled to comprehend what is meant by any slogan. If this principle is sacrificed by the desire to be many-sided, it will dissipate the effectual working of the propaganda, for the people will be unable to digest or retain the material that is offered them. (Hitler, 1933, p. 77)

To his rhetorical devices, Hitler added his coup de grace, a special element of innovation of his part. This was the grand staging, the surrounding of himself with awesome spectacles. You've seen newsreels as well as re-creations in countless movies about Nazi Germany. The thousands of goose-stepping soldiers, the huge red banners hanging above the majestically raised stage on which this little man stood, the eerie spotlights, the Wagner operatic marches. It all elicited spine-chilling emotions and conveyed a great sense of power and historical significance to the German citizens lost as individuals in those enormous rallies. All that emotion and power became attached to Hitler and his ultimately catastrophic ideas. Qualter (1962) describes the spectacle making in his treatise *Propaganda and Psychological Warfare*.

Uniforms, bands, flags, symbols were all part of the German propaganda machine, designed by Hitler and Goebbels to increase the impact of strong words by evidence of strong deeds. Meetings were not just occasions for people to make speeches, they were carefully planned theatrical productions in which settings, lighting, background music, and the timing of entrances and exits were devised to maximize the emotional fervor of an audience already brought to fever pitch by an hour or more given over to singing and the shouting of slogans. (p. 112)

Interestingly, even today Hitler's speeches in the context of grand spectacle have the power to hold people's attention—even among American students with no knowledge of German! And so beyond the words of powerful communicators is the message of their personal power that gets transmitted to the audience.

Fatal persuasion: Jim Jones. Hitler convinced the nation he led to make brutal war which tore the world asunder and caused death and destruction everywhere his message went. More recently, another charismatic leader, a Christian minister, insignificant to world history compared to Hitler, convinced those in his church to do the unthinkable—to poison their own children, commit suicide, and murder their fellows who refused. The mass suicide claimed 913 lives, including more than 200 children. These mind-boggling numbers are unprecedented in the modern history of suicide.

This modern tragedy occurred not long ago, in November 1978 in a remote commune in Guyana, South America. The commune was called Jonestown, and it had been established in 1974 by a preacher and self-proclaimed prophet named Jim Jones. Seeking seclusion and a supportive socialist government, Jones had moved his People's Temple religious cult there from San Francisco. When a U.S. congressman and an entourage of reporters and cult members' concerned relatives visited Jonestown to check out reports that converts were being abused, Jones, already suffering paranoid delusions and ill from jungle disease and drugs, panicked. He envisioned a forcible invasion of the village and a loss of the near total control he had over the thousand people in his "flock" (Galanter, 1989). We'll never know, but in his warped mind, he may have genuinely feared the cold-blooded murder of those people. After entertaining and satisfactorily countering any concerns of the visiting delegation, Jones was nearly successful in disguising the nightmare he had created for his followers in that remote jungle outpost. But when a small group of Temple members asked to return to the United States with Congressman Ryan, Jones' composure became unglued. He dispatched a hit squad to intercept and murder the congressman and his group as they were about to depart Guyana by plane. While this was happening, Jones called his congregation together and, in a masterful speech, first created fears of what the U.S. military would do to them once the murders were known, and then described the glories of "revolutionary suicide," stepping over to the other side where peace and justice would be found. Finally, he ordered the mass suicide to begin. Once his order was obeyed, Jones either shot himself or had an assistant do so.

Imagine for a moment this unimaginable event: the Reverend Jim Jones cajoling and preaching his final sermon and hundreds of people stepping forward to a tub filled with cyanide-laced Kool-Aid, being handed a cupful, and drinking it, with adults voluntarily forcing their children to drink first. It took time for the line to move, for the nearly thousand people to each get their deadly dose. And in that time, people still waiting watched the violent spasms of death of those who preceded them. They could see the contortions and hear the screams—especially of the children, who resisted the bitter-tasting potion and seemed to realize its consequences. Still, people moved forward to the tub of poison in their turn. According to the few who lived to tell of this nightmare, physical coercion in the form of injections of cyanide by Jones' strongmen was applied to some reluctant members. But the great majority of people willingly took their own lives, without having seen external coercion applied. As the line moved along, church members offered moving testimonials to their great leader, to the man they called "Dad," to their "Father, who cares." And then they died for him. How could this happen?

Because Jones had a vision of his place in history, he tape-recorded hundreds of hours of his talks and meetings. That last hour of Jonestown was taped from beginning to bitter end. The surviving tape is chilling. It becomes clear to listeners that the mass suicide could never have occurred without the persuasive pitch Jim Jones delivered as the disaster unfolded. One hears his constant voice, alternately soothing, congratulating, and "clarifying" as needed. One senses how Jones "played the crowd" to perfection. Jones, of course, already had a large hold on his followers. In the language of influence psychology, Jim Jones was a credible, trusted, and expert source. Disaffected with the mainstream culture to begin with, his followers were easily converted to his philosophy—a blend of socialist and biblical ideals. Isolated from contact with nonindoctrinated outsiders, the Jonestown community, by 1978, had totally accepted the world view of Jim Jones. According to this view, "Dad" was a literal reincarnation of Jesus, Buddha, and Lenin, and should rightfully dictate all aspects of one's life (Galanter, 1989). As with the Moonies, the psychological environment of each People's Temple member was carefully controlled—only here the ideas were more extreme and the isolation, thus the control of the total situation, was greater.

But how do you "sell" mass suicide? Jones first used his credibility. As he announced the plan, he reminded the audience how he had never let them down, how he had given them peace and happiness, how he loved them and had tried to give them "the good life." He encouraged others to speak up, but selectively called upon those whom he could count on to eloquently endorse this sentiment. And sure enough, we hear people taking the microphone and thanking "Dad."

The suicidal speech had what communication theorists call a problem-solution organization (Bettinghaus, 1980). Jones first identified the problem. He told the faithful that the congressman was going to be killed by an angered cult member acting on his own (actually Jones had ordered the assassination). As a result, American soldiers would be sent to invade Jonestown and would "butcher" them all, starting with the children and elders. There was no other solution but to commit a mass suicide to prevent this act of vengeance. This picture of things he then worked to great effect. It now became a matter of protecting weaker members of the group. "Be kind to children, be kind to seniors," Jones exhorts. It was now also a matter of controlling one's destiny, rather than having it controlled from without. "It was said by the greatest of prophets, from time immemorial, no man takes my life from me, I lay my life down." Then later, "...we are not committing suicide—it's a revolutionary act." The ringing applause to each of these assertions indicates that Jones' redefinition of the act was both accepted and inspiring. He created a new, shared view of reality, the reality of madness—but he sold his lethal idea as he might make a public health recommendation to exercise more to improve cardiac functioning.

The problem-solution framework also served to intensify a we-they mentality, which had been ingrained in the thinking of all members of the People's Temple. Jones offered a vivid picture of the suffering the American enemies would inflict, stirring passionate emotional acceptance of the need to prevent it. Rational thought declines in an atmosphere of emotional upheaval, and Jones made sure of the upheaval.

Masterfully, Jones destroyed dissent by first inviting it. When a vocal young woman made reasonable arguments for alternative solutions short of suicide, Jones conveyed an air of support and fair-mindedness. "I like you Christina: I've always liked you," he told her. But he refuted her arguments with platitudes that stirred the crowd and ultimately compelled his most committed followers to come forth and publicly question her faith and allegiance. In the end, she was shouted down—and with her defeat, Jones won and the people lost.

As the universal approval for this prophet's visionary "final solution" began carrying people up to the Kool-Aid crucible, Jones began to express displeasure with those who still hesitated. He alternated between a soothing tone ("Go with your child—I think it's humane...it is painless") and the impatient tone of a disappointed parent ("Lay down your life with dignity...stop these hysterics").

In the final analysis, Jim Jones's charismatic speech played a major role in talking nearly a thousand ordinary American citizens into making the ultimate sacrifice. He won credibility with his impressive rhetoric, and used that credibility and rhetoric to influence his followers out of their lives. History gives us few more powerful instances of mass compliance to a communicator. It is vital that we all learn the basic lessons of Jonestown—under the heading of the power of social influence—to prevent a recurrence of such human tragedy. That is one of our goals in writing this book for you.

It is hard to find a better, or worse, example of influence by persuasive communication that was literally a matter of life and death. But as we move to our third and final class of influence settings, the mass media, we will discover that life and death, at least in the long term, may hinge on our reactions to socially sanctioned influence attempts we encounter every day.

Mass Media Influence: Where There's Smoke, There's Fire (and Advertising)

Imagine this. You're at a meeting of managers in a pleasant seminar room of the government office building where you work. There are ten other people present, and six of them have smoked at least one cigarette since the meeting began half an hour ago. At the moment, four people are puffing away, almost in unison. To you, a nonsmoker, it's getting to be a bit much. Normally, cigarette smoke doesn't bother you very much. There are always smokers around, and you usually don't even notice the odor. But this room is small, and the air circulation is poor. Yes, you are uncomfortable with the growing smell and throat irritation. The idea of asking these chimneys not to smoke, however, doesn't even enter your mind. You're in the minority. You're a deviant. And who wants to start a hassle, anyway?

This seems like a strange scenario. Indeed, today it is hard for college students to imagine a time when a majority of adults smoked and when nonsmokers were obliged to keep their mouths (and nostrils!) shut or else risk social rejection. Yet the vignette of the smoke-filled room would be an accurate description of most managerial meetings until quite recently. Smoking was the "in" thing to do; it was fashionable, sexy, and mature. If you don't believe us, rent videos of some old movies—favorites like *Casablanca*, for instance—and count the smoking scenes.

To be sure, since Christopher Columbus brought tobacco leaves from the New World back to Spain, there have been those who vocally opposed the habit. In 1604, King James I of England launched an antismoking campaign. More than two centuries later, cigar smoking flourished in England, over the outspoken criticism of Queen Victoria. From the gay 1890s to the roaring 1920s, antismoking organizations campaigned vigorously for bans on those nasty and unhealthful cigarettes—first mass-produced in the 1860s. Cigarette smoking, these organizations claimed, was bad for your health. Several states outlawed it, and debates over smoking were common in major newspapers and magazines.

But the early antismoking movements never really caught on with the public. In fact, they were roundly defeated in the realm of public opinion. From the 1930s through the early 1960s smoking, particularly cigarette smoking, enjoyed unprecedented popularity in the Western world. Smoking was part of the good life, or so we were told and shown in every segment of the mass media.

From desirable to deviant: smoking loses its cool. It all began to change after the Surgeon General's Report linking smoking and lung cancer appeared in 1964. In the 1950s, about half of all Americans over the age of 18 smoked. A majority of men smoked. By the late 1960s, the overall figure had declined to 42 percent; by the late 1970s, to 35 percent; and by 1985, to 31 percent (Shopland and Brown, 1987). In adult company, nowadays, smoking typically is socially frowned upon. It is prohibited in most indoor public places and on domestic airline flights. And lighting up can bring stares of outrage and even dirty words from zealous advocates of the right to breath fresh air. In two decades, the change has been dramatic. Smokers are now the deviant minority.

This dramatic change illustrates the power of the social influence that can be delivered through the impersonal but ever-present mass media. Unlike earlier antismoking campaigns, the one that began in the 1960s was waged over the television and radio airwaves, as well as in magazine and newspaper ads and public service announcements. Americans repeatedly watched and listened to well-produced messages warning of the health hazards of cigarettes. Moreover, the campaign had the official and highly visible backing of the federal government and the medical profession—highly credible sources to many people. Whereas medical opinion was sharply divided during earlier eras, this time there was total consensus (Troyer and Markle, 1983). The evidence of health risks had simply become too strong to debate.

Against this backdrop of support and legitimacy, the mass media blitz of antismoking messages had a large influence. The hows and whys of media message influences on the human mind will be investigated in depth in Chapters 4, 5, and 9. You can intuit, however, that repeated messages that have the "right stuff" (to be defined later) can shape our images, fears, and attractions. The constant arousal of fear of lung cancer and heart disease proved a strong motivator to quit smoking or not to start. It also eventually made it possible for antismoking groups to attach a label of "deviant" to smokers and make the label stick (Troyer and Markle, 1983). While the American Cancer Society and the American Lung Association tell us "Smoking is bad for you, so *don't do it*," organizations like the Group Against Smoker's Pollution (GASP) have sent the message about the dangers of passive exposure to cigarette smokers: "Smoking is bad for people around smokers, so *don't let them do it.*" If you remember the 1980s, you know that this latter message was heard, believed, and responsible for a significant curtailing of smokers' rights and a tarnishing of their image.

So why are many people still smoking? The decline of smoking, and the role of the mass media in that decline, has been impressive. About 1.5 million Americans quit smoking each year. There may be, however, an even more impressive display of media social influence power in the smoking issue: despite the general decline, cigarette smoking has survived—and the stock market value of cigarette companies has flourished. About 1.25 million Americans *start* smoking each year, newcomers and also old-timers who lost their battle to abstain.

Let us put some things into perspective. With everything in their favor, you would think that the antismoking movement by now would be an irresistible force that has all but eradicated cigarette smoking from our land. It's not as if the movement has its facts wrong. Cigarettes kill, maim, and immobilize. In 1984, the U.S. Public Health Service estimated that cigarette smoking causes 350,000 premature deaths per year in the United States; in 1990, that estimate rose to 390,000 annual deaths caused by smoking, according to the Secretary of Health and Human Services, Louis Sullivan. Other estimates go as high as 485,000 (Ravenholt, 1985). Smoking is the number one cause of preventable deaths in our nation and the only major risk factor that is actively promoted. The amount of cigarette smoking in the United States is the highest in the world, with an average of 3,500 cigarettes smoked each year per adult American. Those who smoke a pack a day spend about 7,000 dollars in 10 years to support that lethal habit. Smoking-related diseases account for over fifty billion dollars in health care and insurance costs, and over forty billion dollars in lost productivity (Davis, 1987; Sullivan report to Congress, 1990). After years of mounting evidence of the dangers of smoking, you would think smoking would now be nearly a thing of the past.

Think again! Tens of millions of Americans continue to smoke, as do people worldwide. About 31 percent of the American population smokes, even though more than 90 percent are aware of the serious health risks (Shopland and Brown, 1987). Of course, you say. It's tough to kick the physical and psychological addiction. Aren't most current smokers longtime users who cannot quit? If only that were true. As it is, thousands *join* the ranks of smokers each day. Many are teenagers being recruited into the army of smokers. One out of every five teens takes up smoking on a daily basis. In the 1980s, there was *no* change in this figure. What has changed is that more and more of the teenagers who do smoke are *female.* For the first time in history, more female than male adolescents smoke (Davis, 1987). Smoking is *increasing* among female adolescents and is holding steady among females in general, even as it declines among men. Soon, in the overall adolescent *and* adult population, female smokers will outnumber male smokers.

This persistence of a deadly habit may be the true mass media influence miracle of our time—a deadly miracle created by a rich and powerful tobacco industry that is able to bankroll the most skillful and creative advertising and marketing programs money can buy. In 1984, cigarette manufacturers spent *2.1 billion dollars* on advertising and promotion—seven times as much as they spent just 10 years earlier (Davis, 1987). By 1989, that figure had expanded to *3 billion dollars* a year, double the amount spent on the next leading advertised products: pharmaceuticals and alcohol (Blum, 1989). We're talking *big* money here, spent by smart people who know how to create *images* that transform reality and guide Americans into suicidal actions—as surely as Jim Jones did on a much more modest scale.

Images of health, fitness, and freedom. Cigarette advertisers began to counter the health warnings by pushing low tar and nicotine cigarettes. Word play ("doublespeak"), as we will see many times in this book, is part and parcel of many social influence strategies. "Less hazardous to health" can very easily be reworded in such a way as to imply (if not say outright) that it is "more healthful" or at least "safe" to smoke this "light" cigarette. A famous ad for Vantage cigarettes had a healthy and handsome man saying that "I hear the things being said against high-tar smoking...and so I started looking for a low-tar smoke." Apparently, nothing can be said against low-tar smokes. That is not so, of course, for they too cause cancer.

Recently, the "low tar and nicotine" pitch has softened (Altman et al., 1987). The ads simply encourage associations between any old brand and the new American values of leading active, healthful lifestyles. Newports are "Alive with pleasure." Judging by the ads, cigarettes go hand in hand with many desirable recreational pursuits. See those people at the ballpark just above the caption "Winston's Winning Taste." Marlboro Menthol has "Spirited Refreshment" for horseback riders. Skiers can discover Alpine's "Peak Refreshment." How can all these healthy looking folks doing such active things be risking their health by smoking?

Women receive special pitches from the cigarette sellers—and their own brands. "You've come a long way baby" was the slogan with which Virginia Slims was introduced. It was a way of linking smoking with the women's movement—with independence from men and the rules designed by men. It was a successful campaign—designed by men, of course. A flood of women's cigarettes followed Virginia Slims: Eve, Silva Thins, Salem Slim Lights, Satin, Ritz—and now, Superslims.

Lethal images: Cigarette advertisers attempt to link smoking with fun, sports, music, sex, romance, glamour, and freedom for "people who like to smoke." *(Both: Annie Hunter/The Image Works)*

They are all distinctive in some way: thinner, stain filter tips, designer logos. The images are clear. Smoking makes you look slim, trim, chic, and fashionable.

Sexiness, of course, is another provocative theme that sells. Scenes that include scantily clad women and romantic backdrops were the second most common, behind recreational ones, in cigarette ads in the 1970s and 1980s (Altman et al., 1987).

Promotions and market savvy. Efforts to encourage smoking go beyond the creation of image-projecting ads. Advertisers are very careful *where* they put their ads. Magazines that youth read (such as *Rolling Stone*) get the recreation-vitality ads. Magazines that adult women read (like *Cosmopolitan*) have the romantic and "be slim and trim and independent" ads. Billboard advertising of cigarettes mostly occurs in blue-collar and ethnic neighborhoods, whose residents smoke in greater numbers. It all seems so calculated. And it is—to make lots of money.

Since the 1960s, there has been a huge increase in the sponsorship of major sporting and cultural events by tobacco companies. The Virginia Slims Women's Professional Tennis Tour was the first to co-opt the concern of raising the prizes and publicity for women's sports by identifying this cigarette with that goal. Why, you might ask, is there a Kool Achiever Award given annually to people involved in inner-city community development? And what about sponsoring of Hispanic street fairs, outdoor jazz festivals, and other worthwhile events that are plastered with the sponsoring company's cigarette logo. Don't we owe it to them to smoke a little if they have given so much to our community? Sponsorship of such events gets brand and corporate names well-exposed in a positive light, much like the Mafia bosses who give big donations to little churches.

With a little help from reporters and celebrities. Cigarette companies get help in their image making from other mass media transmissions. Have you ever noticed all the smoking that goes on in music videos? What does it project to the millions of idolizing teenagers when Madonna and her two sidekicks give out an award on the MTV Music Video Awards show, all the while blatantly smoking? How about Mikhail Baryshnikov incessantly smoking (and dancing) his way through the movie *White Nights?* How much help is it when reporters and commentators speculate about drugs and AIDS as contributors to celebrity deaths, and yet few mentioned baseball commissioner Bart Giamatti's "three pack a day" habit when he died of a massive heart attack at age 51? Even as antismoking messages continue to be transmitted, other mass media messages make it clear to many that smoking has some desirable benefits, that many important people do it, and that compared to the *real* problems of society (drugs, unsafe sex, and the like) cigarette smoking is a small vice. An obvious reason for the collusion of the mass media and the tobacco industry is the enormous amount of money involved in print ads in magazines and newspapers, as well as the political lobbies in Congress that make it clear how much the federal, state, and local governments make from cigarette taxes. They need that revenue and are prepared to resist attempts to get people to stop smoking.

The media sets the stage. We have used the smoking issue to illustrate social influence via the mass media, supporting the notion that people's behavior and thinking can be influenced by information transmitted very impersonally. Of course, there are other influences on smoking, including peer pressure to smoke (especially among adolescents), the addictive quality of nicotine once smoking is done regularly, and the physical enjoyment smoking provides by associating it with desirable activities. But note that the favorable smoking images created on Madison Avenue and in Hollywood have much to do with making smokers who, in turn, become the pressuring peers or self-professed addicts.

The tobacco industry fumes back some more. The Tobacco Institute continues to create ways to keep its business flourishing. Instead of "low tar and nicotine" (ugly words), it's now "low smoke." A recent full-page newspaper ad from Superslims Virginia Slims proclaims: *"The skinny on low smoke.* Kiss that fat smoke goodbye, and say hello to the first low smoke cigarette for women..." (*San Francisco Chronicle,* 2/20/90). They also have embarked on a campaign to discredit the opposition by labeling them as a "coalition of antismoking zealots," as neo-prohibitionists who want to control the lives of freedom-loving Americans. The tobacco industry has recast the issue not in terms of health risks but as a constitutional crisis: smoking is a symbol of free choice that Americans value above all else, and the antismoking agents are trying to deprive smokers of that basic right (Blum, 1989). For a summary of the multilevels on which the new ads for cigarettes operate, see Table 1.1.

The target of these ads has also changed, away from white middle-class males—who have defected in the largest numbers—to women, to adolescents, to homosexuals, to blue-collar workers, and to black and Hispanic consumers. Let's briefly examine a recent campaign targeted at "virile females" before ending this section with a look at what some critics are calling the "genocide of smoking."

An advertising agency recently designed a detailed marketing strategy for RJ Reynolds Tobacco company that "targets young, poorly educated white women whom the company calls 'virile females,'" according to a story in *The Washington Post* (2/17/90). The competition has become intense for the allegiance of the "lucrative market" of 18- to 24-year-old women because their smoking rate is escalating while that of

TABLE 1.1 FUNCTIONS OF CIGARETTE ADVERTISEMENTS

1. Recruits new smokers from "vulnerable groups"
2. Sustains smoking loyalty of committed smokers (resists pressures from antismokers to quit)
3. Tempts former smokers to restart habit
4. Entices smokers to switch to new brands, with new features (only about 10 percent do per year)
5. Creates an illusion of social acceptability of smoking and smokers through association with positive values and the "good life"
6. Fosters complacency of nonsmokers regarding health dangers and societal threats by viewing so many positive images of smokers
7. Buys immunity from critical attack from legislators, journalists, and business interests

SOURCE: Based on data from Alan Blum, 1989.

most other groups is declining. The new Dakota cigarette marketing is aimed at the virile female with no education beyond high school, who wants to get married early, works but has no career, goes cruising and partying, attends hot rod shows and tractor pulls with boyfriends, and likes all-male rock groups. At press time, a possibility under consideration was to form the company's own rock group, aptly named, of course, Dakota.

The genocide of smoking. Systematic attempts to increase smoking rates among American black and Hispanic consumers have been termed "genocide" in a 1981 pamphlet of the American Cancer Society and by critics who cite the insidious attack on the health of minority communities by the tobacco industry (Blum, 1989). Let's look at the statistics of what smoking is doing to the black community, review briefly the various ways that smoking is supported and resistance is stifled by the tobacco industry, and end with an example of an ad campaign targeted for inner-city black consumers for a new product: Uptown cigarettes.

The cancer death rates for black Americans are increasing much faster than those for white Americans, by as much as 20 to 100 times more, according to cancer mortality statistics published by the National Cancer Institute in 1990. Over the past 30 years the cancer death rate for black males has jumped from 189 per 100,000 a year to 250 per 100,000, while for white males the increase is slight, from 174 to 188 per 100,000 white men. The 44 percent higher cancer death rate for black males is matched by a 14 percent higher rate for black women compared with white women. These and other racial differences in cancer-related statistics are explainable by lifestyle factors as well as diet and alcohol use, but differences in increased rates of smoking contribute directly to putting black consumers at risk from cancers of the lung, throat, mouth, and larynx. And so why do they smoke, and why are they smoking more than ever and dying at these alarming rates?

One set of answers has to do with the power of the media campaigns to make smoking attractive to black consumers, by ads designed to appeal to what ad agencies have determined are their basic values. Added to this form of social influence is the secondary factor of the revenues that these ads bring to the black community in various forms. Magazines that cater to black readers—such as *Ebony, Jet,* and *Essence*—carry a large number of color ads for cigarettes. Billboards and posters on public transportation, gas stations, laundromats, movies, and other sites are another source of revenue for many people in the community. It is estimated that 80 to 90 percent of all advertising in minority neighborhoods is for cigarettes. As noted earlier, donations of prizes and the underwriting of community events has been one strategy used by tobacco companies to co-opt potential sources of opposition. And so it is no wonder that the president of a black ad agency worries that "if they kill off cigarette and alcohol advertising, black papers may as well stop printing," while the publisher of a black consumer-marketing publication moans that "everybody will lose big" (*Newsweek,* 2/5/90, p. 46).

The effects of being dependent on these enormous revenues show up in the failure of most publications that reach black audiences to ever report on the smoking-cancer link and to fail to cover public conferences that address the issue of cancer among minorities. This failure to inform their audience results in a lack of recognition of the parasitic nature of smoking, as seen in the results of a 1986 survey of 1,000 Chicago residents which found that 89 percent of the black respondents and 86 percent of the Hispanic respondents did *not* identify cigarette smoking among nine listed cancer-risk factors (Dolecek et al., 1986).

As with the "Dakota" campaign and women, tobacco companies have used "market segmentation" strategies to identify groups of black people who can be reached with specialized advertising and sales campaigns pitched to their needs, values, and self-images. A promotional blitz was recently designed for urban black citizens in Philadelphia to sell a new cigarette, Uptown, with slick ads suggesting glamour, high fashion, and night life. "Uptown. The place. The taste."

Vocal community and national opposition to this targeting strategy forced RJ Reynolds to retreat reluctantly. The community won that battle, but the odds makers are out on who will win the war on cigarette smoking. But, given the tax money and profits involved, don't bet against the tobacco interests. It may be extreme to refer to this influence situation as "genocide," but minority people are being targeted to engage in behavior now known to kill them in large numbers, and the targeting is likely to continue, and the debate likely to rage on, in the United States and throughout the world.

Pitching cigarettes with ads designed especially for urban minorities identified with market segmentation methods. (*Annie Hunter/The Image Works*)

The smoking issue is a persuasion battleground between anti and pro forces (Troyer and Markle, 1983). It illustrates how social influence tactics and processes at a national level affect us all, whether or not we as individuals smoke. We all pay for the health care of those who do smoke and get ill and die from it. We pay through insurance costs, the drain on medical and research resources, and the grief of personal loss. On the other side of the coin, questions of personal freedoms and precedent-setting restrictions on our freedoms hang in the balance of the controversy. If smoking should be restricted, what else might be? Thus, the smoking example, as well as the earlier examples of persuasion and conversion, illustrates that social influence, although studied by academics, is far more than an academic topic. It is part of the fabric of our lives—and in some cases of our deaths.

A BCs OF INFLUENCE: ATTITUDES, BEHAVIOR, AND COGNITIONS

Ultimately, the goal of an influence agent is to change the target's behavior. Cult recruiters want the targets of their recruitment efforts to live, work, and pray in the sect's isolated community. They want recruits to give their money and time to the religious cause. Dr. King sought to move black and white people to nonviolent demonstration and to vote, and he sought to move people in general to more tolerant treatment of members of other races. With the billions they spend on advertising and marketing, cigarette makers seek to get people to start or to keep smoking their brands. Behavioral change is the ideal name of the influence game.

But has an influence attempt totally failed if the target's *behavior* does not change? Not by a long shot. The influence effort may have succeeded in changing the target's *beliefs* or *attitudes*. Consider a Unification Church recruit who goes for a weekend visit to one of the Church's rural retreats. He doesn't stay past Monday and doesn't join the movement. Yet, after listening to the members' descriptions of how they live and what they hope to accomplish, and observing the day-to-day activities of the communal village, let us say that he is compelled to abandon his image of the Moonies as fanatical, dangerous, and un-American. His new belief is that the movement offers a legitimate alternative lifestyle that may be what some people need. Imagine further that he actually came away with a favorable impression of that lifestyle and a measure of liking for the members he met.

These last changes would indicate that our "near recruit" has acquired a more positive attitude toward the Unification Church. In essence, an *attitude* is an *evaluative disposition toward some object.* It's an evaluation of something or someone along a continuum of like-to-dislike or favorable-to-unfavorable. Attitudes are what we like and dislike, our affinities and aversions, the way we evaluate our relationship to our environment. An attitude is a disposition in the sense that it is a learned tendency to think about some object, person, or issue in a particular way.

What does attitude or belief change buy the influence agent? Potentially a lot, because these internal changes often set the stage for later behavior changes. The newly positive attitude about the Moonies may make the person that much more receptive to future pro-Moonie messages, or more likely to consider joining when frustrations mount in his life in the "mainstream," or more likely to talk in favor of the group in ways that encourage others to join.

An even better example may be those relentless cigarette ads. Any given ad—or even a hundred of them—may not cause a 15-year-old girl to take up smoking. But the repeated association of cigarette smoking with fun and glamour and sexy, exciting people like Madonna may create a positive attitude toward smoking (perhaps not of how it tastes, but of how it *looks* to smoke). Plus, the healthy looking people in those ads, and the advertising emphasis on modern "low smoke" cigarettes, may nurture the belief that smoking isn't *that* unhealthy. Now imagine this girl facing tenth-grade-style peer pressure to try smoking. Is she just as likely to resist the pressure now that she has these media-induced attitudes and beliefs than she would if she never acquired them? It's doubt-ful. And so a change in beliefs or attitudes may not have a direct effect on changing behavior, but may "set up" the person to be more vulner-able to subsequent sources of social influence.

Attitude Systems

These examples illustrate five categories of our reactions to social ob-jects. There is *behavior* itself: we vote, buy a product, sign a petition, donate blood. Secondly, there are *behavioral intentions*, expectations, or plans to act in specific ways prior to doing so; like New Year's resolu-tions, these plans are sometimes never acted upon. Then there are the ideas that inform our actions, our beliefs, or (more broadly) our *cogni-tions*, which include both beliefs and pieces of knowledge about the ob-ject and how one "should" behave toward it. Fourth, there are *affective responses*, emotions, or "gut feelings" that reflect one's attitude at the level of physical arousal (sensations of pleasure, sadness, and so on). And, finally, there is the *attitude* itself, the overall, summary evaluation that includes the other components. In this light, we can define an at-titude more broadly as an evaluative disposition that is based upon cog-nitions, affective reactions, behavioral intentions, and past behaviors, and that, as we will see, can itself influence cognitions, affective re-sponses, and future intentions and behavior (Zanna and Rempel, 1988).

This definition implies that the components are not independent or isolated in different corners of the mind. To the contrary, they can be highly interrelated. Cognitions and attitude cohere into what we might call a *mental representation* of the object. Affective responses and overt behavior may result when the object comes to mind, and they may con-tribute new information back to the representation of the object. Hence, the attitude, behaviors, cognitions, and emotions regarding an object or issue constitute a system of responses that characterize the individual. Because the attitude is the overall summary of the system ("I like it"), let's call it an *attitude system*. An example of an attitude system appears in Figure 1.1.

A closer look at mental representations is in order. Let's take some-thing concrete, for example, cameras. You can conjure up an image of the typical camera. Pondering it, you draw up pieces of knowledge (how cameras work, how much they cost) and various beliefs (using good cameras requires complex understanding of light and shadows) about cameras. The image also includes your camera-using inclinations and behavioral experience with cameras (you bring cameras on vaca-tions and have one ready on Christmas morning). Undoubtedly, as you think about cameras, you will realize that you have at least a mild atti-

An Attitude System

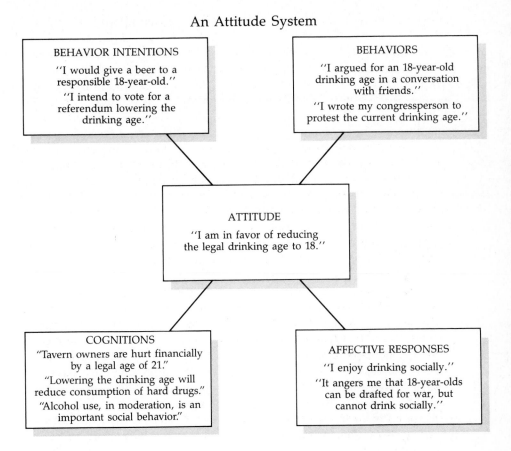

FIGURE 1.1

tude about cameras (you probably like them at least a little; after all, they do capture the moment for posterity).

All together, you have quite a complex mental representation of cameras—an organized set of interrelated thoughts and feelings. Actually, we have mental representations of most objects of our experience, including social issues (abortion, taxes), social groups (Moonies, liberals), and ideals (democracy, free speech). Along with a pro or con attitude about abortion, for example, a person may also have factual knowledge (fetuses aborted in the first trimester have no recognizable human form), various beliefs (life begins at conception), emotional or affective responses (sadness when thinking of a friend who had an abortion), and behavioral inclinations (to vote for pro-life or pro-choice candidates).

An Organizing Theme: Change Begets Change

The interconnectedness of attitudes, cognitions, feelings, intentions, and behaviors into organized systems has a very important implication. It means that change in any one component may lead to change in another. A change in belief may cause revision of the attitude. A new attitude, as already suggested by our earlier examples, may ultimately lead to new behaviors (or as we see in later chapters, a reverse process is possible in which behavior change may cause attitude change). Finally, new attitudes may influence how we think about social objects; and hence, attitude change may cause belief change.

Attitude systems, it should be noted, are not always tightly organized. Some of our attitudes may be based mainly on our feelings and make little contact with beliefs or ideas we hold unless we take pains to think carefully about our attitude (Millar and Tesser, 1986; Wilson et al., 1989). Still, the usual state of affairs is at least some interconnectedness, some "coupling" of attitudinal components.

The usual interconnectedness actually extends further. Attitudes and beliefs about one object may be connected to attitudes and beliefs about another object. For example, one's negative attitude toward free trade with Japan and positive attitude toward giving large companies tax breaks may reflect a common underlying belief that bringing down the domestic unemployment rate is the key to improving the country. If this belief changes, chances are that both attitudes will change as well.

In summary, we have a major theme here, which is a basis for understanding a number of social influence phenomena; specifically, *attitude systems—within and between each other—are organized, such that changes in one facet of a person often cause changes in other facets.*

Further Themes Based On the Central Role of Attitudes

From an influence point of view, attitudes are often the most important component of attitude systems and corresponding mental representations. The tendency to evaluate—to form attitudes—is basic to being human. Indeed, we seem to automatically evaluate just about everything we come across, no matter how brief our encounter or how unimportant the object (Zajonc, 1980). When asked to describe people and objects after a first experience, people almost invariably include some form of good-bad judgment (Osgood et al., 1957). Attitudes, then, are common and pervasive mental reactions. We can have an attitude about something—liking or disliking it—even when the rest of the mental representation is practically devoid of beliefs and actual knowledge. This is true of many of our *prejudices*—the negative attitudes that we may develop about groups of people that we actually know little about.

Attitudes influence perception and thought. In subsequent chapters, we will see that attitudes which initially have little or no basis in knowledge may subsequently affect the acquisition of knowledge and the formation of beliefs that may eventually "fill" the formerly empty mental representation (Pratkanis and Greenwald, 1989). Our overall evaluation of something affects how we interpret what we read and hear about the object. If you have a favorable first impression of a certain new rock artist, for example, you may become especially attentive to subtle aspects of her melodies that fit with your established tastes. If you initially dislike her music, you may hear only what you don't like.

This can be summarized in a second organizing theme (where the first theme stresses mental organization and connectedness). Although it is true that attitudes are shaped by our thinking, the reverse is also true. And so our second basic theme is that *attitudes guide perceptual and cognitive processes.*

Attitudes are easily accessible evaluative summaries. Another important role of attitudes derives from their status as summaries of where we stand on issues. As summary evaluations, they come to mind relatively easily. People don't have the time or mental capacity to think carefully about all of the countless stimuli and situations they encounter. When faced with decisions about social objects, especially decisions that are not earth-shattering, we may not review every belief and fact we have about the object. Rather, we go to the bottom line, conjure up our generalized attitude, and let it guide us.

This role of attitudes as easily accessible summaries brings us to a third theme to be encountered frequently in this book. *Depending on situational and personal circumstances, reactions to influence attempts may range from very thoughtful, analytic, and systematic at one extreme, to superficial, hasty, automatic, and almost "mindless" at the other extreme.* On the "mindless" side, prior attitudes alone may guide reactions. At an even more mindless extreme, we will see behavioral reactions that occur like automatic reflex actions, without even a contemplation of attitude. This often occurs when a prior attitude is weak or nonexistent.

Attitudes are self-defining. Finally, an attitude is a stand about something. ("I dislike this." "I favor that.") As such, our more important attitudes help form our self-definitions (Pratkanis and Greenwald, 1989). That is, they inform the world (and ourselves) what we're all about. Attitudes have "badge value" (Abelson and Prentice, 1989). We are the sum of all our attitudes. As we will learn, self-defining attitudes permeate many behaviors and attitudes on related issues. Moreover, people do not easily give up self-defining attitudes. These facts can have frustrating consequences for would-be influence agents. They also illustrate a final theme: *Since attitudes on important topics may serve and* *sustain one's self-definition and self-esteem, many influence processes involve altering how people perceive themselves—not just the attitude object.* We will see later on that in some instances the goal of social influence goes beyond influencing attitudes and changing behavior; it is no less ambitious than "personality change" or "total mind control," as in some cults and military organizations.

It is for a number of good reasons, then, that attitudes are pivotal attack points in many influence strategies. The ultimately desired goal of influence may be behavioral change, but many paths to this final goal are through the network of attitudes.

A SOCIAL PSYCHOLOGICAL PERSPECTIVE

Although the research material we present in this book is drawn from many fields—including communications, sociology, political science, business management, and consumer behavior—most of it comes from the field of social psychology. In fact, our approach to social influence can be characterized as social-psychological.

What is the social-psychological approach? Basically, it involves four defining characteristics. First, being psychological, the focus is on *individual behavior and mental processes.* Sociologists focus on groups and institutions, and communications researchers tend to concentrate on the structure and content of the communication itself. By contrast, social psychologists are more concerned with what goes on in people's heads and how their thoughts, feelings, and actions are influenced by other people. We have already provided a taste of this focus with our introductory discussion of how attitudes, beliefs, and other mental events form and mutually influence one another.

The second defining feature of the social psychological approach is its emphasis on *situational causes* of behavior. A major principle of social psychology is that what goes on *inside* people (the psychological processes) is primarily determined by factors that are *outside* of them. Particularly important factors are what other people are saying or doing and the features of the immediate situation that, through past learning, trigger specific interpretations and behavior patterns. One of the pioneers of social psychology, Kurt Lewin, long ago presented the simple equation that behavior is a joint function of the person's unique personality and the situation in which he or she is functioning. Social psychologists emphasize the second component—the *power of the situation*—although they still recognize the role that individual dispositions play in the total behavioral scenario. Attitudes, of course, are the favorite dispositional variable of social psychologists. They recognize the important consequences of differences between people in their attitudes. But, primarily, social psychologists are concerned with how attitudes and other dispositions are affected by social situations and with how situations often have such powerful effects on behavior and thought that they override personality differences between people, making different people respond in similar ways to the same situation. Some of our examples earlier in this chapter give graphic illustration to the power of the immediate situation, most notably that of the Jonestown mass suicides.

A third aspect of social psychology is an emphasis on *subjective perception*. How people define social situations is often more important than the objective reality. For example, your positive attitude toward a new acquaintance may depend more on your perception that he has a lot in common with you than on his actual similarity as evaluated by raters. Indeed, should reality prove that he is not so similar, you may wonder why you ever liked him to begin with. The answer is social-psychological: what mattered at the time were personal perceptions, or our social construction of reality.

Fourth, and finally, the social psychological approach is scientific and experimental. Social psychologists, as well as other social scientists, treat human behaviors as natural phenomena. Like other phenomena of the natural world—such as the movement of earthquake faults, chemical reactions in rocket fuel injection, and cell growth in plants—human behavior must be studied under controlled circumstances in order to understand the principles by which it works. "Armchair theorizing" is too subjective, prone to bias (especially when the subject matter is *ourselves!*) and apt to miss causes that are hard to "see." Hence, the social psychological approach is to make controlled observations, that is, observations which are made under strict rules concerning when to observe and how to code behaviors.

The preferred scientific method of social psychology is the *experiment*. The major virtue of an experiment is that it allows for a great deal of *control* over variables. If it is suspected that A causes B, the investigator can design an experiment in which some participants are exposed to A (the experimental group) and others are not (the control group). At the same time, variables C, D, E, and the like, are held equivalent for both groups. If the group exposed to A engages in more B behaviors than the group not exposed to A, logic compels the investigator to conclude that A causes B—at least until better data suggest otherwise.

Practically all of the knowledge and theory about social influence that we will present in this volume is derived from scientific studies. This book's two appendixes review research methods. If you haven't been previously exposed to psychological methodology, or if you think you need a refresher, you may wish to read through the appendixes. Though not absolutely necessary, some familiarity with how social psychological research is done will enrich your understanding and appreciation of the studies we explore.

A LOOK AHEAD

We now have everything in place to begin a journey through the many fascinating paths of social influence in our everyday life. Let us briefly preview this journey. Remember the general idea of an attitude system—that an attitude is the evaluative summary of a personal system of feelings, cognitions, and behaviors regarding an object. Also remember that the system can be entered anywhere, at the level of attitudes, emotions, beliefs, or behaviors. The next four chapters explore three influence pathways through an attitude system. In Chapter 2, we discuss influence forces that are directly aimed at behavior and are capable of changing the influence target's behavior without first enacting any attitude or belief change. You've already heard the labels given to some of these processes, terms such as *obedience, conformity, compliance,* and *conditioning.* In Chapter 3, the interconnected system idea comes prominently into play, for there we will see how direct changes in behavior can trigger a psychological chain reaction of change in attitudes and beliefs. Perhaps you've rationalized things you've *done* with various after-the-fact reasons. That's one part of the "change behavior first to change attitudes" chain. Chapters 4 and 5 are devoted to persuasion—the preferred influence technique of Martin Luther King, Jr., and today's ubiquitous television communications—which tries to change another's attitude by presenting information and arguments aimed at changing beliefs. The general pathway is from beliefs to attitudes (Chapter 4) and, in turn, to behavior (Chapter 5). An additional trick is to make persuasion last (Chapter 5).

We next turn our attention to the theme that some attitudes may be self-defining, to the point where their possessor clings to them in the face of even the most rational appeals—or, paradoxically, is able to be manipulated by influence agents who feign allegiance to the same point of view. More generally, Chapter 6 examines the opposite states of extreme resistance to social influence and extreme susceptibility to it, and how these states can be altered. We take up matters such as the general strategy for getting extremists to moderate their positions, or the specific task of training teenagers to resist the advertising and peer pressure to smoke.

Chapter 7 explores the extent to which influence occurs without the target's awareness of being influenced. Particularly important here are influence techniques and aspects of communication that elicit emotional responses. Conditioning, nonverbal communication (facial expressions and such), and subliminal messages fall into these categories.

By the end of Chapter 7, we will have toured most of the basic theoretical and topical landscape of the world of influence. Along the way, we will have detoured into practical applications and implications at many points. In the final two chapters, the relative emphasis will be reversed. Our sights will be set on practical applications, and we will return to theory as we need to. Chapter 8 is concerned with influence processes in the legal system. The field combining psychology and law is growing rapidly. And no wonder. Social influence is a big part of police interrogation, trial presentation, and jury deliberation, to mention some prominent psychologically loaded legal settings. Chapter 9 focuses on what we might call pro-social influence. You know that psychology can be used to sell products and win votes for politicians. But did you know that it is also being used to influence people to take better care of the environment and of themselves? And further, did you know that influence techniques that work with "normal" people can be adapted for use in psychotherapy to help direct distressed individuals back to better mental health? These applications are explored in Chapter 9.

Finally, we offer a word of caution. Reading this book is designed to change *you!* If you read it wisely and well, you can become more effective in your influence attempts and better able to resist unwanted sources of influence in your life. And so be forewarned that our goal is to change some aspects of your belief system. Whether your behavior also changes accordingly is beyond our control; that's largely a matter between you and the nature of the social contexts in which you will travel after you leave us. Enjoy the journey. We have enjoyed charting the paths we will share in this intellectual adventure.

TO SUM UP...

In this first chapter we defined social influence and presented dramatic influence examples in interpersonal, persuasion, and mass media settings. Then we described how mental and behavioral reactions to a variety of issues, people, and objects can be understood in terms of attitude systems. Finally, our social-psychological approach was outlined along with a preview of the journey to be taken in the upcoming chapters.

- In a social influence process, the behavior of one person has the effect or intention of changing how another person behaves, feels, or thinks about something.
- Social influence is pervasive; advertising, political campaigns, and psychotherapy all involve influence, as do our daily interactions with friends, family, and peer groups. Influence settings can be categorized in terms of how individualized they are and how many people they reach. In *interpersonal settings,* one or a few influence agents have one-to-one communication with one or a few targets of influence. *Persuasion settings* include one influence agent trying to change a larger number of targets. *Mass media settings* involve an impersonal message delivered through a medium such as TV to targets who may number in the millions.

- The recruitment and indoctrination practices of religious cults, like the Moonies, illustrate a powerful version of influence in interpersonal settings. Young people, at transitional life stages, are persuaded to join a cult community by attractive recruiters and become members who spend most of their time recruiting and soliciting funds. In the cult community, a large arsenal of influence techniques—reinforcements, commitment gaining, constant persuasive messages, resource control, and others—encourages some recruits to stay and convert to the dogma of the cult.

- The effective use of words and rhetoric is the essence of persuasion. Although one was fiery and the other low-key, Rev. Martin Luther King, Jr., and Ronald Reagan were very effective communicators who helped bring forth social movements. They both emphasized identification and similarity with their audience, delivered clear and optimistic messages, and communicated sincerity with their vocal and facial expressions. Adolph Hitler and Jim Jones promoted mass destruction and mass suicide by using similar skills of persuasion and by staging powerful emotional scenes to accompany their messages.

- The influence of the mass media is illustrated by the great decrease in cigarette smoking since health messages about the risks of smoking began in the 1960s. Even stronger evidence of mass media impact on "the other side" is the fact that 30 percent of all adult Americans still smoke and that thousands, particularly adolescents and women, take up the habit every day. Advertisers create pervasive images of smoking as healthful, sexy, and a badge of personal freedom, while sponsorship of sporting and cultural events furthers the visibility and attractive associations of smoking. Through sophisticated market segmentation research, promotional blitzes are pitched to the activities and needs of people identified as likely to start or continue to smoke.

- Even if an influence attempt does not immediately affect behavior, it may change beliefs or attitudes, thus "setting the stage" for later changes in behavior. An attitude is an evaluative disposition toward some object that forms the core of one's attitude system regarding the object. There are five components of an attitude system: the attitude, cognitions (beliefs and knowledge), affective responses (feelings), behavioral intentions, and behavior itself.

- Because attitude systems are organized, a change in any one component (e.g., attitude) may cause a change in any other (e.g., behavior). Change in the attitude system about one object (e.g., cigarette smoking) may cause changes in attitude systems about related objects (e.g., advertising companies).

- Attitudes are the most important component of attitude systems. Our attitudes affect our thoughts and perceptions, serve as position summaries that we can access from memory and use with little effort, and sustain our sense of identity.

- The social-psychological approach to influence has four defining features: (1) a focus on individual behavior and mental processes, (2) an emphasis on the power of social situations to cause behavior, (3) an assumption that perception of social situations more strongly affects behavior than does objective reality, and (4) a reliance on scientific methods for generating and evaluating evidence.

QUESTIONS AND EXERCISES

1. Compare and contrast interpersonal, persuasion, and mass media settings using recent occasions in which you feel you were yourself the target of influence in such settings. How were these settings and the corresponding techniques alike? How did they differ?

2. Most of us at one point or another adopt the attitudes, values, and beliefs of a social group (such as a fraternity, sorority, athletic team, or political club). Identify ways in which the influence exerted by these groups resembles and differs from that exerted by cults like the Moonies. What makes cult influence more "coercive" than the influence of the aforementioned groups?

3. List the reasons why public health campaigns were successful in convincing millions of people to quit smoking or not take it up. For each reason, explain how cigarette advertisers have tried to counter it. Why do you think these countermeasures work with some people and not with others?

4. Describe a personal attitude system of your own associated with an issue or object that is important to you. Identify each of the five components, and explain how the attitude component might be self-defining and useful to you.

2

Influencing Behavior:

Taking Direct Approaches

--- ❖ ---

Learning When Actions Pay Off ✦ *Approval and Disapproval: The Power of Social Rewards* ✦ *Conformity: Saving Face and Gaining Grace—and Knowledge* ✦ *Obedience: Basing Behavior on Authority* ✦ *Kneejerk Psychology: Influence through Heuristics* ✦ *Point of Departure: When Inner Changes Flow from External Influence*

What do the following changes in behavior have in common?

- Jason is a young factory worker who enjoys night life and partying; he is also frequently late for work. His company institutes a policy of awarding monthly bonus pay contingent on prompt and perfect attendance. As soon as this happens, Jason punches in early twenty mornings in a row.
- Harvey renamed his economics textbook *Yesdoze,* because it puts him right off to sleep whenever he tries to read it. Yet, he nods in earnest agreement with five classmates who said "yes" when the economics professor asked whether they like the textbook she assigned.
- Hilary does not want to lend Jane any money and told her so when Jane asked to borrow 100 dollars. She knows that Jane takes forever to pay her debts and always needs money because she "loves to shop till she drops."

Nonetheless, the very next day Hilary complies with Jane's tearful request for a 20 dollar loan. And Hilary works hard for her wages.

Each of these not uncommon cases involves social influence. Behavior did not *just change*. It *was changed*—by other people offering money, peer pressure, or (perhaps in Jane's case) a little guilt trip. But the changes in behavior have something else in common. None of them were necessarily preceded by, or even accompanied by, a change in attitudes or beliefs. Instead, in each case there seems to have been a rather *direct* influence on a specific behavior.

You would not be surprised if we told you that Jason can hear his alarm clock only if there is money—the pay bonus—ringing in his ears. He doesn't suddenly *like* being on time and has not developed a positive attitude about punctuality as one of his basic personal traits. Similarly, would you wager that Harvey really likes his economics text, or that Hilary, in the course of a day, has come to see Jane as trustworthy and needy? Probably not. They have not acted out of their personal convictions or upon their prior attitudes, but rather contrary to them in response to situational forces—incentives, group pressure, and a compliance-inducing tactic known as "door in the face," plus a little guilt thrown in for good measure.

In this chapter, we will concentrate on how and why these direct hits on behavior work. First, we will examine *social learning processes*. Influence through social learning processes is based in essence on the power of rewards and punishments. One such process, *instrumental learning*, is behind Jason's newly found promptness. A number of other influence methods are based, in part, on our concerns with real or imagined social rewards and punishments—especially the approval and disapproval of others. We'll get into these next when we examine *conformity* (Harvey's case) and *obedience*. Finally, we will examine *compliance* processes that can explain why Hilary was receptive to a small request after rejecting a large one. Various compliance techniques used in everyday life work because they capitalize on certain "rules" of social interaction that we learn and use automatically as we grow up in a society.

Though the influence processes we examine in this chapter constitute methods of directly controlling behavior while leaving attitudes and beliefs basically untouched, we remind you here that the cluster of related behaviors, behavioral intentions, attitudes, beliefs, and emotions form an attitude system. Since the components of the system are interconnected, a direct influence on behavior may very well trigger a ripple effect that spreads to change later thinking and feeling about the object of the action. These possible *further* consequences of direct influences on behavior are explored only a bit in this chapter, holding off our full discussion of them until Chapter 3. It will be helpful to keep in mind this interconnectedness of the components of the attitude system.

LEARNING WHEN ACTIONS PAY OFF

Learning theorists, such as the late B. F. Skinner, have long championed the idea that situational stimuli—events in the environment—directly influence our behavior. They do so in two ways. As external *consequences* of behavior, they act as *reinforcers* which increase the frequency of any preceding behavior. This reinforcing effect of environmental consequences occurs when the behavior is *contingently* related to the consequence: if behavior X, then consequence Y follows in some predictable fashion. A second way in which situational stimuli come to control behavior is through their *signaling function*; they inform us *when* or *where* our behavior is likely to be followed by a reinforcing event. When stimuli act as discriminative stimuli, they tell us that if we do X here or now, then that desired Y consequence will follow; but when they give off a different signal, that same behavior can be unrewarding or even get us in trouble. We'll have more to say about the discriminating functions of situational stimuli later in this chapter.

As a radical *behaviorist*, Skinner argued that internal events—such as attitudes, intentions, beliefs, and feelings—are little more than by-products of our overt behavior. Attitude or belief change does not necessarily precede or follow a change in behavior; it is overt behavior that is changed by reinforcers. Internal events have a more central role in *social learning theory*, especially as developed by Stanford's Albert Bandura (1977, 1986). We will see that this approach focuses on how people learn behavior patterns both from being directly reinforced and from observing the consequences that follow the actions of other people. In addition, social learning theory has more to say about the way the person, the behavior, and the environment all interact to change one another.

Instrumental Learning and Contingent Reinforcement

When our behavior is a means of changing some aspect of the environment—is instrumental in getting something to change—then we learn a relationship between a specific response and its consequence. In *instrumental learning* (also called *operant learning*) it is the actor's actions that change the environment, that produce consequences which operate on the environment. When the consequences are desirable, good, or pleasurable, those actions get repeated and eventually become a learned habit. When the action that gets reinforced is complex or does not come easily to the person, then it must first be "shaped." *Shaping* is a learning procedure in which we start with low standards and work up to high ones by initially rewarding any actions that resemble the final product we're after. Then we gradually raise our criteria for when a reward is given following a response that is closer and closer to our targeted goal response. Finally, only the real thing gets rewarded. Some teachers use this instrumental shaping procedure to get students to give more thoughtful answers to questions, at first by reinforcing them with verbal praise for just raising their hands and giving almost any answer and then by selectively giving out the "praise goodies" only for better and better responses.

Instrumental learning is a straightforward result of the principle that behaviors that are followed by good things—that are "instrumental" in obtaining good things—tend to be repeated. The good things— life's rewards—are *positive reinforcements*; that is, reinforcement is defined as any stimulus whose presence serves to increase the likelihood of a recurrence of the behavior that preceded it. We learn to do what pays off and to stop doing what has no payoff, or has undesirable payoffs. Simple principles, to be sure—but with widespread and potent applications in our lives.

Social Learning Theory

Much of what we learn does not involve doing an overt action and receiving a tangible reward. We watch others, listen, read, and thus learn indirectly to do those things that have had positive consequences for others and not to do things that get them in trouble, ill, hurt, rejected, or worse. Social learning theory expands on the basic principles of instrumental learning by adding this notion of *observational learning*: observing what particular models do and what consequences follow their actions, and then imitating the behavior of those models. But we also learn what to do in another way, without ever doing it ourselves or watching others doing it—we learn *behavioral rules* via verbal instructions. Rules are behavioral guidelines for the way to act in certain situations, verbally encoded as instructions, commands, suggestions, or in the form of proverbs or stories. Remember the "golden rule" of grammar school that urged us to treat others as we would want them to treat us? It tells us to act toward strangers with kindness even before we get any rewards for doing so. Rule learning involves recognizing the behavioral contexts in which the rules are relevant and then perceiving the reinforcing contingencies for obeying or violating them. Society passes along its accumulated wisdom, as well as prejudices and irrationalities, to future generations through transmission of its rules for behaving appropriately. However, when rules are internalized, and come to function as "my own rules," then they exert powerful influences on our behavior and self-conceptions. Many negative behavior patterns of those who are shy, have low self-esteem, are neurotic, or are overly vulnerable to persuasion attempts can be traced to the self-limiting rules which they impose on themselves regardless of the reality of the situation.

This brings us to another important feature of social learning theory: its emphasis on the powerful role on our behavior of self-expectations and cognitions in general. We each develop a sense of the degree to which we are likely to be effective on certain tasks, in certain settings, and with certain people. When we have high self-efficacy, we predict that we will succeed, we try harder, we persist longer, and we assume that negative feedback means that the task is difficult for everyone and we will have to put in more effort (Bandura, 1982). When we do all that, chances improve that we will succeed, and this provides feedback to further enhance our self-efficacy. Those with low self-efficacy start out assuming that they are not particularly good at math or sports or dancing or debating, for example. They avoid those situations and thus do not get essential practice, or they get anxious when forced to perform. Anticipating failure, they do not work as hard as they should. They get distracted, do not hang in when the going gets tough (for everyone), and assume that difficulties are not in the task but in their lack of ability. Their expectations are also usually fulfilled—with poor performance ("See, I told you so"). When they do succeed, what do they say? "I guess I was lucky." So, success or positive consequences have little impact on changing their negative self-perception.

These self-efficacy examples show us how an internal set of beliefs can affect behavior, which in turn has an impact on the environment. Then the environmental consequences feed back to further influence the person's self-image. The interplay between person, behavior, and environment is a continuous *reciprocal interaction*, in which each affects the other two and is in turn affected by them. What we do has consequences on the environment, which we then perceive as evidence about some aspect of ourselves as agents of those consequences. These thoughts, beliefs, expectations, and emotional reactions may direct our behavior by guiding our choices of activities, tasks, situations, and companions, as well as the nature of our response to them. What we do, the consequences we perceive as behavior-contingent, and how we think and feel about our actions and their consequences form a behavioral system which can work to enhance our personal development or diminish it.

However, it is also true that some of our thoughts and feelings do not get overtly expressed in actions; and likewise, some of our actions we do mindlessly or automatically so that they do not feed back to affect our internal states. Thus some behaviors can be changed directly without first changing internal processes, and similarly, some attitudes and beliefs can be changed without showing up in relevant changes of behavior.

Industrial strength examples. The increase in Jason's rate of getting to work on time is attributable to the new rewards that are contingent upon this new behavior. Whenever he punches in on time, he earns another brownie point toward the real prize of a bonus at the end of the month. Some companies have actually tried this technique and met with success. One innovative hardware company, for example, used the power of reinforcement to effect a positive change in the attendance habits of its secretaries, salespeople, and stock personnel. The company announced a "lottery" plan in which employees who had perfect attendance and punctuality for a given month (excluding absences for vacations and funerals) would become eligible for a drawing at the end of the month. The drawn names would win color TVs and other appliances, and each eligible perfect-attendance employee would have a 1 in 25 chance of winning. According to the company's personnel department, absenteeism and tardiness declined 75 percent during the first year of the lottery (Nord, 1970). There are a lot of Jasons out there in the hardware business nailing down "employee of the month" honors.

And there are many others in the retail world of large department stores. In one field experiment in a large metropolitan retail store, researchers investigated how contingent reinforcement might influence salespeople's performance (Luthans et al., 1981). First, sales employees in sixteen departments were observed for 4 weeks. Sales work, stock work, attendance, and other work behaviors were observed, and the frequency of behaviors that met company standards was recorded. When the time was over, the employees were carefully reminded of the standards—number of sales expected, time off allowable, and the like. However, over the next 4 weeks, employees in eight departments (a randomly selected experimental group) were systematically reinforced for performance that met or exceeded standards. The reinforcements, awarded each week, consisted of (1) time off with pay or the equivalent in cash, the amount contingent on the performance, and (2) an entry into the (ever-popular) lottery—this time for a company-paid vacation for two. Employees in the remaining eight departments (the control group) were offered no such rewards for excellence. Again, during the second period, standard-matching work behaviors were counted. What happened? Figure 2.1 traces the frequency of desirable work behaviors in terms of "aggregate retailing behavior." Though the performance of the two groups of employees was nearly identical during the first (baseline) period of 4 weeks, the reinforced group's performance improved dramatically once the rewards were announced so that they outdistanced the control group.

Kid stuff. The power of positive reinforcement was used in a most unusual way to help "problem students" at a junior high school in California (Gray et al., 1974). Rather than try to influence directly the behavior of the "juvenile delinquents" through contingent rewards, a psychologist and a special education teacher trained the children to

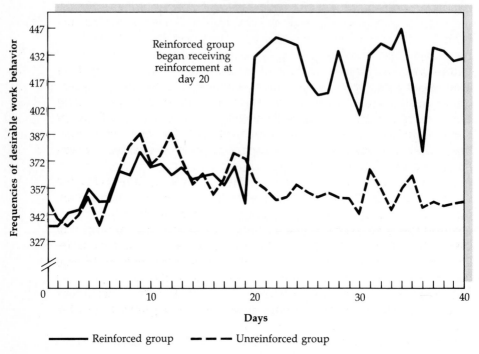

FIGURE 2.1
Systematic reinforcement increases desirable, productive sales behaviors. When department store salespeople began receiving time off and lottery tickets in return for productive
work habits, they quickly became more productive than nonreinforced salespeople.
(Data from Luthans, Paul, and Baker, 1981. Copyright 1981 by the American Psychological Association. Adapted by permission.)

shape their teachers' behavior toward them. The researchers teamed up
with the "problem kids" to teach them how to change the behavior of
teachers who were creating the "problems" for them. The reasoning
was that the children generally had poor social skills and had already
been labeled "incorrigible." Both of these factors, it seemed, led to subtle teacher biases and a not so subtle tendency for the teachers to be
quick to suspend the students and generally give up on them. Accordingly, seven children, ages 12 to 15, were selected from a class of
"incorrigibles" and given training and practice in behavior modification. The students were taught "various reinforcements to use in shaping their teachers' behavior. Rewards included smiling, making eye
contact, and sitting up straight in their seats. They also practiced ways
of praising a teacher, for example, by saying 'I like to work in a room
where the teacher is nice to the kids.' And they learned to discourage

negative teacher behavior with statements like 'It's hard for me to do good work when you're cross with me'" (Gray et al., 1974, p. 44). These techniques, though hard to learn, were eventually mastered, and the children, now armed with their personal reward arsenal, were let loose on the teachers.

As evidenced in records kept by both the children and impartial observers, the number of positive teacher-student contacts increased enormously, whereas the negative contacts decreased. Before the children began their counterattack, they averaged only 8 positive and 18 negative contacts per student in the prior week. After only 5 weeks of applied behavior modification, the average number of positive contacts zoomed to 32 while the negatives vanished to zero!

Perhaps most important from the point of view of educators is that the young behavior modifiers developed self-confidence in their ability to handle the school environment. In other words, the influencers were themselves influenced. They learned they had some control. At a practical level, then, this study demonstrates a powerful way to improve interpersonal relations. But it also shows us that our actions have huge effects on others, even though we may be unaware of it. The demonstration rings quite true to one of your authors, who has often been told that his young daughters "know all the right buttons to push" with him, getting him to do what they want so that he thinks it is what he wants.

Of course, you realize that not all consequences of behavior are positive. Behavior that meets with negative aftereffects, or punishments, tends to become less likely. A *punishment* is a stimulus whose occurrence following a behavior leads to a decrease in that behavior. When you verbally chastise a friend for making a thoughtless remark, chances are (and your hope is) that she will refrain from such remarks in the future.

When the absence of reinforcement following a learned behavior decreases the rate of performing the behavior, this "shutting down" reaction is called *extinction*. When a junior high student in a health education class asks the teacher delicate questions about human sexuality, and the teacher ignores the student, this student will learn that if she wishes to learn about sexuality, asking that teacher will not lead to reinforcement (answers). She is apt to stop asking that teacher. If adults in general shy away from the student's information seeking about this sensitive issue, the behavior may stop altogether, or go "underground."

Modeling Aggression

We noted earlier that people learn by observation as well as by the consequences of their actions. Observational learning is also called *vicarious learning* because we learn indirectly, vicariously through watching what others do and what happens to them as a consequence of their actions. Bandura conducted a classic series of studies exploring the observational learning of violent behavior (Bandura 1965; Bandura et al., 1961; 1963). In a typical experiment, an experimental group of nursery school children watched an adult model badly beating up on a life-size, inflated plastic Bobo doll, while control groups watched either no one or an adult model playing nonaggressively with the Bobo doll. In some cases, the violent model was praised and offered soda and candy as a reward for this behavior. In other cases, the violent model was roundly criticized and even mock spanked. In still other cases, neither reward nor punishment followed the assault on the Bobo doll. These studies showed a reliable result: violence breeds violence. When the children were given the opportunity to play with the Bobo doll and other toys, those who watched a violent model were more violent toward the Bobo doll than those who observed no model or a model who played nonaggressively with the Bobo doll. The most violent children were those who saw the violent model go unpunished.

Interestingly, the children imitated the violent model even when no reinforcement followed his violence. Later research showed that reinforcement of a model does not increase imitation unless the reinforcement is very strong and salient (Rosenkrans and Hartup, 1967). Thus, it seems that observational learning does not require that the observed model be reinforced. All that is necessary is that the observers pay attention to and remember the act, and are able to perform it. According to social learning theorists, reinforcement comes into play in determining the *performance*, not the learning, of the observed behavior. In the Bobo doll aggression studies, the children probably learned how to aggress against the target figure. But they also learned something about what they could expect from doing what they had learned—and this differed depending on the consequences they observed. When the model was rewarded, the children learned that assaulting the Bobo doll in the immediate setting would be apt to get them some decent outcomes. When the model was not extrinsically rewarded but still seemed to enjoy the violence, the children again learned that a good thing—fun—could come from assaulting the Bobo doll in the immediate setting. And when the model was punished, they learned that Bobo bashing *right here* was a no-no, apt to bring down the wrath of big people. But, and here's the catch, the violence might still be performed in another setting in which the child feels safe from punishment yet able to get the same enjoyment the model had. Thus *learning* how, when, and what to do occurs by simply watching. *Performance* depends on the expectation of reinforcement or punishment in the same or related situations. If Bobo bashing is punished across many different circumstances, the observing child may always refrain from this form of violence, despite knowing how to do it.

It may have occurred to you that many children see violent models every day on television—models who go unpunished and even get rewarded for their aggression. Do children learn aggression from watching violent TV programs and movies, with their superheros, cops and robbers, and horror movie slashers? A long history of research on this worrisome matter does suggest that frequent exposure to media violence is associated with greater aggressiveness in some children (Liebert and Sprafkin, 1988; Wood et al., 1990). We will have more to say about this—and influence methods for reducing this social problem of violence—in the next chapter.

The Yin and Yang of Modeling

Observational learning is greater when the model is *powerful*, when he or she is seen as having much control over the observer's environment and its resources. On the plus side for humanity is the second finding about what makes models more influential: when they are perceived as *warm* and *supportive* (Grusec, 1971; Grusec and Skubiski, 1970). These modeling factors, characteristic of many parents, increase the chances that the child will pay attention to the model's behavior and expect positive outcomes from imitating it. Another characteristic of parents is that they often come in twos. Imitative behavior is more likely when there are multiple models doing the same thing (Fehrenbach et al., 1979).

A model of good behavior. Play and destructive activities are not the only behaviors that can be influenced by models. A lovely example of modeling for good is one that induced poor children to donate some of their prize money to charity. In a study of working-class children in London, England, 7- to 11-year-olds played a bowling game with an adult model in which they could win tokens that, in turn, could buy desirable prizes (Rushton, 1975). In one condition of the experiment, the model, who played first, consistently placed some of his or her winnings in a bowl beneath a "Save the Children Fund" poster. In another condition, the model never made such a donation. As the social learning perspective would lead us to expect, children exposed to the generous model donated considerably more of their own winnings than those exposed to the selfish model. In fact, they contributed more than eight times as much! Giving was also greater among children exposed to a generous model than among a group of children who were not exposed to any model, and less among children who saw a selfish model than among the control group children without models. To top it off, differences in giving were still evident 2 months later when the children replayed the game in a different room with a different charity advertised. And so the specific behavior change had some enduring effects over time and place.

Modeling works with adults just as well. Studies have shown that adult models can influence the likelihood that other adults will stop to help someone with a flat tire, will drop money in a Salvation Army kettle at Christmas time (Bryan and Test, 1967), and will agree to donate blood (Rushton and Campbell, 1977).

In everyday life we see aspects of vicarious learning at work, as when bartenders and coatroom attendants "salt" their tip jars—priming the pump with some of their own coins and bills—in the hope that customers will imitate what appears to be the tipping by previous patrons. And evangelical crusades enlist thousands of confederates—planted worshipers who are instructed beforehand to come forward at predetermined times during calls to the altar to serve as heavenly models of those who have been touched, heard the call, or been born again (Altheide and Johnson, 1977).

Conditioned hatred. One of the authors can reach into his store of adolescent memories for a disturbing example of how a young child's behaviors and attitudes toward a minority group can be influenced by social learning processes. At the stag party of a soon-to-be-married high school friend, the author got into a card game with the groom's father and several guys from the old neighborhood. The father, while boasting about his children, told a story that he felt demonstrated the budding intelligence of his youngest son, Davey, then 3 years old. It seems little Davey had been gazing out of his living room window when he saw a black man walk by—a rarity in the all-white ethnic neighborhood. The child came running to his father, gasping, "Daddy, Daddy, I just saw a jungle bunny." The proud father, beaming all the while, went on to tell us that he couldn't help laughing when he heard this and that he praised his son for that "cute" remark. This distressing anecdote illustrates the joint operation of instrumental and observational learning. Davey could have learned the pejorative label only from hearing it used by important role models, like his father. And given the high level of prejudice in the neighborhood (most of the card players were quite amused by the story), the youngster probably also saw his father and others reinforced for their prejudiced remarks. Now the child was being reinforced for making the same statements. Importantly this shaping has a direct influence on behavior. Davey has no personal reasons for referring to black people in this way: at age 3, he probably has no attitude toward black people whatsoever. But sadly, through processes we will examine more closely later, his attitudes and beliefs—the negative preconceptions we call prejudice—are sure to follow once Davey starts thinking about his reinforced negative labeling.

The presence of discriminative stimuli will play an important role in whether or not Davey will put his learned prejudice into practice when he grows up and goes to college. In the local bar, with his childhood chums, the signal is "go": say it, do it, be it—prejudice is accepted and approved. But in the presence of his more liberal college professors and peers, Davey gets the signal that acting the bigot is not appropriate, will not be tolerated, and may be punished. So he refrains, holds his peace, and acts cool. If he then comes into contact with members of other racial and ethnic groups, he may begin to gather new evidence about their positive qualities which challenge his data-less preconceptions. Under these conditions some prejudiced attitudes begin to weaken.

Thus, the presence of discriminative stimuli which set the stage for responding in previously learned ways can induce or suppress the behavior depending on the signals they send out. Your friendly constructive criticism to Tanya may be seen as hostile when given in public, but helpful when in private. The presence of others then is a discriminative stimulus to which you should be sensitive in attempts at counseling this friend. This means that a powerful form of behavior control comes from being able to manipulate those discriminative stimuli once we know how they are functioning in a given setting. Propagandists use symbols as discriminative stimuli for invoking fear and avoidance responses by foes, or patriotism and approach responses in their presence by followers.

APPROVAL AND DISAPPROVAL: THE POWER OF SOCIAL REWARDS

Several of our examples have involved *social* rewards and punishments instead of material or tangible rewards. For little Davey, the approval of his prejudiced father was reinforcing. For sensitive Tanya, being made to "look bad" in front of others is a punishment to be avoided. Indeed, for most human beings, what others think about us and how they act toward us are among the most potent sources of influence over our behavior (Baumeister, 1982). This is not so surprising. Rejection by peers can be devastating to a youngster; it denies the child the satisfaction of basic human needs for social affiliation and stimulation. Rejection by parents or other caretakers is even worse, leaving lasting imprints on the child's psychosocial development. In contrast, social acceptance, early on, is associated with nurturance, being comforted, security, and other reinforcing goodies, such as food. Thus, by association with outcomes as basic as food and security, social approval becomes a robust reward, and its denial an equally powerful punisher.

What about another frequently experienced association, that between deviance and rejection? Disagreeing with others, acting the deviant, typically leads to the much feared social cold shoulder. Have you ever noticed it? Researcher Stanley Schachter did. In a classic demonstration, Schachter (1951) had groups of college students meet to discuss whether a juvenile delinquent, Johnny Rocco, should be treated leniently or harshly. A typical group consisted of nine individuals, three of whom were confederates of the researcher who were trained to play certain roles. One conforming confederate took the same position as expressed by the six real students (either lenient or harsh). The second was a "deviant," who took a position diametrically opposed to what the group felt and stuck to that opposing viewpoint throughout. The third confederate was a "slider," who began by disagreeing with the group, but eventually gave in and let the group convert him to their opinion.

Group after group displayed a similar set of responses. As they discussed the Johnny Rocco case, the real students' comments began to be increasingly directed toward the deviant. The deviant received many more communications than the agreeing confederate. And while pleasant enough at first, these communications became angry as the deviant continued to resist. Some groups finally gave up and ignored the deviant from that point on. You could say that the deviant eventually got the "silent treatment."

Postdiscussion ratings by the real subjects indicated that, of the three confederates, they liked the deviant least and the consistent agreer most. When asked to pick their preferences for assignments to subcommittees for future case evaluations, the students almost never chose the deviant for the more important subcommittees that they themselves preferred. They restructured the boundaries of the group by excluding and isolating the deviant. He had become "an enemy of the people" simply by consistently expressing a different opinion. No such discrimination was leveled at the slider or the consistent agreer. As Schachter later commented in a film interview, this was pretty rough treatment for a person "whose only sin was to disagree."

Rather than sin and risk a sort of earthly hell, we can, of course, "go along with the crowd"—do what others are doing, say what they are saying, comply with their wishes. When we behave this way in order to be accepted or to avoid rejection, we are experiencing what has been labeled *normative social influence* by Morton Deutsch and Harold Gerard (1955). Normative influence involves outwardly adopting the prevailing standard, or *norm*, of a group, going along to gain (or avoid losing) the *positive affect*—the liking, the respect, the acceptance—of the norm-defining group.

This normative social influence can be contrasted with *informational social influence*. Notice the word "informational." None of us has all the information about how to act in all situations, and so we must turn to others to get that information. We may "go along" with others when we are in a novel situation, are unsure of what to do, and rely on these apparently more knowledgeable people for direction. At frosh orientation, upper-class students offer the newcomers the low down on the right courses to take and avoid, and also the correct forms of behavior in various situations. According to this analysis, agreeing with others may yield, not one, but two, reinforcers: social approval *and* a sense of being correct.

In his *Theory of Social Comparison,* Leon Festinger (1954) argued that people have a basic need to evaluate their ideas and attitudes and, in turn, to confirm that they are correct ones. Believing that one's behavior and beliefs are correct or appropriate, among other things, can provide a reassuring sense of control over one's destiny and a satisfying feeling of competence. Festinger went on to note that "correct," in the case of beliefs and social behavior, is a pretty subjective thing, defined by social reality rather than objective absolutes. It is like judging how good a runner you are by comparing yourself with those who can run faster or slower than you instead of using stopwatch times to assess your running ability. In other words, being socially correct is usually best gauged in terms of what others think and do. Driven by the need to be correct, people thus look to the beliefs and behaviors of others—especially in novel or ambiguous social settings.

The concepts of normative and informational social influence aid in understanding conformity and obedience, two phenomena that have been systematically and even dramatically studied by social psychologists. It is to these twin concepts of social control that we now turn.

CONFORMITY: SAVING FACE AND GAINING GRACE—AND KNOWLEDGE

Remember Harvey, the student who professes to love his textbook after hearing the raves of his classmates? Harvey's behavior was an act of *conformity,* which we will define as a change in belief or behavior in response to real or imagined group pressure when there is no direct request to comply with the group nor any reasons given to justify the behavior change. In one of the earliest demonstrations of this process, Muzafer Sherif (1936) showed that conformity can occur even when the group consists of total strangers. Sherif made use of the "autokinetic effect," the illusion of apparent motion by a stationary light when it is observed in an otherwise completely dark room. In a typical study, subjects estimated the direction and distance they perceived the light to move. Different people saw it moving in quite different ways: some said it moved only small amounts, and others claimed that they saw large movement—even elaborate designs being traced by the light. Each subject developed his or her own range of apparent light movements. Then, several subjects were put together and required to make judgments one after the other. In this group context, it wasn't long before a new *group range* developed. Small-movement subjects saw larger movements than they had previously while large-movement subjects saw smaller ones. In short, merely hearing each others' judgments led to more and more agreement among the judges. A new group norm emerged which pulled individual judgments toward it.

We know what you're thinking. Illusions are ambiguous, and in the face of ambiguity, the most independently minded person would make use of the judgment of others. Perhaps the conformity observed by Sherif was quite purely a matter of informational influence. The subject may think, "It's really tough to tell how far that light moved, and so let me see what my fellow subjects think. They may know more than I do." Two decades later, Solomon Asch (1951) set out to demonstrate that conformity to the opinions of strangers is not very likely if the judgment stimulus is straightforward and unambiguous. To his surprise, Asch proved his own hunch wrong. His study of independence turned out to be the classic conformity study of normative influence to group pressure.

Groups of male college students were told they were participants in an experiment on visual judgment. They were shown two cards: one on which three lines were drawn and another on which a single line called the "standard" appeared (see Figure 2.2). Participants were told to judge which one of the three lines was the same length as the standard line. The three lines were different enough in actual length so that everyone could easily pick the line that was objectively the same as the standard. The experimenter would hold up the standard line and the comparison lines, and ask each student in turn to give his answer. However, all but one of the students were confederates. And the sole

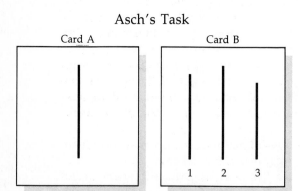

Asch's Task

Card A   Card B

                                      1   2   3

FIGURE 2.2
Sample stimuli used in Asch's studies of conformity. Subjects must pick the line from card B that matches in length the line on Card A. On conformity trials, the subject may learn that other subjects unanimously identify line "1" on card B as the same length as the line on card A.

real subject always answered last. At first, there was agreement among their judgments, but then a curious thing began to happen. Everyone else in the room said they saw a smaller line as the same size as the standard and then a longer line as equal to it. On certain key trials, the confederates all chose the same wrong line. These were the critical "conformity trials." When faced with this discrepancy between his perception of the unambiguous stimuli and the divergent group consensus, what did the subject report?

One-third of those in the critical group gave estimates that were wrong and in line with those of the confederates. A comparison group who gave their answers privately in writing made virtually no errors in this easy judgment task. About 30 percent of all student subjects agreed with the majority on half or more of the twelve critical trials. While about 70 percent conformed at least once, only a minority consistently maintained independence in the face of group pressures—a mere 25 percent never conformed. How do you think you would have acted in this situation?

The Causes of Conformity

Asch's startling findings demonstrate quite clearly that, even in the face of clear, objective standards, a group norm can influence our behavior. Not surprisingly, this conclusion stimulated an enormous amount of research. Asch made some experimental variations that give us good leads into the question of why people conform and how we can learn to resist some conformity pressures.

The approval motive in action. Suppose the lone subject had a little social support—one other person who opposed the majority's false judgment. Then what? To find out, Asch had one confederate buck the trend on some conformity trials and openly disagree with the majority. The real subjects conformed only 6 percent of the time on these trials. A little social support for dissent weakens the stranglehold of conformity. This is a convincing signal that the act of conformity was aimed at avoiding a total loss of social support. Where there is some social support provided by the dissenting partner, the loss of social support of the group is less extreme. But when the supportive partner abandoned the subject and started agreeing with the majority, the power of the majority was restored to its full effect—conformity rose again to nearly 30 percent. Normative social influence is definitely the main force operating in the Asch situation, not informational influence.

The critical role of normative influence is also evident in several other experiments. Conformity is much lower when subjects are al-

Scenes from one of Asch's conformity studies. Person number 6 is the only real subject, and he does a double-take when everyone else gives an obviously incorrect answer about which lines are equal in length. (*William Vandivert*)

lowed to respond privately, that is, out of earshot of the majority (Deutsch and Gerard, 1955; Insko et al., 1985). On the other hand, conformity is greater when the group is attractive to the individual (Sakarai, 1975). If you like the people in the majority, you're bound to conform more because you want them to like you and not turn you out.

The quest for truth. Informational influence also plays a role in conformity, especially when the judgments at stake are not entirely cut-and-dry and there appear to be experts at hand. Social psychologists have devised a number of conformity situations that involve more than judging unambiguous line lengths. After hearing the prearranged responses of others, unsuspecting research participants have been asked to judge the aesthetic quality of women's clothes, to choose among several solutions to a perplexing social problem, and to decide whether a briefly exposed comparison computer screen has the same number of dots as a standard screen. In studies like these, where it makes sense that some people are more expert at the task than others, unanimous majorities compel more conformity when they are perceived to be experts on the matter. And larger groups generally promote more conformity (Campbell et al., 1986), although we will see in Chapter 8 that minorities can sometimes also wield influence.

Self-confidence matters, too. Are you confident in your ability to choose clothing fashions that fit the occasion and suit your own per-

"Well, heck! If all you smart cookies agree, who am I to dissent?"

Conformity through informational influence.
(Drawing by Handelsman; © 1971 The New Yorker Magazine, Inc.)

sonal style? If so, then you may be unmoved by the person-in-the-street TV interviews about "what is in this year." People less secure in their "fashion sense," however, may quickly decide that they need a new wardrobe.

Sex and the single subject. Self-confidence is relevant to male-female differences in conformity. Stereotypes and even early research had it that females yield more readily than males when they are cast as the sole opposition to a unanimous majority. Careful research, however, suggests that this is not the case. Rather, women or men may conform more, depending on which group is likely to be more self-confident. Women tend to conform more than men when the object of conformity is something of more familiarity and interest to men than to women; and men conform more when the object is more familiar and interesting to women (Karabenick, 1983; Sistrunk and McDavid, 1971).

Consider, for example, one study in which male and female college students evaluated photographs of football tackles and women's fashions (Cacioppo and Petty, 1980). The photographs were accompanied by handwritten comments purportedly made by a subject from a previous study. There were always four comments, three factual and a fourth that was both evaluative (for example, "That's a great tackle" or "That's a chic fashion") and either right (it was, in fact, a good tackle) or wrong (it was a missed tackle). Subjects rated the quality of each photograph as well as their level of agreement with the comments of the other subject. When the other subject's evaluation comment was inaccurate, both males and females disagreed with it more often than they conformed to it. But where they did conform, men conformed more than women to the false assertions about the women's fashion photos, and women conformed more than men to the inaccurate evaluations of the tackles. This pattern is a clear demonstration that conformity will be greater when one lacks knowledge and confidence about a topic. In short, informational influence strikes again.

What changes? Our definition of conformity allows for change in behavior, in belief, or in both. Conformity is usually restricted to behavior change, which involves public agreement with a group norm when the reasons for going along are mainly to gain acceptance or keep it (normative influence). But going along may reflect both behavior and belief change when the group has been looked to, at least in part, for needed information about correctness (informational influence). This is a tidy dichotomy. And the whole story is never *that* tidy. Whether for acceptance or for information, conformity can involve "deeper" psychological processes that go beyond behavior, beyond just acting out the conforming actions.

You will recall Sherif's autokinetic-effect conformity study where a group norm developed in which subjects in the group all made similar judgments. Did this social influence have any lasting effect on the individual subject's actual perception, or was it transient? Subjects retested alone following the group judgments, even a year later, persisted in "seeing" movement close to the magnitude of the group norm (Rohrer et al., 1954). The influence effect had endured!

Changes analogous to this perceptual shift can also occur at the cognitive level. Suppose that during a conversation, several of your acquaintances, quite similar to you in many ways, express eager agreement that they would never go out of their way to help another person if it meant giving up some personal pleasure. This stunning revelation would be bound to give you pause. But would you agree with the statement? In one study, university students were confronted with just this sort of situation (Allen and Wilder, 1980). The results suggest that, if you did conform, it would be because the unusual group norm compelled you to "cognitively restructure" the meaning of the norm. For example, you might conclude that, in this context, "going out of your way" means something heavier and more sacrificing than simply being a bit inconvenienced. In conformity situations, then, we often do a "double take," trying to figure out if we have missed something (Campbell et al., 1986). In the process, we may "find" something and then begin to "see things" differently. We may change the meaning of the situation and not just our reaction to it. Or as Asch has described it, we may change how we perceive the object of our judgment and not merely our judgment of the same object.

The difficulty of just saying no. To sum up our main points, we see that people conform to maintain social approval as well as to increase their chances of being right in uncertain situations. The stronger these personal motives are and the more attractive and cohesive the group, the greater the pressure a group can exert on an individual. With much riding on how one reacts to the group, its pressures cannot be easily refused. In this light, consider the "Just say no" campaign against drug use launched by Nancy Reagan, the former first lady. On posters, in TV ads, and in the speeches of Ms. Reagan in schools across the country, the same message was hurled at the nation's youth: Just say no to drugs; when confronted by pushers, peers, or parties, simply decline the invitation to indulge. The wide publicity of the "war against drugs" afforded by this sensible slogan no doubt contributed to a growing awareness of the dangers of drug use and perhaps to some decline in the number of young people who began using cocaine, marijuana, and other controlled substances. Yet, given what you now know about conformity, you can see that the advice to "just say no" is easier heard than heeded. The social reality of many young adolescents includes high-status peers whose very "coolness" proves their expertise and lends huge value to their approval. Plus, they are present in the here and now, not as a remote TV image. Peer pressure is conformity pressure, and it can be intense. It includes gangs on whose acceptance one's social status and personal survival often depend. "No, no, Nancy" campaigns are effective primarily if they lead youngsters to *avoid* peers likely to provide temptations. If influential peers cannot be avoided, "No" may lose out to the chorus of "Yes, let's get down and be bad." Fortunately, as we will see in Chapter 6, children can be taught more effective methods of resisting peer pressure.

Expressive dissent. The desire for approval and the desire to be correct are not the only psychological bases of conformity. In some instances, people will refuse to conform, but instead will dissent openly as a means of expressing their individuality. Dissent as a self-expressive act is particularly likely in social influence situations in which people have more options than simply agreeing or disagreeing with the majority opinion. If there is the option of offering a third opinion—which might or might not incorporate the majority's ideas—a number of people will take it. In a revealing demonstration of this effect, undergraduates at the University of California, Berkeley, were asked to listen to stories depicting specific problems common to college students (Santee and Maslach, 1982). One such story is reproduced in Figure 2.3. After each story, a subject was asked his or her preferred solution to the problem. Three possible solutions were posed, including two good ones that shared some common wisdom and a decidedly poor one. The subject could either choose one of these or provide his or her own solution. However, on conformity trials, the subject learned that one of the good solutions was the unanimous choice of three other subjects. The presence of the majority, as in previous studies we have looked at, clearly influenced decisions. Nearly 70 percent of the time, subjects chose the same solution, compared with only 50 percent of the time when they responded alone.

But what about the 30 percent of the responses that were nonconforming? Very few of them were responses indicating agreement with the poor option. Rather, about half of the nonconforming responses consisted of stating a preference for the other good solution, and another one-third consisted of making up one's own solution. Thus, nonconformity could take different forms and did. Sometimes dissent is basically just an expression of disagreement, refusing to go along with the crowd. At other times, it is more creative—as in, "Here's a better idea, folks." What's more, it seems that it is a certain kind of person who tends to "creatively dissent" by giving a new answer. The experiment-

A Modern Conformity Item

Geraldine and Lennie are college students who have been living in an apartment together near the campus. Lennie's allowance buys the food, and they are sharing the rent. Geraldine has told her parents she is rooming with another girl, and now her parents are coming to visit their daughter. They have never seen her apartment. Geraldine has asked Lennie to move out for the time her parents are in town.

Should he?

1. Yes. His moving out will save a lot of trouble with her parents.

2. No. It would be hypocritical of them to pretend, so Geraldine should tell her parents before they come.

3. Yes, but Geraldine should pay for Lennie's new accommodations and food.

4. _____

FIGURE 2.3
A sample of the items used by Santee and Maslach (1982) to study creative dissent in conformity situations. In this example, the first two solutions had been rated by judges as good and the third one as poor. After learning that the other subjects had chosen one of the good options, a subject makes a selection. Instead of choosing 1, 2, or 3, a subject can create his or her own solution as option 4.

ers had administered a battery of personality inventories to subjects weeks before their conformity study. Analyses of scores on these tests were then related to responses in the conformity situation. A "creative dissenter" profile was revealed: that person had high self-esteem, low anxiety in social situations, and a strong inclination to be *individuated* (Maslach et al., 1985). Individuation here means a willingness to act differently from others so as to stand out. Presumably, people with these characteristics have a strong need for self-expression. Thus, when there is such an opportunity, they take it.

More sex and the single subject. Inclinations toward individuation and self-expression tie into conformity differences between men and women. Earlier, we saw that on the subject of conformity, sex is less important than knowledge and self-confidence. It seems, however, that there may be a tendency for men to conform a bit less overall, because they are more likely to see dissent as a way to express their competence. Men tend to believe that, to "stand out" as competent, they must be independent. Women, in contrast, tend to see cooperation and agreement with others in their group as reflecting competence. And so for women, positive self-expression can be achieved through conformity (Santee and Jackson, 1982). Note, however, that these sex differences are "on the average"; they certainly do not characterize all men and all women. In fact, differences in biological sex are less important than personality style and interests that form learned differences in *gender*. Men with personal qualities and interests that fit the traditional conception of "feminine" conform as much as women with these qualities and interests. Women and men with a more "masculine" orientation conform less (Maslach et al., 1987). This research offers us a fine example of how personality or individual differences can *interact* with situational variables to determine how people will react in conformity settings.

Conformity: Bad or Good?

Constructive dissent and independence are praiseworthy qualities for the most part, especially for Americans who are taught to value such virtues. But what about conformity? Suppose we called you a "conformist" or (worse) a "blind conformist"? How would you react? With something like the sting of a choice four-letter word. Yet conformity in most circumstances serves a valuable social purpose. To run smoothly, societies require that people conform to certain rules. Conformity to social rules and norms lubricates the machinery of social interaction. It enables us to structure our social behavior and predict the reactions of others. Individuals avoid major personal disasters by looking to others for guidance.

Conformity pressures might even serve social causes. In 1986, millions of Filipinos took to peacefully protesting the repressive government of Ferdinand Marcos. There were sit-ins, work stoppages, and nonviolent obstructions of the movement of government soldiers. Ultimately, this awesome outpouring of common behavior was instrumental in the success of a bloodless coup that brought down Marcos in favor of Corazon Aquino. Mass hatred and resentment of the Philippine military dictatorship had existed for years, but it was only when a critical mass of people took to active protest that many, many more joined the crowd—in spite of the ever-present fear of swift punishment. Conformity may not have been a primary trigger, but it helped the cause by bringing in many otherwise recalcitrant or fearful fence sitters. Three years later, in 1989, we saw similar scenes replayed in eastern Europe as one Communist regime after another was overthrown by massive people power. The assist given by conformity processes is this: A large number of people engaged in the same act are sure to attract an even larger number of people so engaged until a critical and ultimately influential mass is reached.

OBEDIENCE: BASING BEHAVIOR ON AUTHORITY

So far, we have looked at conformity, which involves changing behavior to what "everyone else" is doing, even when no one is explicitly requesting such a change. It turns out that it is also hard to say "no" to explicit direct requests from a single person, especially when the person comes packaged as an authority figure. This is the phenomenon of *obedience*, or doing what someone requests even without any internal inclination to do so. Like conformity, obedience is an everyday event. Children usually go to their rooms when their parents instruct them to. Beach-goers turn off their radios when a lifeguard informs them she has deemed the beach too noisy. At the awful extreme, young German soldiers murdered millions of innocent people in the Nazi death camps of World War II when they were ordered to by their superiors. In most of these cases, of course, the consequences of disobedience are severe, because the order giver has an enforceable, sometimes even physical, power over the individual. This is true enough. But a famous and literally shocking series of studies by a student of Solomon Asch, Stanley Milgram (1965; 1974), illustrates that destructive obedience to unjust authority can occur even when there are no negative physical consequences of just saying, "No, I refuse to do what you ask."

Milgram's Scenario: Would You Shock a Stranger If Hitler Asked You?

The best way to look at Milgram's studies is from the subject's perspective. Let's assume that you are the subject. Through a newspaper ad, you sign up for a study on "memory and learning." You show up at the arranged time and are greeted by a rather stern-appearing experimenter in a white lab coat. There is also a second subject. The experimenter frames the purpose of the study in pro-social terms to discover ways of helping people improve their memory. He goes on to explain to both of you that research has already proved the beneficial effects of rewards on memory but that no one has yet studied the possible benefits of selective punishment for errors. This study involves the effects of punishment on learning and verbal memory. One of you will be the "teacher" and the other the "learner" during the session. In turn, you are each asked to draw a slip of paper from a hat, which randomly determines that you will be the teacher and the other subject the learner—your pupil. The teacher is to read word pairs to the learner and then test the

Once social movements reach a critical mass, conformity pressures may help propel them further. This scene is Prague's Wenceslaus Square, November 1989, during the fall of Communist rule in Czechoslovakia and other Eastern European nations. (*Reuters/Bettmann Newsphotos*)

learner's memory by giving the first word of each pair and asking the learner to supply the associated word. Incorrect answers are to be punished with an electric shock, delivered by flipping one of the thirty switches of a "shock generator" that the experimenter shows to you. In units of 15 volts, the switches are labeled with increasing voltage designations, from 15 to 450 volts. The switches also have descriptive labels. For example, "slight shock" describes the 15- to 60-volt range, "very strong shock" describes the 195- to 240-volt range, and "danger: severe shock" the 375- to 420-volt range. The 435 to 450 range is simply labeled "XXX." The experimenter says that you, as the teacher, are to punish the first recall error with a mild 15-volt shock and then increase the shock by 15 volts for each succeeding error.

Next, as you tag along, your fellow subject, the learner—who is a middle-aged, mild-mannered, and likable guy—is escorted to a nearby room where he is strapped to a chair and hooked up to an electrode that transmits the electric shock. However, his skin is first treated with electrode paste—"to avoid blisters and burns." The learner, a bit worriedly, mentions that he has a "slight heart condition," but the experimenter assures him that "although the shocks may be painful, they cause no permanent tissue damage." The experimenter then escorts you to your seat in the main room in front of the shock generator. He gives you a sample shock which makes you flinch a bit. You think it may have been 75 volts, but the experimenter says it was only 45 volts.

Let's begin to help the learner improve his memory with your special teaching aid. The first wrong answer comes along, and an electric buzzer sounds; you flip the switch and correct the error—next trial, please. Wrong answers continue (approximately three of every four responses are wrong), and your shocks are escalating by small steps of 15 volts. At 75 volts, you hear the learner moan "ugh." At 150 volts, the learner starts yelling to be let out, that his heart is bothering him. At 180, he says that he can't stand the pain. At 210, he threatens to stop answering and demands release. At 270, he is screaming in pain. Beyond 300 volts the screams become intensely agonized and increasingly prolonged. Then, after 330 volts, there is silence. You turn to the experimenter and tell him that the learner isn't responding and you think you do not want to go on. He reminds you that the rules state that failure to respond is an error punishable by the next level of shock, and he tells you to continue.

You protest on behalf of your pupil, and the experimenter counters with statements like "It is absolutely essential that you continue" and "You have no other choice, you *must* go on." OK you go a little further, but then ask who is responsible for the other guy? You are reassured that the experimenter assumes responsibility. "Teacher, please continue!" Do you? Will you go on? Where will it all end? How far up the 450-volt scale would ordinary people—like *you*—administer brutal and perhaps lethal shocks, at the mere command of an authority? College students surveyed by Milgram before his experiments figured that normal folks, on average, would go to 135 volts before flatly disobeying the experimenter and quitting their role as teacher. Most said that no one would go all the way to 450 volts. On average, the surveyed students estimated only about 1 in 100

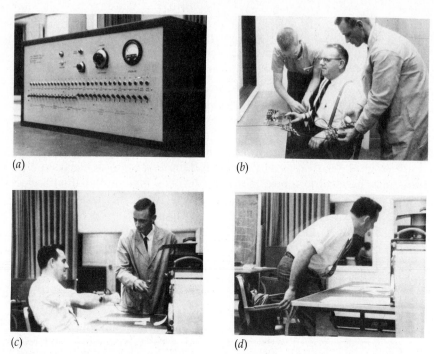

Scenes from Milgram's obedience lab: (*a*) The shock generator, (*b*) the "learner" being "hooked up," (*c*) a subject ("teacher") being instructed by the experimenter, and (*d*) leaving his station. (*From the film* Obedience, *NYU Film Laboratory*)

would go all the way. Forty psychiatrists Milgram surveyed estimated that only 1 in 1000—the sadists—would ever get up to the very end. Milgram himself foresaw little total obedience.

The actual results proved these estimates to be just a bit low—a megabit. Out of the first forty subjects Milgram (1963) tested, all men aged 20 to 50, twenty-five went all the way to 450 volts; 63 percent of the men had given the maximum possible shock to this innocent learner turned victim. In a second experiment, summarized in Figure 2.5, 65 percent gave the maximum shock. The *majority* obeyed totally!

At this point, as your justified horror sets in, let us at least assure you that no shocks were actually received. The learner was an experimental accomplice trained to play a role, and the shouts and screams were preprogrammed on tape. The teacher-learner drawing was rigged. But the actual subjects, those in the role of teachers, did not know this. They believed that everything that was going on was real, judging by postexperimental interviews and by the graphic signs of tension and worry most displayed in film recordings of them carrying out their grim task of helping the helpless student improve his memory, even if it cost him his life in the process.

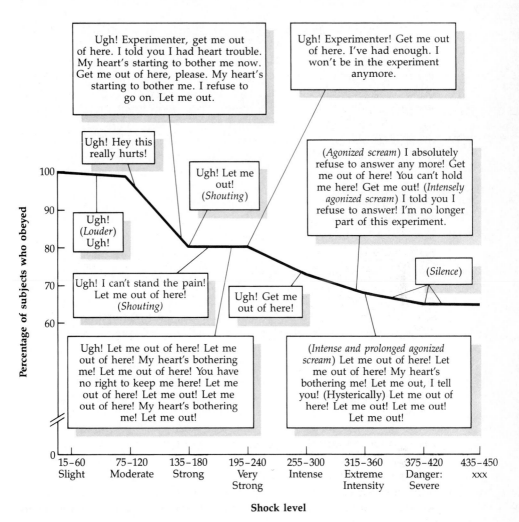

FIGURE 2.4
The shocking results of one of Milgram's early experiments.

Explaining Extraordinary Behavior by Looking At the Ordinary

What accounts for this unexpected and unnerving behavior—inflicting intense, surely dangerous pain on another human being simply because an authority figure said to? A natural immediate reaction is to suspect the subject sample. Maybe they were weird or just happened to be a sadistic bunch? Unlikely, given the suffering and concern the *teachers* themselves expressed. Many subjects showed signs of extreme tension and virtually all complained and verbally dissented, even as they kept flipping the shock switches. Milgram (1963) reported that "subjects were observed to sweat, tremble, stutter, bite their lips, groan, and dig their fingernails into their flesh" and that there was "the regular occurrence of nervous laughing fits." When women subjects were used as teachers in this obedience paradigm, they often cried—while continuing to deliver their painful lessons in memory enhancement. These and other data also rule out the possibility that the experimental scenario was not believable, that the subjects did what they were asked without really buying the story about the other person being harmed (Sheridan and King, 1972).

A "bad apples" explanation is also refuted by the demographic qualities of the subject sample and the fact that the results were repeated with numerous other samples. In general, Milgram's samples were quite representative of the American population. He tested literally thousands of subjects—including postal workers, construction workers, engineers, high school teachers, salespeople, factory workers, college professors, and college students from Yale University. Always, the results were the same: meek obedience to unjust authority.

It seems, then, that we have to treat the obedience observed by Milgram as a "normal" example of social influence. If so, let us see whether normative and informational social influences are at work. To begin with, the subject-teacher is in a very novel situation. It is a laboratory, a scientist is present, and a strange task is involved. Simply put, the subject has little experience or known rules of conduct to rely on as behavioral guides. The "rules" are being provided by a person who has high status and authority and who is presumably an expert on the matters at hand. The situation seems ripe for informational influence. The experimenter has information that the subject needs. This information, moreover, has premium value, as the teacher is rapidly jettisoned into the throes of a serious conflict: to continue hurting this poor man or to stop and spoil an apparently important experiment. There are time pressures to deal with. As Milgram (1963) noted, "the experiment gives the subject little time for reflection." With constant pressure to act, the subject may accept the experimenter's information that it is important for science for him to continue and that physical injury is unlikely. Nagging doubts about the truth of these claims may surface, as questions of morality pop into the subject's consciousness. But these doubts fall on deaf ears since there is no opportunity to confirm them and think about their implications through discussion with others.

On top of all this, normative influence is apt to be at work. Will stopping make the subject appear like an impulsive fool? Will the psychologist-experimenter think that the subject is ignorant, impulsive, overly sensitive, or "unmanly," and express his disfavor? It may be easier to continue without questioning than to risk these interpersonal hassles that are likely if you refuse to go on.

Obedience: Part normative, part informational. Further experiments by Milgram have confirmed that informational and normative pressures—the desires to be correct and to avoid social disgrace—helped compel people to behave against their own wishes in this stunning display of destructive obedience, as can be seen in the summary graph (Figure 2.5) from eighteen different studies he conducted with over a thousand subjects.

The original studies were conducted at Yale University, a revered and respected seat of learning and expertise. When they were repeated in a somewhat shabby downtown building, ostensibly by an outfit

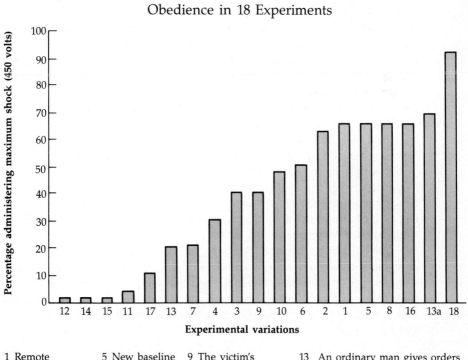

Obedience in 18 Experiments

1 Remote	5 New baseline	9 The victim's	13 An ordinary man gives orders
2 Voice-feedback	6 Change of	limited contract	13a The subject as bystander
3 Proximity	personnel	10 Institutional context	14 Authority as victim—
4 Touch-proximity	7 Closeness of	11 Subjects free to	an ordinary man commanding
	authority	choose shock level	15 Two authorities—
	8 Women as	12 Learner demands	contradictory commands
	subjects	to be shocked	16 Two authorities—one as victim
			17 Two peers rebel
			18 A peer administers shocks

FIGURE 2.5
A profile of weak to strong obedience effects across Milgram's nineteen experimental variations.
(From Miller, 1986.)

called "Research Associates of Bridgeport," the full obedience rate dropped from 63 to 48 percent. When an "ordinary man" gave the orders, obedience fell to about 20 percent. But when the research was conducted at Princeton University using high school students, obedience soared to 80 percent (Rosenhan, 1969). These variations are expected: the declines from the decrease in informational influence pressure that should accompany lessened expertise or authority of the experimenter, and the increase from the increase in those same pressures.

Want to knock out the "obedience effect"? Want to show that the effect is caused by forces in the situation rather than by aspects of the personalities of the subjects? You only have to look at the graph data from conditions 12, 14, 15, 11, and 17. In them, the learner demands to be shocked rather than the experimenter commanding it, and subjects do not obey the learner. Or make the authority the victim, or have two authorities whose status is decreased by giving contradictory commands. Or have two peers rebel and disobey. Simply put, there are a variety of situational forces that increase or decrease the obedience effect. It goes up when aspects of the situation convey that the authority has high status and power (informational), and when peers are first observed administering the shocks as in condition 18 (normative); it goes down when authority weakens and there is social support for dissent and disobedience. Obedience is also greater when the direct contact between the subject and the victim is more *remote*. This allows for the victim to be perceived in less humanized ways. People thus follow authority—its information value and normative power—sometimes for better and sometimes for worse.

It should be apparent that this experiment raises serious ethical concerns about the treatment of human research subjects. It certainly could not be conducted today, given the greater sensitivity of researchers as well as federal and university committees that oversee research; but its merits and faults continue to be debated (Baumrind, 1964, 1985; Miller, 1986).

Obedience to authority as ingrained habit. Explaining Milgram's obedience and Asch's conformity with the same concepts is sensible and points to important similarities in the phenomena. But the desires "to be right" and 'to be liked" (Insko et al., 1985) don't fully account for the obedience of Milgram's teachers. We need to call further upon the power of situations that we discussed in the opening chapter. But why was the situation so powerful? Milgram himself argued that obedience "may be a deeply ingrained tendency, indeed a prepotent impulse overriding training in ethics, sympathy, and social conduct" (Milgram, 1963, p. 371). Roger Brown (1986), a well-known social psychologist, has echoed this sentiment, suggesting "that 'disobedience drills,' comparable to fire drills, may be necessary to break the habit of obedience, the cake of custom" (p. 35).

What Milgram and Brown are suggesting is the role of learning the *prescriptive rules of behavior* in a modern, complex society. One rule we learn is that legitimate authority is to be obeyed without question. We learn this well, through the instrumental and observational learning processes we have already discussed, as well as through the instructions of parents, religious leaders, teachers, and government figures. And the learning normally serves individuals and societies quite well. Like conformity, obedience has its virtues. Society benefits since anarchy and chaos are avoided; order reigns. We also benefit personally by learning certain rules of thumb that help us to avoid certain punishments (among them, unemployment for ignoring the boss and arrest for ignoring a police officer ordering our car to the curb) and acquire certain rewards (such as the sound advice of an expert).

But therein lies the rub. The rule "obey legitimate authority figures" may be so well learned that people are prone to *overapply* it, to *over*generalize the relationship between authority figure and obedience. Social psychologist Robert Cialdini (1988) has an intriguing perspective on this notion. He suggests that social rules like "obey authority" can kick in automatically when the social environment provides certain cues—discriminative stimuli signaling that the stage is set for quick responding, delivering the prepared script without thinking.

Stop! Stop processing what you just read as an abstract principle that has little personal relevance for your life! Let's do a thinking experiment. Think back to the experimental scenario in Milgram's basic paradigm, and assume that you are one of the hardy minority who refuse to obey. You won't go all the way; you quit after giving 300 volts. That makes you a hero of sorts, doesn't it? You have been able to resist pressures that most people have caved into. OK, now what? What is your next move? Do you get up from your assigned seat and go to help or just check on the learner, your pupil, whom you have certainly hurt and maybe seriously injured? It is the humane, sensible thing to do at that moment, isn't it? "Well, of course, sure I would," is what you want to believe you would say. We are so confident that you would not that we would give big odds in a bet that you and virtually everyone else would not get out of the assigned seat. How could we be so sure? Guess how many of the hundreds of people in all these studies reacted in this "heroic" way?

Curious about the answer, your senior author called Stanley Milgram, his high school classmate at Monroe High School in the Bronx, New York. His answer was quick and concise: "Not one, not ever." What's going on here? How could none of those people who had the courage and integrity to quit the experiment, to refuse to obey totally, not do the next reasonable thing and directly help the person they had possibly harmed?

"Stay in your seat, until I tell you that you can leave," is perhaps one of the most lasting lessons of our early childhood education—coming from elementary school teachers. That behavioral rule is so internalized that it controlled the reactions of the "heroes" in the Milgram studies, who disobeyed the experimenter's external command but totally obeyed this more deeply ingrained internal command. In that sense, we argue that obedience to general authority as reflected in Milgram's demonstrations is total, a full 100 percent!

Obedience through heuristics. We encounter a command from someone who appears to be an authority figure and, in kneejerk-like fashion, we obey. This sort of mindless reaction, this habitual reflex springs from our need for mental efficiency. It would be paralyzingly time-consuming to analyze every social encounter before deciding on an action. And so we rely on "rules of thumb" or *judgmental heuristics*, mental shortcuts like "obey authority" that eliminate the need to think and speed up reactions. Usually the shortcut rules work quite well, and that is why we all use them quite often. But they can also get us in trouble. Consider this use by Andy Rooney, a CBS-TV commentator from *60 Minutes* who was suspended in 1990 for allegedly making some stupid prejudiced comments to a magazine interviewer. Ten years earlier, Rooney challenged critics of a CBS program on homosexuality, referred to them as "gays" (which they were not), and said that he knew they were because, in his words: "I am a reporter, and prejudice saves me a great deal of time in making quick judgments over the years" (*San Francisco Chronicle*, 1/29/90).

Sometimes, the problem is that the rules are misapplied. We don't pay attention to critical details in the compliance setting, and so we fail to see that this person is not "legit" or that the order or advice is wrong. Over and beyond normative and informational influence pressures, this may be precisely what happened to Milgram's teacher-subjects. The trappings of authority—the experimenter's white lab coat, his title, the aura of science—led subjects to prematurely apply a rule that has many exceptions.

The misapplication of the obedience rule may have been hastened further by the stress and conflict of the Milgram situation. Rational thinking becomes more difficult when people are anxious. At the same time, the desire to get a bad situation over with grows stronger. "Mindless obedience," asking no questions, is sometimes seen as a way to escape the situation. The individual thinks, "Just let me get this over with," closes his or her mind, and carries out the orders of authority.

Pushing the Disobedience Exit Button

The Milgram situation was high on "obedience cues"—and low on "disobedience cues" to suggest that defying the authority was appropriate and possible. You will recall that teacher-subjects were less obedient when in the company of disobedient models. Besides providing social support for subjects' desires to quit shocking the learner, these models may have "showed them the way" to disobedient action. In effect, isolated subjects may not have known *how* to disobey in such an unusual situation. It has been suggested by social psychologist Lee Ross (1988) that obedience in Milgram's experiments would have been much less had a "quit" button been made visible and within easy reach of subjects. The button would suggest to subjects both the appropriateness and the means of stopping their destructive obedience.

This point can be extended to everyday compliance situations, like telephone solicitors or door-to-door salespeople who get you to listen to their sales pitches because you don't know how to exit easily and gracefully, without hurting their feelings or being impolite. Professional influence peddlers count on those reactions to hook their catches into listening to their message to give or to buy. The cure: (1) Trust your intuition that "something is wrong here"; (2) do not accept the definition of the situation as presented to you by the other party, whose vested interests may be at odds with yours; (3) consider the "worse case" scenario, and act on the possibility; (4) figure out an escape plan, and put it into action as soon as possible; (5) do not care what image the other person may form of you for doing so, and remember that you can always apologize when you are in a safe situation if you made a mistake; (6) think about the above escape hatch scenario, and mentally rehearse it as it applies to different situations in your life.

You will be in many situations throughout your life when authorities of some kind will put pressure on you to comply with their requests, some of which may be unethical, illegal, immoral, or even just unreasonable and inappropriate for you. Many high-level scandals in government, the military, and business boil down to powerful authority figures pressuring their subordinates to do as they are told, to be "team players," not to "rock the boat," and so forth. But the same thing happens at times between doctors and nurses, bosses and workers, teachers and students, parents and children. What should you do about it? Again, there is a set of psychological counterstrategies that must be enacted swiftly. Be alert to aspects of this compliance-gaining situation that do not seem right and are different in some important way from others, where complying is appropriate. When you notice this, question it, and do not accept the answer uncritically. For example, if the Milgram experimenter really wanted to study the effect of different levels of shock on learning and memory, why did he need *you* to deliver the shocks; why couldn't *he* do so—unless of course he was really interested in *you* and your reactions? To begin to think such thoughts, it is essential to step back mentally from the immediate, on-going demands of the situation, to seek a "time out" so that you can try to make sense of it all. Ideally, you should back off and out physically as well, so that you can distance yourself from the direct power of the agent of influence. And so you never sign on the dotted line without going home to think about it, or without talking the decision over with someone whom you trust has your interests at heart.

KNEEJERK PSYCHOLOGY: INFLUENCE THROUGH HEURISTICS

"Obey authority" is not the only guiding rule that is deeply ingrained by socialization. Through training and experience most people learn to associate consensus with correctness, as we have seen in discussing group size effects in conformity studies. The heuristic (or decision-aiding rule) here is, "They can't all be wrong." Two additional social rules abound in the habits of most, if not all, human societies, and normally they help society function smoothly. These rules are central to certain procedures for gaining compliance with our wishes. One is the *reciprocity rule,* which states that we should return the favors or help we receive from others. The other is the *commitment rule,* a belief that once we have given our words or deeds to a cause, we should stick to it. Cialdini (1987, 1988) has argued that these rules will guide behavior in situations that (1) provide a cue that signifies a rule is relevant and (2) prevent or discourage careful thinking.

The Rule of Reciprocity

Anthropologists, moral philosophers, and sociologists alike have expounded on the norm of reciprocity, the social rule to help people who have helped us. Alvin Gouldner (1960), a sociologist, contends that this norm is universal, basic to humanity. And who would argue? Many of us use the norm routinely to influence others. And studies confirming the reciprocity rule abound.

In one experiment, pairs of subjects were put to work making perceptual and aesthetic judgments of pictures (Regan, 1971). In one condition of the experiment, one member of a pair, who was actually an experimental confederate, left the lab during a break and returned several minutes later with two bottles of Coke. He gave one, gratis, to the other member of the pair—the real subject. In another condition, no

Cokes entered the picture at all. Later, as the picture-judging session wound down, the confederate asked the real subject whether he would do him a favor and buy one or more raffle tickets from him at twenty-five cents each. Subjects who had accepted the Coke condition bought nearly twice as many tickets on average as subjects who had been offered no Coke. Receiving a favor incurred a sense of obligation, a motive to reciprocate the good deed.

Door in face, favor in hand. A more mysterious method of winning compliance, known as the *door-in-the-face* technique, also seems to have something to do with the reciprocity norm. This technique refers to a strategy of first making a large request that is almost certain to be refused—to get the door slammed in one's face. Then, when the request is refused, a second, smaller request is made. Research—and the practical wisdom of salespeople the world over—suggests that, under certain circumstances, the smaller request is more likely to be granted if it follows the larger one than if the requester leads right off with it. Remember Hilary's grudging 20 dollar loan to Jane, who had first asked for 100 dollars? Hilary was "door in the faced."

Some field experiments relevant to the business world have demonstrated the door-in-the-face technique (Mowen and Cialdini, 1980). Experimenters approached pedestrians on the walkways of a large university to get them to comply with their request to fill out a "California Mutual Insurance Company" survey on "safety in the home or dorm." The survey, the pedestrians were assured, took only 15 minutes to complete. Some pedestrians were simply asked directly (and very nicely) to complete this short survey. But since universities are pretty busy places and insurance surveys are hardly enjoyable, you will not be surprised to learn that only 29 percent complied with this request. Other pedestrians, however, were made the targets of a door-in-the-face strategy. These prospective survey respondents were first asked to fill out a survey that would take 2 hours to complete. Then, after they predictably refused, they were asked if they would at least complete the more important part of the marathon survey: the 15-minute version. Fifty-three percent complied!

This same no-then-yes effect has been observed in other contexts as well. Why does reciprocity work in this way? One answer is that "the requester's movement from the initial, extreme favor to the second, more moderate one is seen by the target person as a concession. To reciprocate this concession, the target must move from his or her position of noncompliance...to a position of compliance" (Mowen and Cialdini, 1980, p. 254). Consistent with this interpretation, the effect does not work when the smaller request is not perceived as a genuine concession, such as when the person who asks the favor requests a smaller but suspiciously *different* act of the target (Mowen and Cialdini, 1980).

Dagwood probably would have complied if the boy had said it right—and delivered the door-in-the-face.
(Reprinted with permission of King Features Syndicate, Inc.)

This sort of faux pas may trigger the thought, "Hey, this guy wanted this second thing all along."

And that's not all. . . . The norm of reciprocity is also implicated in another compliance tactic that resembles the door-in-the-face technique in some ways, but does not require a "no" before the "yes." One of your authors and his wife were once shopping for carpeting for their family room. A particular rug in the fourth store they visited seemed to fit their needs and budget. This carpet was a good deal: a reasonable price for excellent material, the right color, a reputable store. What more could anyone want? Although inclined to buy, they hesitated and told the salesperson they needed a bit of time to think it over. The salesperson obliged, suggesting that they check out how the carpeting looked under various lighting by taking a sample over to a section of the store set up for that purpose. The salesperson left and returned after 10 minutes or so. Before the author could say anything, the salesperson, in a nice and natural tone said, "I can actually do even better on the sale price. Since we have a full roll of that carpeting right here in stock, I can sell it to you for two dollars less a yard." Sold, on the spot. What a deal!

But your friendly author, who thought he knew all the tricks, puzzled over this unprompted "deal sweetening" for several days. After all, the buyers had expressed genuine interest and had never balked at the price. No bargaining had begun; none seemed necessary. On the other hand, the salesperson could not be sure of a sale. People fall from fences of indecision both ways. Was this intended as the decisive nudge?

Almost surely. Just 2 months after this incident, an article in a social psychology journal described several experiments on a compliance tactic just like the one used by the carpet salesperson. The researcher called it the that's-not-all technique (Burger, 1986). In one experiment, the researcher had students who were working at a bake sale try to sell a package of a cupcake and two cookies for a total of seventy-five cents. One of two approaches was used. One way was a straight offer: simply offer the full package for seventy-five cents right off the bat. The other strategy was to offer first the cupcake alone for seventy-five cents and then, after a brief interruption and conferral with a cosalesperson (before the customer could answer), make a revised offer of throwing in the cookies for the same price. Buying was 40 percent with the straight offer approach; it jumped to 73 percent with the sweetened deal, that's-not-all, approach. *Reciprocal concessions* strike again. Adding something to the deal is perceived as a negotiation, which the potential buyer then feels obligated to reciprocate by purchasing the "better" package.

The reciprocity rule may not be the only factor operating in the door-in-the-face and that's-not-all effects. An additional factor is *perceptual contrast.* Here a second smaller request (or better deal) may look even smaller (or better) when contrasted with the first, larger request (or poorer deal) than when examined by itself (Burger, 1986). Fifteen minutes of survey responding may seem a small sacrifice of time when it could have been two hours.

The Rule of Commitment

Besides the rule of reciprocity, the commitment rule—to stand by what one has said, promised, or done—is another important psychological lever for gaining the compliance of others. The old adage "A man is only as good as his word" reflects a fundamental teaching of our culture. Going back on one's word is a mortal cultural sin. It breeds dislike and distrust. This makes good sense. People whose actions belie their words or (worse) their promises are unpredictable; we call them hypocrites. And it is hard to live in a world of unpredictable inhabitants. Not surprisingly, then, feeling committed to one's freely chosen actions is ingrained in us early. Being *consistent* in words and deeds is a related social value learned young.

The key psychological process at work here is the binding effect of an earlier commitment on subsequent behavior; the second act naturally follows from the first in this consistency play. This is especially true when the initial behavior is public and freely chosen, or people have the illusion that it is. A well-established finding in the realm of persuasion, for example, is that the act of publicly stating a point of view on a social issue serves to make the individual more resistant to messages urging the opposite viewpoint (Kiesler, 1971; Pallak et al., 1972). The push toward consistency compelled by public commitment is also evident in the Asch conformity situation, where it makes a big difference *when* the subject responds. If a subject states his or her judg-

ment about the length of the line first, and then hears a unanimous majority disagree with that judgment, the subject very seldom changes to
the majority view when invited to reconsider (Deutsch and Gerard,
1955).

You can probably relate quite easily to this effect of public commitment. Have you ever told your friends that you're starting a diet, going
to stop drinking, or going to study every night in the hope that an-
nouncing your intention will make you go through with it? Often, it
does—a fact that, as we'll see in Chapter 9, is not lost on those who run
diet workshops, counseling centers, and other self-improvement services, who often insist on public declarations of a commitment to
change.

A stunning and socially significant example of the power of the
commitment principle can be seen in the work of Tom Moriarty (1975),
who used the principle to influence helping behavior among usually
cynical New Yorkers. Beach-goers sunning themselves on a sandy
beach were asked to keep an eye on a nearby radio left on a blanket
while its owner (an experimenting social scientist) was briefly away. In
a control condition, the research made a similar social contact with the
nearby stranger, asking him or her for the time. A few minutes later a
confederate attempted to steal the radio—in full view of the neighboring sunbather. Could a verbal commitment to watch the property of a
total stranger influence the willingness to intervene in a theft? Without
a doubt, it did. Of those who were never asked to watch the radio, only
20 percent stopped the thief. In contrast, fully 95 percent of those who
agreed with a request to watch the radio intervened. Some went so far
as to run after and grab the thief. A similar result was observed in a
companion study, when diners were asked to keep watch over a purse
at a fast-food restaurant. When a stranger tried to steal it, those committed to watching it honored their word—even cynical New Yorkers!
We might take better care of each other if we made more promises in
this society. If you want to change some social behavior, just try asking
directly for a commitment.

Throwing a low ball for a strike. Commitment can work in yet
more subtle ways to bring about compliance. After someone has made
a commitment to buy something for a stated price, the deal is
changed—for the worse for the buyer, of course. *Low balling* refers to
getting someone to agree to a very attractive deal—a sale or business
arrangement, for example—and then, on the basis of some excuse,
making the deal *less* attractive. Car salespeople use the low-ball technique particularly well. Once the customer agrees on a seductively low
price, the salesperson may say that he must check with the manager,
pretend to do so for some time, return, and apologetically inform the
customer, "The boss won't go for it; we have to make at least some

profit to survive." He then may offer a somewhat higher price, still decent but not seductive (Cialdini, 1988). Car dealers know that the
chances are good the unwary customer will accept the higher counter-
offer. Social psychologists know why. The customer has already
agreed—made a commitment—to buy the car, although not at the new
price. The customer has made a decision. To back out now would be
inconsistent, and it would require bucking the entrenched habit of
standing by one's word. The customer's turnaround would feel bad.
And how would it look to the salesperson for the customer to give up
the car of his dreams because of a fairly minor difference in price, perhaps a few hundred dollars on a multithousand-dollar car? After all, the
original price really was a steal, and the new price is both good and realistic. (Little does the customer know that the salesperson never intended to sell the car at the first agreed-on price.)

There have been several research demonstrations that the low-
balling technique is effective. The seminal study, by Cialdini and his
colleagues (1978), found that it was difficult to get college students at
Ohio State University to volunteer for psychology studies that began at
7 a.m.—*unless* they first got the students to agree that they would like
to participate in the studies in general and *then* threw the low ball, men-
tioning the 7 a.m. starting time. Fifty-six percent of the low-balled students volunteered (and nearly all of these showed up for the study), as
opposed to only thirty-one percent of those told up-front about the un-
godly starting time.

A necessary condition for a low-ball effect is that the target of low
balling perceive that he or she *freely* entered into the initial agreement
(Cialdini et al., 1978). It is one's own words and deeds that one commits
to; forced acts are, in a real sense, not one's own. And so what does the
salesperson do to create that conscious state? "I don't know why I let
you talk me into such a deal; but a deal is a deal"—until he comes back
and throws a low-ball to strike a better deal for the company.

A "foot in the door" is worth a bird in the hand. One final tactic of
gaining compliance by securing commitment is called the *foot-in-the-door
technique.* Door-to-door salespeople have a standard proviso: "If I can
just get my foot in the door, I can make a sale." Psychologists have explored—and confirmed—this notion that gaining compliance with a
small request (being allowed into the prospective customer's home) can
increase the chances of obtaining compliance with a larger request (buying something, like a set of encyclopedias) (Beaman et al., 1983). The
first experimental demonstration of the effectiveness of the technique
was made by Jonathan Freedman and Scott Fraser (1966) in the area
around Stanford University.

Door-to-door requests were made of the homemakers in a random
sample of suburban homes to perform a small act of helping: signing a

petition for a good cause—either to keep California beautiful or to promote safe driving. Other randomly selected homes, in the comparison condition, were not approached at this time. A different researcher then visited both sets of homes two weeks later and made a large request. He asked each homemaker to place on her front lawn a large and downright ugly billboard that said "Drive Carefully" and to keep it there for a couple of weeks. Homemakers who had been approached with (and had agreed to) the first, small request were considerably more likely to grant this imposing request than were those who were not approached with the first request.

More recently, researchers found that residents of a middle-class neighborhood in Israel were more likely to donate money to a charity if they had been asked to sign a petition for the same charity—and actually did so—two weeks earlier (Schwarzwald et al., 1983). Of these residents, 95 percent donated, in contrast to only 61 percent of those who had not first been asked to sign the petition. The petition-signing group was also more responsive to the specific amount requested. The greater the size of the suggested donation, the more they gave, whereas those not asked to sign the petition gave about the same (lesser) amount regardless of the amount suggested.

This is a robust compliance effect that works even when the two requests have little in common, and the requesters and their requests are quite different (Snyder and Cunningham, 1975). The key is having the first commitment be to a small, easy-to-agree-with request. This commitment appears to make salient the image people want to have of themselves as good people, willing to respond to worthwhile requests for good deeds by legitimate requesters. Subsequent commitment then is a way of maintaining consistency with that positive self-image. In the next chapter, we will examine in some detail the important links between commitment, consistency, and self-image.

Let us draw this part of our social influence analysis to an end with a very profound conclusion that Robert Cialdini came to after years of observing and experiencing firsthand what a host of different compliance professionals did so well. Cialdini argues that the effectiveness of all compliance-gaining strategies can be boiled down to six psychological principles, each of which works in a given context. The influence agent sets up the right context or setting in which the principle will function best to increase compliance.

We have explored in detail two of them: the context of creating feelings of *obligation*, which enables the *principle* or *rule of reciprocity* to operate, and the context of *commitment*, which invokes the *consistency principle*. Table 2.1 outlines the pairings of contexts and principles that account for most sources of compliance. We have seen that the power of the *authority principle* holds when the context of the influence agent's credibility is created. We are more likely to desire something that is dif-

TABLE 2.1 CIALDINI'S SIX COMPLIANCE CONTEXTS AND PRINCIPLES

Concern Aroused by Influence Context	Psychological Principle That Governs Action
Obligation	Reciprocation
Commitment	Consistency
Credibility	Authority
Friendship	Liking
Competition	Scarcity
Social validation	Consensus

SOURCE: Based on data from Cialdini (1987).

ficult to obtain than something that is easy, something rare as opposed to something ordinary; and so we comply more when a context of *competition* between people is created for limited resources. This perception triggers the operation of the *principle of scarcity*, which makes us value and want to own what is of limited availability, like A grades from tough-grading teachers, antique autos, rare wines, and people who play hard to get. At an obvious level is the link between the *friendship* context and the *liking principle:* we are more willing to do things for people we like, whose friendship we value and fear losing by not complying with their requests.

The final pairing links the *principle of consensus* with the context of *social validation* or social proof. Our sense of identity and self-worth is established in large part by evaluations others make of us. We want other people to think well of us, for them to have the same good opinion of us as we ourselves do. When uncertain about what to do to gain that positive social regard, we can look to what others are doing in that situation, or to what others whom we value are doing, and then imitate them. So when the context arouses our concern for being socially validated, we are more ready to do what we think is expected of us, to follow the in-crowd, to go with the consensus—to respond to normative and informational influence. Think about the everyday situations you encounter where these principles function to elicit your compliance, where you use them to get others to comply, and how this knowledge can lead you to be more effective—as a compliance agent, and a compliance resister.

POINT OF DEPARTURE: WHEN INNER CHANGES FLOW FROM EXTERNAL INFLUENCE

The theme of this chapter has been the power of direct and ordinary influences on behavior. We have seen that rewards, social pressure, clever juxtaposition of various requests, and a number of other situational factors can lead directly to changes in behavior—without our first having to change beliefs or attitudes. Yet, we have hinted that these changes in behavior can themselves trigger internal changes. Complying with a small request, for example, may lead to the belief that one is a generous person. Doing may pave the way for thinking or feeling. In the next chapter, we will see the many and varied ways in which actions translate into attitudes, beliefs, and self-concepts, so that what we do alters who we are.

*T*O SUM UP...

We discussed theories and methods of *directly influencing behavior* without first changing attitudes, beliefs, or feelings. We explained how the offer of rewards or punishments can accomplish this, as can situational manipulations that encourage conformity, obedience, and compliance without any persuasion or reason.

- Behavior may be directly influenced by situational stimuli that suggest a certain action will produce a positive outcome (reinforcement) or a negative outcome (punishment). Conditions suggesting that such a contingency between action and outcome is operative may cause people to perform the behavior that earns the reward or avoids the punishment. People learn contingencies by experiencing the consequences of their own actions (instrumental learning), by watching what others do (observational learning), and by receiving verbal messages about behavioral rules (instructional learning). Expectation of reinforcement is necessary for the later performance of observed behavior, but not for learning by observation.

- *Social approval* is rewarding; rejection is punishing. Deviance leads to rejection, and so "going along with the crowd" wins or keeps its acceptance. This is *normative influence*. Alternatively, we may go along because we assume that they know more about what is appropriate. We agree with others to reap the rewards of being correct. This is *informational influence*.

- *Conformity* is the act of changing one's behavior or belief to that of a group when the group doesn't directly request the change. People conform to incorrect group judgments when the judgment task is ambiguous (Sherif's studies) as well as clear-cut (Asch's studies). Conformity decreases when people have some social support for deviating, suggesting that conformity is a product of normative influence. Conformity increases when the group includes experts or when the person lacks self-confidence, suggesting that informational influence and genuine belief change may also, or alternatively, be at work.

- Though conformity usually entails only change in public behavior, it can lead to changes in private beliefs if the disagreeing majority causes the person to reexamine the situation to find out why the majority disagrees. Dissent from a unanimous majority occurs more often when there is an opportunity to offer a creative alternative and when the person enjoys acting differently—individuating—from others.

- If we conform too readily, we become vulnerable to manipulation by others. Yet conformity serves important personal and societal needs for prediction, order, and even change.

- *Obedience* is the act of doing what someone requests even when you would rather not. In laboratory studies of obedience, Milgram demonstrated that most normal, well-adjusted adults will deliver painful and dangerous electric shocks to a fellow subject at the command of an experimenter–authority figure. Given this, obedience to more powerful authority figures is seen not as a dispositional weakness but as a product of powerful situational forces.

- Obedience results partly from informational and normative pressures. Authority figures are presumed to know more and often give orders in novel contexts devoid of other cues to appropriate behavior. In addition, the target may fear rejection or ridicule by the authority figure. Obedience to authority also occurs because it is an ingrained habit—a judgmental heuristic or "rule of thumb" learned during socialization. To avoid obedience traps, we need to question why we are obeying, step out of a situation, rethink it, and learn to discriminate between just and unjust authorities.

- There are other *judgmental heuristics,* including the *reciprocity rule* to return favors and the *commitment rule* to stick to our words and deeds. "Kneejerk reactions" based on these socially learned rules are behind a number of compliance-gaining techniques.

- In the door-in-the-face technique, compliance with a small request is made more likely by first making a large request that the target refuses. Since the requester reduced the amount, the target feels obligated to reciprocate by acquiescing. The that's-not-all technique gains acceptance of a package deal by gradually "sweetening the deal" instead of offering it all at once. "Adding something" to the deal makes the target feel obligated to reciprocate.

- People tend to stick to positions to which they have made public commitments. The low-ball technique uses a customer's sense of commitment to gain agreement with a poorer deal after withdrawing a previously agreed on better deal. The foot-in-the-door technique parlays commitments to small favors into agreements to do big favors.

QUESTIONS AND EXERCISES

1. How would you use social learning principles to get a college roommate to study more often and conscientiously? Include applications of shaping, instrumental learning, observational learning, and discriminative stimuli.

2. Discuss the similarities and differences between conformity and obedience. To what extent are they based on the same psychological processes?

3. Imagine that your friend is about to buy a car. Illustrate how the low-ball, foot-in-the-door, that's-not-all, and door-in-the-face techniques could be

used on her by a cunning and conniving salesperson. How would you advise your friend to recognize and resist these tactics?

4.   Identify some of the elements of conformity, obedience, commitment, and social learning that seem to be involved in the Moonie recruitment process described in Chapter 1.

3

Influencing Attitudes through Behavior:

When Doing Becomes Believing

--- ❖ ---

Attribution and Self-Attribution ◆ *Self-Persuasion and Role-Playing* ◆ *The Psychology of Self-Justification: Dissonance Theory* ◆ *Dissonance, Self-Attribution, and Self-Affirmation: Similarities and Identities* ◆ *A Concluding Note*

Bill hangs out with a bunch of guys he has known since his family moved into the neighborhood when he was in the fourth grade. These are great guys, true friends with whom he has shared many childhood adventures. Now, in ninth grade and finally accustomed to the huge and confusing high school, Bill and his buddies are getting to know some of the older students. Although they are occasionally bullied by upperclassmen, they are increasingly accepted in various areas of high school social life.

Some of Bill's buddies recently joined the older group in an activity Bill's folks had taught him to avoid—smoking pot. At first, Bill resisted. But his friends, although not taunting, tried to convince him otherwise by describing how much they enjoy getting high, without any downside ill effects. Bill was not convinced, but finally yielded and smoked his first joint. Since then, he has smoked marijuana on three consecutive weekends. He is unlikely to admit it, or even be fully conscious of it, but the main reason Bill took up pot is that it became too socially uncomfortable not to. He didn't fit in until he said "Yes." Close and trusted friends were smoking pot, popular upperclassmen expounded its virtues, and it was readily available.

A familiar scenario—giving in to peer pressure. Bill's drug use is an example of conformity based on both the normative and the informational influence pressures we saw in Chapter 2. Bill feels that he will be part of the "in crowd" if he smokes pot; and his friends assure him that getting high on pot is enjoyable and safe. The evidence suggests that peer influence is the top cause of initiation into marijuana use (Kandel et al., 1978). But will Bill continue to use pot? Yes, most likely. Researchers who followed more than 600 young people in southern California over an eight-year period, from their junior high school years until they were in their early twenties, discovered great stability in the use of drugs (Stein et al., 1987). The best predictor of post–high school drug use was whether or not the individual was using drugs during the later years of high school. This was, in turn, highly related to earlier use of drugs. In short, once they begin to behave in a certain way, people tend to continue to do so. It's an old adage among behavioral scientists: the best predictor of future behavior is past behavior.

But why does this behavioral constancy hold true? Part of the reason has to do with the effects that our behavior can have on our attitudes and cognitions. If doing something a certain way gets us thinking that the behavior is desirable, necessary, or characteristic of our personality, then the chances are good that we'll continue to behave the same way in the future. The influence of behavior on attitudes and thoughts is the focus of this chapter. In Chapter 2, we saw that behavior can be influenced *directly* by certain social stimuli, without first changing attitudes or beliefs. This happens when social stimuli play upon the social and informational needs of people and the tendency for people to rely on judgmental heuristics in deciding a course of action. We also hinted that attitudes and beliefs may change indirectly because of a change in behavior, setting the stage for further or continuing behavior change. You will recall, for example, that the foot-in-the-door effect is partly driven by changes in *self-image*. Reflection on past help-giving makes one feel like the kind of person who is the "helping type." And feeling this way makes the person more prone to help again. Can you imagine a similar self-reflective and, in turn, self-defining course of mental events in Bill's life? "I smoke pot. I am that sort of person (I guess). I like feeling high." By concluding that he smokes pot because he likes the altered state it induces, Bill has made a *self-attribution* of causality. He believes his liking causes his smoking—rather than his need to be liked by others.

Beyond self-attribution, you may also suspect another mental activity that may grow out of behaving in a certain way. You know it as "rationalization"—coming up with reasons for your actions that you find satisfying and rational, after the behavioral fact. Smoking pot is banned by mainstream society, yet Bill does it anyway. This fact may bug Bill, who is normally law-abiding and supportive of the social status quo. He may be bugged enough to come up with reasons for this one big indiscretion. The reasons, of course, will be rationalizations, or *self-justifications*. Still they may be pretty convincing. Bill just may talk himself into becoming a regular pothead. He may succeed at *self-persuasion* using his rationalizations as arguments.

Self-attribution, self-persuasion, self-justification—it is time to take a close look at what social scientists know about these important processes that can shape how we think, feel, and act. The common link among them is that the critical agent of influence is the self—the internalized concept of oneself—and not change induced by an external persuasive agent. The person is thus both target and agent of influence, a dynamic duo within a single mind.

ATTRIBUTION AND SELF-ATTRIBUTION

In many ways, the process of self-attribution is a special case of the more general perceptual and cognitive processes by which we make attributions about what causes others' behavior. Just how do we make decisions about the *kinds* of people with whom we deal in our daily social encounters? How do we infer what others are thinking or feeling? Or what they are really like? More generally, how do we infer the *causes* of people's behavior? Answers to these questions are vital to understanding human behavior and interpersonal influence.

It is clear that people do attempt to "figure out" others. Fritz Heider (1958), a seminal thinker in the area of investigation known as *attribution theory*, proposed that we have a basic need to believe that we control our environment. We seek to understand why people do things in order to be able to predict and control what happens to *us*. In addition, what we figure out about others naturally should affect how we *behave* toward them.

Attribution Theory

Who you are or where you are. Most broadly, when trying to discern why someone did a particular thing—acted generously or violently, bought an expensive stereo, or started taking drugs—we can attribute the cause to either something about that person's disposition or something about his or her situation. *Dispositional* (or internal) *attributions* identify the causes of observed behavior as within the individual. To make a dispositional attribution is to assume that the behavior reflects some unique property of the person. Explanations of someone's hard work in terms of personal attitudes, religious beliefs, or character and personality traits would all be instances of dispositional attributions. The cause is assumed to be inside the person, as in "Tanya worked hard on the project because she enjoys the work."

In contrast, *situational* (or external) *attributions* identify factors in the social and physical environment that are causing the person to behave in a particular way. For example, if we saw someone hard at work and explained this behavior in terms of the money, the grade, or the praise that might be earned, then we would be making a situational attribution. The cause is seen as outside the person, as in "Tanya worked hard on the project because she really wanted the bonus the boss offered." Such an explanation assumes that most other people would act the same way, get the same results in the same situation. In other words, the person's behavior says more about the nature of the situation than about the individual. Also, if we make a situational attribution, we are assuming that without those situational factors, the person would not engage in the behavior we have observed.

Let's nail down the distinction with an example. Suppose Joe Candidate delivers a speech advocating tougher pollution controls for coal-burning factories as a means of eliminating acid rain. One listener, Joan, applauds this pro-environment stance. "I may vote for this guy; he's got the right idea about dealing with the acid rain problem." Marie, Joan's friend and colistener, screws up her face and stares at Joan. "Come on, Joan, the guy is just playing to his audience. He'll promise those controls to woo the votes of all the environmentalists in this college crowd. But don't bet on any real action." Marie has made a situational attribution: the audience made him do it. Joan has made a dispositional attribution: the candidate's pro-environment attitude is behind the speech; and by inference, she predicts that his future stands on other environmental issues will be similar.

A different example shows how this distinction between situational and dispositional analysis of behavior can reveal underlying prejudices. In comparing top professional basketball players, it is often said that player A achieved his status by hard work, while player B has made it because of his natural athletic talents. More often than not, you can bet that the analyst is referring to a white player A and a black player B. In this case, it is being implied that the black star didn't have to practice and work hard to make it to the top; he just had it all to begin with. Tell that to Michael Jordan, or to any other professional athlete of color, and see their reaction to your compliment that their success is "all natural talent."

How we decide. According to prominent attribution theorist Harold Kelley (1967), we consider three factors in deciding whether to make a dispositional or a situational attribution about an observed behavior. We focus on the *person* under three conditions. First, we are especially likely to make dispositional attributions when the behavior is *nonnormative*, that is, when it differs from what we think most people would do. For example, suppose you see a student behaving rudely toward a very well liked and respected professor. You are far more likely to attribute this atypical behavior to something special, and negative, about the student ("an insensitive and self-important boor," "a pathologically hostile guy") than to attribute it to something about the situation (such as a remark made by the professor).

Second, a dispositional attribution is more likely when the actor (behaving person) is known to frequently engage in the observed behavior. *Consistent* behavior over many occasions suggests something about the person, not the situation. For example, you explain the behavior of Terri, who is *always* on time for class, by saying that she is a punctual person or driven by compulsive needs. You see the behavior as reflecting a character trait, rather than occurring in response to situational factors that vary from occasion to occasion. Situational causes are possible: it might be that, for this class, the teacher locks the door once the class begins and takes attendance, dropping students who "cut" class. But the dispositional factor is the most likely attribution in the face of consistent behavior. Personality theorists, in fact, consider consistency of behavior across situations as one defining aspect of personality traits.

A third circumstance that compels dispositional attributions is when the same kinds of behavior occur in many different situations involving very different stimuli, in other words, when the behavior is *nondistinctive* or nonunique to a specific kind of situation. For example, you might really suspect an inner compulsion to be prompt when Terri not only makes all her classes on time but is invariably on time to all kinds of events, even parties where being "fashionably late" is the norm. Since no one situation or stimulus within a situation seems to be causing the behavior, you assume that something within Terri is causing it.

Information about normativeness, consistency, and distinctiveness can be available to an observer all at once. Thus, we usually weigh the various factors to decide the dispositional-or-situational question. Suppose that after you volunteer a comment in class, a classmate of the opposite sex compliments you on your insightfulness. The next two times you speak out, this person again takes time to praise your remarks. You find yourself more than a little curious about why this highly attractive person lavished such praise on you. You think: "No one else has flattered me (nonnormative). And it is the third time this attractive person has complimented me (consistent)." Interesting. But you also recall overhearing the person indiscriminately complimenting many other opposite sex classmates after they participate in classroom dialogue (nondistinctive). All three of your observations—but especially the last one that the person flatters people of the opposite sex indiscriminately—suggest a dispositional attribution that, sadly, does little for your ego. The person is flirtatious, or at least the type who wants to get involved with *anyone* who speaks out—anyone of the opposite sex, that is.

But now consider how a change in one piece of information could change your attribution, and maybe even your subsequent behavior. If the person never seems to compliment others—the flattery is distinctive, unique to you—your most likely conclusion then would be that your flattering classmate likes you. It is the classmate's disposition to like your disposition! OK, now that feels better.

What, specifically, is it about you? In the preceding example, when the compliment was nonnormative, one scenario led to the attribution of a flirtatious personality, and another to the attribution that the person likes you. The distinctiveness of the person's behavior was decisive about the *specific* internal attribution in this case. Other considerations may also rightly or wrongly lead us to conclusions about the specific kind of person we are observing.

We may use information contained in the effects we perceive from the actor's behavior (Jones and Davis, 1965). If the person's behavior has a certain effect and that effect is different from what would have happened had the person chosen a different behavior, we tend to extract clues about the kind of person we are dealing with on the basis of that *noncommon effect*. Consider a busy student with a rare chance to see a movie. To understand why she chose movie A over B, we first discount all common elements they share, such as price, starting time, distance to the theater, and others. The uncommon element is that movie A is science fiction and B is a nominee for an Oscar. We reasonably infer the cause of her decision to be a strong liking for science fiction flicks.

Another "clue" to judging the correct disposition reflected in a behavior gets us back to the idea of judgment heuristics, which we encountered in Chapter 2. Just as we learn certain "rules" of behavior, we also learn certain cause-and-effect relations that we may then apply without much thought. Kelley (1972) refers to these as culturally approved *causal schemata*. Examples: Q. Why is 12-year-old Marty so rebellious all of a sudden? A. It's just a stage he's going through. Q. Why is dad so grouchy tonight? A. He's probably angry about another bad day at the office.

Causal reasoning—not always reasonable. The attribution principles we have described depict rhyme and reason: a human observer who is quite rational. If everyone behaves as the actor does, the observer infers that the situation is a pretty powerful cause. If the actor's behavior has a unique consequence, the observer sees the consequence as a good clue to the actor's motive. These are quite sensible decision rules. And, indeed, people do use normativeness, consistency, distinctiveness, and noncommon effects, as shown by studies in which subjects are presented with various behavioral scenarios (like that of the flattering undergraduate) differing in the presence or absence of these factors and then they decide the most likely cause of the behaviors (e.g., McArthur, 1972; Ferguson and Wells, 1980).

On the other hand, causal attributions can be less than perfectly rational. The information processing involved in making these evaluations can become *biased*, that is, distorted in particular ways. One bias is a tendency to *oversimplify*. This can be the case when we apply a causal schema. It may be more than a stage Marty is experiencing. He may have a new peer group, or be having trouble in school. More generally, people point to one or two causes of behavior when, in fact, there usually are many causes. Another bias is what social psychologists refer to as the *salience effect*. This is the tendency to give more weight to those factors that are most visible and attention getting—like bad news.

In an experimental demonstration of the salience effect, subjects watched a prerehearsed conversation between two female confederates, whom we'll call Ann and Blair (Taylor and Fiske, 1975). One group of subjects watched from a vantage point behind Blair, facing Ann. Their visual attention was just on Ann. A second group had the opposite view: behind Ann, facing Blair. A third group had equal visual access to both Ann and Blair. When later asked who controlled the conversation—caused topic changes, won debates, and the like—the subjects who could see both faces gave Ann and Blair fairly equal marks. Despite hearing *exactly* the same conversation, however, the other groups of subjects interpreted things quite differently. Those whose attention was on Ann attributed greater control to her, while subjects attending mainly to Blair saw her as in charge. Perception of cause is very literally a matter of point of view.

The (apparent) dominance of dispositions. Then there is an attributional bias that is so pervasive and so full of implications that it has been dubbed the *fundamental attribution error* (Ross, 1977). Whenever we observe behavior and try to make sense of it in terms of its source, our judgment may be distorted in two interrelated ways. If the cause is not obvious, we tend to err in the direction of *overestimating* dispositional factors while *underestimating* situational factors. We are too ready to read personality and character traits into the behavioral drama and too resistant to see stage settings as the basis for the action. Our culture emphasizes the "cult of the ego," focusing on individual initiative and personal responsibility for success and failure, for sin and legal culpability. It is no wonder that we tend to look for the person in the situation more than we search for the situation that makes the person. Indeed, one of the major lessons of social psychology is that human behavior is much more under the influence of situational variables than we usually recognize or are willing to admit (e.g., Watson, 1982).

And by failing to account adequately for the power of these subtle situational forces—such as roles, rules, uniforms, symbols, or group consensus—we become vulnerable to those very forces. We do so because we overvalue our dispositional strength to resist undesirable forces and undervalue the situational strength to comply with them. Reconsider Stanley Milgram's classic demonstration of obedience to authority, which we outlined in Chapter 2. As we noted, before the study forty psychiatrists predicted that fewer than 1 percent of the subjects, the "abnormal" ones, would go all the way in delivering the full 450 volts to the helpless victim. They were making a dispositional attribution that their profession had trained them to overuse. And even after the results are in, showing over and over that the majority of people in this obedience paradigm comply with the rules of the game, to give increasingly high levels of shock to the "learner," most students persist in the belief that those subjects are different from them. Again the dispositional tendency overrides the obvious situational attribution, that something powerful in that situation is causing most subjects to react in unusual, atypical ways.

Scientific demonstrations of the fundamental attribution error abound, suggesting just how infrequently an accusing finger is pointed at the situation. In a study, which has relevance to how students judge their own and others' intelligence, students played a *College Bowl* quiz game in which one person asked questions while the other tried to answer them (Ross et al., 1977). The researchers randomly assigned students to their roles as "questioners" and "contestants." If selected as questioners, students were asked to think up ten of the most difficult questions about any topics to which they knew the answers. This, of course, put contestants at a tremendous disadvantage. They hardly could be expected to know a lot about what their questioners were interested in or knowledgeable about. Thus, in session after session, the contestants had to confess weakly "I don't know" to many of the questions. And in session after session, students observing this interaction attributed great intelligence and knowledge to the questioner and less of these virtues to the contestant. This happened despite the fact that they had been made fully aware of the game rules about who decided the question topics. The observers clearly tripped up on the fundamental attribution error. They failed to consider how stacked the situation was in favor of the questioner and against the contestant.

A critical implication of this and many related lines of experimental evidence is that we often *fail to discount* sufficiently for the impact of situational variables on the behavior we observe in others, even when we do acknowledge that the situation did play some role. We see this in the phenomenon of "blaming the victim" for being homeless or unemployed or abused, despite giving lip service to the social or political issues involved (Ryan, 1971). A concise statement of how this point of view becomes part of political philosophy is revealed in a recent article by Mona Charen, a conservative attorney who was a speech writer for President Reagan. She writes about the crack epidemic in America's inner cities: "Conservatives see people destroying their lives by ingesting drugs and conclude that the problem lies not with the society but the lack of self-control on the part of the individuals involved" (Charen, 1990, p. 3).

Self-Perception and Self-Attribution

The actor whose behavior you most frequently encounter is none other than yourself. When you do something, nearly always you are aware of your action, and therefore capable of reflecting on it—just as you might reflect on someone else's action. Do the general attributional principles just outlined apply to self-perception? Certainly, much of our behavior is planned in advance and so does not require the kind of after-the-fact explanation involved in attribution processes. In addition, our internal states, such as our attitudes and emotions, often spur us to behave in a certain way in a given situation. In these cases we know *why* we behaved that certain way. On the other hand, you will recall that the previous chapter featured behaviors that occur without much prior consultation with one's existing attitudes or mental states. In the cases we examined, unconscious habits and subtle situational pressures conspire to produce behavior. According to Daryl Bem's (1972) *self-perception theory*, the behaving person (*actor*) asked to explain this sort of behavior may engage in much the same attributional reasoning as would an *observer* watching the actor.

Bem argued that much of people's behavior is not a product of thinking about internal feelings and attitudes prior to acting. Instead, just the opposite often happens. People *infer* what their internal states and feelings are—or should be—by perceiving their past behavior and the situational forces that surrounded them at the time. For example, consider the Wall Street lawyer who, on a typical day, doles out all her pocket change to the street people who cross her path as she treks to and from work. One day at lunch, conversation centers on life in the Big Apple, and a colleague happens to ask the lawyer how she feels about giving to beggars. This gives her pause, as she has never really thought about it. What she can look back on, however, is the fact that she gives money to them every day (consistent behavior). Moreover, she cannot remember ever being forced to do so; if she wanted to, she could simply avoid eye contact and walk right by (no obvious situational pressures to give). And finally, now that she thinks about it, the situation cannot be very powerful, given that plenty of people walk right by these unfortunate individuals in their midst (no normative pressures on her). It becomes clear to our charitable attorney that, given her behavior, she must have a favorable attitude toward giving to beggars. She is indeed a generous person.

If this example reminds you of one explanation for the foot-in-the-door effect noted in the previous chapter, you are right in making that extension. Self-perception offers a viable account of why people who do small favors often become willing to do bigger ones. They infer from their past helping behavior that they are helpful people.

We are what we do. An ingenious experiment illustrates how beliefs about the self can be shaped by reflecting on past behavior (Salancik and Conway, 1975). College students completed a questionnaire that asked them to indicate whether or not each of twenty-four statements was self-descriptive. Some statements were about pro-religious acts, while others described antireligious acts. The students were randomly divided into two groups, one exposed to slightly different wording of the statements than the other. In the first group, most of the statements of proreligious acts contained the adverb "on occasion" (e.g., "I attend a church or synagogue on occasion"). Most of the statements of antireligious behavior contained the adverb "frequently" (e.g., "I frequently refuse to listen to the religious sermon at the end of the television broadcasting days"). In the second group, just the opposite adverb pairings were made on the questionnaire. Most proreligious statements were phrased with "frequently" ("I frequently refuse to attend classes on the religious holidays") and most antireligious statements with "on occasion" ("I refuse to discuss religion with friends on occasion").

The researchers reasoned that, in general, students would be reluctant to endorse the "frequently" statements as self-descriptive. Most of the listed behaviors simply were not of the type college students frequently do. The "on occasion" statements, in contrast, should more often be judged as self-descriptive. The behaviors were such that most students could readily recall engaging in them at least once in a while. Merely because of the different phrasing of the statements, students in the first group (pro-on-occasion) should answer true ("That's me") to a greater number of proreligious statements than those in the second group (anti-on-occasion).

This is exactly what happened. But that is only part of the story. The real kicker, consistent with self-perception theory, is that students in the first group later rated themselves as more religious than those in the second group. In answering that they occasionally did a lot of proreligious things, students in the first group recalled many of their past religious behaviors. From this remembered evidence of religious behavior, the students inferred that they were pretty religious. Just the opposite occurred among students in the second group, who found themselves recalling a number of occasional antireligious behaviors, leading to the self-perception of low religiosity. Just this brief exposure to a few descriptive terms resulted in very different self-perceptions on this important dimension. College students came to define themselves as more or less religious types of people based on the way this rather minor situational manipulation had altered their self-image.

Getting emotional. Self-attribution processes are particularly likely to play a role in the experience of emotions. Strong emotions have a common feature: they involve heightened physiological arousal characterized by quickened pulse, stomach butterflies, and the like. Normally, we know which emotion we are feeling because we have this queasy arousal, and the cause of this arousal is obvious from the situation. For example: "My heart is racing and my hands are sweating. I am angry and feeling jealous because I just saw the love of my life with someone else." Occasionally, however, we get mixed messages from physical sensations and the situation, yielding an attributional dilemma: What is this feeling? In classic self-attributional form, if the internal state of arousal is ambiguous enough, the experienced emotion will reflect whatever the obvious aspects of the external situation suggest.

And when the situation is misread, the result is what is called *misattribution*. One classic study asked people to take increasing levels of electric shock, ostensibly to study their pain tolerance (Nisbett and Schachter, 1966). Some subjects were first given a drug that supposedly produced heart palpitations and other symptoms of arousal. Actually, the "drug" was a sugar pill. Yet these subjects tolerated more shock than those not given the "drug": the shocks did not hurt them as much. They had mistakenly attributed their arousal not to its actual cause—the anticipated pain and worry of electric shock—but to the alleged "normal" effects of the drug.

Similar misattribution was observed in an experiment on adding arousal to insult (Zillman and Bryant, 1974). Participants either exercised vigorously or engaged in a relaxing task before pausing for a brief period. After the pause, they interacted with an insulting confederate. Those who had vigorously exercised expressed greater anger over the confederate's personal insult than those who had just been relaxing. The leftover arousal from the exercise was apparently "added" to whatever arousal followed the insult, creating an exceptionally strong sense of anger. Take heed from this study. Do you think this principle ever operates in group rallies, where speeches are preceded by marches, singing, and shouting?

Fundamentally wrong—about oneself. One thing you may have noticed about the examples discussed so far is that there is something a bit faulty about the attributional reasoning of self-perceiving people. They seem to ignore the *real* reasons for their behavior. For example, students overlooked the situational prod of cleverly placed adverbs in inferring their religious feelings. They committed the fundamental attribution error of underestimating the causal role of the situation in determining behavior, in this case, *their* behavior of making self-evaluations.

Perhaps more surprising in this regard are some additional results from the *College Bowl* quiz game study. Observers concluded that "contestant-subjects" were appreciably less knowledgeable than "questioner-subjects" after watching the contestants' dismal levels of success at answering the questioners' tough queries. They failed to fully discount for the fact that the game rules were to blame: the questioners got to choose the question topics. We know that even the contestants failed to appreciate this situational constraint because they rated themselves as less knowledgeable than the student who had questioned them. Another victory for situations over people!

We should not be so hard on these people, because situational forces can be easy to miss. But then again, that is precisely the point. One major reason situationally induced behavior can influence our attitudes and self-images is that situations are so powerful, yet seemingly so trivial.

When self-knowledge overrides self-perception. The process of self-perception—with its potential pitfalls—is most likely to occur when, in Bem's (1972) words, "internal cues are weak, ambiguous, or uninterpretable." If you aren't really sure what your favorite color is, because you have never thought much about it, you might have to check out your behavior to figure it out. What color do you wear most often? What seems to be the dominant color you used in decorating your room or apartment? On the other hand, if you *know* your favorite color, it is unnecessary to examine your behavior in order to infer your color preference.

Often "strong internal cues" are nothing more than clear and salient beliefs you have about yourself: self-knowledge. One of the clearest demonstrations of how self-knowledge lessens reliance on self-attributions is provided by a follow-up study to the religious-statements experiment we outlined earlier. The researchers repeated that experiment, using the linguistic magic of adverbs to get subjects to recall either "pro" or "anti" behaviors. They introduced two changes to the procedure: First, the behavioral topic was ecology rather than religion; second, two groups of students were studied who started out with different attitude structures about ecology. One group was known to have consistent and clearly defined attitudes about ecological and environmental issues. The other students had attitudes toward the environment that were not very consistent or well thought out. The results, shown in Figure 3.1, were clear. Both groups were affected by the remarkably powerful linguistic variation of the questionnaires, reporting more pro-ecology behaviors when they rated the self-descriptiveness of pro-ecology statements phrased with "on occasion" than when they rated statements phrased with the more extreme "frequently." Yet it was only the students with initially "weak" attitudes whose later *attitudes* were influenced by how they answered the questionnaire. Those with consistent, "strong" initial attitudes showed no effect, holding fast to their prequestionnaire stances. The researchers concluded that "high consistency subjects possessed strong internal cues regarding their feel-

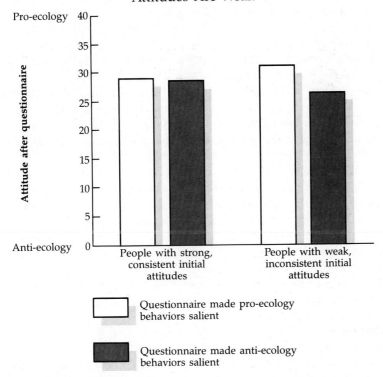

FIGURE 3.1
The wording of a self-report questionnaire encouraged respondents
to report having engaged in either many pro-ecology or many
antiecology behaviors. Respondents whose attitudes about ecology
were weak and poorly thought out later reported attitudes consistent
with the self-perceptions encouraged by the questionnaire. But
respondents with prior strong, clearly defined attitudes about
ecology were not affected by their "questionnaire behavior."
(From Chaiken and Baldwin, 1981. Copyright 1981 by the American
Psychological Association. Adapted by permission.)

ings and self-perceptions about being environmentalists and thus did
not need to 'infer' their attitudes from currently available behavioral information" (Chaiken and Baldwin, 1981, p. 9). Those with weak initial
attitudes did as Bem would have predicted: they let their actions speak
for their new attitudes.

I don't know until you ask me. Clearly, people are not continually
engaged in the formation of new attitudes and beliefs based on self-
perceptions of their current or recent behavior. This self-perception pro-

cess occurs mainly when we have a "need for structure regarding some novel attitude object" (Fazio, 1987). When we are directly asked our opinion about something or when we expect to encounter the object directly in the near future, this is the time we turn to perceptions of our behavior to discover what we believe about the issue. Under these circumstances of needing an attitude "on the spot," past relevant behavior may weigh heavily in its formation.

It is interesting, in this light, to consider once again the Wall Street lawyer. Her behavior toward beggars has always been quite routine and automatic. A cup is extended, a plea is made ("I have no job and I need a meal"), and she drags a quarter from her coat pocket and flips it in the cup. Her *mind* is on other things, like the cases she is preparing. She has really never taken the time to form an attitude about this giving, because she hasn't needed to and requires the mental space for other things. Only when the question was posed did the need to *form* an attitude arise. However, our guess is that she would also have formed an attitude about giving to beggars the following week (it was the summer of 1988) when her copy of *Time* arrived with a cover headline: "Begging in America: To Give or Not To Give?" The media, not just social psychologists, create situations that call for us to form attitudes, to stand up and be counted: for or against.

Religious conversion—acting oneself into it. Our first chapter described recruitment into the Moonies religious cult. People are invited to come voluntarily for a weekend retreat and are encouraged in light and airy ways to join into the group's activities. Once recruits find themselves at a Moonie retreat, acting like Moonies, they may very well infer from their behavior that they like and believe in at least some of the Moonies' ideas. This self-attribution is encouraged further by other factors. The cult people initially make the experience fun and rewarding, what is called "love bombing." Recruits enjoy themselves and infer that the lifestyle of the cult is the source of the pleasure. A positive attitude toward the cult follows. Moreover, they may do little things for the cult: contribute a little labor in the fields, give a small donation. As part of a class exercise, some of our students undergo the "Moonie recruitment treatment." In a break from the past, those students doing so in 1990 reported having to pay a small fee for the dinner and another for the ride to the retreat and for the weekend at the camp—foot-in-the-door-style cult commitment.

*S*ELF-PERSUASION AND ROLE-PLAYING

Self-attribution processes alone can mold our attitudes, feelings, beliefs, and self-images. But there are additional processes as well through

A Moonie lectures a potential recruit on 42nd Street in New York City. (*UPI/Bettmann Newsphotos*)

which outward behaviors can turn into changes in internal states. These additional processes, which may be accompanied by self-attribution, involve acting out or thinking out a new frame of mind to the point of accepting it as yours. During their stay with the Moonies, new recruits are encouraged to act out and think out the idea that their precult lives lacked love and direction, which can all be changed by joining in peaceful coexistence. Acting out is role-playing, thinking out is self-persuasion, and situations that promote them in tandem can profoundly change people.

All the World's a Stage...and We're Just Role-Players

People who are knowledgeable about interpersonal relationships—such as marriage counselors, mediators in labor-management disputes, and wise parents of peer-sensitive teens—commonly advise that it is helpful to try to take the point of view of someone with whom we may disagree. "Imagine yourself in her shoes," we might be instructed, "and maybe you'll see things differently." Therapy groups also employ this technique. *Role-playing*, as it is called, requires participants to adopt actively the role of another person (usually someone with whom they are having interpersonal difficulties). The goal is to produce changes in the participants' perceptions and evaluations of this other person: for example, "Now I see why he always puts me down; he's not very confident about himself." Sometimes just watching another member of the group enact a role may vicariously produce changes in perceptions and attitudes. But when you enact the role personally and experience what it feels like to be on the other side of the fence, that is when you are enmeshed in a powerful attitude change situation.

Role-playing can also be used to make people more tolerant of a given contrary position by having them publicly espouse opinions with which they initially disagree. Indeed, under some conditions, role-playing that requires the person actively to construct and improvise the role can be more effective in changing attitudes than passive exposure to persuasive communications (McGuire, 1985).

Beginning in the 1950s, social psychologist Irving Janis conducted some of the more important studies of how attitudes can be changed by role-playing. The earliest studies pitted the effects of improvising a speech advocating an initially negative position against the effects of listening to or reading verbatim an already prepared speech which came to the same conclusion. The basic finding was that attitudes changed most in the direction of the speech when it was improvised, when the subjects made up and played the part of someone who believed in the unpopular position (Janis and King, 1954; King and Janis, 1956). This was true even when male college students were arguing in favor of military draft for college students. A later study extended the role-playing idea into a setting of more immediate practical significance—getting cigarette smokers to adopt more negative attitudes toward smoking and, ultimately, to kick the habit.

In the smoker study, the researcher recruited college women who smoked at least fifteen cigarettes a day and randomly assigned them to either a role-playing condition or a control condition (Janis and Mann, 1965). Each woman in the role-playing condition was asked to adopt the role of someone who is being treated by her doctor for a "bad cough that was not getting any better" and who is now visiting the doctor a third time to learn the results of a chest x-ray and other tests. In the course of this third visit, she learns that she has lung cancer and needs immediate surgery and that, even with the surgery, there is only a moderate chance for a "successful outcome." She must, of course, quit smoking immediately. Within this frightening context, the experimenter sketched out five scenes (worrying while in the waiting room, conversing with the doctor as he gives the diagnosis, thinking about the news as the doctor phones for a hospital bed, and so on) that the role-player was to act out in her own words as realistically as possible.

Then the minidrama began, with the experimenter as the doctor and the subject talking through the role of someone who is learning that she may die because she smoked heavily. In contrast to this *active involvement* in an uncomfortable role, the women in the control group merely listened to a tape recording of one of the active role-playing sessions. They *passively* obtained the same information as the women in the role-playing condition. But does actually acting out a role make a difference over and above merely getting the new information abut the other side's position?

The results clearly indicated that role-playing made such a difference. Compared with subjects in the control condition, the role-players expressed stronger beliefs that smoking causes lung cancer and greater fear of personal harm from smoking. The role-players also indicated greater intentions to quit smoking. Ah, but talk is cheap, and smoking is addictive. Did the role-players actually change their smoking habits? And did their habits change more than those of the non-role-playing control subjects? Yes and yes. In a telephone follow-up 2 weeks after the experimental sessions, women in the control condition reported smoking an average of 4.8 fewer cigarettes per day. The control subjects were affected by passive exposure to a powerful situation. But active immersion in that situation through role-playing had double the effect. Women in the role-playing condition reported smoking 10.5 fewer cigarettes per day, on average. This difference is remarkable considering that the role-players enacted the role for less than an hour. Even more remarkable is that the difference was still evident in a second follow-up conducted 6 months later (Mann and Janis, 1968).

What gives improvisational role-playing this power to influence subsequent attitudes and behavior? Two factors appear responsible: self-attribution and self-persuasion. Self-attribution processes, by now familiar to you, can be engaged by acting out a role. An individual may have an overall opinion about a topic, but it is unlikely that *all* the knowledge, beliefs, and feelings held about that topic are unambiguously one-sided. Most things are a bit muddier than that. Attitudes toward smoking in the mid-1960s were muddy, if not yet tarred indeed. The Surgeon General's report of compelling evidence that smoking causes lung cancer followed this role-playing study by 3 months, and for years before, the issue had been in the news. These young women—informed college students—were likely to have had some negative feelings and uncomfortable knowledge about smoking. Role-playing the thoughts and emotions of a smoker who had cancer would favor recall of the negatives about smoking. These salient thoughts, coupled with the emotion felt while acting out a horribly traumatic experience, might easily dominate self-reflection. "Gee, I really do believe that smoking is dangerous and dumb. It's time to give it up." In other words, because the role enactment ensured that subjects would generate mostly negative thoughts about smoking, any inferences from self-perception would most likely be negative.

The second factor in role-playing is *self-persuasion*. Remember, the role-players improvised: they constructed their own character and her thoughts and reactions to the situation. In a real sense, they created a convincing portrayal, and they convinced themselves of the ideas and emotions conjured up for the role. As one of the role-players put it, "I heard so much about the dangers of smoking, and then one more thing and that was it" (Janis and Mann, 1965, p. 89). That "one more thing" she provided herself. But the control subjects heard someone else's role enactment. Shouldn't they be persuaded as well? Self-persuasion often has considerably more impact than receiving information from someone else. It's a matter of "getting into it." Creating ideas and feelings for yourself makes them more salient, more personally relevant, and more memorable (Greenwald, 1968). Since you usually know your defenses that bolster a given attitude, you are in the best position to attack them—from the inside out. Also, when actively role-playing, you're fully engaged in generating ideas that support the role. As a result, counterarguments (e.g., "But smoking relaxes me, and some medical researchers dispute the cancer claims") are less likely to come to mind than if you're just sitting there listening. We will have more to say about the impact of *active* thinking and its role in persuasion in Chapter 5.

Fear arousal also may have contributed to role-playing's powerful effect. To be sure, the role enactment aroused fear, and fearful thoughts can be particularly self-persuasive. One could say that the role-players frightened themselves into attitude change. As the next example demonstrates, however, fear is not a necessary ingredient for role-playing to move attitudes.

More Self-Persuasion: TV or Not TV

The self-persuasion component of the role-playing effect, and its potential as an influence tool, can be illustrated by looking at a practical problem: the influence of television on behavior and mental life. Social scientists have done a great deal of research on the subject of TV, since it is a frequent companion to most people—a companion that constantly communicates messages and does not allow back talk. People in Western nations, on average, spend 2 to 3 hours per day watching television—twice as much time as they spend socializing with other people (Liebert and Sprafkin, 1988; McGuire, 1985). Children are among the most avid TV watchers; some watch for as much as half their waking day, and much of what they watch depicts violence. This troublesome fact has prompted much research on the effects of watching TV violence on children's attitudes and behavior. The general conclusion reached by this body of research suggests that a heavy diet of TV violence does contribute to the development of a more aggressive interpersonal style, especially among children whose environments and learning already favor aggressive behavior (Eron, 1980; Wood et al., 1990).

Can anything be done to weaken or break this unfortunate relationship, which adds to the high level of generic violence in the United States? Violence-filled action TV programs are so popular that the networks will certainly not remove them voluntarily. In a free society, censorship is out of the question. A better approach is to work directly with the children who watch violent TV programs. Children learn aggressive responses from TV because they tend to see the depicted violence as a realistic and socially acceptable response to problems. In addition, TV's violent heroes are so attractive that adoring viewers quickly come to identify with them. If children could be taught that society does not accept aggression as a solution to problems, that what TV depicts is very unrealistic and is done with special effects, and that there are usually better ways of solving problems, then perhaps children would not adopt for themselves the aggressive styles of TV stars.

This reasoning led one research team to use a coordinated series of lectures, demonstrations, and small group discussions in an effort to persuade first and third graders that TV violence is faked, that violence leads to social rejection, and that there are more effective ways of solving problems than through violence (Huesmann et al., 1983). There was only one problem: it didn't work. The children given this training showed no changes in attitudes, TV-viewing behavior, or aggressiveness. Indeed, in these respects, they were indistinguishable after their training from children in a control group who had been given no instruction.

Disappointed but not defeated, the researchers did a second study in which they tried self-persuasion. They randomly assigned first and third graders from a school district in suburban Chicago to either an "intervention" or a control group. In the first of two group sessions, the children in the intervention group were asked to volunteer to help make a videotape to show other kids who had been "fooled by television or harmed by television violence or got into trouble because of imitating it." The experimenter continued that "of course you know better than to believe what you see on TV and that imitating what you see may be bad." Accepting this attractive self-perception, all the children readily volunteered. The eager volunteers then composed persuasive essays in which they were instructed to "tell how television is not like real life," "why it is bad to imitate TV violence," and "why it is bad to watch too much TV." Examples were provided to help them with their essays. A week later the children read their essays on camera, and responded to brief questions as if they were guests on a talk show. At the end, the resulting videotape was replayed so that they could see themselves contributing to the story line "Don't be fooled by TV." The children in the control group went through a very similar procedure, except that their essay-videotape topic was "Why everyone should have a hobby," instead of TV violence.

A week before the essay-videotape sessions, children in the two groups had similar scores on an attitude questionnaire tapping the extent to which they thought that things on TV shows were faked and that watching violent shows makes kids meaner. They were also comparable in their level of aggressiveness (as judged by schoolmates) and in their TV viewing habits. This similarity disappeared following the experiment. The children who wrote essays concerning TV violence definitely persuaded themselves, just like the role-playing smokers. When they were again given the attitude measure 2 months after the intervention, they gave responses consistent with the "don't be fooled by TV violence" theme they had written about. The average change was a robust 2.3 points per 5-point attitude scale! In contrast, the control group showed virtually no change. In the months that followed the essay-videotape sessions, children in the control group became more aggressive, which is consistent with observations by developmental psychologists that aggression increases with age during the elementary school years. This was not so with the children in the intervention group: they did not become more aggressive. They had psychologically inoculated themselves against the social virus of video aggression.

Finally, children in both groups continued to watch about the same amount of violent television. But amount watched did not get translated into aggressive behavior among the children in the intervention group. For these youngsters, it seems that watching no longer stimulated doing. In short, they adopted exactly the attitudes and beliefs about TV violence that they had spoken in favor of in their videotaped messages to children. With a little nudging from the experimenters, the children convinced themselves that TV violence, though fun to watch, was pure fantasy, that aggression in real life is "uncool," and that they were smart enough to realize these differences between image and reality.

This is a truly impressive case of self-persuasion. Think about it. In just two short and enjoyable sessions, children took on the roles of teacher and social commentator, and they were meaningfully transformed into knowledgeable critics of gratuitous TV violence. And the simple activities they performed were effective where lecture and group discussion—more traditional educational tools—had failed. Role-playing can achieve positive educational goals, because even 8-year-olds can be effective persuaders—of themselves.

We have now seen in some detail that our behaviors can cause our attitudes. It can happen because we sometimes decide how we feel by reflecting on how we behaved—especially when internal feelings were absent or ambiguous before the behavior. It can also happen because some of our behaviors, like role-playing or communicating a specific point of view, encourage us to think in ways that lead to a new attitude or self-image. These mediators of the behavior-to-attitude causal chain are more or less purely "cognitive": behavior rather naturally instigates thoughts that favor an attitude consistent with the behavior. This sequence typically involves less than perfect reasoning. We fail to recognize situational influences and are overly swayed by whichever of our thoughts are most salient. Nevertheless, there is no necessary bias involved—no motivation or *need* to have an attitude that *justifies* the behavior. We now turn to a final psychological process that can be a potent factor in the behavior-to-attitude chain, the one that does involve motivated self-justification.

*T*HE PSYCHOLOGY OF SELF-JUSTIFICATION: DISSONANCE THEORY

Consider the following situations and the questions they pose.

- Bill was asked to tell a "white lie" and received twenty dollars for doing so. Tom received only one dollar for telling the same lie. One of these fellows ended up believing in the lie he told. Was it Bill or Tom?

- You say you don't like the idea of eating fried grasshoppers? Suppose you are persuaded to try one, and the person persuading you is really nice. Would that affect your actual liking of such an obnoxious food? Would it affect it more or less than if your agent of persuasion was negative—someone you disliked?

There are likely answers to these questions, for the situations described have been created in social psychological experiments. The answers are that (1) Tom, who received only one dollar, will come to believe in his lie; and (2) you will probably like grasshoppers better once you've tried them—but especially if you had complied with the wishes of a *disliked* person to eat one. Are you surprised? Skeptical? Indeed, most newcomers to social psychology would not make these predictions. But they make good sense from the point of view of *cognitive dissonance theory*. Let us first outline some basic aspects of this interesting theory, and then we will return to white lies and fried grasshoppers.

Dissonance theory deals with how people handle the inconsistencies that they experience. We saw in Chapter 2 that people are uncomfortable with inconsistencies in social situations. Disagreement with others who are in many ways similar creates an inconsistency that is often "fixed" by bringing one's beliefs more in line with those of others. That is, of course, one source of conformity in group settings. In another example, a desire to be consistent may compel people to agree to big favors after doing small ones. Leon Festinger (1957) felt that people's discomfort with inconsistencies applies very broadly—that even discrepancies existing entirely within the individual's own cognitive system are sources of psychic unrest. Festinger used the term *cognitive dissonance* to refer to the internal inconsistency between different cognitions in the mind of a person.

Cigarette smokers provide a good example of cognitive dissonance. A person who smokes has the cognition "I am a smoker." Information about the negative consequences of smoking produces a second cognition ("Smoking causes lung cancer") that is inconsistent or dissonant with the first one. After all, if smoking causes lung cancer, and you don't want to die prematurely, why smoke? One cognition does not psychologically follow from the other; it is hard to believe them both at the same time.

In dissonance theory, cognitions are bits of knowledge ("It is raining"), attitudes ("I like the rain"), or beliefs ("The rain makes flowers grow") either about the environment or about oneself. According to the theory, cognitions can be in one of three relationships: dissonant, consonant, or irrelevant. In the smoking example, the cognitions "I like the taste of cigarettes" and "smoking is relaxing" would be consonant with the self-knowledge that the person smokes, while most cognitions concerning rainfall would be irrelevant.

Factors Affecting the Magnitude of Dissonance

Some inconsistencies involve more dissonance than others. One factor that affects the magnitude of dissonance is the *importance* of each of the cognitive elements. "I don't want to die before my time" is dissonant with continuing to smoke. But if it were not important to a smoker that he or she might die of lung cancer (because the person is 80 years old and has already lived a full life), then little dissonance would be produced by the two cognitions "I smoke" and "smoking causes cancer."

A second factor affecting the magnitude of dissonance is the number of dissonant and consonant cognitions a person is experiencing at any one time. The greater the *ratio of dissonant to consonant cognitions*, the greater the dissonance. In the smoker example, only two cognitions were dissonant. Adding a third cognition, "My cigarettes have less tar and nicotine than others," reduces dissonance by increasing the number of consonant cognitions. Any addition of consonant cognitions can dramatically reduce dissonance. But knowing several smokers who recently died of lung cancer tips the ratio in the high dissonance direction.

Since some cognitions are linked to a person's behavior and others to the environment, changes in both the environment and in the person's behavior will change that person's cognitions. If our smoking friend stopped smoking, the cognition "I smoke" would obviously change to "I don't smoke." Thus a critical point of the theory is that one way a person can change a set of dissonant cognitions to a set of consonant cognitions is to change behavior, if behavior is itself the source of a dissonant cognition.

But it isn't always so easy. The behavior may be difficult to modify, as in the case of smoking highly addictive nicotine products. Or the behavior in the dissonant relationship may be a *past* behavior, undeniable yet starkly at odds with the person's current attitude. In this situation of difficult to change *attitude-discrepant behavior*, dissonance theory becomes very relevant to our major theme in this chapter that attitudes can be influenced by behavior. The theory maintains that *something* has to change because cognitive inconsistency is uncomfortable and people are naturally motivated to eliminate it—to reduce dissonance. Festinger's theory assumes that people have a need to maintain cognitive consistency, and that dissonance is an aversive drive state motivating action to reduce it until consistency is again established.

When behavior cannot be changed or revoked, one or more of the beliefs or attitudes with which it is inconsistent might be changed, as in "I do not buy the evidence that links smoking and cancer." Consonant cognitions might be added: "Smoking keeps my weight down." These means of reducing dissonance, of course, are modifications in attitude—changes in a person's view of the world in the service of seeing his or her current or past behavior as consistent, reasonable, and justified.

Dissonance and Insufficient Justification: Less Is More

Consider the following situation. A university, eager to develop an innovative "core" of required courses in the liberal arts, invites input from the faculty. In the psychology department, the general feeling is that, although imperfect, the proposed curriculum put forth by a special committee is the best that is likely to emerge. In addition, since the university administrators who control the purse strings favor it, it would be unwise politically for the department to oppose it. Our hero, young Professor Smith, has some reservations about the proposed curriculum and is leaning toward voting against it. One day, however, the department chair suggests to Smith that he put in "whatever good word he can" about the proposal at a faculty meeting. The chair explains, "Although I know you oppose aspects of the proposal, I would really find it helpful if some of the more thoughtful faculty members said something about what is good with the plan. But say what you want to. After all, you've got tenure, and so you are free to present your own viewpoint."

You probably can guess what Professor Smith did. He spoke mildly in favor of the proposed core curriculum. Through some sense of obligation to his likable chairperson and a nagging fear of what proposals might be offered if the current one were defeated, Smith opted to publicly speak for something he was consciously opposed to. But once this was done, Smith was guilty of attitude-discrepant behavior.

And then something else happened to Smith. In a rather brief time span, he changed his mind about the new core curriculum, which was passed by a narrow margin. In fact, he volunteered to teach one of the new "interdisciplinary" core courses.

According to dissonance theory, Smith got himself into a state of cognitive dissonance. The two clashing cognitions were "I dislike the proposal" and "I said favorable things about it to my colleagues." But the two would *not* be dissonant if Smith somehow felt *forced* to say the favorable things. If he did feel compelled or pressured, he could *justify* the inconsistency. "I had to do it, I had no choice." The catch here is that the chairperson did not twist his arm; the chairperson's push was gentler. Smith did not feel coerced; he was free to act as he felt. If Smith had felt forced to behave inconsistently with his attitude, he probably would not have then changed his attitude. The inconsistency would not need to be justified. "I did it to keep my job, but I don't believe in what I had to say."

Professor Smith's change in attitude about the curriculum proposal illustrates both a major tenet and a major practical implication of dissonance theory. The tenet is this: For attitude-discrepant behavior to produce an uncomfortable state of dissonance that is later eliminated by attitude or behavior change, people must perceive that they *freely chose* to perform that behavior. The implication that follows from this principle involves a crucial distinction between *outward behavioral compliance* and genuine changes in *private attitudes or beliefs*. If you want people to *do* as you wish, the more coercion, or reward, you can supply, the more likely you will get your wish. "Support my policies or you're fired." "Endorse my product and I'll pay you 1,000 dollars." The more the inducement, the more the compliance. On the other hand, if your ultimate goal is to get others to *like* or *agree with* the behavior you've compelled them to do, then the *less* inducement you need to gain behavioral compliance, the better. The less the inducement, the more the private attitude will change in the direction of the induced compliant behavior.

Why? Because big inducements (threats, bribes, begging, money, and what not) are obvious justifications that eliminate any sense of freedom to choose. Thus we have the logic of dissonance theory: Use only as much "force" as necessary to get the person to perform the behavior. The inducement should be *barely sufficient* to get compliance and *insufficient* as an additional cognitive element that would itself justify the attitude-behavior inconsistency. The fewer the reasons for engaging in attitude-discrepant behavior, the greater the dissonance. In short, when asked why he is doing the discrepant deed, the high-dissonant person should not be able to justify it by pointing to situational variables. And so if it wasn't anything easily identifiable out there, it must be something about...me.

As the pegs turn... Which brings us back to little white lies. In one of the classic experimental demonstrations of the less-is-more principle, college students were first put through a full hour of dull, monotonous tasks (Festinger and Carlsmith, 1959). While the experimenter ostensibly monitored their performance, they repeatedly filled a tray with spools, emptied it, and then turned square pegs a quarter-notch at a time. Boring, to say the least. Later, some of the subjects were offered one dollar by the experimenter to describe (for research purposes) the experimental tasks as interesting and enjoyable to the next subject. Other subjects were offered twenty dollars to do the same thing. Despite the difference in the size of the inducement, nearly all subjects agreed to tell this lie, to engage in this attitude-discrepant behavior.

Although the compliance rates were similar, the attitudinal consequences were not. After telling their lie, all subjects were individually interviewed by someone they believed was unaffiliated with the experiment. The interviewer asked them to rate how much they themselves had enjoyed the experimental tasks. The subjects who had been paid twenty dollars rated the tasks as relatively unenjoyable. Their judgments closely resembled those of control subjects who simply engaged in the tasks and then rated them. In contrast, those paid only one dollar expressed a more positive attitude: they rated the tasks as enjoyable. It appears that the subjects paid twenty dollars experienced little dissonance. A twenty dollar payment justified a lie—especially a little one sanctioned by an authority in the form of a researcher. A one dollar payment, however, is more difficult to think of as a sufficient reason to deceive a fellow student. Subjects paid one dollar therefore had dissonance to reduce, and they did so by changing their attitude to fit their dirty deed.

The illusion of choice. Because the one dollar is so paltry a payment, subjects had the all-important impression that they freely chose to deliver false information to another person. In fact, they had an "illusion of choice" created by the researchers, who took advantage of something we have seen time and again in this chapter: people's insensitivity to subtle situational prods. The real reasons for the subjects' be-

THE FAR SIDE   By GARY LARSON

Insufficient justification
misapplied. Less is more if
your goal is attitude change,
but not if your goal is simply
compliant behavior.

Ineffective tools of persuasion

havior are contained in the powerful situational trappings of the experiment—a situation so powerful that 90 percent of the subjects who were paid one dollar complied. Politely but firmly, and with apparent logic, an authority figure (the experimenter) asked a favor (to deceive the next subject for scientific purposes). (Incidentally, you should now be thinking of the Milgram studies.) But the compliance pressure is so subtle that, unless an obvious prod is provided (say twenty dollars), it looks to subjects as if they've freely decided with no pressure. The language of the compliance manipulation typically stresses that "you don't have to do it if *you* do not want to," "it's entirely up to *you*, although it would be appreciated if you did," and so forth.

Many studies have since replicated the basic less-inducement-more-attitude-change finding. These studies are called induced-compliance studies because of their use of barely sufficient nudges to induce attitude-discrepant acts. A more recent study is worth reviewing, because it illustrates further the role of perceived freedom of choice and highlights several additional conditions necessary to arouse cognitive dissonance and make it drive attitude change.

Paying to park—and liking it. In this study, the attitude-discrepant behavior was the writing of an essay endorsing a university parking fee by students who, until then, enjoyed free parking (Elkin and Leippe, 1986). Naturally enough, a preliminary survey revealed that the student subjects strongly opposed a parking fee. Indeed, the average attitude was 1.6 on a 31-point scale in which 1 meant strongly opposed and 31 meant strongly in favor.

During the experiment, these opponents of a parking fee were told that they would each be writing an essay about the "possibilities of a parking fee." These essays would be sent to a university policy making committee collecting arguments on both sides of the issue. To subjects randomly assigned to a low-choice condition, the experimenter said that the best procedure for obtaining arguments on both sides was simply to assign a side regardless of how people personally feel. He went on to assign the subjects to write in support of a parking fee. In contrast, to subjects in a high-choice condition, the experimenter stressed the "voluntary nature of the issue you decide to write on." Subjects could write on either side, even though enough anti-parking-fee essays had been collected and the committee now needed essays on the pro side. The experimenter gave high-choice subjects a pitch much like the one Professor Smith received from the department chairperson. But to really foster the sense of free choice, the experimenter also had high-choice subjects sign a release form indicating their voluntary participation, making it salient to them.

All subjects in both choice conditions wrote an essay in favor of the parking fee—despite the attitude they had previously expressed against such a fee. A few minutes after completing the essay and placing it in an envelope addressed to the committee, subjects again completed an attitude test concerning parking fees. As is shown in Figure 3.2, the only subjects who shifted their attitude were those in the high-choice condition. Their attitudes changed in the direction of a more pro-parking-fee stance. They had dissonance to reduce. Falling for the illusion of choice created by the experimenter, they had no justification for their attitude-discrepant essay. How could they justify writing in favor of paying to park if they were against it? Maybe they weren't really so much against it now that they accentuate some of its positives and eliminate some negatives. Low-choice subjects experienced little dissonance, because they had been *told* what to write.

From discrepant acts to dissonance—the necessary conditions. Again we see in this study the necessity of *perceived free choice* in the creation of cognitive dissonance (Zimbardo, 1969). But there are also some other requirements. The individual must *feel personal responsibility* for the anticipated consequences of the attitude-discrepant act. This means that the person must be committed to the behavior and thus unable to deny he or she did it and knew the consequences at the time. Further, the individual must *anticipate aversive consequences*. In the parking-fee study, the consequences of the students' essays were quite clear before

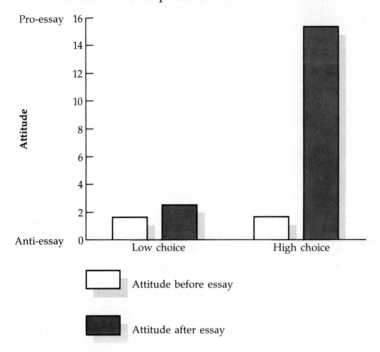

FIGURE 3.2
Attitude change to reduce dissonance. Subjects who perceive that
they freely chose to write the essay endorsing a student parking
fee change their attitudes to agree with the essay. Subjects who
perceive low choice do not change.
(Data from Elkin and Leippe, 1986. Copyright 1986 by the American
Psychological Association. Adapted by permission.)

they wrote them, and these consequences were distinctly negative. By
their supportive essay to a policymaking committee, they could be giving away their own money as well as that of their friends—right down
the (parking lot) drain. Subjects in the high-choice condition, as well,
could hardly deny responsibility for their essay, since they had signed a
release form.

As Joel Cooper and Russell Fazio (1984), two leading dissonance
theorists, have put it, dissonance is aroused if the expected outcome of
behaving inconsistently with one's attitude is "an event that one would
rather not have occur." Other theorists have pointed out that aversive
consequences can also be defined in terms of the individual's self-
concept. Dissonance is aroused, they say, when a person feels responsible for outcomes that don't jibe with his or her self-image—when they

OWIT

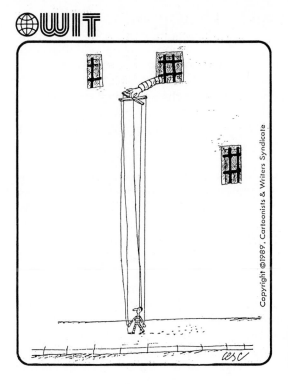

The illusion of choice and control.
(Cesc, © 1990 Cartoonists & Writers Syndicate.)

imply that the person is "bad" or has different values than he or she actually does (Baumeister, 1982; Schlenker, 1982).

Although not strictly necessary for the arousal of dissonance, attitude-discrepant acts are especially dissonance arousing when they are highly *public* (Baumeister and Tice, 1984; Elkin, 1986). There are three reasons for this. First, public behavior may trigger the *commitment heuristic* we saw in Chapter 2. You will recall that people tend to feel obliged to stand by their public deeds. Thus, if the behavior is public, the motivation to bring attitude into line with the behavior will be fueled by both dissonance arousal and the commitment heuristic—a potent one-two punch. A second role of publicity is to increase the implications of the inconsistency for a person's *self-concept*. As if it were not enough that personally unwanted consequences may follow from the behavior, the behavior will also imply a willingness to look either unscrupulous or wishy-washy to others—unless one's attitude changes to concur with the behavior. Indeed, according to some theorists, concern over the impressions that our inconsistencies make (on others and ourselves) can be a stronger force on attitude change than the inconsistency itself (Tedeschi and Rosenfeld, 1981). Finally, there is the *external reality anchoring* of public actions. Public behaviors cannot easily be denied or distorted in the person's mind, as can one's attitudes, beliefs, and feelings. Thus, when dissonance exists between a behavioral cognition ("I just endorsed the curriculum proposal in my address to the faculty") and an attitudinal cognition ("The proposal is not so hot"), the cognition pertaining to the behavior is less likely to change to the extent that it is an undeniable public fact, while the attitudinal cognition can more readily be adjusted so as to agree with the behavior ("The proposal is actually educationally sound"). Representative Private yields the floor to Representative Public.

To know grasshoppers is to love them. Having outlined the role of publicity in dissonance, imagine how you would feel if you had just agreed to eat a fried grasshopper in front of your peers—and then did so. Subjects were induced by an experimenter to do just that in one study, which used both college students and also Army Reserve Training soldiers (Zimbardo et al., 1965). In one condition of the experiment, however, the subjects witnessed a series of events that made the experimenter look like an extremely pleasant and fair-minded fellow. In a second condition, other subjects witnessed events that created the impression of that same experimenter as an unpleasant, two-faced person. Despite his image—whether positive or negative—the experimenter elicited compliance from about half the subjects, who actually ate the ugly grasshoppers. But as we alluded to earlier, a positive change in attitude toward finding the slimy little beasties palatable was only prevalent among those subjects who complied with the unpleasant, negative experimenter. And now you know why: If the experimenter is pleasant and likable, there is clear justification for the literally distasteful act ("I couldn't refuse such a nice guy")—a situational attribution. If the experimenter is not so nice, and people are watching as well, you've got some explaining to do—to yourself and maybe to others ("I sort of like these gourmet treats")—a dispositional attribution. If the subject did not eat the grasshopper because of any good feeling toward the negative experimenter, then how can he or she justify this dissonant munching? Easily, by persuading oneself that they aren't so awful after all, in fact. A more extreme measure of attitude change had subjects endorse eating grasshoppers as a suitable survival food in an alleged new army manual that would identify them personally as soldiers who had tried and liked them.

Religious conversion—revisited. Earlier we noted that the subtle influence techniques of Moonie recruiters may go unnoticed by new recruits. With no strong attitudes regarding religious and social matters, recruits may infer their attitudes from their behaviors of joining into cult activities without obvious outside pressure to do so. Even if new recruits do have an initially anti-Moonie attitude, however, you can

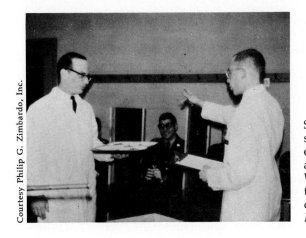

Courtesy Philip G. Zimbardo, Inc.

Scene from the "grasshopper study": The "negative experimenter" criticizing his assistant while a subject looks on. When subjects ate grasshoppers at this experimenter's request, they came to like them. (*Courtesy Philip G. Zimbardo, Inc.*)

now see that, via the principle of insufficient justification, the subtle compliance techniques of the Moonies can win the recruits. The technique may produce considerable dissonance: "I do not believe in this philosophy"; "I am behaving like those who do believe in it"; "No one is forcing me to." An obvious way to reduce the dissonance caused by the inconsistency is to change the first cognition to "I believe in some of this philosophy."

And why is persuading new converts a major cult activity? Here we find dissonance again. Additional justification for becoming a Moonie is obtained by having social support for this major act. Dissonance should be enormous when people join religious cults, given the major change in lifestyle, the rejection of previously valued friendships, and the acceptance of required new ways of behaving. By being "deployable agents" effectively getting other individuals who initially valued the same things as the converts to reject their old ways and join the cult, recent converts can point to this additional support to *rejustify their own decision*. They must have made the right choice, otherwise why would so many people be choosing to join the group?

Modes of Dissonance Reduction

Overall, specific ways to reduce dissonance fall into four general modes. Dissonance can be reduced by (1) attempting to revoke or change decisions, attitudes, or behaviors; (2) lowering the importance of the cognitions, or of the decision; (3) adding consonant elements to change the dissonant-to-consonant ratio; and (4) directly reducing the arousing aspect of dissonance through the use of tranquilizing drugs or alcohol.

Which of these paths will be taken by the person experiencing dissonance from his or her postdecisional conflict? Fortunately, the theory is not silent on this matter. The overall rule is that *people take the path of least resistance.* In other words, the cognitions that are easiest to change are the ones that do change. Some cognitions resist change more than others; they are the ones that are undeniable and that are especially important to the person's way of thinking or self-image.

Undeniability. Normally, it is quite difficult to change one's knowledge of the behavior, especially if the behavior is public. It is simply undeniable that the attitude-discrepant behavior occurred. Private attitude change is easier. Even easier, if the situation permits, are more subtle cognitive changes, such as reducing the importance of the inconsistency ("Sure a parking fee is distasteful, but what's a few more bucks added to the megabucks we pay for tuition"). In a similar way, freely made decisions are often undeniable or irrevocable. You got taken by the confidence man, you agreed to do a worthless or dangerous thing, or you made a major change in your lifestyle by joining the cult. When considering what to change after you have made a decision, reevaluating the chosen and nonchosen alternatives is a much less resistant path than trying to undo the behavior.

Importance. Suppose each of the dissonant cognitions is undeniable. In this case, we would expect the *less important* cognition to change (Hardyck and Kardush, 1968). Importance depends on several factors, including the extent to which the cognition is (1) deeply embedded in a larger network of cognitions and (2) a significant aspect of the individual's positive self-concept (Aronson, 1969).

On the first factor, attitude change is most likely to occur when a given attitude is *not* a central part of a complex attitude structure. Changing a central attitude will create new inconsistencies with all the other components of the attitude system to which it was linked. It is easier to change more isolated, less embedded attitudes and beliefs.

Cognitions that are tied to how people define themselves are highly change-resistant. One study found that individuals who rated being a feminist as their central trait did not become less feminist after engaging in a sexist (dissonant) act. Instead, they increased the ratio of feminist-to-sexist cognitions by making their next act exceptionally pro-feminist (Sherman and Gorkin, 1980). Note here that we seldom find people confessing to "stupidity" or "a mental lapse" following a bad decision or an attitude-discrepant behavior. Adding self-deprecating cognitions like these would hit at an extremely important attitude—that which one holds about oneself. We will have more to say at the end of this chapter about the importance of maintaining an overall positive self-affirming image, and how this need may override even strong needs for cognitive consistency.

Double jeopardy. Needless to say, dissonance is greatest when two inconsistent cognitions are *both* important. Under these circumstances, the most elaborate efforts at dissonance reduction will take place. Rather than a single change in attitude or a slight alteration in one's perception of the world, a person is apt to try a more effortful *cognitive restructuring*. The individual may add cognitions, adjust others, think rather deeply about the topic of his or her inconsistency, and otherwise gradually put everything back "into sync" (Hardyck and Kardush, 1968). In other words, all the means of reducing dissonance may be employed in a thoughtful binge of rationalizing.

Because it requires much mental effort, cognitive restructuring occurs only if there is no easier change possible and if certain situational pressures are present. For example, one researcher found that subjects did the most cognitive restructuring in resolving the inconsistency between their attitude and their behavior when they were publicly committed to their attitude-discrepant behavior, and when they were explicitly asked to make public what their attitude was following the behavior. Without these pressures to "go public," other subjects tended to engage in superficial changes in attitude (Elkin, 1986).

Cognitive restructuring, then, is rare. Yet it is the most meaningful mode of dissonance reduction because restructuring involves the most mental activity. As a result, as we saw with role-playing, the attitude and cognitive changes associated with restructuring are likely to persist and influence subsequent behavior and thought. They are more likely to be *internalized*—integrated into the deeper belief systems of the individual.

Finally we turn to pills and alcohol to deal with dissonance. For some people, the unpleasant arousal associated with cognitive dissonance can be handled by going straight to the source, in this case relieving that negative state by the immediate gratification that comes with turning off the arousal. When one team of researchers gave subjects the opportunity to take a tranquilizing drug after dissonance was aroused in them, dissonance-reducing attitude change was less than in other subjects who did not have the tension-calming drug (Cooper et al., 1978). A second team of researchers also showed that cognitive change is no longer the primary mode of dissonance reduction when it is possible to drink alcohol to reduce the tension experienced by dissonance arousal (Steele et al., 1981). In this second study, subjects drank beer or vodka, supposedly for a taste discrimination study, immediately after dissonance had been aroused by inducing them to write counterattitudinal essays in favor of a tuition increase. Those who did not drink alcohol and those who drank water or coffee all showed the typical dissonance-reducing effect of changing attitudes to be in line with their behavior. They supported tuition increases. But both light and heavy drinkers of alcohol did not change their attitudes to fit their discrepant actions. The alcohol apparently worked directly to lower their dissonance arousal, and so there was no further need to adjust their old cognitions to fit their new actions. The authors speculate that some forms of alcohol abuse may develop through the reinforcement of drinking as a means of reducing dissonance among people with limited cognitive coping skills.

Dissonance and an Unethical Business Decision

A fitting way to end our discussion of cognitive dissonance is with an example from beyond the laboratory that we think illustrates the lengths to which a person might go to justify a poor decision. It's an example of how a bad business decision became an immoral one, with dissonance-inducing justifications paving the descent.

In June 1988, the former vice president and president of the Beech-Nut Nutrition Corporation were convicted of selling millions of bottles of bogus juice for babies, advertised as "100 percent apple juice" but containing cheaper and less healthful contents such as sugar, water, coloring, and flavoring. As reported in *The New York Times* (Traub, 1988), the defendants, even as they were sentenced to 100,000 dollar fines and a year in prison, seemed unmoved by their undeniable and self-serving transgression, and seemed unwilling to shed their perceptions of themselves as virtuous men. It was a curious stance, but no more curious than the whole fiasco.

After the research and development director told the vice president of his suspicions that the concentrate being purchased from a supplier to make the juice was diluted or adulterated, the vice president made his first decision: he agreed to send an inspection team to visit the supplier but ordered Beech-Nut to continue to use the supplier's concentrate in the meantime. The inspection team found no evidence of adulteration—because the "blending facility" the supplier claimed to operate turned out not to exist at the given address. This aroused further suspicions on the part of the research director, as did evidence from an outside lab that the concentrate was more corn syrup than apple juice. Still, the vice president refused to stop buying from the suspect supplier. In fact, his next decision was to sign an agreement *with* the supplier that consumer complaints about the concentrate would be the supplier's responsibility, not Beech-Nut's.

And on it went. When another lab test indicated no adulteration, the vice president felt vindicated. He refused to entertain the suspicion of colleagues that the supplier had switched diluters—from corn syrup to beet juice, which could not be detected by lab tests. For 5 years, under the vice president's direction, Beech-Nut continued to make and sell the phony juice; 5 years during which the vice president, and later the president, on the vice president's advice, justified one bad decision with another.

The descriptions of the reporter who covered this sad story are instructive. He noted that the vice president seemed to have "simply blinded himself to the consequences of his acts," that he "unleashed a cascade of tortuous rationalizations," and that finally both the vice president and president were "still convinced that they committed nothing graver than a mistake in judgment" (Traub, 1988). All they did was to sell damaged goods to millions of America's babies for 5 years!

Are you surprised that a dispositional analysis of the culprit vice president reveals that he is not a sinister character? According to friends and neighbors, he is a "figure of propriety and rectitude." And so how can we explain his willful and unapologetic descent into corporate deception about baby food and, ultimately, his ruined career? We suspect, as we are sure you also do by now, that cognitive dissonance was at work here. The vice president, early on, made a decision based on financial and personal concerns. Beech-Nut was struggling, and the vice president wanted to maintain the profits—and the accompanying glory—gained from using the inexpensive ersatz concentrate.

Faced with a choice between success and morality, the vice president chose success. He was now stuck with all the negative aspects of that decision, including the cognitions "I am taking nutrition from the mouths of babes" and "I'm lying about what's in my products"—cognitions sure to be inconsistent with any conception of himself as a good man. To reduce the dissonance, he downplayed the significance of these negative consequences and "up-played" the corporate need for the act. In the end, dissonance had been reduced to the point where it was cognitively impossible for the vice president to think of himself as anything but a corporate patriot. He could see nothing wrong with his behavior. After all, the "unapple" juice was not actually harmful, was it? And it did take a long time to gain "convincing" proof that it was adulterated? Sure.

DISSONANCE, SELF-ATTRIBUTION, AND SELF-AFFIRMATION: SIMILARITIES AND SEPARATE IDENTITIES

The phenomena of self-attribution and of dissonance reduction share similarities. In particular, they both may contribute to the less-is-more effect of getting people to change their attitudes by giving them barely sufficient incentive to behave as the influence agent desires. In terms of cognitive dissonance, too much incentive adds a consonant cognition that makes attitude change unnecessary. In terms of self-attribution, a large incentive provides a situational explanation for the person's behavior—making a dispositional attribution about oneself less likely.

We pointed to the difficulty in changing cognitions when they support one's self-concept. A new formulation by Claude Steele (1988) goes further in arguing that some forms of dissonance may threaten the integrity of the self-concept by making the person feel stupid, inept, or immoral, or by raising other self-negatives. If given an opportunity to do something that enhances the self-image, or if given other positive input to bolster the self-concept, then there is no need to work to achieve cognitive consistency. Needs for self-affirmation then override those for consistency. Let's briefly examine some of the implications of these three processes of dissonance, self-attribution, and self-affirmation.

Overjustification

You may have noticed that the less-is-more effect has an additional implication that follows from both dissonance and self-attribution perspectives. More can be less, at times. Too much inducement or incentive may lead to even less attitude change than would ordinarily occur with modest inducements. In one study, preschool children were either told or not told that they would receive a prize for making the best drawing with a set of colorful magic markers (Lepper et al., 1973). Two weeks later, the children who had been drawing for a prize were found to be spending less of their free time playing with the magic markers than were the children who had expected no prize and therefore were just drawing for the fun of it. Other studies have found that when rewards or pay are offered for behaviors that were interesting to begin with, both children and adults may come to like them less as a result (Deci and Ryan, 1985). It seems that the reward can become the explanation for the behavior, making the attitude "I like doing this" less apt to be produced via self-observation, self-justification, or both. This *overjustification effect*, resulting in reduced intrinsic interest in a task, is especially likely when the external reward is exceptionally salient and when it is perceived by the recipient as an attempt to control his or her behavior (Deci and Ryan, 1985; Ross, 1975). Under these conditions rewards can transform play into work, and once the reason for that work is no longer present, as when the reward is withdrawn, the "work" stops.

This is not to deny the power of rewards to influence. We saw extensive evidence in the previous chapter of how they shape behavior. The message to parents, teachers, and other social control agents, rather, is that rewards should be used thoughtfully. Rewards can both maintain behavior and actually enhance interest if they are *informative about competence and achievement*, rather than simply controlling. And if the desired behavior is already occurring happily on its own, one might consider a modification of some old-fashioned advice: Simply replace the "something" with "someone" in the old saw, "If something works, don't fix it."

Similar Effects from Different Processes

While both processes contribute to important influence outcomes such as insufficient justification and overjustification effects, dissonance reduction and self-attribution are different processes. Dissonance reduction is primarily a process of motivated *change*—often attitude change. Inconsistencies between existing cognitions create tension, and something must give. Self-attribution, on the other hand, is a cognitive process that occurs when initial attitudes are weak, ambiguous, or nonexistent. It is a process of building consistency—inferring a consistent attitude from behavior—rather than resolving inconsistency. Self-attribution, then, is a process of attitude *formation* or of movement toward believing in more of what one already accepts (Fazio, 1987; Fazio et al., 1977).

Affirming One's Self-Regard

In recent years, a number of psychologists have pointed to a primary process assumed to be a basic function of the human condition: behaving in ways that protect the ego from threat and which attempt to restore self-regard that is under threat. A "totalitarian self" has been proposed that biases information processing to affirm the goodness, strength, and stability of the self-concept (Greenwald, 1980). Steele (1988) has shown in an ingenious series of studies that when dissonance is aroused, subjects do not show typical dissonance-reducing attitude change if they have the opportunity to affirm their self-concept, such as by expressing their most important values on a questionnaire. This process of self-affirmation "appears to have eliminated dissonance by somehow reducing the 'sting to the self' inherent in dissonance-provoking inconsistencies" (Steele, 1988, p. 277).

A CONCLUDING NOTE

The systematic analysis of how behaviors can shape attitudes and self-image is one of the greatest contributions of social psychology to the understanding of social influence. We have seen that very subtle situational and interpersonal nudges on behavior can sometimes translate into profound changes in attitudes, which, in their turn, can influence subsequent behavior. Moreover, as we shall see in Chapter 6, attitudes and self-images, however they come to be, can become tough to budge further. Indeed, an important irony of social psychological processes is that subtle nudges often move beliefs more readily than sledgehammer-strength factors. Finally, we note that influencing attitudes through behavior runs counter to popular conceptions about attitude change. The common view is that you change attitudes not by first changing behavior but with information and persuasive argumentation that appeal to reason. Well, that can also work sometimes, as we shall see in the next chapter.

*T*O SUM UP...

We explored how a change in behavior may feed back to cause a change in attitude or belief. This pathway of change is the reverse of what one intuitively expects, yet it is a pathway well-served by processes of self-attribution, self-persuasion, and self-justification driven by cognitive dissonance.

- We have a natural inclination to figure out people's actions. Making causal attributions about behavior contributes to our sense of control and helps guide our actions. In general, we make either dispositional or situational attributions. A dispositional attribution locates causes for behavior in the actor's personality or motives. A situational attribution locates the causes for behavior in the social and physical environment. In deciding whether behavior has a dispositional or a situational cause, we consider these factors: whether the behavior is unusual (nonnormativeness), whether the actor behaves the same way toward the current stimulus (consistency), and other stimuli (distinctiveness). We infer a specific causative trait by examining the unique outcomes the actor gains from the behavior, or we rely on well-learned "rules of thumb," or heuristics, about causes of certain behaviors.

- Attributional reasoning has certain cognitive biases. We tend to oversimplify and to be overly influenced by what is most salient and vivid in the scenes we observe. We also tend to overestimate dispositional factors while underestimating situational ones. This bias—the fundamental attribution error—is illustrated by the surprise people have about the high rate of obedience in the Milgram studies, and by their refusal to believe that they too would probably obey. The failure to appreciate how situational variables override dispositional factors greatly affects social attitudes.

- Self-attribution, in which we engage in the same attributional analysis of our own behavior as an observer might, occurs when our behavior is unplanned or our attitudes are weak or ambiguous. Because situational influences on behavior can be subtle, we may infer our attitude from our behavior. Self-attribution of emotions may also occur when we use a powerful situational cue to explain arousal that has a hidden cause.

- An effective way to change attitudes and behavior is to get targets to espouse ideas or role-play behaviors that oppose their current attitudes. Counter-attitudinal role-playing works through self-attribution processes as well as self-persuasion—generating one's own arguments for change. People can argue with themselves more effectively, and with more salient images, than others can argue with them.

- Cognitive dissonance exists when there is inconsistency between cognitive elements (beliefs, attitudes, or knowledge of one's behavior). Dissonance is assumed to be a psychologically uncomfortable drive state, which leads the person to reduce or eliminate it by changing one or more cognitions. Hence, dissonance may be at the root of self-justification—changing one's attitudes or beliefs to make them justify (be consistent with) situationally induced behavior.

- People can be induced by rewards or threats to engage in attitude-inconsistent acts. Normally, the larger the inducements, the greater the behavioral compliance. However, to get people to like or agree with the induced behavior, less is more. Attitude-inconsistent behaviors do not cause dissonance if they can be sufficiently justified by situational forces. Dissonance is aroused if the inducement is just sufficient to get compliance without being recognized as an acceptable justification for the behavior. The person must perceive that the attitude-inconsistent behavior was freely chosen. In the absence of perceptible external justification, attitude change becomes the route of self-justification.

- If attitude change is to follow attitude-discrepant behavior, the individual, in addition to perceiving free choice, must feel personally responsible for the consequences of the behavior and anticipate that the consequences will be aversive.

- Attitude change is only one mode of dissonance reduction. Others include lowering the importance of the behavior or another cognition, adding consonant or self-affirming cognitions, and directly reducing dissonance tension with drugs or alcohol. People take the path of least resistance. Undeniable, important, and self-relevant cognitions are highly resistant to change. When all relevant cognitions have these qualities, effortful cognitive restructuring may occur that leads to fundamental changes in the person.

- If less is more, then more can be less. Providing too much external justification for behavior that is already occurring on its own may cause the actor to like the behavior less.

QUESTIONS AND EXERCISES

1. Think about an event in your own life in which you believe your attitude or emotional response was the result of a self-attributional process. Explain why you believe this, and describe the situational factors and personal conditions (your internal state) that promoted a self-attribution process.

2. Using attribution, self-persuasion, and dissonance principles, sketch out a program for getting presently disinterested high school students to (a) work harder on academic tasks and (b) like going to and being in school.

3. Consider two nations—say, the United States and Japan—trying to negotiate a new trade agreement at a highly publicized and controversial economic summit. Discuss some ways in which attribution processes, in particular the fundamental attribution error, may come into play and possibly affect the course of negotiations. Think about, for example, inferences made concerning the motives

of each side, the perceptions of the public and the press in each country, and the negotiators' self-perceptions of their own behavior.

4. Under what conditions do attitudes change following attitude-discrepant behavior? From the perspective of cognitive dissonance theory, what makes these conditions so important?

5. Plan a campaign at your school designed to get donations to the annual blood drive. Analyze sources of resistance to giving blood, means of overcoming those resistances, and a variety of dissonance, compliance, and conformity techniques you will recommend.

4

Changing Attitudes through Persuasion:

Take My Words for It

———— ❖ ————

Seeking Out Influence: Social Comparison Processes ✦ *Being Sought as a Target:*
Persuasive Appeals ✦ *Presentation and Exposure* ✦ *Attention* ✦ *Comprehension*
✦ *Acceptance: The Biggest Hurdle* ✦ *An Interim Stop on the Road to Lasting Persuasion*

S pend a few minutes watching TV the week before a presidential election, and you will see a popular form of influence in action: the persuasive communication. Listen to a salesperson tell you about the virtues of buying a particular hot car or cool stereo, and you will experience the same technique again. That technique is persuasion. It consists of presenting arguments and facts, reasoning, drawing conclusions, and spelling out the positive results of a recommended course of action—all in the hope of convincing an audience to pursue that course of action.

In Chapter 2, we described methods of influence that go directly to behavior, changing it without first changing beliefs or attitudes. In Chapter 3, we saw that, under some conditions, behavior change may lead to attitude change, belief change, or both, as a kind of feedback process. *Persuasion*, in contrast, is a method of influence that begins with changing beliefs and knowledge: the cognitive component of the attitude system. Persuasive messages present information aimed at changing beliefs. Because the system is interconnected—because attitudes are often based on beliefs—the changed beliefs should lead to a change in attitude. In turn, the new attitude may guide the behavior of the target of the persuasive message.

Suppose someone wants to use persuasion to influence your attitude regarding abortion—as, indeed, either pro-choice or anti-abortion activists might. The persuader would construct a message that includes reasons for accepting new beliefs about abortion, for discrediting old beliefs that run counter to the persuader's viewpoint, or both. She might focus on beliefs regarding whether a 3-month-old fetus has a soul and, therefore, whether abortion violates religious rules. The belief about whether a 3-month-old fetus is human might also be addressed. Or she might attempt to establish or change your beliefs about the consequences of an abortion (or not having one) for the mental and physical health of the mother. Again, the idea is that if beliefs change, attitudes will follow (Ajzen and Fishbein, 1980).

It sounds so sensible, which perhaps explains why persuasive communication is what most of us think of when influence is mentioned. In fact, in our highly verbal society, the persuasive appeal is often our influence weapon of first resort. Informed of your disagreement with a cherished friend, another friend will probably advise you to talk to him about it: "He'll see the light, I'm sure." Studies have shown that when asked to indicate what they do to get others to behave as they want, people most often identify strategies involving persuasive appeals: giving logical and personal reasons, lending expertise, and so on. Persuasive communication is reported as more likely than tactics such as bargaining, flattering, threatening, and forcing. Only the simple act of asking for one's wishes is reported as a more popular and socially acceptable way of getting someone to comply (Rule and Bisanz, 1987). Business managers report using "rational persuasion" more than any other single tactic in attempts to influence both their subordinates and their superiors (Yukl and Falbe, 1990). Even partners in long-term romances report commonly using persuasive communication to gain influence over their partner (Falbo and Peplau, 1980). We might say that the power of love frequently depends on the power of positive persuasion.

Belief in the power of persuasive communication is hardly new. Aristotle attempted to set forth principles of persuasion more than 2,000 years ago in his work *Rhetoric*. Aristotle identified components of persuasive appeals whose importance has been well documented by scientific psychology in this century. He eloquently discussed how the "character of the speaker," the "frame of mind" of the audience, and "the speech itself" are factors in whether or not an audience is influenced by a persuasive message (Petty and Cacioppo, 1981). This "who says what to whom" trio of factors—the focus of much modern persuasion research—rightly suggests that persuasion can be a complicated affair. Sensible and simple as persuasion sounds, the fact is that many variables come into play in helping determine whether John Target will change his mind based on Susan Sender's impassioned speech.

We begin to appreciate the complexity of persuasion when we consider how varied persuasive appeals are in their effectiveness. Some speeches are tremendous successes; others, resounding failures. As we saw in Chapter 1, the messages of Martin Luther King, Jr., and Ronald Reagan had a large impact, in part because these communicators understood how to deliver their messages. Persuasion has also worked when a chorus of advocates presents a strong case over the mass media. The messages from the Surgeon General, the American Cancer Society, and other health agencies about the health dangers associated with cigarette smoking have clearly been influential (Surgeon General, 1983). In the late 1970s, it seems that outspoken criticism about the SALT II nuclear arms limitation treaty by military and diplomatic experts was at least partly responsible for the cooling of public opinion toward the treaty (Page et al., 1987). And, of course, we can all think of times when the force of someone's arguments during a friendly conversation compelled us to adopt his or her point of view, and maybe even to later become advocates for our new attitude.

But we can also remember failed persuasion attempts. The authors, for example, are well aware that their speeches about the virtues of hard study have occasionally failed to inspire certain students. We saw in the previous chapter that professing reasons and arguments did little to change children's attitudes about and imitation of TV violence. Finally, at the level of national media, the blitz of TV and radio messages designed to persuade sexually active people to use condoms as a precaution against the AIDS virus has enjoyed only mixed success. Despite the strong, life-and-death arguments, a large segment of the at-risk population has failed to adopt this sane practice (Aronson, 1991).

Is persuasion then a random hit-or-miss phenomenon? Not quite. We can identify a number of principles that can help determine what makes a persuasive appeal effective in one given situation and yet ineffective in another. In this chapter, we will examine those principles that make communications effective sources of social influence.

Our first task will be to examine the principles behind *social comparison*—the processes by which we actively seek out persuasive information from others. Then, we will turn to persuasive messages that seek us out. Although there are countless such messages, only a relatively small number have a major impact on us. We will see that this restricted effectiveness occurs because successful persuasion requires several "processing steps." Generally speaking, if a message is to change our attitude, we must be exposed to it, pay attention to it, comprehend it, and accept it. The conditions necessary for these four steps—some of the "who, what, and to whoms" (as well as "whens")—will be explored in this chapter. In the next chapter, we will continue our analysis of persuasive influence by investigating two further steps: retention of the new attitude and its translation into behavior.

SEEKING OUT INFLUENCE: SOCIAL COMPARISON PROCESSES

We tend to think of persuasive appeals as initiated by others and then directed at people who did not invite the influence attempt. Certainly, this is true much of the time. TV commercials for toilet paper and the next-door neighbor's reasons for opposing our choice of house paint colors may be seen more as nuisances than as welcomed guidance. Yet sometimes people do search for persuasive messages from others. Sometimes they actively try to find out what others think about an attitude, object, or issue.

You will recall that in the previous chapter, we saw that a major assumption of attribution theory is that people have a basic need to predict and control their environment, or at least to believe they can do so. This basic need is behind our attempts to figure out the causes of others' behavior. Social comparison theory, which we encountered only briefly in Chapter 2, sees this same need underlying our concern with having "correct" attitudes and beliefs, or opinions (social comparison theorists refer to opinions as verbalized attitudes and beliefs). Valid opinions lead to accurate predictions about persons and objects; invalid opinions can be disastrous in misleading us. One way to find out if our opinions are valid is to compare them with the opinions of others. In fact, given the subjective nature of many important opinions, social comparison of this sort is often the *only* way to evaluate opinions. There is, of course, no guarantee that the people with whom we seek to compare ourselves will agree with us, and so we may be inviting, or risking, a persuasive appeal for us to change when we go social comparison shopping to buy some correctness for our attitude wardrobe.

To whom do we compare ourselves? In his original formulation of social comparison theory, Leon Festinger (1954) proposed that we are most likely to seek opinion comparisons with others who are *similar* to us. However, he never made it quite clear just what was meant by "similar." Actually, we can think of a comparison seeker and a potential comparison object as being similar in two ways: (1) they can share the same opinion about the topic or object at issue, or (2) they can be similar in other ways—on attributes related to the topic or object. It turns out that both kinds of similarity can serve as magnets for social comparison. Let's look at the second kind of similarity first.

Similarity on Related Attributes

Imagine yourself thinking that you like the latest clothing fashions displayed at a recent show in a local department store. But you are not entirely sure and could use some input from others who also saw the show. Would you ask the opinion of someone who has a lifestyle and tastes similar to yours, or would you ask someone who dresses quite differently because of a different lifestyle or differences in taste? Our guess is that you would seek out the similar person. And this action would make sense. Consider it from an attribution theory angle (Goethals and Darley, 1977). If the similar other agrees with your tentative judgment, you can feel more confident that the judgment is "correct" because both you and your comparison object, with the same fashion sense, like those fashions. Hence, this basic fashion sense of yours, not some passing fancy or irrelevant situational factor, such as the model's good looks, must have caused your positive reaction to the fashions. If the similar other disagrees and expresses dislike for the new fashions, you also learn something. Upon more careful reflection, maybe the fashions are not your style after all; they won't play up your best features.

Contrast this scenario to that of social comparison with a dissimilar other. What do you learn if that person happens to share your initial opinion of the clothes? It may or may not be a correct fashion sense that backs your opinion? It certainly isn't *your* fashion sense that is behind the opinion of this person with such different taste. And if the dissimilar other disagrees, you may or may not consider it relevant to what you should like.

Research bears out the notion that, on subjective matters, we want to know how others feel who are most like us. In one study, when told they could compare their opinions about an upcoming judgment with those of people who either shared or did not share similar personal values, more than 80 percent of the subjects chose to compare with the person who most closely shared their values (Goethals and Ebling, 1975).

This finding, and the social comparison principle behind it, helps explain why, after televised presidential debates, we may be most eager to hear the commentary of similar others—representatives of our political party or those who share our political philosophy. Following such debates, the TV networks parade before us spokespersons from both conservative and liberal organizations, senators and representatives from both major parties, and pollsters who are actually employed by one or the other campaign. The number of partisan analysts usually dwarfs the number of impartial experts on the issues. In the meantime, in the "spin room"—an area set aside for reporters and campaign workers to meet—a curious ritual unfolds. Campaign managers and even famous politicians spin tales of how their candidate "won" the debate and why. Often the impressions they offer fly in the face of the facts, as when Republican "spinners" confidently announced that Dan Quayle had "won" his 1988 vice presidential debate with Lloyd Bentsen. Virtually every less partial observer agreed that the young Quayle had been less impressive and convincing then his seasoned opponent. (Democrat spinners, to be sure, have spun equally "tall tales" after their lost debates.) Yet reporters and the public hang on every word offered by spinners—despite the fact that the statements are often boringly predictable and superfluous.

Why is so much attention paid to the statements of already opinionated people? Social comparison theory provides a sensible clue: many TV viewers and newspaper readers have a political party affiliation. The comments of similar others—those with the same allegiance—supply insights into the opinion implications of the debate for "people like me." Partisan comments provide desired information. It's a lesson the campaign managers and spin doctors know well, and so they keep on spinnin'.

Opinion Similarity

The people who most often seek like-minded opinions on the specific matter are those who are already committed to an opinion. Yes, even committed people seek social comparison. They are not so interested in *evaluating* as in *validating* their opinion (Kruglanski and Mayseless,

Who won the debate? Shall we let the "spin doctors" decide?   (*UPI/Bettmann Newsphotos*)

1987). By "comparing notes" with a specifically like-minded person, committed people can avoid discovering good reasons for holding the opposite opinion—reasons that would be dissonant with their entrenched position. They may also learn additional attitude-supportive reasons—and thereby bolster their confidence.

Dissimilarity as a Basis for Comparison

Do people ever compare themselves with dissimilar others? Two situations in particular encourage comparison with *un*like-minded people. The first is when the opinion is more or less a matter of fact (a verifiable belief) rather than a matter of evaluation and preference (an attitude). Learning that someone with a different "mind set" shares your belief about a fact produces more confidence than knowing that someone similar agrees with you, as you might expect them to. Comparison with a dissimilar person lets you rule out your own bias as responsible for the way you see things. If someone with a different bias sees it the same way, you can attribute the cause of your belief to the object of that belief rather than to your personal bias (Goethals and Darley, 1977). Again, this attraction to dissimilar others is evident mainly when you are seeking verification of facts (such as whether New York City attracts more tourists than Paris). For likes and dislikes (whether New York City is better than Paris for a vacation), we seek similar comparison others to get that quick reflected evaluation of our personal preferences.

We also seek comparison with dissimilar people when we *fear invalidity*. Imagine you are a fashion designer who puts out lines of clothing for a profit. It's how you make a living. In evaluating your designs, it would make sense to seek the opinions not only of designers who you know have the same fashion sense but also of designers who have a different fashion eye. You need a broad perspective because you must be able to predict which designs will sell well and also gain the respect of your colleagues. To be wrong will cost you a loss of money and status.

One interesting study clearly illustrates how *motives* influence whether social comparison is made with similar or dissimilar others (Kruglanski and Mayseless, 1987). Subjects offered their opinion as to which of two candidates was better qualified for graduate study in clinical psychology and were then given the opportunity to examine the written opinion of one other subject. In one condition, subjects were told that their initial opinion was final and that they would have to defend it in front of other subjects. Most (74 percent) chose to inspect the reasons of someone who had selected the same candidate. In another condition, subjects were told that they could change their choice, and if their final choice was correct, they would win some money. Among these subjects, most (67 percent) chose to see the rationale of someone whose choice disagreed with theirs. Committed to their choice and to extolling its virtues, the first group needed to bolster or validate its opinions. The second group, however, needed to be right: they feared invalidity and were motivated to construct the "best" opinion (Fazio, 1979).

Social comparison is a process by which people seek informational influence. But we can see now that people really seek *two* kinds of information, broadly speaking: (1) information that *validates*, or gives comfort that they are already correct or close to it; and (2) information that *evaluates*, or more truly instructs them about the appropriateness of their subjective attitudes. Generally, both kinds of information can be gained by social comparison with like-minded people. Comparison with dissimilar others is common only when evaluation needs are strong and objective truth is attainable.

BEING SOUGHT AS A TARGET: PERSUASIVE APPEALS

Actually, finding suggestions about the "right" attitudes and beliefs isn't hard. Persuasive appeals abound, though many are unwanted or emanate from people with little social comparison value. We inevitably encounter such appeals when we watch TV or turn on the radio, take a Sunday drive, or even have a few drinks with colleagues after work. Advertisements alone are staggering in number. Companies spend fifty billion dollars every year to promote their wares on TV, radio, and roadside billboards, as well as in newspapers and magazines (McGuire, 1985). TV alone presents the average child with 20,000 advertisements per year (Adler et al., 1980). Beyond commercial ads, there are political and public service ads, not to mention the more subtle communications built into the comedies, dramas, and documentaries we watch—that reflect the philosophies of the writers and producers. Finally, even "shooting the breeze" with friends, family, and lovers can involve persuasive communication. The daily exchange of feelings and preferences is part of the habit of verbal socializing that most humans come to enjoy, and others, like the shy, long for.

As we saw in the discussion of cigarette advertising in Chapter 1, persuasion in the media is sophisticated and often successful. It may be no less so in many other settings. Successful advertisers, government officials, company managers, and consumer advocates are all alike in their ability to use the persuasion principles we are discussing here. When you add it all up, according to one estimate, we are exposed to as many as 1,500 persuasive messages a day (Schultz, 1982). Many of these messages do not even enter our conscious awareness, as we flip absentmindedly through the newspaper, speed by signs on the road, and grab another cup of coffee during TV commercials. But even if only 100 or so messages "got through," that would be a lot. If each of them had some influence on us, our beliefs would be ever-changing, pushed and pulled by whatever managed to catch our attention. Or we would be overwhelmed and suffer attitudinal paralysis, not knowing what to believe or to doubt at any given moment. And in short order we could expect that indecision to restrict our actions.

Of course, these frightful outcomes seldom happen. Buy why not? Why are we not overcome by the noisy persuasion attempts that abound all around us, shouting to be noticed? And given our apparent ability to resist most of the potentially persuasive messages hitting on us, what ingredients must a message have to penetrate this resistance—to "get under your skin" and make you think and feel differently about some aspect of your world?

We can begin answering these questions by noting that, as thinking creatures, we are never totally defenseless against a communication. Since many attitudes rest on knowledge, persuasion can be resisted by *counterarguing* ("Hey, I can't buy your argument, Mr. Candidate. Despite your statistics, your plan to reduce the federal deficit won't work, and here's why..."). But counterarguing is just one defense against persuasion. To be persuasive—to change an attitude and, in turn, a behavior—a message must penetrate several levels of passive and active defenses. There are, in effect, a number of steps in the persuasion process, and the recipe for mind-altering persuasion requires adding necessary ingredients at each step. Let's start cooking.

Steps in the Persuasion Process

Systematic analysis of the idea that persuasion involves a series of steps or processes began with the work of Carl Hovland, a social psychologist at Yale University who created the large and productive Yale Communication Research Project in the 1950s (Hovland et al., 1949; 1953; 1957). Hovland took a *learning theory approach* to persuasion. He maintained that a message can succeed in changing an audience's attitude if its arguments promote the belief that adopting the message's position will result in reinforcement. The arguments in the message, for example, might dwell on why the advocated position is correct and on how adopting it will result in rewards like approval from important people.

These arguments, however, can affect beliefs only if they are learned. Learning requires that the audience pay *attention* to the message and, in turn, gain some *comprehension* of it, understanding the new beliefs it proposes. Then, if the message has compelling arguments, *acceptance* of its conclusion and a change in attitude will follow. Of course, actions associated with the changed attitude may be required in the future. Accordingly, there also must be *retention* of the new attitude until the time when the new action is possible. In this way, the Yale approach identifies three mental steps to persuasion, and a fourth if the attitude change is to lead to future action.

Initial and Final Steps

Further consideration suggests two more steps as well, one at the beginning of the process and one at the end (McGuire, 1968; Sherman, 1987). At the beginning is *exposure*. People cannot attend to a message until they are exposed to it. Advertisers, for example, may put their messages out there, but there is no guarantee that people—or the "right people"—will see or hear (be exposed to) them. This is why TV ratings are so important. The more people watching a show, the more people are likely to see the commercials. At the end of the chain, retention alone can't guarantee that attitude change will lead to action. As we have seen, the immediate situation can inhibit the expression of a person's true feelings. The final step, *translation of attitude to behavior*, requires what we might call situational support for the expression of attitude-consistent behavior.

To summarize, in order for a persuasive message to influence *behavior*, six mental steps must occur. Each one of them is an iffy thing. It may or may not happen. Thus, you should not be surprised that, even though there are zillions of persuasion attempts out there in daily life, relatively little persuasion actually happens. For a message to change our behavior, we have to: be exposed to the message, pay attention to it, comprehend at least some of it, accept its conclusion, retain the new attitude over time (without the message being restated), and find ourselves in a situation that reminds and encourages us to let the new attitude guide our behavior (see Figure 4.1).

In the remainder of this chapter, we will deal with the first four steps, which culminate in attitude change. We will look at the details of the rich range of psychological and circumstantial forces that promote or block each step. In Chapter 5, we will discuss the final two steps essential for newly acquired beliefs to give birth to bouncing behaviors with that shared family resemblance.

PRESENTATION AND EXPOSURE

Against good advice, busy people take little time to "stop and smell the roses." Nor do they stop and read the messages very often. But even if you were to be attentive to as many messages as possible for an entire day, or even a month, you would discover something very interesting—at least regarding messages about social, political, religious, and lifestyle issues. Of all the possible points of view in the world on these matters, you receive messages spanning a fairly narrow range of viewpoints, and few offer viewpoints that differ much from your own. In other words, you already mostly agree with the messages to which you are exposed. Although they are lurking out there somewhere, in Jaws-like fashion, highly discrepant messages seldom get the bite on us.

Six Steps in the Persuasion Process

1. **Exposure to message**
   If the target of the message never sees or hears it, the message cannot have influence.

2. **Attention to message**
   The target must pay attention to the message if it is to have influence.

3. **Comprehension of message**
   The target must understand at least the conclusion of the message if it is to be influential.

4. **Acceptance of its conclusion**
   The target must accept the message's conclusion for attitude change to occur.

5. **Retention of new attitude**
   If the new attitude is forgotten, the message will not have influence in the future.

6. **Translation of attitude to behavior**
   If the message is to influence behavior, the new attitude must guide behavior in a relevant situation.

FIGURE 4.1

When was the last time you heard a detailed argument that schoolchildren should be encouraged to experience all forms of sexual activity as soon as they reach the first stage of puberty? Or that college students should constantly challenge all those in authority, especially their parents, their teachers, and the Pope, while they are at it?

The tendency to be exposed mostly to opinions we already agree with is called *selective exposure*. The major reason for it has to do with built-in filtering systems in the structure of our lives and of society. In addition, on rare occasions we deliberately stay away from attitude-discrepant messages we would rather not hear because of the dissonance they would produce (Sweeney and Gruber, 1984).

Idea Filtration

The way we live our lives. Our lifestyle itself leads to selective exposure. The attitudes, values, interests, and personal philosophies we develop as we grow and mature have much to do with our lifestyle. An interest in literature and books may lead an individual to major in English in college and to pursue a career in the publishing field, as a book editor, perhaps. On the job, the person makes friends and colleagues. And they are very likely to have similar interests and points of view.

After all, they were similar enough to have chosen the same field of work.

Even more generally, we choose friends and even marriage partners on the basis of attitude similarity. Other things being equal, we like similar others better than dissimilar others (Byrne, 1971). And we also buy homes in neighborhoods that tend to be populated by people much like ourselves—people of a similar socioeconomic class with similar backgrounds and experiences. The point is that we tend to live in fairly homogeneous environments. The people with whom we interact usually share our views on the issues most important to us. This one-sidedness in the messages we receive is not restricted to spouses, neighbors, and colleagues. If we are liberals, we probably subscribe to liberal-learning magazines, listen to liberal politicians, and get on the mailing lists of liberal organizations. Right-wing messages, even ordinary conservative messages, find their way into our households and mental mailboxes less often. The social clubs we join will not be conservative, nor will the conservative candidate for mayor be invited to speak at the annual banquet of our association.

Censorship—the mild case. The government and media also play a role in insulating us from the most discrepant messages. In general, Western democracies enjoy great freedom of speech and publication. Even so, there are military and foreign affairs secrets—"classified information"—as well as efforts to play down or ignore cultural attitudes judged incompatible with Western values. The media, for their part, do not print or broadcast all available stories, speeches, and events. News reporters and executives *select* which stories and angles to cover. And as successful members of a Western society that socialized them, they can be expected to select material that *makes sense* to Western audiences (like themselves and ourselves). Thus, even though the Western media present a wide range of opinion, the coverage tends to be of variations on Western, capitalistic, materialistic, democratic, Judeo-Christian ideas of relevance to a Caucasian audience. Readers of newspapers write complaints to the editor if Doonesbury's cartoons "go too far" in satirizing some sacred institution, or if a tragic scene is graphically depicted too "up close and personal."

Censorship—the worst case. The importance of exposure in the attitude change process becomes starkly clear when we consider the effects of censorship as exercised in totalitarian states. As the pro-democracy student demonstrations grew in Beijing and a few other large cities in the spring of 1989, the Communist Chinese government blacked out news reports—especially to smaller cities and the countryside. As a result, millions of citizens never learned just how massive the protests were becoming—that tens of thousands of students and workers were occupying Tiananmen Square in Beijing and gaining the vocal support of many more. Many citizens eager for democratic reforms never knew that the unrest was reaching a critical mass to which they might have contributed had they known. Like a river that keeps a forest fire from spreading across it, China's censorship contained the flames of revolution within manageable boundaries.

In Beijing, of course, the mass demonstrations and sit-ins at Tiananmen Square could not be hidden, especially from the world media on hand to cover the visit of Russia's new leader Mikhail Gorbachev. The demonstrations simply got too big, too showy, and too persistent. The government cracked down with a brutal massacre in which thousands of the protesting students and workers died as they fled from tanks and grenades.

Then came another crackdown on exposure. Historically, totalitarian governments have been known to distort events and rewrite history to make them fit the "party line." What seemed an excessive example of this principle when portrayed by George Orwell in his prophetic novel *Nineteen Eighty-Four* was shown to the world of 1989 as all too real in Communist China. After the savage crushing of the peaceful demonstrations, the Chinese government totally distorted the reality shown on television broadcasts and reported by eyewitnesses. The official government line was that thugs and counterrevolutionaries had murdered soldiers of the People's Republic of China, who in self-defense fired back and killed a few of these enemies of the people. Unless the current regime in China eventually falls, future generations in that country may never know what took place in 1989; they may never be exposed to the fact that a peaceful pro-democracy coalition of university students and workers almost brought the government down and that their government attacked its own people. And, of course, "no one died in Tiananmen Square" (Lutz, 1989).

> Reality is not external. Reality exists in the human mind, and nowhere else. Not in the individual mind, which can make mistakes, and in any case soon perishes; only in the mind of the Party, which is collective and immortal. Whatever the Party holds to be truth *is* truth. It is impossible to see reality except by looking through the eyes of the Party. (George Orwell, *Nineteen Eighty-Four*)

Media Mind Management

The news and what's important. Let's head back west, to the more modest, nontotalitarian limits on exposure in our media. By deciding what to present, those who control the mass media help define the range of opinions to which the public is exposed. And they also help set the standards people use in forming opinions. Consider research by one team of political psychologists (Iyengar et al., 1984). They asked Yale undergraduates to watch videotaped recordings of TV network evening news broadcasts that had aired in 1979 and 1980. Each participant watched a tape that ran about 40 minutes and included stories on numerous events and problems of the time. The researchers divided participants into two groups that got different exposure to events of that era. The energy-in group saw a tape with six stories about the energy crisis that was in full swing at the time. These stories included footage of gas lines, updates of meetings of Arab oil ministers to decide oil prices, reports on the booming coal industry, and speeches by then President Jimmy Carter outlining his energy program. The energy-out group viewed a news tape that contained no stories about the energy crisis. After viewing the news video, participants in both groups, among other things, judged President Carter's performance in numerous areas, including energy, and his overall performance as President.

Did the groups differ in their judgments of Carter? Yes, but primarily in terms of the weight they gave to his handling of the oil crisis. Subjects who were heavily exposed to the energy stories made significant use of their opinion about Carter's performance in dealing with the energy crisis when judging the quality of his *overall* performance. If they thought he was dealing well with the crisis, they judged him relatively positively; if they thought he was botching the problem, they gave him a more negative overall rating. This relationship was much less evident among subjects who were not exposed to energy crisis news. Among all the opinions that influenced their assessment of President Carter's overall performance, the one concerning the quality of his dealing with the energy crisis had relatively little input.

This finding was confirmed in related studies using other issues (inflation or national defense instead of energy) and nonstudent participants (residents of New Haven, Connecticut). It seems that, by giving a problem great coverage, newscasters make that problem readily *accessible* in the minds of viewers. Exposure makes viewers more likely to think about a particular problem area when they judge the "bottom line" on a President. It also dictates what issues we should be concerned about. When did *you* last think about the starving children in Ethiopia and send a donation to an African hunger fund? Probably not since there was massive TV exposure of the plight of those unfortunate drought sufferers some years ago, when it was *news*.

Setting the agenda. Consider what this means. To an extent, the electorate's evaluation of an American President will not be based evenly on all of his accomplishments and failures. Instead, performance in those areas that news reporters deem important will contribute inordinately to that judgment. The media may not have big direct effects on public evaluations; rather they have indirect effects by setting the agenda of what is important to evaluate (Becker et al., 1975). When one of your authors was being taken on a tour of the NBC News station in New York's Rockefeller Center, he asked the TV producer who was acting as his guide whether this was where the NBC Nightly News program reported the news. "This is where we *make* the news; we don't just report it," was his pithy reply.

Education or hidden propaganda? What about the role of the educational system in shaping people's values and attitudes? Here, we might be tempted to draw a sharp distinction between propaganda and education. Traditionally, *propaganda* is defined as an attempt to influence public opinion and public behavior through specialized persuasion techniques. One of the most devastating propaganda machines in history was that of Nazi Germany. Joseph Goebbels, Hitler's minister of propaganda, masterminded a blitz of political cartoons, editorials, false rumors, faulty theories of race and genetics, and other devices that caused Germans to accept war and hate Jews.

Propaganda contrasts with *education*, in which the attempt to change attitudes and behavior is through information, evidence, facts, and logical reasoning. In an ideal sense, educators teach students not *what* to think, but only *how* to think. In this way, propagandists differ from educators because they intentionally try to bias what people see, think, and feel in the hope that they will adopt a particular viewpoint—theirs.

But are there concealed, subtle forms of bias or indoctrination in education that cloud these neat distinctions? Consider the complaints of the black community that textbooks in all areas omit reference to the reality of their history, black culture, or even black existence—except as related to slavery and primitive native customs. Such an omission most likely fosters the majority attitude among black and other minority children that their race is insignificant and that they as members of it share the same fate. And the same point can be extended to Latinos, Native Americans, and Asian Americans. If the slighting of minority contributions is not an intentional goal of our educational process, then correctives should be considered promptly to alter those nonintentions.

Consider another example. Was it the bravery, savvy, and yearning for freedom of the American colonists that won the Revolutionary War? Or were the British simply too preoccupied with their major opponent, France, to care much if they lost the Colonies? Detroit youngsters get the former story, while just a few miles away, schoolchildren in Windsor, Ontario, hear a Canadian version much like the latter. Who is right? The point is straightforward: the educational system of any nation helps control and limit the values and perceptions of reality to which people are exposed.

We might find inspiring pictures of revolutionary patriotism like this in any American social studies textbook. Education almost always comes with a dose of cultural propaganda.   (*Courtesy New York Public Library*)

*A*TTENTION

If there is one word, one concept, or one process by which advertisers live and die, it is "attention." Attract it, get it, hold it, extend it, switch it, manage it—and you are in—to first base, at least. Without it, your side has struck out. Sit down. Lots of messages penetrate the various barriers to exposure, although few severely disagreeable ones get through to us. But even if we are exposed to a message, we may not pay attention to what the message says. Gaining attention is crucial, but also difficult. Advertisers raise the volume of TV commercials over that of the programs they accompany to make them more salient and unavoidably noticeable. Sexy women and men are presented in proximity to the object that the advertisers are hawking, because they know that sexual images attract attention and have done so since the dawn of evolution—or else mollusks and not humans would be doing their thing at the beach at Ipanema.

A major, lucrative industry is the selling of "space and time." This involves positioning ads in appropriate magazines, newspapers, billboards, and time slots on TV, by regional preferences so that the largest number of potential buyers will be slithered out of their routine existence and seduced into paying attention to yet one more commercial. In a book titled *Positioning: The Battle for Your Mind,* we are told by the heads of a major ad agency that "in the communication jungle out there, the only hope to score big is to be selective, to concentrate on narrow targets, to practice segmentation. In a word, 'positioning'" (Reis and Trout, 1986, p. 6). To segment a market is to identify the people who have special needs or attributes that your product or service can most readily satisfy. Then you put all or much of your advertising and marketing budget into ads focused on those people. You will recall from Chapter 1 the campaign by R. J. Reynolds to sell menthol cigarettes to inner-city black consumers. Their market research showed that this "target group" overwhelmingly preferred the menthol brand, and that ads could appeal to the sophisticated "Uptown" lifestyle that was allegedly attractive to this consumer type.

Despite all these efforts, people seldom pay close attention to advertisements or to political and public service messages. Attention, after all, is a *limited processing* mental function, according to much research from our colleagues in cognitive psychology (Kahneman, 1973). We can fully attend to only one thing at a time, without special training to divide our attention (Spelke et al., 1976). Media messages face stiff competition for our attention. We watch TV with family and friends, often discussing the plot or the ball score during commercial breaks. We get phone calls, do our homework, daydream, and have sexual fantasies. Push buttons and remote controls make it easy to flip TV and radio stations. Researchers who have filmed living rooms while the residents watch TV (with their consent, of course) have confirmed that people divide their attention between the TV and a host of other activities (Comstock et al., 1978). So many watch, but few really see and listen. This is one of the reasons that, while TV ads and political campaigns do affect public attitudes and behavior, the effects are, in one researcher's words, "remarkably small for the resources expended" (McGuire, 1985).

In our "overcommunicated" society, advertisers spend nearly 400 dollars for each American every year, compared with less than 20 dollars for the rest of the world. And so if your company is planning to spend a million dollars on advertising, it will "bombard" the average consumer with less than a half cent of advertising spread out over the year. Thus even a million dollars is a piddling amount in this massively competitive market to attract and hold consumer attention on the way to getting them—us—to buy a product or service. Media executives know a fundamental truth about how the human mind works. They recognize that "the mind, as a defense against the volume of today's communications, screens and rejects much of the information offered it" (Reis and Trout, 1986, p. 6). But advertisers also count on the power of big numbers that lie behind the small percentages—if only 5 percent of an audience of forty million is affected by a message, that is two million people!

Tuning Out

Cognitive dissonance theory predicts *selective attention*—a tendency to pay closer attention to a presented message that supports our existing attitude compared to one that opposes it. Opposing information creates internal inconsistency—the discomfort of dissonance. By dwelling on positive aspects of our chosen position and the negative aspects of what we have rejected, we eliminate the dissonance: we increase the ratio of consonant to dissonant cognitions. There is nothing like a good old supportive message to accomplish this. With this in mind, consider a situation in which George, a politically opinionated school teacher, sits down to read the *USA Today* editorial page while having a solitary, and somewhat rushed, breakfast. The paper carries several editorials, whose positions are given away by their titles. George, then, is exposed to both agreeable and disagreeable messages, in the sense that they are right in front of him and he gets the gist of each simply by scanning titles and the clear pro-con labels used in the *USA Today* format. But in his short breakfast break, is he just as likely to attend to, or read, any one editorial as opposed to any other?

Research suggests that George will probably attend to those he is most apt to find supportive of his opinions (Frey, 1986). In one study, as a test of their decision-making skills, German high school students were asked to evaluate information relevant to whether the contract of a fictitious store manager should be extended (Frey and Rosch, 1984). After making their final decision, the subjects were told that they would now have a chance to get further information about the manager. They were given the titles of ten descriptions of the store manager supposedly made by people who knew the manager very well. Five titles clearly indicated that the description supported a subject's final decision, whereas five others indicated that the description was nonsupportive. Subjects were then asked to check which of the titles in the "table of contents" they would like to read. As can be seen in Figure 4.2, subjects selected nearly twice as many supportive titles as nonsupportive ones. Here is a clear case of willingness to pay attention to messages, as long as they agree with what is already believed.

This sort of selectivity is not limited to judgments about hypothetical people. Another study found that when college students were asked to write essays about federal funding of abortion or the use of nuclear energy, they tended to select, as support material, magazine articles with titles that supported their own opinion (McPherson, 1983).

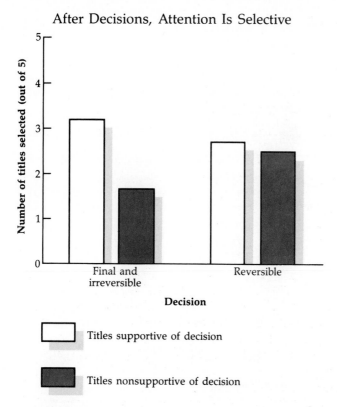

After Decisions, Attention Is Selective

FIGURE 4.2
After making a decision about a case study, subjects were given the opportunity to read additional descriptions relevant to the case. When told that their decision could not be changed, subjects primarily chose to read descriptions whose titles suggested support for their decision. When the decision could be changed, the selective attention to supportive information did not occur.
(Data from Frey and Rosch, 1984. Reprinted by permission of Sage Publications, Inc.)

Intelligent people, of course, do not always slant their attention toward supportive messages. That would be a foolish course, because new information may prove old beliefs wrong. We can understand, therefore, why messages expected to reveal *novel* information tend to draw similar amounts of attention whether or not they support the individual's existing beliefs. This attending to "the news" occurs under two conditions: when being correct is important and when the individual is not irrevocably committed to a given opinion (Frey, 1986). For ex-

Dad knows that gaining attention and "sympathetic" cognitive responses enhance the persuasive impact of a communication.

(© King Features Syndicate, Inc., 1977. Reprinted with permission.)

ample, in the study with German students, a similar number of supportive and nonsupportive descriptions were selected when students were informed that they could change their decision after studying the descriptions and the descriptions presented entirely new information (see Figure 4.2).

Advertisers and editorialists might take heart from this news. It suggests that potentially disagreeable messages may nonetheless be able to "grab" attention if, before the audience tunes out, they announce two things: (1) that they contain useful new information ("New studies reveal that...''), and (2) that a change of mind is desirable and easy ("It isn't too late to get a great deal on our new model, and a good price for your late-model trade-in").

Tuning In and Out

Can captive audiences (adults and especially children)—who must endure exposure to the full message—practice selective attention? An intriguing study illustrates that they can (Kleinhesselink and Edwards, 1975). University students listened to a message that advocated the legalization of marijuana. The message contained fourteen arguments, seven of which were strong and difficult to refute and seven of which were silly and easily refutable. Presented through headphones, the message was accompanied by a constant static that made close listening difficult. Apologetic and concerned, the experimenter explained that the static was the result of problems with the audio equipment, and that they had devised a push-button contraption which would allow students to block out the static for 5 seconds at a time. Subjects were told that they could push the button as often as they pleased. In actuality, the static was there deliberately, and frequency of button pushing was the measure of interest. The researchers reasoned that the more often a subject pushed the button to remove the static, the more he or she was willfully "tuning in"—being attentive.

And button pushing varied systematically in a revealing way. Subjects who favored legalization of marijuana—the position taken by the message—pushed the button significantly more often when the speaker was delivering strong arguments for legalization than when he was delivering weak ones. They listened more closely to the most supportive aspects of the message. In contrast, subjects who opposed the message position did just the reverse. They pushed the button more frequently while the speaker gave the easily refuted pro-legalization arguments than while he presented his more impressive points. For opponents of legalization, "lame" reasons *for* legalization support their beliefs. People on both sides of the message worked harder to pay closer attention to those parts of the message that most bolstered their existing beliefs about an important campus issue of the time.

The elusive attention of an audience is hard to keep, especially when the audience opposes the message. Can the problem be overcome? One approach is to keep reminding the audience that there is "something in it for you"—that the discrepant information is useful and new, and that, if thought about, it may not be so discrepant from the way they "really feel." Some advertising executives admonish their colleagues for thinking in terms of ads as having sledgehammer effects, when they should use the metaphor of a "light fog" that envelops the consumer for a brief moment in persuasive sales time.

COMPREHENSION

Attention without understanding is like eating cotton candy. You see it, but there's no substance, no lasting value. At a minimum, we must understand the *conclusion* of the message. From the perspective of the Yale approach, it is also important to understand the *arguments,* because they make explicit the link between the advocated opinion and the desirable rewards for accepting it. Studies have documented the importance of comprehension. Researchers have compared the influence of a clear message with the influence of the same message presented amid loud background noise that actually interfered with understanding. They have also examined the difference between giving an argument straightforwardly and giving it in a complicated, tough-to-follow fashion. The typical result is that when comprehension is impaired, attitude change is also reduced (Eagly, 1974).

This observation is relevant to the problem of choosing a medium for transmitting a given message. Will a speech or a written presentation have a greater persuasive impact? Advertisers face such a question when they decide whether a TV commercial or a magazine ad should be the primary medium for a campaign. And not a few love-struck souls have agonized over the choice of a love letter or a phone call, or maybe even a dating ad in the personals column.

One factor to consider in deciding between the print and the broadcast media is the *level of complexity* of the message. As an illustration, consider this experiment (Chaiken and Eagly, 1976). College students, after reading the background facts of a legal dispute, were presented with a "law student's case discussion" that advocated one side of the dispute. There were two versions of this message, an easy-to-understand plain English version and a difficult version that said exactly the same thing but in "legalese." In addition, some students read a typewritten copy of one or the other version of the message, whereas the others heard the message, either as an audiotaped or a videotaped speech. Following the message presentation, the students gave their opinion of the case and took a test of message comprehension.

As expected, the easy message was clearly understood no matter how it was presented. Of most interest to us is the difficult message. Comprehension of the difficult message was impaired when it was presented as a speech, but not in printed form. This makes sense since, while reading, one can reread, pause to figure things out and put them together, and so cut through the legal jargon. In contrast, a speech just continues on even if it loses the audience. As it turned out, the speech lost the audience in more than one way. Not only did students who heard the speech fail to fully understand the difficult message, but they were also less swayed by it than were students who read the message. Limited comprehension led to limited persuasion. Hence, clarity is a compelling message quality. But if for some reason a message must be highly complicated, it will probably be most persuasive in written form. The audience needs enough time to read it, enough intelligence to decode it accurately, and motivation to be willing to put in that time and mental effort.

A different dimension that must be considered by the persuasive agent is whether to make the message rational or emotional, to engage the mind or tug at the heart strings. A recent text on message strategies in advertising suggests that the emphasis should be on gaining comprehension of rational arguments when the information in the arguments is (1) important and (2) unfamiliar to the audience (Rothschild, 1987). When importance is low, familiarity is high, and the message will be repeated often, an appeal to emotions is more persuasive according to this account (Rothschild, 1987). The evidence suggests that TV conveys emotional appeals better while print media are better for rational arguments. Emotional images need the sight, sound, and movement quality that TV offers, while rational arguments turn over some control of the pace of presentation to the recipient. Use TV to hit below the cortex, and print to justify things intellectually.

ACCEPTANCE: THE BIGGEST HURDLE

Achieving comprehension is good, but it is no cause for complacency. You're only part way "home"—to eliciting the desired change in attitude. Beyond a certain level at which the audience "gets the point," ever richer understanding of a message's arguments does not necessarily yield greater attitude change. Studies have shown, for example, that persuasive impact is not increased if the audience studies or rehearses arguments that were already understood (Greenwald, 1968). When you think about it, this makes sense. People do not passively accept every word and image they receive, just because they comprehend it. On the contrary, people have this funny habit of thinking about things occasionally.

In this section, we will see what happens to attitude change when people think carefully about a message, what happens when they think less carefully, and what factors determine whether or not they do much thinking. Both the quantity and the quality of thought may prove crucial to message acceptance—the springboard to attitude change.

Cognitive Responses: It's the Thought That Counts

The thoughts people have as they receive a message are pivotal, according to the *cognitive response approach* to persuasion. As outlined by Anthony Greenwald (1968), this approach maintains that we react to persuasive information by relating it to our existing attitudes, knowledge, and feelings about the message topic. In doing so, we generate thoughts, or "cognitive responses," relevant to the message that may or may not include the information in the message and may or may not agree with what the message advocates. What's important is the *evaluative nature* of the cognitive responses ("Hey, that's great!" "Gee, that's stupid"). We will change our attitude to agree with the message position to the extent that the message evokes cognitive responses in us that agree with the position it advocates. But if the cognitive responses support "the other side"—if they are counterarguments or otherwise unfavorable to the message position—our attitude will either remain unchanged or possibly even "boomerang," that is, change away from the message advocated.

Quality messages. This idea that message acceptance hinges less on what the message says than on the cognitive reactions it elicits complicates things considerably for the would-be persuader. For one thing, *message quality*—the validity, strength, and compellingness of the message arguments—becomes important. The arguments need to withstand the scrutiny of comparison with what the audience already knows, and they need to link the recommended position to the audience's existing attitudes. Strong arguments, in general, are those that seem plausible and important, and that add something new to the issue in question (Morley, 1987). Messages with arguments meeting these "quality" criteria are more persuasive than messages that contain implausible or illogical arguments (Leippe and Elkin, 1987; Petty and Cacioppo, 1984). And the more good arguments, the better, since each additional argument may evoke an agreeable cognitive response that further tips the balance of thinking in favor of the message (Calder et al., 1974).

Know your audience. The cognitive response approach also complicates the persuader's life because it implies that, to gain acceptance, he or she must know something about the *prior knowledge and attitudes* of the audience. Remember, our cognitive responses to the message depend on what we already know, remember, believe, or feel about the message topic. In Chapter 1, we noted that part of Martin Luther King, Jr.'s magic as a communicator was drawn from his knowledge of his audience. He spoke in the biblical language familiar to his religious followers, appealed to the patriotism and "love of liberty" of the American middle class, and invoked the words and deeds of heroes and leaders admired by black and white people alike.

In a similar, if less inspiring, fashion, advertisers also need to know the audience. They painstakingly tailor their messages for specific audiences, by including content that agrees with what the audience already finds desirable. According to the Sunday afternoon commercials, brand X beer has all the attributes desired by the typical male "couch potato" football fan. The commercials airing during the Video Hits hour late Friday night, however, clearly inform the viewer that brand X is the perfect brew for singles who want to be a hit on the dance floor.

Compared to their less opinionated peers, people who initially oppose a message's position should have more negative cognitive responses to the message and so should be more likely to resist persuasion. And this should be especially true if they are well informed about the message topic. Knowledge is a great asset to the ability to counterargue the points of a message.

One researcher tested just this hypothesis (Wood, 1982). In an initial testing session, the researcher learned that the college-student subjects virtually all supported environmental preservation. But by having these pro-preservation students list their beliefs and past behaviors relevant to preservation, the researcher also found that the students fell into two groups: (1) those who were quite knowledgeable about preservation issues and were able to recall numerous personal behaviors and beliefs relevant to preservation; and (2) those with less knowledge, beliefs, and experience relevant to preservation. In a second session a week or two later, both the knowledgeable and the less knowledgeable students read a message opposed to environmental preservation. As the cognitive response model would predict, the two groups responded quite differently to the message. The less knowledgeable students were swayed by the message toward a more moderate position. In contrast, the more knowledgeable students held their ground, budging very little from their highly pro-preservation stance. Moreover, they resisted by engaging in solid counterarguing. They used what they knew about the topic to discredit the message.

This pattern—greater resistance to influence by people who have well-articulated attitudes—may remind you of the study we reviewed in Chapter 3. People with clear and strong attitudes were found less likely than others to infer a new attitude from their situationally induced behavior. Indeed, the general principle is the same: if you know how you feel and why, forces outside you have less impact in changing beliefs and emotions. In the case of persuasion, the relevant knowledge and experiences stored in your memory get triggered by the message, and if the message is counter to your attitude, this knowledge helps you generate cognitive responses that refute the message.

But do strong experience-based attitudes always lead to resistance to persuasion? Is there no way to change those tough-minded attitudes once they are formed? An interesting prediction of cognitive response theory is that people with more firsthand experience with an attitude object should be *more* influenced than those with less experience by one kind of message: a message that advocates a position consistent with, but more *extreme*

Argum
vnclw

than, theirs. ("I agree with you, but you don't go far enough; from my point of view...") Research confirms this idea (Wu and Shaffer, 1987). Why? Because the cognitive process of thinking about the new information in a given attitude-consistent message taps into a large memory store of basically agreeing beliefs and experiences that leads people to generate numerous *pro*-message cognitive responses. These, in turn, provide the foundation for endorsing an even more extreme attitude.

Know your audience even better. Persuaders should keep in mind one more thing about the prior knowledge of message recipients. Different people are knowledgeable about different things and have diverse ways of organizing and interpreting their world. He's a religious type, she has a business angle on everything, and that one over there wants to be a lawyer. There is much to be said for the old advice that the persuader should "put it in terms the audience can relate to."

One study identified people who were either "legalistic" or "religious" types, in terms of the traits they identified as self-descriptive. A pro-attitudinal message about abortion that took a legalistic perspective on the issue was rated more persuasive by the legalistic types than by the religious types. But when the message took a religious angle, religious types found it more persuasive (Cacioppo et al., 1982). Thus, before you compose your persuasive pitch, make the effort to know your audience better. Many businesses do this by hiring research agencies to conduct values appraisals of their potential market members, to segment them into different types clustered around unique sets of values. There might be nature lovers, ecology-minded types on one hand, and career-oriented, gourmet food, high-status-interest types on another. They also try to know their audience better by conducting "focus groups" in which a number of small groups of people—a cross-section of the intended market—are brought together for intense personal discussions. They are encouraged to share their feelings and beliefs about the product or service and about its competition. In this way, those who do the marketing and advertising for the company get a firsthand sense of the images, language, metaphors, and types of arguments and counterarguments such people use in relation to what they are trying to sell.

Shortcuts to Acceptance: Using Heuristics Instead of Systematic Analysis

A strong message composed with the audience's perspective in mind has a good change of persuading them, especially an audience not already knowledgeably opposed to the message. Indeed, these are the right ingredients for persuasion—but only if the audience *systematically analyzes* the message. This is a big "if." As described so far, the cognitive response approach implies that we think about the individual arguments in the message or mentally "elaborate on" them, relating the arguments and information to beliefs and knowledge stored in memory. Collectively, these activities are often referred to as *systematic message analysis or message processing.* In reality, sometimes we do systematically analyze or process, and sometimes (probably most often) we don't. There are simply too many messages bombarding us daily about what and who to like, what to buy, what to do or not do, who to say "No" to, who to say "Yes" to. We can't simply leave them all back at persuasion step 2—unattended to—because some of them are valuable to us. But who has time to carefully analyze them all? We do, after all, have busy lives to live each day and textbooks like this one to read and memorize.

What can you do? The problem is the same one we encountered in Chapter 2: too much information to think about carefully. And the psychological solution is also the same. Chapter 2 introduced the concept of the *judgmental heuristic.* As we mature, we learn simple rules of thumb, such as obey authority and return favors; and we let the seemingly appropriate rule guide us in certain situations. Experience also teaches guiding heuristics in persuasion, such as "statements by recognized experts can be trusted," "messages that most people agree with are probably valid," and "the longer the message, the more valid it probably is." Persuasion researchers have discovered that, at the acceptance step, use of heuristics can occur in addition to, or *instead of,* the systematic processing we have so far been describing (Chaiken, 1987; Chaiken et al., 1989; Petty and Cacioppo, 1986).

Here's how it works. You hear or see a message that may cue you into the correct attitude to hold on a topic. You pay enough attention to get the gist of the message, but with other things on your mind, you don't scrutinize its content. Instead, you notice that the source of the message is a famous expert on the message topic. Perhaps unconsciously, you apply the "experts can be trusted" heuristic and accept the message's conclusion, changing your attitude accordingly. All this occurs without systematic message analysis.

The *heuristic "route"* to persuasion, then, involves applying a rule of thumb, usually based on a salient cue—like the source's expertise—that is readily apparent without having to delve into message content. For this reason, some cues that suggest a heuristic have been referred to as *peripheral cues;* they are outside, or on the periphery, of message content (Petty and Cacioppo, 1986). They are to be distinguished from *central message aspects,* such as message quality, which are only knowable if we take the systematic route of careful message analysis.

When will the heuristic route predominate? That depends on *motivation* and *ability.* If the topic is fairly remote from personal interest and we are not motivated to analyze it systematically, the use of heuristics, which requires less effort, will prevail. Ability enters in when the message is difficult to hear or too complicated to judge confidently, or when we lack the skill or training for systematic analysis. Under these circumstances, we may be forced to rely on peripheral cues in deciding whether to accept the message even if we are motivated to take a closer look.

The eloquence of relevance. As usual, a good research study nicely illuminates things. In this case we learn about differences between the heuristic and systematic strategies of responding to persuasive appeals, and also about the role of motivation in determining which strategy is used. Richard Petty and John Cacioppo, two social psychologists who pioneered the "two routes to persuasion" idea, created a persuasion procedure in which it was possible to make the same message seem either highly relevant or quite irrelevant to the university students who heard it. High relevance, as we noted, should be a source of motivation to systematically analyze the message. This procedure was used in a study in which subjects were seated comfortably in small private rooms, where they learned that the administration at their university was considering instituting a requirement that all students pass a "senior comprehensive exam" before being granted a degree (Petty et al., 1981). Their assigned role in the study was to evaluate the "broadcast quality" of a policy statement on this topic. This policy statement was an audiotaped speech endorsing senior comprehensive exams—which were strongly opposed by the student body. Half the subjects eventually heard a version of the message made up of strong and compelling arguments, while the other half heard a version that contained weak and easily countered arguments. In addition, the strong or weak message was said to be based on a report prepared either by experts—the "Carnegie Commission on Higher Education," chaired by a highly respected Princeton education professor—or by clear-cut nonexperts—a local high school class. Thus, subjects heard either a strong or a weak message based on the ideas of either experts or nonexperts.

But before they heard their assigned message, subjects learned one more thing. The experimenter remarked to half the subjects that the university was debating the possibility of instituting comprehensive exams the very next year. To the rest, he stated that the exams were being considered for 10 years hence. Thus, we have a manipulation of personal relevance. Whereas some subjects might be personally touched by the message issue in the very near future, others would never be affected personally because they would graduate long before the comprehensive exams were instituted.

The relevance factor proved critically important, as we can see by studying Figure 4.3. After hearing the message, subjects responded to various attitude questions. Their responses revealed that, for high-relevance subjects, the strong message was far more persuasive than the weak message. Yet the expertise of the message source had virtually

Two Routes to Persuasion

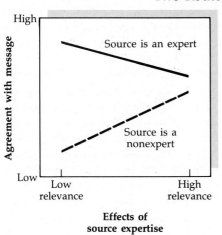

**Effects of
source expertise**

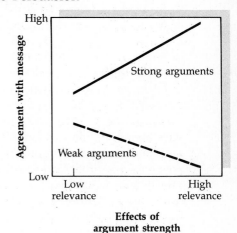

**Effects of
argument strength**

FIGURE 4.3
When college students heard a message advocating senior comprehensive exams, they carefully studied the message when they believed that the exams might be instituted the next year (high relevance). Hence, the attitudes of high relevance subjects were influenced by the strength of the message arguments. In contrast, when they believed that the exams would not be instituted for 10 years (low relevance), they studied the message less and relied on "who said it." Low relevance subjects were persuaded by an expert, but not by a nonexpert.
(From Petty, Cacioppo, and Goldman, 1981. Copyright 1981 by the American Psychological Association. Reprinted by permission.)

no effect on the attitudes of high-relevance subjects. The reverse of this pattern occurred among low-relevance subjects. Message quality had little effect on their attitudes, whereas source expertise had a major influence; the message was far more persuasive when it was attributed to experts than when it was attributed to nonexperts.

A dramatic demonstration! Concerned with the issue, high-relevance subjects were motivated to carefully consider what the message *said*—and did so. When it made strong points, their cognitive responses were largely favorable and they ultimately agreed with the message. When the message was naive and stupid in places, more negative cognitive responses were triggered and the message recommendation was rejected. In contrast, the less motivated low-relevance subjects never picked up on message quality; they took the heuristic route, deciding whether to accept the message recommendation on the basis of *who said it*. ("Experts can be believed; high school students can be ignored.")

When weak works. The pattern this experiment detected has also been found in other studies (Leippe and Elkin, 1987; Petty and Cacioppo,

1984; Sorrentino et al., 1988). It is interesting that this pattern, besides illustrating two different "routes" to persuasion, also indicates one circumstance in which a weak, invalid communication can be persuasive. A credible source can get away with a poor message as long as the audience is not motivated to systematically analyze the arguments.

A second way a weak message might be persuasive is if something interferes with the audience's *ability* to analyze its arguments. If the arguments cannot be carefully scrutinized, their invalidity may go unnoticed and fail to elicit many negative cognitive responses among audience members. Instead, only the superficial main thrust of the message arguments may be comprehended. If so, then they may trigger favorable responses that lead to attitude change. One way to accomplish this interference would be to distract the audience, as with background music or other attention-getting activity. The distraction, of course, should not be so severe as to prevent comprehension; rather, it should be just enough to make counterarguing difficult.

In one test of this idea, subjects listened to either a strong or a weak message advocating a tuition increase at their university (Petty et al., 1976). While listening to the message, they were asked to try to keep track of the number of times an "X" briefly appeared on a TV monitor. As a manipulation of distraction, the experimenters varied the frequency with which the "X" flashed, from never for some subjects (no distraction), to five or ten times per minute for others (low and medium distraction), and up to twenty times per minute for a final group of subjects (high distraction).

After listening to the message and counting the flashes, subjects indicated the extent to which they agreed with the message. Their average responses are graphed in Figure 4.4. When there was no distraction, the strong message was much more persuasive than the weak message. But the advantage disappeared with increasing distraction. Consistent with the idea that distraction would disrupt counterarguing, the weak message was more persuasive the greater the distraction. And the strong message was *less* persuasive the greater the distraction. Why? Because distraction prevented the mental elaboration that would have allowed the strong arguments to trigger positive cognitive responses. Distraction seems to be a great equalizer—a tool that can be used to hide both poor and good ideas.

Let's get back to heuristic cues, for they have further important implications for persuasion, which become clearer when we recognize a couple of additional details about persuasion settings.

Cues by the plenty. One such detail is the fact that for someone with little time, inclination, or ability to analyze a message systematically, any of a number of heuristic cues may be available as a shortcut alternative to *mindful processing*. We have seen one: source expertise.

The Effects of Distraction Depend on Message Strength

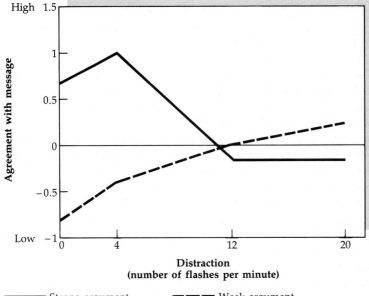

FIGURE 4.4
Subjects monitored computer screen flashes while listening to a
communication about tuition increases. The more flashes they saw
on the screen, the more distracting the task. A strong message
became less persuasive as distraction increased, but a weak message
became more persuasive.
(From Petty, Wells, and Brock, 1976. Copyright 1976 by the American Psychological Association. Reprinted by permission.)

The source of the message may have other apparent attributes that provide a rule of thumb relevant to accepting the message. The source may
appear similar to the audience, thereby encouraging social comparison
and application of the "similar people usually like similar things" rule
(Brock, 1965). Or the source may be known to be very trustworthy.

   Through normative social influence, other members of the audience
may actually provide heuristic persuasion cues, too. Enthusiastic applause, for instance, implies that many others agree with the message
and, in turn, that it must be valid. The same speeches have been found
to be more persuasive when they are accompanied by applause than
when they are not (Axsom et al., 1987; Landy, 1972). In the same vein,
researchers have documented that the "laugh tracks" accompanying
many TV sitcoms increase ratings of how funny the jokes are (Fuller
and Sheehy-Skeffington, 1974).

   Finally, aspects of the message itself may be cues to its validity. A
long-winded speech may win acceptance less because of what it says

than because it is simply long (Petty and Caciappo, 1984; Wood et al., 1985). For the halfhearted listener, the operative rule might be that "with so much to say, the speaker must have a valid idea, even though I've stopped listening." The point is that there is often much to go on *besides the message arguments* when a decision must be made about whether to accept a communication.

Because experience teaches that rules of thumb are usually right, people can be expected to use heuristic cues to some extent even when they have more than passing interest in the message topic. As a result, both the amount and the quality of systematic analysis may be affected by the peripheral cues that are present in a situation. On the amount side, other things being equal, the heuristic route will be used more than systematic analysis when the message setting is rich in peripheral cues (Chaiken et al., 1989). The cues may *eliminate the need* to study the actual arguments. On the quality side, any systematic analysis that does occur may be "tainted" by what is inferred from peripheral cues. Knowledge that the speaker's credibility is suspect, for example, may cause the audience to evaluate message arguments with greater skepticism, leading to more negative cognitive responses (Hass, 1981).

Televised Images

The powerful influences of peripheral persuasion cues have special significance to advertising and campaign messages, especially those transmitted over television. To appreciate this, let us return to the study that compared the persuasive impact of print, audio, and video message presentations (Chaiken and Eagly, 1976). This study found that a complex message was most persuasive when presented in writing, presumably because it could be better comprehended if it was read. On the other hand, an easy-to-understand message was most persuasive when presented via videotape and least persuasive in print. One reason for this reversal is that, in a video presentation that includes a speaker's image, the characteristics of the speaker and his or her delivery are salient and vivid. They constitute a rich source of peripheral cues about such things as the speaker's likability, confidence, and so forth, which might be used as a guide to attitude change as well as message analysis.

This idea was tested in follow-up studies (Chaiken and Eagly, 1983). College students received the same highly comprehensible message in either print or broadcast (audiotape or videotape) form, after first being given information that made the communicator appear either likable or unlikable. The key finding was that the effects of message medium depended on the likability of the communicator. When the communicator was likable, more attitude change occurred when the message was broadcast than when it was read. But when the communicator was unlikable, the opposite pattern prevailed. Putting it somewhat differently, source likability—a peripheral cue—had more influence when the source could be seen, heard, or both.

Under these "broadcast" circumstances, the source is a salient aspect of the persuasion situation. As we saw in Chapter 3, the stimuli that gain the most attention are the ones that dominate our thinking and judgments of causality (Fiske and Taylor, 1984). Thus, a seen-or-heard source will enter more prominently into an audience's cognitive responses. If he or she is liked, positive features of the source will get noticed and produce positive cognitive responses; but if he or she is disliked, negative features become noticeable (remember selective attention). This interpretation is nicely borne out in the cognitive responses that the college students listed following exposure to the message. There was greater thinking about the source when the message was broadcast than when it was written, and the thinking was more positive when the communicator was likable.

Thus, the broadcast media allow peripheral cues to pack a double wallop. They make them more salient and therefore more likely to be used in decisions involving attitude change. And they may distract recipients from systematic message analysis since greater thinking about the communicator (or some other peripheral characteristic) leaves less time and energy available to scrutinize what the message says. Moreover, as we noted earlier, televised images are effective forms of emotional appeals.

Don't think the gist of this conclusion is lost on advertisers. Indeed, the people who compose, direct, and deliver our commercials, campaign speeches, and public service announcements know all about the impact of peripheral cues in the broadcast media and in those print media in which peripheral cues can be highlighted, such as billboards and pictorial magazine ads. They know that a picture can be worth a thousand words when the audience is too busy or disinterested to demand a real argument-based message. And they know that, under those circumstances, the key is the *image*—the attention-grabbing, easily understood, and memorable cue that says, "You need not bother with the details; my message (or my product) is right for you." (In other words, "Don't even listen, just read my lips.")

Presidential images: style replaces substance. There may be no better illustration of the use of images to trigger heuristic thinking than the 1988 U.S. presidential election campaign. The Democratic candidate, Michael Dukakis, had an image problem all along. He looked and acted too much the cool, dispassionate technocrat, and too little the warm and emotional leader. But the campaign of George Bush, his Republican opponent, created an even more damning image of Dukakis, while creating a clean and simple positive image of Bush. Sensing distrust of the left wing by the American public, Bush relentlessly labeled

An image for General Noreiga. This memorable
mugshot appeared on the front page of hundreds
of newspapers and did an effective job of
strengthening the deposed Panamanian dictator's
image as a thug. (*UPI/Bettmann Newsphotos*)

Dukakis a "liberal" and proceeded to define a liberal as someone who is
soft on crime, pro-abortion, pro-taxes, and even unpatriotic. The Bush
campaign staff crystallized these negative connotations via vivid TV
ads. One of these pictured and told the grisly story of a convicted murderer, Willie Horton, who gained release from a Massachusetts prison
through a state furlough program while Dukakis was the governor of
Massachusetts. While on furlough, the prisoner raped a young woman
and assaulted her boyfriend in Maryland. The ad made no bones about
who was to blame for this tragedy.

This tactic apparently worked for the Republicans. A big Dukakis
lead in the polls in the summer of 1988 disappeared before Labor Day,
and by September, Bush was solidly in front. Regarding the ad just de-

scribed, it didn't seem to matter that (1) the Massachusetts prisoner furlough program was instituted before Dukakis became governor, (2)
Dukakis immediately eliminated the program following the Horton incident, and (3) the federal prison system had a similar furlough program during the years of the Reagan administration in which Bush
served as vice president. Many voters never delved far enough into the
campaign messages to learn these facts. Many others knew these facts,
but it didn't matter. Taken together with Dukakis's image as a liberal
and an opponent of the death penalty, the furlough of Willie Horton
was not like other prisoner furloughs: it was a careless mistake guided
by a permissive, "soft on crime" liberal philosophy.

This example vividly illustrates two consequences of the reliance on
heuristics encouraged by the cue-rich medium of television: (1) not
enough thinking about the quality and reasoning of the message, and
(2) some distortion of the thinking that does occur. Dukakis was never
able to shed the negative images created for him. At first, he tried to
refute them by appealing "to the record," failing to realize that the public's responses to his arguments were influenced by his negative image
as much as (or more than) by the content of those arguments.

Not until October did Dukakis start working on his own image making: too little, too late. And Bush already had assumed the image the
public seemed to want—of the patriot and optimist. One campaign
strategist summed it all up in *Time* magazine with a ringing acknowledgment of the power of peripheral images: "If we get the visual that
we want, it doesn't matter as much what words the networks use in
commenting on it."

Optimism wins. A theme that stands out in a message can also
serve as a peripheral cue. If the theme is sufficiently salient and compelling, people may decide to accept the message's conclusion without
digging past the theme into the arguments that purportedly support the
message. George Bush's stump speeches in 1988 contained such a
theme. The theme was *optimism.* It was quite simple, as any persuasion
cue should be. Bush told America what former President Reagan had
told us: You're doing great. Looming problems such as the federal deficit and urban poverty and crime can be corrected and will be. Indeed,
the President-to-be explicitly proclaimed, "I am an optimist." Although
Bush offered few arguments about how to correct these problems, the
voters responded to this bright outlook.

This outcome didn't surprise psychologists who analyzed the nomination speeches of the two major candidates in the ten presidential
election races between 1948 and 1984 (Zullow et al., 1988). In nine of
these ten races, the candidate with the more optimistic outlook won.
Applying the same analysis to the stump speeches of the presidential

contenders *before* the 1988 primaries, the same researchers concluded that Bush was the most optimistic Republican and Dukakis the most optimistic Democrat. Winners think, or at least talk, positive.

Optimism seems to serve as a message acceptance cue in part because of the need people have to believe that they control their own destinies. As a result of this need, the "you and I can do it" message evokes positive cognitive responses. It also implies that the candidate believes in himself or herself. The philosophy that you can do anything if you believe in yourself is deeply ingrained in Western, free enterprise culture. (Consider the perpetual fame of *The Little Engine That Could*.)

Even though persuasion can be accomplished by providing an audience with salient but superficial cues, it is important to keep in mind two things. First, people at times do go beyond the cues and really concentrate on a message's arguments when they have the time, ability, and desire to do so. Second, the heuristic route, like more effortful systematic analysis, usually does produce a *valid* attitude. The rules of thumb that people use are good ones, *on the average*. Systematic analysis is likely to be called into play when the issue at hand is so important that people are unwilling to risk that this time may not be "average."

Objectivity and Bias in Systematic Processing

Whether or not we can be *completely* objective in evaluating message arguments is another story. We are likely to counterargue messages that oppose our existing attitudes, particularly if we are sufficiently knowledgeable to do so. Counterarguing can be objective and based on accurate beliefs. But despite all good intentions to "let the facts speak for themselves," biases based on our existing attitudes can sneak into our perception and interpretation of the "facts." What we notice in a message, how we interpret ambiguous message information, and which beliefs and knowledge are conjured from memory during the cognitive response process are all affected in subtle ways by one's existing point of view.

Imagine two bright people in their twenties who are on opposite sides of the issue of capital punishment. One is a proponent of capital punishment, believing that it is a deterrent to murder. The other opposes capital punishment and believes that it has no effect on the murder rate. What would happen if both of these individuals carefully read detailed scientific reports of two seemingly reputable studies, one which found that the death penalty has a deterrent effect and the other stating that the murder rate is actually higher in states that have a death penalty? In effect, the opposing findings of the two reports suggest that the evidence is inconclusive regarding the deterrent effect of the death penalty. Therefore, you might predict the two recipients of this information to move closer together—toward a neutral position—on the issue. After all, their systematic analysis should make it clear that neither side has compelling arguments that are not countered by evidence for the other side.

You might expect a coming together of attitudes, but you probably wouldn't get it. In a study that carried out exactly this procedure, subjects who disagreed about capital punishment *became even further separated* after reading the mixed evidence (Lord et al., 1979). Those in favor became more pro; those opposed, more con. This peculiar effect appears to be the result of *biased interpretation*. The subjects tended to accept at face value the data that supported their position while actively counterarguing the nonsupportive findings. Flaws in the discrepant study were searched for and alternative explanations conjured up— mental acts that were not difficult for people who entered the study possessing knowledge and beliefs supporting the opposing viewpoint. After all the new data were digested, recipients (to their minds) had an even stronger basis for their original belief: a supportive scientific study and new "evidence" that opposing studies are flawed. In this way, attitudes of opposing camps become polarized and unreconcilable.

The biased perception and interpretation apparent in this study just reviewed lead to other interesting and important outcomes. For example, it is becoming increasingly well documented that voters misjudge the positions of political candidates. Voters who like a candidate typically judge his or her position as closer to theirs than it actually is, whereas voters who dislike the candidate see his or her position as more at odds with theirs than it is. Thus careful analysis of survey data shows that (in 1968) those supporters of Democratic candidate Hubert Humphrey who opposed the Vietnamese war saw Humphrey as considerably more "dovish" than those Humphrey supporters who favored a continued U.S. involvement in Vietnam. Antiwar Humphrey supporters saw his opponent, Richard Nixon, as more "hawkish" than did the more hawkish Humphrey supporters. The mirror image of this pattern was observed among Nixon supporters (Granberg and Brent, 1974).

Part of the misperception can be attributed to the candidates' own behavior—their tendency to tailor their message to the audience they happen to be addressing at the moment. But such selective presentation does not account for the size of the differences in perception that are usually found (Judd et al., 1983). Interpretation within one's own framework and desires is also going on. Interestingly, even a preferred candidate's chances of winning are subject to biased interpretation. Voters have a strong tendency to expect their candidate to win, even when the polls suggest otherwise (Granberg and Brent, 1983).

A major point of this chapter. (Reprinted with permission of Washington Star Syndicate, Inc.)

AN INTERIM STOP ON THE ROAD TO LASTING PERSUASION

The main message of this chapter is that gaining attitude change in response to an argument-based communication is an uncertain result of several perceptual and mental steps, each of which includes obstacles to change. Besides getting the attention and comprehension of a target (who habitually prefers a diet of agreeable, easy-to-digest information), you need powerful peripheral cues (if the heuristic path is likely). Or else, you need arguments strong enough to withstand counterarguing and more subtle biases in judgment and interpretation (if systematic analysis is likely). If your target is exceptionally knowledgeable about his or her position and is committed to it, your persuasion task will be difficult indeed.

We will take up the problem of seemingly unbudgeable attitudes in Chapter 6. In the meantime, we move on to Chapter 5, where we continue through the "steps to persuasion" to the point where the action is. Some behavioral act occurs—a vote is cast, a product is purchased, or perhaps one's lifestyle changes. How can that behavior be channeled into the desired direction, to achieve the objective of the persuasive campaign? Let's see.

TO SUM UP...

We focused on persuasion: using communicated information and argumentation from a given source to change beliefs in a target audience. Changes in beliefs, in turn, may lead to attitude and behavior change in the interconnected attitude system. We examined how, through social comparison, people obtain information relevant to the subjective correctness of their attitudes. We then examined four psychological steps to attitude change through persuasion: exposure, attention, comprehension, and acceptance.

- We all desire to hold correct attitudes and beliefs. Feeling right helps fulfill our sense of predictability and control. Social comparison theory posits that we attempt to assess the validity of our opinions by comparing them with those of others.

- For very subjective opinions, we seek comparison with those who are similar to us on attributes related to the opinion issue. Comparison with dissimilar others leaves it unclear whether disagreement reflects invalidity or just different values. When already committed to an opinion, we may seek to bolster that opinion through comparison with people who are like-minded on related attributes *and* on the issue at hand. Comparison with dissimilar others occurs when being wrong is very costly or when the opinion is a verifiable belief. Under these circumstances, agreement from a different angle is informative about correctness.

- Though we are bombarded daily with persuasive messages, only a few influence us. Six mental steps must occur before a message can change behavior. We must (1) be exposed to the message, (2) pay attention to it, (3) comprehend its gist, (4) accept its conclusion as our new attitude, (5) remember the new attitude, and (6) use it to guide behavior.

- We already agree with most messages we are exposed to. One reason for such selective exposure is that our lifestyles and philosophical preferences lead us into careers and leisure activities in which most people we encounter resemble us. In addition, the values and mental frameworks shaped by society influence what is presented in the media and taught in schools. In effect, both intentional and unintentional censorship occurs even in democracies. Extreme censorship in totalitarian states can keep revolutionary forces in check—for a time.

- Once exposed to a message, we must pay attention for it to have an impact. Internal preferences as well as external stimuli divert attention from messages. We pay closer attention to received messages that support our attitudes than to those that oppose them, unless the message contains novel and useful information and we feel uncommitted to our position.

- Limited message comprehension may lead to limited persuasion. As a result, difficult messages are more persuasive in print—where the target controls the pace of presentation—than when spoken. Appeals to reason require more comprehension and are more effective in print. Appeals to emotion are best in audiovisual media, since they require emotion-eliciting images but little comprehension.

- Comprehension does not guarantee attitude change. Acceptance of the message requires favorable cognitive responses (the products of thinking about the message). Thus, messages with new and compelling arguments that relate to the target's existing knowledge, values, and interests are most persuasive.

- The impact of message quality, however, is strong only if the audience systematically analyzes the message, and systematic analysis is only likely when the audience is motivated and able to do so. When motivation is low (because the message has little personal relevance) or ability is low (e.g., because the audience is distracted), the audience will take a heuristic route—deciding to accept or reject the message based on rules of thumb suggested by peripheral cues ("Experts can be trusted"). Reliance on heuristic cues may also supplement or replace systematic analysis when the message setting is rich in such cues. The availability of certain types of peripheral cues may bias systematic processing.

- Television lends itself to messages rich in peripheral cues, or images. The communicator's looks, delivery style, symbols, "sound bites," musical background, and broad themes (such as optimism) provide cues for heuristic judgments and distract people from the substance of messages.

- If sufficiently motivated, people engage in systematic analysis, but it is difficult to be completely objective—unbiased by existing preferences and beliefs—even when one is trying to be. Opposing factions may each get belief-supportive information from the same middle-of-the-road message.

QUESTIONS AND EXERCISES

1. Analyze your own social comparison habits. To whom do you compare yourself, and what conditions lead you to seek different sorts of people for comparison? How do your habits conform to social comparison theory and research described in this chapter? How (and if so, why) do they differ? When do you compare yourself to someone who is quite different from you? Are there certain classes of people who are "noncomparison" targets for you (by virtue of gender, class, or race, for example)?

2. Imagine that you have the task of composing and arranging for the presentation of a public service message that encourages people to place a greater percentage of their earnings into savings. Using the principles discussed in this chapter, describe the message you would develop. Who would deliver it? What considerations would go into its composition? Who would it be most pitched to and how? What media and "message accompaniments" would be used and why?

3.   "Attitudes are hard to change." Articulate support for this statement by examining the first four steps to persuasion.

4.   Distinguish between persuasion through systematic analysis and persuasion by the heuristic route. When does one occur and not the other? Can they both occur in response to the same message? From the point of view of the *persuader*, what are the advantages and disadvantages of each?

5

Making Persuasion Last:

The Persistence and Behavioral Consequences of Attitude Change

❖

Sowing the Seeds of Retention: Creating Strong, Clear, and Extreme Attitudes ◆ Retention: Persuasion over Time ◆ Translating Attitudes into Behavior: Ultimate Persuasion ◆ The Hard-Earned Rewards of Persuasion

In thinking back, he must have been about 75 miles north of the South Carolina border. As he barreled south on Interstate 95 through the pine forests and July heat of North Carolina, a sign caught his eye, maybe because of its bright colors and homemade look. He doesn't remember what the sign said, yet he was sure that a second sign, a few miles farther down the road, was related to the first one. Its message was completely different, but the colors and the styling were similar. Two miles later, there was another colorful sign with that same homemade look. And then another...and another. The written messages were simple ones, but cryptic and thus curiosity-arousing: "Wow!" "The Good Times Are Here Again," and "You'll Be Tickled Pink" (written in shocking pink). Many of the billboards, the driver noticed, contained a picture of a Mexican sombrero, and some made reference to someone named Pedro or conveyed a Mexican accent in their written message: "Beeg Deal" "Bear Up a Leetle Longer" (beside a picture of a bearlike cartoon character).

Thirty miles north of the border, these colorful billboards increased in number—each one different, yet all the same. Ten miles later the signs started coming rapid fire, as the silver Ford Tempo blazed along. Now they were even more eye-catching; some included moving figures. As the border drew nearer, the driver exclaimed to his wife, "There must have been over a hundred of them already." "Three-Year-Olds Say: 'I Wuv Pedro'" "Awesome!" "Shop Til You Drop (Pedro Weell Catch You)" "Stop Before You Pop!"

Suddenly, looming in the distance, he saw it: a 200-foot tower topped with a sombrero and, underneath it, two huge but lovable carved figures, Pedro and his mule.

The driver, with his wife's eager approval, exited where the last signs instructed all cars to go. He could barely contain his excitement as he rounded the last bend. He found himself in the middle of a vast and, in its gaudy way, unique shopping village called "South of the Border." It had all kinds of stores—fast food, fireworks, souvenirs, exotic clothing—plus rides, arcade games, motels, shows. It was a neat design for an ultra tourist trap.

But the point of this story, experienced by one of the authors, centers on the "over a hundred" billboards that strategically dot the landscape on the way to Pedro's place. If it were not for those signs, both members of the happy couple are certain they would not have stopped. Even several billboards would have been insufficient to get them to stop; they aren't the type to visit tourist traps. Besides, they were hurrying to Myrtle Beach to see their 11-year-old daughter dance in a national competition, and they hadn't seen her in a week. There was no way they would stop for some Pedro or other.

No, it was the sheer number of billboards, the repeated exposure to variations on an amusing theme, that got them to stop. In a word, all those signs were a very effective use of the *repetition* principle, an easy-to-use and thus often-used persuasion tool. As the travelers encountered more and more signs, they found themselves laughing and joking about them and growing increasingly fond of them. Ultimately, the signs accomplished three persuasion goals. The travelers formed a positive attitude toward the source of the signs, the "South of the Border" outfit, and *strongly accepted* the message of the signs—that the place was worth checking out. Second, they did check the place out; they stopped and, it must be confessed, they shopped. (Remember the power of commitment and consistency: "Now that we're off the highway, we might as well...") In other words, the attitude *translated into the behavior* desired by the source of the message. Finally, the message was *memorable*. Of the tens of thousands of billboards the couple has seen, they remember very few. But among those few are a number from the "South of the Border" bunch. They'll probably stop there again next time they travel south.

In the preceding chapter, we discussed the first four necessary steps to persuasion. If you are exposed to a message, pay attention to it, understand it, and accept its conclusion, then you have been persuaded by it. Your attitude has changed.

But how long will the attitude change last? Will you remember the message, or at least your new attitude, tomorrow? Next month? Next year? Will your new attitude withstand assaults of messages from "the other side"? And even if it persists and withstands attacks from the opposition and the forces of forgetting, will your new attitude affect your actions?

These questions will be our central concern in this chapter. What is necessary for the retention, or persistence, of attitude change? And what turns new attitudes into new actions? It seems that both retention and translation to behavior are more likely when the new attitude is strong and extreme. The creation of such an attitude depends on how a message is first presented as well as on how often it is presented. Accordingly, we will first reexamine the issue of how messages are presented—this time with an eye not only on *whether* the steps leading to attitude change occur but on *how strong and extreme* the changed attitude becomes.

Next, we will examine studies that have actually followed the course of persuasion over time. These "persistence of persuasion" studies reveal the importance of extreme and clear attitudes at the retention step. They go on to highlight additional conditions during and following message presentation that promote retention of attitude change over time. Finally, we will take a close look at critical factors operating during the final persuasion step, where changed attitudes are translated into action, into one of the array of recommended behaviors—be it voting, buying, dating, studying, cleaning, drinking, dieting, and anything else humans are capable of doing.

SOWING THE SEEDS OF RETENTION: CREATING STRONG, CLEAR, AND EXTREME ATTITUDES

Why did we begin this chapter with an example of the use of repetition in persuasion? We did it for one solid reason: Repeated presentation of a message is an effective strategy for obtaining lasting attitude change that will guide future behavior. Sometimes, our first response to a message may be nothing more than a fleeting sense of liking or agreement: a "passing fancy" that involves few links to other cognitions. Responses based on heuristic decision rules are often like this, as with "Flush after each use" or "Change your car's oil every 3,000 miles." In addition, a persuasive message may produce only modest agreement or change in our attitude, making us no more than lukewarm toward what the message wants to convey. Such superficial or middle-of-the-road attitudes are less likely to be retained and to guide our behavior than those deeper and more extreme attitudes that are based on numerous mental connections with thoughts and feelings that fit together into a congruent attitude system. And so how can we deepen and firm up flabby attitudes that lack real tone?

Decent Exposure

A major goal of advertising a new product is often simply to expose as many people as possible to it—not just once. There needs to be enough exposure to establish "brand recognition." Similarly, people seeking to become celebrities welcome as much exposure as possible and often go to great lengths to get it. As P. T. Barnum said, and some people believe, there is no such thing as bad publicity. What is bad is no publicity.

As we saw in the preceding chapter, a single presentation of a message makes subsequent persuasion steps leading to attitude change *possible*. Many presentations, however, may be necessary to make those tentative steps highly *probable*.

Familiarity breeds "content." Social psychologists have amassed a great deal of evidence that, up to a point, the more we are exposed to an object, the more we are apt to like it. Robert Zajonc (1968), for example, conducted a series of studies in which bland, novel, or complex stimuli were briefly exposed to viewers. Some were shown only once; others, a few times; and still others were briefly shown (for about 2 seconds) many times. The stimuli shown to American college students were sometimes Chinese words and sometimes nonsense words (e.g., IKTITAF) or other symbols.

For example, in one study subjects saw some Chinese characters once, others twice, and still others five, ten, and twenty-five times. Following the entire presentation, subjects were asked to guess each character's meaning on a bad-to-good scale. Reliably, the more often the stimulus was presented, the more subjects rated it "good." This relationship holds for a diverse range of stimuli, including people and artworks. One reason for the "mere exposure leads to liking" effect seems to be simply that there is comfort in the sense of familiarity (Zajonc, 1968; 1980).

However, there is an additional psychological process at work here. This process, which has special relevance to understanding attitude change, is evident from studies that have used stimuli for which people already have attitudes. A number of these studies have observed *polarization:* repeated exposure to stimuli people already like causes them to rate those stimuli even more positively, whereas repeated exposure to initially disliked stimuli leads to even more negative ratings. In one such experiment, subjects were exposed one, two, five, or ten additional times to abstract paintings they reported either liking or disliking after an initial exposure. The trend was for liked paintings to become more liked and for disliked paintings to become more disliked with increased viewing (Brickman et al., 1972). A similar effect has been found when the stimuli were words whose tone was positive ("bluejay") or negative ("depravity") (Grush, 1976), or were pictures of men who were portrayed in positive or negative roles in photographs (Perlman and Oskamp, 1971).

Polarization occurs because repeated exposure causes people to make an increasing number of mental associations to the stimulus—*cognitive responses,* to use our term from the previous chapter. Most of these associations have an evaluative tone that is consistent with the initial attitude toward the stimulus. This was evident in the experiment with emotionally toned words (Grush, 1976). As each word was presented, subjects made a "verbal association" to the word: they wrote down whatever came to mind. For example, "awful" and "unclean" might be written in response to the word "leprosy," whereas the word "dumpling" might conjure associations like "delicious" or "apple." After being exposed to the words and listing associations, subjects rated their verbal associations on a numerical bad-to-good scale. By examining these ratings, the researchers discovered that the evaluative tone of the verbal associations became more extreme with increasing exposure. The associations became increasingly positive for initially liked words and increasingly negative for initially disliked words.

We saw in Chapter 4 that one's attitude toward a message object or issue depends on the balance of favorable and unfavorable cognitive responses that are generated as a result of the message. The more favorable these responses are, the more the attitude of the target audience will change in the direction of the message. In the case of stimuli that are not part of a persuasive message—as in the mere exposure studies—a cognitive response process is at work as well.

There are two key new points, though, for us to consider. First, cognitive responses—be they complicated thoughts or simple verbal associations—occur *each time* the stimulus is presented. Second, the cognitive responses to later exposures tend to have the *same evaluative tone* as the cognitive responses to earlier exposures. For example, if the stimulus evoked positive thoughts the first time it was presented, then the new thoughts it evokes the second time it is viewed will probably also be positive. With increasing exposure, thoughts on one side of the ledger "build up."

Mere thought. This pattern of *evaluative consistency of cognitive responses* is apparent even when people simply think about a stimulus without the benefit of new repeated exposures. Consider the intriguing "thought polarization" studies conducted by psychologist Abe Tesser. Subjects in one such study rated their agreement or disagreement with one-sentence statements about sociopolitical issues, such as "Prostitution should be legalized." After each rating, they were asked simply to think about the issue for several minutes. Following this period, the experimenter asked for a second agree-disagree rating. What were the results? The attitudes of the majority of subjects polarized. Initial agreers agreed more so after thinking about it, whereas initial disagreers disagreed more after thinking about it (Tesser and Conlee, 1975). In studies using similar procedures, thought has been found to polarize attitudes about objects as diverse as people, artwork, fashions, and football strategies (Tesser, 1978).

A principle of evaluative consistency. Whether or not a stimulus is present, thinking about it seems to involve tendencies to (1) generate cognitions that are evaluatively consistent with an already existing attitude and (2) make existing cognitions more consistent with one another. Tesser (1978) suggests that the reason for these tendencies is that each of our attitudes reflects a part of our mental framework, or what psychologists like to call a *schema,* for understanding the attitude object. Thinking about the object is directed largely by the relevant schema. It creates a thought process that leads to memories and associations that support the attitude and fit nicely into the framework. The more we think or associate, up to a point, the more the consistent thoughts accumulate and the more extreme our attitude becomes.

The upshot is that most human beings are "wired" to think in consistent terms. This basic aspect of human mental processing gets an added boost from the culturally learned *need* for consistency that we have seen manifested in various influence phenomena in previous chapters (Giacalone and Rosenfeld, 1986). You can recognize consistent-thought and associated processes in the (1) enhanced attention to information that supports rather than opposes our decisions, (2) biased interpretation of mixed messages, and (3) counterarguing against disagreeable messages. But what is the practical significance of the principle of evaluative consistency?

It suggests a pragmatic strategy for creating extreme attitudes. The trick is first to elicit in the influence target at least a mildly favorable response to a product, an idea, or some other object. Then, you must somehow get the person to think and reflect further about that object. If the object is a social issue, a favorable response might be obtained by a persuasive message that contains strong and compelling arguments. How can you encourage further thinking? Perhaps you can do this by making the strong message personally relevant to your target, or by removing all distractions that could impede the time and ability to think about the message. Personal relevance and absence of distraction, as we saw in Chapter 4, are two conditions under which strong messages are most persuasive.

Jingle-jangle. If the object is a product, we might get people to like it simply through a pleasant first advertisement. Then it's time for repeated exposure. The key to an effective TV commercial, then, is to couch the product in a context that evokes positive feelings. If this is artfully done, the feelings become associated with the product, and the stage is set for continued exposure and mere thinking about the product to polarize those feelings—to make them even more positive. Thus, ads for men's cologne invariably include a sexy woman who is a plea-

In the never-ending "Cola wars," creating positive associations to the product is a primary goal of advertising.   (*Courtesy of Coca Cola USA*)

sure to look at and a bigger pleasure for many men to fantasize about. The basketball sneaker crowd gets treated to uplifting scenes of heroics by playground superstars wearing Nikes or Reeboks, while car buyers view the "Heartbeat of America" being driven through scenes of Americana guaranteed to prompt patriotic pride.

Nothing seems sacred in the pursuit of positive feelings, or affect. Ads aimed at affluent "baby boomers" frequently use classic rock songs from the 1960s and early 1970s. Indeed, these songs, or modifications of them, seem to have become more popular than original jingles in ads. Cute little California raisins sing and dance to "I Heard It through the Grapevine" as boxes of Post Raisin Bran are filled and emptied. The good life that the American Express credit card signifies is presented in wonderful visual scenes of that life as viewers are serenaded with the Temptations' "My Girl." (Can you see a connection?) Even sanctified Beatles songs now appear in commercials. The approach, though less creative than writing original jingles, may be more effective. For many in the targeted mass audience, these tunes elicit positive, nostalgic emotional responses. There is a risk though; some people become indignant that their favorite song is being perverted as a commercial jingle! So what, advertisers argue. For each such downer and lost sale, there are several uppers who buy the jingled-jangled association and the goodies at the end of the message.

Creating that initial positive response is the first step in introducing a new product. But note: repeated exposure *alone* assists positive affect, since it is known that even neutral stimuli tend to become more liked through repeated exposure. Familiarity leads to contentment, probably because we feel less uncertain toward known objects, which contributes a bit to that basic sense of control and predictability we seem to need at a most fundamental level. Also, a new product may gain a positive first impression through association with the *image* of the company that produces it. Simply because a new product is manufactured by a known, trusted (and thus liked) company—Nabisco, GE, Kodak, for example—it may elicit a favorable first reaction.

There are no absolutes in the world of influence. As important as it can be to create positive emotional associations to a product, we must note that occasionally it is unnecessary. In some cases, in fact, a more effective strategy is to repeat, in a memorable fashion, the simple message that a product is of superior quality. Over the years, many people have been downright annoyed by the "Ring around the collar" (for Wisk liquid detergent) and the "Don't squeeze the Charmin" ads. However, according to advertising executives, these ads have worked because they convince—and remind—people that the products are good ones (Kahn, 1987). Even if they don't like the jingle, the jangle still gets through to influence them, possibly by jangling those associative networks surrounding the attitude schema.

The politics of repeated exposure. If the attitude object is a person, liking can certainly be enhanced by the now-familiar strategy of obtaining initial exposure under positive circumstances (to gain acceptance) and following up with lots of repetition (to gain more extreme and stronger acceptance). Indeed, one research team discovered that the repeated exposure effects found in artificial laboratory studies do generalize to an important real-world phenomenon: political elections. Naturally, you might think. After all, political candidates and parties spend great sums of money on exposure in the form of TV and radio ads, campaign stops, doorknob fliers, and the like. Yet exposure effects should not be strong when both candidates are already well known and likely to get equivalent additional exposure, as in presidential and many senatorial elections. A more likely place to look for political exposure effects is congressional primary elections. These elections often involve more than two candidates, who are all initially unknown and likely to spend different amounts of money advertising themselves. In one study, researchers dug out records from the 1972 primary elections for the U.S. Senate and House of Representatives, and they examined the relationships among three variables: the amount of each candidate's previous exposure (how well known he or she was), how much the candidate spent on advertising before the primary (a pretty good indicator of media exposure), and the percent of the vote the candidate won in the primary (Grush et al., 1978).

*"It was either the knish in Coney Island, the cannoli in Little Italy,
or that divinity fudge in Westchester."*

Exposure gains votes, but not always without costs that are hard to digest.
(Drawing by Levin; © 1976 The New Yorker Magazine, Inc.)

Exposure effects were very much in evidence, in two ways. First, in
those primaries in which all (three or more) candidates were virtual un-
knowns and all spent a good deal on advertising, the strongest determinant of winning was the amount spent on gaining exposure. The biggest spender won in 57 percent of these primaries; and the second
biggest spender, in another 25 percent. The second way in which exposure was found to be important concerns primaries in which one of the
candidates already had great exposure by being an incumbent, by holding a highly visible position, or by being otherwise famous. Pre-
campaign exposure was the best predictor of the winner in these cases,
with the highly visible candidate going into the campaign winning the
race 88 percent of the time.

Repetition of Complex Messages

People, artwork, Chinese characters, and words—mere repeated exposure to them can make them better liked, as long as people don't initially react negatively to them. Will complex messages, with arguments
and reasoning, also produce greater agreement if they are repeated?
The principle of evaluative consistency suggests that this should be so if
the message arguments are strong enough to elicit favorable cognitive
responses and if people are motivated and able to engage in systematic
mental processing each time the message is presented. Under these cir-

cumstances, continuing analysis of the repeated message should yield additional thoughts that are mostly consistent with the initial favorable ones.

Two experiments confirm this prediction, with an added twist (Cacioppo and Petty, 1979). College students listened to a tape-recorded message consisting of eight quite reasonable arguments either once, three consecutive times, or five consecutive times. The same pattern occurred in both experiments, as shown in Figure 5.1. As predicted, agreement with the message was higher after three presentations than after only one presentation. This increased influence effect with increased exposures to the message arguments clearly supports the evaluative consistency principle. The favorable reaction to the high quality of the message arguments snowballed with increasing exposure. This is evident from the message-relevant thoughts subjects listed following their final exposure to the message. Subjects who heard three presentations had the greatest number of favorable cognitive responses.

But what happened when subjects were exposed to the same message five times? As you can also see in Figure 5.1, there was a curvilinear effect of first increased persuasion as presentations went up from

Repetition Increases Persuasion...Up to a Point

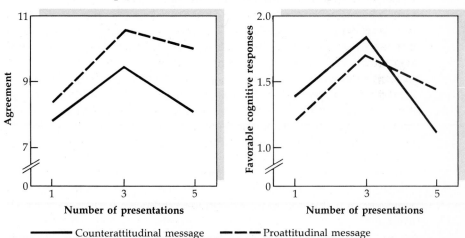

Counterattitudinal message   Proattitudinal message

FIGURE 5.1
Persuasion was greater when a strong message was presented three times compared with once, whether or not subjects initially agreed with (pro-attitudinal) or opposed (counterattitudinal) the message proposal. Persuasion decreased, however, when presentations reached five. Cognitive responses show a similar trend. A second experiment replicated these results.
(From Cacioppo and Petty, 1979. Copyright 1979 by the American Psychological Association. Adapted by permission.)

one to three and then decreased persuasion when they were repeated beyond that.

Why should agreement go down as messages are repeated beyond a certain number? Well, too much of a good thing can be "too much," or at least enough to reappraise it into becoming a bad thing. No doubt you have heard of *overexposure*. People's reactions to messages turn sour if the message is presented too often. There are several reasons for this. One is the possibility of *thought satiation* (Leippe, 1983). Continued analysis of the message may lead to a point at which one can come up with no more evaluatively consistent thoughts, and thinking finally turns to thoughts that are less message-favorable. Between three and five exposures, the subjects in the experiments actually showed an increase in unfavorable cognitive responses and a decrease in positive ones. More than likely, however, this turn to more unfavorable thoughts is assisted by a sense of *tedium:* people simply get sick of the message. Finally, a part of the "turn off" may be what is known as *psychological reactance* (Brehm, 1972). This occurs when people sense that their freedom of choice is being threatened by an external agent. The natural inclination is to reassert that freedom by doing exactly the opposite of what the external agent is thought to want. "Reverse psychology" is what Tom Sawyer would call it. Excessive repeated exposure to the same message may create a sense of having the message "forced down your throat." And your gut response is: "Oh yeah? I'll show you."

How many repetitions are too many? It depends on the message. For example, more complex messages can typically benefit from more exposures. There is more to learn from them and to respond to—in an evaluatively consistent fashion. The turn from positive to negative responses can also be staved off by presenting a slightly different message, a variation on the same theme (McCullough and Ostrom, 1974). Providing some novelty in the repeated presentations keeps things interesting and suggests a need for the repetition—to get across more information. In addition, variations in the message we receive may encourage us to make new associations with our knowledge, beliefs, and remembered experiences. (Think about your college courses where you would have welcomed more repetition and those where once more was too much.)

Let's sum up what we have discussed so far. (You mean you're going to repeat the complex message being transmitted so that we can comprehend and accept it more favorably? Yes, if that's the way you want to put it.) Short of the overexposure effect, the general rule is that the more cognitive responses we make to a simple or complex message, (1) the more extreme our attitude toward the message object becomes, and (2) the greater the number of associative links the new attitude has with our beliefs, knowledge, and related attitudes. Making a point of

Repetition (and other factors!) can cause psychological reactance.
(Rose is Rose, 1988, reprinted by permission of United Features Syndicate, Inc.)

view extreme and strongly embedded (in one's mind) is the hallmark of successful persuasion. (As the old song line goes, "Time after time, you'll hear me say that I'm, so lucky to be loving you..." This holds for "product love" as well as for "person love.") Embedding strong attitudes also lays a solid foundation for the persistence of persuasion through time, which we will now focus on directly.

RETENTION: PERSUASION OVER TIME

What is the direct evidence that messages which produce strong and extreme attitudes have a more lasting impact? To produce such evidence, social psychologists have conducted studies in which people are first exposed to a persuasive message and then have their attitudes measured in the future—days, weeks, or even months after being presented with the message. These studies are well worth our attention. They confirm the importance of creating strong and extreme attitudes. And they also reveal important additional factors that affect retention—factors that agents of persuasion may well be able to control. Keep in mind that, usually, persuasion agents care less about your attitude immediately after exposure to their message than about your attitude down the line at some later time—when you are on the shopping line, casting a vote, supporting a cause, or perhaps deciding on a career.

Hit It Again, Harder, Again and Again

How? Harder! We have already noted that repetition of a compelling message fosters strong and extreme attitudes. If such attitudes are more durable, repetition of a message should serve to prolong its impact on people. In fact, this has been demonstrated in several experiments (Johnson and Watkins, 1971; Ronis et al., 1977; Wilson and Miller, 1968). In one of these, subjects listened either once or five times to a communication that argued against the use of chest x-rays for the detection of tuberculosis (Johnson and Watkins, 1971). The source of the message was said to be either a medical expert on tuberculosis or a medical quack. The attitude responses in the various conditions of this experiment are presented in Figure 5.2.

Not surprisingly, the quack was pretty unconvincing, whereas the expert won strong acceptance of the message. Interestingly, acceptance of the expert's message was not immediately influenced by repetition. Rather, the impact of repetition became evident 4 weeks later, when subjects were questioned a second time about the issue as part of a larger, seemingly different survey. As you can see in Figure 5.2, among

Repeated Messages Have More Lasting Impact

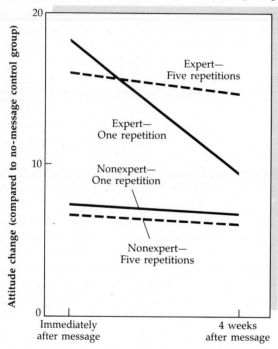

FIGURE 5.2
Subjects heard a message about chest x-rays either one or five times in succession. The source was either a medical expert or a nonexpert. The message had greater persuasive impact when attributed to an expert, but this greater impact persisted over time only when the message had been repeated.
(Data from Johnson and Watkins, 1971.)

those who listened to five presentations attributed to an expert, agreement was just as great after 4 weeks as it had been immediately following the message. In contrast, those who heard one presentation by the expert showed decreased agreement after 4 weeks. To hold on to the initial attitude change required repetition of the message.

Is the absence of a repetition effect on the *immediate* posttest inconsistent with the evaluative consistency principle? Not necessarily so. One exposure to the expert's message in the Johnson and Watkins study seems to have created close to maximal agreement, reaching a "ceiling effect" with little room for a repetition effect to add anything further. Also, some reactance may have been created by the staccato-like quintuple presentation, since each presentation was separated by only a 20-second pause.

The persistence of persuasion brought about by repetition makes sense given that continued thinking about the plausible arguments of a message leads to an attitude that is "well connected" to consistent beliefs and knowledge in memory—and hence readily available and easily retrieved from memory. Practice makes persuasion more perfect. Note, however, that this advantage of repetition requires that the audience engage in some systematic message analysis. Using only quick-and-dirty reliance on heuristic cues is a mindless way of bypassing the thinking necessary for polarization and embedding of attitudinal responses. At best, a bit of a mere exposure effect might occur if the audience takes the heuristic route only. In the experiment just described, subjects were apparently doing some systematic analysis of message presentations beyond the first one, because those who heard the message five times had significantly better recall of message content.

Systematic Analysis: Active Minds Make Durable Attitudes

Whether encouraged by repetition or by some other means, attitude changes that result from active and systematic mental processing are the most durable, persisting changes. We saw in Chapter 3 that some of the most profound and lasting changes in attitudes and behavior can sometimes be achieved through *self-persuasion.* Under the right conditions, smokers can literally talk themselves into quitting. Children can convince themselves that violent TV shows are woefully unrealistic. When self-persuasion works, it does so because the individual struck some internal chords, generating ideas and arguments that are convincing because they originated in the individual's own system of values, beliefs, and knowledge. For that very same reason, self-generated arguments, whether they result from actively thinking about a message or in response to an instruction to act out a role, are also memorable.

By employing a variant of role-playing, one researcher demonstrated that people can be more lastingly convinced by their own ideas than by those of others (Watts, 1967). In the experiment, the control group of subjects passively read a plausible 600-word message arguing a policy position (e.g., "Courts should deal more leniently with juvenile delinquents"). The active, experimental group wrote a "strong convincing argument" for the same policy. In a sense, they played out a role as policy advocate. No immediate differences were found between the attitude change of the reading versus the writing groups. They produced equivalent increases in agreement with the advocated policy. Six weeks later, however, the writers' self-induced agreement had not slipped a bit, in contrast to the readers, most of whom reverted all or part of the way to the attitude they held before reading the message. Moreover, the writers were much more likely than the readers to recall the policy issue and the side taken—"their side."

Creating a message actively engages the mind, and the products of that engagement—the cognitive responses—are memorable. Theoretically, the same effect can be produced by reading a message, but only if the audience does extensive systematic message analysis that results in many cognitive responses. For instance, research has shown that when the amount of systematic mental processing is increased by alerting recipients to the high *personal relevance* of the message, the change in attitude produced by the message is more likely to persist (Chaiken, 1980). It is nearly always true that we remember better our own responses to a message than the literal information that is contained in the message (Greenwald, 1968). Incidentally, this fact is a strong argument for doing *active studying*—self-quizzing, writing summaries and integrations—instead of simply passive reading and listening. In a sense, this type of active involvement enables you "to own" the information, rather than merely borrow it temporarily.

Added to all those self-persuasion and induced compliance studies we reviewed in Chapter 3, does the study on creating versus merely reading a message imply that getting people to play their own devil's advocate will be a more successful long-term persuasion strategy than just "sending them a message"? Not at all. A big advantage of a structured persuasive message is that the sender can control its content. In contrast, even if people can be cajoled into generating a message that goes counter to their current attitudes, they may do an unconvincing job because of lack of knowledge or a sense of coercion (remember the role of free choice in dissonance). The trick with designing the ideal persuasive message is that it has to be of such quality that the recipients' "own cognitive responses" to it are numerous as well as favorable.

Positive and plentiful cognitive responses help persuasion survive events that may occur in the trenches of the influence battlefield—after the message has made it to its source. Let us now consider some of these after-the-message events, including discrediting of the communicator and exposure to opposing arguments.

Attitudes: Autonomous Dependents

Imagine this string of events: In the area where Mary lives, the local cable television company is waging a contract dispute with a certain sports network whose broadcasts include nearly all of the games of the local major league basketball and hockey teams. The cable company wants the sports network to be a "pay service," available only to subscribers who pay extra for it, while the sports network insists it should be part of "basic service," available to all subscribers. The issue is complex, with pros and cons on both sides. But most sports fans, like Mary, see the cable company as the bad guy because it refuses to air the sports network's programs at all during contract negotiations. Like tens of thousands of sports fans, Mary is unable to see her favorite teams. Mary flips on the TV one day and catches a businesslike gentleman explaining why the sports network should be a pay service. The arguments—new to Mary—make sense, and she is impressed. But the phone rings, and she leaves the tube to answer it. When she returns, she finds out who the speaker was: the hated president of the hated cable company. Mary ruminates, "So it was that guy, huh? I thought his points made sense, but he obviously is not to be trusted. I'll have to think more about his points. In the meantime, I'm not buying his line." And there she leaves it.

Weeks pass, and one day Mary finds herself discussing the cable TV dispute with a friend. As the friend (a big basketball fan) makes a case for the sports network's position, Mary interrupts and begins giving the *same arguments* that the detested cable company president had given on TV. She doesn't like the cable company, she says, but she believes that the sports network should be a pay service. Interestingly, Mary doesn't realize that she is giving opinions she has heard only from a disliked source. She is now an advocate for the enemy!

The sleeper effect. An unlikely scenario? Not really. In fact, a delayed persuasion effect just like Mary's has been demonstrated in several experiments. The *sleeper effect,* as it is called, occurs when a message is not immediately persuasive, since no attitude change occurs right after the message; however, it is persuasive after an interval of time—when recipients have had a chance to "sleep on it," so to speak. The effect was discovered by Carl Hovland and his colleagues over 40 years ago (Hovland et al., 1949; Hovland and Weiss, 1951). But the conditions necessary for the sleeper effect to occur were not isolated until several decades later.

In two representative studies, college students read a 1,000-word message that argued against the 4-day workweek, spelling out the many problems it creates and citing evidence that it reduces employee satisfaction (Gruder et al., 1978; Pratkanis et al., 1988). Actually, they read the message twice, complying with the experimenter's instructions to read each paragraph first for content and then again for style. Three different experimental conditions were created. In the first "clean" condition, this message was all that the subjects received before answering various questions about the message and their own attitude. In a second, "cues-before-message" condition, the message was preceded by two "discounting cues" meant to arouse a negative reaction—to get subjects to discount or disregard the message. One cue was a note from the editor of the magazine in which the message had supposedly appeared. It indicated that new evidence, which would be reported in the next issue, strongly suggested that the conclusion of the message was false, that the 4-day workweek produces no problems and is a boon to employee satisfaction. The other discounting cue consisted of obnoxious statements early in the message that were sure to arouse psychological reactance (e.g., "Any intelligent person has no choice but to believe"). In a third "cues-after-message" condition, these two discounting cues followed the message.

Figure 5.3 shows agreement with the message in each condition immediately after it was read, and again 6 weeks later—when agreement was assessed in a telephone interview. You can see that, in the absence of the two discounting cues, the "straight-clean" message was initially highly persuasive. A great deal of this persuasive impact, however, was lost after 6 weeks. But what was the effect of the cues, which were meant to produce the same impression of low credibility and manipulativeness that Mary had of the cable company president? Not surprisingly, the cues suppressed initial persuasion. But check out the situation after 6 weeks. In the cues-after-message condition, but not in the cues-before-message condition, agreement with the message actually *increased* over time. Like Mary, the "bad cues after" subjects were advocating a position they had rejected at the time they were first exposed to the message.

How can we explain the sleeper effect? The first thing we need to know is that attitudes can exist independently of memory for the information and circumstances that created them. In fact, cognitive scientists have argued that attitudes and knowledge (about events, people, and issues) are stored separately in our memory system (Anderson and Hubert, 1963; Tulving, 1983). Given this possible independence in memory of attitudes and message information, let's consider the experience of those subjects who read the discounting cues *after* the message. They learned much from reading the message twice and thus had primarily positive cognitive responses. Then along came discounting cues to mistrust the message. These cues elicited strong negative cog-

The Sleeper Effect

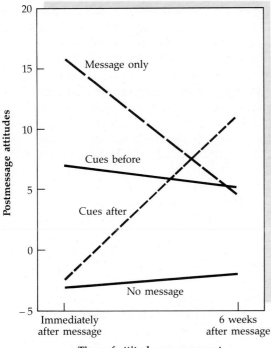

FIGURE 5.3
A message opposing the 4-day workweek was persuasive when presented alone, but not when preceded or followed by "discounting cues" suggesting that it should be rejected. When the cues followed the message, there was a delayed persuasion effect—a sleeper effect, in which attitude change increased over time.
(From Pratkanis, Greenwald, Leippe, and Baumgardner, 1988. Copyright 1988 by the American Psychological Association. Reprinted by permission.)

nitive responses, which carry the most weight in formulating an attitude. Sure enough, subjects did not change their attitude; they stuck to their premessage attitude—in the present case a neutral-to-somewhat-favorable stance on the 4-day workweek. But this doesn't mean that they forgot those information-based, message-favorable responses they had generated while reading the message. Down the road, if these are better remembered than the attitude, they will be called to mind at the next opportunity to consider the issue. At that point, the message will have its delayed, or sleeper, effect.

Separate storage of attitude and cognitive responses to information presented in a communication is the first prong of this explanation, dubbed the *differential decay* hypothesis (Pratkanis et al., 1988). A second prong is necessary to account for why the attitude is forgotten (decays) more rapidly. That one's easy: the content (and favorable responses to it) was better learned. Remember, subjects read the message twice and were explicitly asked to evaluate its content. This fact suggests an important condition for the sleeper effect: the message must be thoughtfully analyzed—systematically processed—so that it (1) is more memorable than the discounting cues and (2) would have been persuasive if it were not for those cues.

A final condition is required for a sleeper effect to work. Notice that no sleeper effect occurred when the cues came before the message. Your new knowledge of how peripheral cues can influence systematic message processing should tell you why. The distrust and indignation created by the cues should have influenced how subjects evaluate the message *as they read it*, encouraging more counterarguments and other unfavorable cognitive responses to it. As a result, both attitudes and cognitive responses should have agreed in opposing the message's position, making irrelevant the possibility that they would be stored separately in memory. The recall of either would yield the same negative response. For a sleeper effect to occur, the discounting cue ordinarily must follow the message.

Can you think of a practical explanation of the sleeper effect? If you have reason to believe that the audience will have a negative attitude to the company or group you represent, withhold that information until after you get your message across. ("...And by the way, I'm from Hated Company, but don't hold that against your new attitude.")

Baseless attitudes. The sleeper effect represents a case where cognitions prevail in memory over emotionally charged attitudes. But often just the reverse is true. Attitudes are retained even though the circumstances, episodes, and information that helped create them have been forgotten. How often have you heard someone say, "I don't know why, but I just can't stand X."

This persistence of attitudes independent of supportive information will concern us in the next chapter, where we will discuss resistance to change in important attitudes. The expression of attitudes without retrieving relevant cognitions is connected to the theme of shortcut thinking evident in the use of judgmental heuristics. As the evaluative summary of a system of feelings, knowledge, and beliefs, an attitude represents an efficient guide to decisions and actions. You can rely on the summary without having to delve into the details. You can use your attitude as an internal heuristic cue for go–no go actions.

Primacy and Recency: Me First or Me Second?

You may have noticed that, in the sleeper effect study, the best predictor of persuasion 6 weeks later was whatever "message" the subjects encountered first. For subjects who got the cue before the message, attitudes 6 weeks later were opposed to the message—the "bad" cue prevailed. For those who got the cue after the message, delayed attitudes favored the message—the message prevailed. This pattern of *primacy*, a greater influence of initially presented information relative to subsequent information, concurs with studies of primacy in many other contexts. Research on impression formation has shown, for example, that the first information people receive about another person weighs more heavily than later information in the impression they form about that person (Anderson and Hubert, 1963; Jones et al., 1968). In one classic study, a person who first appeared extroverted but later behaved in a somewhat withdrawn way was rated by nearly all observers as basically extroverted. When exactly the same behaviors were presented in reverse order for other observers, most rated the person as introverted (Luchins, 1957).

The *primacy effect*, as it is called, is rooted in perceptual and cognitive processes similar to those that produce thought polarization and biased interpretation. Initial impressions form a mental *schema*, a biasing filter, through which subsequent information is selectively noticed and interpreted. Surely, this rings a bell. Few people have escaped receiving advice about the "power of first impressions."

Because of primacy effects, is it better to present your side first in a debate or in a courtroom battle? Research suggests that, if it occurs at all, a primacy effect is mostly likely when there is a time delay between receipt of the opposing messages and when attitudes are measured (Miller and Campbell, 1959). Consider a situation in which the pro side of an issue is given first, followed immediately by the con side. Both sides have made their points. Half of the initially undecided audience is polled on the issue immediately after the second (con) message, whereas the other half is polled one week later. Those polled a week later are apt to slightly favor the first (pro) message: a primacy effect. The immediately polled members of the audience, however, either will show no tendency to be influenced by the order in which they heard the arguments or will tend to favor the second, more recent (con) message, thereby demonstrating a *recency effect* (Wilson and Miller, 1968).

It seems that when attitudes are polled immediately after the second message, the power of the first message to color impressions of the second one is offset by the fact that the second message is more fresh in audience members' minds: it is still in their "working memory." But with delayed measurement, this advantage disappears. Primacy reemerges if a strong schema was established by the first message. This is another example of how cognitions gravitate toward consistency with our schema for an attitude object. We will delve more deeply into primacy and recency effects in Chapter 8, when we discuss the courtroom trial—a persuasion setting in which order effects can be particularly significant.

Now, however, it is time to step up the pace and take the final big step. Imagine that your persuasive message has managed to evoke a strong and extreme, hence durable, attitude response from the audience. Moreover, with the advantage of primacy, the audience can resist counterinfluence. You have achieved the *retention step:* your message has had a lasting influence on audience attitudes. But will the audience *act* as you wish? We now turn to this final *action step*—from attitude change to behavioral action—on the persuasion path.

TRANSLATING ATTITUDES INTO BEHAVIOR: ULTIMATE PERSUASION

In some cases, retention of attitude change is the final goal of a persuader, or even for the target of persuasion who may have sought the input. The psychotherapist and her client, for instance, may feel wonderfully content that the client has a more positive attitude about himself after therapy. The professor may be satisfied that his students have "seen the light." Still, in many other cases, persuaders hope that communication-induced attitudes will translate from internal changes in cognition and affect into some desired behavior. Let us examine the factors relevant to the attitude-behavior link: if, when, and how much it will occur.

The Power of the Situation To Override Attitudes

Although we generally value consistency, we do not always act in ways consistent with our attitudes and beliefs. Indeed, many of the influence processes we have examined depend on the power of situational factors to override personal factors—what is previously believed or valued.

Recall that in Asch's group conformity study, many subjects publicly stated that they judged as equal two lines of very different lengths, in response to the social pressure of the false consensus of their group. But this agreement decreased when they gave the same estimates out of earshot of the group, indicating that their public conformity differed from their private beliefs.

A similar conflict between internal states and overt actions was apparent in Milgram's obedient subjects. They agreed to participate in this research with the understanding that they would be helping the other subject, the "learner," improve his memory. But soon they were hurting, not helping, and they began to dissent. Many showed great distress about delivering the seemingly painful jolts of punishment. However, they dissented verbally, but they did not disobey. Their shocking behavior was more under the control of the powerful situational forces than it was controlled by motivation to hurt the learner, other antisocial attitudes, or the positive values that were relevant at the start of the study.

Significant others. It is the people in a social situation, as we have seen throughout this book, who are typically the most potent influences in that social context. Even strangers can cause us to behave in ways we would not if we merely paid attention to our own attitudes. Allen Funt's *Candid Camera* (the forerunner of *Totally Hidden Video*) exploited this powerful influence principle in many scenarios, the most famous of which revealed how a group of strangers in an elevator could get an unsuspecting rider to face the rear—or any direction—if they all did.

If strangers can have this effect in passing situations, think about the influence of more significant people in our everyday lives. Because his young daughter—a ballerina in the making—loves it so, the father who unequivocally dislikes ballet may buy expensive tickets to ballet performances and sit through them with his wife and daughter, dutifully wearing his best smile and look of interest. A young woman with misgivings about legalized abortion may nevertheless refuse to accept pro-life literature when offered it in the presence of her pro-choice friends. And whether a high school student takes drugs most often depends on whether he or she has friends who do. (In many cases, "a friend in weed is hardly a friend in deed.")

The role of significant others in the attitude-behavior relationship is emphasized in the *theory of reasoned action* (Ajzen and Fishbein, 1980). This theory, graphically presented in Figure 5.4, specifies that a major influence on behavior, naturally enough, is a person's *intentions*. More central to our immediate interest, however, are the two determinants of intentions: (1) attitudes toward the relevant behavior, which are themselves based on beliefs regarding the behavior and its likely outcomes; and (2) subjective norms, which are beliefs about whether significant others approve or disapprove of the behavior. The upshot is that, on any given occasion, attitudes may or may not guide behavior, depending on whether the subjective norm favors or does not favor the behavior and whether it is the norm or the attitude that is more important to the individual. From this point of view, a persuasive message is most likely to cause attitude *and* behavior change if it can shape both beliefs about its topic and beliefs about what important individuals and social groups think about the topic and how they behave toward it.

Timely inconsistencies. Social pressures, subtle or strong, are not the only characteristics of a situation that can encourage behaviors that are inconsistent with attitudes. Inconsistent behaviors can also result from being preoccupied, from trying to do too many things at once, or simply from being in a rush toward some goal other than that involved in doing the attitude-consistent behavior.

As a staunch environmentalist who has a strong positive attitude toward recycling, one of your authors was elated recently when the town

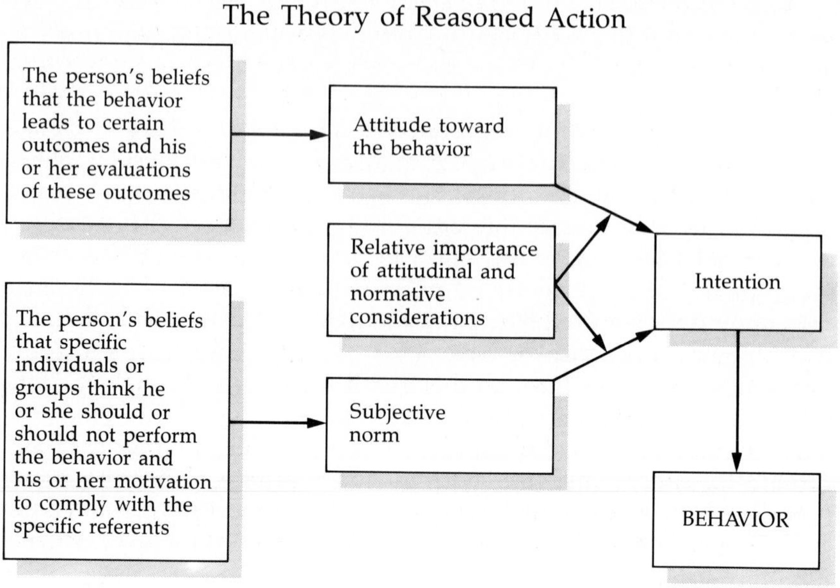

The Theory of Reasoned Action

FIGURE 5.4
A theory of the cognitive chain to behavior. The arrows indicate the direction of influence.
(From Ajzen and Fishbein, © 1980. Adapted by permission of Prentice Hall, Inc., Englewood Cliffs, New Jersey.)

he lives in embarked on an ambitious recycling plan. Each town household received a plastic container in which to place all the newspaper, metal cans, and glass bottles to be disposed of each week. Residents would simply separate these materials from their other garbage and place the container out for pickup once a week. What an excellent idea! The author and his family immediately began engaging in this environmentally conscious behavior. It felt good to be a conscientious citizen.

However, sorting and storing the recyclable items can get tiresome, and the recycling process involves many little hassles and some expenditure of time and effort. The author's occasional failure to recycle goes something like this: He has been in charge of household chores all evening and just when it looks as though he's almost done and can start preparing his notes for a new lecture for tomorrow morning's class, he remembers that he has to pick up and bag various trash, bottles, cans, plastic, newspapers, cardboard, etc. "I'm bushed. The heck with it; it's all going in the same bag this time." And the next time it becomes easier to justify why he isn't doing the right thing, why his good intentions do not translate into "the right stuff" all the time.

Your author's attitude-behavior inconsistency is analogous to, but far less dramatic than, an inconsistency induced by the time pressure created by researchers in a remarkable study on bystander intervention (Darley and Batson, 1973). Subjects were instructed by the experimenter to walk to another building where they were to record a speech concerning material they had thought about in the first phase of the study. Their expectations about how much time they had to cross the campus to get to the recording studio were systematically manipulated by the experimenter's instructions to them. For a randomly selected third of the subjects, he told them that they had plenty of time to get there, while a second group were led to believe that they should hurry over and would be just on time. The final third of the subjects were told that they were already late and had to rush over. While walking from one building to the next, each subject passed a shabbily dressed man sitting in a doorway groaning and coughing. This man—clearly in need of assistance—was actually an accomplice of the researchers. The behavior of interest was whether the subject would stop to offer help. Among those subjects who were not in a hurry, 63 percent stopped to help. In contrast, only 10 percent of those who were "late" helped, with the "on time" people intermediate in their bystander intervention (45 percent helped).

When good Samaritans aren't. Two other facts about this result are needed before you can fully appreciate why we labeled this study "dramatic." First, the subjects were students at the Princeton Theological Seminary, people you would expect to be positively predisposed to helping others—not supposedly calloused big city dwellers. Second, the seminarians were on their way to speak about the parable of the Good Samaritan, in which an ordinary traveler came to the aid of a man injured by the roadside, while a busy priest and a Levite walked right on by. Being reminded of this parable in the first phase of the study was analogous to receiving a message further strengthening a positive attitude toward assisting those in need. And so the failure of almost all the rushed subjects to help the man was a behavior clearly at odds with their attitudes, indeed the basic values that these subjects brought into the experimental setting. Being rushed and preoccupied can do that sort of thing—even to good people.

In defense of the seminarians, though, we should note that they did behave consistently in one sense: their rapid transit time would have been helpful to the experimenter, which was their primary goal in this situation. Conflict between two helping behaviors, rather than personal callousness, may have been behind their unseminarianlike behavior toward the sick man (Batson et al., 1978). And so it is how one defines the situation and the priority of goals and ways of meeting them that plays a big role in whether behavior follows from or is inconsistent with our attitudes, personality, or values.

Much of what makes social psychology interesting rests on the power of situations and people to interfere with what we normally expect will be the behavioral expression of someone's attitudes—and sometimes our own. Time pressures and significant others in a given setting are two components of situations that may override the activation of attitudes. Situations and the people in them can overwhelm us as well when they are novel or strange—different from what we are familiar with. Then neither attitudes nor well-learned habits and cognitive strategies can be readily called forth. Instead there is ambiguity and confusion about how to act appropriately. In our concern to do the right thing when we do not fully understand what is right in the situation, we suspend our usual reaction patterns and allow our behavior to be guided by salient situational cues. We "follow the leader"; we obey the signs, the rules, and what seems to be the consensus response.

When Attitudes Yield Actions: The Conditions of Consistency

If internal states like attitudes were the only determinants of behavior, understanding influence would be much simpler, and probably boring. On the other hand, unless attitudes predict behavior sometimes, we might as well do away with the attitude concept. It would be useless without that behaviorally pragmatic relevance. Happily, attitudes often do predict behavior if they have certain characteristics. Specifically, attitude-behavior consistency is the rule when (1) the attitude is strong and clear, (2) the attitude is relevant to the behavior called for by the situation at hand, (3) the attitude and the behavior have strong links to the same additional component of the attitude system (either cognitions or affective responses), and (4) the attitude is important to the individual. Closer examination of these characteristics tells us something about how and when a persuasive communication will effectively change attitudes and behavior.

Strong and clear attitudes. Attitude change produced by systematic message analysis tends to be more durable and persistent than attitude change that occurs via heuristic decision rules. More cognitive responses result from systematic processing, making the resulting attitude more "well thought out" and "well connected" to beliefs, values, and knowledge. In a situation requiring behavior toward the attitude object, such an attitude should come to mind readily (since there are many associative connections) and should make clear what actions it suggests (since it is well thought out). As long as opposing situational forces are not too strong, attitude-consistent behavior should result.

Evidence supporting this reasoning comes from a study that varied the personal relevance of the message in order to get some subjects to more systematically analyze the message than others (Leippe and Elkin, 1987). Subjects read a message advocating a campus policy (either a parking fee or a mandatory senior exam) and were informed that the policy might take effect next year (high personal relevance) or not for 6 years (low personal relevance). After the message, subjects first expressed their attitude toward the policy, and then later when they thought the experiment was over, they were given an opportunity to act on their feelings by volunteering to write to the university committee deciding on the policy. As in other studies that have manipulated relevance in this way, high-relevance subjects engaged in more systematic thinking about the message than low-relevance subjects.

The majority of the high-relevance subjects, fully 74 percent, acted in accord with their attitude by first volunteering to write to the administrators and then actually writing a viewpoint that concurred with the attitude they had expressed just after the message. In contrast, only 21 percent of the subjects for whom the issue had low relevance acted on their attitude.

Other research also indicates that attitudes rooted in systematic thought more readily predict behavior than superficial attitudes. One study of Wisconsin college students measured both their attitudes toward conservation and their knowledge about it (Kallgren and Wood, 1986). Weeks later, the study's authors observed the following behaviors: (1) whether subjects signed a pro-conservation petition and (2) how much they participated in a new recycling project. The most knowledgeable students behaved significantly more in accord with their earlier stated attitudes than the least knowledgeable students.

Still other studies demonstrate that attitudes formed through *direct experience* with the attitude object or issue are more predictive of behavior than those formed more indirectly (Fazio and Zanna, 1981). One example of this research introduced subjects to five types of intellectual puzzles in one of two ways. They either *directly experienced* the puzzles by being allowed to work them out or *indirectly experienced* the puzzles by watching the experimenter describe them and their solutions. The direct and indirect experiencers then indicated their attitude toward each puzzle type by rating how interesting they thought it was. After that, they were given a 15-minute "free play" period during which they could work on the puzzle types of their choice. The number of times a subject attempted each type of puzzle was observed; this provided a clear-cut measure of behavior toward the attitude object (puzzle type). Among subjects who formed their attitudes through direct experience, attitudes predicted behavior. Generally, direct-experience subjects worked the most on puzzles they had reported liking the most, and least on those they reported liking the least. In contrast, the correspon-dence between attitudes and behavior was much less among subjects who formed their attitudes through indirect experience.

The impact of direct experience is not limited to playing with puz-zles. Attitudes toward smoking better predict intentions to start smok-ing among adolescents who have spent more time around smokers (Sherman et al., 1982). This relationship should extend to behavior, since intentions often guide behavior (see Figure 5.4). Similarly, atti-tudes toward breast feeding better predict whether breast or bottle feed-ing is chosen among mothers who have had personal experience with breast feeding (Manstead et al., 1983).

Why does experiencing the attitude object for oneself make such a difference? Mainly, it seems that attitudes based on direct experience are stronger and clearer than those based on indirect experience. We learn more about the attitude object from directly experiencing it, and most important, much of what we learn has to do with how we should behave and what the consequences will be (Fazio and Zanna, 1981). Personal experience is also likely to include more emotional involve-ment than passive exposure to just the informational features of the sit-uation. An attitude that is tied to this kind of knowledge will be an un-ambiguous guide to behavior.

What do these findings imply for persuasive messages? First, as largely indirect sources of information, messages may be handicapped in their ability to cause attitude changes that translate into behavior. (Notice the possible connection here to the relative inferiority of mes-sages when compared to self-persuasion processes involving role-playing or dissonant essay writing. Though not the real thing, role-playing is closer to direct experience than passive listening.) Second, the reason for the handicap suggests the way to overcome it. Messages should be constructed in ways that get the audience to think about an issue or object in concrete, vivid images that have definite implications for behavior.

That is why TV commercials often use imagery designed to "put you there." You know the behavioral imagery: here is what you would be doing on a Club Med vacation; can you imagine it? Feel the "fine Corinthian leather" as you seat yourself behind the wheel of this fine automobile. Experience the smooth ride (as the camera gives the driv-er's visual perspective). Similarly, a public service message about drunk driving may take you step by step through the behaviors of giving your car keys to the bartender, asking him to call a cab, then being dropped off by the cab at home, safe and sound. You may learn that this respon-sible behavior is not so difficult and embarrassing as it may seem.

When creative ad people can tap it, the capacity of the video me-dium to get the audience to vicariously experience the product of interest is a tremendous advantage that this medium gives the message. The bottom line is that, however obtained, a strong and clear attitude is *spontaneously activated* when the individual encounters the object (Fazio, 1990). This is crucial for obtaining attitude-behavior consistency. Before an attitude can guide behavior, it must be drawn from memory and give a clear cue about how to behave. If a strong and clear attitude is not activated by the object, the door is open for situational factors to have greater impact on behavior.

Relevant attitudes. Attitude objects often present themselves in complex situations. As a result, activation of an attitude may be accompanied by the activation of attitudes toward other objects or issues in the same situation. In other words, complicated situations may arouse complicated considerations which impede the simple, uncluttered translation of a given attitude into specific behavior. For example, a home owner who has positive attitudes toward quality public education and toward big spending of property tax dollars to finance it may still vote against a proposed school budget that includes a hefty increase in property taxes. Is this a glaring instance of attitude-behavior inconsistency? In a sense, yes. On the other hand, other attitudes and beliefs may be involved. The home owner's vote may be based on a negative attitude toward the administration and school board that run the local school district, a belief that the school tax increase mainly benefits a school administration that is already too big and overpaid, or the belief that the big tax increase will be too much of a personal economic burden. Thus, a number of conflicting attitudes and beliefs may be relevant to the behavior in question. The attitude with most influence on behavior is ordinarily the one that is either most important or most salient (most fully activated) in the situation calling for action.

Also, the attitude that is most *specifically* relevant to the behavior in question has a greater influence on behavior (Ajzen and Fishbein, 1980). Generalized attitudes ("I am in favor of quality public education supported by local tax dollars") tend to predict how people behave on the average over many occasions. Specific attitudes ("I am opposed to the Oakland Public School proposed budget") predict specific behaviors—in this case, perhaps voting on that particular budget or at least talking against it at a local school board meeting. Thus, when trying to talk people into forming a specific attitude and acting on it, the persuasive communicator's arguments need to address directly the merits of the specific issue or object and the specific recommended behavior toward it.

Feelings-based attitudes and cognition-based attitudes. As we saw in the concept of an attitude system presented in Chapter 1, attitudes have both an affective or "feelings" basis and a cognitive basis involving beliefs and knowledge. Some attitudes, as you might expect, have a particularly potent affective component. A fan's allegiance to a local sports team, for example, may be mainly an emotional attachment with little cognitive "justification." Other attitudes are based largely on "cold" cognitions and beliefs. You might like a class not because it "turns you on" but because you believe it provides basic knowledge and experience that lead to important personal goals.

It is possible that one component (feelings or cognitions) is the dominant basis for a particular attitude (Millar and Tesser, 1986). This helps explain a certain curiosity in the advertising world. Through appealing and memorable commercials, a product can become better liked by the public yet not show big gains in sales. A good example is Alka-Seltzer. In the early 1970s, several attractive and entertaining commercials for the fizzy effervescent hit the airwaves. These included ads with memorable lines like "I can't believe I ate the whole thing" after a scene where some poor soul had eaten a whole pizza or a full box of chocolates. And there was also "Plop, plop, fizz, fizz, oh what a relief it is." These refrains actually became popular expressions for a time. The public liked the ads, and they reported positive impressions of the product. Yet sales of Alka-Seltzer actually declined throughout the 1970s (Kahn, 1987). Why?

In part, this is a classic case in which the attitude and the behavior (buying) are mainly connected to different components of the attitude system relevant to the product. Consumers had a positive image of Alka-Seltzer, which consisted largely of good feelings that were themselves a product of pleasant advertising and the ultrafamiliar brand name. Their buying habits, however, were based on more cognitive considerations of which bromide works the best for their occasional upset stomachs. Newer products, sounding "newly formulated" and pitching their ads toward more modern causes of stomach upset (daily stress as opposed to overindulgence), were increasingly being seen as the rational choice of medicine. The attitude that guided buying behavior, then, was the one based on the factor most pertinent to the purchasing decision: what works best for today's health problems. It may also have been true that the scenario of overeating made people feel guilty or embarrassed by their own past excessive indulgences. If so, then laughing at those poor souls in the ads struck a negative personal chord, which might associate Alka Seltzer with bad feelings. In recent years, Alka-Seltzer's ad people have caught on. Their latest commercials emphasize the stress of current lifestyles and the only-occasional eating binge.

The larger moral for message makers is that a message should deal with, and encourage, cognitive responses relevant to the attitudinal component that appears most relevant to the behavior. If the behavior is to be based on beliefs and available information, provide the rational reasons or get the audience to generate them. If feelings are important, focus on feelings.

Attitudes about matters that people care about. It seems apparent that messages which are personally important or relevant are more likely to be systematically thought about than less important messages. The attitude that results is likely to be stronger and more likely to translate into consistent behavior. Interestingly, personal importance may enhance attitude-behavior consistency even if it is not associated with a stronger or more knowledgeable attitude. One study examined how well Michigan State University students' attitudes toward a 1978 proposal to raise the legal drinking age in Michigan to 21 predicted their willingness to telephone people and urge them to vote against this proposal (Sivacek and Crano, 1982). Not surprisingly, most of the sampled students (85 percent) opposed the proposal. But willingness to act on their negative attitudes depended strongly on whether or not the students would be personally inconvenienced by the proposed law. Of the opposed students who would be 21 years old anyway by the time the law took effect, only a measly 12 percent volunteered to make phone calls. By contrast, the volunteer rate was 47 percent among opposed students who would not yet be 19 years old by the time the law took effect and would thus "suffer" for 2 years or more if it passed.

A more dramatic example of the fact that people will act in accord with important and deep personal convictions was displayed in China during the pro-democracy demonstrations of 1989 that we discussed briefly in Chapter 4. University students, committed to democratic reform, occupied Tiananmen Square in Beijing for weeks in protest of the repressive Communist regime. They even erected a model of the Statue of Liberty as a symbol of the freedoms they sought for the people of China, parading it in front of crowds, TV cameras, political leaders, and soldiers in riot gear. The students persisted in this action, refusing to leave even when threatened with guns and tanks. Only when those guns and tanks were actually fired in a brutal massacre did the Chinese government succeed in breaking up the demonstration. The remarkable attitude-consistent behavior of the Chinese students—in the face of extreme outside pressures to stop such behavior—created the seeds of a revolution that may someday overthrow the government of the world's most populous nation.

People act in accord with their attitudes on matters that matter, sometimes no matter what. If it doesn't matter much, situational factors like time pressure ("I have better things to do this week than make

Attitude-behavior consistency that amazed the world. A pro-democracy demonstrator stands up for his convictions and stops "traffic" in Beijing, China.   (*Reuters/Bettmann Newsphotos*)

phone calls") and other relevant attitudes and feelings ("I find calling a stranger on the phone embarrassing") loom larger. The wise message maker emphasizes the great personal implications of the attitude issue at hand.

THE HARD-EARNED REWARDS OF PERSUASION

And so we reach the point of ultimate persuasion—meaningful change in behavior in line with what the persuader wants. Getting there isn't easy, which is why clever influence agents often opt for compliance techniques, such as those discussed in Chapters 2 and 3, that try to by-pass the attitude system altogether (at least initially). But persuasion has its special rewards, especially if it involves systematic mental processing of new information or a new perspective. That sort of active thinking results in belief changes and cognitive restructuring through which the new attitude gets firmly embedded. When such *internaliza-*

tion takes place, the new attitude can be counted on to endure and to manifest itself in future behaviors. Not just a single behavior or attitudinal response has been coaxed. Rather, the individual has been changed in fundamental ways. Although we have used advertising examples to illustrate some of our basic points, you should be aware that many of your most profound attitudes—which together form part of your self-identity—were generated by persuasive communications presented in your family, school, friendship groups, and society.

When strong attitudes have been formed that come to guide how you think and feel about many aspects of your daily life, and also come to direct your everyday actions, they serve another function as well. They help you to resist influence pressures to think otherwise, to feel differently, or to behave in counterattitudinal ways. And so they give us a "mental buffer zone" against being readily swayed by new messages and by compliance-gaining strategies used on us. However, while resisting unwanted influence is a desirable goal, strong attitudes can have the downside of making us inflexible, cognitively rigid, and unwilling to consider new, valid information. In the extreme, this leads to being dogmatic, to perceiving the world only through narrowly filtered attitude systems that do not "change with the times" or "go with the flow" when the times and the flow are good and righteous. In the next chapter our focus is on this crucial issue for influence agents and for each of us as potential targets for all forms of social influence. How and why are some people able to resist influence while others are so vulnerable to it? Let's examine both sides of the yin and yang nature of persuasion: resisting and embracing influence.

*T*O SUM UP...

This chapter highlighted the psychological factors that promote the final two persuasion steps: (1) retention of attitude change and (2) translation of the new attitude into behavior. Both steps require the formation of strong, clear, and extreme attitudes. We examined ways to accomplish this goal during message presentation, described how attitudes may change over time, and explored the battle for behavior change often waged between existing attitudes and powerful situational forces.

- Repeated message presentation increases the chances of the exposure, attention, comprehension, and acceptance steps necessary for attitude change. Repetition also fosters strong and extreme attitude responses.

- Repetition effects are evident in "mere exposure" studies. Stimuli that are initially slightly liked or neutral become better liked the more often they are presented. Greater familiarity makes most things more attractive. However, initially disliked stimuli become more disliked the greater the exposure.

- Polarization from slight to great like or dislike reflects a principle of evaluative consistency. We think in consistent terms: initial cognitive responses to a stimulus guide further thoughts, so that new cognitive responses (upon new stimulus presentations) have the same evaluative tone as previous ones. Strong positive attitudes are thus encouraged by creating positive affect and then encouraging further thought through repetition or other means.

- Complex messages benefit from repetition much like simple stimuli, as long as they have compelling arguments. Too many repetitions, though, may lead to a downturn in persuasion if the audience's consistent thoughts run low. They may also be turned off by tedium or by a sense that they are being controlled.

- Besides creating strong and extreme attitudes, message repetition contributes to retention. Continued thinking about plausible message arguments leads to stronger connections to beliefs and knowledge in memory, making future retrieval easier.

- Retention of persuasion is enhanced by techniques that encourage systematic analysis of the message and issue. Active, elaborative thinking yields attitudes and beliefs that are well connected in memory and interrelated attitude systems. Thus, attitudes resulting from self-persuasion or systematic message analysis encouraged by personal relevance are better retained than attitudes resulting from passive or heuristic processing.

- Attitudes may be stored separately in memory from the information and cognitive responses on which they are based. This helps explain the sleeper effect, a delayed increase in the persuasive impact of a compelling message.

- If opposing messages are presented in succession and an attitude must be expressed immediately, the second message, fresher in mind, may be more persuasive: a recency effect. If attitude is not expressed until a future time, the first message is often more influential: a primacy effect. The first message establishes a first impression that guides further thinking.

- New attitudes may be retained over time, yet may still not translate into behavior. Situational forces can override them. Even strangers can cause conformity and obedience against one's better judgments. Subjective norms—beliefs about the standard, approved ways of behaving in a particular group or situation—are even more capable of overriding attitudes. Time pressures and the strangeness of some situations also interfere with the usual behavioral expression of attitudes.

- Despite the power of situations, attitudes do guide behavior under certain conditions. The attitude must be strong and clear, and thus spontaneously activated in relevant situations. This characterizes attitudes that result from systematic processing, that have a strong knowledge base, or that were formed through direct experience with the attitude object.

- A second condition for attitude-behavior consistency is that the attitude be relevant to the behavior at hand. Situations activate many attitudes; the most specifically relevant one will most affect the specific behavior. A third condition is that the attitude and behavior be linked to the same third component of the attitude system. Emotion-based attitudes may not guide action decisions that are cognitive and rational, but they do guide emotional behaviors. Finally, people act in accord with attitudes on issues they find important.

QUESTIONS AND EXERCISES

1. A friend tells you, "The more I see those ads for Beebop sneakers, the less I like them." How can this negative exposure effect be? Analyze your friend's reaction from the perspective of research and theory relevant to repetition effects, and try to figure out how the Beebop sneaker people could turn the effect around and make familiarity breed liking instead.

2. Self-persuasion through essay writing can create strong new attitudes that guide behavior, as can direct experience with the attitude object. But your only influence tool is a persuasive message. How can you reap some of the benefits (in changing your audience) of self-persuasion and direct experience by the way you construct and deliver your persuasive message?

3. Professor Jones is known to be politically liberal, which makes her less than persuasive with conservative students in her school. But she has some ideas for social reform that she wants these students to accept and remember as they assume influential social roles in the future. She knows that the students would like the ideas if only they were not identified with her liberal image. Suggest some strategies for her, based perhaps on the sleeper effect and evaluative consistency principles.

4. Add to your analysis of designing an effective blood drive (from the previous chapter's exercise) your new knowledge of how to get past the attitude-to-behavior roadblock, and to make the donors retain their net attitudes.

6

Resisting and Embracing Influence:

The Yin and Yang of Persuasion

❖

The Stubborn Mind: Resisting and Selective Bending ◆ *Overcoming Resistance: Liberating the Totalitarian Ego* ◆ *The Other Extreme: Persuasion Pushovers* ◆ *Prejudice: An Attitude That Can Kill* ◆ *A Final Note: On Having an Open Mind without Being a Pushover*

Thinking back over the ground we have covered thus far in our journey, you may sense a subtle paradox. On the one hand, we have seen that human beings are quite malleable creatures. Only gentle prodding is necessary to get people to endorse positions that run counter to their personal attitudes. If the prodding is so gentle that people believe they have freely decided to make the endorsement, their private attitudes change in the direction of their public behavior. People also obey experimenters ordering them to punish others, alter their judgments of perceptual realities to conform to inaccurate majorities, and allow themselves to be persuaded by presumed experts even when the experts' arguments are weak. Let's add in the untold number of consumers who buy advertised products that they do not need, they cannot afford, and are bad for their health or safety. And for good measure, we have to include all those who daily join one of the estimated several thousand cults in the United States. Easy pickings for influence agents.

On the other hand, we have also seen that persuasive messages—even powerful ones—are often totally ineffective. People frequently ignore messages that they sense will challenge their beliefs, counterargue messages that they cannot ignore, and possibly distort those that they cannot counterargue. It sure seems as though you can't teach some old attitudes new tricks. And there is always a sizable minority who are able to resist enormous social pressures of status, power, and majority influence. This resistance to influence surfaces among many people even when faced with powerfully orchestrated situational pressures, as in Milgram's obedience studies. Consider, for a moment, American P.O.W.s who refused to collaborate with their Chinese Communist captors in the Korean war.

Thus, reactions to influence attempts vary widely, from staunch resistance—with a willingness to suffer or die for one's beliefs—to a vulnerability and gullibility that put some people "at risk" for almost any attempt to change their minds and behavior. In this chapter, we will examine these extreme opposite ends of a changeability spectrum, focusing especially on those who refuse to buy into persuasive appeals at any cost as well as those who buy them too readily. First, we will examine the psychological processes of motivation and thought that underlie resistance to influence. Then, we will see what can be done to overcome resistance—what influence techniques may succeed in penetrating a closed or stubborn mind. Finally, we will examine the opposite case of oversusceptibility to influence and those factors that help stiffen resistance when it is necessary.

Before venturing forth into this realm of extreme reactors a word of caution is in order. Offhand, it would seem that there is value in being a resister and danger in being a complier, as if they were poles of a good-to-be versus bad-to-be continuum. This is not always so. The virtue in resisting comes from resisting unwanted, undesirable forms of social influence that come from illegitimate authorities, destructive cults, dangerous peer groups, deceptive salespeople, false advertisements, and their many-colored kin in other areas of our lives. But this virtue fades when resistance takes the form of not complying with expert recommendations from one's physician; or refusing to stop engaging in unsafe, unhealthy behavior or racial prejudices. One aspect of resistance can be a rigid, dogmatic closed-mindedness that keeps at bay both negative and positive types of social influence. And we have to make a value judgment that resistance in that form is not good for individuals or for society. Vulnerability to influence can sometimes be OK when that influence comes in the form of socially acceptable agents who have our best interests in mind, like responsive parents and teachers, and responsible role models, among others.

*T*HE STUBBORN MIND: RESISTING AND SELECTIVE BENDING

One of life's more frustrating experiences is the unsuccessful persuasion attempt, especially when you are sure you are correct and still your target fails to bend to, or even see, your point. Logic, data, reality—nothing moves this person you are desperately trying to enlighten. It gets to a point where you doubt if your friend or child or student will listen to anything short of a booming voice out of the sky—and then only if it is accompanied by a bolt of lightning. To be sure, people are typically most unbudgeable on issues that *involve* them personally to the point where their sense of personal identity, accustomed way of life, or sense of social connectedness is tied tightly to their stand on the issue (Krosnick, 1988). Anti-abortion activists, for example, are less likely to alter their beliefs about abortion than their views on the 55 miles per hour speed limit. No amount of argumentation can convince Christian fundamentalists that evolution was "God's tool," yet logic may persuade these same people that the gasoline tax in the United States should be raised. The sources and varieties of *involvement*, and how thinking about persuasive information is affected by involvement, are central to understanding why some attitudes are staunchly held despite persuasive appeals to the contrary.

Before examining the role of involvement in creating resistance to persuasion, we need to develop an important point; namely, that even attitudes toward uninvolving objects or issues that are not self-defining can become deeply etched in mental stone. A look at this seemingly curious fact is instructive because the resistance to change of trivial attitudes reflects the most basic mental mechanisms behind what is called *belief and attitude perseverance*. Resistance to change starts with the *cognitive structure* in which an attitude and its supporting beliefs are embedded.

Strength in Structure: The Cognitive Bases of Perseverance

In an intriguing analogy, Anthony Greenwald (1980) has likened the human mind to a totalitarian state. We have, according to Greenwald, "totalitarian egos." One important basis for this comparison is that, just as nondemocratic totalitarian states resist social and governmental changes, people resist cognitive changes. Totalitarian governments distort events and rewrite history to make them fit the "party line" (as we saw in Chapter 4 in the case of Communist China's 1989 denial of suppressing the student democracy movement). Human minds select and interpret information to make it fit with established beliefs and attitudes, and may "rewrite" memory to make past actions and thoughts cohere with present and anticipated behaviors. People are "cognitive conservatives" in that they resist changing their thoughts and evaluations of the objects of their world. This assertion, of course, fits some of the psychological processes we have seen in past chapters, including selective attention to attitude-consistent messages, interpretation of ambiguous evidence as consistent with our attitudes, and dissonance reduction. The important points to add here are that the conservatism goes further than we have seen so far and that it does not require intention and desire (such as needs for consistency and the value of sustaining a positive self-image). It is the mind-directing effects of our attitude structures that are sufficient for perseverance. Some research examples illustrate this nicely.

Seek and ye shall find (what you believed all along). Despite good intentions to be objective, people tend to *gather* information in such a way as to stack the deck in favor of confirming their beliefs or "working hypotheses" about an object. This principle was first demonstrated in a study of how people go about testing their hunches about other people's personalities (Snyder and Swann, 1978). Female college students were given the task of interviewing a person with the goal of trying to find out if the person possessed a certain trait. For half the students, the suspected or hypothesized personality was that of an extrovert; for the other half, it was that of an introvert. Students were given a list of twenty-six questions and were asked to choose twelve of them to ask the person during the interview. Some questions had been judged beforehand to be the kind you would ask someone you *already knew* was extroverted, such as: What would you do if you wanted to liven things up at a party? Other questions had been judged to be the sort you would ask a *known* introvert, such as: What factors make it hard for you to open up to people?

Which questions did the interviewers ask? They most frequently chose to ask questions that already implied their hypothesis: what they had expected to find out. Those testing the "person is an extrovert" hypothesis asked mainly questions you would ask an extrovert, whereas those testing the "person is an introvert" hypothesis typically asked questions you would ask a known introvert.

This is certainly not a great way to test a hypothesis. If you suspect someone is an introvert and ask questions designed to confirm that suspicion, then the answers you elicit will likely do so—even when you are wrong. Imagine, for instance, how an extroverted young woman might answer the question: What factors make it hard for you to open up to people? Extroverted though she might be, she has undoubtedly been in situations in which "opening up" has not come easily. And so, in an effort to give a thoughtful answer, she might say something like "Well,

I am a bit inhibited around people my parents' age, and I find it harder to open up with a guy once a relationship starts getting serious." Consider this response carefully. Does it suggest introversion? Extroversion? Not really, at least if the listener has no preconception. But if you already suspect that the young woman is an introvert, it can be construed as evidence confirming your hunch. ("Aha, so problems with intimacy and reminders of parental authority are behind her withdrawn nature.") At the very least, the answer will give no clue to the fact that its source is actually extroverted—the opposite of what you believe!

Social psychologists have given the label *confirmatory strategy* to this tendency to ask questions in ways that practically guarantee a belief-supporting answer. The strategy is not a conscious attempt to get a distorted picture of reality. Rather, it is rooted in the role of a belief (or attitude or hypothesis) in directing and structuring thought. The belief naturally brings to mind *positive instances*—behaviors that are consistent with the belief. Because they are most available in a person's thoughts and memories, these positive instances become the objects of his or her questions. This directive influence of the belief is further supported by a natural, but mistaken, tendency to regard positive instances as sufficient evidence for a trait or a relationship (Crocker, 1981). A few introverted behaviors, for example, may serve as "proof" of the personality trait introversion. But real proof also requires knowing the relative frequency of *negative instances*, in this case nonintroverted or extroverted behaviors. To confirm any hypothesis requires evidence of how often it is rejected, doesn't fit, or fails to be supported. This simple fact of what is necessary to "prove" one's hypothesis is too often ignored.

And so we have a normal bias in the way we gather new evidence relevant to our beliefs, a bias that contributes to some confirmatory strategies that we have already encountered. You will recall that people are selectively attentive to supportive messages and generally seek out similar others for social comparison—practices that will also turn up more confirmations than disconfirmations of the accuracy of their beliefs and attitudes.

Memory serves (the current belief). Another study from Mark Snyder's laboratory at the University of Minnesota informs us that confirmatory strategies can work backward as well as forward, in that current beliefs can influence what people remember (Snyder and Uranowitz, 1978). College students first read a biography of a young woman named Betty that outlined her life from childhood through her early career as a medical professional. A week later some subjects learned that Betty eventually adopted a heterosexual lifestyle while the rest found out that she had adopted a lesbian lifestyle. All subjects then reported what they recalled from the biography. They did so on a detailed questionnaire which was specially constructed to pick up memory for bio-

THE FAR SIDE   By GARY LARSON

Given the prevalence of confirmatory strategies, the therapist is not likely to find any evidence to the contrary.
(*The Far Side,* copyright 1987 & 1990 Universal Press Syndicate. Reprinted with permission. All rights reserved.)

graphical facts that could be interpreted as relevant to Betty's eventual sexual preference.

Sure enough, compared with subjects who now believed that Betty was a married heterosexual, those who now believed that Betty was a lesbian with a live-in female partner remembered more biographical details about Betty that were consistent with the popular stereotype of early signs of homosexuality. The new belief directed their memory search so that subjects could now think to themselves, "Well, from what I know of Betty's childhood and young adulthood, I'm not surprised she's gay." Yet, little evidence of impending homosexuality was remembered from the same biography by subjects who believed that Betty was heterosexual. This research also makes us aware that "the past" is not a fixed, immutable series of events, but often involves subjective interpretation and reconstruction of memories in line with what we believe and value.

Go ahead, discredit my data (I've got more). We have saved for last a most dramatic example of "cognitive conservatism." It suggests that people may cling to a belief even when the information that led to the belief is totally discredited—by the very person who provided the information in the first place! Such remarkable perseverance was demonstrated in a series of experiments conducted at Stanford University (Anderson et al., 1980; Ross et al., 1975; Ross and Anderson, 1980). Researchers first had undergraduates read fabricated information that clearly suggested either that risk takers make better fire fighters or that they make worse fire fighters. An intuitively compelling case can be made for either relationship. Thus, it is not surprising that subjects found the information convincing and had no trouble with their next task, writing an explanation for the relationship they had "discovered" in the provided information.

Now it gets interesting. Subjects were next told to forget what they had read. They were told that, in fact, the fire fighter cases and the information they had been given were totally fictitious. They could just as easily have been randomly assigned to receive information suggesting the very opposite, and the experimenter was not aware of what the true relationship was between fire-fighting prowess and risk taking. He said that he was sorry for the deception; he was just using that false case material to study some other psychological process. Guess what? This thorough discrediting did weaken the beliefs that subjects held about the relationship they had discovered—but only a little. The belief that was adopted persevered despite the discrediting. Those who had initially seen evidence that risk takers make better fire fighters continued to believe this; and those who had seen evidence of the opposite continued to believe that. It seems that, in the act of explaining the discovered relationship, subjects concocted all sorts of supportive reasons and theories for it. (Remember from Chapter 5 how thinking tends to yield consistent cognitions.) The belief now had a broad base of "popular internal support," and so it could live without the original, but now discredited, "external evidence" that gave birth to it.

The upshot of the preceding examples is that beliefs and attitudes, as Robert Cialdini (1988) has put it, "grow their own legs." If, by some form of influence or education, an individual adopts a new belief or attitude, he or she has difficulty considering the issue objectively. Explaining, remembering, and testing reality will all yield supportive evidence for one's position, making it all the stronger and able to exist even if the initial "leg" on which it stood is amputated by forgetting, by contrary evidence, or by a contrary persuasive message. And this is simply due to the way the mind and its cognitive structures ordinarily work, without special motivation to be "defensive."

States of Involvement: Motivational Bases of Resistance and Openness to Persuasion

Having observed that attitudes and beliefs will persevere on their own, due to cognitive features of the way people process information, let us now consider how motivation affects resistance to persuasion. In Chapters 4 and 5, persuasion was discussed pretty much without regard to the specific motives of the audience. We did see a general motive to preserve our initial opinion, which may often grow out of our desire to be consistent and feel correct. Thus, whether we start out agreeing or disagreeing with the message can affect the degree of attention we give the message and how we interpret it (Zanna, 1990). We also saw that the amount of systematic message processing depends partly on whether the message issue is or is not personally relevant. If the issue is relevant, systematic analysis is likely; if it is not relevant, heuristic rules of thumb will be used. This general principle, however, ignores two facts: (1) a message can be relevant for different reasons, and (2) the specific reason for relevance affects the way the message is thought about.

Imagine two young men, Jeff and Tony, who attend a lecture on gun control given by a noted expert on crime and civil rights. In the course of the lecture, the expert presents potent arguments for strict gun-control laws that would make illegal the civilian ownership of handguns and certain kinds of automatic rifles. The expert notes that, compared to nations with strict gun-control laws, the number of people killed by handguns in the United States is astronomical. Indeed, the expert points out that in 1985, handguns killed 1 out of every 5 million Canadians, 1 out of every 7 million Englishmen, and 1 out of every 2.6 million people in Japan. In contrast, 1 out of every 28,000 U.S. citizens was killed by a handgun (Church, 1989). The expert also argues that guns such as the AK-47, a semiautomatic assault weapon imported from China that has been used in crazed attacks on a schoolyard full of children and in an auto dealership, have no reasonable recreational uses, that most city police chiefs support gun control, and that the constitutional right to bear arms does not extend to all arms.

Jeff and Tony both oppose gun control. After the lecture, however, Jeff has been swayed somewhat. At least, he is willing to see the civilian sale of some guns (like AK-47s) banned and to support a federal law requiring longer waiting periods between the purchase and the pickup of a gun. In contrast, Tony remains adamantly opposed to any form of gun control. What's the difference between these two men?

They do not differ in the *amount* of their involvement with the issue. Both men find the gun-control issue sufficiently relevant and interesting to take the time to attend the lecture. And both gave rapt attention to the speaker's message, systematically analyzing the arguments. These qualities are the defining characteristics of *attitude involvement.* An individual is involved in an attitude issue to the extent that (1) the issue is in some way personally relevant to the individual, and (2) he or she is willing to actively think about the issue when confronted with information about it.

Where Jeff and Tony may differ is in the *basis* of their high level of involvement. As we said, an issue may be personally relevant for different reasons. Hence, the conscious or unconscious goals that lead a person to think about message information may differ from person to person and from topic to topic. Gun control turns out to be relevant to Jeff because he sees its resolution as critical to the important contemporary dilemma of how to curb violence without limiting constitutional freedoms. Primarily, Jeff seeks an attitude toward gun control that is informed about and consistent with accumulated knowledge regarding guns, crimes, rights, and so on. For Tony, on the other hand, there is a very different basis for the personal relevance of gun control. A long-time member of the NRA (National Rifle Association), Tony believes strongly in the personal liberties guaranteed by the Constitution. Private ownership of guns is a symbol of freedom for Tony, and freedom is the object of greatest value in Tony's world view. Moreover, Tony hunts and belongs to a gun club. All of his close friends share his point of view and proudly display an NRA bumper sticker on their cars. In acquiring information about gun control, Tony's primary motive is to garner support and strength for, and to protect, if need be, his existing anticontrol stance.

What we have here are two individuals seeking very different goals as they think about the lecturer's persuasive message. Their goals are

At this hearing concerning handgun control legislation, it's a good bet the listeners wearing their attitudes on their jackets will not be persuaded by pro-gun-control arguments.   (*AP/Wide World*)

based on two different motives. Jeff has a *construction motive* (Fazio, 1979; Leippe and Elkin, 1987). Although opposed to gun control, he is not married to that stance. His goal is to have an information-based attitude, and he will revise or "reconstruct" his attitude if new information is judged to be better than that which he possesses. In other words, Jeff is relatively open to the message from a credible communicator armed with solid evidence. Tony is not. He is rather closed to new information and seeks to defend or "validate" his existing stance on the issue. Tony has a *validation motive* for this particular attitude.

The relative openness of construction-motivated involvement. In laboratory studies, a sense of personal relevance is created by informing message recipients that the policy addressed by the message may soon take effect and personally touch their lives. College students may learn that, while they are still students, their university's administration may institute compulsory senior exams, a parking fee, or some other new twist for them. As we know, messages with this sort of more or less immediate personal significance are scrutinized more carefully and systematically than messages with personally remote consequences (Petty and Cacioppo, 1986). People who see an issue as relevant change more in response to strong messages and are more likely to reject weak ones.

This sensitivity to message quality, in particular the positive attitude change in response to a strong message, indicates not only systematic thinking about the message but also a willingness to consider the issue objectively. And why not? The issues used in research (senior comprehensive exams, for example) have seldom if ever been thought about previously, and so recipients are not likely to have an established sense of how the issue's resolution would relate to their lives and their values. ("Would a senior exam be beneficial to me in practical terms? Does it fit my personal philosophy? My lifestyle?") Informed now that the issue is actually relevant to their personal outcomes in the near future, message recipients seek objective answers to these questions. In short, they are motivated to adopt the attitude that is most *accurate* in the sense that it best reflects current on-line reality. Thus, it is not surprising that when involvement is based on new-found awareness that the message issue has *outcome relevance*, people engage in systematic and fairly objective thinking (Johnson and Eagly, 1989).

A construction motive, or openness to information, doesn't guarantee total objectivity, however. Indeed, as a state of mind, total objectivity may be impossible given the subtle ways our prior beliefs and attitudes as well as current goals affect how we take in information and think about it. When the goal is an accurate attitude and people are open—as in the outcome-relevant involvement case we just reviewed—objectivity is probably highest. But although people may be relatively open to a message, other personal goals may interfere with pure accuracy. These goals may influence how the message is thought about so that objectivity is lost and ideas that better serve the goal come to mind. One goal that may promote this "biased openness" is social approval, or how the attitude response appears to others (Zimbardo, 1960). When we desire an attitude toward the message issue that will create a positive public impression, the message is involving because it has *impression relevance* (Johnson and Eagly, 1989).

The role of impression-relevant involvement was evident in one recent study (Leippe and Elkin, 1987). Subjects who heard a strong message while expecting to discuss the message issue with a professor of unknown views were less persuaded than subjects who did not expect a discussion (Leippe and Elkin, 1987). Apparently, subjects were concerned with making a favorable impression on the professor, so they analyzed the message in such a way as to form a *moderate* attitude that would not be too disagreeable to the professor no matter what the professor's stance was. Their cognitive responses to the message were only mildly positive, allowing them to "go the other way" if the professor happened to be negative about what the message advocated (Cialdini and Petty, 1981).

Involvement that closes minds. In the impression-relevant involvement case, openness to persuasion is qualified by a preference for moderation. But at least there is some openness. We all know the frustration of dealing with people whose attitudes are *totally* inflexible. We may even have some uncompromising positions of our own. ("Don't confuse me with the facts, my mind's already made up.")

Sometimes, people's resistance to change seems truly amazing. In 1988, the news media disclosed that televangelist Jimmy Swaggart kept company with a prostitute. With tears streaming down his face, Swaggart gave a sermon in which he confessed to his followers, "I am a sinner." The elders of his church promptly removed him from his TV pulpit, forbidding him to preach at all. Watching this scandal unfold, most casual observers probably thought that this was the end of the road for the ex-good reverend. His followers were conservative fundamentalist Christians, fearful of and disgusted with the sexual and intellectual permissiveness of modern America. They related to Swaggart's Bible-inspired moralizing and condemnation of carnal sin in his fire and brimstone Sunday sermons (that may have come after Saturday night festivities). Surely, they would now reject him as hypocritical—the more so because he had recently publicly condemned and ridiculed his rival televangelist, Jim Bakker, for his own sexual antics.

It was thus very surprising to listen to TV interviews with some of Swaggart's followers. Some praised him for his courageous public confession and vows of repentance. ("It is a great and holy man indeed who can admit to falling victim to temptation.") Others saw Swaggart's

The Reverend Jimmy
Swaggart's tearful admission.
Many of his followers simply
couldn't believe he was
un-Christian—especially after
this particular speech.   (*UPI/
Bettmann Newsphotos*)

indiscretion as an ordeal that would make him an even stronger religious leader. And still others stressed the greatest Christian virtue, for-
giveness. The Reverend Swaggart was preaching again within months.
Old involvements resist new facts to the contrary.

A more somber instance of unyielding belief occurred during World
War II, when the U.S. government removed more than 100,000
Japanese-Americans—most of them U.S. citizens—from their homes on
the West Coast and sent them to internment camps in remote desert
areas under armed guard. These people were totally uprooted, usually
at tremendous financial and psychic costs, and spent more than 2 years
in what resembled concentration camps. They were removed because a
few rather paranoid generals and politicians were able to persuade the
"powers that be" that internment was necessary to prevent Japanese-
Americans from spying and collaborating with the enemy. Most rank-
ing officials in the wartime government and armed forces doubted
(rightly) this notion. Yet the voices of a few prevailed, in part by relentlessly highlighting rumors of an impending Japanese invasion and by
playing upon the fears and latent prejudices of an American public still
jittery from Pearl Harbor.

In the context of our present discussion, it is notable that the advocates and architects of the internment plan were unmoved by what should have been a very persuasive communication. The F.B.I., looking carefully for evidence of sabotage and conspiracy in the Japanese-American community, found *none* and reported this negative outcome to the War Department. Amazingly, this report was used by pro-internment policymakers as evidence *in favor* of their plan! For as Lt. General John L. DeWitt, a major advocate of internment, wrote in his own recommendation to the War Department: "The very fact that no sabotage has taken place to date is a disturbing and confirming indication that such action will be taken" (quoted in Hersey, 1988).

Just as extraordinary is a reaction to this issue 44 years later. In August 1988, President Reagan signed a bill that made an official U.S. apology to the Japanese-American community and awarded $20,000 to each living victim of the internment. A month later, an article in a major magazine detailed the reasons why the apology was appropriate. It reviewed accumulated evidence that the whole thing was a stupid, unnecessary, and sad chapter in U.S. history. Nevertheless, the magazine received and published a letter from a man who had been the chief of the Japan branch of the Office of War Information during the war. This gentleman took strong exception to the article, and to the apology of Congress and the President. In direct opposition to the historical evidence, he argued that if Japanese-Americans had not been interned, the war effort would have been seriously hampered by espionage. The writer is proof positive that some wrongheaded attitudes never die, but live on indefinitely, if not always in infamy.

In these examples, we see instances of those quite ordinary and dispassionate cognitive processes associated with belief perseverance. Prior beliefs bias data gathering, interpretation, and reconstructive memory. But doesn't something else seem to be at work? After all, it's much more than a subtle liking for Jimmy Swaggart that remains among his followers. It's full-fledged devotion to his word. And the F.B.I. report was so unconvincing to General DeWitt that he helped send thousands on a 2-year desert "vacation." There is more than cold cognitive bias here; there's a validation motive in thinking about attitude-relevant information.

Three factors help create an involvement state in which there is strong motivation to validate an existing attitude, and thereby resist change in response to credible messages. In general, people will be highly motivated to defend or validate an attitude if (1) they are committed to it, (2) it is tightly interwoven into their basic self-defining values, (3) it is a viewpoint they share with significant others in their lives.

Our old friend, commitment. Previous chapters have often touched on the psychological effects of commitment. Social life teaches most people the value of keeping their word, of holding to a consistent course, so much so that there may be unconscious striving for consistency. Indeed, behavior that runs counter to a freely chosen previous course will create the disquieting state of cognitive dissonance. Not surprisingly, research indicates that subjects who have committed themselves to a position, even by such minimal actions as jotting down their ideas about a topic for the experimenter or simply completing an attitude scale, are less persuaded by an opposing message than uncommitted recipients (Pallak et al., 1972; Rosnow and Suls, 1970). The desire to stay true to one's past word and deeds directs those all-important cognitive responses to the message. The message is scrutinized for flaws, and message-negating thoughts are drawn from memory. And from the principle of evaluative consistency, you can see that, with further appraisal of the message, the subjects develop less, not more, openness to it. Cognitive responses will be increasingly hostile to the message.

Now consider all those followers of the Reverend Swaggart and all the time, money, and trust they invested as his faithful brethren. Clearly, many had enough commitment stored up to prevent them from accepting the message that their spiritual leader is a hypocritical sinner. And what about the man who refuses to acknowledge the mistake of internment for Japanese-Americans? He was committed to his beliefs and to his public acts as a military official for almost half a century; that's aged-in-the-wood enduring commitment.

When attitudes are "value-able." Everyone has a *value system,* an enduring set of beliefs about what kinds of behavior and lifestyle are preferable or "good" (Rokeach, 1973). Admittedly, different people value different things. For some, individual freedom and the pursuit of personal happiness may be the central, most important values; for others, communal harmony and interpersonal trust may be the core values. Or, for example, it has been argued that while women's ethical decisions are heavily based on valuing supportive relationships, for men abstract principles of justice are more dominant values (Gilligan, 1982). But regardless of the specific values involved, our value system forms a big part of how we see and define ourselves in relation to the world. Some issues are highly relevant to our most self-defining values, and we thus form an attitude about them that reflects and reinforces those values. For example, you may recall Tony, whose anti-gun-control attitude was strongly linked to a *self-defining value system* that centered on individual liberty. Because of its self-defining nature, a strong link between an attitude and a value is referred to as *ego involvement* (Sherif and Hovland, 1961).

As Tony's rejection of the pro-gun-control lecture suggested, attitudes with strong links to values are exceptionally difficult to change (Johnson and Eagly, 1989; C. Sherif et al., 1973). Consider a study that induced college students to make connections between their central values and a specific attitude about an obscure issue (Ostrom and Brock,

1968). Subjects heard a speech advocating that Greenland should not be offered membership in something called the Pan-American Bank. This speech was sufficient to convince subjects, who clearly had no previous opinion or at least no commitment to one. After all, can you imagine a more *un*involving issue? Then some subjects were asked to contemplate whether excerpts from the speech reflected certain self-defining values. This opportunity to link their recently constructed attitude to their values effectively cemented the attitude. Compared with control subjects (who had been asked to make linkages to superficial ideas), the subjects who linked the attitude to personal values were less influenced by a second speech that opposed the first one.

Why does linkage with self-defining values make an attitude change resistant? For one thing, deeply held values exist in a network of supportive beliefs. And those beliefs will influence cognitive responses to challenging messages. A second consideration is that changing a value-related attitude can be *threatening to self-esteem*. Agreeing that the attitude is wrong implies that something is amiss in our self-defining value system, which in turn implies that we are not as worthy as we thought. And, of course, it also means that a change in one part of our cognitive network will reverberate, requiring changes elsewhere—a lot of distressing cognitive work. And so, we resist.

What's more, when compared with less involved people, ego-involved message recipients will generally disagree with *more* of what a counter-attitudinal message says, even the moderate, "meet me halfway" arguments. Linked as it is to the value system, the attitude position is clearly defined, and ego-involved individuals make a sharp distinction between those positions that are and those that are not close enough to be acceptable or possibly integrated into the value system. Ego-involved people have a narrower *latitude of noncommitment*. They either sharply agree or sharply disagree with a given attitude position on the ego-involving issue. They are likely to *assimilate* very close positions into their *latitude of acceptance*—to see them, that is, as identical or interchangeable with their position (C. Sherif et al., 1973; Sherif and Hovland, 1961).

But positions any further away, even moderately distant ones, will be rejected. They fall within a *latitude of rejection*. With high ego involvement, latitude of rejection expands. People become more critical and discriminating, and they see nonagreeing messages as more discrepant than they really are. Their own attitude serves as such a vivid and clear anchor that *contrast* occurs: the difference is perceptually magnified. It's like holding a 16-pound bowling ball for 5 minutes and then replacing it with a tennis ball. The tennis ball feels light as a feather—and *very* different (contrast). But a 15-pound bowling ball will be indistinguishable from the 16-pounder (assimilation).

The ties that bind. In everyday life values-linked attitudes also tend to be attitudes that people share with important others—their closest friends, their respected colleagues, their role models, their heroes, and so on. When attitudes have social significance, the motivation to defend them is stronger yet. Numerous studies indicate that perhaps the most unbudgeable attitudes are those of people who are active members of groups that advocate a specific position (Sherif and Hovland, 1961). Members of special-interest groups, such as animal-rights activists, who define their life's meaning in terms of the group's cause (in this case, stopping all laboratory animal research), are not easily "dis-persuaded" from "their cause."

*O*VERCOMING RESISTANCE: LIBERATING THE TOTALITARIAN EGO

We have looked at a formidable set of cognitive and motivational factors that contribute to the human tendency to resist changing established attitudes and beliefs. Can anything be done to break down resistance? In Chapters 4 and 5, we identified some factors that will enhance the persuasiveness of a communication. Are there some additional things that can be done to penetrate the special barriers we have discussed in this chapter? The answer is "Yes, but don't expect miracles."

The willingness of an audience to be objective is an important step in gaining its acceptance of a more accurate and rational attitude position. Outcome-relevant involvement, as we have seen, encourages the sort of systematic thinking that, more often than not, leads to acceptance of a strong message. But audiences fall short of this level of objectivity if they are ego involved or even if they simply have an initial attitude that is salient enough to direct their thinking and memory (Zanna, 1990). Simply put, people are often either unwilling or unable to be objective and open even when they want to be. They may need some help—some nudging.

Several kinds of nudges may work. One strategy is to make the targets of your message feel accountable to an impartial and important source. A second strategy is to somehow cajole them into considering the opposite of what they currently believe. Third, you could pose questions in ways that elicit agreeable answers—and hence changes in self-perception. Fourth, you can make sure your message addresses the needs that are served by the attitudes of your target audience. Let us examine each of these strategies for overcoming resistance.

Facing the Fire (of Accountability)

People can be nudged into effortful and objective consideration of attitude-relevant information by "holding them accountable." This can be accomplished by convincing them of a need to justify their views to others. Now wait a minute, you may say. Doesn't this instigate impression-relevant involvement and, consequently, thinking that is biased toward yielding a moderate attitude that no one can find offensive? Yes, that can happen, as we've seen. The trick is to get people to believe that agreement with others is less important than the goodness or appropriateness of their attitudes or beliefs—qualities that can and will be evaluated against some objective criterion. For example, a chief executive officer may ask each of several subordinate executives to devise and present to her a strategy for marketing a new product, adding that she will go with the "best plan." Each executive is required to personally justify his or her plan to the boss, who also happens to be a seasoned marketing expert. Research on business decision making suggests that not only will the executives work harder on their task than they would if they felt less accountable but they also will be more objective and open-minded. They will consider more options and be more willing to consider and integrate data that run counter to their initial hunches (Janis and Mann, 1977).

Accountability has similar "debiasing" effects in persuasion. In one study, college students anonymously wrote out their thoughts and feelings about affirmative action, capital punishment, and American defense spending. Some subjects had previously been made to feel accountable by being led to believe that they would later be asked to justify their position to another subject. Other subjects were given no accountability requirement. Close analysis of their written thoughts indicated that accountable subjects had considered more different and inconsistent aspects of the issues than subjects not held accountable. Accountability led to more complex thinking and attempted integration of opposing ideas and evidence into a coherent and accurate perspective (Tetlock, 1983).

Of course, accountability does have its limits as a bias adjuster. It is most effective at getting people to be objective when they are forming new attitudes or revising hazy ones. It doesn't work as well at getting people to give up well-formed beliefs that were originally based on false information (Tetlock and Kim, 1987; Tetlock et al., 1989). Though motivated to be objective, opinionated people who are held accountable may still be influenced by the entrenched belief.

Playing Devil's Advocate Is No Sin

The bias of belief may also be countered by applying a "consider the opposite" strategy. How many times have you been in situations like the following? You are part of a group that must decide on a course of action or on a stand to take. As group members confer, it becomes clear that all are rushing headlong in the same direction, toward a unanimous decision. Just before you get there, however, one group member says something like, "Let's slow down a minute. Let me play devil's advocate here and endorse the other side." That member then argues against the decision that everybody thought was obviously right. And things do slow down. The group may take a second look. Occasionally, spelling out the opposite point of view reveals problems that compel the group to revise, or even scrap, its original decision.

It so happens that your judgments may also benefit if you are willing and able to play devil's advocate with yourself. But you must be a special devil. Simply being self-critical is not enough; you have to consider and imagine the possibility that truth and righteousness is the opposite of what you believe.

This was demonstrated in a study that sought cognitive remedies for the biased interpretation effect we encountered in Chapter 4 (Lord et al., 1984). One condition of this experiment exactly repeated the procedure of a study we reviewed earlier. Proponents and opponents of capital punishment examined two studies, one supporting and one refuting the claim that the death penalty deters crime. As in the original study, this information had the curious effect of polarizing subjects. Even though they examined the same inconclusive evidence, the proponents of capital punishment became more extreme proponents, while the opponents became even more opposed to capital punishment. People selectively accepted the study they already agreed with. In two other conditions, the researchers tried to "correct" this bias by giving subjects special instructions. The be-unbiased instructions asked subjects to "be as objective and unbiased as possible" and, like a judge or juror, "to weigh the evidence in a fair and impartial manner." In contrast, the consider-the-opposite instructions explained how biased interpretation might occur and implored subjects to ask themselves at each step whether they "would have made the same high or low evaluation had exactly the same study produced results on the other side of the issue."

The effects of these two kinds of instructions were very different, as you can see in Figure 6.1. Be-unbiased instructions put no dent whatsoever in the polarization effect. Consider-the-opposite instructions, on the other hand, eliminated polarization. Pro-subjects did not increase their belief that capital punishment deters crime nor did their attitudes become more pro. Con-subjects similarly remained unchanged.

Why does one instruction work and not the other? It seems that asking people to be careful and objective simply motivates them to think harder. Thinking harder, however, just exaggerates the built-in tendency to be consistent that comes with already having an attitude. Subjects given the be-unbiased instructions believed that they were being unbiased; but, in fact, they simply were blind to how opinionated minds like theirs naturally work. Indeed, how many of us ever believe

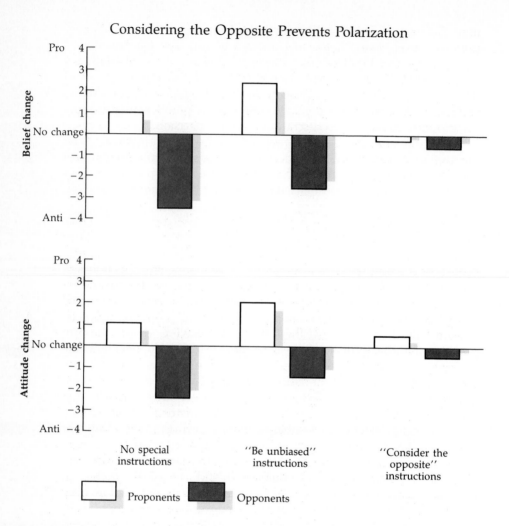

Considering the Opposite Prevents Polarization

FIGURE 6.1
After reading the same inconclusive information about whether capital punishment has a deterrent effect, pro-capital punishment subjects became more pro and anticapital punishment subjects became more anti when they were given no special instructions to be unbiased as they considered the evidence. The only subjects who did not show the polarization pattern were those instructed to "consider the opposite."
(From Lord, Lepper, and Preston, 1984.)

that *we* are biased—isn't it always *they* who are? Subjects asked to consider the opposite may have been no less blind to built-in bias. However, by following instructions, these subjects generated possibilities they would never have considered "naturally." Once brought to mind, these thoughts and ideas exerted an influence on thinking and evaluation. The key was getting opposing thoughts to occur to people in a *salient* fashion in the first place.

As you check out Figure 6.1, you might be thinking that the consider-the-opposite strategy won only half a victory over biased interpretation. Subjects did not polarize, but neither did they moderate. This is true enough, but Rome wasn't destroyed in a day. Polarization is part of the "hardening" process by which attitudes and beliefs get ever more entrenched and unbudgeable. This process was stalled, if not reversed, by the strategy of considering the opposite. As a result, the attitude might still be changeable if stronger opposing evidence came along.

Where Questions Lead, We May Follow—Even to Paradox

In Chapter 3, we discussed how people may come to believe things they were nudged into saying or doing by largely invisible situational forces. We saw, for example, that questionnaire items can be worded so as to prompt certain self-descriptive answers that, via self-attribution, bring people to see themselves differently. A similar procedure, employing leading questions, can be used to change sociopolitical attitudes. The technique takes advantage of a common conversational rule that one should answer questions, not dispute them (Grice, 1975). If questions are asked the right way, people may feel compelled by this rule to provide reasons for positions that actually oppose their own.

Consider the example of Wilma, who has sort of conservative, traditional beliefs about gender roles. One day she is asked by an acquaintance, "Why do you think women make better bosses than men?" Given the conversational rule, her reply is apt to include, at least in part, some reasons that could explain this belief-discrepant possibility: "I don't really know if that's true in general, but let me see. Well, women are, after all, better at reading others' needs and feelings, and at maintaining harmony in groups." In giving this answer, Wilma is confirming the question's premise that women, in fact, are better bosses. And having done so, she is just a small step from inferring that she is not so much of a traditionalist after all—or that her conservative views are perhaps too extreme. It's a little self-perception and a little self-persuasion. A number of studies have confirmed that this sneaky procedure can be effective in changing attitudes (Swann and Ely, 1984; Swann et al., 1988). It's a good way to get someone to bring attitude-inconsistent thoughts to mind without stirring up the cognitive processes that preserve attitudes, and sometimes pickle them permanently.

There's a wrinkle here, however. You probably recall that clear, well-formed attitudes are less susceptible to change through self-attribution. And sure enough, asking leading questions is ineffective

For Better or For Worse®   **by Lynn Johnston**

By expressing her uncertainty, the girl at least avoided getting unmistakedly negative feedback.
(*For Better or for Worse,* copyright 1988 Universal Press Syndicate. Reprinted with permission. All rights reserved.)

with those who are highly certain of their attitude. Wilma, remember, was "sort of" conservative. Connie, on the other hand, is certain of her conservative views about women's roles, and as a result, she will resist leading questions that have a liberal premise. If you ask her why women make better bosses, she'll flatly tell you that they usually don't. If you ask her what she likes best about "sensitive men," she'll tell you it's the fact that "they know I won't date them, and so they don't have to ask." Shall we find another strategy to change Connie? Or could we tinker with the leading questions approach?

The answer is: Tinker. That's what William Swann and his colleagues (1988) did, and the result of their social-psychological tinkering was the paradoxical strategy of asking the "superattitudinal" leading question. They based their strategy on this reasoning: Highly certain people like Connie resist giving confirming answers to *any* questions that imply a different position from theirs. They want you to know exactly how they feel (Swann, 1983). They even resist questions that imply an attitude that is on the same side as theirs but more extreme; for example, if they were a "7" on a 9-point attitude scale and the message they got was a "9." How do they resist? They argue *against* the extreme position. If this happens, highly certain people may be forced into a self-attribution that they are more moderate on the issue than they previously thought. Paradoxically, they will change in the direction opposite to that implied by the question.

That's the reasoning, and now here's the strategy. Ask Connie questions like: "Why do you sympathize with the feelings of some men that women are better kept barefoot and pregnant?" "Why do men *always* make better bosses than women?" Connie will balk at the questions (we hope), find herself sounding almost liberal in the process, and ultimately shift her beliefs toward this "liberal streak" she never knew she had. Now we know the reasoning and the strategy—but what about results? In a pair of studies, the paradoxical strategy was found to have its intended effects on highly certain people, like the Connies of the world (Swann et al., 1988).

This paradoxical effect occurs because people who are certain of their beliefs desire that others know explicitly how they feel. They are not as extreme as the question implies, and they take pains to show it. It may also be that psychological reactance, a process we discussed in Chapter 5, is at work. Highly certain people may take an extreme leading question as an assumption by the questioner that they will subscribe to any old statement on their side of the issue, no matter how inane; and they thus become motivated to assert their freedom to have an individualized and differentiated position.

A combination of the paradoxical effect, psychological reactance, and latitudes of acceptance and rejection can be used to great effect by the clever influence agent. Starting with extreme positions known to be in a person's latitude of rejection, one can make successively less extreme statements which the person verbally disagrees with. Gradually, the person is disagreeing with statements that were formerly in his or her latitude of acceptance, until he or she rejects exactly the position that allows your position to become acceptable (Varela, 1971).

Striking the Right Chord

The preceding strategies have been concerned primarily with getting past the cognitive processes and structures that protect attitudes and beliefs from change. One final strategy that we will mention is concerned more with the motivational aspects of resistance and the needs served by attitudes. We have seen that attitudes are very useful. They serve as evaluative summaries that can guide our behavior, and as organizing points that lend meaning and order to the complex, often confusing world around us.

Some attitudes have even more specialized functions (Katz, 1960; Smith et al., 1956). We observed in chapter 1 and earlier in this chapter that our more important attitudes contribute to our self-identity by defining who we are and by helping us to express our strongly felt ideologies. This has been referred to as the *value-expressive function* of attitudes. An attitude may also serve an *ego-defensive function*. The attitude may be an assertion of some feeling or belief that is incompatible with internal conflicts and anxieties, thereby protecting the individual from consciously recognizing the conflict. A *knowledge function* may be served by an attitude as well. The attitude may provide the individual with a sense of understanding and control—knowledge—regarding the world.

Finally, still another attitude function is *social adjustment;* expressing the attitude allows the individual to fit into important social groups and situations.the other extreme: persuasion pushovers

This functional approach suggests that an attitude will change if the need it serves is satisfied or eliminated by other means, or if it is discovered that an alternative attitude better serves the same need (Herek, 1986). Thus, persuasive messages stand a better chance of getting people to change if they are directed at the functions that the relevant attitudes serve (Snyder and DeBono, 1987).

One series of studies identified two kinds of people: (1) those who strongly value and work at fitting into social situations, and (2) those who strongly value consistently behaving in ways that meaningfully reflect their inner feelings, beliefs, and values. Those in the first group, known as *high self-monitors* (Snyder, 1979) because they carefully monitor situations for cues on how they should present themselves, are apt to hold those attitudes that serve a social-adjustment function. Those in the second group, known as *low self-monitors* because they do not monitor situations for behavioral cues, are likely to hold attitudes for value-expressive reasons. Accordingly, each type should change more in response to persuasive messages that address their specific needs. Consistent with this reasoning, one study found that high self-monitors preferred product advertisements that tried to sell people on the social *image* a user of the product creates, whereas low self-monitors preferred ads that emphasized product quality and value (Snyder and DeBono, 1985). In another study, a message on a sociopolitical issue included credible information about either the position held by people in the recipients' peer group or the position preferred by people who hold desirable personal values. High self-monitors changed more in response to the information about peer opinion (a social-adjustment reason), whereas low self-monitors changed more when the message included information about underlying values (a value-relevant reason) (DeBono, 1987).

Just as the leading-questions strategy requires advance knowledge of the specific position of the persuasion target, a strategy aimed at attitude functions requires the persuader to know the function served by the target's present attitude. One theorist gives this example (Herek, 1986). Two neighborhood residents, Ms. Wagner and Mr. Adams, oppose a plan to build a residential treatment facility in their neighborhood for people with AIDS. Ms. Wagner's negative attitude toward the facility is based on her association of AIDS with homosexuality, which she opposes for religious reasons. Ms. Wagner expresses her self-identity and her values through her religious beliefs. Thus, her opposition to the AIDS facility partly serves a larger value-expressive function. Mr. Adams also associates AIDS with homosexuality, about which he has a psychological "hang-up": he's homophobic. His attitude has an ego-defensive function.

Knowing these facts, would you try to get them to endorse the facility by giving them the same communication? Of course not. The message must be tailored to the needs of the specific target people. Your message to Ms. Wagner might seek to convince her that her religious beliefs would be best expressed by giving strong support to the facility—showing godly love of her neighbor and true Christian charity by providing for unfortunate people who have been shunned by callous, unholy others. You might even have her retell the parable of the Good Samaritan, which she will be modeling by helping those in distress, especially when others "in a hurry" pass them by.

Your message to Mr. Adams might point out that AIDS is by no means unique to gays; it also attacks heterosexuals, intravenous drug users, and even children given contaminated blood transfusions. Or perhaps you might stress that in the process of discovering the cause of AIDS, scientists may learn the secret to combating cancer and other diseases of the immune system, which he and every human being is heir to. Ego involvement and strong cognitive biases on the part of these individuals may still prevail, but you would have gained a fighting chance by aiming at the functions their attitudes serve. Use different strokes for different folks.

THE OTHER EXTREME: PERSUASION PUSHOVERS

If you are persuaded that people are not easily persuaded, get ready to consider the opposite: people can be too easily persuaded. These are opposing, but not incompatible, premises. Resistance is an outgrowth of having set ways of thinking, of having established attitudes that bias cognition and emotion, with no reason to doubt them. Lack of resistance is likely when attitudes and beliefs are still in formative stages, when situational forces, though powerful, are so subtle as to be invisible, when the individual is experiencing a "crisis of belief," or when the individual is cast into a new and vastly different social environment.

Certain kinds of people, as well, are more vulnerable to social influence than others. While it is true that situational and message factors often overwhelm personality differences, it is also the case that the most persuadable people in one situation are also the most persuadable in other situations (see Hovland and Janis, 1959; Janis and Field, 1956).

A common quality of highly persuadable people is *low self-esteem* (McGuire, 1985). Can you see why? Their low regard for themselves includes a low regard for their beliefs and attitudes. Consequently, low self-esteem people may be less motivated to defend their beliefs, and they may give up more easily when they do attempt defense by counter-arguing. But don't think that you can always have your way with those whose self-esteem is depressed. Low self-esteem may lead to poor comprehension of a message—and hence less attitude change—if the individual feels unqualified to figure it out. Also, people with extremely low self-esteem may fail to embrace any position with conviction, as if saying to themselves, "Who am I to be committed to anything, since I'm probably wrong?"

There is a high correlation between low self-esteem and shyness, and so it is no wonder then that under some circumstances shy people are also easy to persuade (Zimbardo, 1977). After being exposed to a persuasive speech advocating a position contrary to their own, shy people are likely to agree with it—but only if they expect to have to defend their own position publicly. If they do not anticipate any public exposure, then they are no more persuasible than nonshy peers.

Lack of Resistance: Cases in Point

Dramatic examples of conversion and change, many of which are socially and personally very costly, are not hard to find. Let us consider three: (1) cult indoctrination, (2) conversion to terrorism, and (3) children's initiation into smoking.

Cult indoctrination. As we discussed in Chapter 1, religious cults such as the Moonies and Hare Krishnas have effective programs of indoctrination. They also know how to pick their targets. They scan the street corners and train stations for adolescents who look "down and out." Hence, the typical convert is in late adolescence and feels alienated and isolated. He or she may feel unloved and lonely. The pressures of transition to adult life, inability to decide on a career course, realization that the "real world" is full of indifference and hypocrisy—all these things may have led the individual to question the beliefs and values of parents and the cultural mainstream. We have here someone whose "resistance is down" and who is therefore prone to "catching a virus" from an agent of influence.

You might wish to review the description of Moonie indoctrination in Chapter 1 as well as the roles played by self-attribution and cognitive dissonance (Chapter 3) in inducing self-change. Here we can add that the persuasive messages that dominate recruitment are designed to capitalize on the weakness and uncertainty of current beliefs, and to break through what's left of the recruit's natural resistances—like confirmatory bias and biased interpretation.

The "love bombs" in these messages are very reinforcing to people who feel deprived of affection, and the motivation to believe them is

very great. Speeches are delivered by skilled lecturers who encourage recruits to listen uncritically. They must "listen with their hearts," not with
their heads. An "open mind" means a vulnerable mind-set of acceptance.
Cardiac comprehension is, after all, rather minimal. Less formal messages
are delivered by attractive similar peers, whose specialized rhetoric and semantic distortions make reality testing hard and reattributions easy.
Agreement is required not with "new" ideas or principles but with familiar
and nice words and phrases (such as peace and tranquility). These messages, along with techniques that tap into virtually all the influence processes we have discussed in this book, can prove irresistible to people who
are unsure and unsettled in their current lifestyles.

Moral disengagement and the cult of terror. People can be converted to beliefs that instigate far more heinous acts than retreating into
a religious cult. The 1980s was a decade of mind-boggling terrorist acts.
Hostage taking; bombings of cars, planes, airports, and abortion clinics;
poisoning of Tylenol, yogurt, and fruit; kamikaze attacks on military
bases—the list could go on and on. How can human beings kill, maim,
and terrorize the innocent public? In responding to this question, we
should remind ourselves of the Milgram obedience studies and the lesson that ordinary, decent people, not just monstrous and evil ones, are
capable of evil deeds. In the case of terrorism, we learn further that ordinary people can be persuaded to *believe* that terrorism is good and appropriate, that under some circumstances taking or risking innocent
lives is morally acceptable.

Psychologist Albert Bandura (1990) refers to such a persuasion process as *moral disengagement* and discusses several influence processes
that make it possible (see Figure 6.2). Most likely, the terrorist-to-be has
strong allegiance to a cause that faces external threat. Repeated messages that emphasize the threat can serve to polarize his or her emotions. In turn, violent acts against innocent people can be morally justified as essential to preserve "our freedom" or as being "God's will."
As further justification for terrorism, indoctrinators use the contrast
principle to alter perceptions of the evil deeds they endorse. The argument is that the deeds, while unfortunate, are trifling compared to the
gross inhumanities perpetrated by "them" on "us." Moreover, by emphasizing the need to protect against external threat, participation in
terrorism can be painted as a *moral responsibility*. In addition, indoctrinators can use euphemisms to minimize the connection between the
endorsed evil deeds and their actual effects on breathing and feeling
human beings. People are not going to be gruesomely murdered by a
terrorist's bomb. Rather, "enemies" or "infidels" are to be "wasted" in
a "clean, surgical strike" by us "freedom fighters."

To be sure, this conversion to the terrorist point of view, to being a
killer, is not instantaneous. Bandura reminds us that it requires "intensive

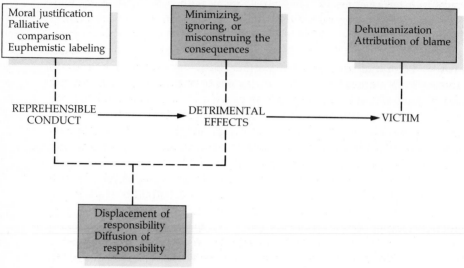

How to Morally Disengage from Destructive Conduct

FIGURE 6.2
The cognitive and emotional steps that lead people to distance themselves morally
from their destructive acts.
(Reprinted from Bandura, 1990, with permission.)

psychological training in moral disengagement" during which recruits
may not even be fully aware of the "transformation they are undergoing."
Once the transformation occurs, though, morally reprehensible actions are
a lot easier to carry out. And once they are carried out, further cognitive
distortion, misplaced emotion, and self-justification will entrench the terrorist attitude even further. Similar processes have been reported in the
training of young Greek soldiers to become cruel torturers—of other Greek
civilians accused of being spies or political enemies (Haritos-Fatouros,
1988). Through techniques of selective desensitization toward physically
beating another human being nearly to death, the military arranged to
have the recruit first watch beatings, then briefly participate in a group effort, then get more fully involved, and finally torture directly one-on-
one—and to do so without guilt, remorse, or any semblance of human
compassion for causing permanent damage to the brain, limbs, or organs
of another person.

Smoking in the boys' and girls' room. It's slower than an act of terrorism, but cigarette smoking also kills. In Chapter 1 we wondered out
loud why so many people—especially young people—are still starting
to smoke. Most smokers start during childhood and adolescence, usually before the age of 19 and quite often at 14 or younger.

Why do so many kids still start smoking? As you might expect, or know from experience, social pressures are the main forces. Early adolescence is a time of great self-consciousness about fitting in, looking good, and no longer being "just a kid." It is also a time when people begin to experience their first "identity crises" and when their thinking grows to include conceptualization of alternative realities and lifestyles (Evans, 1984). Adolescents, therefore, are trying on new roles; they're experimenting. And the roles they stay with are the ones that bring social approval and the most comfortable self-image. Susceptibility to peer pressure peaks in early adolescence, and junior high school students who "hang out" in a group of smokers are very likely to give smoking a try themselves (Mosbach and Leventhal, 1988). Modeling of adult behavior also is to be expected from youngsters shedding their childish self-image. Thus, young teens are considerably more likely to take up smoking if their parents smoke, and more likely still if an older sibling smokes (Flay et al., 1985). Among teenagers with low self-esteem or a sense of powerlessness, these influences to smoke are especially likely to have their unhappy effect (Evans, 1984). Finally, kids are not blind to all those television, print, and billboard cigarette ads picturing attractive adults smoking and happily engaged in life's sexiest and most exciting activities.

Building Resistance

Getting people to be less easily influenced is a straightforward matter in principle. Basically, what is needed is to build into the relevant attitude system all those attributes that underlie the remarkable resistance and resilience we have highlighted in this chapter. In other words, the same psychological factors that must be overcome to obtain change must be nurtured and developed in the person to prevent change. It is a matter of putting persuasion in reverse gear.

There are a number of ways to build resistance to influence in people. They can be (1) encouraged to commit themselves to their existing attitudes, (2) given knowledge, (3) induced into practicing counterarguing persuasive attacks, or (4) forewarned about impending attacks on their lifestyle and attitudes. Let's briefly examine each of these resistance-building strategies.

Standing up to be counted. Taking a stand, especially a public one, is a major resistance builder. As we have seen repeatedly, commitment motivates people to fend off counterattitudinal messages. This is especially true when verbal and behavioral commitments are linked in the individual's mind to his or her personal values (Lydon and Zanna, 1990).

Shoring up knowledge. In previous chapters, we have reviewed research evidence for the notion that people are more resistant to persuasive appeals when their attitudes are well grounded in knowledge about and experience with the object or issue at hand. Knowledge makes counterarguing easier (Wood, 1982). It also contributes to a clear and strong attitude whose ready availability makes it unlikely that the individual will be forced into making self-attributions from situationally influenced behavior (Chaiken and Baldwin, 1981).

In some situations, lack of a knowledge base makes the individual especially susceptible to a persuasive attack on beliefs. In every society, a number of beliefs are subscribed to universally, so much so that they are never attacked. They are called *cultural truisms*. They are simply assumed to be true and are never much thought about. In the West, these include "It is good to brush your teeth after every meal" and "Mental illness is not contagious." Persuasive messages aimed at debunking these cultural truisms are likely to be quite effective because people simply have a weak defense. Their cognitive structure, the fortress in which the belief exists, has such low walls and inept weapons that the attacking message cannot be effectively argued against. It follows that one way to build resistance to attacks on cultural truisms is to provide people with information and arguments that support them. Before hearing an argument against frequent tooth brushing, for example, people could be shown how government-sponsored studies indicate that people who brush more often have fewer cavities. Research has shown that, compared to people simply "hit" with a message attacking a truism, those provided with a *supportive defense* before the message change their attitudes less in response to that message (McGuire and Papageorgis, 1961).

Getting inoculated. There are yet better ways to build defenses against persuasion. William McGuire (1964) made the analogy between building psychological defenses against persuasion and the biological processes involved in defending against germ-borne diseases. We protect ourselves from diseases in two ways. First, we maintain a healthy lifestyle through proper nutrition and exercise, which strengthens and supports our immune system. But second, when we face a strong attack of germs—for example, during a bad flu epidemic—we get inoculated. We receive a shot, consisting of a small amount of the disease-causing germ, which stimulates the body to build up antibodies to fend off full-fledged attacks by the germ in the future.

In attacks on attitudes, the first level of protection, proper nutrition and care, is analogous to providing people with a supportive defense against persuasion. Could a parallel of the second biological defense, inoculation, also be created for defense against persuasion? McGuire reasoned that one *inoculation defense* strategy would be to *weakly* attack a belief and prompt people to refute the attack by suggesting counter-arguments and by encouraging them to think up their own arguments to refute the attack. Having met the challenge of the weak attack, people should now have sufficient "cognitive antibodies" to withstand a full-fledged invasion of persuasion germs. This reasoning has some validity. Several studies have found that people who first receive a mild attack on their tooth-brushing beliefs—an attack which is then refuted—are able to hold their ground later against a full-fledged message attacking those beliefs (McGuire and Papageorgis, 1961; Papageorgis and McGuire, 1961). In fact, as you can see from the results of one study, summarized in Figure 6.3, the inoculation defense strategy confers *more* resistance than a supportive defense strategy.

Self-generated defense. The ability to ward off persuasion can be honed to especially high levels when people are motivated and able to generate their own defense against an impending communication. Thus, research shows that forewarned is forearmed. In one experiment, high school students were told that they would hear a speech that

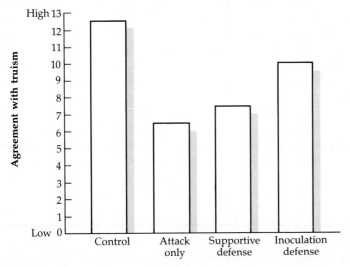

Inoculation Confers Resistance to Attacks on "Truisms"

FIGURE 6.3
A persuasive attack on a cultural truism (e.g., "Frequent tooth brushing is good") caused a considerable decrease in belief in that truism. Subjects were a bit more able to resist when they were first persuaded with arguments that supported the truism (supportive defense). But far more resistance occurred when subjects were first inoculated by receiving a minor attack that they could easily refute. (Data from McGuire and Papageorgis, 1961.)

strongly opposed teenage driving and then heard the speech either immediately or 2 or 10 minutes later. The students' written reactions to the speech revealed that the longer the delay between the forewarning and the speech, the less the persuasive impact of the speech (Freedman and Sears, 1965). As confirmed in later studies, people generate attitude-consistent cognitions in anticipation of an attack, and via the evaluative consistency principle, these cognitions become more numerous and extreme over time (Hass and Grady, 1975; Leippe, 1979; Petty and Cacioppo, 1977). But for all of this to work, people *must* be able to engage in anticipatory counterarguing and must be motivated to do so. Otherwise, forewarning can backfire: people may persuade themselves to accept the attacking position or a neutral position (Cialdini and Petty, 1981; McGuire, 1964).

It may also be possible to get people to generate their own defenses by using reactance. If Ralph Nader were discussing consumerism with children, he might say, "These toy makers think that you kids will run out and buy their toys just because they make them look good in TV commercials." The kids would hopefully respond: "Oh yeah, well we don't need their advice. We'll test those toys out for ourselves."

The concepts of inoculation and self-generated defenses have important societal implications. Of most importance, they argue against systems of socialization and education that teach only the narrowest, most culturally approved ideas and principles while censoring alternative views about lifestyles, social organization, and religion. Left unexposed to other world views, young Americans, for example, may find it difficult to defend their democratic ideals against articulate proponents of different ideologies such as communism. Indeed, this was the situation faced by American prisoners of war in Korea when their Chinese Communist interrogators often knew more about the American Constitution and current events than they did. Education should involve exposure to a wide variety of ideas and ideologies, so as to equip maturing citizens with the means to defend their way of life as well as to recognize where it can be improved.

Marshaling the Forces for Good

The procedures for building resistance to persuasion are being put to use, particularly in programs aimed at teaching children how to deal with negative social pressures. Inoculation and self-generated defense techniques have been used to improve young children's resistance to deceptive TV ads (Feshbach, 1980; Roberts, 1982) and to help sixth and seventh graders resist pressures to start smoking (Evans, 1984; McAlister, 1981). Social psychological techniques are also beginning to be used in training adolescents to resist come-ons to having unsafe sex (Aronson, 1990).

The smoking prevention programs are most developed. Through group discussions led by attractive late-teen role models and careful inducements—adapted from social psychological research—children are encouraged to make a public commitment to not start smoking. Prosmoking arguments likely to be delivered by peers and advertisements are presented, and the kids are taught how to refute them. ("She's not really liberated if she's hooked on tobacco.") The kids may also be asked to think about things themselves—the trusty write-an-essay technique—thereby stimulating self-persuasion. Reactance is aroused by painting peer pressure as constraining freedom of choice.

Another approach to smoking prevention attempts to reach larger groups of kids by using films and posters. The films are a far cry from those in which an adult tells kids to "just say no" (without telling them how to) while rambling on about the long-term dangers of smoking. Instead, recognizing that adolescents are not easily worked up by health ill effects that might occur in 40 years, the films vividly illustrate the immediate effects of smoking, such as measurable amounts of poison (carbon monoxide) on the breath and in the bloodstream. Recognizing as well that adolescents often perceive adults as uninformed about *their* social world, the films also employ poised and attractive adolescent narrators and depict the kinds of situations that adolescents themselves have identified as including great pressure to smoke. As these scenes unfold, the targets of peer and media pressure successfully resist as the narrator explains to the young audience how to be an effective resister (Evans et al., 1981).

A number of studies suggest that these programs are more effective at reducing the proportion of young adolescents who start or continue to experiment with smoking than traditional lecture or informational methods (Flay et al., 1985).

*P*REJUDICE: AN ATTITUDE THAT CAN KILL

We have examined in detail the opposite extremes of overresistance and oversusceptibility to social influence. Both extremes fit into the making and sustaining of the most destructive of all attitudes—those that underlie racial, ethnic, and religious prejudice. Prejudice is usually a product of social influence forces that lay their claim to the minds of the young before they have the ability or motivation to resist them. But once they are prejudiced and all grown up, people staunchly resist liberation from their negative and often hateful views. Let us briefly examine some aspects of this age-old human paradox, of how we can both love and hate our neighbors—today and yesterday.

The Time Is Now

A group of middle-class white youths chase a black youth in a New York neighborhood and brutally murder him because of a false rumor that he is dating one of the neighborhood girls. This incident is only one of a growing number of hate, or "bias," crimes across the United States and throughout the world. In 1989 racial or ethnic incidents were reported on 115 American college campuses (Goleman, 1990).

In Russia, Mikhail Gorbachev relaxes the coercive control that the Soviet Union has exercised over the satellite nations it has annexed since World War II, and we witness the joy of democracies springing up throughout eastern Europe, replacing totalitarian rule with pledges of freedom and equality. But paradoxically, with the return of nationalism comes the resurgence of ancient hostilities between neighboring states and hatred among groups whose religion, culture, or skin color differ. Anti-Semitism comes to the fore as Jews once again are seen as the outsiders. Jewish gravestones are defaced with swastikas.

Japan represents a modern miracle in its transformation from a devastated economy just 40 years ago to a position of economic world supremacy. Despite the affluence that has become a standard for the Japanese, several million live a degraded ghetto life that deprives them of basic civil rights and human dignity. They are the Burakumin, descendants of trades people deemed "impure" in feudal Japan centuries ago. The trades of those once known as *Eta*, meaning "full of filth," included butchering animals to tan their hides and basket weaving. Segregated into designated villages, forced to carry identification marking them as "different," and given inadequate education, these members of Japan's "invisible race" have over the years indeed come to be different from mainstream Japanese society. Their language, manners, customs, and illiteracy set them apart as an inferior caste that is still subjected to scorn as well as economic and political discrimination, which reinforces their ill-deserved status (DeVos and Wagatsuma, 1966).

The Time Is Then

When Thomas Jefferson was drafting the Declaration of Independence, he wrote into his first draft a condemnation of human bondage that denounced George III for propagating slavery in the colonies. But it was omitted from the final version because it was not acceptable to the southern delegation; slavery was just too profitable, despite its immorality.

As late as 1922, there was no federal law against lynching in the United States. An ad in *The New York Times*, seeking to secure passage of such a bill, noted that in the preceding 30 years, over 3,000 Americans had been lynched, and that in the past 4 years, 28 had been burned at the stake by American mobs! The majority of those brutally murdered at the hands of fellow citizens were black men.

Hitler is preparing to assume fascist control of the world and does so not only with military might but with the aid of the most powerful propaganda system ever devised. Through public rallies, films, books, songs, and posters, fear and hopelessness are systematically disseminated to potential enemies of the state. Virulent prejudice is created and intensified against all undesirables of the Fuehrer's so-called "master race," notably Jews. It begins with special texts, like comic books (required reading by all schoolchildren), that portray Jews in the most stereotypically negative manner (Kamenetsky, 1984). When millions of Jews are later rounded up and deported to concentration camps to do slave labor and be gassed, there is no need to justify this suspension of human values; these "enemies" have already been dehumanized in the minds of the German masses.

Prejudice is the bottom line in each of these incidents. It is also at work in less dramatic ways when a child is excluded from play simply because he or she is labeled as unacceptably different, or when a college student is made to feel inadequate because of race, skin color, or religion. Prejudice hurts someone somewhere every day. It can oppress a people, as it does in South Africa where discrimination is institutionalized formally in the laws of the land, and it can demean the human spirit and destroy human life.

Social Psychological Interest in Prejudice

Social psychologists have long been concerned with the dynamics of prejudice. Indeed, modern social psychology can be traced back to World War II, when some psychologists became concerned with understanding how rational individuals could be so readily transformed into mindless masses. Many of these pioneering social psychologists were themselves members of minority groups fleeing to America from the Nazi scourge. Their intellectual interest was in understanding how prejudice develops; their personal goal was to discover strategies for changing prejudiced attitudes and overcoming discrimination.

Prejudice is a puzzle: It seems always to have been part of the human condition even in societies that espouse ideals of equality, fraternity, and democracy. Efforts have also long been made by some groups in those societies to change prejudice, and they have met with only marginal success. While some of the most blatant forms no longer exist in the United States, there is ample evidence that prejudice and discrimination have not disappeared—that they have gone underground, taking on various subtle disguises, especially among the educated.

In the brief space allocated here to this vital topic, all we can do is sketch out some answers to the puzzle of prejudice. (We have touched on aspects of the social learning of prejudice in Chapter 2; and in Chapter 7 we will focus on new research that shows how prejudice can function automatically at nonconscious levels.)

Prejudice is a learned attitude toward a target object that typically involves negative affect, dislike or fear, a set of negative beliefs that support the attitude, and a behavioral intention to avoid, or to control or dominate, those in the target group. It is often a prejudgment based on limited information, which makes the attitude unwarranted and irrational. A prejudiced attitude acts as a biasing filter that influences how individual members of a target group are evaluated. *Stereotypes* are prejudiced beliefs, the set of cognitions that constitute mental schemas about the target group. They support the prejudiced feelings and are invoked by that negative affect or by cues distinctive to the target. Once formed, stereotypes exert powerful influences on how pertinent information is processed, because they serve a basic cognitive goal of simplifying complexity and helping us make our perceived world more predictable and controllable by the act of grouping individual bits of information into categories. In this way, stereotypes influence how information is perceived, organized, stored in memory, and retrieved. When prejudice is acted out, when it becomes overt in various forms of behavior, then *discrimination* is in practice. Because discrimination creates conditions of inequity between citizens, legislation can be enacted to outlaw or punish specific types of discrimination in housing and employment. However, we cannot legislate against holding prejudiced attitudes. Indeed, in recent times, as obvious forms of prejudice in America have declined, racist attitudes have assumed disguised forms that are linked to traditional American values of individualism, self-reliance, and the Protestant work ethic. This new form of prejudice, based on upholding conservative values which are seen as threatened or violated by certain minorities, is known as *symbolic racism* (Kinder and Sears, 1981).

Some Origins of Prejudiced Attitudes

The causes of prejudice are many, complex, and often entwined, thereby explaining some of the difficulty in overcoming prejudice with any single approach. To some extent, prejudice can be analyzed as *dispositional*, as part of the personality and psychoemotional functioning of individuals. A quite different perspective comes from focusing on the *environmental* and *situational* causes (and cures) of prejudice, that is, the role of rewards, punishment, social learning, and conformity pressures. Beyond these twin causes that we have seen operating in most psychological analyses, there are those that operate at a more macro level—the *historical, economic, political* and *sociocultural*. Let's examine and integrate the contributions of each type of analysis (Allport, 1954).

Historical and sociocultural roots. Current discrimination against a target group may represent the carryover of values that were developed years or centuries ago in some particular historical period for reasons that may or may not still prevail. This historical perspective provides a focus for understanding intergroup or even international hostilities that are rooted in ancient traditions, stereotypes, jokes, and belief systems transmitted across generations, without regard for the truth or changing circumstances. The economic advantage accruing to those in power over those they discriminate against is obvious in the institutions of slavery and apartheid, in the treatment of the Burakumin, and in the unequal pay and limits on advancement of women and minorities. Prejudice and discrimination pay off for some people; they did so for the founding fathers of America who were slaveholders, and they still do for those who exploit unskilled and blue-collar laborers in mines and farms and factories. Politics means power, and although economic and political bases of prejudice and discrimination are linked, political causes involve disenfranchising subgroups of the population who might vote against the status quo, attempt to change their lowly state legally, or want ownership of land and property. Finally, a sociocultural analysis of the causes of prejudice informs us about the sociological issues involved: transformation of urban neighborhoods by new immigrants; population density; and cultural values, rituals, and habit patterns that come into conflict when different groups are forced to compete for limited precious resources, jobs, housing, and space.

Dispositions and social environments: A functional analysis. A totally different type of analysis emerges from considering prejudice as part of a distinctive personality style. This view, developed initially by researchers at the University of California's Berkeley campus, highlights a constellation of traits that form the core of the "authoritarian" or "antidemocratic personality" (Adorno et al., 1950). Through questionnaires, interviews, and psychological scales, individuals were identified as being high or low authoritarian personalities, referred to as high-F (fascism) or low-F types. Anti-Semitic prejudice, ethnocentrism, and other values were related to different patterns of child rearing and social learning that fostered a general style of obedience to authority and hostility toward those of lesser status. Such individuals were assumed to be overly susceptible to appeals toward prejudice in the media or by authorities, especially when their sense of security was threatened. This view comes largely from a Freudian orientation in which holding prejudiced attitudes serves the *ego-defensive function* that we discussed earlier in this chapter. The prejudice of some people is a symptom of something wrong with their personality, of repressed hostility and unexpressed conflicts (usually toward their own parents) that are displaced downward onto societally approved scapegoats, the powerless and the "visibly different." These people may then project their own latent impulses toward violence or sexuality onto minority target groups.

If one accepts this view of the origin of prejudice, then the preferred strategy for change involves psychotherapy aimed at gaining insight into the unrecognized link between repressed feelings and prejudiced attitudes and discriminatory actions. However, this view is not accepted by social psychologists as the full explanation of prejudice because it is too narrowly intrapsychic without acknowledging all of the social causes of prejudice. Moreover, if the cure for prejudice depended on getting all the prejudiced people to invest in psychotherapy to rid themselves of a mental problem that they do not know they have, and these people are also the kind who resist opening themselves to personal analysis, then it is an ineffective approach to modifying prejudice in society.

We saw previously that attitudes can serve at least three other functions: knowledge, social adjustment, and value expression. These functions can be served by developing and maintaining prejudiced attitudes. Our basic need for understanding and for meaningfully organizing our personal world of experience in consistent, clear ways is shaped by information and orientations we get from authorities and peers. In many areas they provide accurate information in the form of facts, and so they tend also to be believed when they present their biased opinions about the "facts" of minority groups. This *knowledge function* is open to change when faced with ambiguity provided by new information, that is, when the person changes his or her environment or has positive personal contacts with minority members. Recall from Chapter 5 that exposure in a positive context engages liking and promotes positive cognitive responses.

But often parents, and other influence agents, do more than just transmit information; they create payoffs for believing and acting as they desire. The *social-adjustment function* of attitudes comes into play when we use an attitudinal object to satisfy some need, to get social or tangible rewards and avoid punishments. How can we change prejudice based on the adjustment function? We can change it by changing the reward structure in the situation, by shifting the person to a setting where the payoffs are different, and by refocusing on alternative paths to satisfy those needs and create new levels of aspirations.

Finally, it is central to our daily functioning to maintain a positive self-identity and to act in ways that enhance our self-esteem. Prejudiced attitudes can help to support this *value-expressive function* by giving us a false sense of superiority over those perceived as inferior and less worthy than us. It should be apparent that prejudice based on this function, like the ego-defensive one, is harder to modify than prejudice based on knowledge or the adjustment function. To offset this negative downward form of social comparison, it is essential that the prejudiced person or group be dissatisfied with the current self-image, that the values supporting the old sense of self-superiority be undermined by environmental inputs, and that a new basis be made available for developing a positive self-image not dependent on the suppression of others. This is a tall order, but it means that society and community leaders must be more innovative in finding ways of making their members discover sources of self-esteem within themselves and through their own prosocial activities.

Reducing prejudice and its manifestations in various forms of discrimination, such as apartheid, is one of the most urgent challenges facing our society and our world. It is especially hard because attitudes and social categories form naturally in our mind when people and things seem to fall into natural groupings (Hamilton and Trolier, 1986). Once formed, as we have seen repeatedly, attitudes and other mind-sets affect how we process new information. Biased minds tend to bend objective input into similarly biased "information." Though the task is complex, those armed with a knowledge of social influence and persuasion strategies must be willing to take on a concerted, systematic assault to reduce prejudice and its insidious, pervasively destructive impact on our lives.

A FINAL NOTE: ON HAVING AN OPEN MIND WITHOUT BEING A PUSHOVER

Life's not easy. We can afford to be neither the pushovers discussed in the latter part of this chapter nor the overly stubborn mules of the first part that we all too easily become when established or ego-involved attitudes are on the line. Let us close this chapter with some suggestions on finding the balance: having an open, but not a gullible, mind.

- Be aware of situational and communicator factors known to enhance the chances of influence (see, for example, Andersen and Zimbardo, 1984). And then decide if you are reacting to these cues or to the merits of the message or request. Is the communicator overly emphasizing social consensus or his or her similarity to you? Are the favors being done for you genuine, or possibly designed to make you feel a need to reciprocate? Is the communicator acting overly confident and self-assured? Be sensitive to situational demands however seemingly trivial: role relationships, uniforms, titles, symbols of authority, group pressures, rules, and the language of compliance.

- Practice systematic message analysis so that it becomes a habit in all influence situations of some importance. Look for biases in your thinking. The goal is to be right, not consistent, resistant, or nice. Careful attention to message details increases the chances that "the truth shall win."

- Step back, and take a time-out. Never allow yourself to be pressured to sign on the dotted line *now*. It is always better to take time away from the sales situation to think things over, to get advice from unbiased friends or family before making a costly commitment. Deadlines are rarely fixed and etched in stone. So challenge them.

- Analyze feelings of obligation or guilt in the influence setting. Are they rational? Are they being manipulated by the agent of influence? This will help guard against foot-in-the-door and door-in-the-face sequences of change (see, for example, Cialdini, 1988). Also do what we encourage our students to do: practice being a *victim* or *target* of influence. Put yourself in a vulnerable position in pretending to buy a used car, stereo, expensive sports equipment, or bridal gown; and then note and later analyze the tactics used on you and your feelings toward them. Of course, go with no money, credit cards, or checks in case you lose the war in the influence trenches.

- Practice saying no and dealing with the hassles it invokes. Admit that you are wrong rather than commit a foolish consistency. Be willing to suffer short-term losses in money, time, effort, and even self-esteem, rather than suffer long-term costs of working to reduce dissonance by sticking to a bad commitment. Accept "sunk costs," cut bait, and move out from situations where you made a mistake. Say the three most difficult phrases in the human vocabulary: "I was wrong, I am sorry, and I made a mistake"— and then value the lesson you have learned so that it won't happen again.

- Don't believe in simple solutions to complex personal, social, and political problems; if they were valid, someone would have put them into practice already. Also, in the same vein of reasonable distrust is remembering that instant, unconditional love from strangers can get turned off as fast as it was turned on when you do not do what they want you to. These "microwaved" relationships are suspect; trust takes time to develop and to be earned.

- Avoid "total situations" that are unfamiliar and in which you have little personal control and freedom of action—situations in which you are dependent on others for information, rewards, and direction. Once in one, immediately check out the limits on your independence and authority; discover what the coercive rules are that will imprison you. Check out the physical and psychological exits: be prepared to push the panic button, to shout "help," to accept hassles and threats as the cost of your exiting. This is something that few were able to do in the Milgram studies, or in real-life spouse abusing relationships, cults, and many other settings where the agent of influence has a powerful weapon of "milieu control" (Lifton, 1969).

In short, be a wise consumer of influence. You will certainly be buying a lot of it in your lifetime and will be selling quite a bit directly, and maybe a little on the side. And so the advice outlined here and throughout this book should be taken as more than just "book learning" to be discarded when you do a memory dump right after the course exam. As you will discover, these are vital rules of everyday life, or "street smarts," that can enrich the quality of your life.

*T*O SUM UP . . .

The extremes of influenceability were examined in this chapter. First, we explored why people resist changing their attitudes and beliefs, and we discussed methods by which influence agents can penetrate this resistance. Then we moved on to the opposite situations in which people are overly influenceable, and we discussed how to increase ability to fend off unwanted persuasion. We ended by listing a number of strategies you can use to strike a personal balance between the extremes.

- Resistance to persuasion and to other forms of influence is supported by the "cognitive conservatism" of the human mind. If we have a hypothesis or theory about something, we tend to use a confirmatory strategy as we gather new data to support it. We ask questions whose answers can only "prove" our hunch and take positive instances of the hunch as sufficient evidence for it (without searching for negative instances). This confirmation bias is also evident in how we review past data. We more readily recall what is consistent (versus inconsistent) with current beliefs. Finally, once a belief is shaped by information, we may continue to hold it even if the information is discredited. The belief now rests on ideas we generated through confirmatory thought.

- Motivation may also contribute to resistance to change. Attitude involvement exists when an issue has personal relevance and when the individual is motivated to think about issue-relevant messages. The basis of involvement varies. When the goal is an accurate or socially acceptable belief, and individuals are not invested in an existing viewpoint, they have a construction motive and are open (as far as cognitive conservatism will let them be) to new information relevant to the goal. But people are relatively closed to new information when they have a validation motive: a desire to defend or validate existing viewpoints. A validation motive exists when people are committed to a position and when the attitude is highly self-defining or shared with highly significant others.

- An especially important validation-oriented state is ego involvement, characterized by a tight bond between the attitude at issue and one's self-defining values. Ego involvement is associated with a narrow latitude of noncommitment and a wide latitude of rejection. Close positions are assimilated, seen as identical to one's own; but even mildly discrepant ones are contrasted, distorted to seem very different, and roundly rejected.

- Several influence strategies may help to partially open a closed, validation-oriented mind. First, one can encourage in a message target a sense of accountability to an important other who is interested in belief accuracy. Accountable people evaluate communications in a more complex and balanced fashion. Second, targets can be encouraged to "consider the opposite," to imagine, as they evaluate new information, that truth is the opposite of what they believe. Third, an influence agent can use a linguistic "sleight of tongue." Questions can be posed to the target in ways that prompt an attitude-inconsistent answer, which, through self-attribution and self-persuasion, nudges the attitude into change.

- Knowledge that attitudes serve different functions for different people is the basis of a fourth strategy for overcoming resistance. Attitudes may help express self-defining values, may protect against unconscious conflicts, or may make social acceptance easier. Messages will induce more change if they demonstrate how a different attitude better serves the underlying function, which the influence agent must first discover.

- Whereas established attitudes and beliefs usually resist change, less established ones may be easily swayed. Oversusceptibility to influence is also likely when there is rapid and thorough environmental change, a personal "crisis of belief," or low self-esteem. Cult indoctrination, recruitment into terrorist acts through a process of moral disengagement, and smoking initiation among children are three examples of extraordinary capitulation to influence agents.

- Building resistance into susceptible belief systems entails developing and strengthening the same psychological factors that support our usual cognitive conservatism. This can be done by encouraging people to make a commitment to their existing attitudes and by providing them with attitude-consistent knowledge and experience. People can also be inoculated by weakly attacking their beliefs, or forewarned of impending attacks. Both of these approaches stimulate people to generate their own arguments for their positions—cognitive responses that make counterarguing with full-fledged attacks successful.

- Prejudice is a negative attitude toward some social group. It develops through social and instrumental learning during childhood when individuals are most influenceable. Once formed, prejudiced attitudes are hard to change. They may serve psychic functions (e.g., ego-defense, social adjustment), pay off economically, and be supported by stereotypic beliefs that are repeatedly "confirmed" through biased interpretation of target group information.

QUESTIONS AND EXERCISES

1. Explain why the analogy implied by the term "totalitarian ego" may be an apt one. Now take the analogy further. How is a dramatic conversion or some other capitulation to influence analogous to what can happen to a totalitarian state? (*Hint:* Think about why an attitude might "fall" when there is a total environmental change or a massive attack in comparison to why totalitarian states sometimes suddenly fall—as in eastern Europe in recent years.)

2. Think about the individual you currently most want to change in some way, but who is resisting. Describe previous efforts to change the person that have failed, and analyze why they failed, by using the ideas developed in this chapter. Outline new strategies that, after reading the chapter, you now think may succeed. (If the goal is pro-social or will benefit the target person, try putting them into practice.)

3. Describe a situation in which you were persuaded or otherwise influenced by another person or a group into a behavior or a belief that you later regretted. Analyze this situation in terms of the forces and factors associated with being a "persuasion pushover." In other words, why did you succumb to the social influence attempt?

4. Describe how motives and goals affect the processing of attitude-relevant and belief-relevant information. Identify at least four different motives, and categorize each as either a construction motive or a validation motive.

7

Influence, Awareness, and the Unconscious:

When What You Don't Know May Change You

❖

Awareness and Consciousness of Influence ◆ *Nonverbal (and Not Necessarily Conscious) Messages* ◆ *Subliminals: Inconspicuous Influence* ◆ *Awareness and Consciousness: A Closing Perspective*

*A*s the meeting ended, Bill felt assured that the group decision reached during the meeting was a good one. True enough, when he first entered the meeting, he was not completely sold on the idea of withdrawing corporate sponsorship from the controversial TV show. But Susan Johnson's survey data did prove rather clearly that the kinds of people who are offended by the sexual themes of the show are just the types who buy his company's products. And you can trust Tim Glanville's perceptive sense of critical issues a lot more than the self-serving opinions of Cromwell and Curtis.

So went Bill's justifications for his crucial support for the decision. But then Jean Morano walked up to him and said, "Bill, why do you let Glanville influence you so? Sometimes his control over you is so obvious. Like today, I know you felt differently when the meeting began, but you caved in to his position."

Bill was taken aback. "What do you mean? Johnson's survey was the clincher. Pulling our ads makes sense, regardless of what Glanville thinks. My decision was my own. I wasn't influenced by him at all."

"Come on, Bill. You've known about the survey for days. Once Glanville told us his opinion, you started leaning in his direction. And then he began to bolster your remarks in support of him with praise, a wink of the eye, and his Machiavellian smile which signaled 'You and I know better than these guys, don't we?' And knowing how critical you've been of Cromwell, he made sure to highlight for your benefit just how much he and Cromwell disagree. Although you're usually an independent guy who thinks for himself, it is apparent that Tim Glanville definitely knows how to push your buttons."

Bill continued to protest that the facts alone dictated his decisions. He and Glanville happen to think alike on many matters, that's all. But he'll never convince Jean. To make matters worse, just about every one of Bill's friends agrees with Jean that, on certain matters, Bill is influenced by Glanville.

We all know people like Bill who are regularly influenced by certain others or by certain experiences: yet they do not realize it. But Bill's case also introduces a more general, and more important, point: at times we are all unaware of the forces that shape our attitudes and behaviors. Do you always know when a speaker's sincere smile helped win you over? Or when a commercial jingle aroused a pleasant association that later came to mind and influenced a purchasing decision? Or what it was about the person's style that encouraged you to accept the date?

Influence often occurs at a level below our conscious awareness. Influence tactics may have a predictable effect on how someone thinks, feels, or acts, yet the person is not aware of how those tactics affected his or her state of mind or behavior. For example, you will recall from Chapter 2 that both the low-ball and the foot-in-the-door techniques work in part because they arouse a sense of commitment. But you may not be consciously aware that the reason you are complying is *because* you feel committed. And even if you do consciously feel committed, you probably won't recognize that your sense of commitment was caused by prior compliance with a *deliberately* small request by the person with his little foot in your big door. If you did, we bet you wouldn't agree with the second, larger request. You'd probably angrily revolt against this "obvious" attempt at manipulating you. More often than not, once we are aware that there is a planned attempt to influence us, the influence doesn't happen. Reactance is activated, and we resist—or rebel.

It's the same with cognitive dissonance. We saw in Chapter 3 that situational pressures may occasionally compel you to act contrary to your attitude. When this happens, your attitude may change to conform to the new behavior if you *believe* that you freely chose to engage in the attitude-discrepant behavior. But you did not really have free choice; that was an *illusion* created by the experimenter or the salesperson to provide inducements sufficiently subtle that you do not consciously recognize them, yet powerful enough that they do come to guide your thinking and direct your behavior. The situation made you comply, but you take credit for having made a personal, dispositionally based decision. Researchers have remarked that, in postexperimental interviews, subjects in dissonance studies seldom show any inkling of having been "induced" into doing something. Many are not even aware that they changed their mind about anything, even though they did exactly what the theory and researchers predicted they would do (Bem and McConnell, 1970; Nisbett and Wilson, 1977a).

How can persuasive messages influence us without our full awareness that they are getting to us? One way is through our reliance on heuristic cues. We may not always realize it when we decide to accept or reject the message based on source credibility, audience applause, or some other cue. It is interesting that we tend to be more persuaded by messages that we "overhear"—that do not seem intended for us—than by messages clearly aimed at us (Walster and Festinger, 1962). Apparently, if a message is not seen as a deliberate influence attempt, we cannot make the attribution that the communicator is "just saying that to persuade me." And so we more readily believe the message. Yet we are not always aware when overheard information affects us or that we used perceived intentions as an acceptance cue. "When E. F. Hutton talks, people listen"—especially if he is not talking to them.

We may also not recognize the influence of cognitive *priming*. In a priming procedure, stimuli are first presented that bring to mind a certain idea or mood. Then another stimulus—say, a persuasive message—is presented. Attention may be unconsciously and automatically drawn to certain aspects of the message based on what you are "primed" or "ready" to think about (Sherman, 1987).

In this chapter, we will explore the fascinating interplay between conscious and unconscious perception and thought processes, and the important implications this interplay has for social influence.

First, we will describe how psychologists believe the conscious and unconscious mind works. Then we will apply their theories to such matters as how we come to like or dislike people and things without knowing why. We will consider how some of our responses—even some very important ones—are "mindless" and "automatic." Next we will examine nonverbal communication. It's not just what your words say; it's what your tone of voice, your face, your eyes, and your posture say. Very often, we are not aware of sending nonverbal messages—or of reading and being influenced by them. Last, we will delve into the controversial topic of subliminal influence. Can advertisers send messages to the consumer's unconscious mind and expect more purchases as a return on this hidden investment? We'll see what scientific research has to say about that, and whether this kind of ethically questionable influence really works.

Before we explore unconscious influence, let us note that although we are often unaware of influence forces, there are times when we are very aware of them. In persuasion, for instance, people sometimes consciously choose to use a heuristic rule of thumb to make a decision. You may very seriously reason: "I have no time to analyze this complex message. But I'll trust the source since she is an expert with impressive credentials" (Chaiken et al., 1989). In the preceding chapter, we recommended that, to guard against being too open or too closed to influence, we should try to "get in touch" with what we are reacting to in influence situations. This is possible only within limits imposed by the nature of human consciousness, which enables us to get into "mental touch" with the world around us and its impact on us. But it is what may happen outside those limits—what happens unconsciously—that concerns us in this chapter.

AWARENESS AND CONSCIOUSNESS OF INFLUENCE

So what is consciousness? In general, to be conscious of something is to be aware of it. During our normal waking hours, our consciousness includes visual, auditory, and other sensory perceptions, bodily sensations, emotions, and thoughts. To this we must add our awareness of being aware of these things. We speak of a "stream of consciousness" to describe the sensations and thoughts that move into and out of consciousness as we go through daily life. We do, of course, have some control over the contents of consciousness. We can focus our awareness; we can pay attention to certain stimuli in the external world or to internally generated memories or ideas. And we can hold that attention and concentrate—on a spoken message, for example. This quality of consciousness makes possible "thought out" reactions to stimuli.

Though awareness helps, we need not be aware of stimuli in the environment for them to be registered mentally. Our sensory systems capture a very large amount of external information every waking second. Because we are limited in how much we can pay attention to at once, only some of this vast body of stimulation is consciously noticed. Attention is a limited capacity process. Totally unattended information is held briefly in a "sensory store" or "buffer," and unless attention is shifted to it, this information dissipates rapidly (Broadbent, 1958; 1971).

Researchers have discovered, however, that attention can be *divided* somewhat and that there are *degrees of attention*. What's more, mental analysis of more than one stimulus may go on simultaneously, in a manner referred to as *parallel processing* (Kihlstrom, 1987). Thus, while most of our attention and all our awareness are consumed by one salient piece of environmental stimulation, some unconscious analysis of information in the buffer zone may occur at the same time and then be processed even further to a point where it can enter into decision making and memory. For example, while you are reading this passage and concentrating on those aspects of it that are most important for you to note, there may be music in the background that you "recognize," that you evaluate as your kind of music or not. You may recall when you first heard it, notice you are hungry, realize it is not time for dinner, and try to get back to the ideas you were processing before being so rudely interrupted by your multiple awareness, which interfered with giving this chapter your "undivided attention."

Many cognitive psychologists believe that information need not be noticed before it influences thoughts and behaviors (Bowers, 1984; Mandler and Nakamura, 1987). It is also the case that *higher-order mental processes*—whatever the mind does in the course of judging, evaluating, solving problems, comprehending, and integrating information—are beyond our awareness (Kihlstrom, 1987). As one cognitive scientist noted, "It is the result of thinking, not the process of thinking that appears spontaneously in consciousness" (Miller, 1962, p. 56). Thus, we may not be consciously aware of inconspicuous stimuli that affect us or even of *how* more obvious stimuli enter into our judgments.

Let's look to the world of influence for some evidence of these qualities of consciousness, and for some appreciation of their implications for influence. Specifically, let's examine how (1) emotional attachments (or repulsions) to certain stimuli can be acquired through conditioning and through other processes that we are not even aware are happening; (2) we may be very aware of some stimuli yet unaware of how they are affecting our thoughts and judgments; and (3) some responses to our environment can become automatic habits we perform without the slightest thought.

Awareness, Associations, and Affect

Awareness is not a necessary component in developing emotions. Consider Pavlovian classical conditioning. Given enough pairings of a neutral stimulus (the conditioned stimulus) with one that naturally stirs the emotion (the unconditioned stimulus), the neutral stimulus will gain the power to elicit the same strong emotional response even when later presented alone. Indeed, a strong argument can be advanced that any stimulus a person is capable of perceiving can come to elicit any response he or she is capable of making by proper arrangement of the presentation of conditioned and unconditioned stimuli—any response from a muscle twitch to heart palpitations to anxiety reactions and likes and dislikes.

The father of behaviorism, John Watson, used this notion to make a once fearless infant afraid of anything furry. He demonstrated that strong emotions like fear could be conditioned quickly by pairing any neutral stimulus, like a white rat, with an unconditioned stimulus, like a loud noise that startled the child. Once established, this conditioned fear then generalized to monkeys, dogs, fur coats, and even a bearded mask that had not been directly conditioned to the startle stimulus.

Applied classical conditioning is a favorite technique of advertisers, who often present their products in the context of powerful emotional images like sexually alluring people and nostalgic songs. Controlled laboratory experiments confirm that these conditioning strategies can be powerful and enduring. People have been conditioned to like or dislike neutral words, nonsense syllables (like "wuj"), names, and concepts by repeatedly pairing them with stimuli that are already emotionally charged. In one well-known study, college students rated national names like "Swedish" and "Dutch" more positively when visual displays of these names had previously coincided repeatedly with pleasant spoken words ("happy") than when they had coincided with unpleasant words ("bitter") (Staats and Staats, 1958).

In studies like this, some subjects notice the systematic arrangement of stimuli and some do not (Page, 1969; 1974). But conditioning may occur even among those who do not notice the arrangement. Moreover, whether or not they notice the repeated pairings of the conditioned and unconditioned stimuli, subjects are not necessarily aware that their attitudes (for example, nationality ratings) have been influenced by the pairings (Petty and Cacioppo, 1981).

If the name Pavlov rings a bell with you, what associations does Sigmund Freud evoke? Couches, conflicts, slips of the tongue, and secret selves, for starters. Freud's psychoanalytic theory implies that certain attitudes that have significant behavioral consequences have their basis in associations formed in childhood. The theory states that intense psychic conflicts (often associated with unacceptable sexual and aggressive drives) are *repressed*—kept out of awareness, where they would cause anxiety and threats to our self-worth. They are buried in the deep recesses of the unconscious mind. Certain stimuli were originally associated with the conflict as it developed. When these stimuli are encountered now, they may trigger the association, creating strong anxiety. To ward off that anxiety and continue to keep the conflict under unconscious wraps, the individual employs any one of a variety of ego defense mechanisms, such as denial or projection or rationalization. One form this may take is the development of a conscious reaction in the guise of an ego-defensive attitude toward the stimulus.

Consider Joe Antismut, who is the community leader against any and all forms of pornographic "filth," which he proclaims is polluting the world and making life intolerable for decent citizens. Some such Joes may have an unconscious hang-up about sexuality, so that any sexual stimuli trigger anxiety that the dreaded conflict will emerge into consciousness. How does he keep it in the mental basement where it belongs instead of strutting its stuff in the daylight? *Reaction formation* will work as an ego defense that makes Joe behave in ways opposite to his unconscious inclination. And so he now experiences disgust over anything that is sexually explicit, such as pornography. He develops a belief system to support the perspective that porn harms society. He acts on his new attitude by leading campaigns against allowing "adult bookstores" in his community. He knows how insidious and terrible they are because he personally examined hundreds of these disgusting magazines and 25-cents-per-peek XXX-rated videos. In no way does Joe ever see his dedicated vigilante behavior as related to his personal problems with sexuality.

In terms of the functional theory of attitudes we described in Chapter 6, this "antiporn" attitude is serving an ego-defensive function, allowing partial expression of the sexual part of the conflict yet concealing its true nature. Another person with an unconscious sexual conflict may simply acquire negative attitudes toward products that use advertising themes with sexual connotations. Again, because the conflict is repressed, the individual will not be aware of why he or she dislikes the product.

Commercial music. *Jaws.* Before we even saw the great white shark, we felt fear bordering on panic. The audience had been "set up" by the pulsating bass notes that build to a crescendo in anticipation of something ominous. The first pairing was the music with the sudden disappearance of a young swimmer. Then it was connected with other upsetting events. Finally, *it* was upsetting—upsetting the audience—all by itself.

Commercial films, in movies or television, use music as a vehicle for stirring our emotions—in both positive and negative directions. Advertisements do the same, as we saw in Chapter 5. Here we must emphasize that the conditioning of affect using music can occur unconsciously, even among allegedly sophisticated consumers, such as students in schools of business.

Students in management classes watched what was said to be an ad agency's pilot version of a commercial for a ballpoint pen (Gorn, 1982). In one group of classes, the visual—which contained minimal information about product quality—was accompanied by well-liked rock-and-roll music. In other classes, the same visual was displayed to the tune of disliked (classical Indian) music. There was one more incidental feature: the pen in the commercial was either light blue or beige. After watching and rating the commercial, students were told that, as a reward for their help in evaluating the ad, they had earned a free pen, either a light blue or a beige one. The choice was theirs and, it turned out, was very much a matter of music. The advertised pen—regardless of its color—was chosen by nearly 80 percent of the students exposed to the commercial that had the liked music. In contrast, 70 percent of the students *rejected* the advertised pen when it had been paired with disliked music, choosing instead the pen of the other color. Despite this exceptionally strong effect of the music on choice behavior, only 5 of the 205 participants mentioned the music when later asked to list reasons for their choice of pen.

Music isn't the only stimulus that can be used to condition positive responses to persuasive pitches. Research has shown that subjects were more persuaded by a message when they were given tasty snacks to eat as they listened to it (Janis et al., 1965). The positive quality of the eating experience carried over to evaluations of the message associated with it, even though there was nothing in the message related to food or eating.

The forces of light and dark. A most fascinating study will serve to illustrate further that classical conditioning does not require awareness to have an effect (Zanna et al., 1970). In this study, physiological recordings, such as heart rate, were taken as subjects anticipated and then received mild electric shocks. Subjects believed that the experimenter was interested in developing better measures of physiological arousal. They were told that the onset of a series of one to nine shocks would be signaled by a certain spoken word, whereas the end or offset of a series of shocks would be signaled by a second word. For one group, the word "light" preceded each shock series, whereas the word "dark" followed the final shock in the series. For a second group, the signals were reversed: "dark" was the onset signal, and "light" was the arbitrary offset signal.

Now electric shock is unquestionably an unconditioned stimulus: getting shocked heightens arousal naturally, without any prior learning. The test of conditioning came late in the session when the onset word—light or dark—was presented but was not followed by any shocks. Was there heightened arousal anyway? For nearly three-fourths of the subjects this was indeed the case. The onset word had become a conditioned stimulus for them; its mere presentation elicited arousal.

By itself, this result is no more remarkable than the drooling of Pavlov's dogs when they heard a bell that had formerly signaled the presentation of food. What is most remarkable came in part two of the study. Later that same day, the conditioned subjects participated in a second, seemingly unrelated study. Supposedly as part of a study of meaning, a different experimenter asked them to rate twenty words on several bipolar scales, including good-bad, pleasant-unpleasant, and beautiful-ugly. You guessed it. "Light" and "dark" were among those words. Figure 7.1 presents the mean ratings of these words by conditioned subjects. Subjects for whom the word "light" had been a signal

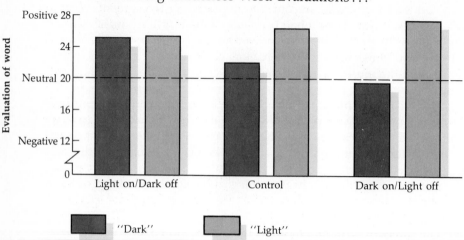

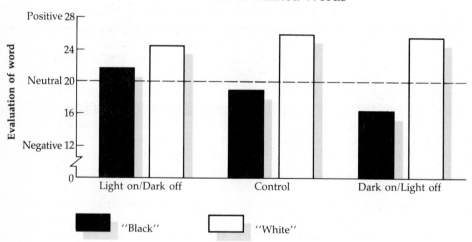

FIGURE 7.1

Normally, "light" is a better-liked word than "dark" (control condition). But when "light" repeatedly preceded the onset of an electric shock, it became less positively evaluated, while "dark" became more positively evaluated when it repeatedly followed the offset of the shock (light on/dark off). When the positioning of the words was reversed, "dark" became less liked and "light" more liked (dark on/light off). These conditioned changes in liking generalized to the related words "black" and "white," which were evaluated in a completely unrelated context. Conditioning can be unconscious.

(Data from "conditionable" subjects reported by Zanna, Kiesler, and Pilkonis, 1970. Copyright 1970 by the American Psychological Association. Adapted by permission.)

of shock on the way rated "light" less positively than those for whom it was an end-of-shock signal. Similarly, "dark" received lower ratings when it had been an onset signal than when it was an offset signal. Both arousal and affect had been conditioned. Subjects *liked a word less* when it had been repeatedly associated with electric shock. This conditioned affect even generalized to similar stimuli, to two closely related words. "White" and "black" were also among the words rated in the "second study." Subjects conditioned to like "light" less also liked "white" less and "black" more, compared with subjects conditioned to like "dark" less.

These shifts in liking for common words were neither deliberate nor conscious. Interviews revealed that not one subject saw a connection between the two studies, and it is unlikely that conscious processes were at work in changing likes and dislikes for shock-related words. It appears that, without conscious awareness, affective associations are readily formed and enter into choices and decisions.

Unexposed exposure. Another line of evidence that we can be unaware of why we like or dislike something comes from research on the "mere exposure leads to liking" relationship we discussed in Chapter 5. You will recall that in a typical study, numerous novel stimuli, such as Chinese ideographs, are presented, some more often than others. Later, subjects rate how much they like these and other (never seen) items. Generally, the more often an item was presented, the more it was liked. A slight modification of this procedure has subjects indicate not only their level of liking for each item but also whether or not they remember having seen the item previously. An intriguing outcome is that the "exposure leads to liking" effect occurs even for items that subjects do not recognize having seen before. An item presented ten times but not recognized as familiar is preferred over a similarly unrecognized item that was presented only once or twice (Moreland and Zajonc, 1979). Subjects seem unaware of how they developed their preferences. Preferences need no conscious awareness.

Preferences may even form for stimuli whose presentation was *subliminal*. The word is taken from the Latin *limen*, which means "threshold." Adding the prefix *sub*, we have "below threshold." Subliminal perception refers to a stimulus being mentally encoded at some level—even though it was presented with less than the minimum duration of time or sensory energy necessary to be consciously noticed—below the threshold of awareness. Later, we will examine subliminal processing and its broader implications for influence in some detail. But for now let's just focus on the link between awareness and affect—the beneath-the-surface link.

In one study, stimulus items (irregular octagons) were presented for only a single millisecond (one one-thousandth of a second): too briefly to be consciously perceived (Kunst-Wilson and Zajonc, 1980). In the first phase of the experiment, ten octagons were presented on a screen for 1 millisecond each. All the subjects could see was a flash, but they were instructed to watch the screen carefully and to acknowledge verbally the occurrence of each flash. In the second phase, each subliminally presented "old" octagon was displayed for a full second, alongside a "new" octagon that had never been presented. Subjects were asked which octagon they recognized as having seen before and which one they preferred. They did no better than pure guessing at the first question, correctly identifying the true "old" item only half of the time. Yet, averaging over subjects, the "old" subliminally presented item was liked better than the "new" one 60 percent of the time. And 75 percent of the subjects showed a significant overall preference for the old octagons they had no memory of having seen!

As Robert Zajonc (1980) puts it, in reviewing this and related literature, "preferences need no inferences." He suggests that the human brain and senses are composed of two relatively separate systems: one for thought and one for feeling. While the former plods along figuring things out, the affective system "gets a feel" for incoming stimuli quickly and efficiently. Is something good or bad? Pleasant or unpleasant? Harmful or harmless? Friend or foe? A speedy affective system would have well served our preverbal ancestors, whose chances for survival depended on the ability to rapidly identify and classify things as likely to bring pleasure (then approach and feast safely) or harm (then flee with alacrity).

Of course, humans eventually evolved language and language-based thought and, with these, more flexible and diverse ways of making decisions. But the propensity to make automatic affective responses still exists—because speed and simplicity still have survival value in our complex and wordy world. The central point is that we humans seem to be equipped with sensory and neurological mechanisms that allow us to respond swiftly with feeling to a stimulus even before we can articulate the stimulus in words and so become consciously aware of it. In this way, we can play the music first, get the dance started, and save the lyrics for later.

Awareness and "Higher-Order" Mental Processes

It is not only simple associations that can be formed without awareness. As noted earlier, the *processes* involved in higher-order cognitive activities, by which information is comprehended and integrated, are not conscious. It is not thinking but the *products* of thought that appear in the mind and direct behavior. Because we have no conscious access to

Some ads are neither subtle nor subliminal in their efforts to condition associations and elicit emotions. Someone "got the message" projected by this ad, and didn't like it.   (*Bruce Kliewe/The Picture Cube*)

how the mind acts on stimuli and integrates them, we typically cannot accurately report how particular stimuli affected our behavior. And so even the complex effects of quite salient and visible stimuli may be unknown to us, because we have no conscious access to the cognitive processes those stimuli trigger. Unawareness extends far beyond conditioning and mere exposure to the most fundamental processes which human beings rely on to cope with the complexities of their world.

Our lack of access to higher-order mental processes has several implications. For one thing, it helps explain why cognitive dissonance and compliance effects occur only when influence targets do not know how and by what they are being manipulated.

One research team conducted tests of the hypothesis that influence targets typically "don't know what hit them" when they make seemingly rational decisions (Nisbett and Wilson, 1977a). In one study, shoppers took part in what was described as a consumer survey. They were asked to compare four pairs of nylon stockings arranged from left to right on a table, and to choose which pair was the best quality. In actuality, the four pairs were all the same brand. Yet there was a clear pattern to the shoppers' choices: the further to the right a pair of stockings was, the more often it was declared the best. In fact, *four times* as many shoppers chose the right-most pair as opposed to the left-most pair. However, they were unaware of the influence that position played in their decisions and even rejected that notion when it was suggested to them.

In another demonstration of how people are unaware of what has actually influenced them, psychology students watched one of two versions of a videotaped interview of a college professor (Nisbett and Wilson, 1977b). In the *warm* version, the professor answered questions pleasantly and enthusiastically, and he was complimentary to students. In the *cold* version, the same professor was unpleasant—rigid, intolerant, and insulting to students. Quite understandably, students who saw the warm interview reported greater liking for the professor than those who watched the cold interview. More interesting, however, is how students rated the professor's physical attributes. In both interviews, the professor was dressed exactly the same way, had the same mannerisms, and spoke with the same European accent. Even so, huge differences in ratings of appearance, mannerisms, and accent were evidenced. Most subjects who saw the professor behaving warmly also found him handsome and suave, with a charming accent. In contrast, those who saw his cold version generally found him unattractive and were annoyed by his mannerisms and accent—same qualities *in*, opposite impressions *out*. This is a most dramatic example of what we have seen many times: perception can be much influenced by attitudes. People see and interpret things in evaluatively consistent ways. Those who study impression formation call this phenomenon the *halo effect*, a tendency to evaluate all components of a target person in the same way once a general evaluation, positive or negative, is formed.

But the real punch line of this experiment is what subjects reported about their judgments of the professor's physical attributes according to their association with liking or disliking this warm or cold teacher. Most subjects believed that it was his physical attributes that contributed to their liking or disliking of the man. This was impossible, of course, since the attributes were exactly the same in the warm and cold conditions. It appears that, because of this unconscious halo effect, beauty is more than skin deep. In a way, beauty is as "deep" as the target's personality and as bright as the eye of the beholder. Likable people look more beautiful *because* they are perceived to be likable (and cold professors become ugly in the eyes of their students).

When we venture out of the laboratory and away from the world of college student subjects, we still find that ordinary people—your mother, my brother, his uncle—are often unaware of the causes of their own judgments and behavior. Yet when asked, people readily explain the causes of their behavior. Sometimes these explanations are accurate; often they are not. Yet the explanations are always ready and available. Why?

According to Richard Nisbett and Timothy Wilson (1977a), the explanations are nothing more than *plausible attributions*. Based on a lifetime of watching our own and others' behavior, of articulating attitudes, values, and beliefs, and of hearing and reading stories of human responses to the social and physical environment, we develop theories about what causes what for whom under what circumstances. Recalling our discussion of culturally approved causal schemas in Chapter 3 may give you another basis for appreciating this human universal reaction of making causal sense of our reactions and those observed in others. From this wellspring of naive personal theories we devise an explanation of what stimuli were influencing us at any given time and predict what stimuli will affect us in the future. Sometimes our theories are right on; and sometimes they are off base. The trouble is that we usually cannot discriminate the right from the wrong times and don't collect the kind of evidence that will help us know how to improve our ability to make such important evaluations.

This analysis suggests that, by being careful observers of our own and others' behavior, we can improve the accuracy of our explanations. In addition, there is a way to increase the influence of factors you believe *should* influence you. You can approach important decisions mindfully and with systematic thought, as recommended in the last chapter. You might not be aware of all the "churning wheels" of your mind, but you can consciously place what you consider important into the works, and more mindfully contemplate the products of those unconscious intermediate thought processes. Perhaps most important is to sustain a kind of "mental flexibility" and not rush to rigidity in coming up with explanations or attributions for why you did or did not do something. Most behaviors have several contributing factors: some in the present setting, some activated from your memories of past situations, and some that are part of your anticipation of future consequences or payoffs. Think provisionally, as scientists do, by generating likely hypotheses—to be evaluated first by attempting to find *disconfirming evidence* before seeking confirmation. Be mindful.

Shifting into Automatic

Speaking of mindfulness, let's now consider another aspect of consciousness. With practice and repetition, patterns of behavior become automatic: they can be executed "without a thought." Driving a car is a good example. While first learning to do it, you must pay close and deliberate attention. You are conscious of everything you are doing, and the slightest distraction may cause a major mistake. After a while, however, driving is a cinch. You gab with your passenger, change radio stations, sing along, or get lost in contemplation of how to frame that paper you must write this week. Driving is the furthest thing from your conscious mind. But, unconsciously, you're giving some attention to driving. Should a car suddenly whip in front of you, your foot goes to the brake—automatically.

Psychologists refer to this state of affairs as *divided consciousness*. Consciously, you're tuned into one thing; unconsciously, to another, in such a way that your behavior seems to be on automatic pilot.

There is every reason to expect the same kind of arrangement with *cognitive* responses to social influence. Given enough "practice" listening to or reading persuasive messages and such, we learn the routine. Unconsciously, we respond to influence stimuli in routinized, automatic ways, even as we talk, daydream, or consciously think about something else. This is precisely the basis of the heuristic rules of thumb described in previous chapters. Certain cues (such as an authority figure) automatically suggest certain responses (such as obedience).

Sweet nothings in a mindless ear. Some responses to social stimuli are so automatic they have been labeled *mindless* (Langer, 1989). In one field experiment, a confederate approached students waiting in line to use a library photocopier and asked if she could go ahead of them. When she simply asked the favor (May I use the copier?), 60 percent let her cut in. This shows that the majority of these students comply with the basic compliance-gaining strategy of merely requesting a favor. How could that effect be increased? She then asked the favor of other students with a slight change in wording: "May I use the copier because I have to make some copies?" Compliance went wild with a whopping 93 percent complying (Langer et al., 1978). Mysterious, isn't it? How was this increase in "favor doing" accomplished by simply adding an idiotic redundancy? Apparently, the word "because" evoked its magic. It's a catchword. "Because" implies a reason for the request, and such "evidence" of a reason on its way triggers an automatic response—just as a suddenly changing traffic light triggers the shifting of the driver's foot to the brake. Such mindlessness happens when we're not processing systematically; and it obviously happens outside our consciousness.

People who are cruising on automatic, going through a routine that requires no focused awareness, can be easily influenced. Harvard psychologist Ellen Langer, who has conducted extensive investigations of the mindless state, adds a cogent anecdotal example:

> Once I was walking in midtown Manhattan when my attention was drawn to a large sign in the window of a tourist shop that for the past twenty years or so has been "going out of business." This sign announced "Candles That Burn!" Thinking that special candles make nice presents, I was about to go in and take advantage of this novel offering when it occurred to me that all candles burn (1989, pp. 50–51).

Langer was rescued by a sudden lapse into mind*ful*ness from an entrepreneur who clearly understands "mindless shoppers."

The difference a category makes. Langer characterizes the state of mindlessness as a passive and reactive one in which overly learned rules and categories are automatically imposed on a situation, or to some structural features of it, like "because." To be mindless is to be unable to think beyond a mind-*set*, to be "trapped by categories." In one study, a rigid categorical label stunted creativity. People who were told in no uncertain terms what an object was ("This is a hair dryer") later could think of fewer alternative uses for it than other subjects who were given only tentative labels for the object ("This could be a hair dryer") (Langer and Piper, 1987). In another study, professional psychotherapists saw a lot of abnormality and maladjustment in the filmed interview responses of a man who was said to be a "patient" on a psychiatric ward. This is interesting, because another group of therapists watched the same interview and concluded that the man was well adjusted. The difference was that the "normal" man was introduced to these therapists as a "job applicant" (Langer and Abelson, 1974).

This consciousness-limiting aspect of preset categories has important implications for influence. If you want to maintain the status quo, nurture a sense that "this is the way it was, is, and always will be." Chances are the habitual behavior will continue unquestioningly. If your goal is to have people "see things in a new light," the trick is to get them out of their established mind-sets. People become more mindful when they encounter novel stimuli that do *not* fit established categories, when their teachers and preachers instruct and guide conditionally ("It depends" instead of "It is certain"), and when they are motivated to engage in systematic thinking, rather than lapse into mindless processing.

We have now seen that much mental processing of influence stimuli occurs unconsciously. And so our moods, likes and dislikes, and decisions may be readily manipulated by influence agents without our awareness through applications of conditioning, repeated exposure, and catching us in a mindless state. With these thoughts consciously in mind, let us move to a discussion of a class of communication stimuli whose influence is especially likely to be unconscious and automatic: the nonverbal behaviors that accompany people's words.

*N*ONVERBAL (AND NOT NECESSARILY CONSCIOUS) MESSAGES

"Remove her gag," Paul commanded.

Jessica felt the words rolling in the air. The tone, the timbre excellent—imperative, very sharp. A slightly lower pitch would have been better, but it could still fall within this man's spectrum.

Czigo shifted his hand up to the band around Jessica's mouth, slipped the knot on the gag.

"Stop that!" Kinet ordered.

"Aw, shut your trap," Czigo said. "Her hands're tied." He freed the knot and the binding dropped. His eyes glittered as he studied Jessica.

Kinet put a hand on the pilot's arm. "Look, Czigo, no need to..."

Jessica twisted her neck, spat out the gag. She pitched her voice in low intimate tones. "Gentlemen! No need to fight over me." At the same time, she writhed sinuously for Kinet's benefit.

She saw them grow tense, knowing that in this instant they were convinced of the need to fight over her. Their disagreement required no other reason. In their minds, they were fighting over her.

She held her face high in the instrument glow to be sure Kinet would read her lips, and said: "You musn't disagree." They drew further apart, glanced warily at each other. "Is any woman worth fighting over?" She asked.

By uttering the words, by being there, she made herself infinitely worth their fighting.

Paul clamped his lips tightly closed, forced himself to be silent. There had been the one chance for him to succeed with the Voice. Now—everything depended on his mother whose experience went so far beyond his own.

Frank Herbert, *Dune*

In this scene from Frank Herbert's science fiction classic, the heroine eventually escapes death by controlling her unsuspecting captors with the way she uses her voice and her body. According to the *Dune* story she was genetically bred and trained in these nonverbal skills. At one point, Jessica's movements and tone of voice communicate the opposite ("Fight over me") of what her words said ("Don't fight over me"), and her nonverbal gestures prevailed. Science fiction writers have long been fascinated with the possibility of a sophisticated science of nonverbal communication in which precise use of voice tone and eye contact would allow social control, as Jessica exercised. One reason for this fascination with the nonverbal is that control with spoken words is often difficult. Words evoke conscious thought—and possibly counterarguments. But the eyes and the nuances of voice can be outside the word stream that dominates the listener's consciousness. While people attend to the words, these nonverbal stimuli may sneak in the side door; while they are trying to comprehend the lyrics, the beat goes on and in.

Farfetched? Frankly, in the extreme forms and potency of science fiction, yes. But judging from the research of social scientists, more modest claims for the influence of nonverbal communication aren't at all "other worldly." By *nonverbal communication* is meant everything *besides the words* that comes across from one person to another in a social exchange (Harper et al., 1978). There are two channels of nonverbal transmission. The *paralinguistic channel*, emphasized in the science fiction scene, includes the auditory characteristics of speech other than the words and sentences. Speech rate, pitch, and loudness are qualities of paralanguage, as are tone of voice and the placing of inflections. In the last case, consider the difference in meaning conveyed when you say, flatly, "good job" as opposed to "go-o-o-d job!" with an emphasis on the drawn out "good." The *visible channel* includes aspects of communication that we can see: gestures, posture, facial expressions, eye movements and contact, and even clothing and makeup.

How important, really, are nonverbal messages? Well, scan your memory for the most dramatic persuader you have ever come across. Chances are that person had a dynamic nonverbal style that got you excited, kept you interested, and convinced you of the person's sincerity. Anyone who has ever fallen asleep during a lecture knows that it takes more than words to keep attention, much less persuade.

Former President Ronald Reagan represents a vivid testimonial to the power of the nonverbal. Reagan acquired a revealing nickname during his presidency. Political and media analysts dubbed him "The Great Communicator." Yet the *content* of Reagan's speeches reveals few great insights— arguably no more than the average U.S. President, and in many cases less. His presidential speeches were neither flowery nor poetic. His vocabulary was rather simple. And he often made great leaps of logic or lost his train of thought when he stopped referring to his 3 × 5 index cards.

But his speeches were certainly effective. This was a President who, for a long time, enjoyed a record high approval rating from the public, even from Democrats. This President was also a modestly successful Hollywood actor for several decades. And accordingly, it was less what he said than *how he said it* that made Reagan both popular and capable of eliciting agreement and support from the American public. We noted back in Chapter 1 that Reagan's speech, voice, and facial expressions revealed a sincere, as well as humble, "I'm just relying on good old common sense" persona. The smiles and the eye contact with the audience were typically perfectly in synchrony with the spoken sentiment. The audience never got the sense that Mr. Reagan was "putting on appearances." He was being "himself," being "real," although one Washington correspondent has argued that Reagan's great skill was imagining himself as an actor, playing the role of President.

Nonverbal communication is a big part of the *image* factor we mentioned in Chapter 4. "Image processing" of political candidates for TV tries to exploit audience responsiveness to nonverbal cues. On the visual side, former President Richard Nixon was advised to have better posture because his stooping shoulders were thought to make him look old and unenergetic. In his televised debates with President George Bush, the 1988 Democratic candidate Michael Dukakis stood on a platform to make him look taller.

On the paralanguage side, Dukakis learned the hard way that tone can matter a lot more than words. In his final televised debate with

Bush, Dukakis was asked if he might come to favor the death penalty if his own wife, Kitty, was brutally raped and murdered. Dukakis answered that he would still oppose the death penalty, noting that there is no evidence that capital punishment is a deterrent to violent crime and that killing Kitty's assailant would not bring her back. Reasonable arguments. But they fell flatter than a week-old beer in the bar at *Cheers*. Dukakis was widely criticized for his answer, even by Democratic opponents of capital punishment. Why? Because the answer was totally without passion. Dukakis expressed no emotion over the thought of his wife meeting a horrible fate; or did he give any nonverbal sign that he knew how worried Americans were about violent crime. Regardless of how he felt, there was no emotion at all in his voice or pain on his face. The audience was forced to ask: Where is the passion behind the logic? What kind of man is this? No doubt a very good man, who would be terribly pained by any harm that befell a loved one. But no such impression came across; the damage was done to his image, and that impression contributed to his downfall.

Now that you have conjured up some famous images, let's add a few more. Visualize and "replay" the audio of John F. Kennedy, Martin Luther King, Jr., Mikhail Gorbachev, and Jesse Jackson. With the nonverbal styles of powerful communicators in mind, let us look at the revealing research about nonverbal communication as a factor in influence. In the following sections we will discover that *how* something is said can have as significant an impact as *what* is said, and that this effect often occurs without our awareness of the cues that are turning us on or off to social influence. We will see that aspects of voice (such as loudness) and eye contact affect impressions and attributions about control in social exchanges; emotions may be revealed in facial expressions and may, in turn, influence the emotions of the perceiver; lies may be "given away" by nonverbal cues; and certain vocal and gestural qualities affect persuasion and even self-perception.

People Reading: Forming Impressions from Voice and Face

Visual and paralinguistic components of speech affect the impressions we form of others, and usually we are fully aware of the nonverbal qualities that will create a specific impression. We may use them to manage our own impressions, and we read them in other people's nonverbal signs to us. A person who blushes easily and avoids eye contact with new acquaintances probably will be considered shy. Someone who (in turning to talk to you) moves his or her head, neck, and shoulders as though they were a single unit and whose hands, wrist, and arm likewise move in the same "unitized" fashion conveys the message of being a high-status person. Transient emotions as well, such as anger, each have telltale nonverbal signs that we can consciously look for, such as a glaring stare and a suddenly raised voice. Theatrical coaches and directors can teach actors the specific gestures and expressions needed to elicit specific emotions in the audience. Our awareness of these signals reflects the fact that within a culture certain expressive behaviors become norms: we all, early on, develop quite similar habits of emotional and trait expression, and learn to recognize and identify these expressions in others (Mehrabian, 1981).

Moreover, at least seven basic emotions seem to be experienced across cultures and are associated in all cultures with the same facial expressions (Ekman and Friesen, 1971; 1986). These *universal expressions* of emotion are pictured in Figure 7.2. When these facial poses have been presented to American college students, members of a preliterate culture in New Guinea, children as young as 6 years of age, as well as other disparate groups, they all agree on which emotion each expression conveys. When members of various cultures and age groups are asked to "make a face" to convey the emotions, they basically make the same faces.

Our *use* of nonverbal cues to infer someone's characteristics is often an instance of applying a judgmental heuristic. Because nonverbal behavior often does accurately reflect a certain trait, a shortcut method of "figuring out" people is to look at what they do instead of systematically analyzing what they say. If a speaker is speaking smoothly and rapidly, she must "know her stuff." If your friend breaks out in a smile when he sees little babies, he must like babies. Most interesting for our present concern in this chapter are those occasions when we make inferences from nonverbal behavior unconsciously—automatically—without deliberate intent to "read" the person.

Who's in charge? The louder one. Such unconscious, subtle influence is well illustrated in a study of the paralinguistic variable of speech loudness. When we describe a person as "loud," the next word that often comes to mind is "obnoxious." Nobody likes a loudmouth. On the other hand, nobody pays attention to those who are too soft-spoken. As we saw in Chapter 3, research indicates that observers attribute more causal power and control to the people in a social exchange who attract their attention. Drawing on this relationship, one pair of researchers reasoned that if people pay more attention to the louder voice in a two-person conversation, they should attribute more conversational influence to the owner of that voice, provided the voice is not obnoxiously loud (Robinson and McArthur, 1982).

To test this idea, they had subjects listen to a 5-minute conversation in which the two participants' voices emanated from different speakers. Speaker A's voice was put through at 75 decibels; and speaker B's, at 70

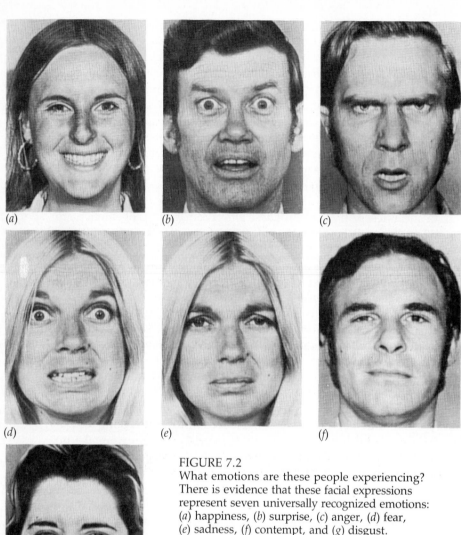

FIGURE 7.2
What emotions are these people experiencing?
There is evidence that these facial expressions
represent seven universally recognized emotions:
(a) happiness, (b) surprise, (c) anger, (d) fear,
(e) sadness, (f) contempt, and (g) disgust.
(From Ekman and Friesen, 1986.)

decibels. This difference is a slight one, just barely noticeable. But it was large enough to get subjects to attend more to the louder voice. And sure enough, subjects consistently rated the conversation partner with the louder voice—speaker A—as having played a greater causal and controlling role in the conversation, and as being more friendly and logical. The mean ratings are presented in Figure 7.3. Note that this impact of loudness has nothing to do with who was speaking or what was said. When it was switched and speaker B owned the louder voice, but all other aspects of the conversation remained the same, the impression of speaker A as the stronger causal influence was greatly reduced (it seems to have persisted a tiny bit because A was a slightly more forceful speaker). Now who was judged as more friendly and logical? The louder speaker B, of course.

Five decibels went a long way in shaping how college students judged other people. If you now told them that their "sensitive, perceptive" evaluations of social and cognitive attributes of others were being manipulated by the variable of speech volume, what do you think they would say? No way! In reply we can say that there is a way: no awareness!

Powerful displays of power. This study suggests that power and influence can be communicated by the intensity or loudness of one's voice. The message to women is clear: talk up or get judged as less influential than louder-talking, less expert men. When students rate their teachers, both sexes judge female professors to be less "dynamic/enthusiastic" than male professors. But then only male students allow this judgment, based heavily on behavioral style, to bias their evaluations of female teachers as also being less scholarly, clear, and organized (Basow, 1986).

A variety of nonverbal behaviors signal who is dominant in face-to-face encounters and who is more credible in speaker-to-audience situations. As gaze toward an audience increased, a speaker was viewed as more skilled, informed, and experienced, as well as more honest, friendly, and kind (Beebe, 1974). So you should not only look before you leap; you should look while you speak. In a two-person exchange, the person who is dominant—because of higher status, greater expertise, or some other asset—typically has the higher *visual dominance ratio* (Exline et al., 1975). Compared with the partner, the dominant person spends proportionately more time looking at the partner while talking than looking while listening. Powerful people look at you when they speak but aren't obliged to look when you're speaking. In addition, the dominant person tends to smile less, gesture more, and make more chin thrusts than the less dominant person. A fascinating series of studies has shown that young adults make these nonverbal displays of power automatically and unconsciously, and that observers infer power differences from these displays (Dovidio and Ellyson, 1982; Dovidio et al., 1988a and 1988b).

Loudness (and thus Salience) Influences Impressions

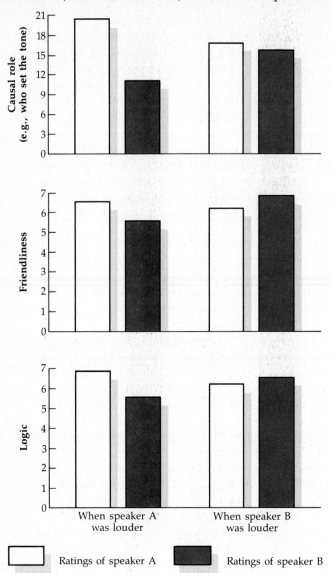

FIGURE 7.3
Subjects heard a tape-recorded exchange between two people, speaker A and speaker B. The exchange was exactly the same except that either speaker A or speaker B spoke 5 decibels louder than the other. Whoever spoke louder was rated as more friendly and logical. Speaker A generally was seen as having more causal influence over the conversation, but the difference was much greater when speaker A spoke louder. (Data from Robinson and McArthur, 1982. Copyright 1982 by the American Psychological Association. Adapted by permission.)

In one of these studies, mixed-sex pairs of college students discussed, in a random order, three topics: one traditionally more familiar to men (automotive oil changing), one traditionally more familiar to women (pattern sewing), and one more or less "gender neutral" (vegetable gardening). The conversations were videotaped, and each participant's verbal and nonverbal behavior was later coded from these tapes. When the conversation topic was a masculine one, the male conversation partners dominated the conversation, initiating more conversation and generally talking more, all of which is consistent with the higher status they had by virtue of greater expertise. They also displayed their power nonverbally. Compared with their female partners, males had a higher visual dominance ratio, smiled less, gestured more, and thrust out their chins more frequently.

On the feminine task, where the status difference was reversed, the opposite pattern prevailed. Females dominated conversation and engaged in more nonverbal power displays. What do you think should have happened in the discussion of the gender-neutral activity (vegetable gardening)? In the absence of expertise on either side, will dominance displays emerge? Well, they did, and right along sexist lines. The males assumed dominance in the discussion of vegetable gardening, showing it in their visual, gestural, and facial behavior. Subjects seem to have slipped right into traditional sex roles. When neither partner had the edge on prior knowledge or experience, the man took the dominant role and displayed his dominance for the woman, and all other observers, to see. Both the men and the women in this study were unaware that their nonverbal behavior was so sensitive to both expertise and culturally conditioned sexism. One implication of this line of research is that "nonverbal sex and gender differences in behavior may be subtle but significant variables in shaping power relationships between men and women" (Dovidio et al., 1988b, p. 586).

Differences in *behavioral styles* between people help create different cognitive structures in the minds of observers as well as in the minds of those who are interacting. Evaluative judgments and attitudes are then formed such that those with high status and power are perceived to be more competent and intelligent. What they say gets listened to more and has greater potential impact; and thus a self-fulfilling prophecy cycle is formed.

To demonstrate this effect, researchers systematically varied the behavioral style of a person who role-played a juror in a personal injury lawsuit. This juror argued an extremely deviant position on how much money should be awarded in the case. His arguments were videotaped and watched by subjects who had to make the final monetary judgment. They were most influenced when the juror displayed a high-status behavioral style—deference demanding—and least influenced when he acted out the low-status role—deferential. What is most important for us to note is that the juror gave identical arguments in each version of the video: the content was held constant, and only the styles were varied. Finally, the juror's impact was greater when displaying high-status behaviors than when described to the subjects as having a high-status occupation but not acting as a high-status person (Lee and Ofshe, 1981).

Confident displays of confidence. Central to persuasion, especially in two-person interactions, is the *expression of confidence.* In a series of studies using pairs of subjects who acted as jurors deliberating a law case, a researcher found that persuaders (those who got the other person to change her verdict) used words expressing confidence, while those who were persuaded in these dyadic persuasive interactions tended to use words expressing doubt (London, 1973). Then confidence, which was naturally expressed in the initial research, was experimentally manipulated to demonstrate that it was the causal variable in this persuasion process. The researcher separated the words from the behavioral style by having the actor mouth the same words, which were dubbed onto the three video tracks with different amounts of expressed confidence.

The results are clear: expressed confidence is a key predictor of persuasion in interpersonal situations, whether expressed in language or paralinguistically. However, too much wordy confidence can backfire to generate antagonism in the other person. In general, the strategy used by those female subjects who were the most effective persuaders was to change the persuadee but also maintain the social bond with her. They used two tactics to achieve this complex goal: (1) expressing confidence in their ability and cause but (2) decreasing the persuasive pressure and ingratiating themselves as soon as it was clear that the victory was about to be won. And so they influenced people and won friends as well. Usually neither party was consciously aware of the interplay of this "deep" strategy and the mechanisms by which it was being expressed.

The Sights and Sounds of Feelings and Lies

Some theorists have suggested that *most* of the useful information for forming impressions and reading emotions may come from nonverbal messages rather than from the words (Mehrabian, 1972). But is this really the case?

In one study, subjects were exposed to segments of a political debate in which the speaker was clearly expressing positive or negative emotions (Krauss et al., 1981). Some subjects saw unadulterated (all-channel) videotapes of these segments and quite easily discerned the emotional tone of the various speech segments. For other subjects, the researchers set up a contest pitting communication channels against each other, by removing one or more channels from the segments. One group read transcripts of the segments; they got the words but no visual and very little paralinguistic information. Another group of subjects got only visual information because they watched the videotape with the sound turned off, causing loss of both language and paralanguage. Yet another group listened to a filtered audiotape in which the speech was unintelligible but paralinguistic features like pitch and loudness remained. Which channel would best communicate emotion? The written word? Visual only? Paralinguistic only? By far the best judgments of emotion occurred in the *transcript* condition, where almost no nonverbal information was available. It was subjects who read transcripts whose judgments best matched the highly accurate judgments made in the all-channel condition.

Surprising? Not when you think about it. Popular claims and the emphasis of this chapter to the contrary, nothing exceeds language as a vehicle for communicating emotion (Brown, 1986). Words and the rules of language are incredibly flexible and extensive tools. Still, the nonverbal channels do assist, in important ways, in reading emotions. In the study just reviewed, the language channel (the transcript) was the best *single* channel for detecting emotion, yet it wasn't as good as having *all* channels available. Getting nonverbal cues in addition to words helped.

Visual and paralinguistic cues are critical in conveying emotions in circumstances where the words themselves offer no cues or misleading cues. When the spoken content is thoroughly, and perhaps intentionally, without emotional references, there is little to go on besides whatever "leaks out" nonverbally. When there is a "mixed message," as when nonverbal cues convey a feeling that contradicts what is said, greater trust tends to be accorded to what the face and body, rather than the words, are "saying." Apparently, people recognize that communicators are less conscious of and less able to control visible nonverbal behaviors than their words. A little later we will examine a specific case in which nonverbal cues may communicate more than (or differently from) the words: the case of lies and deception. First, however, we must examine another basis for the importance of nonverbal communication in influence—the role of nonverbal behaviors in causing emotions, again often without awareness of their impact.

Face work. The face provides particularly rich cues about emotion. Moreover, facial expressions may trigger emotions in others. A good demonstration comes from a study that examined emotional reactions to silent film clips of speeches by the Great Communicator himself, Ronald Reagan (McHugo et al., 1985). Both Reagan supporters and opponents watched 1-minute-long head-and-shoulder clips of the President. Each clip caught him in one of four categories of emotional states: neutral, happy and reassured, fearful and evasive, or angered and threatened (see Figure 7.4). As they watched each clip, physiological recordings were taken of the subjects, including a measure of facial muscular tension. And after each clip, subjects reported *their own* emotions. All the nonneutral emotional clips elicited physiological arousal from subjects—increased heart rate and the like. In addition, the facial tension measures indicated an empathic "mimicking" of the emotion Reagan was expressing. At the physiological level, Reagan's facially communicated emotion produced the same response in subjects. For example, happiness or reassurance displays by Reagan brought smiling from subjects, whereas his anger and fear displays elicited frowning. This held true for both pro- and anti-Reagan viewers.

Attitude toward the President did, however, have an effect on how subjects reported feeling following a particular clip of him. Reagan supporters reported feeling positive and warm when Reagan nonverbally expressed happiness, and rather negative and angry when he looked angered or threatened. In contrast, nonsupporters, especially extreme ones on the Democratic side, reported somewhat negative feelings regardless of what Reagan expressed.

FIGURE 7.4
A study of face work. Former President Reagan displaying (clockwise from upper left) happiness/ reassurance, fear/evasion, and anger/ threat.
(From McHugo, Lanzetta, Sullivan, Masters, and Englis, 1985.)

What do these results mean? Basically, they show that emotional facial expressions by a speaker can *cause* emotional reactions in the audience. The "gut reactions" at the physiological level match the speaker's, an effect much like the common experiences of contagious smiling and the pained expressions we have when we see someone suffering pain. Once these automatic reactions connect with thought and prior attitudes, however, the emotion that is consciously experienced may or may not resemble the speaker's—but it is an emotion nonetheless.

In the world of TV images, this research is very significant. Public figures who are adept at controlling their facial expressions can shape impressions of themselves by eliciting positive emotions in those watching their brief TV appearances on the nightly news—as long as the viewers are not already opposed to the image seeker. Indeed, follow-up studies to the one just described found that previously neutral students reported more positive attitudes toward Reagan after watching his happy and reassuring expressions (Lanzetta et al., 1985).

Image-conscious candidates may do even better if the anchor persons on the nightly news think highly of them. This is not because the anchors will deliver verbal endorsements, since they cannot take sides on the air, but because newscasters may unwittingly wear their candidate preferences on their faces and transmit those preferences to some of their audience, much as Reagan communicated from his face to subjects' affective systems in the studies just described. We know this to be so according to some intriguing field research.

From Mona Lisa to Peter Jennings. The study focused on the 1984 presidential election between incumbent Ronald Reagan and Democrat Walter Mondale (Mullen et al., 1986). In a first phase of the research, videotapes were made of the nightly newscasts of the three major TV networks during the 8 days preceding the election. In a second phase, the researchers had college students rate the facial expressions of the three regular TV network anchormen during those segments of the tapes in which they were reporting on either Reagan or Mondale. The ratings revealed that neither CBS's Dan Rather nor NBC's Tom Brokaw differed in the pleasantness of their facial expressions while reporting on Reagan or Mondale. Each wore an equally (and modestly) pleasant face when talking about either candidate. ABC's Peter Jennings, however, showed a strong positive expressive bias in favor of Reagan; his face "lit up" more when he talked about Reagan than when he reported on Mondale. The significance of this "Jennings smile" was revealed in the final phase of the study, carried out the spring after the election. About 200 voters in five midwestern and eastern cities were surveyed by telephone. They were asked which network nightly news broadcast they most often watch and for whom they had voted. Among those who actually did vote, 63 percent of the regular watchers of CBS and NBC voted for Reagan. In contrast, 75 percent of the regular ABC—Peter Jennings—watchers went for Reagan. Did a newscaster's smile help elect a President?

The investigators believe so. They argue that Jennings' positive facial expressions elicited positive affect in his viewers that became associated with Reagan, the object that coincided with those positive expressions. An alternative possibility is that those already predisposed to Reagan simply tuned to ABC more *because of* the apparent pro-Reagan bias. But this seems unlikely. Independent research suggests that in terms of news *content*, ABC was actually less pro-Reagan than the other networks (Clancey and Robinson, 1985). Thus, the idea that a newscaster's facial bias influenced voters' attitudes is the most likely account of the results—an account that deserves more research attention given its political implications. It gives new meaning to the phrase "being taken at face value."

To lie is dishonest, detecting it is human. Central to the credibility we attribute to any communicator is honesty and truthfulness, along with expertise. When we sense someone is "not telling it like it is," or is covering up something, credibility plummets. Judgments of when people are being deceptive are sometimes guided by nonverbal cues, because people talk and behave differently when they are trying to deceive someone, although the differences are usually subtle (Ekman, 1985). In studies comparing subjects who are instructed to lie about themselves or about a witnessed event with subjects who are asked to be truthful, the liars tend to speak more slowly and in a higher pitch, shift posture more often, smile less, and avoid eye contact (Apple et al., 1979; Zuckerman et al., 1981). In addition, liars make more speech errors and hesitations in responding to questions.

Why do we have these "side shows" of deception? Two of the most important reasons are *leakage* and cognitive interference. Leakage involves the idea that, try as we might to look and sound truthful while lying, we typically find the act anxiety-provoking. We may be able to control one or more channels of our communication, but evidence of our nervousness or of our true feelings is likely to "leak out" of another channel (Ekman and Friesen, 1969). The "leaky" channel, of course, will be the one that is least *controllable*. The verbal channel, the words we consciously choose, is the most controllable. Interestingly, facial expressions are also fairly controllable, but not completely so (Ekman et al., 1988). What research suggests is least controllable are body movements and vocal quality (Scherer et al., 1986). A popular rock ballad of the mid-1970s warns an unfaithful wife that "you can't hide your lyin' eyes." Research suggests she will have greater difficulty hiding her fidgeting feet and shaky voice.

Deception also involves mental effort. Lies are seldom spontaneous; they require fabrication and careful attention to whether they are logical and consistent. These requirements may tax the mind's capacity and thus interfere with the delivery of a smooth report. This helps explain the more hesitating speech that accompanies deception and the observation that descriptions of fabricated events often have a stiff, forced organization (Koehnken, 1985).

We know from careful research, then, which nonverbal behaviors usually accompany lies. But can people identify lies and so defeat influence attempts based on them? It turns out that many of the nonverbal characteristics of lies are the same qualities that people report they use as cues to detect deception. In fact, when they suspect deception, people appear to place the most trust in what they pick up from the less controllable channels of posture and paralanguage and the least trust in highly controllable words—a sensible strategy. Unfortunately, however, human performance at lie detection is not that good. It is better than guessing, but not by much (Brown, 1986). A careful review of deception detection studies found that correct yes-no judgments of whether a stimulus person was lying were made about 57 percent of the time (Kraut, 1980). Guessing would have produced 50 percent accuracy.

Let us hasten to put these discouraging results into perspective. They summarize skill at detecting a stranger's deception in the absence of much context. Under these circumstances, people may look for the right cues to deception but fail to take into account other reasons for those nonverbal behaviors. Maybe the person is simply shy, in a hurry, or generally the "nervous type." A good example is a realistic study carried out at the airport in Syracuse, New York (Kraut and Poe, 1980). Travelers waiting for planes were asked to participate in a simulation in which they would try to get through a customs official without being detained and searched. Half of the volunteers were given contraband (for example, a pouch of white powder) to "smuggle" through and were offered a prize of up to 100 dollars for succeeding. Neither customs officials (supposed experts) nor upstate New York residents who watched videotapes of the customs interviews (nonexperts) could accurately identify who was smuggling and who wasn't. In fact, there was less suspicion of smugglers than of innocent people. Still, judges agreed about who looked suspicious. Most chose to stop nervous-looking people who "hesitated before answering, gave short answers, shifted their bodies, and avoided eye contact (p. 794). All of these behaviors are known to be linked to deception in some cases. The judges apparently failed to consider, though, that the behaviors may not be particularly valid signals of deception in *this* case (smuggling), and that the behaviors are also linked to other personal and situational qualities about which they could not know.

Contrast this with a case in which you are involved and familiar with the situation surrounding someone's possible deceptive statements, and you also know something about the personality style and possible motives of the person. Under these circumstances, you probably would fare better as a human lie detector than laboratory and airport judges of a single, isolated act of a total stranger.

Persuasion and Nonverbal Communication

Impressions of and feelings toward communicators are clearly influenced by nonverbal aspects of their messages. Quickly and unconsciously, we respond to certain nonverbal displays with attributions about power and trustworthiness, as well as with feelings of attraction or repulsion. These reactions to the communicator may influence the degree to which the attitude change advocated by the message occurs. Research supports this notion that nonverbal cues may affect persuasion by shaping impressions of the speaker. One study found that when asked to try to change someone's attitude, as opposed to simply conveying information, college students spoke faster, louder, and more smoothly, and made more pleasant facial expressions and eye contact with the audience (Mehrabian and Williams, 1969)—just what you'd expect from our preceding discussion. What's more, judges rated the messages with these features as more convincing. More effective counseling psychologists have been shown to counsel in a slightly louder voice than their less effective colleagues (Packwood, 1974). Physically attractive people tend to be more persuasive, and perhaps not coincidentally, they speak with above-average speed and smoothness when trying to influence others (Chaiken, 1979).

Speed of speaking appears to be a particularly potent nonverbal persuasion cue. Notice how often it has been mentioned in the preceding paragraphs. Now consider what a team of researchers observed when they trekked to a Los Angeles shopping mall and asked people to listen to, rate, and indicate their agreement with an audiotaped message about the danger of drinking coffee (Miller et al., 1976). Shoppers rated the speaker more credible and agreed more with the message when they heard a tape in which the speaker delivered the message at an above-average rate of speed. The same result occurred in a second experiment conducted in a university laboratory.

Fast speech communicates credibility and knowledgeability, and thus may serve as a heuristic cue to accept the message. It may also make systematic processing more difficult; but that's not an effect of nonverbal communication, and so we won't pursue it here. Hold on, you say; how can this be? We have been warned about "fast-talking salespeople," and so how can fast speech serve as a credibility cue? The answer lies in the phrase itself. Knowledge that the person is trying to *sell* you something is itself a cue—to distrust. Fast talk is persuasive when the talker is not making blatant his or her intent to manipulate you.

The Self-Perception of Nonverbal Acts: I Nod, Therefore I Agree

We saw in Chapter 3 that, in certain circumstances, we infer how we feel from how we behave. In a somewhat related way, our nonverbal behaviors may also give us feedback and influence our attitudes and emotions. This was demonstrated in a very clever experiment (Wells and Petty, 1980). On the pretense that they were testing stereo headphones for "comfort while you're moving," the researchers asked college students to either nod their heads ("Move your head up and down") or shake their heads ("Move your head back and forth") while listening to a radio broadcast. Sandwiched between the music of this broadcast was a 90-second persuasive message on the topic of tuition increases at the subjects' university. This message was introduced by the disc jockey as a station editorial comment. Postmessage opinion measures revealed a clear-cut case of movement over mind. Compared with a listen-only control group, subjects instructed to nod while listening agreed more with the message and subjects instructed to shake their heads (as in a "No" gesture) agreed less with the message.

Revealingly, no subjects expressed the slightest suspicion that the head movements had any effect on their attitudes. Once again we see unconscious processes at work. But how does it work? The researchers' theory is that when we nod, we are almost always thinking positive thoughts, whereas when we shake our heads, we almost always have a negative frame of mind. These associations are so well learned that, for example, "nodding disagreement" is very difficult to do: the bodily response and the cognitive one are incompatible. Basically, then, incompatible cognitive responses are inhibited by the physical head movements, whereas compatible ones are augmented and increased. Nodding promotes mental agreeing responses; head shaking promotes mental disagreeing ones.

Consider the practical implications. Having learned of the head movement study, do you think you might get a little suspicious about a TV commercial that visually features a vertically bouncing ball while the audio portion expounds the product's virtues?

Nonverbal cues, from others and from ourselves, can objectively be seen, heard, or felt. They are noticeable. But as we have seen, they may influence emotions and impressions even when they are not consciously noticed. In the final part of this chapter, we turn to influence cues that may be neither noticed nor noticeable: they are aimed to hit below the mental belt.

SUBLIMINALS: INCONSPICUOUS INFLUENCE

The 1950s produced rock-and-roll music, hula hoops, and a new car by Ford called the Edsel. Rock and roll persists; it's "here to stay," as the song goes. The hula hoop faded fast, but occasionally makes a comeback. Edsels were made in 1958, and never again. Another development in the 1950s was the first commercial experimentation with subliminal influence techniques. In the fall of 1957, moviegoers in Fort Lee, New Jersey, watched flicks that had been tinkered with. At numerous points in a film, single frames were inserted that included the words "Hungry? Eat Popcorn" and "Drink Coca-Cola." The frames zipped by too quickly to be seen, yet the marketing firm that designed this attempt at hidden suggestion reported a 50 percent increase in popcorn sales and an 18 percent jump in soft drink consumption during intermission. Seeking to scare rather than sell, a movie producer used a similar technique to flash, undetectably, pictures of a skull and the word "blood" at key points in a pair of horror movies (Packard, 1957).

When news of these subliminal influence attempts reached the public, reactions were predictable: public outrage and new laws restricting the use of subliminals in advertising. Thus subliminals were abandoned even before it was clearly established whether they really worked. But like hula hoops, subliminals made a comeback in the mid-1970s and are with us still. In the 1974 movie *The Exorcist*, a death mask was flashed on the screen for too-short-to-notice durations. In recent years, to counter thefts, a number of department stores in North America began piping in, along with their easy-listening Muzak goop, some barely audible and rapidly repeated whispers like, "I am honest. I will not steal." Many reported a dramatic decrease in shoplifting (*Time*, 1979). Popular books such as *Subliminal Seduction* (Key, 1973) allege that print advertisements have hidden messages and suggestions, usually sexual— things like penises in the ice cubes of a glass of gin and the tip of a distant ocean wave projected toward the parted legs of bikini-clad women sunning on the beach. And nowadays, you can buy cassette tapes that supposedly cure you of stress with soothing subaudible messages that are covered by mood music and the ambient sounds of nature.

Do these subliminal techniques work? Do they influence their unaware targets as their proponents claim? Given what you have read in this chapter, you may be open to consider that possibility. We have seen that detectable but unnoticed stimuli can influence attitudes and behavior without our awareness. In other instances, we cannot explain how stimuli have influenced us. And one study we examined went even further—not only undetected stimuli but also undetec*table* (that is, subliminal) repeated stimuli had attitudinal effects (Kunst-Wilson and Zajonc, 1980). On the whole, what we have seen so far suggests an open mind about the potential impact of stimuli presented in ways so that we do not "see" or "hear" them.

But open minds should also be discriminating minds. Subliminal processing has been drawing considerable scientific attention in recent years, and so far none of the more fabulous claims for subliminals have been borne out by well-controlled and replicable studies. And while some of the touted subliminal techniques merit scientific study, others are simply not possible given what is known about the functioning of the human mind. Let's sort through the various attempts at subliminal influence, connecting them with relevant insights from recent psychological research and theory.

The Mind-Altering Possibilities of Subliminal "Visuals"

The promoters of the New Jersey popcorn ad claimed that their famous subliminals caused a large increase in sales at the theater's refreshment stand. In reality, however, no controlled study was done, making it impossible to determine what caused the increase or if an increase even occurred. Without a clear definition of "sales" and a clearly defined comparison baseline of sales prior to exposure to the subliminal messages we don't know whether the "increase" was due to the subliminals, an unusually hungry audience, a larger audience, a chance fluctuation, or something else. Some evidence, moreover, suggests the results of the study were made up (Weir, 1984).

If we discount some poorly done studies of the 1960s (Moore 1982), the study reported earlier involving 1-millisecond exposures to octagons provides the first direct evidence that briefly flashed stimuli can influence feelings even when they cannot be consciously attended (Kunst-Wilson and Zajonc, 1980). As we saw, on average, the octagons presented "too fast to see" were liked better than never-presented octagons.

Can the octagon study be generalized to influence cues? Not by itself. One limitation is that the subliminal stimuli were isolated from other stimuli and subjects were focused in their direction. Subjects carefully watched a screen—even though they did not see anything but brief light bursts. In contrast, in advertising uses, the subliminals would be *superimposed* on the audiovisual content of a TV commercial or movie that has the audience's conscious attention. If consciously attending to one thing undermines the impact of a simultaneous subliminal, there is little practical use of subliminals (Dixon, 1971; Moore, 1982).

A second limitation is that the octagon study showed that only stimuli themselves become better liked through subliminal presentation. The popcorn pushers who inserted their famous subliminals were not interested in having the specific physical stimulus (the words "Hungry? Eat Popcorn") liked more. They wanted a more *general* effect: an implanted desire to eat popcorn that produces the action they desire, buying the product. Similarly, the producers of *The Exorcist* sought more than a reaction to their death mask. They, too, sought a more general effect—fear. Pragmatic uses are limited if the effect of a subliminal stimulus is restricted to specific reactions to the stimulus itself.

A third limitation is that the octagon study, by measuring liking within minutes of stimulus presentation, fails to tell us if the induced feeling is strong and persistent enough to affect the mental processes that lead to subsequent directed behavior. The bottom line in advertising is behavior change. Moviegoers must get up and buy that popcorn. Couch potatoes must retain the attitude shaped by the subliminal message about a product until they visit the store, and the attitude must be strong enough to be activated at that time.

Do these constraints mean that subliminal persuasion cannot be effective? Or can subliminals (1) be superimposed on attended-to material and (2) still elicit general emotions and attitudes that (3) are strong enough to influence specific target behaviors? Recent research suggests yes, yes, and yes—within limits. Let's examine some of this research.

Subliminals influence judgments even if superimposed. Several studies demonstrate that subliminal stimuli have an impact even when presented right along with something that dominates conscious attention (Greenwald et al., 1989; Marcel, 1983). These studies employ a tachistoscope, an apparatus that presents stimuli for short, precisely calibrated durations to each eye separately, or to different areas of the visual field of each eye. In one study, an emotionally loaded word was presented to subjects' nondominant eye for only 30 milliseconds at the same time that a "masking" stimulus—a mishmash pattern—was presented to their dominant eye (Greenwald et al., 1989). All that the subjects reported seeing was a blurry flash of the mishmash mask. Less than a second later, another emotionally loaded word was presented for 2 seconds, and subjects were asked to judge whether the word connoted something good or bad. Their judgments were faster when the preceding subliminal word (such as "grief") connoted the same emotion as the target word (in this case, "detest") than when the emotional connotations were different (such as "happy" and "detest"). Thus, even when presented simultaneously with a stronger stimulus, the subliminal got through to subjects: it *primed* them to recognize the emotion more quickly in another stimulus.

Subliminals affect general reactions. Subliminal priming studies also illustrate that evaluations of *other* stimuli are influenced by subliminal ones (Bargh and Pietromonaco, 1982). One study used a tachistoscope to present word pairs to either the left or the right of the subject's focus point, too briefly to detect their meaning (Erdley and D'Agostino, 1988). The words appeared as dark flashes, and subjects were asked to indicate whether each flash appeared on the left or on the right. For some subjects, one word in most subliminal pairs was a synonym of *honest*—"sincere," "upright." For others, most pairs included a synonym of *mean*—"rude," "hostile." A third group of subjects was presented with neutral words. Thus, if subliminal stimuli "get through," some subjects should have been primed to think about honesty as a trait while others should have been primed to think about meanness.

And primed they were. A few minutes after the subliminal phase, all subjects read a short story about the shopping trip of a young woman named Donna who behaved both somewhat honestly and also meanly on several occasions. Compared with the control group, subjects for whom honesty was unconsciously primed later described Donna as more honest and truthful. Subjects unconsciously primed for meanness, in contrast, described Donna as meaner, ruder, and more selfish. What was primed unconsciously spread to conscious judgments of objectively unrelated stimuli.

A slight twist of this priming procedure illustrates dramatically the range of associations that can be triggered subliminally. Instead of words connoting a trait, the primes in one study were words associated with the stereotype of black people held by most Americans, including labels ("Negroes" and "blacks"), qualities ("athletic," "poor," and "lazy"), places ("Africa" and "ghetto"), and activities ("jazz" and "basketball") (Devine, 1989). White subjects were "hit" with 100 subliminal primes. In one group, 80 of these were stereotype-associated words (12 words presented six to seven times each); while in another group, only 20 subliminals were stereotype-associated. Minutes afterward, subjects read a paragraph describing a man (race unspecified) engaged in some "ambiguously hostile behaviors" like demanding money back from a store clerk just after a purchase and refusing to pay rent until his apartment was repainted. They were asked to rate the man's behavior on several dimensions, including hostility.

Here are the stunning results: White subjects who had the heavy dose of black stereotype subliminals rated the man as more *hostile* than white subjects who had the light dose, but they did not rate him any differently on the other trait dimensions. This pattern held whether or not the subjects were prejudiced according to a racism scale administered months earlier.

What's the connection here? How can unconscious reminders of a stereotype cause even unprejudiced white subjects to see greater hostility in a stranger than may be objectively warranted? Stereotypes about black people are learned in early childhood by nearly all white Americans. Part of this stereotype is the assumption that black people are hostile (Brigham, 1971; Devine, 1989). Prejudiced people consciously buy into the stereotype and react emotionally to its negative elements. Less prejudiced people consciously reject the stereotype, but being so well learned, it lives on unconsciously, dormant until some reminder of black people or the black stereotype activates it. When that happens, the person is primed to see qualities associated with the stereotype in the immediate situation. In this study, the reminders were subliminal, yet sufficient to activate the stereotype so strongly that a mere component of it—hostility—was projected into the focus of conscious interest.

On a more benign note, let us briefly describe a study that brought subliminals at the movies into the laboratory and again found an effect that went beyond the subliminals themselves. The researchers had students watch a 2-minute video of rather impressive computer graphics (Robles et al., 1987). Images and angles of furniture-filled rooms rotated vertically and horizontally on the screen in vivid colors. Unbeknownst to the viewers, single-frame "subliminal inserts" lasting one-sixtieth of a second were added in more than a dozen places. These were either positive (popular cartoon characters like Bugs Bunny), negative (bloodied faces, monsters, and devils taken from horror movies), or neutral (gray featureless images). Following the presentation, standard measures of anxiety were administered. The effects of the inserted images on anxiety were unmistakable. Those exposed to the gory images reported greater anxiety than those exposed to neutral images, while those exposed to playful cartoon images reported considerably less anxiety than even the control group.

Subliminals may influence behavior (but more evidence is needed). There is little good research on whether subliminal influence can achieve the ultimate goal of behavior change, but one laboratory study provides a positive hint (Bornstein et al., 1987). This study observed that, over the course of several evaluative tasks, subjects publicly agreed more often with a confederate whose face had previously been subliminally presented to them than with a never before "seen" confederate. The effect was not strong, however, and was not accompanied by other behavioral evidence of greater liking for the "familiar" confederate. But it does suggest that there might be a link to simple acts directly related to the state induced by the subliminals.

And so part of the verdict is in. Short of behavior change, subliminal presentations in moving visual media can at the very least arouse emotions and activate mental categories to the extent that ratings are affected of completely different stimuli (including the self). In explaining these effects, psychologists begin with what we learned about the mind early in this chapter. Stimuli that we are not consciously attending to may still be registered and superficially processed unconsciously. In the case of subliminals, additional assumptions about human information processing must be made, but they are not at all farfetched. It may be necessary, for example, for only a portion of a stimulus to be registered in order to activate an emotion or a specific mental category, such as "honesty," that is relevant to the evaluation. Zajonc (1980), as we have seen, has suggested that stimuli may have attributes that allow for "affective recognition" far faster than the stimulus can be verbally identified. Subliminal processing, in sum, seems to be a by-product of a brain that can pick up things rapidly—on the run, so to say—while it is doing something else much more slowly, like finding meaning in the plot of the movie being watched.

Perhaps, then, those flashed death masks did make *The Exorcist* scarier. Whether subliminals can sell popcorn—or cars and beer, for that matter—remains to be seen, because there is insufficient research using behavioral measures or tracking subliminal effects over periods greater than a few minutes. The smart money suggests that the subliminal stimulation experienced in brief laboratory studies is itself short-lived. But consider these questions: Might subliminally generated emotional reactions grow stronger with the repeated subliminal exposures built into a TV commercial that you see several times a day, several days a week? Could subliminal effects be used as a setup for later persuasion? Or to build resistance to counterpersuasion? One recent study found that attitudes toward Chinese ideographs shaped by subliminal exposure resisted change when later attacked by short persuasive messages by experts on ideograph art (Edwards, 1990). Could an advertiser "get 'em while they're hot," by presenting a persuasive message about a product while the audience is in a subliminally induced good mood? In light of the recent empirical evidence, and the endless quest of advertisers to find a "hook" on which to hang higher product profits, these questions deserve serious study.

Subaudible and Print-Embedded Messages: Less Likely Influences

Subliminal influence via channels other than the visual might also work to produce a desired effect. Let's consider subliminal sounds. On the downside, strictly subliminal influence is far less likely through the ears than through the eyes. Subaudible, or too faint to hear, messages are apt to go *totally* unregistered if attention is riveted to other sounds. Unlike the eye, which receives information from different areas of a visual field all at once, the ear deals with input sequentially, basically one stimulus at a time. When several sounds occur at once, they *blend*; and the effect can range from a blurry blare to an integrated symphony of sound—music. Unless we listen specifically to one of several simultaneous signals, most of that signal will be lost in the blend. And if we can in fact listen to the signal, by definition, it is not subliminal.

On the other hand, a simple supraliminal ("above threshold") signal could be softly repeated to us while our attention to it drifts in and out. We may never become fully conscious of the signal, but through repeated exposure, we might come to experience positive feeling toward the signal or toward its simple suggestion. Though largely untested, this mental mechanism could help make relaxation tapes effective. The simple messages—"Relax," "You're good," "Don't worry, be happy"—are heard, but just barely; and with the help of New Age music, they trigger the appropriate emotional associations.

Recent evidence from a well-designed experiment suggests that subliminal "self-help" tapes have little, if any, therapeutic effect, even though Americans spend fifty million dollars on them annually (Pratkanis et al., 1990). Subjects ranging in age from 18 to 60 years old listened daily for a five-week period to subliminal tapes aimed at improving either their memories or self-esteem. Prior and following exposure to these commercial tapes, each person's memory and self-esteem were assessed along a variety of dimensions. In addition, half the subjects who received the memory tape were led to believe it would improve their memory while the others were falsely told it was a self-esteem booster. The reverse held for those who heard the self-esteem tape.

Two clear results emerged from this study. First, perceptions of self-improvement were significantly affected by what the subjects expected to happen; they reported memory enhancement if they were told the tapes would do that and self-esteem enhancement if they expected that effect. However, this "self-deception" effect was strongest when they got the memory tape and believed it was the self-esteem tape! Second, although what the subjects expected is what they believed they got, in fact, it was not what they actually got for their money. What they got was *nothing*. On none of fourteen objective measures was there any hint of improvement in memory or self-esteem. These results suggest that subliminal therapeutic tapes do not even have a potentially beneficial placebo effect in which expectations alone cause personal changes.

Stimuli embedded in print advertisements are least likely to be effective subliminals. In fact, such embedded stimuli may not even exist. The champion of uncovering Madison Avenue's alleged sinister picture doctoring, Wilson Brian Key, goes to great pains to find erotic objects in magazine ads, including magnification and viewing at cockeyed angles.

PEOPLE HAVE BEEN TRYING TO FIND THE BREASTS IN THESE ICE CUBES SINCE 1957.

The advertising industry is sometimes charged with sneaking seductive little pictures into ads.

Supposedly, these pictures can get you to buy a product without your even seeing them.

Consider the photograph above. According to some people, there's a pair of female breasts hidden in the patterns of light refracted by the ice cubes.

Well, if you really searched you probably *could* see the breasts. For that matter, you could also see Millard Fillmore, a stuffed pork chop and a 1946 Dodge.

The point is that so-called "subliminal advertising" simply doesn't exist. Overactive imaginations, however, most certainly do.

So if anyone claims to see breasts in that drink up there, they aren't in the ice cubes.

They're in the eye of the beholder.

ADVERTISING
ANOTHER WORD FOR FREEDOM OF CHOICE.
American Association of Advertising Agencies

Suggestive stimuli are probably not hidden in print ads. Even if they were, they would need to be discovered ("unhidden") to have any influence. This is very unlikely. (*Courtesy of the American Association of Advertising Agencies*)

Perhaps what he is really seeing with his magnifying glass is precisely what he expects to see. If you look hard enough at any ambiguous stimulus—be it clouds, magnified ice cubes, or Rorschach inkblots—you'll see something. And that something will be shaped in part by what's on your mind.

But even if print ads did contain embedded symbols, they would not influence people subliminally. There simply is no known process by which a stimulus that requires a magnifying glass or careful study to see at a conscious level can be picked up unconsciously by someone casually looking over an ad.

The Ethics of Influence—In and Out of Awareness

Is the commercial use of subliminal influence unethical? In trying to answer this, let's consider the ethical issues associated with influence and persuasion in general and locate subliminals within the context of these issues. Ethical questions are complex and partly a matter of opinion. But many people would agree on at least three defining qualities of an unethical influence technique (excluding coercive physical force, which is beyond the scope of this book). Generally, an influence method could be considered unethical if it relies on deception, prohibits exposure to opposing messages, or unfairly prevents efforts to resist it.

Reliance on deception. As used in selling cars, the low-ball procedure we described in Chapter 2 is unethical because it works only by lying to the target. The salesperson gains a commitment to a low-price deal he or she never intends to make and uses the commitment to clinch agreement to a revised, higher-price deal. Without the lie, you have no technique. (No lie, no sale.) Similarly, subliminals are deceptive, and hence unethical, to the extent that their users keep their use a secret. Conceivably, however, subliminals might exert influence even when it is openly announced that they are present—for example, in a TV commercial that had conscious content of obvious persuasive intent. Under these circumstances it could be argued that subliminals would "pass" at least the deception test of ethics. Both their presence and the message's persuasive intent are openly admitted.

Presenting one side while forbidding the other. Some influence strategies are unethical because they involve actively blocking exposure to opposing viewpoints or behavioral options. The Moonie indoctrination system is often criticized on this basis. As we've seen, cult members keep recruits constantly busy with *their* messages and very deliberately squeeze out time and opportunity to hear—or even think about—the other side. The "denial of the other side" criterion does not really apply to any one influence technique, such as subliminal presentation, per se. It has more to do with the influence agent's more general ability and power to censor and limit the freedom of access to alternative views (as in totalitarian states). In an environment filled with messages on both sides, a one-sided subliminal message does not seem unethical according to this criterion.

Preventing defense. It would seem unethical when the influence procedure somehow strips people of their defenses, of their motivation or ability to counterargue or simply walk away. This can be accomplished by sleep and food deprivation, as in some cult recruitment and prisoner-of-war camps. Defensive will and ability can also be worn down by more purely psychological means: by distracting attention and causing confusion. We'll see a graphic example of preventing defense in Chapter 8 when we discuss how police sometimes coerce confessions to crimes—by innocent suspects. Or targets may be made defenseless by using influence stimuli that work without the target's awareness.

Here is where subliminals can be viewed as unethical in the extreme. You can't defend against something you don't know about, and by definition, you can't know about subliminal messages. But what about classical conditioning? Or the image packaging of candidates and products that deflects attention from substance and suppresses systematic thought by encouraging the audience to respond emotionally and unconsciously to symbols, images, and other affect-loaded stimuli? As we have seen, these tactics instigate processes of change that people are unaware of.

But there is a very important difference between these methods and subliminals. In image processing and conditioning, the operative stimuli and tactics are detectable, even though many people may miss them because they are not sufficiently sophisticated in the use of those techniques. But by being observant and thoughtful, we have at least a fighting chance to resist their influence. We can protect ourselves with mindfulness and with the strategies for analyzing influence situations that we identified in Chapter 6 and elsewhere. This is not the case with subliminals. We cannot be aware of them, and so there is nothing to remind us to be mindful. Our only defense would be later, at the time of behavioral decision. At that point, we could ask ourselves why we feel a certain way. Finding no clue, we might back away from the subliminally shaped inclination. This is a defense, but it's a last defense. Moreover, it would not be a defense against the subtle influence of subliminals on the "little things"—the ongoing on-line judgments we must continuously make without worrying about what contributed to them. Remember the hostility people saw in an innocent stranger after being bombarded with subliminal reminders of a racial stereotype?

And so we must conclude that if subliminal influence should prove to work outside the laboratory in advertising contexts, it would seem highly unethical to use it—mainly because it deprives people of much of their opportunity to resist it.

AWARENESS AND CONSCIOUSNESS: A CLOSING PERSPECTIVE

Two extraordinary distinguishing features evolved in the human species: (1) language, which allows for tremendous complexity and nuance in communication; and (2) consciousness, an ability to be aware of the world subjectively—to observe, *with awareness of observing*, one's own thoughts and exchanges with the outside world. Consciousness largely makes our sophisticated language possible. These hallmarks of humanity represent our dominant modes of communicating and making choices. People live in a verbal, subjectively experienced world. And so it is that verbal and conscious signals are the most powerful, efficient, and common vehicles by which we influence one another.

In this chapter, we have discussed useful supplements to conscious and deliberate communication. First, it doesn't take conscious awareness to register all signals. The mind processes some signals unconsciously while working consciously on others. Second, consciously communicated and received verbal messages are often combined and reacted to at an unconscious level. These "qualities of mind" are crucial because they allow the mind to get around the bottleneck that would be created if everything had to proceed through the slow process of one show at a time in the spotlight of conscious contemplation. Unconscious or unaware information processing necessarily occurs along with, not instead of, conscious or aware processing. They are part of the same system.

It is the task of the psychoanalyst to help guide patients to discover for themselves how unconscious influences are operating on their daily thoughts, feelings, and actions and how they become expressed in overt symptoms. These insights then form the foundation for personal change in more healthful directions. Our task in this chapter has been to make *you*, a potential target of influence, more aware of how and when and why some types of stimulation and messages may work below the level of your conscious awareness to control some of what you do and think and feel. That knowledge needs to be translated into more mindful ways of coping with such pervasive sources of "underground" persuasions and social influence. That is your task.

TO SUM UP...

We discussed the ways in which people may be changed via social influence without being aware of it, or aware of what influenced them. Some influence techniques do not even work if the target notices the subtle social pressures on which those tactics rely. Among other things, we saw that people may be unaware of forming associations, may unconsciously rely on nonverbal cues from others, and may react to subliminal messages.

- To be conscious of something is to be aware of it. Normally we are conscious of only a small portion of the incoming stimulation on which we focus attention, although attention can be divided among several stimulus events. Unconscious processing of one stimulus may occur while conscious attention is occupied by something else.

- Emotions and like-dislike reactions to stimuli often develop through processes we are unaware of. One process is classical conditioning, in which, after repeated pairings of a neutral stimulus with a significant stimulus that elicits a positive or negative response, the neutral stimulus will come to elicit the same response. This can occur without the target's realization that the pairings caused the change in responding. In addition, the mere repeated exposure to a neutral stimulus alone leads to liking it even when we do not recognize having seen the stimulus before. This means that we are mentally equipped to respond to a stimulus with feelings and preferences before we consciously think about it.

- Our conscious thoughts are products of higher-order processes of comprehension, evaluation, and integration that occur beyond awareness. As a result, even salient stimuli may influence us in ways we cannot know, through the unconscious processing of them that underlies attitudes and decisions. In research, subjects often give reasons for their behavior that differ from the influences known to have been operating on them.

- Influence also occurs unconsciously through mindlessness. With practice and repetition, certain responses to social stimuli become automatic: we make them without thinking. We are likely to give mindless responses (such as obedience) to stimuli (such as authority figures) when we are preoccupied or when a rigid categorical label can be applied to the stimulus.

- We often react unconsciously to nonverbal behaviors. Nonverbal cues can be paralinguistic—as in speech rate, inflections, voice tone—or visual, as with facial expressions and body movements. They guide impressions of others' traits and emotions.

- Words can best communicate emotion, but when speech is emotionless or seems to contradict nonverbal behavior, we infer emotions from the nonverbal cues. In addition, facial expressions automatically elicit emotions in observers, usually the same ones conveyed by the communicator. People who are adept at controlling their facial expressions may thus be able to control emotional reactions to themselves and their causes.

- Telling a lie is anxiety-provoking, and the anxiety may leak out through nonverbal channels that are less controllable than words. Deception may show up in posture shifts, voice tremors, and reduced eye contact. Lying is cognitively effortful, and so deception also may show up in more hesitating, awkward statements. We use these nonverbal cues to detect deception but usually require information from the communication context for valid detection.

- Persuasion depends partly on attributes of communicators inferred from their nonverbal behavior. By speaking fast and loud, communicators sound more credible. Pleasant facial expressions and frequent eye contact enhance likability. We may even be influenced by our own nonverbal behavior: nodding as if we were agreeing actually facilitates agreeable thoughts.

- A dramatic form of unconscious influence is subliminal influence—changes in affect and cognition caused by stimuli too weak to be consciously detected. There is no scientific support for the more fantastic claims for subliminals. But laboratory research indicates that visual stimuli flashed too briefly to be seen, or masked from consciousness by stronger stimuli, have an impact. The stimuli themselves become better liked. Further, subliminal presentation of stimuli with strong emotional or thematic associations primes receivers to define and interpret later events in terms of the emotion or theme. Whether the effects persist, can be built up, or influence behavior is not yet known.

- A social influence technique seems unethical if it relies on deception, actively censors the other side, or destroys motivation or ability to defend against it. Unacknowledged subliminals qualify as deceptive. And because they are not noticed, they cannot be counterargued or otherwise resisted.

QUESTIONS AND EXERCISES

1. Pick out a product that gets heavily advertised nowadays. Study the various TV, radio, and print ads for the product. What components of the ads are we likely to attend to consciously? What components may "slip in" and influence us unconsciously (such as music, nonverbal behaviors of models or spokespersons, heuristic cues). What kinds of associations and conditioning do the ads encourage, and how?

2. Your friend is about to go on an intense job interview in which he will undergo much individual questioning and also participate in a group discussion with other interviewees as evaluators watch. He knows his stuff, and so he's not worried about what to say. His concern is with the nonverbal impression he will make. He wants to pick your brain about this. Articulate a short lecture for him about the face, the voice, the body, and how they may enter into impression formation. What could he do to manage the optimal impression he wants to create?

3. Describe the several ways that social influence occurs outside of conscious awareness. In what ways does the unconsciousness of influence create problems for targets of influence? On the other hand, can you think of ways in which the unconsciousness of influence (such as mindlessness, the automatic use of heuristics, emotional conditioning) may be functional?

4. Drawing from the present chapter and salient points from previous chapters, evaluate the assertion that the modern, ultrasophisticated video media have succeeded in making the public more reliant on images, heuristic cues, and emotional appeals that can be processed mindlessly without much conscious attention. What aspects of the media and of society in general may promote this? Is it good or bad? What could be done on a societywide basis to turn things around and get

people to react to influence more mindfully and with an eye toward substance instead of style?

5. Argue the ethics of using subliminal ads for a pro-social message, such as antidrugs, safe sex, or energy conservation. Argue against the use of nonconscious influence techniques by a well-intentioned parent who wants to use persuasive messages while her child is sleeping to promote positive attitudes that will help make the nonresisting child become more patriotic and more religious, and clean his room while he is doing those other good things.

8

Influence and the Legal System:

Trying Experiences

❖

The Adversarial Approach: Does Competitive Persuasion Yield Justice? ◆ The Police Station: Gathering Evidence from People ◆ In the Courtroom: The Persuasion Battleground ◆ The Jury Room ◆ The Case of Psychology and Law: A Closing Statement

*I*t's a hot summer night in New York City, which means that there are many people roaming the streets to escape the stifling heat of their apartments. Among them, out for their evening stroll as well, is the army of criminals who committed 169,407 crimes of all kinds against people and 121,320 burglaries in 1989 (*The New York Times*, 3/31/90). Mom and pop grocery stores are hit regularly because they are defenseless, and liquor stores are targeted because they have lots of cash from their brisk weekend business.

Quicker Liquor is robbed tonight, the third time this month. A squad car from the 41st Precinct arrives on the scene in timely fashion, but not making quite as dramatic an entrance as we used to see on *Hill Street Blues* TV reruns. Its arrival at the crime scene triggers the first in a cascading series of events, each with the potential for *influence processes* to be at work. At what point in this chain of proceedings might some of the social influence processes we have studied thus far play a significant role in shaping the outcome?

- The police take a report from eyewitnesses. Could they influence what the witnesses remember, or think they remember, by the way they ask questions?

- On the basis of witness reports and other evidence, the police develop a theory about the crime: how, why, and who. Could that theory influence their search for more evidence and their interpretation of the new evidence they do uncover?

- A suspect is positively identified out of a lineup by an eyewitness. Could the witness have been subtly pressured to make an identification despite feeling uncertain?

- The suspect, now defendant, is given the opportunity to confess. Can people be influenced, psychologically coerced or tricked, into making confessions that may cost them their freedom or their very lives—sometimes even whey they are innocent?

- A grand jury hearing is held to determine if there is enough evidence against the defendant to pursue the case. Can evidence be "packaged" in particular ways to ensure a grand jury indictment?

- A bail hearing follows the grand jury indictment. In setting the bail amount, will the judge be influenced by the prosecuting and defense attorneys' arguments about whether the defendant represents a "clear and present danger to society" or is likely to jump bail?

- Plea bargaining is attempted; the parties try to negotiate a deal in which the defendant will plead guilty to a lesser offense in exchange for a lighter penalty. Will persuasion and compliance principles operate in the negotiations?

- Plea bargaining fails, a juried trial is held—we go to court. The prosecution and defense lawyers present their cases, and a jury decides on a verdict. Will the lawyers' persuasive skills influence the jury beyond the evidence? What role will the characteristics of the defendant, the victim, and the witnesses play? Are there compliance, conformity, and persuasion processes operating among jurors in the deliberation chambers?

If you've answered "Yes" to each of our queries, you're on the right track. Social influence processes may have a bearing on the outcome at each and every step in the resolution of a legal case. Several factors contribute to the great potential for social influence to operate in or on the legal system.

First, most *evidence is subjective,* a matter of interpretation. For example, gunpowder tests on the hands of the accused might indicate a 50–50 probability that he fired a gun within the preceding 24 hours. Are these high enough odds to warrant further suspicion? Ambiguous information like this, as seen in previous chapters, will be interpreted differently depending on prior beliefs, suspicions, and goals of those making the inferences.

A second factor is that much *evidence is verbal*, in the form of people's words; thus, influence enters into the very production of such evidence. Verbal statements such as eyewitness reports, lineup identifications, and defendant confessions are made in the context of two-way communications in which self-attribution, verbal and nonverbal persuasion, conformity, obedience, and compliance processes are likely to be at work.

Finally, the role of social influence is magnified by the fact that the justice system runs on an *adversarial model* in which two sides investigate and present competing versions of the "truth" and alternate views on what are the "facts." In a real sense, the judge and jury often have to decide between two very different social constructions of reality. On one side is the prosecution; on the other, the defense.

Space does not permit us to cover all the legal settings in which social influence plays a substantial role. But we can focus on some of the more important ways and places in which social influence may affect legal outcomes. In this chapter, we will first examine how the adversarial system of justice may affect the judgments and perceptions of fact finders such as police officers, lawyers, judges, and jurors. Then, we will focus on, in succession, the social influence possibilities inherent in three crucial legal settings. We will examine social influence in the police station (during interrogation of witnesses and suspects), in the courtroom, and in the jury deliberation room.

THE ADVERSARIAL APPROACH: DOES COMPETITIVE PERSUASION YIELD JUSTICE?

In the United States, Canada, and Great Britain, legal cases are decided in a competitive environment known as the *adversarial system* of legal procedure. There are two sides. On one side is the prosecution. Led by a district attorney and aided by the police department, the prosecution tries to get a conviction by proving that the accused is guilty beyond reasonable doubt. On the other side is the defense. Led by a defense attorney, this side attempts to gain an acquittal by showing that such proof is not at hand. Each attorney has wide discretion concerning what evidence to present, which witnesses and experts to call, how to question witnesses, and what version of truth to frame to the judge and jury in opening and closing arguments. Within the limits of law and courtroom rules, the attorneys for the dueling sides call the shots regarding evidence presentation.

Can you see how the adversarial system encourages a selective, biased approach to the gathering, interpretation, and presentation of evidence? Case-supporting evidence, obviously, is sought and advanced. In addition, the system makes persuasion a significant factor in the courtroom. A verdict may depend on which side is most convincing—something which, as we saw in Chapter 4, is a matter not only of what is said but of who said it, when it was said, how it was said, and to whom.

The adversarial approach may be contrasted with the trial system of nations on the European continent, a system called the *inquisitorial approach*, where legal disputes are investigated by *impartial* representatives of the court. In the courtroom, though each side may have an attorney, the presiding judge, working from a report prepared by the court investigator, does the questioning of witnesses and controls the presentation of evidence. All witnesses testify for the court, rather than for one side or the other, and the opposing attorneys cannot coach or otherwise prepare witnesses before their courtroom testimony (Lind, 1982). The goal is to reach the truth through disinterested, objective, and systematic appraisal of the evidence.

At first glance, you might think that the inquisitorial approach serves justice better than the adversarial one. After all, the adversarial system forces jurors to choose between two contesting versions of the truth, both tainted by the biased case building needed to "win." On the other hand, the competitive nature of the adversarial approach may get everyone to try harder. Also, court investigators in inquisitorial trials are not immune to some memory and value biases. And the inquisitorial judge is a human being with personal beliefs, and sometimes also burdened by heavy political pressures and career ambitions that affect objectivity. Remember the religious Inquisition of the sixteenth and seventeenth centuries, where with the best of intentions to rid the world of evil, untold thousands of innocent people were tortured and executed as witches, after "due legal process." So what's the verdict here?

Fairness and Bias: A Question of Balance

Interestingly, it is the adversarial procedure that people see as fairer, be they Americans or continental Europeans (Lind, 1982; Thibault and Walker, 1975). This is evident in studies that have put participants through simulated, but highly involving, mock trials employing either an adversarial or an inquisitorial approach. Even the losers in these simulated disputes feel less dissatisfied with the outcome if it was decided via an adversarial process.

But are cases *actually* decided more fairly under the adversarial system? It really depends on one's conception of fairness. Does fair mean "perfectly consistent with the facts"? Or could it mean giving the underdog a good shot at winning, or at least not losing badly? For better or worse, the biggest difference between the adversarial and the inquisitorial approaches appears to be that the adversarial approach creates greater opportunity to narrow large gaps in the advantage of one side over the other.

This is a good virtue when one side's advantage is based on some irrational preconception, such as jurors' stereotypic beliefs about the crime. ("Drug dealers aren't prosecuted unless the police nailed them red-handed." "Children don't lie about sexual abuse.") As we know, people have a tendency to seek, interpret, and remember information that confirms their prior beliefs and hypotheses (for review, see Chapter 6). Simulated jury studies, in which subjects render a verdict about a hypothetical case, have found that prior beliefs have weaker impact when case evidence is presented in an adversarial format as opposed to an inquisitorial format (Lind, 1982).

But when the *facts*—not preconceptions—give an advantage to one side, reducing the advantage is of more questionable merit. Yet adversarial methods may foster this as well. One study found that law students assigned to the very weak side of a practice case worked harder at investigating the case and arguing their side when adversarial, as opposed to inquisitorial, procedures were used (Lind et al., 1973). As a result, the lopsided case looked much more balanced to impartial observers than it actually was.

When cases are made to seem more balanced than they really are, sometimes dangerous criminals may occasionally go free. On the other hand, the American legal system operates on the assumption that wrongful conviction and imprisonment is the worst kind of mistake. By encouraging the weak side to try harder, the adversarial approach may strike a suitable, if imperfect, balance between giving the benefit of the doubt to defendants and yet still granting powerful investigatory powers to law enforcers.

The More Subtle Social Psychology of the Adversarial System

The adversarial procedure has some compelling selling points. But there are negative consequences of the adversarial system that might be preventable through minor adjustments to legal procedures. Consider the subtle effects of adversarial advocacy uncovered by two recent studies.

What happened depends on who's asking. It is common in the adversarial system for the prosecution to seek out and call (subpoena) its own witnesses, while the defense does the same. Could simply knowing the side that called them affect what witnesses report? To find out, researchers at a Canadian university had students watch a filmed barroom brawl that resulted in a blow to the head with a wine bottle (Vidmar and Laird, 1983). These "witnesses" were then given an authentic-looking subpoena that ordered them to appear for questioning on behalf of either "the Plaintiff, R. Zemp," or "the Defendant, W. Adams," or as "a witness of the court." Each witness was then individually escorted to a private "trial chamber," where he or she was sworn in and questioned by "judges" about what had occurred in the barroom incident.

The results were remarkable. The judges (graduate students) who took the witnesses' statements, as well as an independent group of raters who watched videotapes of the statements, were not made aware of the nature of any subject's subpoena. Nevertheless, both the judges and the raters found the statements of those who testified for the prosecution to be more incriminating than the statements of those who testified as witnesses for the defense. The statements of those who testified for the neutral court fell in between. As the authors put it, "Whereas the witnesses in neutral roles relayed relatively objective accounts, the adversary witnesses tended to describe the factual events with words or phrases that were not affectively neutral but biased in favor of their adversary role" (Vidmar and Laird, 1983, p. 895). And judges and raters picked up on this subtle bias.

Interestingly, the witnesses themselves were probably unaware that their eyewitness accounts were biased in favor of the side that subpoenaed them. After giving their descriptions, witnesses rated the extent of the defendant's responsibility for the incident. The ratings were the same no matter which side had served the witness the subpoena. *Without even realizing it*, people may adopt the adversarial slant implicit in the role spelled out in the subpoena: "You are to testify on behalf of...."

Could this problem be avoided? Perhaps the *court* could call those witnesses whose names are submitted by the contending parties—as in the neutral condition of the preceding study. This might eliminate the unintended bias prompted by the subpoena, but it could not prevent bias produced when attorneys for a given side track down the witnesses to question as they build the case for "their side" of the truth.

Sounding guilty and sounding innocent—all at once. Nowadays, police departments often videotape their interrogations of criminal suspects. If they can secure a confession, the videotape will clearly play well for the prosecution in court. One study recently examined whether the impressions gained from a videotaped interrogation are subject to the interpretive biases of adversarial procedures (Kassin et al., 1990). Subjects read a summary of an actual murder case and watched a 45-

minute interrogation of the female defendant in the case. (The video was courtesy of the Bronx District Attorney's Office.) During the interrogation, the defendant maintained her innocence throughout, yet made some rather implausible assertions. Her statement, then, was rather ambiguous. As such, could it be interpreted as evidence of guilt *or* innocence? To find out, the researchers created two conditions, which were identical except for one variation: the attorney who introduced the tape as evidence. In the defense condition, the defense attorney introduced the tape, citing the defendant's consistent story in the face of heavy pressure to confess. The tape was then played, followed by counterarguments by the prosecuting attorney, who cited the serious flaws in the defendant's account. In the prosecution condition, things were reversed. The prosecution introduced the "flawed" account as evidence of guilt, the tape followed, and the defense gave its counterarguments.

As shown in Figure 8.1, impressions were clearly influenced by which attorney introduced the tape. However, the direction of influence was different for two different types of subjects. Subjects were divided according to their scores on the Need for Cognition Scale, a mea-

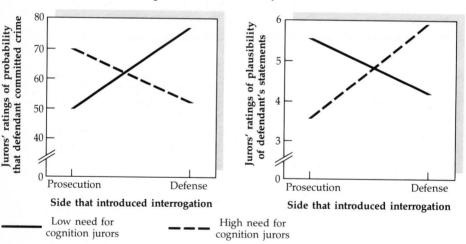

Primacy and Recency in the Courtroom
Depend on Who the Jurors Are

FIGURE 8.1
A videotape of a police interrogation of the defendant was introduced by either the prosecution (as evidence of guilt) or the defense (as evidence of innocence). The other side then rebutted the claim. High need-for-cognition jurors were swayed by the side that introduced the tape (a primacy effect), while low need-for-cognition jurors agreed with the side that had the last word (a recency effect).
(Data from Kassin, Reddy, and Tulloch, 1990.)

sure of how much a person enjoys and spends time thinking (Cacioppo and Petty, 1982). High need-for-cognition subjects showed a strong *primacy effect*, sharing the perspective of whoever introduced the defendant's statement. If the defense introduced the tape, they found the defendant's statement plausible and indicative of innocence. If the prosecution introduced the tape, they saw the statements as implausible and incriminating. Low need-for-cognition subjects, in contrast, showed just the opposite pattern—a *recency effect*. Their interpretation agreed with whoever had the last word about the tape.

It seems that high need-for-cognition people actively form a first impression that guides their subsequent perception and interpretation. In contrast, less cognitively active people wait until the end to think things over and open themselves to be more influenced by the person whose account they hear last.

But it is the larger point that's crucial: *Exactly* the same piece of evidence takes on a highly different meaning depending on which side introduces it in a courtroom trial. This may be another circumstance in which a particular type of evidence—police records—should be introduced by the neutral court and not by one of the biased adversaries.

Here in these two examples of the adversarial procedure we have our first instance of how influence processes may affect judgments and actions of actors in our criminal justice system. With this initial lesson in mind, let's go down to the police station and see what social influence factors might be at work there—as they begin to work up the case of the suspects of the Quicker Liquor Store robbery, among the many they deal with daily.

*T*HE POLICE STATION: GATHERING EVIDENCE FROM PEOPLE

Two crucial forms of evidence are obtained at the police station: eyewitness reports and suspect confessions. Both of these are defined by what people say, and as such, they can be strongly influenced by the tactics and techniques used to secure them—tactics and techniques that, consciously or not, are often guided by the desire to find the criminal as quickly as possible and get him or her convicted.

Eyewitness Testimony: But I Saw It with My Own Eyes

An eyewitness report is extremely important. In many cases it provides the only real leads for the police. If the eyewitness also identifies a suspect as the crime doer, this is usually enough to arrest the suspect. Indeed, a case without a positively identifying eyewitness may be considered too weak to try. In a courtroom trial, eyewitness identification tends to play very well with jurors. One study of English cases found that, in a typical year, convictions were obtained in 74 percent of the court cases in which the *only* evidence was eyewitness testimony (Loftus, 1979).

Eyewitness evidence is powerful, but is it really reliable? On a California campus, an attack on a college professor was once staged in front of 141 witnesses (Buckhout, 1974). Sworn statements taken from all witnesses the same day revealed great inaccuracy as a rule, including overestimation of the passage of time by an average of 150 percent, overestimation of the attacker's weight by 14 percent, and underestimation of his age by more than 2 years. Overall, the average witness achieved a score of only 25 percent correct on a test of recall covering the attacker's appearance, clothing, and actions. Seven weeks later, only 40 percent of the eyewitnesses identified the attacker from a photo spread of six faces. A full 25 percent identified an innocent bystander who had been placed at the scene by the researchers!

In another study, only 30 percent of the witnesses to a staged theft correctly identified the thief a brief 20 minutes after the theft, even though the thief clumsily dropped his bag of stolen goods within a few feet and in full view of the witnesses, and then looked right at them before running off (Leippe et al., 1978). Once he was out of sight, he was out of memory.

This unreliability of eyewitness memory has real consequences. Many cases of wrongful conviction based on mistaken identification have been documented (Loftus, 1984). One of the more notorious is the case of the "Gentleman Bandit" robberies that occurred near Wilmington, Delaware, in 1979. The gentlemanly robber frequently apologized to his victims and treated them quite kindly—except that he robbed them. Local newspapers published a composite police drawing of the robber based on victims' descriptions. Through an anonymous tip, the police learned that the drawing closely resembled a Catholic priest, Father Bernard Pagano. Father Pagano, in turn, was arrested and tried for the robberies. Seven victims identified him in court as the robber, and a conviction based almost solely on this eyewitness evidence seemed all but certain (Wrightsman, 1987). It is likely that the priest thanked heaven that the true robber (already in jail for another crime) came forward with a confession at the trial's eleventh hour.

A number of factors are responsible for false identifications. Of concern to us here are those aspects of *social influence* that can be potent sources of error in eyewitness reports. Memory is an active, constructive process in which what we have seen or heard may become integrated with our other stored memories and expectations as well as with

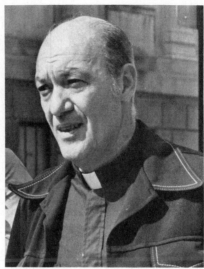

Seven witnesses mistook Father Bernard Pagano (right) for Ronald Clouser (left), the real armed robber dubbed the "Gentleman Bandit." Father Pagano was almost convicted before Clouser turned up.   (*UPI/Bettmann Newsphotos*)

later information that other people communicate to us in questions and suggestions. Memory consists of three separate stages, and distortion and bias may enter at each of them. Information must first be *encoded* (that is, put into a memorable form or code), then it is *stored* in a particular format, and finally it must be *retrieved* with the help of some kind of retrieval cues.

How willing we are to trust or act on our memory can also be influenced by social pressures. Thus, police interrogators can often influence memory reports just by the way they take them. Let us see how.

Where you lead, I will follow. A body of experimental research by cognitive psychologist Elizabeth Loftus has demonstrated that subtle aspects of how a question is asked can have distorting effects on what witnesses report having seen. The general paradigm used by her research team involves subjects first seeing a critical scene (in a slide or videotape). Then they are asked questions about some details in the scene. The researchers systematically vary how the questions are worded, or they mislead the subjects by distorting some detail and then seeing if the reported memory changes to incorporate these suggested false details.

In one series of studies, subjects saw a slide show depicting a pedestrian-car accident (Loftus et al., 1978). During the sequence, the car (a red Datsun) was seen at a yellow yield sign. After viewing the slides, subjects were asked a variety of questions, including a critical one. The control group was asked whether another car passed the red Datsun while it was stopped at the *yield sign*. The biased recall group was asked the same question except that misleading information was planted in it: the yield sign was replaced by a *stop sign*. Later, when asked to identify slides of what they originally saw, most of the misled subjects identified a slide showing the Datsun at a *stop sign*. The verbal information contained in the question seems to have been incorporated into the visual memory of those in the misleading question group.

In light of this rather remarkable control of memory by a few words, consider the many ways in which leading questions could creep into a police officer's interviewing plan. In investigating a crime, the police (quite naturally) will form a theory of what happened and infer certain things that "must have been." A question to the eyewitness, in turn, may imply the inference as a fact. If there are multiple eyewitnesses, a police officer may incorporate what one witness told him ("The holdup man had a tattoo with writing on his arm") into the questions he asks a second witness ("Could you see what the man's tattoo said?"). Notice that the question asked of the second witness assumes the presence of the tattoo. This multiple witness situation may also include the risk of normative conformity pressures ("According to the other two witnesses..."). It probably occurs to you that the interest of justice might be better served by having different police officers interview each witness.

It is also possible that accurate and seemingly innocent cues in a question can be suggestive and can alter memory. Conjure up images of a male truck driver and a male dancer. Which one is heavier? When asked to describe a stranger who had strolled leisurely across the stage during a lecture, students estimated his weight as 172 pounds on average when they were informed during interrogation that he was a truck driver, and as 159 pounds when informed that he was a dancer (Christiaansen et al., 1983). In addition, if the questioner described the stranger as a "man," age estimates averaged 27 years, whereas the descriptor "young man" yielded age estimates of about 24 years. (The stranger, by the way, was 19 years old and weighed 140 pounds). Sticks and stones may break your bones, but a well-placed word may imprison you.

Identification, please. Besides its ability to shape verbal recall, the power of suggestion can affect face recognition and willingness to trust a hazy sense of familiarity. Bringing in a suspect "to the station" is a major advance in the casework of a police investigator. It moves the case to within one step—a positive witness identification—of arraignment and prosecution. And so the police become very motivated to secure a positive identification of the suspect from an eyewitness.

Unless the police are careful, this motivation may translate into influence behaviors that heighten the risks of a false identification. One rather blatant biasing behavior is the construction of an *unfair lineup*. Ideally, a police lineup should include the suspect and several innocent others (foils) who closely resemble eyewitness descriptions of the criminal (Luus and Wells, 1991). Occasionally, this rule is grossly violated, and the suspect sticks out like a sore thumb (see Figure 8.2). In one case in Wisconsin, the victim reported that a black man had committed the crime. The police assembled a lineup consisting of one black suspect and five white men and proceeded to ask the victim if any of the men resembled the criminal (Ellison and Buckhout, 1981)!

A more subtle form of influence is the use of *biased lineup instructions*. By declaring their confidence that the criminal is in the lineup, or by instructing the witness to "indicate which one of the six men before you committed the crime"—without explicitly providing a "none of the above" option—police officers bring several forms of influence to bear on the already cooperative witness. They imply that there is a suspect and that the suspect's probable guilt is backed up by a great deal of evidence gathered by experts. Even aside from this implication, the biased instructions make it less likely that the witness will reject the whole lineup (that is, identify no one). Some witnesses may not even realize that they have the option; others may be unwilling to inquire about it. Finally, in an unfamiliar setting dominated by a classic authority figure (a police officer or detective), some witnesses (despite great uncertainty) may obey, in Milgram-like fashion, the officer's implicit command and choose the most familiar-looking member of the lineup in spite of their considerable uncertainty.

Just how much can biased instructions heighten the risk of a false identification? Consider a well-known study in which witnesses to a

FIGURE 8.2
The risk of false identifications increases when lineups fail to include foils who resemble the description of the suspect.

staged act of vandalism were led to believe either that the vandal was definitely in a five-person lineup (biased instructions) or that he only "might be" (unbiased instructions) (Malpass and Devine, 1981). In reality, the lineup did not even include the vandal. Yet 78 percent of the witnesses given biased instructions identified an *innocent* lineup member as the vandal. In contrast, only 33 percent of those given unbiased instructions did so. This alarming false-alarm effect of biased instructions was replicated in a study in which the witnesses actually thought that they were identifying a real thief for real police officers (Hosch et al., 1984).

Police in many jurisdictions, but far from all of them, are legally required to mention explicitly the "can't decide" or "none of them" options to witnesses. Suspects are also entitled to have their lawyer present at an identification. (Do you have a personal lawyer you could call quickly? We don't and assume that most people do not.) In any case, these rules provide a good starting point, from an influence perspective.

Confidence boosters. Would you agree that eyewitnesses who are confident of their memory are likely to be more accurate than hesitant, uncertain eyewitnesses? It sounds reasonable, doesn't it? Yet an important and surprising finding of eyewitness research is that accuracy and confidence are often only weakly related (Deffenbacher, 1980; Wells and Murray, 1984). Inaccurate witnesses tend to be as confident as accurate ones. It seems that the factors that influence memory are not the same ones that influence "confidence in memory." Moreover, people may not be aware of changes in memory or confidence, or of the factors that caused those changes (Leippe, 1980). As we saw in the previous chapter, the mental processes that lead to conscious thoughts take place unconsciously. The result is that memory and confidence may go their separate ways.

Consider the consequences of this mental state of affairs. Certain procedures of interrogation may bolster witness confidence without improving memory for the critical event or person. For instance, having learned about self-attribution and cognitive dissonance (in Chapter 3), would it surprise you that a witness might become more committed to and confident in her lineup choice after being subtly shoved into the choice via biased lineup instructions? Once a choice is made, particularly an important one that may send someone to jail, postdecisional dissonance reduction will set in. And the freedom-constraining effect of the biased instructions may go unnoticed thanks to the fundamental attribution error: we underestimate the forces operating in the external situation while overestimating the internal forces, in this case, belief in the accuracy of our own memory.

Repeated questioning may also bolster confidence. A witness may be questioned several times during a police investigation. And there may indeed be some gains in amount recalled (Scrivner and Safer, 1988). But it is possible, as well, that an unwarranted escalation in one's confidence about the accuracy of memory may result from the repeated public commitment to one's testimony (Leippe, 1980). Worse yet, the guesses encouraged or the "missing pieces" suggested by the interrogator in Interview One may be confidently "remembered" as part of what one saw in Interview Two (Hastie et al., 1978; Loftus et al., 1978). The safest and most informative police procedure is to first take a *free narrative* report in which the witness simply tells his or her story without interruption. Then more directed questions may be asked, with care taken to avoid "feeding" suspected details to the witness and to include always an "I don't know" option. Further questioning follows the same rules and occurs only when necessary.

The general point of this section has been that *eyewitness reports*, though indispensable, are highly subject to interpersonal influence. Procedures to minimize such influence should be followed—particularly since, as we will see, jurors give confident eyewitness testimony more credence than it deserves. Now let us look at avoidable influence that can be directed at another target—suspects.

What's A Little Confession between Friends?

"Please your majesty," said the knave, "I didn't write it and they can't prove I did; there's no name signed at the end." "If you didn't sign it," said the King, "that only makes the matter worse. You must have meant some mischief, or else you'd have signed your name like an honest man."

Lewis Carroll, *Alice's Adventures in Wonderland*

In New York City in 1964, after extensive interrogation by the police, George Whitmore, Jr., gave a sixty-one-page typewritten confession to the murder of two socialites. He was subsequently proved innocent. How can a man be made to incriminate himself like this when he knows he may forfeit his life as a result? If this occurs frequently, we must surely be dealing with a powerful set of attitude and behavior change techniques. As a matter of fact, about 80 percent of all arraigned suspects confess, after some period of police interrogation, to having committed a crime. Interestingly, this same level of "success" occurred when police were allowed to use third-degree physical abuse, which was later legally prohibited. Apparently, some psychological tactics may be as effective as physical force.

A recent study identified 350 instances of miscarriages of justice in the United States in which innocent persons were convicted of capital crimes. In 49 of these cases, the conviction was obtained primarily on the basis of false confessions, all elicited in response to coercion (Bedau and Radelet, 1987). A case study of four instances of false confessions to criminal acts by innocent suspects for brutal murders or substantial theft notes that the confession was the only evidence linking crime and suspect (Ofshe, 1990).

Not all confessions are the direct result of interrogation tactics; *plea bargaining* often involves confession to a lesser offense in the hope of getting a lesser sentence. Still police routinely encourage suspects to confess. Disputed confessions—those that are later retracted by a defendant now pleading not guilty—may be involved in up to 20 percent of cases that reach the courtroom (Kalven and Zeisel, 1966; Wrightsman, 1987).

Like an eyewitness report, a confession is "drawn" from a person by police officers. As in the case in the interrogation of witnesses, the interrogation of suspects has developed not through systematic research but by trial and error over a long period of time, and "tried and true" on-line practice by detective interrogators. The result has been a highly sophisticated array of techniques, most of which have found their way into the police manuals that police departments may use for training purposes (e.g., Inbau et al., 1986; Inbau and Reid, 1962; Mulbar, 1951). The general approach of the manuals is expressed in the following excerpts:

> If one...has a layman's knowledge of practical psychology, and uses the salesman's approach, he can be successful in reaching into a man's brain and pulling out the facts he wants (Mulbar, 1951).

> ...Candidates for a detective's post undergo an intensive six-week course that stresses the interrogation of prisoners. Most detectives have a built-in psychology based on instinct and experience in which a man's weak points are exploited. They can get prisoners to talk as a result of this. (Michael Murphy, former New York Police Commissioner, quoted in *The New York Times*, November 7, 1963.)

In short, the leading text on interrogation tactics outlines the elicitation of confessions as a tour de force of social influence, in which presumably guilty suspects are "persuaded" to confess (Inbau et al., 1986). What means of drawing confessions do police manuals tout for their interrogators in training? And what influence principles do they rely on? Let's look at some of the major categories of techniques employed by the seasoned interrogator (as determined from a detailed content analysis of many detective manuals, corroborated in interviews with police detectives, by one of your authors, Zimbardo, 1971).

To facilitate the impact of this information, and your memory for it, we'd like you to imagine that *you* are the suspect. You are accused of a crime you know you did not commit; but you do not have a good alibi, and you are the only suspect of the crime that the police have been able to round up.

Control of the psychological situation. The manuals suggest that the interrogator should be alone with the suspect and stand or sit physically close to him or her. Authority is to be established by small gestures like prohibiting smoking, telling the suspect where to sit, or offering to provide a drink of water. The interrogation should take place in an environment unfamiliar to the suspect, thereby destroying all psychological support that familiar things provide. The room should be quite sparsely furnished and free of all distractions. There should be no objects for the suspect to fiddle with (like paper clips) or that remind the suspect of links to life outside (like telephones).

We can identify several influence forces launched into action by these austere arrangements. The interrogator has established himself as an authority figure who is operating in *his own* ballpark. The "obey authority" heuristic may be engaged in the suspect as a result. The interrogator also clearly controls all rewards: a drink to quench thirst, permission to smoke, release from the unpleasant room. As time wears on, these become powerful inducements to just fess up. Because self-distraction is denied, the message repetition will be relentless and inescapable. Counterarguing and other forms of mental and verbal resistance, handicapped already by the absence of reminders of social support, will become more difficult as anxiety and fatigue build up.

Perceptual and judgmental distortion techniques. Interrogators encourage a cognitive restructuring similar to that which occurs in laboratory studies of conformity and obedience. They will either minimize the seriousness of the offense and allow the suspect a face-saving out or use the opposite tactic of exaggerating the seriousness of the crime. In the first case, the investigator suggests that the suspect's indiscretion is not too serious, since there have been thousands of others in the same situation. Or the interrogator may shift the blame to circumstances (such as the environment or the suspect's weaknesses). These suggestions may compel a confession by making the suspect feel less guilty or shameful. We can recognize exploitation of a contrast effect here. Also, by fostering a situational attribution or a sense that the behavior was somewhat normative ("Hey, we know that any normal guy would have been turned on by that little slut's come on"), the suspect may be led to expect that his confession will be greeted with understanding and leniency.

The opposite distortion—that it's worse than the suspect thinks— uses fear to elicit a confession and may be done by blatant misrepresentation of facts. The interrogator may falsely claim to possess certain in-

criminating evidence, making the suspect feel that "the game is up." Or
the interrogator may use a "bluff on a split pair" to pretend, quite elab-
orately, that a suspect's partner who is being questioned separately
next door has just confessed. And guess who he has ratted on—*you*, of
course. Now it's your turn to get even with that rat.

Illusion of empathy. There are several devices for making the prisoner want to confide in the interrogator. Flattery and small favors (offering a cup of coffee, water, a smoke) may be used to encourage liking.
More sophisticated is the *Mutt and Jeff* ruse. Two investigators work in
tandem: Mutt, a cruel and relentless investigator, and Jeff, a kind-
hearted family man, perhaps with a brother who was once in a similar
scrape. Jeff keeps telling Mutt to lay off the prisoner and gets angry
with him. Eventually Mutt leaves the room. Jeff then confides that he,
too, detests Mutt's tactics but suggests that the suspect's only hope is to
cooperate quickly with good ol' Jeff by telling the truth. Together they
will report Mutt to his superiors. The angered suspect sides with Jeff,
buys his story—and sells away his freedom.

Encouraging self-attributions of guilt. The interrogation expert's
intuitive grasp of self-attribution of emotion is evident in another technique. To make prisoners feel highly anxious—and perhaps guilty—interrogators point out supposed symptoms of guilt in their demeanor.
Attention may be directed to pulsation of the carotid artery in the neck,
movement of the Adam's apple, "cotton mouth," fidgeting limbs, and a
"peculiar feeling inside" that could reflect a troubled conscience (Inbau
et al., 1986).

The polygraph prop: scientific lying. Then there is the lie detector,
or polygraph. Lie detectors are machines that measure physiological
arousal—things like changes in heart rate, electrodermal activity (sweating), and respiration. Lying makes us nervous (see Chapter 7), and this
may show up as heightened arousal. There are various procedures used
to assess lying, but the basic method of a lie detector test is to see
whether the suspect shows unusually heightened arousal when responding to questions that are relevant to the crime—especially questions that directly ask whether he committed the crime ("Did you rape
Alice Brown?") or refer to specific behaviors the police know were part
of the crime ("Did you threaten to kill her?"). The assumption is that a
guilty suspect will show greater arousal while lying about these critical
questions than when responding to noncritical "control questions."

Do lie detectors detect lies? In laboratory studies in which subjects
are asked to commit "crimes" and then deny them, polygraph tests reveal their "guilt," on average, in about three-fourths of the cases
(Kircher et al., 1988). "Innocent" subjects who were put up to no crime

are found "innocent" about two-thirds of the time. In some real crime cases in which guilt or innocence was later established without the polygraph, the average rates of accurate detection are about the same (Saxe et al., 1985). But if you were doing a little math in your head, you might have noted that these tests have a significant rate of error, finding innocent people guilty and guilty ones innocent.

In general, polygraph conclusions beat guessing. However, when it comes to criminal justice, we are talking about individual cases—*you*—not generalities. But there is more to the story of lie detectors. They can be beaten by guilty people to give false readings. You can tense your muscles, squeeze your toes, or fidget restlessly, thereby creating a constant heightened arousal that makes changes created by the questions hard to detect (Saxe et al., 1985). A worse problem is that "guilt shows" primarily among people who *believe in* the validity of polygraphs (Saxe et al., 1985). Lies among nonbelievers are harder to detect. As a result, police officers may go to great lengths to convince suspects that the lie detector is foolproof, often staging rigged tricks with playing cards to demonstrate its magical detection skill. Sometimes the police force a confession by only threatening to use a lie detector. ("You may as well confess if you're guilty. The polygraph will find you out anyway.") In the final analysis, lie detector tests are not accurate enough to trust for determining a suspect's guilt or innocence; they usually end up being used as just another powerful situational "stage prop" for coercing confessions.

With their arsenal of influence weapons, police success at inducing confessions should not be surprising. Yet the power of interrogation-room persuasion is not intuitively obvious to a great many judges and jurors. Disputed confessions are often allowed as evidence, on the assumption that jurors can generally determine whether a confession was voluntary or coerced. But the research evidence on the fundamental attribution error—how people underestimate situational causes of behavior, particularly verbal statements—casts doubt on this assumption. Who is more credible, a detective or a suspect fighting for his life, when the issue is what induced the suspect's confession? Moreover, mock-trial studies suggest that jurors are less likely to discount confessions induced by positive psychological ploys (such as a promise of leniency) than confessions induced by threats of punishment (Kassin and Wrightsman, 1980, 1981). People generally believe that punishment is a more powerful "inducer" than reward (Wells, 1980). Isn't it ironic that involuntary confessions can be coerced at least as successfully—and maybe more so—by techniques that use a "velvet glove" as opposed to an "iron fist"?

Coercing confessions by exploiting near-total control over the psychological environment is of questionable ethics. There is evidence that, actually, few *indictments* require confessions to supplement the "hard" evidence (Zimbardo, 1971). Perhaps confession tactics are not needed at all.

IN THE COURTROOM: THE PERSUASION BATTLEGROUND

A courtroom trial is a persuasion setting, if ever there was one. When you think about a trial, what is the first thing that comes to mind? Do you see a lawyer pacing back and forth in front of a jury box, speaking in alternately passionate and somber tones, imploring an intensely attentive jury to return a guilty verdict? A trial lawyer is clearly a persuasive communicator, whose goal is to get an audience (a jury or judge) to adopt a certain belief (guilty or innocent) about an attitude object (the defendant). To get to this belief, the lawyer must influence numerous attitudes and perceptions—about the defendant, supporting and opposing witnesses, the circumstances of the crime, and the strength of physical evidence, alibis, and the like.

However, in contrast to communicators in radio and TV ads, political speeches, and sales pitches, the trial room lawyer must deal with two additional realities: *on the spot* competition with an opposing side and reliance on the performance of other people—his or her witnesses. The courtroom is a *persuasion battleground* with dueling sides and numerous soldiers engaged in verbal warfare. This makes for complex persuasion processes.

Trial Lawyers on Trial

Volumes could be written on the persuasive techniques of trial lawyers. We'll sample some that both psychological research and lawyer lore have addressed in detail.

Order of presentation and what to do about it. We learned in Chapter 5 that the first of two opposing messages has the persuasive edge (a primacy effect) if there is a delay between when each of the messages is presented and when the test of attitudes is taken. To give the second message the advantage (a recency effect) it must be separated in time from the first message, but then the attitude test must come soon after the second message. When neither of these conditions is met, as in a trial where opposing arguments alternate with little delay, an order effect is not as likely. This is fortunate because, in a trial, the prosecution has the first *and* the last word. The prosecution gives its opening statement, followed by the defense. After all evidence is heard, the prosecution makes its closing arguments, the defense follows with its summation, and then the prosecution is allowed a rebuttal—the last word.

Although this rather unbalanced arrangement may not be biasing *generally*, special circumstances do increase the likelihood of an order effect. The last word, for example, may provide a slight, yet decisive, nudge in an extremely close case. Or the defense may have a powerful summation that will be difficult to rebut. In his book *My Life in Court*, trial lawyer Louis Nizer (1961) describes how he fends off a recency effect using variants of the forewarning and inoculation techniques we encountered in Chapter 6. For good measure, he adds dashes of flattery, favor asking, and assumed consensus (that his opponent is a snake):

> When I am required to sum up first, I endeavor to prepare the jury so that it will not yield to the blandishments of my adversary. I remind the jury that he will have the last word and that I will not be permitted to reply. I tell them that I must depend on their recollections to correct any misstatement of fact which my opponent, who follows me, may make. I must rely on their discriminating judgment to reject any false arguments. Then, as I proceed to build my own case, I anticipate the contentions of my adversary. I announce his slogans and attempt to destroy them, asking jurors to become my watchmen when they hear such sophistry, and reject it as an insult to their intelligence (p. 434).

At the other end of the trial, the beginning, the prosecution can enjoy a primacy advantage in a close case if the defense takes no steps to neutralize it. In mock trials of ambiguous cases, a primacy effect—more guilty verdicts—occurred when the prosecution made an expansive opening statement (Pyszczynski and Wrightsman, 1981). It appears that, when the evidence is truly ambiguous, the theory or framework created in jurors' minds by a detailed opening statement can *persistently* bias jurors' interpretations of that evidence.

Put yourself in the role of a juror (you're no longer a suspect under interrogation). What is going to persuade you? What do you want to discover? As the trial progresses, jurors pick up a "story line," or a scenario of a coherent plot. From that they develop "their theory" about what happened (Pennington and Hastie, 1986). It is the lawyer's job to make sure jurors hear—and believe—his or her story.

The prosecution usually opens by summarizing the "State's case" against the defendant. ("We intend to prove...that the defendant did this...and is guilty.") What the defense doesn't want to do is to follow with a brief opening statement that lays out no alternative story, or to forgo its opening statement until after the prosecution presents its evidence and witnesses. Trial simulation studies have found stronger impressions of guilt among jurors when the defense chooses such options (Pyszczynski and Wrightsman, 1981; Wells et al., 1985). Unless the defense provides you, the juror, with a reasonable hypothesis about the crime or expectations about evidence *before* you begin studying the evidence, you may be unwittingly guided in your consideration of the evidence by the only hypothesis you have—the prosecution's.

Stating conclusions. As she presents her case—introducing evidence, calling and questioning witnesses and such—should the attorney "let the evidence speak for itself" or summarize it and explicitly state her conclusions about it? Persuasion studies suggest building in *explicit conclusions*, unless the jury is exceptionally intelligent (Hovland and Mandell, 1952; Weiss and Steenbock, 1965). Attorneys appear to follow this advice regularly and state the conclusion they wish the jury to make (Saks and Hastie, 1978). When there are two sides to a story, leaving the audience to draw its own conclusions is a risky venture.

Mixing it up. Trial practice manuals recommend that attorneys employ vivid audio, visual, and olfactory ("smelly") aids in their presentation of evidence (e.g., Keeton, 1973). Psychologically, this is sound advice. Consider lectures, which are like trials in their continuous stream of words. Even on your best days, you may have difficulty maintaining close attention to the long-winded, uninterrupted flow of the lecturer's words. Films and demonstrations are welcome changes in the classroom action. Against the monotonous verbal background of a courtroom trial, most nonverbally presented evidence—an audiotape of a crucial conversation, a blown-up picture of physical injuries, a simple picture or flowchart drawn on a blackboard—will be highly salient. And as we know, perceptually salient stimuli can dominate attributions. They also may be better remembered during jury deliberation (Reyes et al., 1980). The better trial lawyers make their evidence memorable: eye-, ear-, or nose-catching.

Word wars. Audiovisuals are necessary and sometimes pivotal attention-getters, but ultimately the courtroom is a battlefield of language. Words can be highly salient, or not. Other things being equal, trial lawyers who can verbally "paint" the more vivid pictures of their view of the case win more cases in the long run. Studies indicate that, in actual cases, winning prosecutors speak longer and make more assertive statements than losing prosecutors (Andrews, 1984). This isn't too surprising given the evidence we've seen that impressions of "who's in control" lead naturally to attributions about "who knows more" (see Chapter 3).

Especially important in the courtroom word war is the interaction between the lawyers and the witnesses on the stand. As psycho-legal researchers Michael Saks and Reid Hastie (1978) observed, "much of a lawyer's case is delivered from the mouths of witnesses. The lawyer, however, is in a position to exercise considerable influence over what comes out" (p. 114). Practice manuals spell out many strategies for shaping witnesses' verbal behavior. One common recommendation is to give one's own witness "space" to articulate smooth narrative answers to one's questions—answers that should convey the impression that the witness is assertive and self-confident and that the lawyer trusts the witness enough to relinquish control to him or her (O'Barr, 1982). A narrative style sounds like this:

QUESTION: Now, prior to his being at the store, did you have any customers?

NARRATIVE ANSWER: Oh, yes, customers came in the store, but after 9 there was no one in the store but me. And I was talking on the telephone to my sister in Georgia for about 20 minutes. I was still talking on the phone to my sister and then no one came in then until about 20 after 9 and this man came in, that man, John Barnes. I was still talking. He just walked in. (O'Barr, 1982, p. 145)

Notice the wordy, uninterrupted flow. Now contrast this style with the fragmented delivery that lawyers are advised to "encourage" from opposing witnesses by frequently interrupting and requesting that the witness just answer the question asked:

FRAGMENTED ANSWER: Oh, yes, customers came in the store, but after 9 there was no one in the store but me.

QUESTION: What were you doing at the time?

ANSWER: I was talking on the telephone to my sister in Georgia.

QUESTION: And how long did that conversation run?

ANSWER: It, about, uh, close to 20 minutes.

QUESTION: ...etc. (O'Barr, 1982, p. 139)

Which witness response sounds better? Anthropologist William O'Barr (1982) and his colleagues presented subjects with a lawyer-witness exchange characterized by either a narrative or a fragmented style (Lind et al., 1978). When the style was *narrative* and the witness was a *man*, the witness was seen as more competent and the lawyer was judged as *perceiving the witness* as more competent than when the style was fragmented—confirming the hunches of some good legal minds. Interestingly, though, a *fragmented style* by a *female witness* did not adversely affect impressions of her. O'Barr speculates that fragmented exchanges are expected of females by those who hold the old stereotype that women are unassertive.

"Powerless speech" is also unbecoming of witnesses. By "powerless," we refer to a style of talking that includes lots of verbal hedges (e.g., "I sort of felt uncomfortable"), polite forms (e.g., "Would you please speak louder"), tag questions (e.g., "John is home, isn't he?" instead of "Is John home?"), and empty adjectives (e.g., cute, adorable). Witnesses with a powerless speech style are rated as less convincing, less competent, and less trustworthy than those who speak more "powerfully," apparently because powerless speech conveys low social status (Erickson et al., 1978; O'Barr, 1982). Trial lawyers often coach their witnesses to speak assertively and lose those unbecoming hedges and needless adjectives.

Leading questions and the careful ordering and timing of questions to get the desired answer—these are the stock and trade of successful trial lawyers, particularly when they cross-examine witnesses. We have already seen how leading questions, or questions that subtly suggest the answer or imply a disputed fact, can affect memory reports. Building on this basic idea, a lawyer can get witnesses to say, or sound like they're saying, things they would never admit to in response to a straightforward question.

F. Lee Bailey, the celebrated defense lawyer whose famous clients include the Boston Strangler and Patty Hearst, offers this snippet from a cross-examination in which the victim-witness in an armed robbery case is trapped—by his own words—into giving the impression that his nervousness while being held up clouded his perception and memory. Up to this point he had insisted that fear had not prevented him from getting a memorable look at the perpetrator. We pick up where the witness has just addressed some differences between his report to the police and the actual physical appearance of the defendant.

WITNESS: That was my best recollection at the time I talked with the inspector.

CROSS-EXAMINER: That was less than an hour after the incident, wasn't it, when your recollection was fresh?

WITNESS: Yes, but I was nervous then.

CROSS-EXAMINER: And that nervousness may have somewhat impaired the description you gave the inspector?

WITNESS: Yes, that's right.

CROSS-EXAMINER: But certainly, sir, sitting with the inspector in a lighted room in the security of a police station, you had no fear for your life, did you?

WITNESS: No, I was just nervous.

CROSS-EXAMINER: But surely, sir, you must have been *more* nervous during the few seconds you were being robbed than during your talk with the inspector—isn't that so?

WITNESS: I was nervous both times.

CROSS-EXAMINER: But more so during the robbery, yes?

WITNESS: I might have been. (Bailey, 1985, p. 153)

The cross-examiner used one admission by the witness to force him into a logical necessity of admitting to another, much more important, admission. The witness could either retract his earlier statement and look wishy-washy and disingenuous, or fall into the lawyer's trap of logical implication. Either way, he loses.

A close cousin to the logical trap is the psycho-logical trap of self-attribution (Saks and Hastie, 1978). If the witness will not admit to an emotion, a motive, or a trait, perhaps he can be induced to make self-statements from which he, himself, will infer the characteristic. Consider this "cross-examination" of a student complaining that he did not deserve the poor grade he received on a test. Then think about how it could be applied in a courtroom.

PROFESSOR: You really put very little effort into preparing for this exam, didn't you?

STUDENT: That's not true. I studied. The test was just unfairly hard.

PROFESSOR: Didn't I overhear you tell John that, on the night before the exam, you went to a movie with your girlfriend?

STUDENT: Yes, I did go, but...

PROFESSOR: On Monday, two days before the exam, had you read all the assigned chapters?

STUDENT: No.

PROFESSOR: Did you finally read everything, and then review it?

STUDENT: Yes, I read everything, and went over it once.

PROFESSOR: Is once enough for even your hardest courses?

STUDENT: No.

PROFESSOR: Well, wouldn't you say that your own actions suggest you're giving my course less than your best effort?

STUDENT: Yeah, maybe I'm not giving it my best. (*And to himself:* Is this prof a lawyer or something?)

PROFESSOR: So, you seem to be saying that maybe the test was fair, though hard, for those who studied properly and unfair and difficult for those who did not.

STUDENT: I guess so, sorry to disturb you, I'm outta here before it gets worse.

Identifying Witnesses

Earlier, we observed that eyewitness memory is often unreliable and easily influenced by questioning. In lamenting how poor eyewitness testimony can be, trial lawyer F. Lee Bailey (1985) adds the troubling opinion that "juries take great stock in such testimony, unaware as they are that wrongful eyewitness identifications have put more innocent people behind bars than all other jury mistakes combined" (p. 148). In fact, Bailey considers the discrediting of an identifying witness "the toughest, meanest, most dangerous and exasperating job a trial lawyer ever has to undertake" (p. 145).

Studies of reactions to eyewitness testimony offer nothing to contradict Bailey's ominous observations that jurors overestimate eyewitness accuracy (Brigham and Bothwell, 1983). After reading a summary of an armed robbery court case, mock jurors in one study voted to convict the defendant only 18 percent of the time—when the prosecution supplied no eyewitness. But when an eyewitness was presented—the only addition to the case—the conviction rate soared to 72 percent (Loftus, 1974).

Let's discredit the credibility of the eyewitness and see what happens. One researcher did just that by describing him as badly nearsighted and without his glasses while witnessing the robbery. How far did the conviction rate drop then? Only down to 68 percent! (Loftus, 1974).

A two-phase procedure has been used in some studies of reactions to testimony. In phase one, subject-witnesses observe a staged crime and give an eyewitness report and lineup identification. In phase two, subject-jurors watch videotapes of these memory reports and guess at their accuracy. Subject-jurors guess that false identifications were accurate at an alarmingly high rate (Wells et al., 1979; Lindsay et al., 1981). If people are skeptical of human ability to correctly recognize a once-seen face, they do a good job of hiding it from researchers.

That confident look. How do you decide if you can trust a memory report? Chances are that you check out a number of things. Reports that appear to be internally consistent are more readily believed (Leippe et al., 1990). More detailed reports are also more trusted, even when the details are trivial. Jurors in one trial simulation were more likely to accept the account of a witness to a store robbery when she reported that a bystander to the robbery bought Milk Duds and a Diet Pepsi rather than simply "a few store items" (Bell and Loftus, 1989).

But if we had to select the one variable most likely to influence your belief in the accuracy of another's memory, it would be the degree of *confidence* or *certainty* expressed by the person. In the two-phase staged-crime studies, the more confident the witness looks, the more often subject-jurors guess that he or she has a strong, accurate recollection of the perpetrator (Wells et al., 1979; Leippe et al., 1990). It seems very sensible. The Supreme Court has even identified "confidence in testimony" as one indicator jurors should use to judge courtroom testimony (*Neil v. Biggers*, 1972).

Would that it were true, but it just isn't so. As we noted earlier, confidence and accuracy are only weakly related. Yet the look of confidence (or uncertainty) is so compelling it can easily determine belief (or disbelief) in incriminating eyewitness testimony when the stakes are nothing less than the liberty of the accused. Trial lawyers know this well and invariably advise and even train their witnesses to project a confident demeanor on the witness stand. They also brief witnesses about the antagonistic cross-examination they may face. And what do you think the effects of such briefings are? Accurate or not, eyewitnesses "psych themselves up" and project heightened confidence on the stand (Wells et al., 1981).

Confidence busters. But don't forget the other side. Good cross-examiners can turn the persuasive power of confidence to their advantage by "shaking the confidence" of the witness. Hold on, though, and remember the principles of attribution. If the cross-examiner's tactics are obvious, or if she looks like a bully, jurors will attribute the witness's unconfident testimony to the cross-examiner, not to the witness's poor memory. In the words of the Wicked Witch of the West (late of the Land of Oz), "These things must be done del-i-cate-ly." We are already familiar with one method for doing this. The cross-examiner can (and usually does) question at a fast enough pace to force witnesses into a fragmented style, which may make them look not only less competent but also tentative and unsure. A second method is to induce a *self-perception* of poor memory. Ask enough questions about minute details that prompt "I don't recall" answers and the witness may begin to doubt his or her own memory. Such self-doubt will show up and be duly noted by judge and jury.

Making good memory look bad. Repeated failures to recall details lead jurors to suspect a faulty memory—the flip side of the "lots of details mean good memory" heuristic we saw earlier. Under certain circumstances, recall of trivial details may be an absolutely awful cue to the accuracy of important aspects of testimony, such as facial identification of the criminal. Consider this: An eyewitness can look at only one thing at a time, and so the more she looks at the criminal, the less time she has to study the surrounding scenery. It follows from this that those eyewitnesses with better memory of the criminal's face may have poorer memory for peripheral details. This is exactly what was found in one staged-crime study (Wells and Leippe, 1981).

But much more interesting were the impressions that subject-witnesses projected when they were cross-examined rather mercilessly about unimportant peripheral details. Witnesses with the poorest memory for these details looked pretty bad under such grilling, and subject-jurors who watched the cross-examinations judged their memory reports—*including their lineup identifications*—to be untrustworthy. In fact, they trusted their identifications less than they trusted those of witnesses who had good memory for trivial detail. This was true even though it was the witnesses with poor memory for details who most often correctly identified the culprit in the lineup! (See Figure 8.3.) We have here a clear case of misapplication of a rule of thumb about memory credibility.

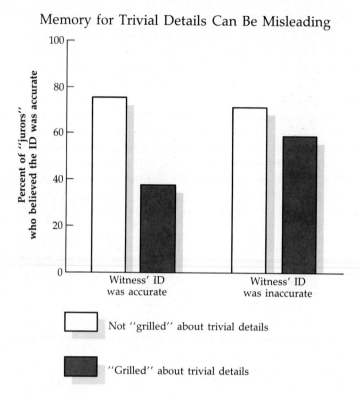

Memory for Trivial Details Can Be Misleading

FIGURE 8.3
Eyewitnesses to a staged theft made either an accurate or an inaccurate identification of the thief from a lineup. They were then cross-examined about their memory and either grilled or not grilled about trivial details of what they saw. Subject-jurors who watched the not-grilled cross-examinations believed the identifications of inaccurate eyewitnesses as often as they believed the identifications of accurate ones. Those who watched eyewitnesses being grilled about trivial details believed the *in*accurate identifications *more* than the accurate ones! Eyewitnesses with good face memory had poorer memory for surroundings (trivial details) and showed it under cross-examination.
(Data from Wells and Leippe, 1981. Copyright 1981 by the American Psychological Association. Adapted by permission.)

The inaccuracy of judging accuracy. We've painted a bleak picture of generally poor ability to make valid judgments of the accuracy of memory reports. Jurors (and police interrogators, we might add) rely on intuitive but often invalid cues like confidence and memory for trivial details. Can anything be done to improve this state of affairs? People can probably never achieve great skill at judging memories. After all, we tend to trust *our own* memories, faulty as they are. There may be few differences between the reports of accurate and inaccurate memories, and those that do exist may be barely perceptible to others.

Yet some improvement is possible. Cognitive psychologists have established that there are systematic differences between reports of real memories and reports of things people are asked to imagine; furthermore, other people may be trained to watch out for these differences (Johnson and Raye, 1981; Schooler et al., 1986). Reports of real memories, for example, convey richer sensory images. And although we have seen that it may compel incorrect inferences about unquestioned aspects of memory, the opportunity to watch witness responses to cross-examination questions may improve detection of the accuracy of those aspects of memory which the cross-examination specifically deals with (Turtle and Wells, 1988).

*T*HE JURY ROOM

We now come to the final topic of this chapter, the deliberation of juries. The jury is the ultimate symbol of democratic justice in our society. In film and television, the jury usually delivers the punch line: Did the hero-lawyer's brilliant defense and impassioned summation persuade the jury to acquit the innocent accused? Will the jury send the evil mob leader "up the river?"

Juries usually consist of twelve citizens who have two highly interrelated tasks. First, they must listen to the evidence presented at trial and evaluate it. Second, they must communicate their impressions to other jurors, with the goal of reaching a unanimous agreement about guilt. During their first task, jurors are targets of many influence attempts, some of which we've discussed. Once in the jury room, however, they are both sources and targets of interpersonal influence—active ingredients in an influence-rich stew of opinion and discussion that hopefully will congeal into a verdict.

Most of the time it does, and quickly. Verdicts are reached in 95 percent of all American trials, by juries that typically deliberate less than 2 hours (Kalven and Zeisel, 1966). Furthermore, most jury verdicts are highly sensitive to the evidence (Saks and Hastie, 1978; Visher, 1987). The defendant may be beautiful and nice, or the weird victim may be hard to relate to. Yet, laboratory simulations and reviews of real court cases suggest that biasing factors like these are usually overridden by legitimate admitted evidence, *provided the evidence is clear.*

It is heartening to know that at times evidence controls inference and generalizations. Does this mean that jury deliberations are uninteresting from an influence perspective? The answer is "No." First, there is the issue of *how* twelve people manage to agree on a basically good decision most of the time. Second, there is the situation in which the evidence is very mixed. That's where the psychological action is. It is the crevice where factors like the lawyer and witness behaviors discussed in the preceding section seep into the judgments of juries.

Majorities Rule Most of the Time

In the 1957 movie *Twelve Angry Men,* eleven jurors quickly conclude that a boy is guilty of murdering his father. One juror, played by Henry Fonda, holds out for acquittal and suffers through the kind of focused and eventually hostile group pressures to "come around" that we described in Chapter 2. But in the end, this courageous minority of one eventually turns around the others, saving the defendant from hanging. Is this a common scenario? Though not unheard of, such persuasive influence by a single dissenting juror is extremely rare. Most often, the eventual verdict is the one favored by the majority of jurors when they *entered* deliberation, especially if the majority consists of at least two-thirds of the jurors (Davis, 1980; Kalven and Zeisel, 1966). This majority-rule relationship concurs with our earlier observation that the weight of the admitted trial evidence is usually decisive. If, say, ten of twelve jurors vote not guilty on the first ballot taken before deliberations, it is likely that defense evidence was stronger than prosecution evidence.

But *how* do majorities usually get their way? According to surveys of former jurors, as well as mock trials in which the investigators eavesdrop on mock juries, minority members do not immediately give in when they discover that they are outnumbered (Stasser et al., 1982). Rather, they must be won over through social influence processes. You will recall that earlier (Chapter 2) we identified two generic forms of influence: *informational influence,* in which people adopt the behavior or attitudes of others because they perceive that the others have more, and more valid, information; and *normative influence,* in which people conform or comply in order to maintain harmonious social relations. Both influence processes are operative in jury deliberations.

More people, more arguments. First consider informational influence. During deliberation, the individual jurors present their opinions and their arguments for it. Assume that ten jurors favor a guilty verdict, while two believe that there is enough reasonable doubt to acquit the defendant. Will the ten members of the majority all present the same argument? Probably not. Each proponent of guilt may contribute his or her own angle on the evidence, perhaps adding information that the others do not remember. Of course, the two holdouts may have somewhat separate arguments as well. But each of those minority members with only one new set of supportive arguments must go head to head against ten opposing sets. What we have is a *persuasion* situation in which the message with a greater number of reasonable arguments creates the attitude change. This is usually the message of the majority.

To hang is to fail. Normative influence may result from the minority's "selfish attempt to gain social approval and avoid social disapproval" (Stasser et al., 1982). Members of a large majority become disgruntled when their calm attempts at persuasion fail to move a dissenting minority, and their communications become tinged with hints of rejection, dislike, and incredulity (see Chapter 2). It takes a brave, firmly convinced, and almost heroic type of person to bear the brunt of such sustained social pressure. Normative influence may work at another level as well (Stasser et al., 1982). A jury's goal is to reach a verdict. If it does not, if it becomes a hung jury, it has failed to reach that goal. It has frustrated justice—and, in a sense, wasted everyone's time except, of course, the defendant's. The desire to avoid this failure to reach a socially desirable group goal may compel many minority members to become increasingly receptive to the majority viewpoint.

As a member of a jury who needed to do some persuading, would you pitch your appeals to the informational or normative concerns of those who oppose you? Your characteristic style surely matters here. You could be a moralizer or a "just the facts" sort of person. Beyond preferred style, however, the case itself may determine which basis of social influence you exploit. In one study, mock jurors deliberated in groups of six after reading a civil case involving injuries caused when a poorly constructed furnace exploded (Kaplan and Miller, 1987). Jurors were told that another jury had reached a verdict against the defendant (the furnace manufacturer) and in favor of the plaintiff (the injured home owner). Their task was to agree on a damage award. Half the juries were to decide *compensatory damages,* which are to compensate the plaintiff for actual losses resulting from the defendant's negligence. The remaining juries were to decide on *exemplary damages,* awarded over and beyond compensation with the intent of punishing the defendant and deterring others from similar indiscretions.

Note that an award for compensatory damages more or less involves looking at the facts. How much did this unfortunate accident cost the plaintiff? In contrast, the award for exemplary damages is more subjective and judgmental; it reflects social values (pro- or antibusiness), sense of moral responsibility, and the like. Given these differences, we might expect more attempts at informational persuasion (stating the facts) in the former (compensatory damages) case and more attempts at normative pressure (moralizing) in the latter (exemplary damages) case. This is exactly what the researchers found when they studied the content of the juries' deliberations. Jurors faced with a fact-based decision (compensatory damages) appealed to facts and evidence in most of their statements ("Just the hospital bills alone would be enormous"), whereas jurors faced with a values-based decision (exemplary damages) most often made statements suggestive of social approval and disapproval ("It is wrong to..." "Do what the majority thinks is right") (see Figure 8.4). In general, then, we can expect a majority to focus on whatever "pressure points" are most relevant to winning others over to "their side" of a case.

Group polarization. The preceding example reminds us that jury decisions are not always dichotomous guilty or not guilty choices. Juries may also make quantitative decisions. In civil suits, the jury may decide how much money to award. In criminal cases, it may have the task of deciding what the defendant is guilty of, if at all. Often the alternatives are ordered according to increasing seriousness and corresponding punishment: for example, manslaughter (a prison term), second-degree murder (a longer prison term), and first-degree murder (life imprisonment or death). Research suggests that, in these situations, it is quite

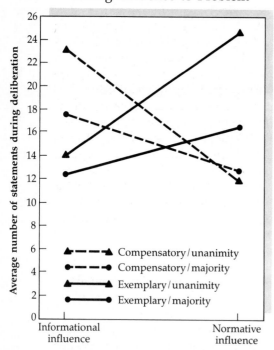

Fitting Influence to Problem

y-axis: Average number of statements during deliberation

26, 24, 22, 20, 18, 16, 14, 12, 10, 8, 6, 4, 2, 0

▲ – – – ▲ Compensatory/unanimity
● – – – ● Compensatory/majority
▲———▲ Exemplary/unanimity
●———● Exemplary/majority

x-axis: Informational influence — Normative influence

Type of statement

FIGURE 8.4
When mock jurors had to decide how much a plaintiff in a civil case should be compensated for actual losses, they tried to influence one another during deliberation by appealing primarily to the facts of the case (informational influence). When they had to decide how much to award in exemplary damages, to punish the guilty party, they appealed primarily to values and morals during deliberation (normative influence). These tendencies were stronger when jurors faced the pressure of reaching a unanimous decision (instead of needing only a majority vote).
(Data from Kaplan and Miller, 1987. Copyright 1987 by the American Psychological Association. Adapted by permission.)

possible that from the first to the last ballot the jury may grow more extreme in its judgments. The majority itself may move—toward greater extremity. *Group polarization* occurs.

To get a better feel for this phenomenon, let us briefly review some observations about how groups become more extreme over time in settings other than those involving injuries, and then turn to jury settings. Polarization was discovered in the early 1960s in studies of business decisions (Stoner, 1961) and was later verified in other studies in which subjects were asked to advise a person or business in the throes of a dilemma (Myers and Lamm, 1976). For example, should Charlie quit that safe and comfortable, but dead end, job and start the business he always wanted? Subjects read background information about the case and then indicated privately what minimal probability of success Charlie should require before he makes his move. The lower the required probability, the riskier they are in encouraging Charlie to be daring. Subjects then got together in a group to discuss Charlie's dilemma, after which they again expressed their opinion of the minimal probability for making a change.

The typical result can be summarized as follows: If, at first, the members of the group individually all tend to favor a risky course of action ("Charlie, go for it even if you've only got a 30 percent chance of making it"), group discussion makes them even riskier ("Go for it if you've only got a 20 percent chance"). If the trend is toward caution at first ("You'd better be 70 percent sure"), discussion makes them even more cautious ("Make that 80 percent"). Group discussion moves the group further out in the direction it was leaning toward initially.

The same effect has been found for attitude issues. French students who at first only mildly liked their president liked him more after talking about him, while their original dislike for Americans was intensified by discussion (Moscovici and Zavalloni, 1969).

Why does group polarization occur? There are two major reasons. First, if all group members are leaning on one side of the issue, most of the ideas and arguments they voice during discussion will also favor that side (Burnstein and Vinokur, 1973). The individual who liked something for two reasons may have five good reasons after hearing others express their views—informational influence again. Second, many people value being a little more extreme—in the right direction of course—than the average person. To be a little extreme is to appear unique, an often desirable quality. As opinions are exchanged in the group, individuals learn that they are not noticeably more extreme, and they shift to become so (Brown, 1965; Goethals and Zanna, 1979). You may recognize this as a special case of normative influence (again) in which those who want to individuate themselves from similar others in a given group setting must behave in ways that are more extreme, if not qualitatively different.

Can polarization occur in juries? It would seem so. Mock jurors in one study deliberated over traffic cases that contained either strong or weak evidence against the defendant. When the case was weak, jurors entered deliberation leaning toward "not guilty" and became further convinced of innocence during deliberation. When the case was strong, jurors' initial leanings toward "guilty" became stronger during deliberation (Myers and Kaplan, 1976).

The propensity for groups to polarize makes the huge damages awarded in some malpractice and personal injury cases seem less surprising. A solid majority, sympathetic to the permanently injured plaintiff, gets on a roll as it discusses how much it should punish the negligent physician or corporation while perhaps sending a message to other potential wrongdoers. This is majority rule—in no moderate terms.

Majorities prevail in *most* jury decisions; and *most* jury decisions are largely based on the weight of acceptable evidence. But then there are the rest of the jury decisions. Verdicts occasionally turn on an irrelevant factor or an errant social psychological process. And sometimes just one or a few jury members can exercise a disproportionate amount of control over the deliberations. Usually, these exceptional influences occur when the case is very close or has some unusual characteristics. Let us look first at how minorities sometimes influence the group verdicts. Then, in the final section, we'll consider extralegal (nonevidence) influences.

The Occasional Power of the Few

The lean to leniency. What happens when the jury is initially evenly split, with six favoring a guilty verdict and six favoring not guilty? Most often, the verdict will be not guilty, reflecting what has been called a *leniency bias* (Davis et al., 1981; MacCoun and Kerr, 1988; Tindale et al., 1990). In fact, even juries initially split seven to five in favor of guilty frequently end up acquitting the defendant (Stasser et al., 1982). Why? Does the pro-acquittal faction generally have more influential arguments? As a matter of fact, it probably does. For one thing, American law works under the assumption of innocent until proved guilty and requires the prosecution to prove guilt beyond a reasonable doubt. If a sizable number of jurors favor acquittal, there is clearly some doubt. All these jurors must do is convince the rest that their doubt is reasonable. In the meantime, the pro-guilt faction must discredit all doubts—a formidable task. Consider also that pro-acquittal jurors can point to the awful risk of a wrongful conviction—depriving an innocent person of his or her liberty. With a faction of five or six, it may be relatively easy to convince pro-guilt jurors that this risk is worse than that of freeing a guilty person (Stasser et al., 1982).

Persistence pays. A minority always has the potential for influence, even if it is a very small minority and is not pro-acquittal. Social psychologists, who have spent decades documenting the "strength in numbers" which creates conformity pressures, have recently begun studying whether there is any "power of the few" dissidents to influence the group's decision. The power exists—but it requires the few to be vocal and persistent.

Here's why. If we examine the ways in which majorities influence human behavior, we see that most processes of majority rule are based in good measure on heuristic processing. The individual, without much thought, applies the rule of thumb that "everyone can't be wrong" and accepts the information provided by the contingent that includes "almost everyone." This is informational influence, but it involves only superficial thought. Majorities also have tremendous normative power; rejection by "everyone who's anyone" could be devastating, and faced with the prospect, people may conform without thinking things through. These qualities of majorities suggest that, unless there is salient opposition, decisions shaped by majority influences may not engage the full *systematic thinking skills* of the individuals in a group.

Enter the vocal minority that calmly articulates its alternative viewpoint, and sticks with it, in the face of all that majority pressure. Shouldn't this get people thinking, and thinking more deeply? ("Hey, maybe this issue is more complicated than I thought. Maybe these few oddballs see something I've missed.") Research in several areas of group decision making has found exactly this. When a minority persists in its judgment, the group as a whole tends to make more thoughtful and more creative decisions compared with when there is no minority (Moscovici, 1980; Nemeth, 1986). Minority dissent seems to stimulate a reconsideration of the issue under consideration and encourages the group to engage in more divergent thinking processes by examining the issue from multiple perspectives. The minority may not prevail—it may even be wrong—but it may have this beneficial effect nonetheless of forcing the majority to process relevant information "mindfully" (Langer, 1989). Recent research has demonstrated that when subjects were exposed to a *consistent minority* view, they recalled the information better than when exposed to the majority view or to an inconsistent minority (Nemeth et al., 1990). Stick to your beliefs, but get a comrade in arms to share your vision. Even if you can't persuade the group to accept your view, at least you can make their final decision more thoughtful and of better quality.

Viewed against these findings, Henry Fonda's role in *Twelve Angry Men* is more believable. But in a jury especially, it isn't enough for a minority simply to disagree persistently. Three qualities are necessary: the minority must appear confident, it must avoid appearing rigid and dogmatic, and it must be skilled at social influence. These qualities fit to a tee the single juror whose influence turned a two-thirds majority for conviction into an acquittal in the celebrated Mitchell-Stans conspiracy trial during the Watergate era.

John Mitchell and Maurice Stans, chairman and treasurer of then President Richard Nixon's 1972 reelection campaign, respectively, were charged with conspiring to impede a federal investigation of a major financial contributor to the campaign. According to the jurors' recollections, only four of the twelve jurors favored acquittal when jury deliberation began (Zeisel and Diamond, 1976). One of those jurors was Andrew Choa, the well-educated vice president of a large bank. During the 10 weeks of the trial, Choa had befriended jurors with favors and good cheer. When deliberations began, he quietly declared his belief in the innocence of Mitchell and Stans. Then, consistently, confidently, and articulately, he argued his minority position. Choa was by far the best-educated and most successful of the jurors; and these qualities enhanced his credibility. Ultimately, he swayed the entire jury. The verdict was not guilty—and unanimous. Regarding the juror-extraordinaire Choa, psycho-legal scholar Lawrence Wrightsman (1987) concludes that "he and he alone appears to have been the cause for the shift of the majority from conviction to acquittal" (p. 224).

When Things That Shouldn't Influence Do Influence

With so much information and so many participants in the courtroom and jury room, there is always the possibility that a jury's decision will be affected by factors that, ideally, should not matter. Such factors are called "extralegal" because they are outside the realm of legal evidence and procedure. As we've noted, if extralegal factors do influence jurors, it is mainly when the evidence is unclear. Let's briefly examine two of these variables.

Inadmissible evidence. We have all watched courtroom dramas on television in which the judge instructs the jury to disregard a witness's statement or a piece of evidence that the lawyer slips in—on the grounds that it is legally inadmissible. And you may have asked yourself: "Come on! How can they possibly ignore, let alone forget, what they saw or heard?" You're right, they cannot. Mock trial studies suggest that disallowed evidence influences jury decisions, perhaps *even more* than it would if it hadn't been disallowed (Sue et al., 1973; Wolf and Montgomery, 1977). By disallowing it, the judge calls attention to the legal evidence, makes it salient, and thus gives it a special memory tag when the jurors are encoding all the massive amount of trial information for later retrieval. The judge may also arouse psychological reactance: jurors may feel that their freedom to consider all evidence of importance is being constrained and may respond by affording the disallowed evidence more weight than it deserves (see Chapter 5).

Not all jurors are created equal. Not infrequently, two or three jurors dominate deliberations. If we can trust highly realistic and involving simulations, complemented by recollections of actual jurors, it appears that, in most twelve-person juries, three jurors do more than half of the talking while three others may do no talking at all (Stasser et al., 1982, 1989; Strodtbeck et al., 1957). This unevenness in participation, in fact, is evident in all types of small group interactions (Bales, 1958). In the jury, it allows the occasional Andrew Choa (or Henry Fonda)—a single individual—to have basically a "single-handed" impact on the verdict. It also means that the unique biases of one or a few jurors could dictate a verdict.

To improve on your chances of having a bigger say in the deliberations, you must get elected foreperson. This isn't so hard: either speak first, get nominated first, or simply volunteer. Take your pick; that is enough to get you elected. To really cinch election, if the deliberation table is rectangular, sit in the "power seat"—the end, or head of the table. Even if sitting there does not get you elected foreperson, you may be able to wield extra influence through nonverbal dynamics. The person at the end is visible to all others and can speak to everyone while also looking at them. Not surprisingly, jurors at the end of the table both initiate and receive the most communicative acts (Strodtbeck and Hook, 1961). Part of this relationship, though, is probably due to the fact that jurors already experienced at taking control (such as managers and entrepreneurs) *choose* the end seats in the first place. Some people, you might say, can take power sitting down.

Our point here is that there is always the possibility that a jury verdict will reflect the bias and orientation of a few jurors who wield extraordinary influence. The chances of this happening are increased in more ambiguous cases that are open to alternative interpretations.

Jury selection: Can juries be "stacked"? The possible power of just a few jurors raises the issue of influence through jury selection. The opposing attorneys in a case are allowed to question potential jurors during a pretrial selection hearing. If either one feels that a potential juror may be predisposed against his or her client or case, the attorney can reject the person as a juror. Thus, to an extent, lawyers have a say about *who* is on a jury during this process, known as voir dire. Can the sharp attorney gain an influence advantage by choosing the audience— by "stacking" a jury with people sympathetic to his or her cause?

It certainly is possible under some circumstances to identify jurors with traits and backgrounds that make it likely they will be biased toward a certain verdict. For example, people with rigid, authoritarian views might be predisposed to see as guilty an accused murderer of a well-respected police officer (Mitchell, 1979). Politically liberal jurors may have a bias that favors acquittal of antigovernment demonstrators accused of inciting a riot. Studies indicate that if you get the people with the relevant traits on the jury, your side might enjoy an advantage in some cases (Horowitz, 1980; Wrightsman, 1987). However, the odds are that your opposing lawyer will also be trying to select the "right" juror. Together, your efforts may cancel each other out. Moreover, it isn't always easy to intuit which kind of person will be sympathetic to what side. These factors limit the likelihood that lawyers, on their own, can select a jury that is especially partial to their side.

Scientific jury selection may fare somewhat better. This is a consulting service provided by some social scientists. They survey people with various backgrounds and traits and ask them their opinions about the upcoming case. From the responses they get, they find out which traits are related to the verdict the attorney seeks and advise the attorney to select as jurors those who appear to share those traits (Schulman et al., 1973).

Even when attorneys use scientific methods, though, the number of cases that can be influenced by jury selection probably is small. Unless the case is very close, it is the weight of the solid evidence that rules judgments. Most jurors—regardless of their backgrounds, traits, and prejudices—let the evidence be their main decision-making guide.

THE CASE OF PSYCHOLOGY AND LAW: A CLOSING STATEMENT

The legal system is comprised of rules and procedures for handling disputes between people. The handling of a dispute, be it a crime or a civil lawsuit, involves a series of decisions, all made by people about people (Ebbesen and Konecni, 1982). Their decisions, inferences, and judgments are subject to a host of cognitive biases that we are all prone to: human intuition is fallible and often wrong, despite good intentions and confidence in its accuracy (Tversky and Kahneman, 1974). Disputes are never totally cut-and-dried, involving as they normally do more subjective evidence than indisputable facts. And the adversarial process guarantees that decision-makers have to contend with persuasive arguments from at least two sides. So what in theory is a legal matter, in practice is a psycho-legal issue.

In conclusion, ladies and gentlemen, we have submitted for your consideration a wealth of social scientific evidence that confirms some common sense notions, challenges others, and (hopefully) has given you new insight into where and how social influence manifests itself in every stage in the legal system—sometimes for better, sometimes for worse. In our next and final chapter, we will extend our focus to areas in everyday life where attitude change and social influence processes operate—and could be made to work for us to promote our health and enhance our happiness.

*T*O SUM UP...

Our examination of how social influence processes operate throughout the legal system concentrated on three major criminal justice settings: the police station, the courtroom, and the jury deliberation room.

- Social influence is prevalent because evidence is subjective and often verbal, and because of the adversarial nature of the Anglo-American justice system. Two sides compete in investigating and arguing for different versions of the truth.

- People perceive the adversarial system as fairer than the European inquisitorial system of impartial, court-administered investigations. Perhaps because it motivates both sides to "win," the adversarial system succeeds in reducing large advantages on one side—whether or not the advantage is undeserved. Adversarial procedures can create perceptual and interpretive biases. Witness testimony can be influenced by which side requests it, and the same evidence may be interpreted differently depending on which side introduces it.

- Eyewitness reports and identifications can be highly inaccurate, partly because of social influences on memory and the willingness of those in the criminal justice system to put undue trust in the accuracy of memory. Misleading or suggestive information in interrogation questions can become incorporated into the witness's memory and later remembered as part of the witnessed event. In lineup identifications, unfair lineups (where nobody looks like the suspect) and biased instructions (where it is strongly suggested that an identification is expected or required) may cause people to act on poor memory and thus increase the false identification rate. Making choices or repeatedly answering questions may boost confidence in one's memory, but they do nothing to improve the memory itself.

- Suspect confessions are a second type of verbal evidence that is highly susceptible to social manipulation. A high percentage of suspects confess during police interrogation; some are false confessions by innocent people. Police use a number of social influence techniques to gain confessions. They make use of their ability to control and distort the psychological situation and so wear down suspects' defenses or manipulate their perceptions.

- The threat of a lie detector test is also used to coerce confessions. Polygraph results, in general, are not trustworthy; they have a significant error rate, can be "beaten," and work better on suspects who believe in them (a placebo effect).

- Courtrooms are persuasion battlegrounds. Research suggests that primacy or recency effects are not likely as long as both sides deliver decent opening statements and summations. Trial lawyers are advised to state conclusions explicitly, include vivid audiovisual aids, and speak longer with more assertive statements.

- The impressions witnesses make on jurors are also crucial. Through coaching and leading questions, lawyers can shape impressions of witnesses to their advantage. Smooth narrative statements and a powerful assertive style with few hedges and qualifiers enhance perceived witness credibility.

- Eyewitness testimony tends to be overbelieved by jurors, especially if it is consistent, detailed, and (above all) delivered confidently. Confidence and memory for details are relied on heavily by jurors and other fact finders, but they are poor predictors of accuracy and are readily manipulable by questioning.

- Juries usually reach verdicts quickly. Most often, the strength of evidence determines verdicts, but extralegal factors may enter in when the evidence is not clear. Majorities usually prevail in jury deliberations, through informational influence (persuasion) and normative influence (social and societal approval measures). The same processes mediate group polarization, increasing extremity (in the direction jurors were initially leaning) as deliberation continues.

- Minorities, however, can prevail over majorities—sometimes. When a sizable minority favors acquittal, it may sway the majority. This is the result of a leniency bias fostered by a normative aversion to wrongful conviction. More generally, even small, vocal, and persistent minorities can cause the entire group to think more carefully about the evidence, thus leading to better decisions.

- In close cases, the chance exists that extralegal (nonevidence) matters will influence jurors. For example, evidence deemed "inadmissible" can often have an influence. Because group discussions are normally dominated by just a few participants, a single juror may have an undue influence, or lawyers may succeed at "stacking" a jury during jury selection; but this is uncommon.

QUESTIONS AND EXERCISES

1. What are the advantages of the adversarial trial system? What are the disadvantages? Which would you prefer to have, an adversarial system or an inquisitorial system, if you were tried for a crime you knew you did not commit but for which there was considerable circumstantial evidence against you? Think of a celebrated criminal case in or near your community in which the adversarial system led to what you regard as the wrong verdict. What influence processes contributed to this, and how would you change the system to avoid the malfunction?

2. On the basis of discussions concerning eyewitness testimony in various places in this chapter, outline a procedure for how eyewitnesses should be "processed" through the criminal justice system. The goals of the procedure you devise are to preserve memory and to avoid undue social influence on the reporting of it. Describe the procedure from initial questioning through courtroom testimony. Justify your plan with influence principles at each step along the way.

3. Aware of your interest in and significant knowledge of social psychology, a law student friend asks for some psychological advice concerning her first moot court assignment. She is playing the role of prosecutor in a date rape case. What advice do you have for her regarding case presentation, direct and cross-examination of witnesses, dealing with juror preconceptions, and so on?

4. Analyze jury deliberations from a normative and an informational influence perspective. Bring in concepts such as heuristic and systematic processing, societal norms, social support, and minority influence, especially as they can be understood in terms of these two major bases of attitude and belief change.

9

Social Influence in the Service of Health and Happiness

———— ❖ ————

Pro-Environmental Influence: Can Persuasion Preserve the Planet? ✦ *The Promotion of Health* ✦ *Social Psychological Roads to Mental Health* ✦ *Social Influence, the Good Life, and Your Future*

To achieve our personal and collective goals, there are times when each of us tries to change or shape the behaviors, beliefs, and feelings of other people. And most of us are pretty good at it, most of the time, even though we are nonprofessional influence agents. Centuries of trial and error, practice, and experience in the laboratory of human life have produced a rich cultural understanding of the psychology of practical influence. We have already examined a good deal of this heritage.

We have also examined the more systematic knowledge of influence gained through scientific research. Some of this general knowledge is sophisticated enough to have been translated into effective strategies that get fashioned into some powerful influence tactics and tools. These tools, as we have seen, are often put to use in advertising, marketing, and sales pitches designed to get us to part with our money, or in the political arena to give some candidates the media presence and style that cover over their lack of substance. It is sad to say,

330

but social psychology is sometimes misapplied to serve unsavory or pernicious goals of those in power—to maintain or extend it.

Fortunately, as we have also observed, social psychology can likewise be used to promote positive and pro-social causes, and to give direction to efforts aimed at improving the quality of life. We devote this final chapter to pro-social influence that can be utilized by ordinary people for their own good and, thereby, for the good of society. We will concentrate on three quality-of-life domains:

- Promoting pro-environmental attitudes and behavior that can help improve the ecology of our communities and our planet
- Getting people to acquire and maintain habits conducive to physical health and wellness
- Helping those with mental problems to achieve mental health through psychotherapy

In short, we will concern ourselves with better living through the chemistry of social influence.

PRO-ENVIRONMENTAL INFLUENCE: CAN PERSUASION PRESERVE THE PLANET?

The winter of 1976–1977 was a very cold one. It was also darker than usual for the residents of Columbus, Ohio. The Arab oil embargo and OPEC price fixing forced gas and oil prices up and created severe shortages of these energy sources. The City of Columbus kept off its streetlights for weeks to hold down its costs and to help the local gas and electric utilities conserve. One of the authors, then a graduate student at Ohio State University, recalls walking through eerily dark, deserted streets at 8 p.m. It was depressing, especially during the holidays since community leaders had urged people to refrain from putting up outdoor Christmas lights—and most people cooperated. In January, the situation reached a peak when the governor of Ohio led the State Assembly in a prayer session to end the energy crisis. The prayer session gained the attention it was expected to, making news nationwide.

There are many stories like this from the 1970s. In California, where "freedom of the road" and "the car as castle" are not just metaphors but basic values for many drivers, the frustrations of waiting in long lines to get a little gas sometimes erupted into violent encounters between neighbors. It was not surprising to see conservation and other environmental problems suddenly become "hot issues." The effects of decades of unchecked industrial pollution had at last become widely and highly visible. Beaches closed, rivers burned, the air stunk. The ugly environmental results of strip mining, excessive lumbering, and other for-profit-only industrial practices were increasingly apparent. The 1973 Arab oil embargo had created widespread worry about Western dependence on foreign oil.

These converging factors fueled the start of a pro-environmental movement. On college campuses, "ecology flags"—green, white, and green versions of the American flag—become a popular symbol, and a modest amount of pro-environmental activism was heard in the land. Stiffer federal and state regulations concerning industrial pollution and waste were enacted. Catalytic converters on cars and the use of unleaded gasoline became legal requirements. The government created funds to clean up toxic waste sites. The strongest movement, however, was for *energy conservation.* The highway speed limit was reduced to 55 miles per hour. Tax credits were provided for home installation of energy-conserving devices such as solar panels. The government mandated that utilities provide free home energy audits. Insulation and caulking mania afflicted many a home owner. Investing in companies that were focusing on solutions to ecological problems was touted as a sound financial strategy. We were on the way!

And then one day the human energy behind the energy conservation movement seemed to vanish, to go up in smoke. Oil prices stabilized and even declined a bit in the early 1980s. Energy supplies seemed abundant again. The new regulations on auto and factory emissions led to enough reduction in urban pollution to make it less visibly obvious. Faced with a recession, the Reagan administration gave high priority to business growth, downplayed environmental problems, and deregulated essential control on many industries. Tax credits for energy conservation were eliminated, while corporations received extensions to deadlines for achieving cleaner production—and foot-dragging slowed all progress. As the environment fell out of style and out of the news, the public seemed to forget about ecological problems. Among other things, energy consumption went back up while car pooling, use of mass transit, and recycling failed to take hold as popular personal habits. People who were fastidious about the cleanliness of their homes, offices, and other private places felt no responsibility for keeping their public spaces litter-free and graffiti-free.

What goes around comes around. In the final decade of this century, concern about the environment is making a comeback in many countries throughout the world. People are becoming concerned by much-publicized news about global heating, called the "greenhouse effect"; the big pollution-caused hole in the ozone layer, which is increasing our risk of skin cancer; acid rain, which destroys our vegetation; the destruction of the Amazon rain forest, which may affect the climate on the entire planet; and the seemingly endless waste—some toxic—piling up everywhere. It's ironic that these very problems were building to crisis levels during the 1980s period of unconcern, and won't go away if we just ignore them and carry on business as usual.

Environmental Attitudes: Weak Links in the Action Chain

The swings in public concern with environmental issues illustrate the major problem regarding environmental attitudes and behaviors. Concern about the environment is all too much a matter of "out of sight, out of mind." People get nervous about pollution, landscape devastation, or running out of natural resources when the problems are publicly visible—when the air turns yellowish brown and smells like a sewer or when the home heating bill suddenly doubles. But when the outward appearances of a problem disappear, so does inward concern with the obviously persistent problem.

This pattern is analogous to what is called the *crisis effect* in the perception of natural disasters such as floods and droughts (Kates, 1976). Concern and action are high during and just after a disaster. As a drought worsens, people rise to action and call for studies and programs to prevent future droughts. Water conservation, finding alternative water sources, and limiting population growth in drought-prone areas are seriously entertained. Yet, as time passes and there is no new drought, restrictions ease, "crises amnesia" clouds memories, and people and governments resort to old habits—of living in a fantasy of paradise with limitless clean, cheap resources.

A problem of low salience. We're sure you see the underlying psychological principles here. As seen in past chapters, we tend to think about and act on stimuli which we are readily aware of. Moreover, we attribute causal significance to stimuli that are salient and attention-getting. Unfortunately, environmental harm is often very hard to see. We do not readily see our personal behavior as a contributing cause of harm to the environment unless the harm clearly reveals itself. Personal waste simply disappears; it's carted away or flushed down the toilet: out of sight, out of mind—underground and underconcerned. Biologists tell us that when pollutants are spewed into a lake for decades, 95 percent of the damage is already done before it is apparent to untrained eyes that the lake is dying. By then it's too late to reverse the process to save the lake and its plant and animal life.

A problem of low motivation. Another barrier to pro-environmental behavior is that pro-environmental motives must compete with stronger needs and desires. Can your pocketbook afford organic vegetables grown without pesticides? How about that fuel-efficient new furnace?

Can you fit recycling into your busy schedule? Are you willing to drive less even when you can easily afford gasoline? This is also a salience issue of sorts. Your money and your convenience are often tangible, salient, and immediate outcomes compared with your small, delayed contribution to preventing or cleaning up a large-scale environmental problem you can't even see.

More generally, in human interaction with the environment, we have many of the ingredients of a weak attitude-behavior relationship discussed in Chapter 5. Because people do not often see the consequences of environmentally destructive behavior or realize which of *their* current behaviors has a destructive delayed effect, three factors are missing that contribute to a strong attitude-behavior relationship: (1) knowledge, (2) clarity, and (3) direct experience with the attitude object. In a given situation, pressures of time and the counterinfluence of other energy-wasteful people may override pro-environment inclinations. When the situation pushes one way and attitude the other, the situation usually wins unless the attitude is held with conviction. Even then, it is possible that those competing motives we mentioned may be more relevant to a given environment-related behavioral choice. We may really mean well, but continue to act badly. Our values may lead to good behavioral *intentions,* but not to meaningful actions.

Can social science help? It certainly is trying. Social scientists have devised techniques for influencing many environmental behaviors. These behaviors have been as diverse as littering, home energy conservation, recycling, and carpooling. Although the environmental behaviors differ, the techniques employed have important similarities. They attack directly either the low motivation problem or the low salience problem. Let us look at some examples of each strategy.

Enhancing Motivation: Pro-Environmental Acts Whose Rewards Outweigh Costs

If pro-environmental acts can be made either more rewarding or less costly, the motivation to perform them should become a stronger psychic force against competing concerns involving time, money, effort, and convenience. This seems like an ideal situation in which to apply principles of instrumental learning, the shaping of behavior through the systematic application of rewards.

Money, buses, bottles, and thermostats. What's a powerful reward? For many of us, money fits the bill. If people were paid to conserve heat in the winter, to use public transportation, or to return their aluminum cans, would they do these things more often? Of course they would. Consider this sampling of research findings. Laws requiring a redeemable deposit on all bottles and cans have led to a 75 percent reduction in bottle and can litter (Osborne and Powers, 1980). Notice that this is a reinforcement-based strategy: people get a nickel or a dime (often their own deposit) for every bottle they return. Similarly, giving people a coupon for free fast food whenever they rode a bus substantially increased the rider volume of a university bus system, thereby decreasing traffic congestion on campus (Everett et al., 1974). When apartment dwellers whose electricity usage was included in their rent were given cash payments according to how much they reduced their weekly usage, they used an average of 36 percent less electricity (Hayes and Cone, 1977). Private home owners have also been found to reduce electricity use in return for monthly cash rebates tied to the size of the reduction (Winett et al., 1978).

It pays to pay people. But money is no cure-all. One obvious drawback is the cost. A metropolitan bus company may not be able to finance coupon rewards on a regular basis. Local governments, already pushing people's tolerance for taxes, can ill afford to subsidize a utility company's reward system.

Another problem is that when payments stop completely, the rate of pro-environmental behaviors declines. This means that those behaviors were never "taken to heart," or internalized as a strong behavior-directing attitude. And no wonder. Remember the self-attribution phenomenon of *overjustification*. If paid to do something, people tend to see the pay (the extrinsic factor) and not their own attitudes (the intrinsic factor) as causing their behavior. Take away the cause, and you stand to lose the effect.

Feedback. Are there alternatives to using money to reinforce energy conservation? Yes, in the area of home energy conservation, providing residents with informative and vivid feedback about their conservation efforts can also serve as a powerful reinforcer with lasting effects. A clear demonstration of this energy feedback comes from a study of upper-middle-class residents living in all-electric townhouses in suburban Washington, D.C. (Winett et al., 1979). Each household in a feedback condition received daily feedback for a month about how much its electricity consumption had gone up or down compared with the previous day. The feedback sheet was colorful and easy to read, and related the day's usage, in dollars-and-cents terms, to the conservation goals the household itself had previously set. The feedback households ended up reducing electricity use 13 percent more than comparison households given no feedback, conserving at a rate that saved them an average of $23 per month. Moreover, 10 weeks after the daily feedback was discontinued, the feedback households were still using less electricity than the comparison households. The motivation directing the conservation behavior had become intrinsic and was no longer tied to the external feedback system.

What makes feedback effective? First, note that just any feedback won't do. In the preceding study, residents were first given detailed reasons for conservation and tips about how to do it. Reducing energy use was also seen, at the time, as a highly desirable, pro-social act; and there was a contestlike spirit that defined conserving as "a skill you can master." Under these circumstances, feedback is effective for four reasons: (1) it provides a rewarding sense of achievement; (2) this rewarding sense comes from within, thus helping to generate the attribution that one conserves because it is personally satisfying to do so; (3) when regularly used, feedback informs one about how specific behaviors relate to consumption outcomes ("I left the window open last night, and my consumption rate was way up on today's reading"); and (4) externally charting the daily fluctuations in the target outcome provides an ongoing record that is clear evidence of success.

With such good reviews, it is heartening to know that technology exists to make massive use of feedback to shape good environmental habits. In home energy conservation, for example, recently developed, easy-to-read indoor monitors allow for the easy self-application of feedback-based reinforcement.

In recent years, utilities have begun to provide a different form of feedback on gas and electric bills. The bills tell customers how their energy use *compares* with that of others. This is a good idea because it utilizes the principle of social comparison (Festinger, 1954). Indeed, let people know how they compare with other people. Utilities are advised, however, that social comparison feedback is an effective reinforcer only if the comparison group is perceived as *relevant*.

Enhancing Salience: Keeping Pro-Environmental Behavior in Mind

We suggested earlier that most of us do not spontaneously think about environmental behaviors and their consequences. The environment offers few vivid, mind-catching reminders about itself. The environment is usually the background; it must be made the figure, pushed into the foreground, if we are to notice it. To do so requires influence strategies based on striking reminders, either of how to behave or of the difference that an individual's behavior makes to the total problem—or its solution.

Doing it promptly. Reminders, signs, or cues about how to behave are called *prompts*. You see a lot of them. ("Save energy." "Please turn the lights off when you leave." "Pitch in.") Do they work? In general, prompts do influence behavior, although some work better than others. Prompts, moreover, are not limited to stickers beside light switches or signs on garbage cans. Consider those advertising ("Specials of the Day") fliers you are often handed as you walk into a retail store. Zillions of these sheets end up as ugly litter. Yet one study conducted at a large supermarket found that a simple but prominent prompt written on the flier put a significant dent in this pollution problem (Geller et al., 1977). The prompt asked people not to litter and to dispose of the flier "for recycling in the green trash can located in aisle one." This instructive reminder increased the percentage of fliers placed in the green can from 9 to 30 percent.

To be especially effective, prompts must attract attention. The familiar "Pitch In" sign on public trash receptacles may have lost effectiveness by being so familiar that it stops being a salient figure and it soon blends into the background. Why not change the signs every 6 months in interesting ways? For that matter, painting trash receptacles in dayglow colors might also increase antilittering "cue value." Prompts are also effective when they instruct people *specifically* and *concretely* what to do, where, and sometimes when, as did the supermarket flier (Fisher et al., 1984).

Prompted by a clean environment. Maybe it's because they are pleasing, or maybe it's that they're rare. But we notice clean surroundings. Hence, the *absence* of litter is itself a prompt. In another supermarket study, littering the aisles with advertising fliers was quite common when the store was already full of litter; but it almost never occurred when special care was taken to make the store spotlessly clean (Geller et al., 1977). A clean environment makes salient the "no littering" norm that we all learned in school and at home, but often forget elsewhere.

Putting two and two together—that norms prescribe proenvironmental behaviors and that reminders like prompts heighten the salience of these norms—creates a strong case for high-frequency media reminders about "environmental hygiene" (see Cialdini et al., 1990). Catchy messages need to be delivered regularly enough to have an impact at crucial moments. For example, some of those knaves who toss empty fast-food bags and cigarette packs out of their car windows might refrain from doing so if they had just heard their celebrity hero give an antilittering message over the car radio.

Energy images. Prompts and reminders just scratch the surface of salience-enhancing devices that can be applied to environmental problems. Suzanne Yates and Elliot Aronson (1983) offer several simple techniques that, if applied together, could add up to big increases in home energy conservation.

First, Yates and Aronson repeat the now-familiar "make it vivid" advice. Dry statistical information has less effect than vivid and concrete examples (Nisbett and Ross, 1980). For example, imagine receiv-

Cleaning up a neighborhood lot. Chances are good that the pleasant change will stay that way because people litter less in already-clean environments that make the "don't litter" norm salient.   (*Eric A. Roth/The Picture Cube*)

ing conservation advice from a home energy auditor. Hearing him drone on about the average percentage ratio of heat loss through windows and cracks might be pretty unmoving. But you might stand up and take notice (and do some caulking and insulating) if the auditor pointed out that, "if we add up all the drafty places in your house, you've got a hole the size of a basketball" (Aronson, 1990).

A second technique is to emphasize loss instead of gain. Most people are "loss averse"—the prospect of losing what they already have ("money thrown out the window") is more motivating than the prospect of gaining a smaller energy bill (Tversky and Kahneman, 1986). This translates into informing people how much they stand to lose each year by not taking some energy-saving actions.

A third technique is to promote a positive image of the conserving, environmentally conscious citizen. Habits like keeping the thermostat low and carpooling conjure up for some people negative images—of miserliness or of being unable to afford small luxuries. Consequently, they avoid these self-images by avoiding the behaviors. To counter this thinking, we could show well-to-do, trim-and-fit, attractive people engaging in conservation activities, thus creating an image of the energy saver as successful, efficient, and sexy. In the same vein, companies can have recognition and award campaigns for the energy-saving employee of the month.

Finally, the principles of commitment and consistency can be put to good use. The little things count. If people can be convinced to do small pro-environmental acts, the foot-in-the-door process may lead to bigger acts (recall the Freedman and Fraser, 1966, study described in Chapter 2). Also, cognitive dissonance can be aroused by revealing their environmentally destructive acts to people who claim to be environmentalists. One study pointed out to some people how wasteful of energy they were despite their endorsement (on a survey) of the importance of conservation. Apparently to resolve the inconsistency, these individuals reduced their electricity usage more than individuals whose inconsistencies were not made apparent to them (Kantola et al., 1984).

From Personal Habits to Global Pollution: The Generalization Gap

If every litter bit hurts, then every little bit of behavior change helps. Clearly, social influence techniques can be applied to changing the environmental behaviors of individuals. But what about the environmentally destructive behaviors that occur to sustain the global economic system? What about the pollution and destruction caused by the ways we produce, distribute, and consume goods? Can these behaviors be changed?

To do so will require more than inducing pro-environmental habits at the individual level. That foot in the door is only so big compared with the massive size of the door. And our investment in our current way of self-centered living is gigantic. Most important, it is the *big* environmental problems that are most prone to out-of-sight, out-of-mind mentality. Have you visited a toxic waste dump recently? Have you checked out the Amazon rain forest this month to witness its deliberate destruction by land developers, ranchers, and others? Hardly. And how does you hair spray pump, which makes your new hairstyle look so good, increase your risk of skin cancer by creating a hole in the ozone layer of the atmosphere?

The solution to what many believe is a global environmental crisis rests in passionately nurturing pro-environmental attitudes and beliefs throughout the culture. Future executives and political leaders must be environmentalists through and through. This is a very hard task. But it can be done. There is evidence that educational programs beginning in early childhood that "immerse" students in environmental consciousness-raising may lead to pro-environment attitudes that people are willing to act on (Asch and Shore, 1975). This involves more than an "ecology section" of a science course. Children must directly experience nature under the

guidance of teachers who can reveal its beauties and teach the consequences of environmental abuse in enough vivid detail to create a sharp
contrast with this beauty. The ecology "out there" must get internalized as
starting "in here," within each of us.

On another front, the mass media can help keep environmental
problems "in sight." The nightly news coverage of the 1989 *Exxon
Valdez* oil tanker spill in Alaska, with its graphic scenes of oil-soaked
seals and spoiled shores, did much to heighten environmental concern.
Similar impact may have been achieved by *Time* magazine's pro-
environmental campaign the same year. Using striking artwork, *Time*
put environmental issues on several covers, which are seen by tens of
millions every week at supermarket checkout counters alone. Another
valuable force comes from the music and movie celebrities who are increasingly vocal about environmental issues and whose influence on
the MTV generation reaches many not touched by traditional educational or media campaigns. Earth Day 1990 was another positive step.
In a nutshell, the more the media are dominated by vivid pro-
environmental ideas, the more these ideas will find their way into attitudes and behaviors—even of corporate executives.

On this optimistic note that social influence can help us improve the
quality of our environment, or save our planet, let us move on to see if
it can help us improve our personal health and save collective health.

THE PROMOTION OF HEALTH

In the late twentieth century, physical health has become a whole new
ball game in our society. Infectious diseases like pneumonia, polio, and
tuberculosis, once major health threats, have been largely overcome by
immunizations, widespread advanced medical care, sophisticated sani-
tation systems, and readily available nutritious foods. Technology,
medical knowledge, and public health programs provide most of us in
industrialized nations with an excellent prospect for living long, healthful lives.

But that desirable prospect never materializes for many. Nowadays,
heart disease and cancer are the number one and number two killers
(Harris, 1980). These illnesses account for nearly 60 percent of all deaths
in the United States and often take their victims "before their time." To
a significant extent, they are *preventable* diseases. They are the products
of lifestyle factors such as stress, overeating, and smoking. Drug and
alcohol abuse contribute to the "big two" disease categories as well,
and also to preventable deaths from traffic accidents, AIDS, and suicide. Today, health professionals understand that the primary cause of
death is *lifestyle*—our patterns of everyday habits. If people would only
make a habit of healthful behavior, they would extend their years of vi-
brant living.

Pro-environmental attitudes must become the cultural norm, guiding the behavior of corporate executives as well as consumers. Salient images of environmental harm in the service of economic gain—like this one—may help shape those attitudes.

Health professionals are at no loss to describe healthful behaviors. Using a public health model in place of the traditional medical-illness model, health scientists and practitioners are spurred by a modern conception of *wellness* that views sickness not as something to treat but as something to prevent. These health specialists have accumulated vast knowledge about what people can do to maintain and enhance health. (A list of the most basic "health behaviors" is provided in Table 9.1. How many describe your lifestyle?) The trick is to spread the word, to influence people to behave healthfully. Despite the stylishness of certain "healthy habits" like aerobics and eating high-fiber foods, this influence task has proved to be no easy feat.

"Healthy influence" attempts take place in several settings. At a *macro* level, the mass media are popular conduits for messages about healthful behavior. Important influence efforts regarding health, however, occur even more often in *micro*, or hands-on, settings. Physicians try to persuade their patients to follow healthy regimens or to take proper medications. Many people attend workshops and clinics designed to help them improve their health habits regarding food, drugs,

TABLE 9.1 THE "WELLNESS" LIFESTYLE

1. Do not smoke cigarettes.
2. Get some regular exercise.
3. Use alcohol moderately or not at all.
4. Get 7 or 8 hours of sleep nightly.
5. Maintain proper weight.
6. Eat breakfast.
7. Do not eat between meals.

SOURCE: Belloc and Breslow (1972).

alcohol, tobacco, and exercise. The goal in these settings, quite simply, is behavioral change through direct social influence. Let us first examine how the psychology of influence is or can be applied to media efforts to promote healthy lifestyles via *mediated influence*; then we'll go to the doctor's office and the clinic to learn how more effective influence strategies can be utilized.

Mass Persuasion: Is an Informed Public a Healthier One?

You have seen hundreds of public service ads that promote health behaviors. In the 1960s, Americans were blitzed by a campaign encouraging the use of seat belts. Most people over 35 can still sing the jingle they heard as they watched (on TV) an attractive family of four buckling up in their station wagon. ("Buckle up for safety, buckle up. Buckle up for safety, always buckle up...") The new TV ads for seat-belt use are directed at young drivers. You've probably seen the "don't be a dummy" series in which the life-size dummies used in car-crash tests come to life in the form of rock musicians. Antismoking ads were big in the 1970s and early 1980s ("It's a matter of life and breath"). More recent campaigns promote safe sex to guard against AIDS and plead with people not to take drugs: "This (fried egg) is your brain on drugs."

These messages reach many people, but do they succeed in changing their attitudes and behavior? There is little doubt that well-designed mass media health campaigns increase the health *knowledge* of the millions who are exposed to them (Atkin, 1979; Roberts and Maccoby, 1985). *Attitudes* are a tougher nut to crack, but here too, health campaigns often make at least modest inroads.

Then there is *behavior change,* the ultimate goal. By themselves, mass media health campaigns usually have weak effects on actual health behaviors. Despite years of mass media promotion, it took state laws to get the rate of seat belt use up to over 50 percent (Kalfus et al., 1987). Enforceable laws are less than thoroughly persuasive, but they tend to beat suggestions. Smokers who swear they hate it keep on puffing (and coughing). And although we all know that American children consume too much sugar, doughnuts and sugar-laden cereals are still found on millions of breakfast tables every morning.

Roadblocks on the road to effective health advertising.   The fact is that there are great natural obstacles, sociological and psychological, that limit the persuasive force of health messages. In this section, we describe four of the obstacles that might be overcome by social psychological solutions. These obstacles include: the pleasure one may get from some unhealthy habits, unrealistic optimism about one's

health, cynicism about health messages, and competition from opposing messages.

Unhealthy attractions. The largest obstacle to successful health persuasion is the very strength of the existing attitudes and habits that the
messages seek to change. Many smokers enjoy smoking. Fried and sug-
ary foods taste very good. And yes, quite a few people enjoy altered
states of consciousness. Mere messages may be insufficient to change
strong, and possibly desirable, habits. Something more is needed—
some new-style interventions that we'll describe later on.

It can't happen to me. In addition to specific likes and preferences, a
media health message must overcome more general health-related attitudes and cognitions. One of these we could call the safer-than-thou
syndrome. People seem to be unrealistically optimistic about their
health prospects. Numerous surveys indicate that the average person
sees himself or herself as "above average" in general health and "below
average" in the risk of disease, injury, and premature death. In one
study, students at Rutgers University were asked to compare their
chances of succumbing to 45 different health hazards with the chances
of "other Rutgers students of your sex." They rated their chances as significantly lower than average for the majority of these hazards (34 out of
45), including venereal disease, heart attacks, lung cancer, migraine
headaches, obesity, gum disease, and tooth decay (Weinstein, 1982).
On none of the hazards did the students see their personal risks as
higher than those of others.

Optimism about one's health and an illusion of personal invulnerability are nice defenses against anxiety and worry. But if *over*optimism is
the rule, many of us may fail to perceive the self-relevance of important
health advice, and hence fail to systematically analyze it. This false
sense of our invulnerability must be overcome; without panicking the
target audience, health messages must instill the recognition that "it
could be me, unless I do something right now."

Ego defense is not the only factor behind unrealistic optimism. The
safer-than-thou mentality is also a consequence of a failure to fully realize that illness and injury can strike people whose habits and lifestyles
closely resemble ours (Weinstein and Lachendro, 1982). To overcome
this cognitive shortcoming, health ads might employ (as spokespersons) recovered or reformed individuals whom people perceive as having highly similar lifestyles (Atkin, 1980). Health campaigners might
also personalize messages as much as possible: "We're talking to *you!*
You're 21, you feel great...just like hundreds of young people who
have high blood pressure. Do yourself a favor, get it checked."

Paralysis of analysis. If overoptimism about health risks doesn't dull
attention to health messages, cynicism and defeatism might. We are hit

almost daily with news of some new health hazard. This causes cancer. That contributes to heart disease. Something else (no, not the news) causes ulcers. Modern scientific research can pick up the smallest hints of disease-causing agents, which the news media broadcast to the world (often prematurely and in exaggerated fashion). The endless bad news compels some people to give up, to see conscientious health behaviors as a "hopeless battle." Consequently, they tune out health messages. Have you ever made health suggestions to friends only to hear them say "Hey, so what *is* good for you?" or "Everything causes cancer" or the classic "If this doesn't kill me, something else will"? Would you expect such a person to react to a TV health message any more constructively?

How do you keep cynics and defeatists from tuning out? For one thing, you make health messages especially attention-getting and attention-keeping, with interesting video or audio components and catchy slogans that trigger positive heuristic judgments. You also need strong arguments to defeat defeatism or cynicism. Health messages must stress *efficacy*—the ideas that, without much hassle, people can be effective at reducing their health risks and that being effective in that domain is part of one's more general effectiveness or self-efficacy.

Messages about controversial health topics need to be accurate as well. If they do tune in, cynical people counterargue. Antimarijuana messages had little impact on teenagers in the early 1970s, mainly because they presented information that was inconsistent with the actual experiences of those familiar with marijuana's effects. The ads evoked ridicule and vehement counterarguing (Ray and Ward, 1976; Smart and Feger, 1974). Unfortunately, the latest efforts to sour attitudes toward pot have fallen into the same mistake of making assertions of questionable validity. Have you seen the one that shows a cessation of brain waves on an EEG monitor and identifies the pattern as that of a teenager's "brain activity after smoking marijuana"? Anyone with firsthand

Cynical reactions to health messages are for the birds.
(*Kudzu*, 3/27/90, reprinted by permission of Doug Marlette and Creators Syndicate.)

experience with marijuana knows that the brain doesn't simply shut down. Only death does that. The tragic thing is that, if this message is discredited, chances are that other valid messages about serious drug hazards will be greeted with inappropriate skepticism. Teenagers will lump them into the same "discredited" category of propaganda by adults against the fun of youth.

Competition. Health messages must often compete with opposing messages. In the first chapter of this book, we used cigarette advertising as a classic example of powerfully effective mass media influence. Remember the millions of dollars that cigarette companies spend on market research and advertising each year? Health organizations can't match these big bucks. Nor, in the case of juvenile smoking, can health ads match the pressure that can be applied by those highly adept influence agents known as peers. Again we see a need for thoughtful message design, in this case, one that teaches defenses and inoculation against counterpersuasion.

Getting specific: A sampling of applications from the science of influence. At this point, let us examine a few specific approaches to overcoming the psychological barriers to changing health behaviors.

Fear you can live with. A popular form of health message is the *fear appeal*, a message that seemingly scares people into change. Fear appeals are among the most effective vehicles of persuasion—but only if they are properly designed so as to avoid scaring people right into a state of denial and tune-out. Proper design begins with the recognition that a fear appeal must do more than frighten. It must also inform the audience about the concrete, detailed, and effective actions they can take to change their unhealthy habits (Leventhal, 1970). Stark and vivid evidence linking cigarette smoking to lung disease may increase a smoker's desire to quite smoking. But the smoker may not know how to quit. Adding specific quitting tips to messages increases the rate at which people translate their desire into actual decreases in smoking (Leventhal et al., 1967).

Still, many people do not use this knowledge of *how* to behave heathfully, often because they doubt that the behaviors will matter *in their case.* Long-term heavy smokers often mutter, "If the damage is done, it's done. It's too late to save myself by quitting or cutting down." We're back to defeatist thinking. To cut it off, a fear appeal must ensure *response efficacy.* The message must present strong arguments that the recommended actions work in preventing the feared outcome. Antismoking campaigns clearly recognized this when, in the 1970s, they ran ads with lines like "The minute you stop smoking, your lungs begin to heal." One (ex-smoker) author still remembers the first time he heard this particular message. And the imagery of healing lungs did much to firm up his resolve to finally kick the habit.

And kick it he did—a few years later. Perhaps the final nudge was an increase in confidence that he could, in fact, quit. In your author's case, this sense of *self-efficacy* was aroused through watching colleagues successfully quit ("If they can do it, so can I"). A fear-arousing message can also convince people of self-efficacy. ("People just like yourself have succeeded in quitting by following these steps." "Studies indicate that, of those who are serious about it, more than 75 percent succeed in quitting.")

This matter of efficacy is a big one. Psychologists recognize that there is trouble when people develop a sense of helplessness, when they feel that what happens to them is beyond their control. This fatalistic belief is associated with chronic depression, heightened difficulty in recovering from an illness, and (among other things) underachievement in academic and job performance (Seligman, 1975; Seligman and Schulman, 1986; Taylor, 1986). In the case of health behaviors, if people don't *believe* that they are capable of success in dieting, quitting cigarettes, or exercising, they just don't do it, or give up too easily (Bandura, 1986).

The ingredients for an effective fear appeal are nicely summarized in the *protection motivation theory* developed by Ronald Rogers (1983). According to this theory, people become motivated to take action to protect themselves from a health threat to the extent that they believe (1) the threat is noxious (fearful), (2) they are vulnerable to it, (3) certain healthful behaviors effectively overcome the threat (response efficacy), and (4) they have, within themselves, the ability to perform those behaviors (self-efficacy). The trick, then, is not to scare people but rather to advise them, in no uncertain terms, of a danger and get them thinking about how *they* can control it—and taking some specific, immediate actions to exercise that control.

Research suggests that the effectiveness of a health message is enhanced by addressing all four beliefs, but especially those involving efficacy. In one study, college students watched either a bland film or a fear-arousing film about health topics such as venereal diseases and cigarette smoking (Rogers and Mewborn, 1976). The fear-arousing versions were quite graphic, showing actual surgery on diseased testicles or lungs while citing statistics suggesting high personal vulnerability to the malady. Generally, the more fearful films had far stronger effects on intentions to adopt healthful behaviors—but *only* when the message also gave assurance that the recommended behaviors do prevent the feared outcome. A subsequent study demonstrated that an antismoking message addressing both response efficacy and self-efficacy—this works and you can do it—had strong effects on intentions to quit smoking even when it included no fearful scenes or scary statistics (Maddux and Rogers, 1983).

New research results from a longitudinal experiment to curb drug use during the junior high school years reveal that education programs based on a social influence model using a combination of tactics can prevent or reduce the use of cigarettes and marijuana (Ellickson and Bell, 1990). Twenty schools were randomly assigned to receive the Project Alert curriculum, which consisted of eight sessions, plus three booster sessions when they reached eighth grade. The remaining ten control schools did not get any formal training other than what the schools normally provide. The impact of the curriculum was assessed at 3-, 12-, and 15-month follow-ups. The Project Alert curriculum aims to help students develop reasons not to use drugs, identify pressures to use them, counter pro-drug messages, learn how to say no to external and internal pressures, understand that most people do not use drugs, and recognize the benefits of resisting undesirable influence pressures. The program involves small group exercises, role modeling, and repeated skills practice, all with high degrees of ·student participation. This innovative social influence program had positive results with both low- and high-risk students, as well as with minority and nonminority students. However, it did not help previously confirmed smokers to stop, nor were its effects on adolescent drinking more than short-lived.

The frame makes the picture. In addition to isolating the specific types of beliefs that messages should target, mass media health campaigns can benefit from adopting psychological approaches that emphasize principles of social perception and social judgment. A good example comes from research aimed at convincing women to perform breast self-examinations. Breast cancer strikes nearly 10 percent of all American women, but the disease is highly curable if detected and treated early. One way to detect it is through self-administered breast exams, which take about 5 minutes to perform. Yet the percentage of women who regularly perform the simple exam is quite low, even among those who are aware of the American Cancer Society's recommendation that it be performed monthly.

How can we explain this *noncompliance?* After all, 5 minutes a month is a tiny sacrifice to save your life. The researchers suspected that the positive outcomes usually touted by messages that promote breast self-exams are too meager to offset a tendency to avoid the risk of actually discovering a lump on one's breast (Meyerowitz and Chaiken, 1987). Outcomes such as the treatment benefits of early detection or becoming skilled at noticing a lump if there is one—these *appear* as very modest and pallid gains, especially to young women who *assume* that they are healthy (remember the optimism bias). Accordingly, the researchers reasoned that messages might have more impact if they presented these benefits not as gains but as *losses* that could be avoided by performing breast exams. As we mentioned in our discussion of environmental attitudes, the threat of a small loss often has more impact than the promise of a small gain (Tversky and Kahneman, 1986). No one likes to lose benefits they already have. Thus, a message phrased, or "framed," in the negative (loss) should be more salient and thought-provoking.

To test these ideas, female college students were presented with foldout pamphlets that included information about breast cancer and how to perform breast self-examinations. While some were randomly assigned to a condition where they got only that input, others were in conditions where they also received six persuasive arguments for monthly breast exams framed in the usual gain terms, or six arguments for monthly breast exams framed in loss terms. For example, two of the *gain arguments* read as follows:

> By doing breast self-examinations now, you can learn what your normal, healthy breasts feel like so that you will be better prepared to notice any small, abnormal changes that might occur as you get older.
>
> Research shows that women who do breast self-examinations have an increased chance of finding a tumor in the early, more treatable stages of the disease.

Now check out the same arguments framed in *loss language:*

> By not doing breast self-examinations, you will not learn what your normal, healthy breasts feel like so you will be ill-prepared to notice any small, abnormal changes that might occur as you get older.
>
> Research shows that women who do not do breast self-examinations have a decreased chance of finding a tumor in the early, more treatable stages of the disease.

The results of this very subtle manipulation, presented in Figure 9.1, were anything but subtle. The women who received the loss arguments later expressed more positive attitudes toward breast self-exams and stronger intentions to begin performing the exams regularly than those who received either no arguments or the gain arguments. These differences were still evident in a telephone survey 4 months later. And during the intervening 4 months, those given loss arguments reported having actually *performed* breast self-exams significantly more often than the others.

When you think about it, this study is remarkable. A slight variation in language achieved an increase in the number of people engaging in a healthful behavior that could prevent future suffering and even prolong life. Health messages should routinely be analyzed in terms of how the targeted audiences *perceive* the health benefits they promise. Perceptions matter.

Gaining Compliance by Emphasizing Losses

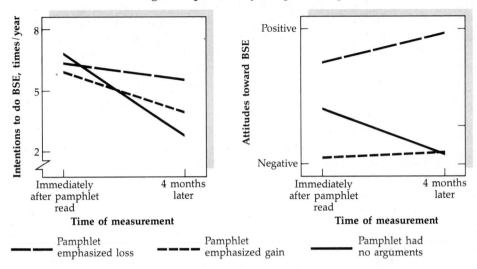

FIGURE 9.1

Female college students were given pamphlets about how to do breast self-examinations (BSE) for cancer. The pamphlets included either no arguments promoting BSE, arguments emphasizing what one gains from doing BSE, or arguments emphasizing what one loses from not doing BSE. The pamphlet emphasizing loss had greater and more lasting impact. (A no-pamphlet control group, not shown, resembled the no-argument group in intentions and behavior.)
(Data from Meyerowitz and Chaiken, 1987. Copyright 1987 by the American Psychological Association. Adapted by permission.)

Making "safe" sexy. With our eye on perceptions, let us turn briefly to the grave health problem of AIDS. Do radio spots which dryly inform the public that using condoms helps prevent the spread of AIDS and other sexually transmitted diseases have their desired impact? Do they compel most teenagers and college students to invariably use condoms during sex? Do more dramatic TV spots showing a young woman sending this same message to a potential sexual partner increase this healthful behavior? We don't have enough evidence to know yet, but there are some promising, if mixed, signs.

A recent survey and personal interview study found that condom use among teenage boys had doubled between 1979 and 1988 (reported by Landers, 1990). Condom use among 17- to 19-year-olds reportedly increased from a low of 21 percent in 1979 to 58 percent in 1988. It appears that it was fear of AIDS and not fear of fathering a child that was responsible for much of this increase. On the negative side were the related findings that two-thirds of the 1979 sample (609 boys) were sexually active compared with three-quarters (of 742 boys) in 1988, and 42 percent of the latter did not use condoms. Most distressing is the finding that most groups at greatest risk of contracting AIDS were still not practicing safe sex. Only 21 percent of teen intravenous drug users (or those who had partners who were intravenous drug users) used condoms, as did only 17 percent of those who had sex with prostitutes. Also on the downside is the evidence that a mere 37 percent of the most sexually active teen males, those who had sex with five or more partners, reported using condoms. Of course, all these data are likely to be overestimates since they are reports given to survey researchers in a context where the teens know that they should have been using condoms.

Social psychologist Elliot Aronson worries that most of the ad campaigns for safe sex may create in people's minds an association between condoms and sterile hygiene practices, coldly planned "bad" sex, and the threat of death. As a result, many sexually active adolescents and young adults may tune out entirely or counterargue the message ("Hey, no one I would have sex with could possibly carry AIDS"). Even those who "get the message" may not spontaneously think of stopping the action to do the "right thing" and put on that good news condom in the heat of their passionate encounter. A device associated with death and dulled sensation is hard to incorporate into one's passion-filled sexual script, which for males (at least) includes a subplot of "strike while the iron is hot."

Aronson (1991) offers an interesting remedy: persuade people that condoms are sexy. This could be accomplished by public service ads showing erotically arousing but tasteful lovemaking scenes which suggest that having both parties engage in putting on and using a condom as an enjoyable, integral part of the foreplay experience. Theoretically, a racy ad like this might achieve two ends. First, it encourages the perception that using a condom is itself an appealing, immediately satisfying act. Second, through the classical conditioning process we discussed in Chapter 7, the audience may acquire a positive attitude about condoms because of their association with sexual arousal elicited by the love scene.

Pulling out all the stops. The mass media message is but one social influence weapon. Why not aim the entire arsenal more directly at unhealthy behaviors? This was exactly the thinking of the researchers who launched the Stanford Heart Disease Prevention Program (Farquhar et al., 1984; Maccoby et al., 1977; Meyer et al., 1980). They conducted an important long-term field experiment to find out how best to educate adults about cardiovascular health and get them to engage in health behaviors that reduce their risk of heart disease. The targeted behaviors ran the gamut of cardiovascular health: eat right, don't smoke, exercise, have frequent cholesterol and blood pressure checks, and reduce cholesterol intake. The targeted people were not the usual laboratory subjects but rather the residents of three California towns with a population of about 14,000 each.

Town A was the control town; it received no special influence interventions beyond those routinely presented in the local mass media. Town B received an intense 2-year mass media campaign consisting of educational messages about the causes of cardiovascular disease and the behavior patterns that influence risk. Town C received the same mass media informational campaign, and in addition, a sample of 100 recruited volunteers from this town participated in a series of instruction sessions and workshops over a period of several months during the media blitz.

These volunteers, ranging in age from 35 to 59 years, were all at high risk for heart disease as a result of poor health habits. The instruction they received involved a variety of influence and educational methods. Participants watched films about smoking, dieting, and exercising. They were taught how to self-monitor healthy and unhealthy behaviors, and how to shop, cook, and store the "right" foods. Cognitive and behavioral aids for quitting smoking were introduced and practiced. Various forms of reinforcement (praise and feedback) were administered for smoking reduction and weight loss. Opportunities for commitment and self-persuasion were provided.

The Town C volunteers, and comparable groups of high-risk citizens of Town A and Town B, were tracked for 3 years, beginning just before the interventions and continuing for a year after the interventions were over. Yearly measures of the participants' knowledge about cardiovascular health, their health behaviors, and their weight, blood pressure, and cholesterol levels were taken.

The major results are presented in Figure 9.2. Looking at the graphs, we can see that, compared with high-risk citizens in the control town (Town A), citizens of the town that received only the media blitz (Town B) showed a lasting increase in knowledge and a lasting decrease in behaviors and indicators associated with high risk. A heavy dose of mass media messages had a clearly positive health impact. However, there was clearly a much bigger impact among the Town C residents who received both the media messages and hands-on training.

This study is encouraging on two counts. First, it suggests that well-executed mass media campaigns do influence health behaviors. Second, it demonstrates that, if money and resources are available to do so, *personalizing* these campaigns with interpersonal direct influence and education adds considerably to their power. Health campaigns, then, get what they pay for. And even the less expensive (mass media) approach can help to some degree.

Psychological know-how can make a difference in effectively communicating health advice to a large, faceless audience through the me-

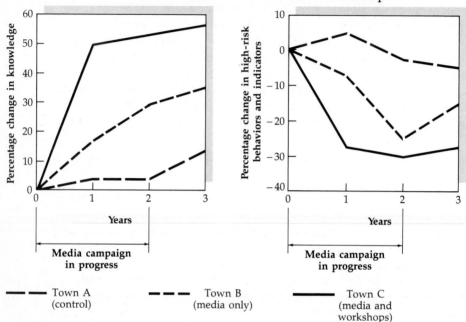

People Respect to Media Health Messages and Even Moreso to Hands-On Workshops

Town A (control)

Town B (media only)

Town C (media and workshops)

FIGURE 9.2

Knowledge of cardiovascular disease risk factors was greater among residents of Town B, who were exposed to a 2-year mass media health campaign, than among residents of Town A, who were not exposed to a campaign. Knowledge gain was greater still when residents (of Town C) participated in intense workshops and instruction sessions for several months during the media blitz. As knowledge increased, bad health habits (risk behaviors) and signs (indicators) decreased, with Town C again leading the way followed by Town B.

(Data from Meyer, Nash, McAlister, Maccoby, and Farquhar, 1980. Copyright 1980 by the American Psychological Association. Adapted by permission.)

dia. Can it make a difference in one-to-one communications that take place in the doctor's office? Let us see.

Doctor's Orders: Why Don't Patients Do As They're Told?

At first glance, you might think that few people fail to follow the advice they receive from their physicians, particularly paid-for, easy-to-follow advice like "Take two pills and call me in the morning." They often take none and can't find the doctor's phone number. It is one thing for healthy people to fail to comply with preventive health messages. But do patients with diagnosed illnesses disobey direct and personal instructions concerning what they must do to keep from getting worse or dying? You'd be surprised.

Consider these findings listed by health psychologists who have reviewed the medical research literature on patient noncompliance (DiNicola and DiMatteo, 1984; Janis, 1984).

- As many as half of the patients with active illnesses fail to take the medications prescribed by physicians at medical clinics.
- About half of all such patients also fail to show up for scheduled treatment appointments.
- The majority of hypertensive patients ignore the diet and slower pace regimens specified by their doctors.
- Even people with acute and painful illnesses, like gastrointestinal ulcers, ignore prescribed regimens.
- *While in the hospital,* patients with ulcers, on average, take less than half the prescribed liquid medication. Patients who are initially compliant tend to slack off within 3 to 5 days.

Of course, patients should not blindly agree with a person just because "M.D." follows the person's name. Medical doctors are not infallible, and legitimate differences of opinion are certainly possible in modern medicine. Milgram's research is a potent reminder of the dangers of kneejerk obedience to someone wearing the cloak of authority. Still, these rates of noncompliance are too large to reflect only rejection of faulty diagnoses by highly intelligent patients. Look at it this way: People are more likely to disobey their own doctor's orders than to disobey an unknown experimenter's instructions to deliver painful shocks to a fellow subject in Milgram's experiments!

Why? One factor is that the image of the medical establishment is not very positive nowadays (Gibbs, 1989). In an era of specialists, cold and imposing technology, and clinic-based care, close doctor-patient relationships are less common than they once were. The threat of medical malpractice suits makes many physicians uneasy with patients, while increasing patient loads make them sometimes curt. For its part, the public, aware of the advances of modern medicine, often expects miracles from doctors. And caught up in a culture of consumerism, some people are inclined to second-guess and comparison-shop for a doctor who says what they want to hear. All these trends conspire to undermine the perceived attractiveness, trustworthiness, and expertise of doctors—the very factors that contribute to their effectiveness as influence agents.

Lack of trust in the doctors is a major cause of patient noncompliance with medical advice. Beyond the poor image of the medical establishment, some doctors are just not persuasive or well-liked. Another related cause of noncompliance is the possible failure of the physician to make the patient clearly understand his or her instructions. Patients may not comply with instructions only because they misunderstand the medical jargon or other ambiguous language of the doctor's instructions (often given in haste). A clear example of this is the quite common problem of patients failing to take a required medicine, such as penicillin, for the prescribed number of days. They stop prematurely because they feel better (DiNicola and DiMatteo, 1984). This noncompliance problem could be greatly alleviated by a clear and explicit instruction ("John, you must take this medicine for 10 days, whether or not you feel better before that") supplemented with a printed reminder.

Finally, patient stress contributes to nonresponsiveness to doctors' influence attempts. When ill, people should ideally make rational decisions about what actions to take and what advice to follow, based on careful consideration of the severity of the illness, the likely effectiveness of the advised treatment, and the costs of the advised treatment (Hochbaum, 1958; Janis, 1984). But serious sickness or injury can be seriously stressful. And decision making under stress often leaves much to be desired. Facing the fact that one's disease is very serious, for example, may cause so much anxiety that the person engages in *defensive avoidance,* denying and downplaying the severity (Janis, 1984). The patient may ignore the doctor's advice as a means of reinforcing this denial. In other cases, the recommended treatment becomes perceived as

It can be surprisingly difficult for doctors to persuade their patients to follow their orders and take their prescriptions.   (*Mark Antman/The Image Works*)

too costly, even when the cost of not undergoing it could be one's life. Smaller, immediate costs loom greater than larger, distant ones.

Defense avoidance of medical advice may also occur if self-defining beliefs and values are threatened by the admission that one is ill. The steadfast resistance of some patients to do what the doctor ordered because it challenges personal beliefs or cultural values is the opposite side of the coin to another stress-related style of responding to physicians' instructions. Instead of defensive avoidance, stress might cause an irrational response to medical advice known as *hypervigilance* (Janis, 1984). This occurs when patients panic over their malady and overreact to their symptoms and any piece of symptom-relevant information they come across. They accept uncritically all they read or hear about their illness—every magazine article, every rumor, every anecdote provided by an acquaintance. ("You know, Fred, my cousin had what you have, and he was cured by...") The doctor's advice, too, is eagerly followed. But if it doesn't work immediately, the hypervigilant patient begins second-guessing or mixing medically prescribed treatments with "home remedies." He is likely to jump from doctor to doctor, from doctor to faith healer, or to guaranteed "miracle cures" promoted in *The National Enquirer*.

In sum, lack of trust in doctors, misunderstanding of instructions, and patient stress contribute to the rather common inability of doctors to influence their patients. Fortunately, these are human relations problems that can be overcome through more effective social influence. Recognizing this, more and more medical schools are including course work on interpersonal relationships in their curricula (Gibbs, 1989). We might recommend adding in a bit about strategies and tactics of social influence. Physicians could be taught how to design effective fear appeals, how to solicit public commitments from patients to follow recommended treatments, and how to show that they are more caring, responsive human beings and concerned, persuasive communicators.

Lessons from fear appeals. In discussing social influence remedies for patient noncompliance, let us start with what is perhaps the most difficult problem: that of patient stress and the poor judgments it may engender. A physician might be able to break through the wall of defensive avoidance by delivering a well-crafted fear appeal. Remember that fear appeals are effective to the extent that they make it clear how personally serious the health threat is, while also stressing that the person who adopts the prescribed treatment behaviors will gain hope and personal control. In effect, the doctor must tell the anxious patient: "Make no mistake about the costs of not following my advice, but be assured that you can handle this treatment and it will help you."

If fear appeals have some success through the mass media, they can be even more effective when they are "up close and personal" in the doctor's office. Doctors can personalize their messages for the individual patient. They also can supplement them by teaching and encouraging the patient to think positively. For example, doctors can teach "positive self-talk," which involves making a habit of giving oneself confidence-boosting messages like "I can meet this challenge" or "I can call upon lots of different strategies to get through this." In so doing, the patient mentally redefines the situation into one of hope and confidence. As we learned in Chapter 3, behaviors readily flow from self-attributions.

Getting a commitment. It should come as no surprise to you that patients are more likely to comply with medical treatments if they make a verbal or behavioral commitment to comply. Doctors can do lots of little things to encourage that commitment. They can remind the patient that it was her decision to begin treatment. They can identify improvements that have already taken place and can attribute them to the patient's cooperative behavior (Janis, 1984). Even taking simple care to extract a verbal commitment ("Yes, I'll do it") from the patient before she or he leaves the office might provide that little extra psychic pressure to ensure compliance. For extended treatments, doctors might even get the patient to sign a *behavioral contract* to engage in the recommended health behaviors (Nelson and Mowrey, 1976).

People more often resist psychologically binding commitments when the medical recommendations concern *preventing* a future health problem rather than *curing* an existing one. Physicians commonly complain about stressed-out executives who won't relax or take a vacation, aging heavy smokers who just won't quit, and almost-obese patients who won't exercise or eat less. In these cases, we must call upon more drastic influence techniques. Do you recall from Chapter 3 the classic study in which emotional role-playing (receiving the news that one has lung cancer) led many smokers to commit to quitting? Enterprising physicians can incorporate small doses of role-playing into their influence arsenal.

To break down resistances to commitment based on unconscious defensive avoidance, doctors can apply the *awareness-of-rationalizations* technique (Reed and Janis, 1974). A doctor might keep a list of common patient excuses for not following health recommendations and hand it out to resisting patients with a somber message: "Betty, these are excuses some of my other patients have used.... Do you recognize any of them in yourself? By the way, several of the authors of these excuses are no longer with us."

Office (and bedside) manners. These are just a sampling of the psychological influence techniques to increase patient compliance with doctors' orders. Did you notice, however, that the success of all these methods, to an extent, rests on the *communication skills* of the practitioner? Physicians must be able to give instructions and medical reasons for them using language that is understandable and tailored to the needs and educational level of their clients. But the fear appeals and verbal manipulations we have suggested require much more than clarity of words. In fact, they require more than words themselves. They require (1) nonverbal styles of communication that convey warmth, trustworthiness, and self-confident expertise, and (2) the ability to read the patient's nonverbal signals of resistance or compliance. Remember (from Chapter 7) the important impact of facial and vocal expressions on emotions and attributions? Communication in the doctor's office is no different.

A study of nonverbal physician influence demonstrated that one can predict which patients will follow their doctor's recommendation to attend a therapy clinic for alcoholism solely on the basis of *how* the doctor makes the recommendation (Milmoe et al., 1967). Doctor-patient interactions were tape-recorded, and the tapes were processed on a special device that filtered out the content of what was said, leaving only the variations in vocal pitch of the physician—that is, how it was being said. Judges rated the tapes on a number of dimensions, including the nonverbal expression of hostility. When hostility ratings were compared with whether or not patients complied, a clear pattern emerged. Those patients least likely to follow the recommendation to go to the alcoholism clinic were those whose doctor prescribed that action in a tone that was hostile. This nonverbal style of expressing hostility was detected by the patient, possibly at an unconscious level, and could have been directed toward the patient, toward alcoholism, or toward the likelihood that the prescribed therapy would actually work.

In any case, the patients who did not comply with the word content of the doctor's message ("go to therapy") were responding to the nonverbal subtext of his or her message ("Don't go, I do not think that it will work for you"). This study also illustrates another reason for noncompliance, namely, awareness that the doctor doesn't really believe in the value of the prescribed treatment or doesn't really care if the patient follows the advice.

There are tests that measure ability to express or "send" emotion through nonverbal behaviors and to "read" the emotions of others from their nonverbal cues. Several studies have shown that physicians who score as good "senders," compared with those who are less adept at nonverbal communication, have patients who are more satisfied with the medical care they are receiving (DiMatteo and Taranta, 1979; DiMatteo et al., 1980). In one study, greater satisfaction with medical care was reported by people who described their doctors as communicating composure, empathy, and immediacy (as opposed to distance and detachment); dissatisfaction was reported when the doctor was seen as conveying an air of dominance and superiority (Burgoon et al., 1987).

Satisfaction provides the fertile groundwork for the seeds of compliance to grow strong roots. This same study found that more satisfied patients more often reported that they followed their doctor's orders. Another study found that physicians skilled at sending positive nonverbal cues had patients who were both more satisfied and less likely to cancel or fail to show up for future appointments (DiMatteo et al., 1986).

The data force the general conclusion that physicians must go beyond being authority figures dispensing unquestionable expertise to become persuasive communicators. They can do so most effectively by using influence principles adapted from social psychology, along with conveying a personal genuineness in their voices, their gestures, and their emotional expressions.

In this discussion of how to get people to follow expert advice that is good for them, we have left out one obvious social tactic. When the fatter of your two authors fails in his quest for waist reduction through diet and exercise unless his wife jogs along, we see the value of social support. *Social support* has been found to be one of the most powerful antidotes to all types of pathology of body and mind, while *social isolation* is one of the strong predictors of physical and mental illness. Being part of a responsive social support network builds resistance to stress and disease (Cohen and Syme, 1985; Pilisuk and Parks, 1986). Behavioral intentions translate into behavior modification when others are there to check up on our commitments and to provide feedback on progress toward our goals—reminding, praising, shaming us on the way. In one study of patients with high blood pressure, the key to their adhering with medical treatments was found in the combination of social support of their spouse coupled with high self-esteem (Caplan et al., 1976).

Having seen that the psychology of social influence can help promote physical health, let us see in the final section of this chapter what it can do for our mental health.

SOCIAL PSYCHOLOGICAL ROADS TO MENTAL HEALTH

To the general public, psychology is best known as the field concerned with understanding and treating mental disorders. Through various forms of therapy, clinical and counseling psychologists attempt to help people overcome severe anxiety, depression, phobias, and more devastating disorders such as paranoia and schizophrenia. The need for psychotherapy has never been greater. It is estimated that more than 20 percent of all American adults suffer from some form of diagnosed mental disorder (Shapiro et al., 1984). That's thirty million people. The stresses and strains of competitive, fast-paced living; the social displacements, poverty, and isolation brought about by changes in family and economic structure—in the United States, these factors and many more contribute to a toll of fourteen million cases of anxieties, obsessions, and phobias; ten million cases of substance abuse; and twenty-five million females and twelve million males experiencing a major depression at some time in their lives (Zimbardo, 1988). It's depressing to think about all of it, let alone to experience any part of it.

But it is not hopeless. Our understanding of the causes and cures of mental disorders is growing rapidly. Quite effective therapies exist for many modern maladies of the mind. However, only about 1 out of every 5 people in need of mental health care actually gets it—even where it is readily available (Shapiro et al., 1984). A major barrier to improving society's collective mental health is the difficulty of communicating the availability and social acceptability of treatment to the masses. It is really a problem of persuasion—of reaching and then convincing people that psychological difficulties are not stigmas to be hidden, that they happen even to good, "normal" people, and that people can get help in dealing with and overcoming them.

Perhaps you've seen the ads of the American Mental Health Fund explaining that depression is not always something people just "get over" without treatment, or the large billboards that inform passing motorists that schizophrenia is a "treatable disease that strikes 1 in 100 Americans" and to call a specific number for information. These mass media messages are often built on sound persuasion techniques: vivid images, repetition, encouraging notes about the efficacy of action ("a treatable disease"). Yet widely held misperceptions of mental illness cannot be dislodged solely through the media. More early exposure to facts about mental illness in the schools would help. People, as we know, can better process messages when they already have a knowledge base and don't have preconceived attitudes that encourage cynical counterarguing.

Therapy by Any Other Name...Is Influence

Our main purpose in the last section of this final chapter is to examine some of the ways in which the social-psychological forms of influence we have analyzed throughout our journey together are, or can be, incorporated into psychotherapy. All psychotherapies involve influence. They are interventions designed to change the client's behaviors, thoughts, attitudes, or feelings in some way. Covering all of the mental health field, however, is beyond the scope of this book. Some psycho-pathologies, like schizophrenia, are profoundly severe, involving loss of touch with reality and often a partial basis in heredity and biological dysfunction. Such disorders are not fully treatable with "normal" social influence techniques. Also, therapies that probe for deep-seated uncon-scious conflicts, such as psychoanalysis, are not within our present focus.

On the other hand, many psychological problems boil down to (1) habits of maladaptive behavior developed as a means of coping with stress and anxiety, (2) conditioned emotional responses that prevent effective ac-tions, or (3) cognitive styles that involve a preponderance of negative thinking. In these cases, improved mental health may be achieved by en-gaging the behavior and attitude change processes that by now must be quite familiar to you. We will look at how applying procedures that in-volve systematic message processing, reward and punishment, self-attribution, commitment gaining, and self-justification can help move peo-ple along the road to mental health.

Therapy as Persuasive Communication

In some psychotherapies, therapists communicate messages to the cli-ent. For example, a therapist might attempt to convince those suffering from depression that their attributions are invalid. Or a marriage coun-selor might attempt to talk couples into trying certain new or alternative behaviors in their interactions. It goes without saying that therapists must have the qualities of good communicators.

High therapist credibility based on perceived expertise may compel the patient to agree with the therapist's message. But if the acceptance is superficial, based solely on the heuristic cue of source expertise, it will not go very far in changing behaviors and deeply embedded atti-tudes, especially when the authority figure is not around. The therapist must get the client to process his messages *systematically,* so that they strike deep cognitive chords and are well understood in terms of their behavioral and emotional implications (Heesacker, 1986). One quality that encourages deep thinking about the therapist's suggestions is the client's perception that the therapist is *similar* to the client on various status and values dimensions. This implies an ability to relate to and empathize with the client. The most important therapist trait, though, is what humanistic psychologist Carl Rogers (1951) has termed *therapeu-tic genuineness.* Therapists must project that they are "together" and "up front"—in touch with their own feelings and concealing them from neither themselves nor the client. There must be trust in their shared goal of changing the client's functioning and outlook in directions that are desirable and beneficial.

Cognitive-Behavioral Therapy and Attribution Therapy: Think and Do Yourself Better

Behavior therapy, or *behavior modification* as it is often called, uses principles of instrumental and classical conditioning to change disturbing or maladaptive behavior patterns. An instrumental conditioning approach to problem drinking, for example, might include systematically punishing the client with electric shocks whenever he orders or sips a drink during sessions at a "therapy bar," and rewarding with praise or a partial rebate on fees when weekly blood tests reveal no evidence of recent alcohol consumption.

Classical conditioning procedures may be employed to treat irrational fears or anxieties. To overcome fear of flying, a client may be trained in relaxation methods and then, while in a relaxed state, paced through gradually more anxiety-provoking situations that elicit the fear: thinking about flying, driving to an airport, sitting in an airport, touring a plane—and ultimately traveling by plane. Since relaxation and fearful anxiety are incompatible responses, if the client can stay relaxed while experiencing the fear-arousing stimuli, the stimulus-to-fear link will weaken and then disappear. Such *counterconditioning* is among the most successful methods for changing irrational emotional responses that prevent adaptive behavior.

Behavior modification is directed exclusively at changing behavior. Many maladaptive behavior patterns, however, are influenced by the habitual ways in which troubled individuals perceive and think about themselves and their social world. Some problems, moreover, are mainly "head problems": behavior is OK, one's work gets done, relationships are generally satisfactory, but the person feels lousy or anxious. In these cases, efforts to shape behavior directly may not, by themselves, be effective therapy. They may need to be supplemented by a therapy focused on those faulty perceptions, beliefs, and attitudes. The combination is called *cognitive-behavioral therapy.*

The dark thoughts of depression. Cognitive-behavioral therapy is a particularly effective treatment for depression. We normally think of depression as a mood state. But it is also a behavioral problem. Chronically depressed people often fail to take actions that could give them the reinforcement, the "lift," they need. In the absence of success experiences that they themselves produce, they become more depressed, which makes them more inactive, which leads to more depression, and so on. It's a vicious cycle.

The inaction (lack of trying) portion of this cycle has its source in cognition. Depressed people are pessimistic thinkers. They make "depressive attributions." When bad things happen, they make internal attributions ("It's my fault...") and see future improvements as beyond their control ("...and I can't make it any better"). Good outcomes are chalked up to temporary luck or someone else's doing. This attributional style leads to a sense of hopelessness and, hence, a lack of trying to improve one's lot (Peterson and Seligman, 1984).

To go along with their depressive attributions, depressed people tend to think too many negative thoughts in general. Remember the role of positive self-talk in patient compliance with difficult medical regimens? Self-talk goes on most of the time in most of our heads. We talk to ourselves, in Hamlet-like monologues, more than we dialogue with anyone else. Research suggests that well-adjusted people average about two positive thoughts for every negative one (Schwartz and Garamoni, 1986).

Depressed people, in contrast, have *less than one* positive thought for every negative one. A study found that about 55 percent of their thoughts were negative (Kendall, 1987). Negative thinking becomes practically automatic in depression (Beck, 1976). ("I'm just not smart enough to cut it at this school." "Nobody finds me very interesting." "I feel like an old toilet brush.") Their thoughts are filled with doom and gloom. They feel that they are going down and being counted out—by the referee aspect of self.

Cognitive-behavioral therapy attacks depression on both the cognitive and behavioral fronts. On the cognitive side, the therapist points out the negative thinking and self-blaming attributions, and argues that this negativism is invalid. Using negative events described in a log kept by the client, the therapist recasts negative outcomes as products of *situational* factors rather than personal, *dispositional* shortcomings. In effect, the therapist delivers highly personalized persuasive arguments meant to change the client's beliefs about the world.

On the behavioral side, the client is given "activity assignments" to go out and do something positive. But first there is training in carefully planning one's actions to ensure success. Compared with the client's current passivity, almost any outcome of these actions is bound to be positive. This sets the stage for classic self-attribution effects. From their successful actions, clients should infer that they are, in fact, efficacious agents who can control what happens to them. Be assured that the therapist pumps successful behaviors for every ounce of self-attributional potential. For example, hearing his patient express just the slightest sense of satisfaction about a recent party she hosted, the therapist might remark, "You must be a rather well-organized person to put a successful dinner party together in such a short time." This self-attributional process of inference from one's own behavior may, in fact, be the most important one (Bandura, 1986).

Cognitive-behavioral therapy for depression has a solid track record of success, particularly for clients who want to change and are receptive to therapy in its early stages (Baker and Wilson, 1985; Kendall, 1987). And depression is not the only psychological problem that can be alleviated through interventions that change attributional styles. Short-term variants of cognitive-behavioral therapy, often called *attribution therapy*, are used in various kinds of counseling.

Do it in the name of love. Partners in unhappy marriages and dating relationships quite often have adopted a "negative attribution bias" about their partner (Fincham and O'Leary, 1983; Kyle and Falbo, 1985). Positive behaviors by the partner are attributed to situational causes or seen as one-time actions with possible ulterior motives. Negative behaviors are attributed to the partner's personality. In fact, distressed couples see less positive causes in the partner's behavior than in their own behavior even when the behaviors are the same (Fincham et al., 1987). It goes something like this: "I put my arm around you at a party because I care for you; you do it for the impression it makes." Or: "I didn't pay attention to you last night because I was preoccupied with my problem at work; you ignore me because I bore you." To go with this, the partner's positive acts are seen as resulting from primarily uncontrollable causes. This kind of reasoning prevails: "She's affectionate only when she needs a shoulder to lean on. Therefore, I cannot 'win' her affections."

Of course, these attributions could be accurate. But when both partners express their love and good intentions and their partner's lack of these, it becomes clear that faulty attributions are going on at least in one mind, and probably in both. Effective marriage counselors bring the attributional biases of their "dynamic duo" into the open, encourage the partners to refute faulty impressions, and engage the couple in mutual "attributional retraining."

Being the new kid on campus is tough for all of us. Before they ever face a marriage crisis, many people face their first year of college—something they so desired in high school and worked so hard to achieve, yet so scary when it is finally realized. Big, impersonal, and difficult classes; possibly being away from home and living with a roommate; going from being a "senior hot shot" to a frosh nobody who has to prove to everyone that you really belong there and you are not a fraud—these are realities that most new students face. The adjustment can be hard and stressful. When students experience difficulty adjusting to college life, they commonly blame themselves. They attribute poor academic performance or a slow-moving social adjustment to their own personal inadequacies. This leads to depression, to the depression cycle that can further deteriorate performance, and also to expectancy-confirming behavior. If you conclude that you're dumb, why study? So you study less, and lo and behold, you fail the test. There is the hard evidence that you were right: *you are dumb!*

One attributional approach to dealing with this syndrome of freshman self-blame is to convince students that *they* are *not to blame.* Mood and motivation often improve if counselors and faculty advisers (highly credible sources) assure new students that first-year difficulties are, in fact, the norm and that grade point averages and personal comfort in school improve over time (Wilson and Linville, 1982). Attention is thereby turned to situational causes that are clearly surmountable (self-efficacy strikes again in the service of health). Armed with optimism and freed of the awful inference that "I *can't* make it," the student is less likely to let his or her behavior be frozen by depression and defeatism.

There is a general principle here that you may find useful yourself. Your psychological well-being often benefits more by seeking out the situational causes of your problems (that you share with others) than by obsessing over idiosyncratic dispositional causes (that set you apart as weird or inferior).

The helpful lies of misattribution. In an ideal sense, attribution therapies attempt to *correct* "faulty" attributions fraught with inaccurate, self-defeating biases that exacerbate the client's problems. Sometimes, however, therapists may use attribution-based tactics that encourage people to replace a set of unhealthy and badly distorted attributions with a set of healthy but still mildly distorted ones. Depressed people are taught to acquire the optimistic sense of personal control displayed by well-adjusted people.

Yet research suggests, and therapists know, that well-adjusted people share a healthy *illusion* of greater control than they really have. The depressed person may have a more accurate view of reality, but it leads to pessimism, passivity, and giving up rather than maintaining the rosy glow of false optimism that encourages the nondepressed among us to try harder, thereby increasing their chances of succeeding and thus validating their optimistic outlook (Lewisohn et al., 1980; Barthe and Hammen, 1981).

Similarly, the freshman with an F, four D's, and a low C on his first six exams may really have inadequate academic potential. Yet the counselor oriented to attribution therapy still encourages the student to put some blame on his difficult situation. The hope is that some minor attribution distortions that *favor* clients are worth it if they emancipate them from beliefs that keep them in the paralyzing clutches of self-blame or steadily worsening social relationships.

Dissonance and Therapy: Commitment, Choice, and Effort

The principles of commitment and consistency emerge time and time again across the varied domains and forms of social influence. Not surprisingly, they are highly applicable in psychotherapy. As a matter of course, psychotherapists seek committing promises of effort and cooperation from their patients. And the earlier in therapy they receive them, the better.

People feel more pressure to behave consistently with prior acts and commitments when they feel that they freely chose them—and they weren't coerced. Recognizing this, some therapists actually ask clients to choose the type of treatment they will receive. The therapist will point out various problem behaviors and list alternative therapeutic techniques that can be used for those problems. The client and therapist then sit down and plan the therapy, with the client explicitly making some of the choices. To make this choosing role salient and to commit the client, the therapist may then ask the client to sign a therapy "contract" describing the chosen treatments. There is evidence that clients in high-choice therapy show faster improvements than low-choice control groups (Brehm and Smith, 1986). Apparently, even in therapy, people become motivated to avoid or eliminate the dissonance associated with failing at something they had a hand in designing in the first place.

Beyond dissonance, making choices enhances the client's sense of personal control and responsibility. This fosters feelings of self-worth and self-efficacy, and nurtures the realization that one cannot simply be cured by passive exposure to an omnipotent therapist. The message is that therapy helps those who help themselves.

A stunning example of the role of choice in therapy is found in research by Joel Cooper (1980). Through campus newspaper ads, people were recruited who described themselves as highly fearful of snakes. When they showed up for a 1-hour therapy session at the laboratory, the recruits were randomly assigned to receive either a *real* short-term therapy or a *bogus* therapy. The real therapy was a variant of "implosive therapy" in which the snake phobic visualizes anxiety-provoking scenes involving snakes to the point where the anxiety basically wears off.

The bogus therapy was called "exercise therapy" and involved running in place, winding a weight-laden yo-yo, and other irrelevant activities. It was explained that the arousal caused by exercise helps people

This method might work—through punishment or maybe even effort justification!
(*B. C.*, 3/26/90, reprinted by permission of Johnny Hart and Creators Syndicate.)

become sensitive to the causes of fearful emotions. Subjects were further divided into high- and low-choice groups. High-choice subjects were told that their therapy "could be very effortful and anxiety-provoking" and that it was up to them whether or not they wanted to continue with the session. Low-choice subjects were told about the effort but were never asked whether they wanted to continue. The experimenter simply proceeded without involving them in that decision.

After the real or bogus therapy, all subjects were tested for improvement. Specifically, they were given the opportunity to walk up to and touch a 6-foot boa constrictor in a glass tank. Before the therapy session, the average subject moved only about 1 foot of the 20-foot distance toward the snake. And after the therapy? Well, you can see the results in Figure 9.3. Whether they received a real or bogus intervention, low-choice subjects went about a foot further on average. None touched the snake. High-choice subjects, in contrast, got an average of 10 feet closer to the snake, to within a distance of 9 feet of it. Three actually walked up and touched the big guy. And that dramatic improvement—this evidence of reduced fear—occurred equally for recipients of both implosive therapy and make-believe exercise therapy. The decision to have therapy mattered, not the content of the therapy.

Cooper argues that two psychological forces were at work in the success of the bogus therapy: (1) the committing effect of perceived choice, as we've been discussing, and (2) *effort justification.* You will recall that both the bogus and the real interventions involved considerable physical and psychological work. At the brink of failure, the wavering subject would experience considerable dissonance: all that hard and freely chosen effort would be inconsistent with failing to achieve the goals of therapy. "It was all for nothing" is a dissonance lament.

Choose To Touch a Scary Boa—and You Might

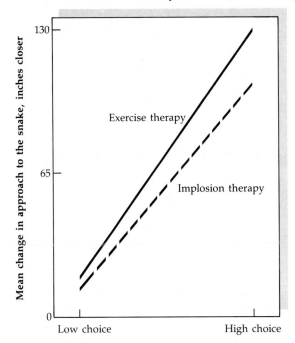

FIGURE 9.3
Whether the therapy for a
snake phobia was real
(implosive therapy) or bogus
(exercise therapy), it worked if
and only if subject-clients freely
chose to undergo the therapy
after learning how effortful it
would be.
(Data from Cooper, 1980.)

One way to reduce this dissonance, to justify one's effort, would be to
get past the brink—to succeed. And so subjects did.

Recent studies have replicated these findings and also found that
merely expecting a freely chosen therapy to be effortful can lead to improvement (Axsom, 1989). Please note, however, that we should not
take these findings to mean that the actual *content* of therapy is never
important. This is not true. Rather, these studies—which involved
short-term interventions into fairly minor disorders—provide strong evidence that therapies can be enhanced by subtle influence techniques
that engage the processes of self-justification.

SOCIAL INFLUENCE, THE GOOD LIFE, AND YOUR FUTURE

There is, of course, no escape from a world of influence. We all control
and are controlled. In this chapter, we discussed some ways in which
psychology is put to use to influence people for their own good, and we
hope that you, the reader, will think of other positive applications in

various domains of your own life. It is interesting and important to note, however, that these forms of benevolent social control are likely to have the most positive effects on those who, themselves, have a strong sense of being *in control*. Self-efficacy, knowledge of how influence works, and knowing how to differentiate sound advice from pop-psych claptrap—these are the traits that help make both the successful person and the good consumer of social influence. In that spirit, we hope this book has helped you enrich those qualities in yourself.

Now you are ready to go forth and face the brave new world, to make friends, to influence worthy causes, and to resist unwanted pressures from groups to conform, from peers to comply, and from the media to be persuaded. The new theoretical and practical information provided here should be a booster rocket for your self-competence in the area of social influence. But temper your newfound sense of "influence smarts" with the stark awareness that there are people out there—and agencies and corporations—whose livelihood and survival depend on developing ever new, more subtle, more effective techniques of mind and behavior control to use on *you* and *us*. Our journey with you is ending, but yours with them is just beginning. We hope that we have prepared you to be as independent and autonomous as possible and have armed you with the best weapon in the encounter—the force of psychological knowledge. Let that force be with you always; use it with integrity and honesty, but use it now that you have it.

*T*O SUM UP...

This final chapter focused on applying social influence principles to a variety of significant pro-social causes. We examined how social psychology can be used to promote pro-environmental behavior, healthful living habits, and mental health.

- One obstacle to widespread pro-environmental behavior is the low salience of pollution, waste, and many types of destruction. Often they are invisible or distant, and hence "out of mind." A second obstacle is low motivation. Pro-environmental motives must compete with stronger economic and personal convenience motives.

- To enhance motivation, instrumental learning can be used. Coupons, rebates, and cash rewards do work to get people to reduce energy consumption, littering, and automobile use. The reward of intrinsically satisfying and informative feedback has been used successfully to get people to conserve energy at home.

- To enhance the salience of the environment as something to care for, prompts and reminders can be used. Media messages can also vividly describe the personal costs of harming the environment, foster positive images of environmentally conscientious people, and encourage commitments to pro-environmental acts. The media, government, and educational system must synchronize their new efforts at more effective environmental persuasion. Consciousness-raising must begin in childhood, while the media must work to keep daily environmental problems and solutions "in sight" and thus in mind, not only during Earth Week.

- Unhealthy lifestyle habits are the primary causes of premature death. Poor health habits persist despite health advice from the media and in doctors' offices, workshops, and clinics.

- Mass media health messages increase health knowledge and positive attitudes but often fail to change health-related behaviors involving tobacco, drugs, alcohol, stress, diet, and exercise. People may fail to change because they enjoy their unhealthy habits or are swayed by the countermessages of peers and advertisers. Also, people are overly optimistic about their health and become cynical about continual health warnings. To overcome these factors, messages should discuss health risks at the personal level, assure people that behavior change is not difficult, accurately describe risks, and alter perceptions of health behaviors by either emphasizing losses avoided by the recommended behavior or associating the behavior with positive emotions.

- Fear appeals can also be effective, if they stress that (1) the target's current behavior poses a noxious health threat, (2) the target is highly vulnerable to the threat, (3) a change in behavior will remove the threat (response efficacy), and (4) the target is capable of the change (self-efficacy).

- Noncompliance with medical advice is common even among patients with serious illnesses. The reasons include the patients' lack of trust in physicians, poor communication skills of physicians, and high patient stress levels that lead to defensive avoidance (denying the severity of illness) or hypervigilance (uncritical acceptance of all "remedies"). To overcome patient resistance, physicians and nurses must be willing and able to give effective fear appeals, gain patient commitments, make patients aware of their rationalizations, and give positive nonverbal signals of concern to their patients.

- Many mental health problems involve maladaptive habits for coping with stress, conditioned emotions, and negative thinking styles—problems amenable to normal change processes.

- Effective psychotherapy requires persuasive communications. Therapists must prompt systematic processing and be perceived as genuine ("together" and "up front") and as holding values similar to those of the client.

- Depression involves a vicious cycle: negative thinking leads to reduced activity, which leads to more negative thinking, and so on. To break this cycle, cognitive-behavior therapy encourages situational attributions for negative outcomes, guides clients into successful actions, and encourages dispositional self-attributions for those successes.

- Counseling aimed at changing attributions can also be effective for marriage and adjustment problems. Therapists may seek to correct "faulty" attributions. But they may also promote slight attributional distortions, such as the overoptimistic sense of control characteristic of well-adjusted people.

- Gaining commitments from clients, allowing them to choose aspects of their treatment, and making treatment somewhat effortful often have positive therapeutic outcomes. These procedures bring into action self-attribution and self-justification.

QUESTIONS AND EXERCISES

1. Go back to Chapter 5, and review the conditions necessary for translating attitudes into behavior. Now consider the discussion of pro-environmental behaviors in this chapter. Put the two sets of information together to analyze the paradoxical reality that most people have positive attitudes toward a clean and healthy natural environment, yet behave in environmentally destructive ways.

2. Using your knowledge of social influence and of the psychological obstacles described in this chapter, design a campaign for your college campus to encourage students (1) to become more environmentally aware and active or (2) to engage in a more healthful lifestyle. Feel free to use all the media outlets and interpersonal settings available on your campus.

3. Discuss three psychological reasons why patients fail to comply with the advice and prescriptions of their doctors. For each one, try to think of an actual example concerning yourself or someone you know, and apply a social influence solution to the examples to help you and your friends or family adhere to those recommendations. If you were hired as a consultant for the local hospital, what steps would you recommend be taken to increase the rate of patient adherence to medical recommendations?

4. Chronic depression, severe shyness, and other states of unhappiness often reflect the extremes of normal cognitive and emotional processes. As such, the influence techniques of social psychology—applicable to the average or "normal" person—can be applied to treating these psychological problems. Assume that you have been hired as a therapist's consultant to outline how social influence tactics and strategies can be integrated into the therapeutic process. Select one type of mental health problem, and outline your treatment recommendations, giving the scientific bases for each of your prescribed actions to be taken by the therapist.

A

Research and the Experimental Method

❖

*B*roadly speaking, social-psychological research on social influence employs either correlational methods or, more commonly, experimental methods. In this appendix we will concentrate primarily on experimental methods, after briefly describing correlational methods.

Correlational Methods in Field Research

In psychology, all research involves making observations of behavior. Some research, called *field research,* observes phenomena or the operation of variables as they exist naturally. That is, the researcher attempts to make systematic, relatively objective, and unbiased observations of things "as they are." The researcher does not interfere with their functioning or try to change or control any of the variables. The researcher's task is to establish whether, and to what degree, two or more variables are corelated.[1] For example, one field researcher showed that college women at Bennington College in Vermont became increasingly liberal in their political and social attitudes from freshman to senior year (Newcomb, 1961). Another study demonstrated that school desegregation was associated with decreased prejudice among elementary school children whose parents were nonauthoritarian and practiced nonpunitive child-rearing practices; however, this was not the case among children whose parents were authoritarian and punitive (Stephan and Rosenfield, 1978).

---

[1]When the variation in one set of data is related to the variation in a corresponding second set (for example, two test scores for each person), the conclusion can be expressed mathematically as the coefficient of correlation, or r. This value may range from -1.0 through 0 to $+1.0$. When $r = 0$, the two distributions of data bear no relation to each other. A positive value of r indicates that variation in each set of data is in a common direction: as A increases, so does B. A negative value of r indicates that A and B go in opposite directions. As r approaches either $+1.0$ or -1.0, it becomes more likely to predict one event knowing the other, that is, to explain the variation in one set of observations from knowledge of the variation in the other.

Field studies like these, and others that employ surveys and polls, are valuable in discovering and analyzing behavioral relationships, and in suggesting variables that might play a vital role in these relationships. Because the observations are made in the everyday world, with minimal interference, their application to everyday life may often be greater than that of observations taken in the more contrived confines of the laboratory. Most field studies, however, are *correlational*. Variables are simply observed, not controlled or changed. Two events or behaviors (*A* and *B*) may turn out to be highly related, or correlated; yet if they have simply been observed, we cannot be certain whether *A* caused *B*, *B* caused *A*, the relation was coincidental, one indirectly caused the other through the operation of an intermediate (unknown variable), or a third variable caused the occurrence of both *A* and *B*.

For example, studies of marital relationships sometimes report that happy couples have sexual relations more often than unhappy couples. Does sex cause happiness? Or does happiness cause sex? Probably both causal sequences occur, but we cannot be sure just from observing the co-occurrence of sex and marital bliss. We also cannot be sure whether a third variable causes the relationship. Perhaps the busy work schedules of some couples cause them to be apart most of the time. This may serve as both a source of unhappiness and an obvious impediment to sexual encounters.

Sometimes correlational studies can provide strong (but still not definitive) insight into causation by varying the times in which variables are measured. It might be observed that whereas changes in variable *A* at time 1 are correlated with changes in variable *B* at time 2, changes in variable *B* at time 1 have little to do with changes in variable *A* at time 2. This pattern implies that *A* has a causative influence on *B*. It is also possible to use certain statistical procedures to tease out suggestions about causation.

The Experiment as a Source of Information about Causation

To truly get at causation, you need an experiment. Most social psychological research, in fact, is experimental. The key to an experiment is *control*. The variable hypothesized to be the causative one, called the *independent variable*, is controlled by the experimenter. He or she manipulates it, giving one level, amount, or type of the variable to the subjects in one treatment condition, another level, amount, or type to those in a second condition, and so on. At the same time, the experimenter attempts to hold constant all other variables to which subjects might be responsive but that are irrelevant for testing the hypothesis at hand.

The experimenter further controls variables through *random assignment* of subjects to the different treatment conditions. This involves using some random method (e.g., coin tosses or consulting a table of computer-generated random numbers) to decide the condition that each subject will be in. Because assignment to conditions is based solely on chance, it will be unlikely that the subjects receiving different levels of the independent variable will differ in any systematic way prior to their exposure to the independent variable. Random assignment usually ensures that any of the multitude of factors that make people differ will be equally distributed among the conditions.

After the presumed causative factor—the independent variable—is introduced, the behavior hypothesized to be the effect, called the *dependent variable*, is observed in subjects. If subjects who receive different levels of the independent variable behave differently on the dependent variable, the logic of experimental control dictates that the independent variable must be the cause. All other variables were held constant, and the independent variable was manipulated *before* the dependent variable was measured.

Thus, you can see that the experimenter does not wait for behavior to occur naturally, but creates the conditions which he or she believes will elicit its occurrence. In this sense, the experimenter creates an artificial environment or interferes with a natural process. This is done in order to (1) make the event occur under known conditions which can be independently replicated on subsequent occasions, (2) make it occur when the experimenter is prepared to make accurate observations (of the dependent variables), (3) make it possible to determine the direction and magnitude of the effect that the independent variable has upon the dependent one, and (4) eliminate the possibility that the relationship between the independent and dependent variable is the result of something other than a direct causal link (for example, *Y* causes both *A* and *B*).

An experiment begins with three basic decisions. From among the infinite array of stimuli that a variety of subjects could perceive and respond to at many levels in numerous dimensions, the experimenter selects a specific stimulus, organism (or subject), and response mode. An experiment can be conceived graphically as a set of three overlapping circles representing the population of all (1) stimuli (independent variables), (2) subjects, and (3) responses (dependent variables) relevant to the general problem under investigation. What the researcher studies is a very small area or point of their intersection. For example, in a study of the effects of the comprehensibility of a persuasive message on attitude change, the independent variable might be four amounts of static accompanying a tape-recorded message, ranging from a tiny amount that does not interfere with comprehension up to an extreme amount of static that makes much of the message very difficult to understand. The subjects might be sixty students taking introductory psychology at a given college. And the dependent variable might be circling a number on a ten-point scale of agreement with the message conclusion.

The set of all stimuli are placed into categories according to theoretically meaningful distinctions. For example, in the Yale Communication Research Project in persuasion undertaken in the 1950s and 1960s (see Chapter 4), the set of all possible communications were categorized according to whether they were two-sided or one-sided, were fear-arousing or not, stated their conclusions explicitly or implicitly, and so on. When stimuli are categorized in this way, the experimenter consciously decides to *ignore* certain properties of the stimuli and emphasize others. For example, the length of the sentences in the message or even the message topic may be irrelevant. This means that the experimenter will select from a large category of one-sided, fear-arousing communications that draw explicit conclusions. The particular one he or she chooses may use twenty-five-word sentences more or less frequently than other communications, and may be about gun control rather than birth control. The hope is that the *same* results will hold across all of these irrelevant characteristics (that is, content, length, syntax, and so on, will not change the basic relationships being examined).

The identical points can be made about the experimenter's selection of types of subjects and responses. Researchers who study college students (or, say, factory workers) to find out about "people in general" often assume that the many differences between different groups do *not* affect the basic causal relationships established in the research. Much research on conformity (see Chapter 2), for instance, studies college students. The possibility that college students may be, on average, more or less "independent thinkers" compared with other adults in the population should not matter when the researcher's interest is focused on how the size of a unanimous majority (e.g., one, two, or three people) affects how often subjects conform to the majority opinion. The relationship between majority size and conformity should be the same regardless of the overall level of conformity of a particular subject group. Similarly, it should not matter whether the conformity response is pushing a button or nodding one's head to indicate agreement.

Of course, if there is some reason to think that basic relationships are not the same for people of different educational levels, social status, ages, genders, or other attributes, additional research can be done comparing different categories of people.

Given that experimenters can select from a large number of specific instances in broad categories of variables and subjects, the decision as to which ones to use is often made on the grounds of convenience, ease and accuracy of measurement, and the extent to which control is possible. Two issues naturally arise: (1) Can the selected instance really be measured in such a way that the same outcome will result regardless of who does the measurement or when it is made? (2) Does the selected instance accurately portray the process or conceptual variable of interest? The first issue is concerned with *reliability,* and the second. with *validity.*

Reliability can be equated with consistency or stability. Will the selected response measure yield the same value on repeated occasions if everything else is the same? Can the same results be obtained under very similar circumstances of testing?

Validity is a more complex issue to demonstrate and has several meanings, only two of which will be mentioned. *Conceptual validity* implies that the treatments, observations, and measurements made by the experimenter are adequate, concrete representations of the broader abstract class that the experimenter really wants to learn something about. An attitude researcher is interested in attitudes, not a check mark on a ten-point questionnaire scale. Ideally, what is desired is a specific set of operations that anchors the abstract concept to events in the real world, but is at the same time as pure an instance of the concept as possible.

The validity of a measure can also be thought of in another way, which we will call *content validity.* Any variation in dependent variable scores has two components: true variance and error variance. As the obtained score is closer to the (hypothetical) true score, it becomes a more valid measure. As its variation is influenced not only by variation in the relevant response being studied but also by extraneous sources of error, it loses its status as a valid representation of the underlying true response system. *Systematic errors* bias the score in a given direction, while *random errors* can cause the score to deviate from its true value in any direction.

Systematic errors may arise, for example, when the experimenter unintentionally gives the subject cues as to what response is predicted, or when an experimenter who knows which subject received a given treatment (such as a drug) is also responsible for making subjective ratings of his or her behavior. Random errors result from environmental disturbances or methodological inadequacies. A transient event could alter the response to the manipulated stimulus on any given occasion (as when an unexpected noise occurs during a conditioning procedure). Similarly, the score could be elevated or depressed in unsystematic and unknown ways if the experimenter presents the stimulus differently to each subject within the same condition. Systematic errors may be minimized by use of controlled procedures, objective scoring methods, randomization, and control groups. Elimination of random errors depends largely upon standard methodology and use of an environment not subject to random changes in features that could affect the subject's response.

To recast the goal of research in light of the present discussion, we might say that an experiment is a set of objective procedures for isolating a signal from a background of noise. The true score, or signal, must be conceptually purified to distinguish it from similar signals. The treatment procedures are designed to amplify the signal, while the measurement procedures should be able to detect even a weak signal. This is possible only when adequate control can be exercised over competing signals and background noise, either by minimizing them or by being able to precisely evaluate their contribution to the observed value of the primary signal.

But what about the generalizability of the findings of an experiment? Few scientists are satisfied with conclusions limited to the details of the specific stimuli and operations used with a unique sample of subjects who gave a particular response. We want our conclusions to be at a higher level of abstraction. We have already seen that, when studying *basic* psychological processes, researchers may be able to assume that their results will hold in the "big picture" of the larger population. But there are a number of factors involved in experimental research that are relevant to ensuring that this assumption is reasonable. We examine these in the following sections.

Generalizing from Experiments: Statistical Inference

There is always a risk involved in making inferences from a study, even if it is well designed and carefully executed. However, the extent of this risk can be calculated by means of statistically objective procedures that evaluate the probability that a given conclusion from a particular set of observations may be false. Suppose we wished to evaluate whether participation in a group discussion changed attitudes toward drug use. We might measure the opinions of the participants both before and after the discussion. The opinion scale ratings of our sample of subjects would first be summarized in a convenient and efficient manner by certain *descriptive statistics*. "What is the typical or average score before the discussion and after?" is a question answerable by computing means, medians, or modes. "How much do individual subjects deviate from this representative value?" can be answered by establishing the variability of response (the range, or the standard deviation).

However, in order to determine whether it was group discussion that changed attitudes in the direction advocated, it is necessary to compare the obtained descriptive statistics with the estimated change that might have occurred from the mere act of repeated measurement of opinions, in the absence of the discussion. Comparison of the obtained distribution of scores with different types of *theoretical* distributions allows one to estimate the probability that the data are not due to chance but to a statistically reliable relationship (*inferential statistics*). Different behavior (between groups of initially comparable subjects) in response to the treatment variable is more likely to be a "real" difference, as a direct function of three factors: number of observations, magnitude of the difference, and variability of the response. An obtained difference is more likely to be a significant one as the number (N) of observations increases, as the difference between groups in performance (measured by some descriptive statistic) is greater, and as the variation within each separate group decreases.

The concept of *significance* is defined in psychology as the minimum criterion for establishing that a given result is due to treatment effects rather than chance fluctuation (error variance) in the observations. A probability level, arbitrarily set at $p < .05$ (p is less than .05, or 5 percent), is this minimum standard. This means that the difference found would occur only 5 times in 100 by chance alone. Therefore, we may infer that this occasion is one of the 95 times when the difference is not attributable to chance. Under certain circumstances, the researcher may demand a more stringent rejection probability, such as $p < .01$ or even $p < .001$ (that is, only 1 time in 1,000 will the experimenter draw a false conclusion by accepting the obtained difference as a real one).

Although the risk involved in drawing an inference is reduced by couching the conclusion in probabilistic rather than absolute terms, there is still considerable risk involved in making inferences in either of two directions from the sample of behavior observed. One can make inferences upward to a more abstract, conceptual level of explanation, or downward to a more concrete, specific instance. In the former case, there may be an error in extrapolation in that the particular results do not reveal the presumed general relationship or theoretical process. In the latter, there is the problem of assuming that a general relationship can predict a specific person's behavior.

For each of these cases there are two types of errors possible. If the significance of an obtained difference is $p < .05$, then the experimenter will be wrong 5 times in 100 in concluding that he or she has found a real effect. This is because chance alone can generate differences of that magnitude, and a particular experiment may represent one of those five possible chance occurrences. Here we have a type 1 (or alpha) error: inferring that a relationship exists when it does not. Looking at our probability and decision-making process differently, suppose the significance of a difference is rejected because it is at the .06 level of probability (beyond the conventional limit of scientific acceptability). Then 94 times out of 100 the investigator will conclude that no relationship exists when, to the contrary, it does. This is a type 2 (or beta) error.

How does the psychologist decide whether to be more risky (type 1 error) or more conservative (type 2 error)? Clearly, his or her strategy should be determined by the action implications of each type of conclusion, by the relative costs or dangers of each type of error, and finally by the stimulation or inhibition of creative thinking each may cause. For example, in making upward inferences to generate conceptual, theoretical statements about physical or psychological reality, progress may be more impaired by a type 2 error (which could serve to close off an area of investigation prematurely) than by a type 1 error (which ought to be readily discovered by others in independent replications). However, if replication studies are rare, then a type 1 error may be perpetuated, resulting in much wasted effort testing derivatives of the original, unsubstantiated hypothesis.

Generalizing from the Laboratory to the Real World

What faces the experimentalist is the dilemma of gaining control while losing power. The full range and intensity of psychological variables cannot be achieved in the laboratory setting. This is because there is only a relatively brief exposure to the independent variable in an experiment. The subject's task is often of limited relevance to other life experiences and has minimal implications for his or her future functioning. In addition, the nature and intensity of the experimental manipulations are limited by legal, ethical, and moral considerations. But while the power of variables is often best demonstrated under uncontrolled natural circumstances, studying phenomena at this level risks a loss of understanding of the processes involved, a lack of specification of causality, and the inability to analyze the complex network of factors into relevant component variables. On the other hand, the gains achieved by the superior control of an experiment may be offset by its trivial content. As a result of purifying, standardizing, controlling, and selecting certain stimulus and response dimensions, the experimenter may have created a very distant, watered-down version of the phenomena or problems he or she set out to study. Under such conditions the results of the investigation may have little practical significance.

It is possible to get around some of these limitations in any particular experiment by *combining* research strategies and by conducting several different experiments on the same topic. For example, suppose an experimenter is worried that the use of monetary rewards to vary "justification" in an induced-compliance dissonance experiment (see Chapter 3) may not be the same as varying "justification" by giving subjects social reasons for complying. He or she can assess this possibility by including *conceptual replications* of "justification" in the experiment or by conducting several different experiments that *systematically replicate* the conceptual variables being studied.

Experimental and mundane realism. To bridge the gap from lab to reality, experimental researchers generally strive to make their experiments realistic. The most important kind of realism is *experimental realism*, which in essence refers to "bringing the experiment to life" (Aronson and Carlsmith, 1968; Aronson et al., 1990). Care must be taken to make the procedure engaging and interesting and to make the independent variables attention-getting and attention-keeping. Subjects should be "caught up" in the laboratory experience, responding (naturally) to the events taking place rather than being bored, thinking (and maybe worrying) about themselves as objects being scrutinized, or trying to figure out what the experimenter's theory is. If an experiment does not have experimental realism, there is a risk that the observed causal relationships are limited only to when people know they are in an experiment. Hence we may learn little about psychological processes in general.

In some cases, the experimenter also seeks *mundane realism,* which refers to manipulating and measuring variables in the same way they exist in the everyday world (Aronson and Carlsmith, 1968). A researcher interested specifically in how questioning style influences eyewitness memory for criminal events (see Chapter 8) might have subjects watch a live staged crime and then report their memories of it under various kinds of questioning conditions. This would have more mundane realism than having subjects view a series of slides and then questioning them. Mundane realism is especially important when generalization is sought to a specific setting or psychological process in the everyday world rather than to a broad class of settings or processes.

Experimental validity. We saw earlier that dependent variables must be valid. The concept of validity also applies to the experiment as a whole, and it is the concept that summarizes well the main issues we have been concerned with in our discussion of experimentation. The conclusions we draw from experiments can be invalid—and thus not generalize—in two different ways. We can erroneously conclude that a causal relationship exists between the specific manipulations and the specific measures being used, when in fact the observed relationship is due to some other factor, an artifact, or confounding variable. In this case we would be drawing an incorrect conclusion about the *internal validity* of the experiment. In addition, it is also possible to conclude erroneously that the specific causal relationship applies across *all other* instances of the conceptual variables not assessed in the study; that is, it generalizes to other people, settings, measures, and conceptually equivalent manipulations. In this second case the *external validity* of the experiment is at issue. One way to avoid drawing both kinds of invalid conclusions is to be aware of the more common sources of invalidity that crop up in experimental research, and then examine different ways of designing experiments that overcome each type of fault.

Let us first consider what some of the sources of *internal invalidity* might be.[2]

1. *Internal artifacts:* It is possible that an uncontrolled event which the experimenter did not want to occur caused the effect the experimenter observed. If this happened, a conclusion that the independent variable was causing the effect would be incorrect.

2. *Subject changes:* Rather than stimulus events (the independent variable) occurring outside of the subject, it is possible that they occurred inside of him or her. For example, the subject may have been sick or worried about a personal problem.

---

[2]The remaining parts of this appendix are largely derived from a book by Campbell and Stanley (1963).

3. *Testing sensitization:* Taking an initial test (premeasure) may affect how the subject reacts to a second test (postmeasure).

4. *Subject selection biases:* If subjects are not assigned to experimental groups at *random,* then there is always a possibility that differences between experimental groups are caused not by differences in the independent variable, but rather by preexisting differences between the subjects in the various groups.

5. *Attrition:* If, after subjects have been randomly assigned to conditions, an uncontrollable factor eliminates some of the subjects from the final analysis of the results, valid conclusions about the effect of the independent variable on the dependent variable cannot be drawn. One uncontrolled factor might be the subject's choice not to continue in the experiment. Another might be some feature inherent in the experiment itself.

Before the sources of *external validity*—or generalizability to other people, settings, and such—can be understood, the concept of *interaction* must be discussed. Let us suppose that we are concerned with the effects that the amount of vicarious reinforcement has on imitation (see Chapter 2). To study this, we expose young children to a film of an adult male model who beats up a bobo doll. After doing so, the model receives none, one, two, four, or ten candy bars. The children are then given the opportunity to "play" with the bobo doll, and the researcher records the frequency with which they engage in the same types of "aggressive" activities as the model. Suppose the average number of imitated responses increased as the size of the reward given to the model increased. The researcher concludes that an increase in the amount of vicarious reinforcement causes people to imitate more.

Note that the above conclusion is not qualified. It implies that the same *relationship* between amount of vicarious reward and amount of imitation will hold across all types of models, all types of subjects, all types of rewards, all types of responses, all settings, and all media used to present the model's actions. The conclusion did not say that the relationship applied only to children in a particular age group from a given school, who observed a particular male model in a film doing certain specific things to a bobo doll and receiving candy bars afterward. What if the relationship is different when a female model hits the bobo doll? Let us suppose the amount of imitation actually decreases with increasing rewards to female models. If the relationship between an independent variable (amount of vicarious reinforcement) and a dependent variable (amount of imitation) changes as a function of some other variable (in this example, sex of model), it is said that the two variables *interact* to determine the outcome.

Interactions can be of many types. The amount of imitation could increase for *both* models, but at different rates. Alternatively, the relation might be reversed (increasing for one, decreasing for another). It might even be that the relationship holds in one case but fails to emerge (amount of vicarious reinforcement has no effect at all) in the second case. In short, the presence of an interaction limits the range of situations, settings, subjects, and so forth, to which the result or relationship of interest can be generalized. In the study of social influence and attitude change it is rare to find variables that are not limited or qualified by their interaction with other variables. Researchers, in fact, often design studies expressly to discover interactions, because interactions inform us about the all important question of when a causal relationship exists and when it does not.

We can now examine some of the more common factors which may limit external validity.

1. *Reactive effects of measurement:* When subjects are given a test, say a self-rating attitude scale, it may be that taking the test itself influences how the subject will behave. In an attitude measurement study, the test may become the stimulus condition that elicits the attitude; the subject either did not have the attitude before or changes his or her true response after realizing the intent of the test or experiment. Thus, any findings would be limited to subjects who had taken the test.

2. *Interaction of selection bias and experimental variable:* The effect of an experimental variable may show up only on certain kinds of subjects. For example, if only subjects with extreme attitudes were studied, it is possible that variables that normally change the attitudes of more moderate subjects would not have an effect on these extreme ones.

3. *Reactive effects of experiment:* Specific differences between the conditions existing in the experimental setting and the conditions existing outside of it may be crucial in determining whether or not the results of the experiment can be applied. For example, experimental subjects might always be highly motivated to attend to the communication, a condition that would not occur naturally.

4. *Multiple treatment effects:* Sometimes each subject is measured with and without the experimental variable present. It is thus possible for sequential effects to occur; that is, the first manipulation affects how the second manipulation will influence the subject's behavior. The results would apply only to subjects who had been exposed to more than one treatment and possibly only one order of treatment.

Experimental Designs

Now that we have presented a few of the more common sources of internal and external invalidity, let us see how well these sources of error can be eliminated by various experimental designs.

Table A.1 presents, in summary form, a set of five highly sophisticated experimental designs. The symbol O in the table refers to observation or measurement, while the symbol M is used to refer to an experimental manipulation of an independent variable that is presented in that condition. In each of these experiments there are at least two groups of subjects. Some of the subjects experience the manipulation; others do not. Those subjects who experience the manipulation and those who do not are always determined randomly. This random assignment of subjects to conditions is indicated by an R in front of

TABLE A.1 SOME EXPERIMENTAL DESIGNS WHICH MINIMIZE SOURCES OF INVALIDITY

	External sources of invalidity			
Experimental Designs	*Reactive Measurement*	*Interaction of Selection Biases and Experimental Variable*	*Reactive Effects of Experiment*	*Multiple Treatment Effects*
	1	2	3	4
1. *Pretest-posttest design* Group 1 R O O 2 R O M O	Yes	Maybe	Maybe	No
2. *Solomon four-group design* 1 R O M O 2 R O O 3 R M O 4 R O	No	Maybe	Maybe	No
3. *Posttest-only design* Group 1 R M O 2 R O	No	Maybe	Maybe	No
4. *Time series with control* Group: Time → 1 R OOOOOOO 2 R OOOMOOO	Yes	No	Maybe	No
5. *Separate sample pretest-posttest design* Group 1 ⎧ R O 2 ⎪ R M₁ O R* ⎨ 3 ⎪ R O 4 ⎩ R O 5 ⎧ R O 6 ⎪ R M₂ O R* ⎨ 7 ⎪ R O 8 ⎩ R O	No	No	No	No

*Here one randomizes both by assignment of individuals to groups and by whether or not comparison groups experience the manipulation.

each group. For example, the simplest design presented in Table A.1 is a two-group design in which the subjects are randomly assigned to one or the other group. Only subjects in group 1 experience the manipulation, after which both groups are observed.

Group 1	R	M	O
Group 2	R		O

Also in the table is a list of the various sources of external invalidity previously described. For each design, if a "yes" appears in the column for the particular source of invalidity, it means that the design is not able to remove that particular kind of error. A "No" means that it does not have that problem. (Internal sources of invalidity are not shown in the table. None of them are a problem with any of these designs *as long as* the investigator properly designs and monitors the experimental procedure.)

The "best" design to use to minimize sources of invalidity is the separate sample pretest-posttest design. Here the experimenter randomly assigns subjects to a number of conditions. The experimenter initially measures the pretreatment responses of only half of all the subjects. The remaining half are measured some time later. However, those subjects who are measured later are also divided in half so that one group experiences the manipulation and the other does not. Furthermore, the reader should note a very distinctive feature of this design. It is possible to demonstrate that the conceptual status of the independent variable is not limited to a single set of specific operations. By using two different sets of operations (M_1 and M_2), both derived from the same conceptual independent variable, general conclusions can be drawn from concrete observations to abstract variables.

From this description you can see that, in any design, randomization is very important. It is also important that the *observations* made of the subjects do not interfere with the behavioral effects of the experimental *manipulations*.

B

Measuring Attitudes and Their Components

❖

*I*n experimental and field studies, people's responses are measured. In this text, we examine many studies, giving brief descriptions of how the dependent variable was measured. In this appendix, we describe some basic measurement techniques in greater detail. These techniques often form the basis from which specific measures are fine-tuned to fit the needs of a specific study. Mostly we will concentrate on measuring attitudes, the central concept of this text. We will also briefly note how other components of attitude systems may be measured.

If you stop to think about it, you will realize that measuring an attitude is not an easy task. How do you measure something that is inside a person's mind? As you might guess, the only solution to that problem is to get the person to make the internal attitude external, so that you can then assess it. Put another way, you must get the person to translate an internal *attitude* into an external *behavior*. This behavior might involve completing a paper-and-pencil test or questionnaire.

Attitude Scales

Several different paper-and-pencil tests have been developed to measure attitudes. Of these tests, four have been fairly highly refined. These major techniques are Thurstone's method of equal-appearing intervals, Likert's method of summated ratings, Guttman's scalogram, and Osgood's semantic differential. A brief review of each of these methods will hopefully provide you with a clearer understanding of how the social psychologist obtains the data from which he or she so elegantly extrapolates.

Each of the techniques to be discussed makes different assumptions about the nature of the test items that are used and the kind of information they provide about a person's attitudes. However, there are certain basic assumptions that are common to all of these methods. First of all, it is assumed that subjective attitudes can be measured by a quantitative technique, so that each person's opinion can be represented by some numerical score. Secondly, all of these methods assume that a particular test item has the same meaning for all respondents, and thus a given response will be scored identically for everyone making it. Such assumptions may not always be justified, but as yet no measurement technique has been developed that does not include them.

Thurstone's method of equal-appearing intervals. The first major technique of attitude measurement was developed in 1929 by Thurstone in his study of attitudes toward religion. The scale he constructed introduced precise measurement to an area of research where it had never been used before. Thurstone assumed that one could obtain statements of opinion about a particular issue and could order them according to a dimension of expressed favorableness-unfavorableness toward the issue. Furthermore, the ordering of these statements could be such that there appeared to be an equal distance between adjacent statements on the continuum. Because of the latter assumption, one can make judgments about the degree of discrepancy among different people's attitudes. Thurstone also assumed that the statements are uncorrelated and that each statement has a position that is independent of the others. That is, acceptance of one statement does not necessarily imply the acceptance of any others.

A Thurstone scale is made up of about twenty independent statements of opinion about a particular issue. Each statement has a numerical scale value determined by its average judged position on the continuum. People's *attitudes* on the issue are measured by asking them to check those statements with which they agree. Each person's *score* is the mean scale value of those items which he or she checked. An example of a shortened version of such a scale follows.

Trait: Attitude toward Desegregated Housing

Scale Value		Statement
Least favorable	1.5	A. A person should refuse to rent to anyone he or she doesn't like.
	3.0	B. Federal laws enforcing open housing should apply only to public housing, not to private neighborhoods.
	4.5	C. Local governments should publicly urge people to engage in fair housing practices.
	6.0	D. Only in extreme cases of discrimination in housing should there be some sort of legal intervention.
Most favorable	7.5	E. A person must rent to the first eligible applicant, regardless of race, color, or creed.

The hallmark of a Thurstone scale is that the intervals between the statements are approximately equal. This property of the scale is achieved by the method in which it is constructed. The first step is to collect a large number of opinion statements about some particular issue. Any statements that are confusing, ambiguous, double-barreled, or likely to be approved by individuals with opposed attitudes are immediately discarded. Each of the remaining statements is then sorted into one of eleven categories by a group of judges, according to the degree of favorableness or unfavorableness toward the issue expressed by the statement, *regardless* of the judges' own attitudes. These categories thus make up a scale that ranges from very favorable, through neutral, to extremely unfavorable opinions about the issue. By tabulating the ratings of all the judges, it is possible to calculate both the numerical scale position of each statement (its average scale value) and the extent to which the judges agreed in its placement (its spread of ratings). The statements that are selected for use on the final scale are those that have high interjudge agreement and fall at relatively equally spaced intervals along the continuum. A person's attitude on the particular issue is then derived from his or her responses to this final set of scale items.

Likert's method of summated ratings.   One of the practical drawbacks of the Thurstone scale is that its construction is extremely laborious and time-consuming. To cope with this problem, Likert developed a different technique, which could produce an equally reliable attitude scale with relative ease. The Likert scale is made up of a series of opinion statements about some issue. However, in contrast to the Thurstone scale, a person's attitude is measured by asking him or her to indicate the *extent* of agreement or disagreement with each item. This is done by having the person rate each item on a five-point scale of response (strongly agree, agree, undecided, disagree, strongly disagree). A person's attitude score is the sum of his or her individual ratings. An example of a single scale item is the following:

A.   "The death penalty for first-degree murder is a good thing"

Rating Value	
1	(*a*) Strongly agree
2	(*b*) Agree
3	(*c*) Undecided
4	(*d*) Disagree
5	(*e*) Strongly disagree

Likert assumes that each statement which is used in the scale is a linear function of the same attitude dimension. This assumption is the basis for the operation of adding up a person's individual scores (or summating the ratings, to put it more formally) to obtain the final score. A further implication is that the items in a scale must be highly correlated with a common attribute and thus with each other, as opposed to Thurstone's distinct and independent items. It is important to note that at no point does Likert assume equal intervals between scale values. For example, it is quite possible that the difference between "agree" and "strongly agree" is much larger than the difference between "agree" and "undecided." This means that a Likert scale can provide information on the *ordering* of people's attitudes on a continuum, but cannot precisely indicate how close or how far apart different attitudes might be.

Likert's method of scale construction is similar to Thurstone's in the initial collecting and editing of a variety of opinion statements. The remaining statements are then rated by a sample group of subjects on the five-point response scale in terms of their *own* opinions about the statements. This is in contrast to the Thurstone technique, where the ratings are made by trained judges and are based not on personal opinions but on some relatively objective evaluation of where the statements fall on a continuum. The Likert scale is composed of those items that best differentiate between sample subjects with the highest and lowest total scores.

Guttman's scalogram. A third scaling technique is based on the assumption that a single, unidimensional trait can be measured by a set of statements that are ordered along a continuum of "difficulty of acceptance." That is, the statements range from those that are easy for most people to accept to those that few persons would endorse. Such scale items are *cumulative*, since the acceptance of one item implies that the person accepts all those of lesser magnitude (those less difficult to accept). To the extent that this is true, one can predict a person's attitude toward other statements on the basis of knowing the most difficult item he or she will accept. An example of such a scale might be the following:

Trait: Attitude toward Desegregated Housing

Acceptability	*Statement*
Least difficult to accept	A. Generally speaking, people should be able to live anywhere they want.
	B. Real estate agencies should not discriminate against minority groups.
	C. The city should actively support the idea of desegregated housing.
	D. There should be a local review board that would pass on cases of extreme discrimination in housing.
Most difficult to accept	E. There should be federal laws to enforce desegregated housing.

In order to obtain a scale that represents a single dimension, Guttman presents sample subjects with an initial set of items and records the extent to which they respond to the items with specified answer patterns. These patterns, which are referred to as *scale types*, follow a certain steplike order. The subject may accept none of the items in the set (score 0), may accept item A only (score 1), may accept items A and B only (score 2), may accept items A, B, and C only (score 3), and so on. If the subject gives a nonscale response pattern (for example, accepts item C only and not those of lesser magnitude), it is assumed that he or she has made one or more response errors. By analyzing the number of response errors made, Guttman is able to determine the degree to which the initial set of items reflects a unidimensional attribute (that is, the extent to which they are scalable). The final scale is obtained by eliminating poor items and retesting sample subjects until a scalable set of items has been developed.

A person's attitude is then measured by having him or her check all the statements on the scale that are acceptable. Variations of Guttman scales are used in research on attitude involvement to determine people's latitudes of acceptance and rejection (see Chapter 6). The final score is that of the appropriate scale type or (if the person has given a nonscale response pattern) that of the scale type closest to his or her response. As the latter scoring procedure implies, it is almost impossible to develop a perfect unidimensional scale. This may be because people are actually responding not on the single dimension hypothesized but rather on a different one, or on multiple dimensions.

Osgood's semantic differential. The three methods just described attempt to measure attitudes by having people indicate the extent of their agreement with various opinion statements. In contrast to this approach, Osgood has studied attitudes by focusing on the *meaning* that people give to a word or concept. Underlying this technique is the basic assumption of a hypothetical semantic space of an unknown number of dimensions, in which the meaning of any word or concept can be represented as a particular point. Osgood's procedure is to have people judge a particular concept on a set of semantic scales. These scales are defined by verbal opposites with a midpoint of neutrality, and are usually composed of seven discriminable steps. For example, a particular person's meaning of the concept of "nuclear power" is measured by his or her ratings of it on a set of semantic scales:

Good	____	____	____	____	____	____	____	Bad
Strong	____	____	____	____	____	____	____	Weak
Fast	____	____	____	____	____	____	____	Slow
Active	____	____	____	____	____	____	____	Passive

and so on.

An analysis of the ratings collected by this method may reveal the particular dimensions that people use to qualify their experience, the types of concepts that are regarded as similar or different in meaning, and the intensity of the meaning given to a particular concept. Osgood's own research has indicated that there are three dominant, independent dimensions that people use in judging concepts (Osgood et al., 1957). He refers to these dimensions as the evaluative factor (such as good-bad), the potency factor (such as strong-weak), and the activity factor (such as active-passive). Although this method can provide a lot of information about a concept, it is not exactly clear how the concept's *meaning* for a person is related to the person's attitudes.

Single-item and few-item scales in experiments. In most studies of attitudes or attitude change, particularly laboratory experiments, the attitude measure is composed of only one or a few items. Typically, the measure uses a Likert scale format, but not a systematically developed multiple-item questionnaire. In a persuasion study, for example, the first item following the persuasive message might restate the message conclusion and ask the subject to rate his or her agreement with it on a Likert scale. It may have five, ten, or even thirty or more points, and descriptive labels attached to a subset of the points. For example:

The university should institute a student parking fee
of \$50 per semester:

1	2	3	4	5	6	7	8	9	10	11	12	13	14	15
Disagree			*Disagree*			*Undecided*				*Agree*			*Agree*	
Strongly			*Moderately*							*Moderately*			*Strongly*	

The semantic differential may also be used in modified form. Often the semantic scales are chosen to emphasize the good-bad dimension, which best captures the definition of an attitude as an evaluative summary. For instance, after hearing a message advocating a student parking fee, the subjects might be asked to "rate the concept of a parking fee for students on the following four dimensions." The dimensions might be good-bad, wise-foolish, favorable-unfavorable, and beneficial-harmful. In some cases, each subject's ratings would be added together and the sum taken as the subject's attitude score.

Beyond these common approaches, specific self-rating scales have been employed. For example, subjects may be asked to rate themselves on a scale of "like to dislike" for an attitude object.

Attitude measurement: To each one's own.   Actually, there is much variation across studies on how attitudes are measured. This lack of uniformity creates problems of interpretation and comparability. In fact, it isn't only the scale or the subject's response task that varies. It is also true that, even when very similar measurement systems are used, the experiments may use different techniques of translating these common responses into quantitatively derived independent variables. An example of the latter problem can be seen when two studies ask the subject to give his or her opinion by checking one point along a pro-con, like-dislike scale. Attitude change may then be described in terms of any one of the following measures: (1) percentage of subjects showing any positive change at all; (2) percentage of subjects showing "large," "moderate," "small," or "no" change (categories arbitrarily defined); (3) net percentage change (positive minus negative changes); (4) any of the above for an arbitrarily determined combination of opinion items; (5) the absolute mean scale distance changed; and (6) distance changed relative to amount of change possible.

There is a plus side to the diversity in attitude measurement. First, if similar findings keep occurring even when different measurement techniques are used, we can be more confident that the findings are valid and generalizable—that the independent variables in question really do influence attitudes in the observed way (Campbell and Fiske, 1959). If the dependent variable was measured only in precisely the same way, the possibility would exist that the measurement procedure itself contributed to the observed effects. Second, scores on carefully chosen and developed attitude measures (even few-item scales) are usually quite highly correlated, suggesting that they are measuring highly similar aspects of attitude. Third, we note that different researchers and different studies may not all be focused on precisely the same conceptualization of attitude. Some theoretical treatments or applied research problems, for example, may be concerned primarily with attitude as a summary of beliefs and cognitions, while other treatments and problems may be concerned primarily with the affective component of attitude. In the former case, a Thurstone scale might be most appropriate; in the latter, ratings on like-dislike and good-bad scales might be called for. Both concerns are with attitudes, but the measurements are neither conceptually nor operationally identical—nor should they be.

Measuring Other Components of Attitude Systems

Throughout the course of this text, we see cases in which the actual behavior that should follow from one's attitude is measured. In some persuasion studies, for example, the experimenter is able to provide an opportunity for subjects to act on a new attitude instilled by the persuasive message: to sign a petition, donate blood, purchase a product, or engage in some other response recommended by the message. In compliance and dissonance studies, behaviors such as buying raffle tickets, lying to another subject, and openly refusing to go along with a group decision have been observed. When behavior cannot actually be observed, researchers may measure behavioral intentions, which usually correlate with future behavior, but by no means perfectly (see Chapters 1 and 5). The researcher may ask subjects to rate on a numerical scale how likely they are to do something (e.g., purchase a product or quit smoking).

In recent years, social psychologists have developed a growing interest in measuring the cognitive component of attitude systems. One popular technique, commonly used in persuasion studies, is the *thought-listing* method (Greenwald, 1968; Petty and Cacioppo, 1981). After hearing or reading a message, subjects are asked to write down all the thoughts they have that are pertinent to the issue and message in question. They are instructed to sort their thoughts into "individual ideas" and are given response sheets blocked off into sections for writing their thoughts idea by idea. A time limit is placed on the task (often 3 minutes). Later, two or more judges rate and categorize the thoughts (the judges are kept blind to the experimental condition that the subjects were in). Depending on the focus of the experiment, each thought may be categorized according to whether it agrees or disagrees with the message position, reflects something the message said or an idea generated by the subject, deals with the message itself or the communicator, and so on. By looking at certain kinds of thoughts, the researcher can often learn much about the belief and knowledge bases of the attitude and how the message or other manipulation influenced these mental variables.

There are also *content analysis* techniques for analyzing written essays, group deliberations, and other verbal responses according to such dimensions as complexity of thought, evaluative consistency of thought, and knowledge of a topic.

Time and physiological measures have also been used to measure attitude-relevant concepts. The time it takes people to signal agree or disagree to brief attitude statements (called reaction time) has been used to study the accessibility and strength of attitudes.

Physiological measures such as heart rate and galvanic skin response (akin to sweating) have long been used to tap into emotions and the affective component of attitudes. Traditional physiological measurement procedures can validly gauge changes in the intensity of feelings and emotions but they do not reveal whether those responses reflect positive or negative attitudes. More recently, however, researchers are examining very specific bodily reactions to social stimuli that, with further testing, may prove to reflect one's actual attitude orientation to a social stimulus. For example, in one careful program of research, it has been observed that small but measurable changes in the activity of the facial muscles around the mouth occur as people listen to and think about persuasive messages (Cacioppo and Petty, 1987). One pattern occurs when the recipient is known to be counterarguing, and another when the message is evoking positive, agreeing cognitive responses. This work builds on the relationships known to exist between emotions and facial expressions (see Chapter 7).

All in all, it may be said that measurement techniques in the study of attitude change and social influence are many and varied, with some approaches more developed than others.

References

___ ❖ ___

Abelson, R. P., and Prentice, D. A. (1989). Beliefs as possessions: A functional perspective. In A. R. Pratkanis, S. J. Breckler, and A. G. Greenwald (Eds.), *Attitude structure and function* (pp. 361–381). Hillsdale, NJ: Erlbaum.

Adler, R. P., Lesser, G. S., Meringoff, L. K., Robertson, T. S., and Ward, S. (1980). *The effects of television advertising on children.* Lexington, MA: D. C. Heath.

Adorno, T. W., Frenkel-Brunswick, E., Levinson, D. J., and Sanford, R. N. (1950). *The authoritarian personality.* New York: Harper.

Ajzen, I., and Fishbein, M. (1980). *Understanding attitudes and predicting social behavior.* Englewood Cliffs, NJ: Prentice-Hall.

Allen, V. L., and Wilder, D. A. (1980). Impact of group consensus and social support on stimulus meaning: Mediation of conformity by cognitive restructuring. *Journal of Personality and Social Psychology, 39,* 1116–1124.

Allport, G. W. (1954). *The nature of prejudice.* Cambridge, MA: Addison-Wesley.

Altheide, D. L., and Johnson, J. M. (1977). Counting souls: A study of counseling at evangelical crusades. *Pacific Sociological Review, 20,* 323–348.

Altman, D. G., Slater, M. D., Albright, C. L., and Maccoby, N. (1987). How an unhealthy product is sold: Cigarette advertising in magazines, 1960–1985. *Journal of Communications, 37,* 95–106.

Andersen, S. M., and Zimbardo, P. G. (1984). On resisting social influence. *Cultic Studies Journal, 1,* 196–219.

Anderson, C. A., Lepper, M. R., and Ross, L. (1980). Perseverance of social theories: The role of explanation in the persistence of discredited information. *Journal of Personality and Social Psychology, 39,* 1037–1049.

Anderson, N. H., and Hubert, S. (1963). Effects of concomitant verbal recall on order effects in personality impression formation. *Journal of Verbal Learning and Verbal Behavior, 2,* 379–391.

Andrews, L. B. (1984). Exhibit A: Language. *Psychology Today,* Feb., 28–33.

Apple, W., Streeter, L. A., and Krauss, R. M. (1979). Effects of pitch and speech rate on personal attributions. *Journal of Personality and Social Psychology, 37,* 715–727.

Aronson, E. (1969). The theory of cognitive dissonance: A current perspective. In L. Berkowitz (Ed.), *Advances in experimental social psychology* (vol. 4, pp. 1–34). New York: Academic Press.

Aronson, E. (1991). How to change behavior. In R. C. Curtis and G. Stricker (Eds.), *How people change: Inside and outside therapy*. New York: Plenum.

Aronson, E., and Carlsmith, J. M. (1968). Experimentation in social psychology. In G. Lindzey and E. Aronson (Eds.), *The handbook of social psychology* (2d ed., Vol. 2, pp. 1–79). Reading, MA: Addison-Wesley.

Aronson, E., Ellsworth, P. C., Carlsmith, J. M., and Gonzales, M. H. (1990). *Methods of research in social psychology* (2d ed.). New York: McGraw-Hill.

Asch, J., and Shore, B. M. (1975). Conservation behavior as the outcome of environmental education. *Journal of Environmental Education, 6*, 25–33.

Asch, S. E. (1951). Effects of group pressure upon the modification and distortion of judgements. In H. Guetzkow (Ed.), *Groups, leadership, and men*. Pittsburg, PA: Carnegie Press.

Asch, S. E. (1952). *Social psychology*. Englewood Cliffs, NJ: Prentice-Hall.

Atkin, C. K. (1979). Research evidence on mass mediated health communication campaigns. In D. Nimmo (Ed.), *Communication yearbook 3*. New Brunswick, NJ: Transaction Books.

Atkin, C. K. (1980). *Effects of the mass media*. New York: Holt, Rinehart & Winston.

Axsom, D. (1989). Cognitive dissonance and behavior change in psychotherapy. *Journal of Experimental Social Psychology, 25*, 234–252.

Axsom, D., Yates, S., and Chaiken, S. (1987). Audience response as a heuristic cue in persuasion. *Journal of Personality and Social Psychology, 53*, 30–40.

Bailey, F. L. (1985). *To be a trial lawyer*. New York: Wiley.

Baker, A. L., and Wilson, P. H. (1985). Cognitive-behavior therapy for depression: The effects of booster sessions on relapse. *Behavior Therapy, 16*, 335–344.

Bales, R. F. (1958). Task roles and social roles in problem-solving groups. In E. E. Maccoby, T. M. Newcomb, and E. L. Hartley (Eds.), *Readings in social psychology* (3d ed., pp. 437–447). New York: Holt, Rinehart & Winston.

Bandura, A. (1965). Influence of models' reinforcement contingencies on the acquisition of imitative responses. *Journal of Personality and Social Psychology, 1*, 589–595.

Bandura, A. (1977). *Social learning theory*. Englewood Cliffs, NJ: Prentice-Hall.

Bandura, A. (1982). Self-efficacy mechanism in human agency. *American Psychologist, 37*, 122–147.

Bandura, A. (1986). *Social foundations of thought and action: A social-cognitive theory*. Englewood Cliffs, NJ: Prentice-Hall.

Bandura, A. (1990). Mechanisms of moral disengagement in terrorism. In W. Reich (Ed.), *Origins of terrorism: Psychologies, ideologies, theologies, states of mind* (pp. 161–191). New York: Cambridge University Press.

Bandura, A., Ross, D., and Ross, S. A. (1961). Transmission of aggression through imitation of aggressive models. *Journal of Abnormal and Social Psychology, 63*, 575–582.

Bandura, A., Ross, D., and Ross, S. A. (1963). Imitation of film-mediated aggressive models. *Journal of Abnormal and Social Psychology, 66*, 3–11.

Bargh, J. A., and Pietromonaco, P. (1982). Automatic information processing and social perception: The influence of trait information presented outside of conscious awareness on impression formation. *Journal of Personality and Social Psychology, 43*, 437–449.

Barker, E. (1984). *The making of a Moonie: Choice or brainwashing.* Oxford, England: Basil Blackwell.

Baron, R. A., and Byrne, D. (1981). *Social psychology: Understanding human interaction* (3d ed.). Boston, MA: Allyn & Bacon.

Barthe, D. G., and Hammen, C. L. (1981). The attributional model of depression: A naturalistic extension. *Personality and Social Psychology Bulletin, 7,* 53–58.

Basow, S. A. (1986). *Gender stereotypes: Traditions and alternatives* (2d ed.). Belmont, CA: Brooks/Cole.

Batson, C. D. (1975). Rational processing or rationalization? The effect of disconfirming information on a stated religious belief. *Journal of Personality and Social Psychology, 32,* 176–184.

Batson, C. D., Cochran, P. J., Biederman, M. F., Blosser, J. L., Ryan, M. J., and Vogt, B. (1978). Failure to help when in a hurry: Callousness or conflict? *Personality and Social Psychology Bulletin, 4,* 97–101.

Baumeister, R. F. (1982). A self-presentational view of social phenomena. *Psychological Bulletin, 91,* 3–26.

Baumeister, R. F., and Tice, D. M. (1984). Role of self-presentation and choice in cognitive dissonance under forced compliance: Necessary or sufficient causes? *Journal of Personality and Social Psychology, 46,* 5–13.

Baumrind, D. (1964). Some thoughts on the ethics of research after reading Milgram's *Behavioral Study of Obedience. American Psychologist, 19,* 421–423.

Baumrind, D. (1985). Research using intentional deception: Ethical issues revisited. *American Psychologist, 40,* 165–174.

Beaman, A. L., Cole, C. M., Preston, M., Klentz, B., and Steblay, N. M. (1983). Fifteen years of foot-in-the-door research: A meta-analysis. *Personality and Social Psychology Bulletin, 9,* 181–196.

Beck, A. T. (1976). *Cognitive therapy and emotional disorders.* New York: International Universities Press.

Becker, L. B., McCombs, M. E., and McLeod, J. M. (1975). The development of political cognitions. In S. H. Chaffee (Ed.), *Political communication: Issues and strategies for research* (pp. 21–63). Beverly Hills, CA: Sage.

Bedau, H., and Radelet, M. (1987). Miscarriages of justice in potentially capital cases. *Stanford Law Review, 40,* 21–179.

Beebe, S. A. (1974). Eye contact: A nonverbal determinant of speaker credibility. *The Speech Teacher, 23,* 21–25.

Bell, B. E., and Loftus, E. F. (1989). Trivial persuasion in the courtroom: The power of (a few) minor details. *Journal of Personality and Social Psychology, 56,* 669–679.

Belloc, N. B., and Breslow, L. (1972). Relationship of physical health status and family practice. *Preventive Medicine, 1,* 409–421.

Bem, D. J. (1972). Self-perception theory. In L. Berkowitz (Ed.), *Advances in experimental social psychology* (vol. 6, pp. 1–62). New York: Academic Press.

Bem, D. J., and McConnell, H. K. (1970). Testing the self-perception explanation of dissonance phenomena: On the salience of premanipulation attitudes. *Journal of Personality and Social Psychology, 14,* 23–31.

Bettinghaus, E. P. (1980). *Persuasive communication* (3d ed.). New York: Holt, Rinehart & Winston.

Blum, A. (1989). The targeting of minority groups by the tobacco industry. In L. A. Jones (Ed.), *Minorities and cancer* (pp. 153–162). New York: Springer-Verlag.

Bornstein, R. F., Leone, D. R., and Galley, D. J. (1987). The generalizability of subliminal mere exposure effects: Influence of stimuli perceived without awareness on social behavior. *Journal of Personality and Social Psychology, 53,* 1070–1079.

Bowers, K. S. (1984). On being unconsciously influenced and informed. In K. S. Bowers and D. Meichenbaum (Eds.), *The unconscious reconsidered.* New York: Wiley.

Brehm, J. W. (1972). *Responses to loss of freedom: A theory of psychological reactance.* Morristown, NJ: General Learning Press.

Brehm, S. S., and Smith, T. W. (1986). Social psychological approaches to psychotherapy and behavior change. In S. L. Garfield, and A. E. Bergin (Eds.), *Handbook of psychotherapy and behavior change* (3d ed., pp. 69–115). New York: Wiley.

Brickman, P., Redfield, J., Harrison, A. A., and Crandell, R. (1972). Drive and predisposition as factors in the attitudinal effects of mere exposure. *Journal of Experimental Social Psychology, 8,* 31–44.

Brigham, J. C. (1971). Ethnic stereotypes. *Psychological Bulletin, 76,* 15–33.

Brigham, J. C., and Bothwell, R. K. (1983). The ability of prospective jurors to estimate the accuracy of eyewitness identifications. *Law and Human Behavior, 7,* 19–30.

Broadbent, D. E. (1958). *Perception and communication.* London: Pergamon Press.

Broadbent, D. E. (1971). *Decision and stress.* New York: Academic Press.

Brock, T. C. (1965). Communicator-recipient similarity and decision change. *Journal of Personality and Social Psychology, 1,* 650–654.

Brown, R. (1974). Further comments on the risky shift. *American Psychologist, 29,* 468–470.

Brown, R. (1986). *Social psychology: The second edition.* New York: Free Press.

Bryan, J. H., and Test, N. A. (1967). Models and helping: Naturalistic studies in aiding behavior. *Journal of Personality and Social Psychology, 6,* 400–407.

Buckhout, R. (1974). Eyewitness testimony. *Scientific American, 231,* 23–31.

Burger, J. (1986). Increasing compliance by improving the deal: The that's-not-all technique. *Journal of Personality and Social Psychology, 51,* 277–283.

Burgoon, J. K., Pfau, M., Parrott, R., Birk, T., Coker, R., and Burgoon, M. (1987). Relational communication, satisfaction, compliance-gaining strategies, and compliance in communication between physicians and patients. *Communication Monographs, 54,* 307–324.

Burnstein, E., and Vinokur, A. (1973). Testing two classes of theories about group induced shifts in individual choice. *Journal of Experimental Social Psychology, 9,* 123–137.

Byrne, D. (1971). *The attraction paradigm.* New York: Academic Press.

Cacioppo, J. T., and Petty, R. E. (1979). Effects of message repetition and position on cognitive response, recall, and persuasion. *Journal of Personality and Social Psychology, 37,* 97–109.

Cacioppo, J. T., and Petty, R. E. (1980). Sex differences in influenceability: Toward specifying the underlying processes. *Personality and Social Psychology Bulletin, 6,* 651–656.

Cacioppo, J. T., and Petty, R. E. (1982). The need for cognition. *Journal of Personality and Social Psychology, 42,* 116–131.

Cacioppo, J. T., and Petty, R. E. (1987). Stalking rudimentary processes of social influence: A psychophysiological approach. In M. P. Zanna, J. M. Olson, and C. P. Herman (Eds.), *Social influence: The Ontario Symposium* (vol. 5, pp. 41–74). Hillsdale, NJ: Erlbaum.

Cacioppo, J. T., Petty, R. E., and Sidera, J. A. (1982). The effects of a salient self-schema on the evaluation of proattitudenal editorials: Top-down versus bottom-up message processing. *Journal of Experimental Social Psychology, 18,* 324–338.

Calder, B. J., Insko, C. A., and Yandell, B. (1974). The relation of cognitive and memorial processes to persuasion in a simulated jury trial. *Journal of Applied Social Psychology, 4,* 62–93.

Campbell, D. T., and Fiske, D. W. (1959). Convergent and discriminant validation by the multitrait-multimethod matrix. *Psychological Bulletin, 56,* 81–105.

Campbell, D. T., and Stanley, J. C. (1966). *Experimental and quasi-experimental designs for research.* Chicago: Rand McNally.

Campbell, J. D., Tesser, A., and Fairey, P. J. (1986). Conformity and attention to the stimulus: Temporal and contextual dynamics. *Journal of Personality and Social Psychology, 51,* 315–324.

Caplan, R. D., Robinson, E. A. R., French, J. R. P., Caldwell, J. R., and Shinn, M. (1976). *Adhering to medical regimens: Pilot experiments in patient education and social support.* Ann Arbor, MI: Institute for Social Research, University of Michigan.

Chaiken, S. (1979). Communicator physical attractiveness and persuasion. *Journal of Personality and Social Psychology, 37,* 1387–1397.

Chaiken, S. (1980). Heuristic versus systematic information processing and the use of source versus message cues in persuasion. *Journal of Personality and Social Psychology, 39,* 752–766.

Chaiken, S. (1987). The heuristic model of persuasion. In M. P. Zanna, J. M. Olson, and C. P. Herman (Eds.), *Social influence: The Ontario symposium* (vol. 5, pp. 3–39). Hillsdale, NJ: Erlbaum.

Chaiken, S., Liberman, A., and Eagly, A. H. (1989). Heuristic and systematic information processing within and beyond the persuasion context. In J. S. Uleman and J. A. Bargh (Eds.), *Unintended thought: Limits of awareness, intention, and control.* New York: Guilford.

Chaiken, S., and Baldwin, M. W. (1981). Affective-cognitive consistency and the effect of salient behavioral information on the self-perception of attitudes. *Journal of Personality and Social Psychology, 41,* 1–12.

Chaiken, S., and Eagly, A. H. (1976). Communication modality as a determinant of message persuasiveness and message comprehensibility. *Journal of Personality and Social Psychology, 34,* 605–614.

Chaiken, S., and Eagly, A. H. (1983). Communication modality as a determinant of persuasion: The role of communicator salience. *Journal of Personality and Social Psychology, 45,* 241–256.

Charen, M. (1990). Say no way: Time for good old self-control. *San Francisco Examiner, Chronicle,* This World Section, p. 3.

Christiaansen, R. E., Sweeney, J. D., and Ochalek, K. (1983). Influencing eyewitness descriptions. *Law and Human Behavior, 7,* 59–65.

Church, G. J. (1989). The other arms race. *Time,* Feb. 6, 20–26.

Cialdini, R. B. (1987). Compliance principles of compliance professionals: Psychologists of necessity. In M. P. Zanna, J. M. Olson, and C. P. Herman (Eds.), *Social influence: The Ontario symposium* (vol. 5, pp. 165–184). Hillsdale, NJ: Erlbaum.

Cialdini, R. B. (1988). *Influence: Science and practice* (2d ed.). Glenview, IL: Scott, Foresman.

Cialdini, R. B., Cacioppo, J. T., Bassett, R., and Miller, J. A. (1978). Low-ball procedure for producing compliance: Commitment then cost. *Journal of Personality and Social Psychology, 36*, 463–476.

Cialdini, R. B., and Petty, R. E., (1981). Anticipatory opinion effects. In R. E. Petty, T. M. Ostrom, and T. C. Brock (Eds.), *Cognitive responses in persuasion.* Hillsdale, NJ: Erlbaum.

Cialdini, R. B., Reno, R. R., and Kallgren, C. A. (1990). A focus theory of normative conduct: Recycling the concept of norms to reduce littering in public places. *Journal of Personality and Social Psychology, 58*, 1015–1026.

Clancey, M., and Robinson, M. J. (1985). General election coverage: Part I. *Public Opinion, 7*, 49–54, 59.

Cohen, R. E., and Syme, S. L. (Eds.) (1985). *Social support and health.* Orlando, FL: Academic Press.

Comstock, G., Chaffee, S., Katzman, N., McCoombs, M., and Roberts, D. (1978). *Television and human behavior.* New York: Columbia University Press.

Cooper, J. (1980). Reducing fears and increasing assertiveness: The role of dissonance reduction. *Journal of Experimental Social Psychology, 16*, 199–213.

Cooper, J., and Fazio, R. H. (1984). A new look at dissonance theory. In L. Berkowitz (Ed.), *Advances in experimental social psychology* (vol. 17, pp. 229–266). New York: Academic Press.

Cooper, J., Zanna, M. P., and Taves, P. A. (1978). Arousal as a necessary condition for attitude change following induced compliance. *Journal of Personality and Social Psychology, 36*, 1101–1106.

Crocker, J. (1981). Judgment of covariation by social perceivers. *Psychological Bulletin, 90*, 272–292.

Darley, J. M., and Batson, C. D. (1973). From Jerusalem to Jericho: A study of situational and dispositional variables in helping behavior. *Journal of Personality and Social Psychology, 27*, 100–108.

Davis, J. H. (1980). Group decision and procedural justice. In M. Fishbein (Ed.), *Progress in social psychology.* Hillsdale, NJ: Erlbaum.

Davis, J. H., Holt, R. W., Spitzer, C. E., and Stasser, G. (1981). The effects of consensus requirements and multiple decisions on mock juror verdict preferences. *Journal of Experimental Social Psychology, 17*, 1–15.

Davis, R. M. (1987). Current trends in cigarette advertising. *The New England Journal of Medicine, 316*, 725–732.

DeBono, K. G. (1987). Investigating the social-adjustive and value-expressive functions of attitudes: Implications for persuasion processes. *Journal of Personality and Social Psychology, 52*, 279–287.

Deci, E. L., and Ryan, R. M. (1985). *Intrinsic motivation and self-determination in human behavior.* New York: Plenum.

Deffenbacher, K. (1980). Eyewitness accuracy and confidence: Can we infer anything about their relationship? *Law and Human Behavior, 4*, 243–260.

Deutsch, M., and Gerard, H. B. (1955). A study of normative and informational social influences upon individual judgment. *Journal of Abnormal and Social Psychology, 51*, 629–636.

DeVos, G. and Wagatsuma, H. (1966). *Japan's invisible race.* Berkeley: University of California Press.

Devine, P. G. (1989). Stereotypes and prejudice: Their automatic and controlled components. *Journal of Personality and Social Psychology, 56,* 5–18.

DiMatteo, M. R., and Taranta, A. (1979). Nonverbal communication and physician-patient rapport: An empirical study, *Professional Psychology 10,* 540–547.

DiMatteo, R. M., Hays, R. D., and Prince, L. M. (1986). Relationship of physicians' nonverbal communication skill to patient satisfaction, appointment noncompliance, and physician workload. *Health Psychology, 5,* 581–594.

DiMatteo, R. M., Taranta, A., Friedman, H. S., and Prince, L. M. (1980). Predicting patient satisfaction from physicians' nonverbal communication skills. *Medical Care, 18,* 376–387.

DiNicola, D. D., and DiMatteo, R. M. (1984). Practitioners, patients, and compliance with medical regimens: A social psychological perspective. In A. Baum, S. E. Taylor, and J. E. Singer (Eds.), *Handbook of psychology and health* (vol. 4, pp. 55–84). Hillsdale, NJ: Erlbaum.

Dixon, N. F. (1971). *Subliminal perception: The nature of a controversy.* London: McGraw-Hill.

Dolecek, T. A., Schoenberger, J. A., Omam, J. K., Kremer, B. K., Sunseri, A. J., and Alberti, J. M. (1986). Cardiovascular risk factor knowledge and beliefs in prevention among adults in Chicago. *American Journal of Preventive Medicine, 2,* 262–267.

Dovidio, J. F., and Ellyson, S. L. (1982). Decoding visual dominance behavior: Attributions of power based on the relative percentages of looking while speaking and looking while listening. *Social Psychology Quarterly, 45,* 106–113.

Dovidio, J. F., Ellyson, S. L., Keating, C. F., Heltman, K., and Brown, C. E. (1988a). The relationship of social power to visual displays of dominance between men and women. *Journal of Personality and Social Psychology, 54,* 233–242.

Dovidio, J. F., Brown, C. E., Heltman, K., Ellyson, S. L., and Keating, C. F. (1988b). Power displays between women and men in discussions of gender-linked tasks: A multichannel study. *Journal of Personality and Social Psychology, 55,* 580–587.

Eagly, A. H. (1974). Comprehensibility of persuasive arguments as a determinant of opinion change. *Journal of Personality and Social Psychology, 29,* 758–773.

Ebbesen, E. B., and Konecni, V. J. (1982). Social psychology and the law: A decision-making approach to the criminal justice system. In V. J. Konecni and E. B. Ebbesen (Eds.), *The criminal justice system: A social-psychological analysis.* San Francisco: W. H. Freeman.

Edwards, K. (1990). The interplay of affect and cognition in attitude formation and change. *Journal of Personality and Social Psychology, 59,* 202–216.

Ekman, P. (1985). *Telling lies: Clues to deceit in the marketplace, politics, and marriage.* New York: Norton.

Ekman, P., and Friesen, W. V. (1969). Nonverbal leakage and clues to deception. *Psychiatry, 32,* 88–106.

Ekman, P., and Friesen, W. V. (1971). Constants across cultures in the face and emotion. *Journal of Personality and Social Psychology, 17,* 124–129.

Ekman, P., and Friesen, W. V. (1986). A new pan-cultural facial expression of emotion. *Motivation and Emotion, 10,* 159–168.

Ekman, P., Friesen, W. V., and O'Sullivan, M. (1988). Smiles when lying. *Journal of Personality and Social Psychology, 54,* 414–420.

Elkin, R. A. (1986). *Self-presentation and attitude assessment effects on cognitive processes following attitude-discrepant behavior.* Unpublished doctoral dissertation, Adelphi University.

Elkin, R. A., and Leippe, M. R. (1986). Physiological arousal, dissonance, and attitude change: Evidence for a dissonance-arousal link and a "don't remind me" effect. *Journal of Personality and Social Psychology, 51,* 55–65.

Ellickson, P. L., and Bell, R. M. (1990). Drug prevention in junior high: A multisite longitudinal test. *Science, 247,* 1299–1305.

Ellison, K. W., and Buckhout, R. (1981). *Psychology and criminal justice.* Cambridge, MA: Harper & Row.

Erdley, C. A., and D'Agostino, P. R. (1988). Cognitive and affective components of automatic priming effects. *Journal of Personality and Social Psychology, 54,* 741–747.

Erickson, B., Lind, E. A., Johnson, B. C., and O'Barr, W. M. (1978). Speech style and impression formation in a court setting: The effects of "powerful" and "powerless" speech. *Journal of Experimental Social Psychology, 14,* 266–279.

Eron, L. D. (1980). Prescription for the reduction of aggression. *American Psychologist, 35,* 244–252.

Evans, R. I. (1984). A social inoculation strategy to deter smoking in adolescents. In J. D. Matarazzo, S. M. Weiss, J. A. Herd, N. E. Miller, and S. M. Weiss (Eds.), *Behavioral health: A handbook of health enhancement and disease prevention.* New York: Wiley.

Evans, R. I., Rozelle, R. M., Maxwell, S. E., Raines, B. E., Dill, C. A., Guthrie, T. J., Henderson, A. H., and Hill, P. C. (1981). Social modeling films to deter smoking in adolescents: Results of a three-year field investigation. *Journal of Applied Psychology, 66,* 399–414.

Everett, P. B., Hayward, S. C., and Meyers, A. W. (1974). The effects of a token reinforcement procedure on bus ridership. *Journal of Applied Behavior Analysis, 7,* 1–9.

Exline, R. V., Ellyson, S. L., and Long, B. (1975). Visual behavior as an aspect of power role relationships. In P. Pliner, L. Krames, and T. Alloway (Eds.), *Nonverbal communication of aggression* (pp. 21–52). New York: Plenum.

Falbo, T., and Peplau, L. A. (1980). Power strategies in intimate relationships. *Journal of Personality and Social Psychology, 38,* 618–628.

Farquhar, J. W., Maccoby, N., and Solomon, D. S. (1984). Community applications of behavioral medicine. In W. D. Gentry (Ed.), *Handbook of behavioral medicine* (pp. 437–478). New York: Guilford.

Fazio, R. H. (1979). Motives for social comparison: The construction-validation distinction. *Journal of Personality and Social Psychology, 37,* 1683–1698.

Fazio, R. H. (1987). Self-perception theory: A current perspective. In M. P. Zanna, J. M. Olson, and C. P. Herman (Eds.), *Social influence: The Ontario symposium* (vol. 5, pp. 129–150). Hillsdale, NJ: Erlbaum.

Fazio, R. H. (1990). Multiple processes by which attitudes guide behavior: The MODE model as an integrative framework. In M. P. Zanna (Ed.), *Advances in experimental social psychology* (vol. 23, pp. 75–109). New York: Academic Press.

Fazio, R. H., Sanbonmatsu, D. M., Powell, M. C., and Kardes, F. R. (1986). On the automatic activation of attitudes. *Journal of Personality and Social Psychology, 50,* 229–238.

Fazio, R. H., and Zanna, M. P. (1981). Direct experience and attitude-behavior consistency. In L. Berkowitz (Ed.), *Advances in experimental social psychology* (vol. 14, pp. 162–202). New York: Academic Press.

Fazio, R. H., Zanna, M. P., and Cooper, J. (1977). Dissonance and self-perception: An integrative view of each theory's proper domain of application. *Journal of Experimental Social Psychology, 13,* 464–479.

Fehrenbach, P. A., Miller, D. J., and Thelen, M. H. (1979). The importance of consistency of modeling behavior upon imitation: A comparison of single and multiple models. *Journal of Personality and Social Psychology, 37,* 1412–1417.

Ferguson, T. J., and Wells, G. L. (1980). Priming of mediators in causal attribution. *Journal of Personality and Social Psychology, 38,* 461–470.

Feshbach, S. (1980). Television advertising and children: Policy issues and alternatives. Paper presented at the American Psychological Association convention.

Festinger, L. (1954). A theory of social comparison processes. *Human Relations, 7,* 117–140.

Festinger, L. (1957). *A theory of cognitive dissonance.* Stanford, CA: Stanford University Press.

Festinger, L., and Carlsmith, J. M. (1959). Cognitive consequences of forced compliance. *Journal of Abnormal and Social Psychology, 58,* 203–211.

Fincham, F. D., Beach, S. R., and Baucom, D. H. (1987). Attribution processes in distressed and nondistressed couples: 4. Self-partner attribution differences. *Journal of Personality and Social Psychology, 52,* 739–748.

Fincham, F. D., and O'Leary, K. D. (1983). Causal inferences for spouse behavior in maritally distressed and nondistressed couples. *Journal of Social and Clinical Psychology, 1,* 42–57.

Fisher, J. D., Bell, P. A., and Baum, A. (1984). *Environmental psychology* (2d ed.). New York: Holt, Rinehart & Winston.

Fiske, S. T., Taylor, S. E. (1984). *Social cognition.* Reading, MA: Addison-Wesley.

Flay, B. R., Ryan, K. B., Best, J. A., Brown, K. S., Kersell, M. W., d'Avernas, J. R., and Zanna, M. P. (1985). Are social-psychological smoking prevention programs effective? The Waterloo study. *Journal of Behavioral Medicine, 8,* 37–59.

Freedman, J. L., and Fraser, S. C. (1966). Compliance without pressure: The foot-in-the-door technique. *Journal of Experimental Social Psychology, 4,* 195–203.

Freedman, J. L., and Sears, D. O. (1965). Warning, distraction, and resistance to influence. *Journal of Personality and Social Psychology, 1,* 145–155.

Frey, D. (1986). Recent research on selective exposure to information. In L. Berkowitz (Ed.), *Advances in experimental social psychology* (vol. 19, pp. 41–80). New York: Academic Press.

Frey, D., and Rosch, M. (1984). Information seeking after decisions: The roles of novelty of information and decision reversibility. *Personality and Social Psychology Bulletin, 10,* 91–98.

Fuller, R. G. C., and Sheehy-Skeffington, A. (1974). Effects of group laughter on responses to humorous materials: A replication and extension. *Psychological Reports, 35,* 531–534.

Galanter, H. (1989). *Cults: Faith, healing, and coercion.* New York: Oxford University Press.

Geller, E. S., Witmer, J. F., and Tuso, M. A. (1977). Environmental interventions for litter control. *Journal of Applied Psychology, 62,* 344–351.

Giacalone, R., and Rosenfeld, P. (1986). Self-presentation and self-promotion in an organizational setting. *Journal of Social Psychology, 126,* 321–326.

Gibbs, N. (1989). Sick and tired. *Time,* July 31, 48–53.

Gilligan, C. (1982). *In a different voice: Psychological theory and women's development.* Cambridge, MA: Harvard University Press.

Goethals, G. R., and Darley, J. (1977). Social comparison theory: An attributional perspective. In J. Suls and R. Miller (Eds.), *Social comparison processes: Theoretical and empirical perspectives* (pp. 259–278). Washington, DC: Hemisphere.

Goethals, G. R., and Ebling, T. (1975). *A study of opinion comparison.* Unpublished manuscript, Williams College.

Goethals, G. R., and Zanna, M. P. (1979). The role of social comparison in choice shifts. *Journal of Personality and Social Psychology, 37,* 1469–1476.

Goleman, D. (May 29, 1990). As bias crime seems to rise, scientists study roots of racism. *The New York Times,* pp. B5, B7.

Gorn, G. J. (1982). The effects of music in advertising on choice behavior: A classical conditioning approach. *Journal of Marketing, 46,* 94–101.

Gouldner, A. W. (1960). The norm of reciprocity: A preliminary statement. *American Sociological Review, 25,* 161–178.

Granberg, D., and Brent, E. (1983). When prophecy bends: The preference-expectation link in U. S. presidential elections, 1952–1980. *Journal of Personality and Social Psychology, 45,* 477–491.

Granberg, D., and Brent, E. E. (1974). Dove-hawk placements in the 1968 election: Application of social judgment and balance theories. *Journal of Personality and Social Psychology, 29,* 687–695.

Gray, F., Graubard, P. S., and Rosenberg, H. (1974). Little brother is changing you. *Psychology Today,* March, 42–46.

Greenwald, A. G. (1968). Cognitive learning, cognitive response to persuasion, and attitude change. In A. G. Greenwald, T. C. Brock, and T. M. Ostrom (Eds.), *Psychological foundations of attitudes* (pp. 147–170). New York: Academic Press.

Greenwald, A. G. (1980). The totalitarian ego: Fabrication and revision of personal history. *American Psychologist, 35,* 603–618.

Greenwald, A. G., Klinger, M. R., and Liu, T. J. (1989). Unconscious processing of dichoptically masked words. *Memory & Cognition, 17,* 35–47.

Grice, H. P. (1986). Logic in conversation. In I. P. Cole and J. L. Morgan (Eds.), *Syntax and Semantics* (vol. 3, pp. 41–58). New York: Academic Press.

Gruder, C. L., Cook, T. D., Hennigan, K. M., Flay, B. R., Alessis, C., and Halamaj, J. (1978). Empirical tests of the absolute sleeper effect predicted from the discounting cue hypothesis. *Journal of Personality and Social Psychology, 36,* 1061–1074.

Grusec, J. E. (1971). Power and the internalization of self-denial. *Child Development, 42,* 93–105.

Grusec, J. E., and Skubiski, S. (1970). Model nurturance, demand characteristics of the modeling experiment and altruism. *Journal of Personality and Social Psychology, 14,* 353–359.

Grush, J. E. (1976). Attitude formation and mere exposure phenomena: A nonartifactual explanation of empirical findings. *Journal of Personality and Social Psychology, 33,* 281–290.

Grush, J. E., McKeough, K. L., and Ahlering, R. F. (1978). Extrapolating laboratory exposure research to actual political elections. *Journal of Personality and Social Psychology, 36,* 257–270.

Hamilton, D. L., and Trolier, T. K. (1986). Stereotypes and stereotyping: An overview of the cognitive approach. In J. F. Dovidio and S. L. Gaertner (Eds.), *Prejudice, discrimination, and racism* (pp. 127–164). New York: Academic Press.

Hardyck, J. A., and Kardush, M. (1968). A modest, modish model for dissonance reduction. In R. Abelson et al. (Eds.), *Theories of cognitive consistency: A sourcebook.* Chicago: Rand McNally.

Haritos-Fatouros, M. (1988). The official torturer: A learning model for obedience to the authority of violence. *Journal of Applied Social Psychology, 18,* 1107–1120.

Harper, R. G., Weins, A. N., and Matarazzo, J. D. (1978). *Nonverbal communications: The state of the art.* New York: Wiley.

Harris, P. R. (1980). *Promoting health—preventing disease: Objectives for the nation.* Washington, DC: U.S. Government Printing Office.

Hass, R. G. (1981). Effects of source characteristics on cognitive responses and persuasion. In R. E. Petty, T. M. Ostrom, and T. C. Brock (Eds.), *Cognitive responses in persuasion* (pp. 141–172). Hillsdale, NJ: Erlbaum.

Hass, R. G., and Grady, K. (1975). Temporal delay, type of forewarning, and resistance to influence. *Journal of Experimental Social Psychology, 11,* 459–469.

Hastie, R., Landsman, R., and Loftus, E. F. (1978). Eyewitness testimony: The dangers of guessing. *Jurimetrics Journal, 19,* 1–8.

Hayes, S. C., and Cone, J. D. (1977). Reducing residential electrical energy use: Payments, information, and feedback. *Journal of Applied Behavior Analysis, 10,* 425–435.

Heesacker, M. (1986). Counseling pretreatment and the elaboration likelihood model of attitude change. *Journal of Counseling Psychology, 33,* 107–114.

Heider, F. (1958). *The psychology of interpersonal relations.* New York: Wiley.

Herbert, F. (1965). *Dune.* Philadelphia: Chilton.

Herek, G. M. (1986). The instrumentality of attitudes: Toward a neofunctional theory. *Journal of Social Issues, 42,* 99–114.

Hersey, J. (1988). Behind barbed wire. *The New York Times Magazine,* Sept., 57–59, 73–76, 120–121.

Hitler, A. (1933). *Mein Kampf.* Trans. by E. T. S. Dugdale. Cambridge, MA: Riverside.

Hochbaum, G. (1958). *Public participation in medical screening programs.* DHEW Publication No. 572, Public Health Service. Washington, DC: U.S. Government Printing Office.

Horowitz, I. A. (1980). Juror selection: A comparison of two methods in several criminal cases. *Journal of Applied Social Psychology, 10,* 86–99.

Hosch, H. M., Leippe, M. R., Marchioni, P. M., and Cooper, D. S. (1984). Victimization, self-monitoring, and eyewitness identification. *Journal of Applied Psychology, 64,* 280–288.

Hovland, C. I. (Ed.) (1957). *Order of presentation in persuasion.* New Haven, CT: Yale University Press.

Hovland, C. I., and Janis, I. L. (1959). *Personality and persuasibility.* New Haven, CT: Yale University Press.

Hovland, C. I., Janis, I. L., and Kelley, H. H. (1953). *Communication and persuasion*. New Haven, CT: Yale University Press.

Hovland, C. I., Lumsdaine, A. A., and Sheffield, F. D. (1949). *Studies in social psychology in World War II.* Vol. 3: *Experiments in mass communication.* Princeton, NJ: Princeton University Press.

Hovland, C. I., and Mandell, W. (1952). An experimental demonstration of conclusion-drawing by the communicator and by the audience. *Journal of Abnormal and Social Psychology, 47,* 581–588.

Hovland, C. I., and Weiss, W. (1951). The influence of source credibility on communication effectiveness. *Public Opinion Quarterly, 15,* 635–650.

Huesmann, L. R., Eron, L. D., Klein, R., Brice, P., and Fischer, P. (1983). Mitigating the imitation of aggressive behaviors by changing children's attitudes about media violence. *Journal of Personality and Social Psychology, 44,* 899–910.

Inbau, F. E., and Reid, J. E. (1962). *Criminal interrogation and confessions.* Baltimore: Williams and Wilkins.

Inbau, F. E., Reid, J. E., and Buckley, J. (1986). *Criminal interrogation and confessions.* Baltimore: Williams and Wilkins.

Insko, C. A., Smith, R. H., Alicke, M. D., Wade, J., and Taylor, S. (1985). Conformity and group size: The concern with being right and the concern with being liked. *Personality and Social Psychology Bulletin, 11,* 41–50.

Iyengar, S., Kinder, D. R., Peters, M. D., and Krosnick, J. A. (1984). The evening news and presidential evaluations. *Journal of Personality and Social Psychology, 46,* 778–787.

Janis, I. L. (1984). Improving adherence to medical recommendations: Prescriptive hypotheses derived from recent research in social psychology. In A. Baum, S. E. Taylor, and J. E. Singer (Eds.), *Handbook of psychology and health* (vol. 4, pp. 113–148). Hillsdale, NJ: Erlbaum.

Janis, I. L., and Field, P. B. (1956). A behavioral assessment of persuasibility: Consistency of individual differences. *Sociometry, 19,* 241–259.

Janis, I. L., Kaye, D., and Kirschner, P. (1965). Facilitating effects of "eating-while-reading" on responsiveness to persuasive communications. *Journal of Personality and Social Psychology, 1,* 181–186.

Janis, I. L., and King, B. T. (1954). The influence of role-playing on opinion change. *Journal of Abnormal and Social Psychology, 49,* 211–218.

Janis, I. L., and Mann, L. (1965). Effectiveness of emotional role-playing in modifying smoking habits and attitudes. *Journal of Experimental Research in Personality, 1,* 84–90.

Janis, I. L., and Mann, L. (1977). *Decision making.* New York: Free Press.

Johnson, B. T., and Eagly, A. H. (1989). Effects of involvement on persuasion: A meta-analysis. *Psychological Bulletin, 104,* 290–314.

Johnson, H. H., and Watkins, T. A. (1971). The effects of message repetition on immediate and delayed attitude change. *Psychonomic Science, 22,* 101–103.

Johnson, M. K., and Raye, C. L. (1981). Reality monitoring. *Psychological Review, 88,* 67–85.

Jones, E. E., and Davis, K. E. (1965). From acts to dispositions: The attribution process in person perception. In L. Berkowitz (Ed.), *Advances in experimental social psychology* (vol. 2). New York: Academic Press.

Jones, E. E., and Harris, V. A. (1967). The attribution of attitudes. *Journal of Experimental Social Psychology, 3,* 2–24.

Jones, E. E., Rock, L., Shaver, K. G., Goethals, G. R., and Ward, L. M. (1968). Pattern of performance and ability attribution: An unexpected primacy effect. *Journal of Personality and Social Psychology, 10,* 317–340.

Judd, C. M., Kenny, D. A., and Krosnick, J. A. (1983). Judging the positions of political candidates: Models of assimilation and contrast. *Journal of Personality and Social Psychology, 44,* 952–963.

Kahn, D. (1987). It's a great ad, but will it sell? *Newsday,* Mar. 29, 80, 77.

Kahneman, D. (1973). *Attention and effort.* Englewood Cliffs, NJ: Prentice-Hall.

Kahneman, D., and Tversky, A. (1979). Prospect theory: An analysis of decision under risk. *Econometrica, 47,* 263–291.

Kalfus, G. R., Ferrari, J. R., Arean, P., Balser, D., Cotronea, R., Franco, M., and Hill, W. (1987). An examination of the New York mandatory seat belt law on a university campus. *Law and Human Behavior, 11,* 63–67.

Kallgren, C. A., and Wood, W. (1986). Access to attitude-relevant information in memory as a determinant of attitude-behavior consistency. *Journal of Experimental Social Psychology, 22,* 328–338.

Kalven, H., and Zeisel, H. (1966). *The American jury.* Boston: Little, Brown.

Kamenetsky, C. (1984). *Children's literature in Hitler's Germany: The cultural policy of National Socialism.* Athens, OH: Ohio University Press.

Kandel, D. B., Kessler, R. C., and Margulies, R. L. (1978). Antecedents of adolescent initiation into stages of drug use: A developmental analysis. *Journal of Youth and Adolescence, 7,* 13–40.

Kantola, S. J., Syme, G. J., and Campbell, N. A. (1984). Cognitive dissonance and energy conservation. *Journal of Applied Psychology, 69,* 416–421.

Kaplan, M. F., and Miller, C. E. (1987). Group decision making and normative versus informational influence: Effects of type of issue and assigned decision rule. *Journal of Personality and Social Psychology, 53,* 306–313.

Karabenick, S. A. (1983). Sex-relevance of context and influenceability, Sistrunk and McDavid revisited. *Personality and Social Psychology Bulletin, 9,* 243–252.

Kassin, S. M., and Wrightsman, L. S. (1980). Prior confessions and mock jury verdicts. *Journal of Applied Social Psychology, 10,* 133–146.

Kassin, S. M., and Wrightsman, L. S. (1981). Coerced confessions, judicial instruction, mock juror verdicts. *Journal of Applied Social Psychology, 11,* 489–506.

Kassin, S. M., Reddy, M. E., and Tulloch, W. F. (1990). Juror interpretations of ambiguous evidence: The need for cognition, presentation order, and persuasion. *Law and Human Behavior, 14,* 43–55.

Kates, R. W. (1976). Experiencing the environment as hazard. In H. M. Proshansky, W. H. Ittelson, and L. G. Rivlin (Eds.), *Environmental psychology: People and their physical settings* (2d ed.). New York: Holt, Rinehart & Winston.

Katz, D. (1960). The functional approach to the study of attitudes. *Public Opinion Quarterly, 24,* 163–204.

Keeton, R. E. (1973). *Trial tactics and methods* (2d ed.). Boston: Little, Brown.

Kelley, H. H. (1967). Attribution theory in social psychology. In D. Levine (Ed.), *Nebraska symposium on motivation* (vol. 51). Lincoln: University of Nebraska Press.

Kelley, H. H. (1972). Causal schemata and the attribution process. In E. E. Jones, D. E. Kanouse, H. H. Kelley, R. E. Nisbett, S. Valins, and B. Weiner (Eds.), *Attribution: Perceiving the causes of behavior.* Morristown, NJ: General Learning Press.

Kendall, P. C. (1987). Cognitive processes and procedures in behavior therapy. In G. T. Wilson, C. M. Franks, P. C. Kendall, and J. P. Foreyt (Eds.), *Review of behavior therapy, theory and practice* (vol. 11). New York: Guilford.

Key, W. B. (1973). *Subliminal seduction.* Englewood Cliffs, NJ: Signet.

Kiesler, C. A. (1971). *The psychology of commitment: Experiments linking behavior to belief.* New York: Academic Press.

Kihlstrom, J. F. (1987). The cognitive unconscious. *Science, 237,* 1445–1452.

Kinder, D. R., and Sears, D. O. (1981). Prejudice and politics: Symbolic racism versus racial threats to the good life. *Journal of Personality and Social Psychology, 40,* 414–431.

King, B. T., and Janis, I. L. (1956). Comparison of the effectiveness of improvised versus non-improvised role-playing in producing opinion change. *Human Relations, 9,* 177–186.

Kircher, J. C., Horowitz, S. W., and Raskin, D. C. (1988). Meta-analysis of mock crime studies of the control question polygraph technique. *Law and Human Behavior, 12,* 79–90.

Kleinhesselink, R. R., and Edwards, R. E. (1975). Seeking and avoiding belief-discrepant information as a function of its perceived refutability. *Journal of Personality and Social Psychology, 31,* 787–790.

Koehnken, G. (1985). Speech and deception of eyewitnesses: An information processing approach. In F. L. Denmark (Ed.), *Social/ecological psychology and the psychology of women* (pp. 117–139). New York: Elsevier Science Publishers.

Krauss, R. M., Apple, W., Morency, N., Wenzel, C., and Winton, W. (1981). Verbal, vocal, and visible factors in judgments of another's affect. *Journal of Personality and Social Psychology, 40,* 312–320.

Kraut, R. (1980). Humans as lie detectors: Some second thoughts. *Journal of Communications, 30*(4), 209–216.

Kraut, R. E., and Poe, D. (1980). Behavioral routes of person perception: The deception judgments of customs inspectors and laymen. *Journal of Personality and Social Psychology, 39,* 784–798.

Krosnick, J. A. (1988). The role of attitude importance in social evaluation: A study of policy preferences, presidential candidate evaluations, and voting behavior. *Journal of Personality and Social Psychology, 55,* 196–210.

Kruglanski, A. W., and Mayseless, O. (1987). Motivational effects in the social comparison of opinions. *Journal of Personality and Social Psychology, 53,* 834–842.

Kunst-Wilson, W. R., and Zajonc, R. B. (1980). Affective discrimination of stimuli that cannot be recognized. *Science, 207,* 557–558.

Kyle, S. O., and Falbo, T. (1985). Relationships between marital stress and attributional preferences for own and spouse behavior. *Journal of Social and Clinical Psychology, 3,* 339–351.

Landers, S. (1990). Sex, condom use up among teenage boys. *APA Monitor,* Apr., 25.

Landy, D. (1972). The effects of an overheard audience's reaction and attractiveness on opinion change. *Journal of Experimental Social Psychology, 8,* 276–288.

Langer, E. (1989). *Mindfulness.* Reading, MA: Addison-Wesley.

Langer, E., and Abelson, R. P. (1974). A patient by any other name...: Clinical group differences in labelling bias. *Journal of Consulting and Clinical Psychology, 42,* 4–9.

Langer, E., Blank, A., and Chanowitz, B. (1978). The mindlessness of ostensibly thoughtful action: The role of "placebic" information in interpersonal interaction. *Journal of Personality and Social Psychology, 36,* 635–642.

Langer, E., and Piper, A. (1987). The prevention of mindlessness. *Journal of Personality and Social Psychology, 53,* 280–287.

Lanzetta, J. T., Sullivan, D. G., Masters, R. D., and McHugo, G. J. (1985). Viewers' emotional and cognitive responses to televised images of political leaders. In S. Kraus and R. M. Perloff (Eds.), *Mass media and political thought: An information processing approach* (pp. 85–115). Beverly Hills, CA: Sage.

Lee, M. T., and Ofshe, R. (1981). The impact of behavioral style and status characteristics on social influence: A test of two competing theories. *Social Psychology Quarterly, 44,* 73–82.

Leippe, M. R. (1979). *Message exposure duration and attitude change: An information processing analysis of persuasion.* Unpublished doctoral dissertation, Ohio State University.

Leippe, M. R. (1980). Effects of integrative memorial and cognitive processes on the correspondence of eyewitness accuracy and confidence. *Law and Human Behavior, 4,* 261–274.

Leippe, M. R. (1983). *Persuasion, cognitive responses, and message exposure duration: Evidence for thought reversal.* Paper presented at the meeting of the Eastern Psychological Association.

Leippe, M. R., and Elkin, R. A. (1987). When motives clash: Issue involvement and response involvement as determinants of persuasion. *Journal of Personality and Social Psychology, 52,* 269–278.

Leippe, M. R., and Romanczyk, A. (1989). Reactions to child (versus adult) eyewitnesses: The influence of jurors' preconceptions and witness behavior. *Law and Human Behavior, 13,* 103–131.

Leippe, M. R., Romanczyk, A., and Manion, A. P. (1990). *Eyewitness persuasion: How and how well do factfinders judge the accuracy of adults' and children's memory reports.* Manuscript submitted for publication, Adelphi University.

Leippe, M. R., Wells, G. L., and Ostrom, T. M. (1978). Crime seriousness as a determinant of accuracy in eyewitness identification. *Journal of Applied Psychology, 63,* 345–351.

Lepper, M. R., Greene, D., and Nisbett, R. E. (1973). Undermining children's intrinsic interest with extrinsic reward: A test of the overjustification hypothesis. *Journal of Personality and Social Psychology, 28,* 129–137.

Leventhal, H. (1970). Findings and theory in the study of fear communications. In L. Berkowitz (Ed.), *Advances in experimental social psychology* (vol. 5). New York: Academic Press.

Leventhal, H., Watts, J. C., and Pagano, F. (1967). Effects of fear and instructions on how to cope with danger. *Journal of Personality and Social Psychology, 6,* 313–321.

Lewisohn, P. M., Mischel, W., Chapline, W., and Barton, R. (1980). Social competence and depression: The role of illusory self-perceptions. *Journal of Abnormal Psychology, 89,* 203–212.

Liebert, R. M., and Sprafkin, J. (1988). *The early window: Effects of television on children and youth* (3d ed.). New York: Pergamon.

Lifton, R. K. (1969). *Thought reform and the psychology of totalism.* New York: Norton.

Lind, E. A. (1982). The psychology of courtroom procedure. In N. L. Kerr and R. M. Bray (Eds.), *The psychology of the courtroom* (pp. 13–38). New York: Academic Press.

Lind, E. A., Erickson, B., Conley, J. M., and O'Barr, W. M. (1978). Social attributions and conversational style in trial testimony. *Journal of Personality and Social Psychology, 36,* 1558–1567.

Lind, E. A., Thibault, J., and Walker, L. (1973). Discovery and presentation of evidence in adversary and nonadversary proceedings. *Michigan Law Review, 71,* 1129–1144.

Lindsay, R. C. L., Wells, G. L., and Rumpel, C. (1981). Can people detect eyewitness identification accuracy within and between situations? *Journal of Applied Psychology, 66,* 79–89.

Loftus, E. F. (1979). *Eyewitness testimony.* Cambridge, MA: Harvard University Press.

Loftus, E. F. (1974). Reconstructing memory: The incredible witness. *Psychology Today,* Dec., 116–119.

Loftus, E. F. (1984). Eyewitnesses: Essential but unreliable. *Psychology Today,* Feb., 22–26.

Loftus, E. F., Miller, D. G., and Burns, H. J. (1978). Semantic integration of verbal information into a visual memory. *Journal of Experimental Psychology: Human Learning and Memory, 4,* 19–31.

London, H. (1973). *Psychology of the persuader.* Morristown, NJ: General Learning Press.

Lord, C. G., Lepper, M. R., and Preston, E. (1984). Considering the opposite: A corrective strategy for social judgment. *Journal of Personality and Social Psychology, 47,* 1231–1243.

Lord, C. G., Ross, L., and Lepper, M. R. (1979). Biased assimilation and attitude polarization: The effects of prior theories on subsequently considered evidence. *Journal of Personality and Social Psychology, 37,* 2098–2109.

Luchins, A. (1957). Primacy-recency in impression formation. In C. I. Hovland (Ed.), *The order of presentation in persuasion.* New Haven, CT: Yale University Press.

Luthans, F., Paul, R., and Baker, D. (1981). An experimental analysis of the impact of contingent reinforcement on salespersons' performance behavior. *Journal of Applied Psychology, 66,* 314–323.

Lutz, W. (1989). No one died in Tiananmen Square. *The New York Times,* July 12, A1, A9.

Luus, C. A. E., and Wells, G. L. (1991). Eyewitness identification and the selection of distractors for lineups. *Law and Human Behavior,* in press.

Lydon, J. E., and Zanna, M. P. (1990). Commitment in the face of adversity: A value-affirmation approach. *Journal of Personality and Social Psychology, 58,* 1040–1047.

Maccoby, N., Farquhar, J. W., Wood, P. D., and Alexander, J. (1977). Reducing the risk of cardiovascular disease: Effects of a community-based campaign on knowledge and behavior. *Journal of Community Health, 3,* 100–114.

MacCoun, R. J., and Kerr, N. L. (1988). Asymmetric influence in mock jury deliberations: Jurors' bias toward leniency. *Journal of Personality and Social Psychology, 54,* 21–33.

Maddux, J. E., and Rogers, R. W. (1983). Protection motivation and self-efficacy: A revised theory of fear appeals and attitude change. *Journal of Experimental Social Psychology, 19,* 469–479.

Malpass, R. S., and Devine, P. G. (1981). Eyewitness identification: Lineup instructions and the absence of the offender. *Journal of Applied Psychology*, 66, 345–351.

Mandler, G., and Nakamura, Y. (1987). Aspects of consciousness. *Personality and Social Psychology Bulletin*, 13, 299–313.

Mann, L., and Janis, I. L. (1968). A follow-up study on the long-term effects of emotional role playing. *Journal of Personality and Social Psychology*, 8, 339–342.

Manstead, A. S. R., Proffitt, C., and Smart, J. L. (1983). Predicting and understanding mothers' infant-feeding intentions and behavior: Testing the theory of reasoned action. *Journal of Personality and Social Psychology*, 44, 657–671.

Marbury, C. H. (1989). An excursus on the biblical and theological rhetoric of Martin Luther King. In D. J. Garrow (Ed.), *Martin Luther King, Jr.: Civil rights leader, theologian, orator* (vol. 3). New York: Carlson.

Marcel, A. J. (1983). Conscious and unconscious perception: Experiments on visual masking and word recognition. *Cognitive Psychology*, 15, 197–237.

Maslach, C., Santee, R. T., and Wade, C. (1987). Individuation, gender role, and dissent: Personality mediators of situational forces. *Journal of Personality and Social Psychology*, 53, 1088–1093.

Maslach, C., Stapp, J., and Santee, R. T. (1985). Individuation: Conceptual analysis and assessment. *Journal of Personality and Social Psychology*, 49, 729–738.

McAlister, A. (1981). Antismoking campaigns: Progress in developing effective communications. In R. E. Rice and W. J. Paisley (Eds.), *Public communication campaigns* (pp. 91–103). Beverly Hills, CA: Sage.

McArthur, L. A. (1972). The how and what of why: Some determinants and consequences of causal attribution. *Journal of Personality and Social Psychology*, 22, 171–193.

McCullough, J. L., and Ostrom, T. M. (1974). Repetition of highly similar messages and attitude change. *Journal of Applied Psychology*, 59, 395–397.

McGuire, W. J. (1964). Inducing resistance to persuasion: Some contemporary approaches. In L. Berkowitz (Ed.), *Advances in experimental social psychology* (vol. 1). New York: Academic Press.

McGuire, W. J. (1968). Personality and attitude change: An information processing theory. In A. G. Greenwald, T. C. Brock, and T. M. Ostrom (Eds.), *Psychological foundations of attitudes* (pp. 171–196). New York: Academic Press.

McGuire, W. J. (1985). Attitudes and attitude change. In G. Lindzey and E. Aronson (Eds.), *Handbook of social psychology: Volume II* (3d ed., pp. 233–346). New York: Random House.

McGuire, W. J., and Papageorgis, D. (1961). The relative efficacy of various types of prior belief-defense in producing immunity against persuasion. *Journal of Abnormal and Social Psychology*, 62, 327–337.

McHugo, G. J., Lanzetta, J. T., Sullivan, D. G., Masters, R. D., and Englis, B. G. (1985). Emotional reactions to a political leader's expressive displays. *Journal of Personality and Social Psychology*, 49, 1513–1529.

McPherson, K. (1983). Opinion-related information seeking: Personal and situational variables. *Personality and Social Psychology Bulletin*, 9, 116–124.

Mehrabian, A. (1972). *Nonverbal communication.* Chicago: Aldine-Atherton.

Mehrabian, A. (1981). *Silent messages: Implicit communication of emotions and attitudes* (2d ed.). Belmont, CA: Wadsworth.

Mehrabian, A., and Williams, M. (1969). Nonverbal concomitants of perceived and intended persuasiveness. *Journal of Personality and Social Psychology, 13,* 37–58.

Meyer, A. J., Nash, J. D., McAlister, A. L., Maccoby, N., and Farquhar, J. W. (1980). Skills training in a cardiovascular health education campaign. *Journal of Consulting and Clinical Psychology, 48,* 129–142.

Meyerowitz, B. E., and Chaiken, S. (1987). The effect of message framing on breast self examination attitudes, intentions, and behavior. *Journal of Personality and Social Psychology, 52,* 500–510.

Milgram, S. (1963). Behavioral study of obedience. *Journal of Abnormal and Social Psychology, 67,* 371–378.

Milgram, S. (1965). Some conditions of obedience to authority. *Human Relations, 18,* 57–76.

Milgram, S. (1974). *Obedience to authority.* New York: Harper & Row.

Millar, M. G., and Tesser, A. (1986). Effects of affective and cognitive focus on the attitude-behavior relationship. *Journal of Personality and Social Psychology, 51,* 270–276.

Miller, A. G. (1986). *The obedience experiments: A case study of controversy in the social sciences.* New York: Praeger.

Miller, G. A. (1962). *Psychology: The science of mental life.* New York: Harper & Row.

Miller, K. D. (1986). Martin Luther King, Jr., borrows a revolution: Argument, audience, and implications of a secondhand universe. *College English, 48,* 249–265.

Miller, N. E. (1978). Biofeedback and visceral learning. *Annual Review of Psychology, 29,* 373–404.

Miller, N., and Campbell, D. T. (1959). Recency and primacy in persuasion as a function of the timing of speeches and measurement. *Journal of Abnormal and Social Psychology, 59,* 1–9.

Miller, N., Maruyama, G., Beaber, R. J., and Valone, K. (1976). Speed of speech and persuasion. *Journal of Personality and Social Psychology, 34,* 615–624.

Milmoe, S., Rosenthal, R., Blane, H. T., Chafetz, M. E., and Wolf, E. (1967). The doctor's voice: Predictor of successful referral of alcoholic patients. *Journal of Abnormal Psychology, 72,* 78–84.

Mitchell, H. E. (1979). *Informational and affective determinants of juror decision making.* Unpublished doctoral dissertation, Purdue University.

Molko v. Holy Spirit Association, 179 Cal. 3d 450; Daily Journal D. A. R. 13197 (1988).

Mooney, H., Bradbury, C., and Folmer, K. (1990). *The efficacy of four persuasion techniques in four conceptually different situations.* Paper presented at the meeting of the Western Psychological Association, Los Angeles, CA.

Moore, T. E. (1982). Subliminal advertising: What you see is what you get. *Journal of Marketing, 46,* 38–47.

Moreland, R. L., and Zajonc, R. B. (1979). Exposure effects may not depend on stimulus recognition. *Journal of Personality and Social Psychology, 37,* 1085–1089.

Moriarty, T. (1975). Crime, commitment and the responsive bystander: Two field experiments. *Journal of Personality and Social Psychology, 31,* 370–376.

Morley, D. D. (1987). Subjective message constructs: A theory of persuasion. *Communication Monographs, 54,* 183–203.

Mosbach, P., and Leventhal, H. (1988). Peer group identification and smoking: Implications for intervention. *Journal of Abnormal Psychology, 97,* 238–245.

Moscovici, S. (1976). *Social influence and social change.* London: Academic Press.

Moscovici, S. (1980). Toward a theory of conversion behavior. In L. Berkowitz (Ed.), *Advances in experimental social psychology* (vol. 13, pp. 209–239). New York: Academic Press.

Moscovici, S., and Zavalloni, M. (1969). The group as a polarizer of attitudes. *Journal of Personality and Social Psychology, 12,* 125–135.

Mowen, J. C., and Cialdini, R. B. (1980). On implementing the door-in-the-face compliance technique in a business context. *Journal of Marketing Research, 17,* 253–258.

Mulbar, H. (1951). *Interrogation.* Springfield, IL: Thomas.

Mullen, B., Futrell, D., Stairs, D., Tice, D. M., Baumeister, R. F., Dawson, K. E., Riordan, C. A., Radloff, C. E., Goethals, G. R., Kennedy, J. G., and Rosenfeld, P. (1986). Newscasters' facial expressions and voting behavior of viewers: Can a smile elect a president? *Journal of Personality and Social Psychology, 51,* 291–295.

Myers, D. G., and Kaplan, M. F. (1976). Group-induced polarization in simulated juries. *Personality and Social Psychology Bulletin, 2,* 63–66.

Myers, D. G., and Lamm, H. (1975). The group polarization phenomenon. *Psychological Bulletin, 83,* 602–627.

Neil v. Biggers, 409 U.S. 188 (1972).

Nelson, Z. P., and Mowry, D. D. (1976). Contracting in crisis intervention. *Community Mental Health Journal, 12,* 37–43.

Nemeth, C. J. (1986). Differential contributions of majority and minority influence. *Psychological Review, 93,* 23–32.

Nemeth, C. J., Mayseless, O., Sherman, J., and Brown, Y. (1990). Exposure to dissent and recall of information. *Journal of Personality and Social Psychology, 58,* 429–437.

Newcomb, T. M. (1961). *The acquaintance process.* New York: Holt, Rinehart & Winston.

The New York Times (1990). U.S. tobacco ads in Asia faulted. P. J. Hilts (writer), May 5, p. 19.

The New York Times (1990). Killings in '89 set a record in New York. J. C. McKinley (writer), Mar. 31, L27, L30.

Newsday (1990). Mar. 28.

Newsweek (1990). Feb. 5.

Nisbett, R. E., and Ross, L. (1980). *Human inference: Strategies and shortcomings of social judgment.* Englewood Cliffs, NJ: Prentice-Hall.

Nisbett, R. E., and Schachter, S. (1966). Cognitive manipulation of pain. *Journal of Experimental Social Psychology, 2,* 227–236.

Nisbett, R. E., and Wilson, T. D. (1977a). Telling more than we can know: Verbal reports on mental processes. *Psychological Review, 84,* 231–259.

Nisbett, R. E., and Wilson, T. D. (1977b). The halo effect: Evidence for unconscious alteration of judgments. *Journal of Personality and Social Psychology, 35,* 250–256.

Nix, S. (1989). Weekend with the Moonies. *San Francisco Chronicle*, Aug. 10, B1, B3, B6.

Nizer, L. (1961). *My life in court.* New York: Pyramid.

Nord, W. (1970). Improving attendance through rewards. *Personnel Administration, 33,* 37–41.

O'Barr, W. M. (1982). *Linguistic evidence.* New York: Academic Press.

Ofshe, R. (1990). Coerced confessions: The logic of seemingly irrational action. *Cultic Studies Journal, 6,* 1–15.

Oldenburg, D. (1990). High-tech subliminals: You are what you hear. *The Washington Post,* Apr. 19, B3, B5.

Osborne, J. G., and Powers, R. B. (1980). Controlling the litter problem. In G. L. Martin and J. G. Osborne (Eds.), *Helping the community: Behavioral applications.* New York: Plenum.

Osgood, C. E., Suci, G. J., and Tannenbaum, P. G. (1957). *The measurement of meaning.* Urbana: University of Illinois Press.

Ostrom, T. M., and Brock, T. C. (1968). A cognitive model of attitudinal involvement. In R. P. Abelson, E. Aronson, W. J. McGuire, T. M. Newcomb, M. J. Rosenberg, and P. H. Tannenbaum (Eds.), *Theories of cognitive consistency: A sourcebook* (pp. 373–389). Chicago: Rand McNally.

Packard, V. (1957). *The hidden persuaders.* New York: McKay.

Packwood, W. T. (1974). Loudness as a variable in persuasion. *Journal of Counseling Psychology, 21,* 1–2.

Page, B. I., Shapiro, R. Y., and Dempsey, G. R. (1987). What moves public opinion? *American Political Science Review, 81,* 23–43.

Page, M. M. (1969). Social psychology of a classical conditioning of attitudes experiment. *Journal of Personality and Social Psychology, 11,* 177–186.

Page, M. M. (1974). Demand characteristics and the classical conditioning of attitudes experiment. *Journal of Personality and Social Psychology, 30,* 468–476.

Pallak, M. S., Mueller, M., Dollar, K., and Pallak, J. (1972). Effects of commitment on responsiveness to an extreme consonant communication. *Journal of Personality and Social Psychology, 23,* 429–436.

Papageorgis, D., and McGuire, W. (1961). The generality of immunity to persuasion produced by pre-exposure to weakened counterarguments. *Journal of Abnormal and Social Psychology, 62,* 475–481.

Pennington, N., and Hastie, R. (1986). Evidence evaluation in complex decision making. *Journal of Personality and Social Psychology, 51,* 242–258.

Perlman, D., and Oskamp, S. (1971). The effects of picture content and exposure frequency on evaluations of negroes and whites. *Journal of Experimental Social Psychology, 7,* 503–514.

Peterson, C., and Seligman, M. E. P. (1984). Causal explanations as a risk factor for depression: Theory and evidence. *Psychological Review, 91,* 347–374.

Petty, R. E., and Cacioppo, J. T. (1977). Forewarning, cognitive responding, and resistance to persuasion. *Journal of Personality and Social Psychology, 35,* 645–655.

Petty, R. E., and Cacioppo, J. T. (1981). *Attitudes and persuasion: Classic and contemporary approaches.* Dubuque, IA: Wm. C. Brown.

Petty, R. E., and Cacioppo, J. T. (1984). The effects of issue involvement on responses to argument quantity and quality: Central and peripheral routes to persuasion. *Journal of Personality and Social Psychology, 46,* 69–81.

Petty, R. E., and Cacioppo, J. T. (1986). The elaboration likelihood model of persuasion. In L. Berkowitz (Ed.), *Advances in experimental social psychology* (vol. 19, pp. 123–205). New York: Academic Press.

Petty, R. E., Cacioppo, J. T., and Goldman, R. (1981). Personal involvement as a determinant of argument based persuasion. *Journal of Personality and Social Psychology, 41,* 847–855.

Petty, R. E., Wells, G. L., and Brock, T. C. (1976). Distraction can enhance or reduce yielding to propaganda: Thought disruption versus effort justification. *Journal of Personality and Social Psychology, 34,* 874–884.

Pilisuk, M., and Parks, S. H. (1986). *The healing web: Social networks and human survival.* Hanover, NH: University Press of New England.

Pratkanis, A. R., Eskenazi, J., and Greenwald, A. G. (1990). What you expect is what you believe (but not necessarily what you get): On the ineffectiveness of subliminal self-help audiotapes. Paper presented at the Western Psychological Association, Los Angeles, CA, April 1990.

Pratkanis, A. R., and Greenwald, A. G. (1988). Recent perspectives on unconscious processing: Still no marketing applications. *Psychology and Marketing, 5,* 337–353.

Pratkanis, A. R., and Greenwald, A. G. (1989). A sociocognitive model of attitude structure and function. In L. Berkowitz (Ed.), *Advances in experimental social psychology* (vol. 22, pp. 245–285). New York: Academic Press.

Pratkanis, A. R., Greenwald, A. G., Leippe, M. R., and Baumgardner, M. H. (1988). In search of reliable persuasion effects: III. The sleeper effect is dead. Long live the sleeper effect. *Journal of Personality and Social Psychology, 54,* 203–218.

Pyszczynski, T., and Wrightsman, L. S. (1981). The effects of opening statements on mock jurors' verdicts in a simulated court case. *Journal of Applied Social Psychology, 11,* 301–313.

Qualter, T. H. (1962). *Propaganda and psychological warfare.* New York: Random House.

Ravenholt, R. T. (1985). Tobacco's impact on twentieth-century U.S. mortality patterns. *American Journal of Preventive Medicine, 1,* 4–17.

Ray, M., and Ward, S. (1976). Experimentation for pretesting public health programs: The case of the anti-drug abuse campaigns. *Advances in Consumer Research, 3,* 278–286.

Reed, H. B., and Janis, I. L. (1974). Effects of a new type of psychological treatment on smokers' resistance to warnings about health hazards. *Journal of Consulting and Clinical Psychology, 42,* 748.

Regan, D. T. (1971). Effects of a favor and liking on compliance. *Journal of Experimental Social Psychology, 7,* 627–639.

Reis, A., and Trout, J. (1986). *Positioning: The battle for your mind.* New York: Warner.

Reyes, R. M., Thompson, W. C., and Bower, G. H. (1980). Judgmental biases resulting from differing availability of arguments. *Journal of Personality and Social Psychology, 39,* 2–12.

Roberts, D. F. (1982). Children and commercials: Issues, evidence, interventions. *Prevention in Human Services, 2,* 19–36.

Roberts, D. F., and Maccoby, N. (1985). Effects of mass communication. In G. Lindzey and E. Aronson (Eds.), *Handbook of social psychology: Volume II* (3d ed., pp. 539–598). New York: Random House.

Robinson, J., and McArthur, L. Z. (1982). Impact of salient vocal qualities on causal attributions for a speaker's behavior. *Journal of Personality and Social Psychology, 43,* 236–247.

Robles, R., Smith, R., Carver, C. S., and Wellens, A. R. (1987). Influence of subliminal visual images on the experience of anxiety. *Personality and Social Psychology Bulletin, 13,* 399–410.

Rogers, C. R. (1951). *Client-centered therapy: Its current practice, implications and theory.* Boston: Houghton-Mifflin.

Rogers, R. W. (1983). Cognitive and physiological processes in fear appeals and attitude change: A revised theory of protection motivation. In J. T. Cacioppo and R. E. Petty (Eds.), *Social psychophysiology.* New York: Guilford.

Rogers, R. W., and Mewborn, C. R. (1976). Fear appeals and attitude change: Effects of a threat's noxiousness, probability of occurrence, and the efficacy of coping responses. *Journal of Personality and Social Psychology, 34,* 54–61.

Rohrer, J. H., Baron, S. H., Hoffman, E. L., and Swander, D. V. (1954). The stability of autokinetic judgments. *Journal of Abnormal and Social Psychology, 49,* 595–597.

Rokeach, M. (1973). *The nature of human values.* New York: Free Press.

Ronis, D. L., Baumgardner, M. H., Leippe, M. R., Cacioppo, J. T., and Greenwald, A. G. (1977). In search of reliable persuasion effects: I. A computer-controlled procedure for studying persuasion. *Journal of Personality and Social Psychology, 35,* 548–569.

Rosenhan, D. L. (1969). Some origins of the concerns for others. In P. Mussen and M. Covington (Eds.), *Trends and issues in developmental psychology.* New York: Holt, Rinehart & Winston.

Rosenkrans, M. A., and Hartup, W. W. (1967). Imitative influences of consistent and inconsistent response consequences to a model on aggressive behavior in children. *Journal of Personality and Social Psychology, 7,* 429–434.

Rosnow, R. L., and Suls, J. M. (1970). Reactive effects of pretesting in attitude research. *Journal of Personality and Social Psychology, 15,* 338–343.

Ross, L. (1977). The intuitive psychologist and his shortcomings. In L. Berkowitz (Ed.), *Advances in experimental social psychology* (vol. 10, pp. 173–220). New York: Academic Press.

Ross, L. (1988). Situationist perspectives on the obedience experiments. Review of A. G. Miller's *The obedience experiments. Contemporary Psychology, 33,* 101–104.

Ross, L., Amabile, T. M., and Steinmetz, J. L. (1977). Social roles, social control, and biases in social-perception processes. *Journal of Personality and Social Psychology, 35,* 485–494.

Ross, L., and Anderson, C. A. (1980). Shortcomings in the attribution process: On the origins and maintenance of erroneous social assessments. In A. Tversky, D. Kahneman, and P. Slovic (Eds.), *Judgment under uncertainty: Heuristics and biases.* New York: Cambridge University Press.

Ross, L., Lepper, M. R., and Hubbard, M. (1975). Perseverance in self perception and social perception: Biased attributional processes in the debriefing paradigm. *Journal of Personality and Social Psychology, 32,* 880–892.

Ross, M. (1975). Salience of reward and intrinsic motivation. *Journal of Personality and Social Psychology, 32,* 245–254.

Rothschild, M. L. (1987). *Advertising.* Lexington, MA: Heath.

Rule, B. G., and Bisanz, G. L. (1987). Goals and strategies of persuasion: A cognitive schema for understanding social events. In M. P. Zanna, J. M.

Olson, and C. P. Herman (Eds.), *Social influence: The Ontario symposium* (vol. 5, pp. 185–206). Hillsdale, NJ: Erlbaum.

Rushton, J. P. (1975). Generosity in children: Immediate and long-term effects of modeling, preaching and moral judgment. *Journal of Personality and Social Psychology, 31,* 459–466.

Rushton, J. P., and Campbell, A. C. (1977). Modeling, vicarious reinforcement and extraversion on blood donating in adults: Immediate and long-term effects. *European Journal of Social Psychology, 7,* 297–306.

Ryan, W. (1971). *Blaming the victim.* New York: Pantheon.

Sakarai, M. M. (1975). Small group cohesiveness and detrimental conformity. *Sociometry, 38,* 340–357.

Saks, M. J., and Hastie, R. (1978). *Social psychology in court.* New York: Van Nostrand Reinhold.

Salancik, G. R., and Conway, M. (1975). Attitude inferences from salient and relevant cognitive content about behavior. *Journal of Personality and Social Psychology, 32,* 829–840.

San Francisco Chronicle (1990). Jan. 29.

San Francisco Chronicle (1990). Feb. 20.

San Francisco Examiner and Chronicle (1990). Feb. 12.

Santee, R. T., and Jackson, S. E. (1982). Sex differences in the evaluative implications of conformity and dissent. *Social Psychology Quarterly, 45,* 121–125.

Santee, R. T., and Maslach, C. (1982). To agree or not to agree: Personal dissent amid social pressure to conform. *Journal of Personality and Social Psychology, 42,* 690–700.

Saxe, L., Dougherty, D., and Cross, T. (1985). The validity of polygraph testing: Scientific analysis and public controversy. *American Psychologist, 40,* 355–366.

Schachter, S. (1951). Deviation, rejection, and communication. *Journal of Abnormal and Social Psychology, 46,* 190–207.

Scherer, K. R., Feldstein, S., Bond, R. N., and Rosenthal, R. (1985). Vocal cues to deception: A comparative channel approach. *Journal of Psycholinguistic Research, 14,* 409–425.

Schlenker, B. R. (1982). Translating actions into attitudes: An identity-analytic approach to the explanation of social conduct. In L. Berkowitz (Ed.), *Advances in experimental social psychology* (vol. 15, pp. 151–181). New York: Academic Press.

Schooler, J. W., Gerhard, D., and Loftus, E. F. (1986). Qualities of the unreal. *Journal of Experimental Psychology: Learning, Memory and Cognition, 12,* 171–181.

Schulman, J., Shaver, P., Colman, R., Emrich, B., and Christie, R. (1973). Recipe for a jury. *Psychology Today,* May, 37–44, 77–84.

Schultz, D. P. (1982). *Psychology and industry today: An introduction to industrial and organizational psychology* (3d ed.). New York: Macmillan.

Schwartz, R. M., and Garamoni, G. L. (1986). A structural model of positive and negative states of mind: Asymmetry in the internal dialogue. In P. C. Kendall (Ed.), *Advances in cognitive-behavioral research and therapy* (vol. 5, pp. 2–63). New York: Academic Press.

Schwarzwald, J., Bizman, A., and Raz, M. (1983). The foot-in-the-door paradigm: Effects of second request size on donation probability and donor generosity. *Personality and Social Psychology Bulletin, 9,* 443–450.

Scrivner, E., and Safer, M. A. (1988). Eyewitnesses show hypermnesia for details about a violent event. *Journal of Applied Psychology, 73,* 371–377.

Sears, D. O., and Freedman, J. L. (1967). Selective exposure to information: A critical review. *Public Opinion Quarterly, 31,* 194–213.

Seligman, M. E. P. (1975). *Helplessness: On depression, development, and death.* San Francisco: Freeman.

Seligman, M. E. P., and Schulman, P. (1986). Explanatory style as predictor of productivity and quitting among life insurance agents. *Journal of Personality and Social Psychology, 50,* 832–838.

Shapiro, S., Skinner, E. A., Kessler, L. G., Korff, M., Von German, P. S., Tischler, F. L., Leaf, P. J., Benham, L., Cottler, L., and Regier, D. A. (1984). Utilization of health and mental health services. *Archives of General Psychiatry, 41,* 971–978.

Sheridan, C. L., and King, R. G. (1972). Obedience to authority with a genuine victim. *Proceedings of the 80th annual convention of the American Psychological Association,* Los Angeles.

Sherif, C. W., Kelly, M., Rodgers, H. L., Jr., Sarup, G., and Tittler, B. I. (1973). Personal involvement, social judgment, and action. *Journal of Personality and Social Psychology, 27,* 311–328.

Sherif, M. (1936). *The psychology of social norms.* New York: Harper & Row.

Sherif, M., and Hovland, C. I. (1961). *Social judgment: Assimilation and contrast effects in communication and attitude change.* New Haven, CT: Yale University Press.

Sherman, S. J. (1987). Cognitive processes in the formation, change, and expression of attitudes. In M. P. Zanna, J. M. Olson, and C. P. Herman (Eds.), *Social influence: The Ontario symposium* (vol. 5, pp. 75–106). Hillsdale, NJ: Erlbaum.

Sherman, S. J., and Gorkin, L. (1980). Attitude bolstering when behavior is inconsistent with central attitudes. *Journal of Experimental Social Psychology, 16,* 388–403.

Sherman, S. J., Presson, C. C., Chassin, L., Bensenberg, M., Corty, E., and Olshavsky, R. W. (1982). Smoking intentions in adolescents. *Personality and Social Psychology Bulletin, 8,* 376–383.

Shopland, D. R., and Brown, C. (1987). Toward the 1990 objectives for smoking: Measuring the progress with 1985 NHIS data. *Public Health Reports, 102,* 68–73.

Sistrunk, F., and McDavid, J. W. (1971). Sex variable in conformity behavior. *Journal of Personality and Social Psychology, 17,* 200–207.

Sivacek, J., and Crano, W. D. (1982). Vested interest as a moderator of attitude-behavior consistency. *Journal of Personality and Social Psychology, 43,* 210–221.

Smart, R. G., and Feger, D. (1974). The effects of high and low fear messages about drugs. *Journal of Drug Education, 4,* 225–235.

Smith, M., Bruner, J., and White, R. (1956). *Opinions and personality.* New York: Wiley.

Snyder, M. (1979). Self-monitoring processes. In L. Berkowitz (Ed.), *Advances in experimental social psychology* (vol. 12, pp. 85–128). New York: Academic Press.

Snyder, M., and Cunningham, M. R. (1975). To comply or not to comply: Testing the self-perception explanation of the "foot-in-the-door" phenomenon. *Journal of Personality and Social Psychology, 31,* 64–67.

Snyder, M., and DeBono, K. G. (1985). Appeals to image and claims about quality: Understanding the psychology of advertising. *Journal of Personality and Social Psychology, 49,* 586–597.

Snyder, M., and Debono, K. G. (1987). A functional approach to attitudes and persuasion. In M. P. Zanna, J. M. Olson, and C. P. Herman (Eds.), *Social influence: The Ontario symposium* (vol. 5, pp. 107–128). Hillsdale, NJ: Erlbaum.

Snyder, M., and Swann, W. B., Jr. (1978). Hypothesis-testing processes in social interaction. *Journal of Personality and Social Psychology, 36,* 1202–1212.

Snyder, M., and Uranowitz, S. W. (1978). Reconstructing the past: Some cognitive consequences of person perception. *Journal of Personality and Social Psychology, 36,* 941–950.

Sorrentino, R. M., Bobocel, D. R., Gitta, M. Z., Olson, J. M., and Hewitt, E. C. (1988). Uncertainty orientation and persuasion: Individual differences in the effects of personal relevance on social judgments. *Journal of Personality and Social Psychology, 55,* 357–371.

Spelke, E., Hirst, W., and Neisser, U. (1976). Skills of divided attention. *Cognition, 4,* 215–230.

Staats, A. W., and Staats, C. K. (1958). Attitudes established by classical conditioning. *Journal of Abnormal and Social Psychology,* 37–40.

Stasser, G., Kerr, N. L., and Bray, R. M. (1982). The social psychology of jury deliberations: Structure, process, and products. In N. L. Kerr and R. M. Bray (Eds.), *The psychology of the courtroom* (pp. 221–256). New York: Academic Press.

Stasser, G., Kerr, N. L., and Davis, J. H. (1989). Influence processes and consensus models in decision-making groups. In P. B. Paulus (Ed.), *Psychology of group influence* (2d ed., pp. 279–326). Hillsdale, NJ: Erlbaum.

Steele, C. M. (1988). The psychology of self-affirmation: Sustaining the integrity of the self. In L. Berkowitz (Ed.), *Advances in experimental social psychology* (vol. 21, pp. 261–302). New York: Academic Press.

Steele, C. M., Southwick, L. L., and Critchlow, B. (1981). Dissonance and alcohol: Drinking your troubles away. *Journal of Personality and Social Psychology, 41,* 831–846.

Stein, J. A., Newcomb, M. D., and Bentler, P. M. (1987). An 8-year study of multiple influences on drug use and drug consequences. *Journal of Personality and Social Psychology, 53,* 1094–1105.

Stephan, W. G., and Rosenfield, D. (1978). Effects of school desegregation on racial attitudes. *Journal of Personality and Social Psychology, 36,* 795–804.

Stoner, J. A. (1961). *A comparison of individual and group decisions involving risk.* Unpublished master's thesis. School of Industrial Management, Massachusetts Institute of Technology.

Strodtbeck, F. L., and Hook, L. H. (1961). The social dimensions of a twelve-man jury table. *Sociometry, 24,* 397–415.

Strodtbeck, F. L., James, R. M., and Hawkins, D. (1957). Social status in jury deliberations. *American Sociological Review, 22,* 713–719.

Sue, S., Smith, R. E., and Caldwell, C. (1973). Effects of inadmissible evidence on the decisions of simulated jurors: A moral dilemma. *Journal of Applied Social Psychology, 3,* 345–353.

Sullivan Report to Congress (1990).

Surgeon General (1983). *The health consequences of smoking: Cardiovascular disease: A report of the Surgeon General.* DHHS Publication No. PHS 84-50204. Rockville, MD: Office of Smoking and Health.

Swann, W. B., Jr. (1983). Self-verification: Bringing social reality into harmony with the self. In J. Suls and A. G. Greenwald (Eds.), *Social psychological perspectives on the self* (vol. 2, pp. 33–66). Hillsdale, NJ: Erlbaum.

Swann, W. B., Jr., and Ely, R. J. (1984). A battle of wills: Self-verification versus behavioral confirmation. *Journal of Personality and Social Psychology, 46,* 1287–1302.

Swann, W. B., Jr., Pelham, B. W., and Chidester, T. R. (1988). Change through paradox: Using self-verification to alter beliefs. *Journal of Personality and Social Psychology, 54,* 268–273.

Sweeney, P. D., and Gruber, K. L. (1984). Selective exposure: Voter information preferences and the Watergate affair. *Journal of Personality and Social Psychology, 46,* 1208–1221.

Taylor, S. E. (1986). *Health psychology.* New York: Random House.

Taylor, S. E., and Fiske, S. T. (1975). Point of view and perceptions of causality. *Journal of Personality and Social Psychology, 32,* 439–445.

Tedeschi, J. T., and Rosenfeld, P. (1981). Impression management theory and the forced compliance situation. In J. T. Tedeschi (Ed.), *Impression management theory and social psychological research.* New York: Academic Press.

Tedeschi, J. T., Schlenker, B. R., and Bonoma, T. V. (1971). Cognitive dissonance: Private ratiocination or public spectacle. *American Psychologist, 26,* 685–695.

Tesser, A. (1978). Self-generated attitude change. In L. Berkowitz (Ed.), *Advances in experimental social psychology* (vol. 11). New York: Academic Press.

Tesser, A., and Conlee, M. C. (1975). Some effects of time and thought on attitude polarization. *Journal of Personality and Social Psychology, 31,* 262–270.

Tetlock, P. E. (1983). Accountability and complexity of thought. *Journal of Personality and Social Psychology, 45,* 74–83.

Tetlock, P. E., and Kim, J. I. (1987). Accountability and judgment processes in a personality prediction task. *Journal of Personality and Social Psychology, 52,* 700–709.

Tetlock, P. E., Skitka, L., and Boettger, R. (1989). Social and cognitive strategies for coping with accountability: Conformity, complexity, and bolstering. *Journal of Personality and Social Psychology, 57,* 632–640.

Thibaut, J., and Walker, L. (1975). *Procedural justice: A psychological analysis.* Hillsdale, NJ: Erlbaum.

Time (1979). Secret voices: Messages that manipulate. Sept. 10, 71.

Tindale, R. S., Vollrath, D. A., Davis, J. H., Nagao, D. H., and Hinsz, V. B. (1990). Asymmetric social influence in freely interacting groups. A test of three models. *Journal of Personality and Social Psychology, 58,* 438–449.

Traub, J. (1988). Into the mouths of babes. *The New York Times Magazine,* July 24, 18–20, 37–38, 52–53.

Troyer, R. J., and Markle, G. E. (1983). *Cigarettes: The battle over smoking.* New Brunswick, NJ: Rutgers University Press.

Tulving, E. (1983). *Elements of episodic memory.* Oxford: Clarendon Press.

Turtle, J. W., and Wells, G. L. (1988). Children versus adults as eyewitnesses: Whose testimony holds up under cross-examination? In Gruneberg et al. (Eds.), *Practical aspects of memory*. London: Wiley.

Tversky, A., and Kahneman, D. (1974). Judgment under uncertainty: Heuristics and biases. *Science, 185,* 1124–1131.

Tversky, A., and Kahneman, D. (1986). Rational choice and the framing of decisions: *Journal of Business, 59,* S251–S278.

Varela, J. A. (1971). *Psychological solutions to social problems: An introduction to social technology.* New York: Academic Press.

Vidmar, N., and Laird, N. M. (1983). Adversary social roles: Their effects on witnesses' communication of evidence and the assessments of adjudicators. *Journal of Personality and Social Psychology, 44,* 888–898.

Visher, C. A. (1987). Juror decision making: The importance of evidence. *Law and Human Behavior, 11,* 1–17.

Walster, E., and Festinger, L. (1962). The effectiveness of "overheard" persuasive communications. *Journal of Abnormal and Social Psychology, 65,* 395–402.

The Washington Post (1990). Feb. 17.

Watson, D. (1982). The actor and the observer: How are their perceptions of causality different. *Psychological Bulletin, 92,* 682–700.

Watts, W. A. (1967). Relative persistence of opinion change induced by active compared to passive participation. *Journal of Personality and Social Psychology, 5,* 4–15.

Weinstein, N. D. (1982). Unrealistic optimism about susceptibility to health problems. *Journal of Behavioral Medicine, 5,* 441–460.

Weinstein, N. D., and Lachendro, E. (1982). Egocentrism as a source of unrealistic optimism. *Personality and Social Psychology Bulletin, 8,* 195–200.

Weir, W. (1984). Another look at subliminal "facts." *Advertising Age, 46,* October 15.

Weiss, W., and Steenbock, S. (1965). The influence on communication effectiveness of explicitly urging action and policy consequences. *Journal of Experimental Social Psychology, 1,* 396–406.

Wells, G. L. (1980). Asymmetric attributions for compliance: Reward versus punishment. *Journal of Experimental Social Psychology, 16,* 47–60.

Wells, G. L., Ferguson, T. J., and Lindsay, R. C. L. (1981). The tractability of eyewitness confidence and its implications for triers of fact. *Journal of Applied Psychology, 66,* 688–696.

Wells, G. L., and Leippe, M. R. (1981). How do triers of fact infer the accuracy of eyewitness identification? Using memory for detail can be misleading. *Journal of Applied Psychology, 66,* 682–687.

Wells, G. L., Leippe, M. R., and Ostrom, T. M. (1979). Guidelines for empirically assessing the fairness of a lineup. *Law and Human Behavior, 3,* 285–293.

Wells, G. L., Lindsay, R. C. L., and Ferguson, T. J. (1979). Accuracy, confidence, and juror perceptions in eyewitness identification. *Journal of Applied Psychology, 64,* 440–448.

Wells, G. L., and Murray, D. M. (1984). Eyewitness confidence. In G. L. Wells and E. F. Loftus (Eds.), *Eyewitness testimony: Psychological perspectives.* New York: Cambridge University Press.

Wells, G. L., and Petty, R. E. (1980). The effects of overt head movements on persuasion: Compatibility and incompatibility of responses. *Basic and Applied Social Psychology, 1,* 219–230.

Wells, G. L., Wrightsman, L. S., and Miene, P. K. (1985). The timing of the defense opening statement: Don't wait until the evidence is in. *Journal of Applied Social Psychology, 15,* 758–772.

Wilson, T. D., Dunn, D. S., Kraft, D., and Lisle, D. J. (1989). Introspection, attitude change, and attitude-behavior consistency: The disruptive effects of explaining why we feel the way we do. In L. Berkowitz (Ed.), *Advances in experimental social psychology* (vol. 22, pp. 287–343). New York: Academic Press.

Wilson, T. D., and Linville, P. W. (1982). Improving the academic performance of college freshmen: Attribution therapy revisited. *Journal of Personality and Social Psychology, 42,* 367–376.

Wilson, W., and Miller, H. (1968). Repetition, order of presentation, and timing of arguments and measures as determinants of opinion change. *Journal of Personality and Social Psychology, 9,* 184–188.

Winett, R. A., Kagel, J. H., Battalio, R. C., and Winkler, R. C. (1978). Effects of monetary rebates, feedback, and information on residential electricity conservation. *Journal of Applied Psychology, 65,* 73–80.

Winett, R. A., Neale, M. S., and Grier, H. C. (1979). Effects of self-monitoring and feedback on residential electricity consumption. *Journal of Applied Behavior Analysis, 12,* 173–184.

Wolf, S., and Montgomery, D. A. (1977). Effects of inadmissible evidence and level of judicial admonishment. *Journal of Applied Social Psychology, 7,* 205–219.

Wood, W. (1982). Retrieval of attitude relevant information from memory: Effects on susceptibility to persuasion and on intrinsic motivation. *Journal of Personality and Social Psychology, 42,* 798–810.

Wood, W., Kallgren, C. A., and Priesler, R. M. (1985). Access to attitude-relevant information in memory as a determinant of persuasion: The role of message attributes. *Journal of Experimental Social Psychology, 21,* 73–85.

Wood, W., Wong, F. Y., and Chachere, J. G. (1990). Effects of media violence on viewers' aggression in unconstrained social interaction. *Psychological Bulletin,* in press.

Wrightsman, L. S. (1987). *Psychology and the legal system.* Monterey, CA: Brooks/Cole.

Wu, C., and Shaffer, D. R. (1987). Susceptibility to persuasive appeals as a function of source credibility and prior experience with attitude object. *Journal of Personality and Social Psychology, 52,* 677–688.

Yates, S. M., and Aronson, E. (1983). A social psychological perspective on energy conservation in residential buildings. *American Psychologist, 38,* 435–444.

Yukl, G., and Falbe, C. M. (1990). Influence tactics and objectives in upward, downward, and lateral influence. *Journal of Applied Psychology, 75,* 132–140.

Zajonc, R. B. (1968). Attitude effects of mere exposure. *Journal of Personality and Social Psychology Monograph, 9* (2, pt. 2).

Zajonc, R. B. (1980). Feeling and thinking: Preferences need no inferences. *American Psychologist, 35,* 151–175.

Zanna, M. P. (1990). Message receptivity: A new look at the old problem of open- vs. closed-mindedness. In A. Mitchell (Ed.), *Advertising exposure, memory, and choice*. Hillsdale, NJ: Erlbaum.

Zanna, M. P., Kiesler, C. A., and Pilkonis, P. A. (1970). Positive and negative attitudinal affect established by classical conditioning. *Journal of Personality and Social Psychology, 14*, 321–328.

Zanna, M. P., and Rempel, J. K. (1988). Attitudes: A new look at an old concept. In D. Bar-Tal and A. W. Kruglanski (Eds.), *The social psychology of knowledge*. New York: Cambridge University Press.

Ziesel, H., and Diamond, S. S. (1976). The jury selection in the Mitchell-Stans conspiracy trial. *American Bar Foundation Research Journal, 1*, 151–174.

Zillman, D., and Bryant, J. (1974). Effect of residual excitation on the motivational response to provocation and delayed aggressive behavior. *Journal of Personality and Social Psychology, 30*, 782–791.

Zimbardo, P. G. (1960). Involvement and communication discrepancy as determinants of opinion conformity. *Journal of Abnormal and Social Psychology, 60*, 86–94.

Zimbardo, P. G. (1969). *The cognitive control of motivation*. Glenview, IL: Scott, Foresman.

Zimbardo, P. G. (1971). Coercion and compliance. The psychology of police confessions. In C. Perruci and M. Pilisuk (Eds.), *The triple revolution emerging* (pp. 492–508). Boston: Little, Brown.

Zimbardo, P. G. (1977). *Shyness: What is it, what to do about it*. Reading, MA: Addison-Wesley.

Zimbardo, P. G. (1988). *Psychology and life* (12th ed.). Glenview, IL: Scott, Foresman.

Zimbardo, P. G., Weisenberg, M., Firestone, I., and Levy, B. (1965). Communicator effectiveness in producing public conformity and private attitude change. *Journal of Personality, 33*, 233–256.

Zuckerman, M., DePaulo, B., Rosenthal, R. (1981). Verbal and nonverbal communication of deception. In L. Berkowitz (Ed.), *Advances in experimental social psychology* (vol. 14, pp. 1–59). New York: Academic Press.

Zullow, H. M., Oettingen, G., Peterson, C., and Seligman, M. E. P. (1988). Pessimistic explanatory style in the historical record. *American Psychologist, 43*, 673–682.

Name Index

❖

Abelson, R. P., 35, 259
Adler, R. P., 134
Adorno, T. W., 237
Ahlering, R. F., 175
Ajzen, I., 128, 189, 190
Alberti, J. M., 29
Albright, C. L., 24, 26
Alessis, C., 184
Alexander, J., 350
Alicke, M. D., 59, 72
Allen, V. L., 61
Allport, G. W., 237
Altheide, D. L., 52
Altman, D. G., 24, 26
Amabile, T. M., 94, 208
Andersen, S. M., 239
Anderson, C., 208
Anderson, N. H., 184, 187
Andrews, L. B., 310
Apple, W., 268, 272
Arean, P., 342
Aronson, E., 118, 129, 233, 337–338, 350,
    A.7–A.8
Asch, J., 339
Asch, S. E., 56–57, 61, 79, 188
Atkin, C. K., 342, 343
Axsom, D., 157, 367

Bailey, F. L., 312, 313
Baker, A. L., 363

Baker, D., 47, 48
Baldwin, M. W., 99, 230
Bales, R. F., 325
Balser, D., 342
Bandura, A., 44, 46, 50, 227, 346, 363
Bargh, J. A., 279
Barker, E., 11
Baron, R. A., 16
Baron, S. H., 61
Barthe, D. G., 364
Barton, R., 364
Basow, S. A., 265
Bassett, R., 81
Batson, C. D., 191
Battalio, R. C., 335
Baucom, D. H., 363
Baum, A., 337
Baumeister, R. F., 53, 115, 271
Baumgardner, M. H., 179, 184, 185
Baumrind, D., 72
Beaber, R. J., 274
Beach, S. R., 363
Beaman, A. L., 81
Beck, A. T., 362
Becker, L. B., 141
Bedau, H., 304
Beebe, S. A., 265
Bell, B. E., 314
Bell, P. A., 337
Bell, R. M., 347
Belloc, N. B., 341

Bem, D. J., 95, 98, 246
Benham, L., 359
Bensenberg, M., 194
Bentler, P. M., 88
Best, J. A., 229, 233
Bettinghaus, E. P., 14, 20
Biederman, M. F., 191
Birk, T., 358
Bisanz, G. L., 128
Bizman, A., 82
Blane, H. T., 357
Blank, A., 258
Blosser, J. L., 191
Blum, A., 24, 27, 28
Bobocel, D. R., 156
Boettger, R., 218
Bond, R. N., 272
Bonoma, T. V., 115
Bornstein, R. F., 280
Bothwell, R. K., 314
Bower, G. H., 310
Bowers, K. S., 248
Bray, R. M., 318, 319, 322, 325
Brehm, J. W., 178
Brehm, S. S., 365
Brent, E. E., 163
Breslow, L., 341
Brice, P., 105–106
Brickman, P., 171
Brigham, J. C., 280, 314
Broadbent, D. E., 247
Brock, T. C., 156, 157, 215
Brown, C., 22, 23
Brown, C. E., 265, 267
Brown, K. S., 229, 233
Brown, R., 72–73, 269, 273, 321
Brown, Y., 323
Bruner, J., 223
Bryan, J. H., 52
Bryant, J., 97
Buckhout, R., 298, 301
Buckley, J., 304
Burger, J., 78, 79
Burgoon, J. K., 358
Burgoon, M., 358
Burns, H. J., 299, 303
Burnstein, E., 321
Byrne, D., 16, 138

Cacioppo, J. T., 60, 81, 128, 150, 152–158, 177,
    179, 211, 232, 249, 297, B.7, B.8
Calder, B. J., 150
Caldwell, C., 324
Caldwell, J. R., 358
Campbell, A. C., 52

Campbell, D. T., 187, A.8, B.6
Campbell, J. D., 59, 61
Campbell, N. A., 339
Caplan, R. D., 358
Carlsmith, J. M., 111, A.7–A.8
Carver, C. S., 280
Chachere, J. G., 51, 105
Chafetz, M. E., 357
Chaffee, S., 143
Chaiken, S., 99, 148, 153, 157, 158, 182, 230,
    247, 274, 347, 349
Chanowitz, B., 258
Chapline, W., 364
Charen, M., 95
Chassin, L., 194
Chidester, T. R., 222–223
Christiaansen, R. E., 300
Christie, R., 326
Church, G. J., 209
Cialdini, R. B., 73, 76, 77, 81–83, 208, 212, 232,
    240, 337
Clancey, M., 272
Cochran, P. J., 191
Cohen, R. E., 358
Coker, R., 358
Cole, C. M., 81
Coleman, R., 326
Comstock, G., 143
Cone, J. D., 335
Conlee, M. C., 172
Conley, J. M., 311
Conway, M., 96
Cook, T. D., 184
Cooper, D. S., 302
Cooper, J., 114, 119, 123, 365–367
Corty, E., 194
Cotronea, R., 342
Cottler, L., 359
Crandell, R., 171
Crano, W. D., 197
Critchlow, B., 119
Crocker, J., 206
Cross, T., 307
Cunningham, M. R., 82

D'Agostino, P. R., 279
Darley, J. M., 131, 133, 191
d'Avernas, J., 229, 233
Davis, J. H., 318, 319, 322, 325
Davis, K. E., 92
Davis, R. M., 23, 24
Dawson, K. E., 271
DeBono, K. G., 224
Deci, E. L., 122
Deffenbacher, K., 302

Dempsey, G. R., 129
DePaulo, B., 272
Deutsch, M., 54, 59, 80
Devine, P. G., 279–280, 302
DeVos, G., 234
Diamond, S. S., 324
Dill, C. A., 233
DiMatteo, R. M., 353, 354, 357–358
DiNicola, D. D., 353, 354
Dixon, N. F., 277
Dolecek, T. A., 29
Dollar, K., 79, 215
Dougherty, D., 307
Dovidio, J. F., 265, 267
Dunn, D. S., 34

Eagly, A. H., 148, 153, 158, 211, 212, 215, 247
Ebbeson, E. B., 326
Ebling, T., 131
Edwards, K., 281
Edwards, R. E., 147
Ekman, P., 263, 264, 272
Elkin, R. A., 113, 114, 115, 119, 150, 155, 193, 211, 212
Ellickson, P. L., 347
Ellison, K. W., 301
Ellsworth, P. C., A.7
Ellyson, S. L., 265, 267
Ely, R. J., 222
Emrich, B., 326
Englis, B. G., 269–271
Erdley, C. A., 279
Erickson, B., 311, 312
Eron, L. D., 105–106
Eskenazi, J., 282
Evans, R. I., 229, 232, 233
Everett, P. B., 335
Exline, R. V., 265

Fairey, P. J., 59, 61
Falbe, C. M., 128
Falbo, T., 128, 363
Farquhar, J. W., 350, 352
Fazio, R. H., 100, 114, 123, 134, 193, 194, 195, 211
Feger, D., 344
Fehrenbach, P. A., 51
Feldstein, S., 272
Ferguson, T. J., 92, 314, 315
Ferrari, J. R., 342
Feshbach, S., 232
Festinger, L., 55, 108, 111, 130, 246, 336
Field, P. B., 225
Fincham, F. D., 363

Firestone, I., 116
Fischer, P., 105–106
Fishbein, M., 128, 189, 190
Fisher, J. D., 337
Fiske, D. W., B.6
Fiske, S. T., 93, 159
Flay, B. R., 184, 229, 233
Franco, M., 342
Fraser, S. C., 81, 339
Freedman, J. L., 81, 232, 339
French, J. R. P., 358
Frenkel-Brunswick, E., 237
Frey, D., 144–146
Friedman, H. S., 357
Friesen, W. V., 263, 264, 272
Fuller, R. G. C., 157
Futrell, D., 271

Galanter, H., 7, 10, 18, 19
Galley, D. J., 280
Garamoni, G. L., 362
Geller, E. S., 337
Gerard, H. B., 54, 59, 80
Gerhard, D., 317
Giacalone, R., 173
Gibbs, N., 353, 355
Gilligan, C., 215
Gitta, M. Z., 156
Goethals, G. R., 131, 133, 187, 271, 321
Goldman, R., 154, 155
Goleman, D., 234
Gonzales, M. H., A.7
Gorkin, L., 118
Gorn, G. J., 250
Gouldner, A. W., 76
Grady, K., 232
Granberg, D., 163
Graubard, P. S., 47–48
Gray, F., 47–48
Greene, D., 122
Greenwald, A. G., 35, 104, 123, 149, 179, 182, 184, 185, 204, 278, 282, B.7
Grice, H. P., 221
Grier, H. C., 335
Gruder, C. L., 184
Grusec, J. E., 51
Grush, J. E., 171, 172, 175
Guthrie, T. J., 233
Guttman, L., B.4

Halamaj, J., 184
Hamilton, D. L., 239
Hammen, C. L., 364
Hardyck, J. A., 118, 119

Haritos-Fatouros, M., 228
Harper, R. G., 260
Harris, P. R., 340
Harrison, A. A., 171
Hartup, W. W., 50
Hass, R. G., 158, 232
Hastie, R., 303, 309, 310, 313, 317
Hawkins, D., 325
Hayes, S. C., 335
Hays, R. D., 358
Hayward, S. C., 335
Heesacker, M., 360
Heider, F., 89
Heltman, K., 265, 267
Henderson, A. H., 233
Hennigan, K. M., 184
Herbert, F., 260
Herek, G. M., 224
Hersey, J., 214
Hewitt, E. C., 156
Hill, P. C., 233
Hill, W., 342
Hinsz, V. B., 322
Hirst, W., 143
Hitler, A., 17
Hochbaum, G., 354
Hoffman, E. L., 61
Holt, R. W., 322
Hook, L. H., 325
Horowitz, I. A., 326
Horowitz, S. W., 306
Hosch, H. M., 302
Hovland, C. I., 135, 183, 216, 217, 225, 310
Hubert, S., 184, 187
Huesmann, L. R., 105–106

Inbau, F. E., 304, 306
Insko, C. A., 59, 72, 150
Iyengar, S., 140

Jackson, S. E., 64
James, R. M., 325
Janis, I. L., 102–104, 135, 218, 225, 251, 353–356
Johnson, B. C., 312
Johnson, B. T., 211, 212, 215
Johnson, H. H., 179–180
Johnson, J. M., 52
Johnson, M. K., 317
Jones, E. E., 92, 187
Judd, C. M., 163

Kagel, J. H., 335
Kahn, D., 175, 196

Kahneman, D., 143, 326, 338, 348
Kalfus, G. R., 342
Kallgren, C. A., 158, 193, 337
Kalven, H., 304, 317, 318
Kamenetsky, C., 235
Kandel, D. B., 88
Kantola, S. J., 339
Kaplan, M. F., 319, 320, 322
Karabenick, S. A., 60
Kardush, M., 118, 119
Kassin, S. M., 295–296, 307
Kates, R. W., 333
Katz, D., 223
Katzman, N., 143
Kaye, D., 251
Keating, C. F., 265, 267
Keeton, R. E., 310
Kelley, H. H., 90, 92, 135
Kelly, M., 215
Kendall, P. C., 362, 363
Kennedy, J. G., 271
Kenney, D. A., 163
Kerr, N. L., 318, 319, 322, 325
Kersell, M. W., 229, 233
Kessler, L. G., 359
Kessler, R. C., 88
Key, W. B., 276, 282
Kiesler, C. A., 79, 251, 252
Kihlstrom, J. F., 247, 248
Kim, J. I., 218
Kinder, D. R., 140, 236
King, B. T., 102
King, R. G., 70
Kircher, J. C., 306
Kirschner, P., 251
Klein, R., 105–106
Kleinhesselink, R. R., 147
Klentz, B., 81
Klinger, M. R., 278
Koehnken, G., 273
Konecni, V. J., 326
Korff, M., 359
Kraft, D., 34
Krauss, R. M., 268, 272
Kraut, R. E., 273
Kremer, B. K., 29
Krosnick, J. A., 140, 163, 204
Kruglanski, A. W., 133
Kunst-Wilson, W. R., 254, 277
Kyle, S. O., 363

Lachendro, E., 343
Laird, N. M., 295
Lamm, H., 321
Landers, S., 349

Landsman, R., 303
Landy, D., 157
Langer, E., 258, 259, 323
Lanzetta, J. T., 269–271
Leaf, P. J., 359
Leippe, M. R., 113, 114, 150, 155, 178, 179,
    184, 185, 193, 211, 212, 232, 298, 302,
    303, 314–316
Leone, D. R., 280
Lepper, M. R., 122, 163, 219, 220
Lesser, G. S., 134
Leventhal, H., 229, 345
Levey, B., 116
Levinson, D. J., 237
Lewisohn, P. M., 364
Liberman, A., 153, 158, 247
Liebert, R. M., 51, 104
Lifton, R. K., 241
Likert, R., B.3–B.4
Lind, E. A., 293–294, 311, 312
Lindsay, R. C. L., 314, 315
Linville, P. W., 364
Lisle, D. J., 34
Liu, T. J., 278
Loftus, E. F., 298, 299, 303, 314, 317
London, H., 268
Long, B., 265
Lord, C. G., 163, 219, 220
Luchins, A., 187
Lumsdaine, A. A., 135, 183
Luthans, F., 47, 48
Lutz, W., 139
Luus, C. A. E., 301
Lydon, J. E., 229

McAlister, A. L., 232, 352
McArthur, L. A., 92, 263, 266
McArthur, L. Z., 264–266
Maccoby, N., 24, 26, 342, 350, 352
McCombs, M. E., 141
McConnell, H. K., 246
McCoombs, M., 143
MacCoun, R. J., 322
McCullough, J. L., 178
McDavid, J. W., 60
McGuire, W. J., 102, 104, 134, 136, 143, 225,
    230–232
McHugo, G. J., 269–271
McKeough, K. L., 175
McLeod, J. M., 141
McPherson, K., 144
Maddux, J. E., 347
Malpass, R. S., 302
Mandell, W., 310
Mandler, G., 248

Manion, A. P., 314
Mann, L., 102–104, 218
Manstead, A. S. R., 194
Marbury, C. H., 15
Marcel, A. J., 278
Marchioni, P. M., 302
Margulies, R. L., 88
Markle, G. E., 22, 30
Maruyama, G., 274
Maslach, C., 62, 63, 64
Masters, R. D., 269–271
Matarazzo, J. D., 260
Maxwell, S. E., 233
Mayseless, O., 133, 323
Mehrabian, A., 263, 268, 274
Meringoff, L. K., 134
Mewborn, C. R., 346
Meyer, A. J., 352
Meyerowitz, B. E., 347, 349
Meyers, A. W., 335
Miene, P. K., 309
Milgram, S., 65, 67–75, 94, 188, 240, 353
Millar, M. G., 34, 196
Miller, A. G., 71, 72
Miller, C. E., 319, 320
Miller, D. G., 299, 303
Miller, D. J., 51
Miller, G. A., 248
Miller, H., 179, 187
Miller, K. D., 14
Miller, J. A., 81
Miller, N., 187, 274
Milmoe, S., 357
Mischel, W., 364
Mitchell, H. E., 326
Molko/Leal v. Holy Spirit Association, 11
Montgomery, D. A., 324
Moore, T. E., 277
Moreland, R. L., 253
Morency, N., 268
Moriarty, T., 80
Morley, D. D., 150
Mosbach, P., 229
Moscovici, S., 321, 323
Mowen, J. C., 77
Mowry, D. D., 356
Mueller, M., 79, 215
Mulbar, H., 304
Mullen, B., 271
Murray, D. M., 302
Myers, D. G., 321, 322

Nagao, D. H., 322
Nakamura, Y., 248
Nash, J. D., 352

Neale, M. S., 335
Neil v. Biggers, 314
Neisser, U., 143
Nelson, Z. P., 356
Nemeth, C. J., 323
New York Times, The, 290, 304
Newcomb, M. D., 88
Newcomb, T. M., A.1
Newsweek, 29
Nisbett, R. E., 97, 122, 246, 255, 256, 337
Nix, S., 9
Nizer, L., 309
Nord, W., 47

O'Barr, W. M., 311, 312
Ochalek, K., 300
Oettingen, G., 16, 161
Ofshe, R., 304
O'Leary, K. D., 363
Olshavsky, R. W., 194
Olson, J. M., 156
Oman, J. K., 29
Osborne, J. G., 335
Osgood, C. E., 34, B.5
Oskamp, S., 171
Ostrom, T. M., 178, 215, 298
O'Sullivan, M., 272

Packard, V., 276
Packwood, W. T., 274
Pagano, F., 345
Page, B. I., 129
Page, M. M., 249
Pallak, J., 79, 215
Pallak, M. S., 79, 215
Papageorgis, D., 230, 231
Parks, S. H., 358
Parrott, R., 358
Paul, R., 47, 48
Pelham, B. W., 222, 223
Pennington, N., 309
Peplau, L. A., 128
Perlman, D., 171
Peters, M. D., 140
Peterson, C., 16, 161, 362
Petty, R. E., 60, 128, 150, 152–158, 177, 211,
　　212, 232, 249, 275, 297, B.7, B.8
Pfau, M., 358
Pietromonaco, P., 279
Pilisuk, M., 358
Pilkonis, P. A., 251, 252
Piper, A., 259
Poe, D., 273
Powers, R. B., 335

Pratkanis, A. R., 35, 184, 185, 282
Prentice, D. A., 35
Presson, C. C., 194
Preston, E., 219, 220
Preston, M., 81
Priesler, R. M., 158
Prince, L. M., 357–358
Proffitt, C., 194
Pyszczynski, T., 309

Qualter, T. H., 17–18

Radelet, M., 304
Radloff, C. E., 271
Raines, B. E., 233
Raskin, D. C., 306
Ravenholt, R. T., 23
Ray, M., 344
Raye, C. L., 317
Raz, M., 82
Reddy, M. E., 295–296
Redfield, J., 171
Reed, H. B., 356
Regan, D. T., 76
Regier, D. A., 359
Reid, J. E., 304, 306
Reis, A., 143
Rempel, J. K., 32
Reno, R. R., 337
Reyes, R. M., 310
Riordan, C. A., 271
Roberts, D., 143
Roberts, D. F., 232, 342
Robertson, T. S., 134
Robinson, E. A. R., 358
Robinson, J., 263, 266
Robinson, M. J., 272
Robles, R., 280
Rock, L., 187
Rodgers, H. L., Jr., 215
Rogers, C. R., 360
Rogers, R. W., 346, 347
Rohrer, J. H., 61
Rokeach, M., 215
Romanczyk, A., 314
Ronis, D. L., 179
Rosch, M., 144, 146
Rosenberg, H., 47–48
Rosenfeld, P., 115, 173, 271
Rosenfield, D., A.1
Rosenhan, D. L., 72
Rosenkrans, M. A., 50
Rosenthal, R., 272, 357
Rosnow, R. L., 215

Ross, D., 50
Ross, L., 75, 93, 94, 163, 208, 337
Ross, M., 122
Ross, S. A., 50
Rothschild, M. L., 149
Rozelle, R. M., 233
Rule, B. G., 128
Rumpel, C., 314
Rushton, J. P., 51, 52
Ryan, K. B., 229, 233
Ryan, M. J., 191
Ryan, R. M., 122
Ryan, W., 94

Safer, M. A., 303
Sakarai, M. M., 59
Saks, M. J., 310, 313, 317
Salancik, G. R., 96
San Francisco Chronicle, 11, 27, 74
San Francisco Examiner and Chronicle, 8
Sanford, R. N., 237
Santee, R. T., 62, 63, 64
Sarup, G., 215
Saxe, L., 307
Schachter, S., 53–54, 97
Scherer, K. R., 272
Schlenker, B. R., 115
Schoenberger, J. A., 29
Schooler, J. W., 317
Schulman, J., 326
Schulman, P., 346
Schultz, D. P., 134
Schwartz, R. M., 362
Schwarzwald, J., 82
Scrivner, E., 303
Sears, D. O., 232, 236
Seligman, M. E. P., 16, 161, 346, 362
Shaffer, D. R., 152
Shapiro, R. Y., 129
Shapiro, S., 359
Shaver, K. G., 187
Shaver, P., 326
Sheehy-Skeffington, A., 157
Sheffield, F. D., 135, 183
Sheridan, C. L., 70
Sherif, C. W., 215
Sherif, M., 55–56, 61, 216, 217
Sherman, J., 323
Sherman, S. J., 118, 136, 194, 246
Shinn, M., 358
Shopland, D. R., 22, 23
Shore, B. M., 339
Sidera, J. A., 152
Sistrunk, F., 60
Sivacek, J., 197

Skinner, E. A., 359
Skitka, L., 218
Skubiski, S., 51
Slater, M. D., 24, 26
Smart, J. L., 194
Smart, R. G., 344
Smith, M., 223
Smith, R., 280
Smith, R. E., 324
Smith, R. H., 59, 72
Smith, T. W., 365
Snyder, M., 82, 205, 206, 224
Solomon, D. S., 350
Sorrentino, R. M., 156
Southwick, L. L., 119
Spelke, E., 143
Spitzer, C. E., 322
Sprafkin, J., 51, 104
Staats, A. W., 249
Staats, C. K., 249
Stairs, D., 271
Stanley, J. C., A.8
Stapp, J., 63
Stasser, G., 318, 319, 322, 325
Steblay, N. M., 81
Steele, C. M., 119, 121, 123
Steenbock, S., 310
Stein, J. A., 88
Steinmetz, J. L., 94, 208
Stephan, W. G., A.1
Stoner, J. A., 321
Streeter, L. A., 272
Strodtbeck, F. L., 325
Suci, G. J., 34, B.5
Sue, S., 324
Sullivan, D. G., 269–271
Sullivan, L., 23
Suls, J. M., 215
Sunseri, A. J., 29
Surgeon General, 129
Swander, D. V., 61
Swann, W. B., Jr., 205, 222–223
Sweeney, J. D., 300
Syme, G. J., 339
Syme, S. L., 358

Tannenbaum, P. G., 34, B.5
Taranta, A., 357
Taves, P. A., 119
Taylor, S., 59, 72
Taylor, S. E., 93, 159, 346
Tedeschi, J. T., 115
Tesser, A., 34, 59, 61, 172, 173, 196
Test, M. A., 52
Tetlock, P. E., 218

Thelen, M. H., 51
Thibaut, M., 293, 294
Thompson, W. C., 310
Thurstone, L. L., B.2, B.4
Tice, D. M., 115, 271
Time, 276
Tindale, R. S., 322
Tischler, F. L., 359
Tittler, B. I., 215
Traub, J., 120, 121
Trolier, T. K., 239
Trout, J., 143
Troyer, R. J., 22, 30
Tulloch, W. F., 295–296
Tulving, E., 184
Turtle, J. W., 317
Tuso, M. A., 337
Tversky, A., 326, 338, 348

Uranowitz, S. W., 206

Valone, K., 274
Varela, J. A., 223
Vidmar, N., 295
Vinokur, A., 321
Visher, C. A., 317
Vogt, B., 191
Vollrath, D. A., 322
Von German, P. S., 358

Wade, C., 64
Wade, J., 59, 72
Wagatsuma, H., 234
Walker, L., 293, 294
Walster, E., 246
Ward, L. M., 187
Ward, S., 134, 344
Washington Post, The, 27
Watkins, T. A., 179, 180
Watson, D., 93
Watson, J. B., 248
Watts, J. C., 345

Watts, W. A., 182
Weins, A. N., 260
Weinstein, N. D., 343
Weir, W., 277
Weisenberg, M., 116
Weiss, W., 183, 310
Wellens, A. R., 280
Wells, G. L., 92, 156, 157, 275, 298, 301, 302,
    307, 309, 314–317
Wenzel, C., 268
White, R., 223
Wilder, D. A., 61
Williams, M., 274
Wilson, P. H., 363
Wilson, T. D., 34, 246, 255, 256, 364
Wilson, W., 179, 187
Winett, R. A., 335
Winkler, R. C., 335
Winton, W., 268
Witmer, J. F., 337
Wolf, E., 357
Wolf, S., 324
Wong, F. Y., 51, 105
Wood, P. D., 350
Wood, W., 51, 105, 151, 158, 193, 230
Wrightsman, L. S., 298, 304, 307, 309, 324, 326
Wu, C., 152

Yandell, B., 150
Yates, S., 157
Yates, S. M., 337
Yukl, G., 128

Zajonc, R. B., 34, 171, 253, 254, 277
Zanna, M. P., 32, 119, 123, 193, 194, 209, 217,
    229, 233, 251, 252, 281, 321
Zavalloni, M., 321
Zeisel, H., 304, 317, 318, 324
Zillman, D., 97
Zimbardo, P. G., 113, 116, 212, 226, 239, 304,
    308, 359
Zuckerman, M., 272
Zullow, H. M., 16, 161

Subject Index

❖

Acceptance step in persuasion, 135, 137, 149–163

Accountability:
in business decision making, 218
effect of, on attitude change, 217–218

Activation of attitudes, 194

Active vs. passive participation, 103–104, 182

Adversarial system of legal procedure, 292–297
effects of, on jurors and witnesses, 294–297
fairness and bias of, 293–294
vs. inquisitorial approach, 293–294

Advertising:
attention and, 142–143
behavioral imagery and, 194
behavior-relevant attitude and, 196
brand recognition in, 171
choice of medium for, 149, 158–159
classical conditioning and, 249–251
creating positive associations in, 174–175
image making in, 24–26
market segmentation in, 26–29, 152
money spent on, 143
nonverbal behavior and, 275
number of advertisements and, 134–135
repeated exposure and, 170–171
self-monitoring variable and, 224
smoking and, 21–30
(See also Cigarette advertising)

Affective responses:
in attitude systems, 32
thoughts and, separate brain systems for, 254

Aggression:
modeling of, 49–51
television violence and, 50, 104–107

AIDS, health messages about, 129, 349–350

Alcohol consumption and cognitive dissonance, 119

Alcoholics Anonymous, 10

Altruism:
modeling of, 51–52
time pressures and, 191–192

Antidemocratic personality, 237

Aquino, Corazon, 64

Aristotle, 128

Assimilation, 216

Attention:
awareness and, 247
divided, 247, 257–258
as limited processing mental function, 143
selective, 144–147

Attention step in persuasion, 135, 137, 142–147

Attitude(s), 31, 32
activation of, 194
in attitude systems, 32
central role of, 34
toward environment, 333–340
as evaluative summaries, 32, 35
toward health behaviors, 342–352
influence of, on perception and thought, 35
memory and, 183–185
relation of, to behavior, 30–32, 188–198

Attitude(s) (*Cont.*):
  self-defining nature of, 35–36
  similarity of, 137–138
  sleeper effect and, 183–185
  strength and clarity of, 192–195
    as goals in persuasion, 169–170, 173–174
Attitude-behavior relationship:
  attitude sets stage for later behavior
    change, 31
  behavior-to-attitude link in, 88–89, 123–124
  behavior toward the environment and, 334
  direct experience with attitude object and,
    193–194
  feelings-based or cognition-based attitudes
    and, 195–197
  knowledgeability and, 193
  novelty of situation and, 192
  personal importance of issue and, 197
  relevance of attitude to behavior and, 195
  social pressures and, 189
  spontaneous attitude activation and, 195
  strength and clarity of attitudes in, 192–195
  systematic message processing and,
    192–193
  theory of reasoned action in, 189–190
  time pressures and, 189–192
Attitude functions (*see* Functional theories of
    attitudes)
Attitude involvement (*see* Involvement)
Attitude measurement techniques, B.1–B.7
  factors in choice of, B.6–B.7
  Guttman's scalogram as, B.4–B.5
  Likert's method of summated ratings as,
    B.3–B.4
  Osgood's semantic differential as, B.5
  physiological measures of, B.8
  single or few-item scales as, B.5–B.6
  Thurstone's method of equal-appearing
    intervals as, B.2–B.3
Attitude perseverance (*see* Belief
    perseverance)
Attitude systems, 32–33
  interconnectedness of components and, 34
Attribution (*see* Causal attribution)
Attribution therapy, 361–365
Attributional biases, 92–95
Audience factors in persuasion:
  knowledgeability as, 150–152, 230
  personal relevance of message as, 154–155
  prior attitudes as, 150–152
  self-esteem as, 225–226
  self-monitoring as, 224
  shyness as, 226
  systematic message analysis and, 153–155
Audience-approved language in persuasion,
  14

Authoritarian personality, 237, 326
Awareness:
  of being influenced, 244–254
  of conditioning, 248, 250–253
  of higher-order mental processes, 248,
    254–257
  mere exposure effect and, 253–254

Bakker, Jim, 212
Beech-Nut baby juice incident, 120–121
Begging, reactions to, 95, 100
Behavior:
  attitudes and, 30–32
  in attitude systems, 32
  (*See also* Attitude-behavior relationship)
Behavioral intentions:
  in attitude systems, 32
  regarding the environment, 334
  in theory of reasoned action, 189
Belief perseverance:
  cognitive conservatism and, 204–205
  cognitive structure and, 204–208
  confirmatory strategy and, 205–206
  involvement and, 212–217
  selective attention and, 206
  selective memory and, 206–207
  techniques to overcome, 217–225
Beliefs as cognitions in an attitude system, 32
Bentsen, Lloyd, 131
Biased interpretation:
  by audience, 162–163
  consider-the-opposite strategy and, 218–221
Brand recognition, 171
Brokaw, Tom, 271
Bush, George, 159–161, 261

Candid Camera, 189
Carter, Jimmy, 140
Causal attribution:
  biases in, 92–95
  of corresponding traits, 92
  dispositional vs. situational, 89–90
    factors in deciding between, 90–92
  explanations of unconscious influence and,
    256–257
  judgmental heuristics in, 92
  theories of, 89–92
  (*See also* Self-attribution)
Censorship, 138–139, 284–285
Charismatic communication, 4, 16
China, People's Republic of, 1
  attitude-behavior consistency of
    demonstrators in, 197–198
  censorship in, 138–139, 204

Choa, Andrew, 324
Choice (see Perception of choice)
Cigarette advertising, 21–30
  functions of, 28
  image making and, 24–26
  market segmentation and, 26–29
Classical conditioning:
  behavior modification therapy in, 361
  of emotion and attitudes, 248–253
Cognition, need for, 296–297
Cognitions in attitude systems, 32
Cognitive-behavioral therapy, 361–365
Cognitive conservatism, 204–205, 207
Cognitive dissonance, 107–109
  attitude-discrepant behavior and, 109
  Beech-Nut baby juice incident and, 120–121
  conditions necessary for, 113–115
  consciousness of dissonance manipulations
    and, 245–246, 255
  effort justification and, 366–367
  eyewitness identification and, 302
  factors affecting magnitude of, 108–109
  impression management and, 115
  insufficient justification and, 109–113
  modes of reduction of, 117–120
  pro-environmental behavior and, 339
  in psychotherapy, 365–367
  religious conversion and, 116–117
  self-affirmation, self-attribution and,
    121–123
Cognitive priming (see Priming)
Cognitive psychology, attention processes
    and, 143
Cognitive response approach, 149–152
Cognitive restructuring:
  in confessions to police, 305
  in conformity situations, 61
  as mode of dissonance reduction, 119
Commitment:
  cognitive dissonance and, 115
  consistency and, 79
  cult influence and, 10
  eyewitness testimony and, 302
  foot-in-the-door technique and, 81–82
  healthful behavior and, 351, 356
  low-ball technique and, 80–81
  pro-environmental behavior and, 339
  in psychotherapy, 365
  resistance to persuasion and, 214–215, 229,
    233, 240
  rule of, as judgmental heuristic, 76
  as source of involvement, 214–215
Compliance:
  awareness by target and, 245, 255
  contexts and principles of, 76–83
  with medical regimens, 352–358

Comprehension:
  medium of transmission and, 148
  of persuasive messages, 135, 137, 148–149
Conditioning (see Classical conditioning;
    Instrumental learning)
Confessions to police, 303–308
  effects of, on jurors, 307
  plea bargaining and, 304
  polygraphs and, 306–307
  social influence techniques in, 305–308
Confirmatory strategy, 205–206
Conformity, 55–65, A.4
  Asch studies of, 56–59, 188
  pressures for, on eyewitnesses, 300
  Sherif studies of, 55–56
Consciousness, 247
  awareness and, 247
  divided, 257–258
  (See also Attention; Awareness)
Consensus heuristic, 76, 192
Conservation of energy and resources,
    334–339
Consider-the-opposite strategy, 218–221
Consistency:
  culturally learned need for, 79, 173
  of drug-using behaviors, 88
  of thought and cognitive responses,
    172–173, 187, 208, 219
  (See also Attitude-behavior relationship;
    Cognitive dissonance; Commitment)
Contrast:
  assimilation and, 216
  in compliance techniques, 79
Control (see Personal control)
Correlational methods of research, A.1–A.2
Courtroom:
  effects of subpoena on witness statements
    in, 294–295
  introduction of evidence in, 295–297
  presentation strategies of lawyers in,
    308–310
  primacy vs. recency in, 296–297, 308–310
  witness questioning strategies and, 310–316
  witness speech styles and, 311–313
  (See also Eyewitness testimony; Juries)
Crisis effect, 333
Cues (see Persuasion cues)
Cults:
  conversion to: cognitive dissonance and,
    116–117
    self-attribution, self-persuasion and, 100–
    101
  statistics on, 7, 11
  techniques of Moonies for, 5–12, 226–227
  deprogramming of converts and, 8
  ethics of, 284–285

Cults (*Cont.*):
  heavenly deception technique and, 9, 11
  legality of conversion techniques of, 10–12
  "love bombing" and, 9
  types of people susceptible to influence of, 9
Cultural truisms, 230

Death penalty, 162–163
Deception, detection of:
  from nonverbal cues, 272–274
  with polygraphs, 306–307
Defense mechanisms, 249–250
Dependent variable, A.3
Depression, 361–363
  cognitive-behavioral therapy for, 361–363
  depressive attributions in, 362
DeWitt, John L., 214
Discriminative stimuli, 44, 52–53
Dissent, 62–64
Dissonance (*see* Cognitive dissonance)
Doctors:
  patient noncompliance and, 352–358
  perceptions of, by patients, 353–354
Door-in-the-face technique, 77–78, 240
Drug use:
  cognitive dissonance and, 119
  just-say-no campaign against, 61–62
  peer influence and, 87–88
Dukakis, Michael, 159–161, 261–262

Earth Day 1990, 340
Education:
  as propaganda for establishment, 141
  social learning processes in, 46–49
Efficacy (*see* Self-efficacy)
Effort justification, 366–367
Ego defensive function, 223, 237, 250
Ego involvement (*see* Involvement)
Emotions:
  as affective responses, 32
  conditioning of, 248–249
Energy crisis of 1970s, 331–333
Environmental influence, 331–340
  instrumental learning and, 334–336
  motivation for pro-environmental behavior
    and, 333–336
  prompts and, 336–337
  salience of environmental problems and,
    333, 336–338
  self-attribution and, 335–336
  social comparison and, 336
Ethics of influence, 284–286, 307
Europe, eastern, Communist downfall in, 1,
  64–66, 234

Evaluative consistency principle, 172–173,
  176–177
Exorcist, The, 276, 281
Experimental realism, A.7–A.8
Experiments, A.2–A.12
  causation and, A.2
  control and, A.2
  dependent and independent variables in,
    A.2–A.3
  experimental designs in, A.10–A.12
  generalizing from, A.5–A.10
  random assignment in, A.2
  realism in, experimental and mundane,
    A.7–A.8
  validity: conceptual and content, A.4–A.5
    external and internal, A.8–A.12
Extinction in social and instrumental
    learning, 49
Exxon Valdez oil tanker spill, 340
Eyewitness testimony:
  ability of jurors to validly judge, 316–317
  accuracy and confidence relationship in,
    302–303, 314–316
  factors affecting belief in by jurors and,
    314–317
  importance of, 297
  leading questions and, 299–300
  reliability of, 298–299
  repeated questioning and, 303
  social influences on lineup identifications
    and, 300–302

Facial expressions (*see* Nonverbal
    communication)
Fear appeals, 345–347, 355–356
Feedback, 335–336
Field research, A.1–A.2
Fonda, Henry, 318, 323
Foot-in-the-door technique, 81–82, 95, 100,
    240, 245
Forewarning, 231–232, 309
Fragmented vs. narrative speech style, 311,
    315
Freud, Sigmund, 249
Functional theories of attitudes, 223–225
  applied to prejudice, 237–239
  awareness of influence and, 250
Fundamental attribution error, 93
  applied to Milgram obedience studies, 94
  blaming the victim and, 94–95
Funt, Allen, 189

Gorbachev, Mikhail, 139, 234, 262
Group polarization (*see* Polarization)

Gun control, attitude issue of, 209–210
Guttman scalogram, B.4–B.5

Halo effect, 256
Health knowledge, 342, 350–352
Health psychology, 340–358
    fear appeals and, 345–347, 355–356
    mass media health campaigns and, 342–352
        cynicism about, 343–345
    message framing in, 347–349
    patient compliance and, 352–358
    unrealistic optimism and, 343, 349
    workshops teaching health behaviors and,
        350–352
Helplessness, sense of, 346
Heuristics (see Judgmental heuristics;
        Persuasion cues)
Hitler, Adolph, 16–18, 235

Image-making:
    of corporate names, 175
    of environmentally conscious citizens, 338
    ethics and, 285
    nonverbal communication and, 261
    of U.S. presidents, 159–162
    (See also Advertising; Television)
Inadmissible evidence, 324–325
Independent variable, A.2
Individual differences:
    authoritarian personality and prejudice,
        237
    experimental methods and, A.4
    individuation and conformity, 63–64
    among jurors, 325–326
    need for cognition and primacy-recency,
        296–297
    self-confidence and conformity, 59–60
    self-esteem and persuasion, 225–226
    self-monitoring and persuasion, 224
    sex: conformity and, 60, 63–64
        nonverbal communication and, 267–268
    (See also Audience factors in persuasion)
Individuation, 63–64
Induced compliance studies, 110–116
Informational social influence, 54
    conformity and, 59–61
    drug use and, 87–88
    in juries, 318–320
    obedience and, 70–72
Inoculation defense, 230–232, 309
Instrumental learning:
    in behavior modification therapy, 361
    in business settings, 46–47
    contingent reinforcement and, 44–45

Instrumental learning (Cont.):
    in education settings, 45, 47–49
    health behaviors and, 351–352
    obedience to authority and, 73
    prejudice and, 52–53
    shaping and, 44–45
    shaping pro-environmental habits and,
        334–336
Insufficient justification, 109–113
Intentions (see Behavioral intentions)
Internalization of attitudes, 198–199
Interpersonal influence settings:
    definition of, 4
    religious cults as examples of, 5–12
Involvement, 208–217
    basis of vs. degree of, 210
    commitment and, 214–215
    construction-motivated, 211–212
    ego, 215
    impression relevance of message and, 212,
        218
    outcome relevance of message and, 211,
        217
    role of, in resistance to persuasion, 204,
        212–217
    self-defining values and, 215–216
    significant others and, 216–217
    validation-motivated, 211, 212–217

Jackson, Jesse, 262
Japanese-Americans, internment of, 213–214
Japanese Burakumin, 234
Jennings, Peter, 271–272
Jonestown mass suicide:
    description of, 18–19
    persuasion skills of Rev. Jim Jones as
        factor, 19–21
Judgmental heuristics:
    attitudes as, 186
    awareness of using, 246
    causal attribution and, 92
    commitment heuristic in dissonance, 115
    compliance-gaining techniques and, 76–83
    about eyewitness memory, 315–316
    majority influence and, 323
    mindlessness and, 258
    nonverbal cues as, 263, 274
    obedience to authority and, 74
    persuasion and, 153–162
Juries, 317–327
    group polarization and, 320–322
    inadmissible evidence and, 324–325
    informational influence and, 318–320
    juror participation rates and, 325
    juror selection and, 324–326

Juries (*Cont.*):
  leniency bias of, 322
  majority rule and, 318–322
  minority influence and, 322–324
  normative influence and, 318–320
Just say no to drugs campaign, 61–62

Kennedy, John F., 262
King, Martin Luther, Jr., 12–15, 262
Knowledge function, 223, 238
Korean prisoners of war, 232

Latitude of acceptance, 216, 223
Latitude of noncommitment, 216
Latitude of rejection, 216, 223
Laugh tracks, 157
Lawyer strategies (*see* Courtroom)
Leading questions:
  as attitude-change technique, 221–223
  witness testimony and, 299–310, 312
Learning:
  of prescriptive rules of behavior, 73
  versus performance, 50
  (*See also* Classical conditioning;
      Instrumental learning; Social learning
      theory)
Learning theory approach, to persuasion, 135
Leniency bias of juries, 322
Lewin, Kurt, 36
Lie detection (*see* Deception, detection of)
Likert summated ratings attitude scales,
  B.3–B.4
Littering, 336–337
Loss-averseness, 338, 347–349
Low-ball technique, 80–81, 245, 284

Mass media:
  role in promoting healthy lifestyles,
    342–352
  role in raising environmental conscience,
    340
Mass media settings, 4
  cigarette advertising as example of, 21–30
  number of messages in, 134–135
  (*See also* Advertising; News broadcasts)
Measurement:
  of attitudes (*see* Attitude measurement
    techniques)
  of behavior and intentions, B.7
  of facial muscle activity, B.8
  of physiological responses, B.7–B.8
  of reaction time, B.7–B.8
  of thoughts, B.7

Memory:
  selective, 206–207
  in sleeper effect, 184–186
  stages of, and susceptibility to distortion,
    299
Mental health:
  mass media and consciousness of, 359
  statistics on, 358–359
  (*See also* Psychotherapy)
Mental representation:
  in attitude systems, 32
  example of, 33
Mere-exposure-leads-to-liking effect, 171–172,
  253–254
Mere thought, 172
Messages, persuasive:
  advantages over self-persuasion, 182
  problem-solution organization of, 20
  quality/strength of, 150, 154–156
  rational vs. emotional, 149
  (*See also* Persuasion)
Milgram studies of obedience, 65–69, 188,
  227, 240
Mindlessness vs. mindfulness, 257–259
Minority influence, 322–324
Misattribution:
  of emotions, 97
  as technique in psychotherapy, 364–365
Mitchell-Stans conspiracy trial, 324
Modeling (*see* Observational learning; Social
  learning theory)
Moonies (*see* Cults)
Moral disengagement, 227–228
Mundane realism, A.8
Music, conditioning of attitudes and, 250–251

Narrative vs. fragmented speech style, 311,
  315
Nazi Germany, 65, 141, 235
Need for cognition, 296–297
News broadcasts:
  nonverbal communication of newscasters
    and, 271–272
  selective exposure and, 140–141
Nixon, Richard, 261
Nonverbal communication:
  channels of, 260–261
  detecting deception and, 272–274
  in expression of confidence, 268
  facial cues in: audience emotions and,
    269–271
    inferences about power from, 266–268
  loudness of speech as, 263, 266–267, 274
  patient compliance and satisfaction and,
    357–358

Nonverbal communication (*Cont.*):
  persuasion and, 274–275
  self-perception and, 275–276
  sex differences in, 267–268
  skills of great orators in, 14, 261
  speed of speaking as, 274
  television and, 158–159, 271–272
  unconscious reading of, 263
  universal facial expressions as, 263–264
Noreiga, Manuel, 160
Normative social influence, 54
  conformity and, 57–59
  drug use and, 87–88
  in juries, 318–320
  obedience and, 70–72
Norms:
  development of, in groups, 56
  regarding expressive behaviors, 263
  regarding littering, 337
  subjective, in theory of reasoned action,
    189

Obedience to authority:
  causes of, 69–74
  confessions to police and, 305
  Milgram studies of, 65–69, 188, 227, 240
  reducing, 72, 75–76
Observational learning:
  factors affecting, 51
  obedience to authority and, 73
  (*See also* Social learning theory)
Optimism:
  health prospects and unrealistic, 343
  in persuasive communication, 15–16,
    161–162
Orwell, George, 139
Overjustification effect, 122

Pagano, Bernard, 298–299
Paradoxical strategy, 222–223
Paralinguistic channel of nonverbal
    communication, 260–261, 269
  (*See also* Nonverbal communication)
Parallel processing, 247
Participation, active vs. passive, 103–104, 182
Pavlov, I., 248, 249
Perception of choice:
  effectiveness of psychotherapy and,
    365–367
  as illusion, 111–112, 245
  low-ball technique and, 81
  as necessary condition for dissonance,
    110–113
Perseverance (*see* Belief perseverance)

Persistence of persuasion (*see* Retention step
    in persuasion)
Personal control:
  over life events, 1–2
  as motive in causal attribution, 89
  as motive in social comparison, 55, 130
  sense of, as factor in mental health, 364–365
  (*See also* Helplessness)
Personality factors:
  cult influence and, 9
  (*See also* Audience factors in persuasion;
    Individual differences)
Persuasion, 127, 135–137
  acceptance step in, 135, 137, 149–163
  attention step in, 135, 137, 142–147
  biased interpretation and, 163–164
  changeability spectrum and, 203
  cognitive response approach to, 149–152
  comprehension step in, 135, 137, 148–149
  cult influence and, 10
  distraction and, 155–156
  forewarning and, 231–232
  nonverbal communication in, 274–275
  optimism theme and, 15–16
  overheard communications and, 246
  peripheral cues (*see* Persuasion cues)
  popularity of, as compliance-gaining
    strategy, 128
  presentation (exposure) step in, 135–142
  in psychotherapy, 360–362
  repetition and, 170–172, 176–179
  resistance to, 204–217
  retention step in, 136–137, 179–188
  similarity to audience and, 14–16
  sincerity of communicator and, 16
  stating conclusions and, 310
  steps in process of, 135–137
  susceptibility to, 225–233
  systematic vs. heuristic processing in,
    152–155
  translation-to-behavior step in, 136–137,
    169, 189, 192–196
  ubiquity of persuasive messages and, 134
  (*See also* Audience factors in persuasion;
    Messages, persuasive; Persuasion cues;
    Resistance to persuasion and
    influence; Source factors in persuasion)
Persuasion cues:
  applause as, 157
  discounting, in sleeper effect, 184–186
  effects of, on systematic processing, 158, 159
  as judgmental heuristics, 153
  message length as, 158
  optimism of source as, 161–162
  source similarity as, 157
  televised images as, 158–162

Persuasion settings:
  definition of, 4
  famous communicators and, 12–21
Philippines, revolution in, 64
Physiological measures of attitudes, B.7
Plea bargaining, 291, 304
Polarization:
  of cognitive responses: during repeated
        exposure, 171–172
    during thinking, 172–173
  group, 320–322
  in juries, 322
  principle of evaluative consistency and, 173
Political candidates, perception of, 159–163
Pollution (see Environmental influence)
Polygraphs (see Deception, detection of)
Positioning in advertising, 142–143
Positive instances, overreliance on, 206
Powerless speech style, 311–312
Prejudice, 34, 52–53, 233–239, 279–280
  against black people: in South Africa, 235
    in United States, 234–235
  anti-Semitic, in eastern Europe, 234
  in contemporary world, 234
  functional analysis of, 237–239
  historical, 234–235, 237
  in Japan, 234
  learning of, 52–53
  as negative attitude, 34
  stereotyping and categorization and, 236,
        239
  symbolic racism and, 236
  unconscious activation of stereotypes and,
        279–280
Presentation step in persuasion, 135–144
Presidential election campaign of 1988, 131,
        159–162
Primacy effect, 186–187, 296–297, 308–310
Priming:
  in persuasion, 246
  subliminal, 278–280
Pro-environmental influence (see
        Environmental influence)
Project Alert, 347
Prompts, 336–337
Propaganda, 141
  for establishment, through education, 141
  Nazi propaganda machine and, 141, 235
Protection motivation theory, 346
Psychoanalytic theory, 249
Psychological reactance, 178, 181, 223, 233,
        245
Psychotherapy:
  attribution therapy in, 363–365
    for college freshmen, 363–364
    for unhappy marriages, 363

Psychotherapy (Cont.):
  behavior modification in, 361
  cognitive-behavioral therapy in, 361–365
    for depression, 361–363
  role of persuasion in, 360–362
Punishment:
  social disapproval as, 53–55
  in social and instrumental learning, 49

Quayle, J. Danforth, 131

Random assignment, A.2
Rather, Dan, 271
Reactance (see Psychological reactance)
Reagan, Nancy, 61
Reagan, Ronald, 15–16, 261, 269–270
Reasoned action, theory of, 189–190
Recency effect, 186–187, 296–297, 308–310
Reciprocity, rule of:
  door-in-the-face technique and, 77–78
  as judgmental heuristic, 76
  that's-not-all technique and, 78–79
Reinforcement:
  cult influence and, 10
  overjustification and, 122
  social approval as, 53–55
  social influence and, 44–49
  (See also Instrumental learning; Social
        learning theory)
Reliability in experiments, A.4
Repeated exposure:
  to complex persuasive messages, 176–179
  overexposure and, 178
  in persuasion, 169
  political elections and, 175–176
  retention of persuasion and, 179–181
  to simple stimuli, 170–172
Repetition (see Repeated exposure)
Resistance to persuasion and influence:
  building: 229–233, 239–241
  overcoming, 217–225
  sources of, 204–217
  (See also Belief perseverance; Commitment;
        Involvement)
Retention step in persuasion, 136–137, 179–188
  message repetition and, 179–181
  personal relevance of message and, 182
  sleeper effect and, 183–186
  systematic processing and, 181–183
Role-playing:
  active vs. passive participation in, 103–104
  psychotherapy groups and, 101
  as self-persuasion and self-attribution,
        101–104

Role-playing (*Cont.*):
  smoking cessation and, 102–104
  as strategy for patient compliance, 356
  (*See also* Self-persuasion)
Rooney, Andy, 74

Salience and vividness:
  causal attribution and, 93
  courtroom presentation and, 310
  of environmental problems, 333, 336–338
  of source characteristics in broadcast
    media, 159
SALT II nuclear arms treaty, 125
Schemas, 92, 173, 187, 256–257
Scientific jury selection, 326
Selective attention:
  belief perseverance and, 206
  after decisions, 142–146
  to persuasive messages, 147
Selective exposure:
  censorship and, 138–139
  education and, 141
  lifestyle and, 137–138
  media and, 139–141
Selective memory, 206–207
Self as agent of influence, 89
Self-affirmation, 121–123
Self-attribution, 88, 95–100
  cognitive dissonance and, 121–123
  confessions to police and, 306
  of emotions, 97
  environmental influence and, 335–336
  fundamental attribution error and,
    97–98
  leading questions influence technique and,
    221–223
  misattribution and, 97
  nonverbal acts and, 275–276
  psychotherapy and, 362, 364
  question-asking and, 100
  religious conversion and, 100
  self-knowledge and, 98–99
  witness testimony and, 302, 313
  (*See also* Self-perception)
Self-definition:
  attitudes and, 35–36
  involvement and, 215–216
  values and, 215–216
  (*See also* Self-image)
Self-efficacy:
  effectiveness of psychotherapy and, 365
  fear appeals about health behaviors and,
    346–347
  social learning theory and, 46
Self-esteem, 216, 225–226

Self-fulfilling prophecy, 267
  (*See also* Confirmatory strategy)
Self-image:
  behavior-to-attitude link and, 88
  cognitive dissonance and, 114–115
  (*See also* Self-definition)
Self-justification, 88–89, 107
  (*See also* Cognitive dissonance)
Self-monitoring:
  advertising and, 224
  attitude functions and, 224
Self-perception:
  Bem's theory of, 95–96
  question-asking and, 100
  religious conversion and, 100
  (*See also* Self-attribution)
Self-persuasion, 88–89
  religious conversion and, 100–101
  retention of persuasion and, 181–182
  role-playing and, 101–104
Semantic differential, B.5
Sex differences (*see* Individual differences)
Sexual behavior, health messages about,
    349–350
Situational factors, power of, 37, 188
  due to fundamental attribution error, 97–98
  to override attitudes: social pressures and,
    189
    time pressures and, 189–192
Skinner, B. F., 44
Sleeper effect, 183–186
Smoking behavior:
  adolescent susceptibility to influence and,
    228–229
  health risks of, 23, 28
  history of, 21–23
  prevalence of, social groups and, 22–23
  prevention programs for adolescents,
    232–233
  relation of, to attitudes and intentions, 194
  role of mass media ads and, 21–30
Social adjustment function, 224, 238
Social comparison:
  Festinger's theory of, 55, 130
  motives for, 133–134
  similarity of others and, 130–134
  "spin control" and, 131–132
Social influence, 2, 3
  lifestyles and (*see* Health psychology)
  mental health and (*see* Mental health;
    Psychotherapy)
  pathways of, through attitude systems, 38
  possibilities for, in criminal cases, 290–292
  pro-environmental behavior and (*see*
    Environmental influence)
  processes and settings for, 3–4

Social learning theory:
  aggression and, 49–51
  altruism and, 51–52
  examples of, in business and education
    settings, 46–49
  prejudice and, 52–53
  self-efficacy and, 46
Social psychology:
  perspective of, 36–37
  scientific method and, 37, A.1–A.2
Social support, health behaviors and, 358
Source factors in persuasion:
  expertise as, 154–155
  optimism as, 15–16, 161–162
  of psychotherapist, 360–361
  salience in broadcast media and, 159
  similarity to audience as, 14–16, 157
  trustworthiness as, 16, 157
Speech style:
  narrative vs. fragmented, 311, 315
  powerless, 311–312
Spin control in political contests, 131–132
Stanford Heart Disease Prevention Program,
    350–352
Statistical inference procedures, A.5–A.7
Stereotypes, role of, in prejudice, 236
Subliminal influence, 276–286
  behavior and, 280–281
  ethics of, 284–286
  print-embedded messages as, 282–283
  self-help audiotapes and, 282
  subaudible messages as, 281–282
  subliminal priming in, 278–280
  in visual media, 277–281
Subliminal perception, 253
  and mere exposure effect, 253–254
  (See also Subliminal influence)
Supportive defense against influence, 230–231
Susceptibility to persuasion, 225–233
Swaggart, Jimmy, 212–213, 215
Symbolic racism, 236

Television:
  degree of attention to, 143
  images as persuasion cues and, 158–162

Television (Cont.):
  violent programming and: link to
    aggression, 50, 104–105
  reducing effects of, on children,
    105–107
That's-not-all technique, 78–79
Theory of reasoned action, 189–190
Thought vs. affect, separate brain systems
  for, 254
Thought-listing method, B.7
Thurstone equal-appearing intervals attitude
  scales, B.2–B.3
Totalitarian ego, 204
Totally Hidden Video, 189
Trials (see Courtroom)
Twelve Angry Men, 318, 323

Unconscious influence (see Awareness;
  Consciousness)
Unification Church (see Cults)

Validity in experiments:
  conceptual, A.4
  content, A.4
  errors and, A.4
  external and internal, A.8–A.12
Value expressive function, 223–224, 238
Values, 215–216
Victim blaming, 94–95
Visible channel of nonverbal communication,
  261, 269
  (See also Nonverbal communication)
Vividness (see Salience and vividness)
Voir dire, 325

Wellness, 341
Witnesses (see Courtroom; Eyewitness
  testimony)
Working memory, 187

Yale Communication Research Project, 135,
  A.3